My Life In Percussion
Five Decades in the Music Products Industry

Karl Dustman

ISBN 9781888408539

Library of Congress Control Number: 2021905246

edited by Rob Cook

Rebeats Publications
P.O. Box 6, Alma, Michigan 48801
www.Rebeats.com

Printed in the United States of America

THROW 'EM TO THE WOLVES TOUR 1990
DIO
VIP
VIP
GFM
Phil Collins
The Serious Tour
1990
IM-SICK
Quite Serious
GUEST
AFTER SHOW
JAMES TAYLOR
WORLD TOUR
1987-88
AUG 13 1988
AFTER SHOW
7-5
1991
DOOBIE BROTHERS
BROTHERHOOD
Genesis
MAMA
tour 1983-84
BACKSTAGE
EXCEPT DURING SHOW
VENUE:
OTTO
GUEST
CHARMED LIFE
FAREWELL TOUR '91
THE Judds
Crew
SOUND SEVENTY
TOM JONES
AA
Lionel Richie
WORLD TOUR
BACKSTAGE
LIMITED ACCESS
10/19
SAMMY
RED
ROCKER
HAGAR
January 12, 1996

Acknowledgements

Thank you to my parents for their unconditional support and encouragement in allowing me to pursue music as a dream and profession. I am grateful to all those in our family-tree who surrounded me with patience, understanding and determination to see me through the good and bad times.

INTRODUCTION

by Karl Dustman

This story is not much different than many others. I have been truly blessed to work and earn a living in an industry filled with gifted people, creative individuals and companies and an opportunity to build relationships and friendships with so many marvelous people. The Music Products Industry is all about making music, achieved with musical instruments that are an extension of our personalities, our souls, and our character founded on a common connection that all humanity loves music. Being part of that equation has been an honor and a dream.

Careers are built on experiences, experimentation and adapting to the circumstances we are faced with. The stories and insights contained in this book represent fifty five years of a learning process that will never stop. There is as much joy written about as there is disappointment. There are wonderful people who have become life-long friends and there are those I have tried to forget for a variety of reasons. But this history needs to be shared with anyone who loves music, shares a passion for the musical instruments that make that music in any genre, and has a thirst for learning some rules of survival in an industry unlike any other.

Very few people in the drum business or the music products industry have the opportunity to work with and for an American, an Asian, and a European manufacturer. They are vastly different from each other,…as is working for a family-owned business or an international corporation. I guess I am what is referred to as "A LIFER". meaning I remained working and connected with a single industry my entire career,..versus those that were "passing through" looking for fame, fortune or artistic identity. Lifers outlast and endure through the darkest years of an industry or company, as you will read. While you will learn about some of these, you will also have insights to the many wonderful people, places, events and opportunities that I have treasured and illustrate in each chapter.

Little did I, or my parents for that matter, know or anticipate the importance music would have on shaping my life, my life's work, and whatever recognition I may have received along the way within this music industry journey. The Music Products Industry is all about cause, effect, reaction, and outcome to the market, economy, popular music, trends, and who's in-charge. You will experience this as you read about the ever changing demands for creativity, profits and market share. Part of what makes *this* story unique are the multiple insights in to this industry's Retail, Wholesale-Distribution, and Manufacturing environments and workplaces. My journey is not limited to just percussion, but includes direct connections and experiences in acoustic, electronic and digital pianos, acoustic, electric, and classical guitars, and even some sound reinforcement excursion. Then there is the experience of having clients in professional development, healthcare equipment, music instruction publishing, commercial real-estate, and even a nineteen-year leadership of a non-profit trade association in the percussion industry.

For most of my professional life, I have had only very few regrets. It was a privilege to contribute my part to a company, client, project, product-line, educational event, or promotion that enhanced the musical products for the people that buy and play them.

It is my hope and intention that this journey through my on-going and still-in-development career will be of some encouragement to those considering the music products industry as a viable career path. For those industry colleagues reading this, I hope this will instill a "stick with it" attitude about your future.

I have been called a legend, an ambassador, and a life-long music advocate. The most valued reference I have is probably being thought of as a professional and friend to everyone I worked with or for, and whoever worked for me.

Fasten your seat belts for a journey that I hope you will find more than "interesting".

KARL DUSTMAN

Phil Collins
The Serious Tour
1990
FORUM
Quite Serious
1
NELSON
after the rain
world tour 90-91
VIP
MAR 11 1991
ROBERT PLANT
13
Manic
Nirvana
VIP·GUEST
AFTER SHOW ONLY
11-17-90
Linda Ronstadt
Cry like a rainstorm
TOUR 1990
GUEST
B 30
DH
PAUL
SIMON
TOUR 1991
3/7
AFTER SHOW ONLY
HARRY
CONNICK,
Jr.
ALABAMA
TOUR 1990's
HOUSE
9/15 Mark
Randy
TRAVIS
NO HOLDIN' BACK
GUEST PASS

Forward
William F. Ludwig III

It's not very often that we encounter a person in our working lives that can be called an associate, a business partner, confidant, mentor, fellow-employee,...and friend. Karl Dustman is one of those rare individuals who is qualified for each description.

When I started working for the family business in 1976, Karl had already been working for Ludwig for five years and had himself fully entrenched in the company, running the Educational Department. His presence in every aspect of the marketing, promotion, and trade-show exhibit areas was quickly seen and experienced. I found Karl to be an extremely detailed, organized, and professional leader in all aspects of his life. He was a joy to work with as he always had his projects and assignments prepared and ready in advance of any deadline.

As Ludwig's Advertising Manager/Artist Relations, I saw firsthand Karl's interaction with all the artists in every instrument category, the annual clinic programs with over three-hundred events, week-long international percussion symposiums on various college campuses and wuth all of the outside Ludwig Sales Representatives. Karl's passion for everything in percussion was contagious, which helped Ludwig achieve unprecedented success during the summer symposiums. I truly believe Karl's success rate is better than NASA's. He orchestrated everything like a well-oiled machine. At the same time, all the internal Ludwig administrative and production departments respected "KD", as he was referred to, including all levels of company management and the Ludwig family.

Anyone reading this book who already knows KD will thoroughly enjoy this snapshot of his lifelong career in percussion and the music products industry. For those meeting Karl through this book for the first time, you will have valuable insights to the drum business, the music products industry, working within American, Asian and European drum manufacturers,... while being encouraged to pursue a career in the music products field. I am certain this book will reflect many of the attributes that define an industry leader while being a friend to anyone he can help or assist.

Today, I continue to receive and value KD's continued support and encouragement with my own company. He has always been available for discussion, interested in guiding and creating multiple options and solutions for any situation.

Thank you, Karl, for sharing your LIFE IN PERCUSSION story with everyone who loves music, business, and percussion.

William F. Ludwig III
Founder & President
WFL III Drums & Percussion

JB0705 ORCH H 41 @ G-TYPE
25.00 ORCH / GATE D 25.00
COCA COLA AT JONES BEACH
THE DOOBIE BROTHERS
JOE WALSH
FRI JULY 5,1991 8:00PM
WBAB * RAIN OR SHINE
5JUL91 NO REF/EX/CAM/REC/BOT/CAN

DOOBIE BROTHERS
GUEST
7/20
GUEST
DOOBIE BROTHERS

SPECIAL GUEST
JAN 22 1990
PUMP
WORLD TOUR
1989 - 1991

WANTED
LIVE•IN•CONCERT
WARRANT
LAST SEEN WITH
SALOON
Tuesday, March 28 • 8PM
Nashville Center Stage
741-2787
KDF

Lionel Hampton/Chevron
JAZZ FESTIVAL 1990
BACK STAGE PASS

cellar door
PRODUCTIONS
PRESENTS
Los Lobos
Bont 4.
8·29·87

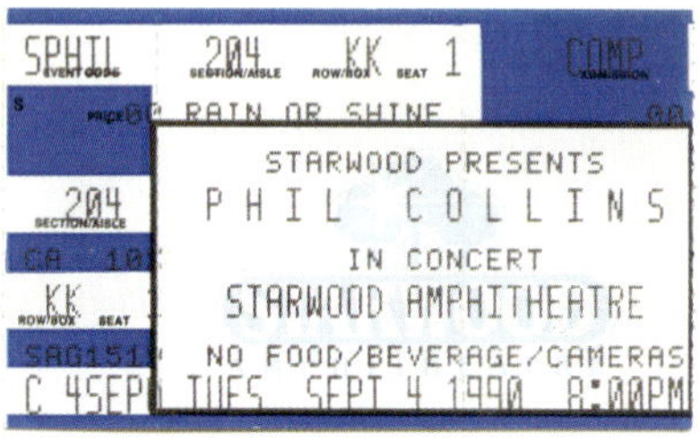

SPHIL 204 KK 1 COMP
RAIN OR SHINE
STARWOOD PRESENTS
PHIL COLLINS
IN CONCERT
STARWOOD AMPHITHEATRE
NO FOOD/BEVERAGE/CAMERAS
TUES SEPT 4 1990 8:00PM

WORKING
GUEST
CL8
JUL 15 1999
PRESS/PHOTO
PROMOTER
VANS
WARPED
TOUR 1999

AMATEUR HOUR IS OVER.
SHURE
WIRELESS SYSTEMS
ALL ACCESS

Chapter 1

It All Started With Elvis Presley and Learning the Guitar

MUSIC,.... Can be a lifelong friend, companion and motivation. It is there to celebrate the most wonderful times and occasions in life,. and yet music can also console a hurting heart filled with pain and sorrow. My family always had music in and around the house, my father played the Lowrey organ and my mother would sing along to Dad playing popular tunes they grew up with.

Something must have rubbed off on me.

This story begins in 1957 when the Dustman family had just relocated to Boardman, Ohio, during the summer of 1956. I was adjusting to a new school, new friends, neighbors, teachers and the popular music that was playing on the radio and black & white televisions throughout the country. Receiving an Arvin portable radio as a birthday present, music was around me all the time. The Elvis Presley craze was on. It was sweeping the country like a wildfire. I was an impressionable 8 year old and one of the millions of youngsters who wanted to be Elvis Presley. I was infatuated with his playing the guitar and shaking around on stage with everyone yelling and screaming. While maybe I didn't like all of the Presley music at that time, I liked his guitar playing, stage presence, and the national dominance he had on the music scene and young people. If he can do this... so can I.

I was a typical boy with interests in baseball, archery, bicycles, Topps baseball cards and particularly go-carts. Adjusting to a new home and school was traumatic at that young age, so when I gravitated to playing a musical instrument, regardless of my internal ambitions to emulate Elvis Presley, my parents agreed. They rented an acoustic folk guitar from the corner music store and I was signed up for weekly guitar lessons. It was a challenge to get me motivated to practice in between the private lessons. Despite the kind guitar teacher's honest efforts and even allowing me to test-play beautiful Gibson electric guitars from the display in the music store, I soon began to feel that this was more work than fun. The lessons were stopped and the rental guitar was returned to the music store. This was a learning expedition for me and my parents.

Going into the third grade at West Boulevard Elementary School in Boardman, I attended one of those beginning band student recruitment programs conducted on the small stage in the school's little gymnasium-auditorium. It was very much like we still do today, where the school has their concert band perform for all the students, they have the instruments on display and the whole program is basically a recruitment tool. It was then and there that I got bit by the drum bug. The school's band director, Mr. Mould, seemed to recognize my interest in drums and drumming. The road to drums and playing percussion began. I received some very basic drum lessons at school, and started participating in the third-grade band. The first pair of drum sticks and the small angled rubber practice pad were purchased to get me started. As the interest increased, so did the need for a beginning snare drum rental kit. My parents started with the instrument rental program and private beginning drum lessons at Dusi Music in Youngstown, Ohio. We rented a Slingerland white marine pearl snare drum in one of those accordion-style square cases and for the rest of my school days (all the way through high school) I was always involved in the school bands. The next-door neighbor boy of the same age attended the same school, but he was learning accordion at that same time, so we would occasionally play some duets for our parents. This made everyone happy to see the investment in private lessons paying off with some simple music be-

ing played.

By the end of 1959, it was decided that the family was moving back to our home in Northbrook, Illinois. This was traumatic once again, as each of us had started establishing connections. My mother was active in a number of community activities and my brother had just been confirmed in the local Lutheran Church and was in high school. We prepared to move immediately after Christmas vacation started and would resume our schooling in Northbrook right at the beginning of the New Year (1960).

I feel like my real commitment to drumming started

Northbrook family home rendering by Jerry Owings of Ludwig Industries

that Christmas season. My one-and-only Christmas gift wish was to visit to Karnes Music Store on Davis Street in Evanston, Illinois, to look into a drum. While I really wanted a blue sparkle drum we settled on an in-stock Ludwig Super Classic 5"x14" with the usual accordion-style suitcase containing the stand, pad and sticks, etc. This was the best Christmas gift ever for 1959. This started the sequence of drums and related equipment becoming the "wished for" gift for every birthday and Christmas present thereafter. Every gift from then on had something to do with more drums; sticks, pedals, cowbell holders, etc.

It felt good to be in the fifth grade back in North-

A Memorable Moment:

I was too young at the time to realize the sacrifice my parents were making at that time, as we returned to Northbrook in early December without my father having a job to come back to. The $150.00 new Ludwig Snare Drum Kit purchase was probably a real financial strain for the family budget at that time.

brook, Illinois, where my family was from. My parents were recognizing my deep interest and commitment to playing drums. Clearly I was thoroughly enjoying my participation in the school's concert band. My mother had made certain that I could get into the fifth grade band at Crestwood Elementary School immediately upon my return to classes in Northbrook in January. Stuart Ludlow was the band director for the elementary schools in Northbrook. He covered both the Northbrook and Glenview schools as an independent music educator rather than an employee of the school districts. I was intent on putting together a Ludwig drum set, one drum at a time and the Christmas wish list for December 1960 was a matching Ludwig 14"x22" Super Classic bass drum with Speed King Pedal and shell-mount cymbal arm. My parents granted that

Christmas wish once again and included a used 14" Zildjian cymbal. I was now "playing drum set" for real.

By random coincidence, a fifth-grade teacher at my school, Bill Olive, was a prior professional drummer in the Navy band. He was not my fifth grade teacher, but he saw me rehearsing with the fifth grade band in the gymnasium and took an interest in helping me out. Bill Olive had a private drum lesson teaching studio called Drum Specialist in his home in Glenview, the next town over. He agreed to give me private lessons on drum set and took this very seriously. My parents drove me over to his basement teaching studio once a week for help developing my reading and 4-way coordination skills. He had all the drum company posters on the walls, he sold sticks, heads and accessories, and this was a very cool place to come to for lessons. I continued there for as long as I felt I was getting better and could start taking these basic drumming skills further on my own.

Like most young drummers of that time I was of course studying every Ludwig catalog that came out. I had the pages memorized, the product model numbers were branded into my head. I was well aware that the Ludwig Drum factory was only a few miles away in Chicago. My father agreed to my request to visit Ludwig for a factory tour. That visit fueled my enthusiasm for drumming even more and I came away from the factory feeling that someday working for Ludwig would be the ultimate dream job. While I don't remember the name of the person who gave us the factory tour, it was amazing, about two hours long, and we went through every manufacturing department on every floor. I remember to this very day my enthusiasm for seeing where my drums were made. The smell of wood, sawdust everywhere, glue, sounds of drilling, sanding…. all brought to life the building of drums.

I was immersed in every school band or orchestra performing group I could get into. Sixth grade had begun and the snazzy blue concert band uniforms with white contrasting braids and waist-belts with gold buckles were really cool. I was so focused on making music that my academic subject grades were slipping and my parents were not happy when report cards came out. I recall vividly the threat to take me out of all music programs unless I get my grades up. This did not happen overnight and the wished-for Christmas present of the 9"x13" Ludwig mounted tom to match my bass and snare was in question.

I played in all the various school bands and orchestras, and believed it was only a matter of time before I would be performing in other settings. I set my sights on what looked like a perfect launching pad, the nationally televised Ted Mack Amateur Hour which was taped in Chicago. The show featured all

A Memorable Moment:

By now I was working and saving my money by cutting lawns and doing yard work around the neighborhood to fund my planned drum and accessory purchases. As Christmas of 1961 approached it was apparent that the "must have 9x13" Mounted Tom with holder" was not going to arrive for Christmas, as my grades had not met my parent's requirements. My brother agreed to help me take matters into my own hands by ordering the Ludwig tom on my own. That involved taking the bass drum I had received the year before to Karnes Music in Evanston, to have the tom mount installed on it. Unnoticed by our parents, we carried this huge bass drum on the blue Glenview Bus Co. bus into downtown Evanston, stopping at Karnes Music. We ordered the Ludwig tom, provided the bass drum for Karnes Music to drill and mount the tom holder, and paid for the complete purchase transaction in full. We returned home and waited for word from Karnes Music as to when the drums would be delivered to our home. The Karnes salesman, Ted Dolan, lived in Northbrook, and had agreed to deliver it. Somehow the two drums and receipt were delivered to the house when I was NOT home to secretly receive my order. Our mother answered the door, now learning that Karl had ordered the drum, had the tom holder mounted, and the order was completed and paid for. My brother and I each caught our own version of hell from both parents. I was informed that "we ruined Christmas" and that BOTH drums were confiscated until further notice.

sorts of performers; singers, dancers, mimes, magicians, and of course musicians. My parents agreed to help me apply for the audition and get my drum kit to the studio. The show provided professional musician accompanists so I had a pianist and bassist. We played three or four standards, they thanked me and said they would call. They never called, which was part of that whole learning experience. It did not dampen my enthusiasm for drumming. This was a time when I was listening to a lot of Dave Brubeck Quartet, the Oscar Peterson trio and Ramsey Lewis; primarily jazz and popular standards along with big bands. I did not get caught up in the "British Invasion" that was happening at that time (Not that I was opposed to that, it just wasn't my thing.)

I was expanding my 33 1/3 LP record collection. I received an album for Christmas titled HI FI DRUMS, featuring Buddy Rich, Louis Bellson, and four other leading drummers. This Capitol Records monaural recording introduced me to the magic of Buddy Rich, and I played this album over and over, learning the rhythms, the various licks, and sounds coming from Buddy's solos and his backing of Woody Herman's Herd Big Band. Before long I learned that Buddy was coming to Chicago with his band for a performance at the Scotch Mist Club in downtown Chicago. A Buddy Rich CLINIC was being also promoted on a Sunday afternoon. I convinced my parents that I *had* to be there to see and experience Buddy Rich. We went into the city, my mother accompanied my brother and I, while my father went around the corner to a movie theater to see Never On Sunday.

Buddy apparently was angry at the poor attendance for the clinic and decided to start the event two hours late. My parents were not happy, but this event ignited the determination that I could spend the rest of my life playing drums even though I could never become as good as Buddy. Buddy autographed my HI FI DRUMS album, which I still have on display in my office.

By the middle of junior high school I began to feel the urge to expand my percussion awareness and start playing a melodic instrument like vibraphone. While I loved drums, I did not want to always be relegated to the drummer position behind the band. I liked the sound of a vibraphone which was prominent in a lot of the music that I was listening to. Once again, my parents supported my ambition and we went down to Franks Drum Shop on Wabash Avenue in downtown Chicago to look at Vibes, new and used. This was a fantastic drum shop where they had every vibe imaginable; Deagan, Musser, Jenco.... some were new, some were used, some were consignments... That was my first introduction to Maurie Lishon and he was very accommodating to my interest and appreciated my parent's support and encouragement while finding a way to provide this percussion instrument. We ultimately decided that a Musser M45 One-Niter from Karnes Music in Des Plaines, Illinois, was the way to go. When the instrument arrived at the store from Musser and we were advised that we should come and pick-up the instrument, I felt the same excitement and anticipation as I did with each instrument in building my drum set over the years.

Initially, I made little one-inch square index-card note-labels for each of the bars to identify the correct notes. By the time the labels vibrated off, I'd learned the keyboard and had a basic grasp of reading treble-clef music. Karnes Music had a percussion vibe instructor, Joe Zawierucka, who would come to our house to give me lessons for thirty minutes every week, then we changed the schedule to every two weeks to allow for more time to practice between lessons. Joe was a young starting-out musician, but took the time and effort to see that I got started correctly on this new Musser Vibe, He would arrive at each lesson with new mallet reading exercises, scales and simple tunes. This was all done on the purple-ink mimeograph paper at that time. This foundation in mallet keyboard (Vibes) opened many doors in my percussion studies and education. I could now read and thoroughly understand both bass and treble clef music.

A Memorable Moment:

For a short time, my father was employed by Karnes Music Company as an electrical engineer, making house calls for repairing various brands of electronic organs. Marian Karnes mentioned at some point during the Vibraphone purchase that I might enjoy attending the NAMM convention (National Association of Music Merchants) in June held at the Palmer House Hotel on State Street in downtown Chicago. He arranged for two guest passes for my Mother and I and we took the Milwaukee Road train into Union Station. At the Palmer House I experienced my first introduction to the vast music products industry, seeing all the various brands of drums and all music instruments on display in the hundreds of various guest suites. The displaying companies took all the furniture out of the rooms and set up massive displays in the parlors and sleeping rooms. All the boxes were thrown in the bathrooms for storage. Ludwig, Slingerland, Rogers, Camco, Trixon, Remo etc. were there and welcomed my visit through their exhibit area, wearing my Karnes Music Co. NAMM Guest Badge. My mother had problems walking long distances so she would wait in the grand lobby of the hotel while I would go to every floor in the hotel, walking through all the percussion instrument display rooms. Absolutely amazing to an enthusiastic twelve year old boy…attending his first NAMM convention and getting his introduction to the music products industry.

I listened to all the recordings of Cal Tjader/Solar Heat, Milt Jackson of the Modern Jazz Quartet, Red Norvo, Lionel Hampton, and of course Gary Burton. Sergio Mendez and Brazil 66 was extremely popular and I was listening to and purchasing all their albums. I regularly received a new album or two for Christmas or Birthday which included the wonderful series of Persuasive Percussion and Provocative Percussion albums on the Command label. The diversity of percussive sounds, rhythms and textures hypnotized me into wanting to learn and play ALL these wonderful percussion instruments I heard. The interest in anything percussive was like a powerful magnet that took over my entire life and ambition.

I had a junior high band director, Stuart Ludlow, that recognized my thirst for making music and love of drums. I wanted to start my own small dance band (then called jazz ensemble) which would perform mostly at school events. Ted Collison had the largest living room, so we rehearsed at his house. We had simple ensemble books scored for all the different instruments, but we needed professional rehearsal direction. My parents created a letter that asked each band member's parents if they would contribute $10.00 a month towards hiring a suitable music director that would help the band progress. Director Mr. Ludlow had a son that was in college pursuing a music education degree. He was hired to rehearse the band every other week. That was the beginning of my "band leader days".

(L-R) Bill Kuhlin, Craig Smith, Lee Arbetman, Karl

(L-R) Craig Smith, Karl, Jim Goettsche

I was getting somewhat proficient on Vibes, and wanted to try a more simple approach to creating various small combos. It was no problem to find a pianist/organist, a clarinet/sax player, and a drummer at school. We occasionally used a bass also, but generally the organist played the bass parts. We were known as the Karl Dustman Trio, then a quartet, The Four Sharps. I promoted the group as entertainment for classmates, which went over quite well as there were not many student combos at the time. There was the school orchestra, the marching band and the concert band, but this was different.

Onward to Glenbrook North High School in Northbrook. I was thrilled to be accepted in the "Spartan Varsity Band"…. as a Freshman. Very few from the Jr. High band went directly into the Varsity band for their first year. Coming into high school, the treble clef experience I'd gotten on the vibraphone came in very useful in the school band where I was called on to play orchestra bells/chimes and related melodic percussion instruments. This also extended my Timpani performance starting in my 2nd year. The high school band director, Harold Smith, had a military background and of course had a profound impact on my musical development. I played in every possible school band, orchestra, group, ensemble, and marching band that I could arrange to join. I enrolled in every possible music class that was offered; Music Theory, Western Civilization Music, and Music Appreciation, for all four years of high school. Some of this I enjoyed, some not. I kept wanting the teachers to use and play Jazz in these mostly classical music-oriented classes. I survived and got through it. Today, I occasionally use and refer to those very same textbooks kept in my library all these years, to help with a music question or foreign language musical interpretation.

During these high school years I continued to stay in contact regularly with Karnes Music Company and they continued to send me invitations for various Ludwig Drum Company key dealer events that they provide me dealer guest passes for. These were primarily percussion concerts, produced by Ludwig for their dealer guest attending the summer NAMM convention annually in Chicago. SOUND SPECTACULAR 63' was produced by Dick Schory under the promotional and financial banner of Ludwig at Orchestra Hall in downtown Chicago. An Evening With Dick Schory and His Percussion Pops Orchestra in June of 1964 at Orchestra Hall was another momentous event underwritten by Ludwig and Zildjian. New Dimensions in Sound, MUSIC 66' in July at the Conrad Hilton Grand Ballroom featured Dick Schory and his Percussion Pops Orchestra along with Dave Brubeck and the Quartet. All three of these live music percussion performance features had deep impact on my appreciation for the diversity of percussion sounds and instruments. The ability of the musicians and the showcasing of percussion making a full concert a memorable experience stays with me to this day. I don't believe there has been anything like these Ludwig dealer concert events that created as much recognition for the company.

My grades began to slip (again) because I was too busy with all of the musical opportunities to spend time studying. Of course my parents were not too happy that I was getting A's and B's in all of my music classes but was slipping in math, science, history etc. I was given the ultimatum that either the grades would come up in those other disciplines, or I would be removed from every single music program. That got my attention very quickly and I knuckled down and got back into balance between the music making, music classes and academics.

A Memorable Moment:

Organist Craig Smith was expanding his connection in the area for public performances with my combo, The Four Sharps. Somehow he was able to get us booked playing the DesPlaines Moose Lodge on a Saturday evening. We weren't even old enough to drive,no less performing as minors in a BAR! The manager kept reminding us to not tell anyone in the place our age as it was against the law for minors to be IN the bar, no less playing music in the place. We were paid $25.00 per person for a three-hour gig and thought we had made the big time. My father volunteered to drive me to the venue, and decided to stay for the entire three hours, grabbing a seat in the bar, listening to the band. We didn't get home till 1am. What a Father!

(L-R) Bill Durling, Rob Rennix, Karl, Jim Bovinet, Steve Summers

Rock and Roll was not a favorite of mine, but THE SEMIS, which was a little out of character for me, invited me to be their drummer. I was not keen at playing *Louie, Louie* and but I played it- along with *Wipeout* at every performance. The band became very popular at high school, playing all the hot rock tunes and occasionally some Sandy Nelson, *Let There Be Drums* renditions.

The combos I was leading and playing Vibes in were getting pretty good local exposure, playing on stages at the local annual summer Northbrook Days Carnival, and for local school plays. Organist Craig Smith was starting to get associated with Karnes Music Company by assisting with some light teaching, product demonstration, and beginning his keyboard sales career.

As a result, over the course of our four years of high school, Craig got the band invited to headline or perform at four Karnes Organ Club open-to-the-public Concert demo events. These were designed to demonstrate the use of the home organ for combo use and enjoyment. I used these spotlight appearances to "sell and book the band" at private events to those in the audience.

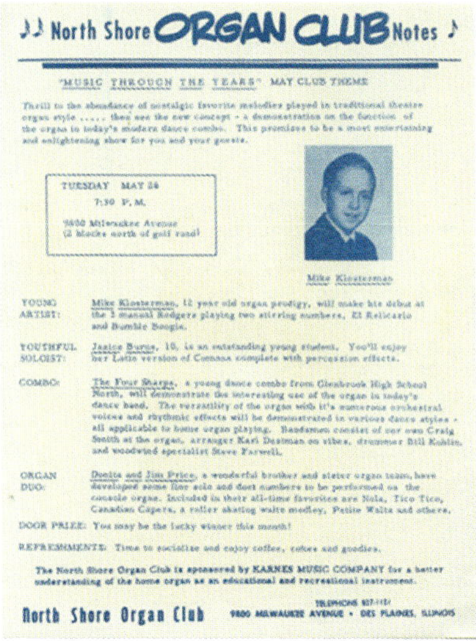

North Shore ORGAN CLUB Notes

"MUSIC THROUGH THE YEARS" MAY CLUB THEME

Thrill to the abundance of nostalgic favorite melodies played in traditional theatre organ style ..... then see the new concept - a demonstration on the function of the organ in today's modern dance combo. This promises to be a most entertaining and enlightening show for you and your guests.

TUESDAY MAY 24
7:30 P. M.
9800 Milwaukee Avenue
(2 blocks north of golf road)

Mike Klosterman

YOUNG ARTIST: Mike Klosterman, 12 year old organ prodigy, will make his debut at the 3 manual Rodgers playing two stirring numbers, El Relicario and Bumble Boogie.

YOUTHFUL SOLOIST: Janice Burns, 10, is an outstanding young student. You'll enjoy her Latin version of Comanna complete with percussion effects.

COMBO: The Four Sharps, a young dance combo from Glenbrook High School North, will demonstrate the interesting use of the organ in today's dance band. The versatility of the organ with it's numerous orchestral voices and rhythmic effects will be demonstrated in various dance styles - all applicable to home organ playing. Bandsmen consist of our own Craig Smith at the organ, arranger Karl Dustman on vibes, drummer Bill Kuhlin, and woodwind specialist Steve Farwell.

ORGAN DUO: Donita and Jim Price, a wonderful brother and sister organ team, have developed some fine solo and duet numbers to be performed on the console organ. Included in their all-time favorites are Nola, Tico Tico, Canadian Capers, a roller skating waltz medley, Petite Waltz and others.

DOOR PRIZE: You may be the lucky winner this month!

REFRESHMENTS: Time to socialize and enjoy coffee, cakes and goodies.

The North Shore Organ Club is sponsored by KARNES MUSIC COMPANY for a better understanding of the home organ as an educational and recreational instrument.

North Shore Organ Club TELEPHONE 827-1151 9800 MILWAUKEE AVENUE • DES PLAINES, ILLINOIS

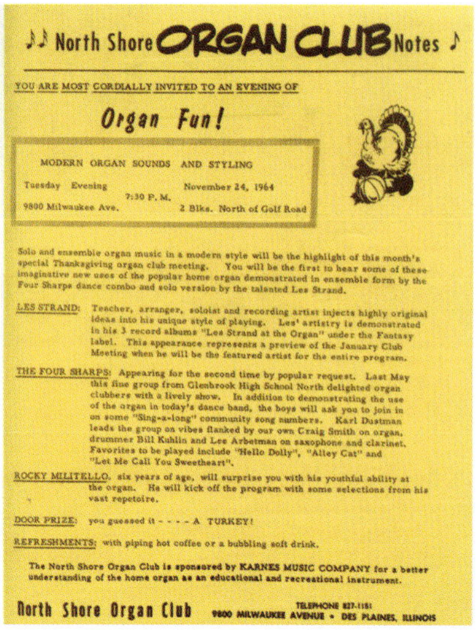

North Shore ORGAN CLUB Notes

YOU ARE MOST CORDIALLY INVITED TO AN EVENING OF

Organ Fun!

MODERN ORGAN SOUNDS AND STYLING
Tuesday Evening 7:30 P. M. November 24, 1964
9800 Milwaukee Ave. 2 Blks. North of Golf Road

Solo and ensemble organ music in a modern style will be the highlight of this month's special Thanksgiving organ club meeting. You will be the first to hear some of these imaginative new uses of the popular home organ demonstrated in ensemble form by the Four Sharps dance combo and solo version by the talented Les Strand.

LES STRAND: Teacher, arranger, soloist and recording artist injects highly original ideas into his unique style of playing. Les' artistry is demonstrated in his 3 record albums "Les Strand at the Organ" under the Fantasy label. This appearance represents a preview of the January Club Meeting when he will be the featured artist for the entire program.

THE FOUR SHARPS: Appearing for the second time by popular request. Last May this fine group from Glenbrook High School North delighted organ clubbers with a lively show. In addition to demonstrating the use of the organ in today's dance band, the boys will ask you to join in on some "Sing-a-long" community song numbers. Karl Dustman leads the group on vibes flanked by our own Craig Smith on organ, drummer Bill Kuhlin and Lee Arbetman on saxophone and clarinet. Favorites to be played include "Hello Dolly", "Alley Cat" and "Let Me Call You Sweetheart".

ROCKY MILITELLO, six years of age, will surprise you with his youthful ability at the organ. He will kick off the program with some selections from his vast repetoire.

DOOR PRIZE: you guessed it - - - - A TURKEY!

REFRESHMENTS: with piping hot coffee or a bubbling soft drink.

The North Shore Organ Club is sponsored by KARNES MUSIC COMPANY for a better understanding of the home organ as an educational and recreational instrument.

North Shore Organ Club TELEPHONE 827-1151 9800 MILWAUKEE AVENUE • DES PLAINES, ILLINOIS

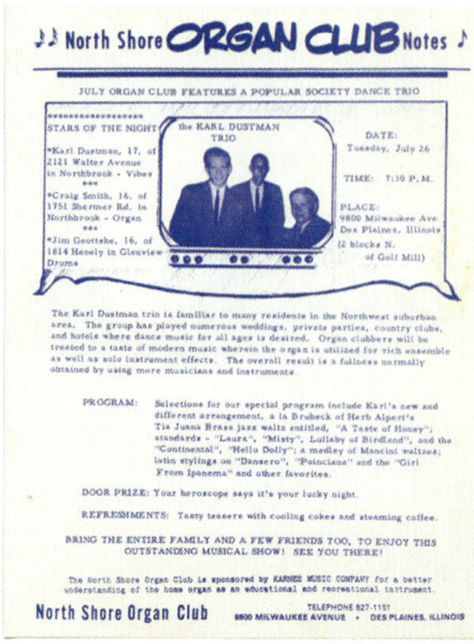

North Shore ORGAN CLUB Notes

JULY ORGAN CLUB FEATURES A POPULAR SOCIETY DANCE TRIO

STARS OF THE NIGHT
*Karl Dustman, 17, of 2121 Walter Avenue in Northbrook - Vibes
*Craig Smith, 16, of 1751 Shermer Rd. in Northbrook - Organ
*Jim Geottshe, 16, of 1814 Henely in Glenview Drums

the KARL DUSTMAN TRIO

DATE: Tuesday, July 26
TIME: 7:30 P. M.
PLACE: 9800 Milwaukee Ave. Des Plaines, Illinois (2 blocks N. of Golf Mill)

The Karl Dustman trio is familiar to many residents in the Northwest suburban area. The group has played numerous weddings, private parties, country clubs, and hotels where dance music for all ages is desired. Organ clubbers will be treated to a taste of modern music wherein the organ is utilized for rich ensemble as well as solo instrument effects. The overall result is a fullness normally obtained by using more musicians and instruments.

PROGRAM: Selections for our special program include Karl's new and different arrangement, a la Brubeck of Herb Alpert's Tia Juana Brass jazz waltz entitled, "A Taste of Honey"; standards - "Laura", "Misty", Lullaby of Birdland", and the "Continental", "Hello Dolly"; a medley of Mancini waltzes; latin stylings on "Dansero", "Poinciana" and the "Girl From Ipanema" and other favorites.

DOOR PRIZE: Your horoscope says it's your lucky night.

REFRESHMENTS: Tasty teasers with cooling cokes and steaming coffee.

BRING THE ENTIRE FAMILY AND A FEW FRIENDS TOO, TO ENJOY THIS OUTSTANDING MUSICAL SHOW! SEE YOU THERE!

The North Shore Organ Club is sponsored by KARNES MUSIC COMPANY for a better understanding of the home organ as an educational and recreational instrument.

North Shore Organ Club TELEPHONE 827-1151 9800 MILWAUKEE AVENUE • DES PLAINES, ILLINOIS

North Shore ORGAN CLUB Notes

TEEN-AGERS WILL BE IN THE SPOTLIGHT AT MAY 25th MEETING

An annual favorite among Organ Clubbers, the May "Teen Special" program will be a very lively and entertaining show. The Four Sharps, last year's headliners, will be back along with a strong supporting cast. The selections will range from classical to swing and should appeal to all Organ Clubbers regardless of age and musical tastes. Plan now to attend and give your support to these youthful performers who have worked hard in preparing their numbers.

TUESDAY MAY 25th

7:30 P. M.

9800 Milwaukee Ave., Des Plaines
(2 blocks north of golf road)

THE FOUR SHARPS

As my junior year in high school began, I tried to talk to the school counselors about career options in music, but they really had no suggestions. (It seemed like they never experienced anyone seeking a career in music and were at a loss as to where to begin). It was pretty much up to my parents to figure out "What are we going to do with Karl?" Music was all I talked about, all I seemed to be interested in. I seemed to have some natural talent at it, so my parents began to investigate music schools that we could consider after High School. We narrowed it down to Eastman, New England Conservatory, Berklee, and Juilliard. During the summer of 1966 we took a long distance driving tour to each school mentioned, stopping at the school, meeting the percussion instructor and each school's Registrar. I had an aunt and uncle living in Astoria, New York, who offered to help with the logistics of an audition at Julliard School of Music in New York if I chose to pursue that for an application and or attendance in the fall of 1967. My entire junior year of high school was spent preparing for the Julliard audition. The result was a cordial "Thanks, but no thanks." from Julliard. I was of course extremely disappointed. The family decision was pretty much that I would remain in Chicago, continue teaching, continue playing in combos, and continue studying percussion- all while considering some other new career path. The career path that I eventually discovered was marketing.

JUILLIARD SCHOOL OF MUSIC
PETER MENNIN, President
120 Claremont Avenue, New York, N. Y. 10027

OFFICE OF THE REGISTRAR

March 9, 1967

Mr. Karl Dustman
2131 Walter Avenue
Northbrook, Illinois 60062

Dear Mr. Dustman:

I regret to inform you that, on the basis of the entrance examinations, we are unable to admit you to Juilliard School of Music at this time.

While this decision will undoubtedly be a disappointment to you, I hope that you will bear in mind that the results of the examinations are in no way to be construed as an attempt to predict your future success in your chosen field, but rather as an attempt to determine by faculty judgment whether or not you are ready to study at this particular school at this time.

Juilliard School of Music is limited in the number of students it can accept each year on the basis of the number of vacancies in each departent. Therefore, the purpose of the examinations is to select those students who now seem best prepared to enter into and make progress in a program of study at the School in the year ahead. Students not admitted for the approaching school year are free to make reapplication at some future time with every assurance that they will again be considered without prejudice.

If you feel that you would profit by a personal interview regarding the results of the entrance examinations, we shall be glad to have you call MOnument 3-7200, Extension 88, in approximately two weeks and make an appointment for an interview with Miss Irene Anderson, Assistant to the Registrar.

Sincerely,

Judson Ehrbar
Registrar

JE:rob

1961
Ludwig

Chapter 2

Music Center of Deerfield, Entry to the Music Industry

By the time I was fourteen years old, I was trying to earn money through a variety of revenue-producing activities. Knowing that my sixteenth birthday was approaching and with it came the ability to have a driver's license, I was intent on purchasing my first automobile immediately after I got my Illinois state driver's license. My under-age working included working Saturdays at the local bicycle shop fixing flat tires for $1.00 an hour, under-the-table. And at the same time, I developed a beginner drum teaching practice for the local kids who wanted to learn drums. Little did I know I was about to enter the music products industry.

A Memorable Moment:

Within two months after qualifying for my drivers license we started looking for a suitable automobile for Karl. The perfect 1963 Chevrolet Impala Convertible showed up on the Jennings Chevrolet used-car lot. Since the age of 14 I had been saving money that I earned cutting lawns, doing yard work for neighbors, and working in the bicycle shop. The $3000 I had saved was a little short, but my parents agreed to loan me the additional $600 that I needed.

As a result of giving private lessons on drum set in my parent's living room, I realized there was a greater money-making opportunity to be realized. I approached Carl Bernardi who owned and operated the Music Center of Deerfield along with his wife, Wanda. I was sixteen years old in 1965 but looked twenty-something. I asked about a teaching position at the store, as this was the only real music store around my home. I taught in the evenings during the week and started out with four to five 30 minute private lessons. Before long I had 40 private lesson students a week. Saturdays became so busy that I had to eat my lunch during a lesson as the scheduling was constant from 9 am to 5 pm, which meant sixteen thirty-minute lessons in one day. The fact that I was also playing Saturday nights with one band or another compounded the intensity that I had created for myself. And of course this was all while I was going to high school at the same time. I was young and full of energy and ambition. I was eager to sort out what I saw as many different musical opportunities in my future. While the rejection from entering Juilliard School of Music in New York was a disappointment, I realized I had a lot of good things going on in my life during my senior year of high school here in Chicago and I was making excellent money combining all the different things I was working on.

Music Center today, Waukegan Road, Deerfield, IL

Carl and Wanda Bernardi were wonderful "first bosses" at the Music Center. I believe Carl saw himself in my youthful can-do character, my professionalism, and my determination to grow-up quickly. I truly enjoyed working with the drum students I was teaching as well as my conversations with their parents in the store environment. By the middle of my senior year, I had left the Sales position at the Schwinn bicycle shop in Northbrook and concentrated exclusively on working at the Music Center of Deerfield. I advised Carl Bernardi of my intention to stay in the area after high school, starting a Marketing-Business Administration major at DePaul University in downtown Chicago. By now I was already helping with the ordering of Ludwig, Gretsch, and Slingerland drum sets, accessories, drum instruction books and even using my early experiences with guitar playing to help with the sales and service of the huge guitar student population going through the store on a weekly basis.

After graduation, I got my own apartment in Deerfield less than a half-mile from the Music Center. Now I was going to classes at DePaul in the city full time five days a week. I would take the 7 am train into Union Station and scheduled myself to be back in the Deerfield at the Music Center by 3:30 in the afternoon to start the many after-school drum lessons that were scheduled. Sometimes the private lesson schedule would end at 9 pm when the store closed. Anyone who has ever taught a musical instrument with 35-40 lessons a week knows you can burn-out quickly from giving these many lessons. The store owners saw this developing and sought a solution that would serve everyone. They came up with a combination that involved less private teaching and more of helping with staffing and other managerial duties. This included placing purchase orders, interviewing and selecting new private teachers, and doing anything that was necessary to run the store and business during the hours I was there; afternoons during the week and all day on Saturday. I became the store manager at the age of 19.

Whether I knew it or not,… I was IN the MUSIC PRODUCTS INDUSTRY now. The experiences were life-changing and the business side of my sales, people-skills and professionalism seemed to override the performance element of music making.

While I was still either leading a combo or playing in multiple bands, I had begun taking orchestral percussion private lessons through DePaul University where I met percussion legend Bob Tilles. Tilles was the widely recognized percussion director at DePaul and I studied all aspects of percussion under him. This was not through the school of music at DePaul, I studied privately with him while I was completing my marketing major. I had no idea that down the road I would learn that Bob Tilles was one of the most in-demand clinicians that the Ludwig drum company had.

In total, the Music Center of Deerfield had between 300 and 350 students per week, so there were a lot of administrative duties to keep me busy while I was working there. I was responsible for helping in organizing group bus trips to regional competitions in Chicago, working on the student ensemble registration documents, orchestrating parent chaperones, transportation, and so forth. This was primarily Accordion, Guitar and Percussion competition events.

I loved what I was doing at the music store. I was experiencing and immersed in almost facet of the retail store and teaching studio operation. I was learning and absorbing everything I could. This learning curve dramatically increased when the store started offering private lessons for band instrument lessons. Now the store was stocking, selling, and servicing saxophones, flutes, clarinets, and trumpets and related accessories. Orchestral string instruments were not taught, but the store did offer replacement strings and professional servicing for violins, violas, cellos and string basses. WOW!

The Music Center farmed-out the repair, service, and adjustment work to a local band instrument repair technician in Libertyville, Sage Band Instrument. Gary Sage was the principle repair man and I found myself making one or two trips per week up to his repair shop to drop-off or pick-up repaired instruments. This forced me to quickly learn the various parts needing repair-service, the names of the parts, writing the customer repair tickets, figuring the gross margin mark-up the Music Center owners required, and all the necessary vocabulary associated with selling and servicing these band and orchestral instruments to the Music Center's customers. Little did I realize the foundation and wealth of knowledge and experience I was gaining each and every day… just by being in this work environment and willing to do whatever was required. The Music Center owners recognized my grasp of how everything was connected in this retail setting and the extremely broad reach of knowledge, experience and people-personality that is required to run a profitable music store with a sizable private lesson program. By now I had hired a talented young man, Jim Hunt, to take all the percussion students, as my time and energy was completely focused on helping to run the Music Center's operations.

This retail experience also allowed me to create some interesting music making opportunities with various private teachers at the Music Center. Michael Conforti was an excellent jazz guitarist and we knew all the same tunes which resulted in a few opportunities to perform professionally around the area. Bob Dehm was the instructor for sax-clarinet and flute, finishing his degree from Northwestern University as a performance major, He eventually worked at learning, playing, and teaching the electronic guitar, really well. Bill Putney was another gifted guitar instructor with ambitions of composing music that would become a number one Billboard chart hit. He formed a "recording band" that recorded demos of his tunes for presentation to *The Association*, *Bread,* and similar popular recording bands, hoping they would "record one of his tunes". I went with him a couple times when he arranged meetings with these celebrity bands to "pitch" his tune through the recorded demo. Unfortunately, nothing really developed for this newly composed music or the band recording the demo with all the vocals.

Life was good for a twenty-three year old young man that was going to college, studying percussion with a dedicated professional instructor, working in a music store 30-40 hours a week, and gigging with some of the store's private teachers in between everything else. I had my own car, my own apartment in Deerfield and I was making more money than I could have ever imagined.

In spite of the financial success I was enjoying, I could see that I did not want to spend the next 50 years running a music store. I knew I had decades of work ahead of me and I really wanted to try some different things. I wanted to find out what big business was all about, how corporate American worked. At the same time I guess I was ready for a change and a self-inflicted test of ability in applying everything I thought I knew in a totally different structure.

I started sending out confidential letters of interest with a resume to a number of very large corporations that were either headquartered in Chicagoland or had sizable presence in the area. I selectively pursued the usual Xerox, Pitney Bowes, and IBM as a starting point. Much to my surprise I heard back from the IBM branch office in Evanston, Illinois, on Central street. This was just down the street from Dyke Stadium where the Northwestern University Wildcat Marching Band would perform and rehearse for their football games. Administrative Operations Manager Bob Underwood interviewed me along with his assistant, Sherwin Geitner. They must have seen enough personality and determination to overshadow whatever I was lacking in related experience. They offered me an administrative position. That required a twenty-five percent pay-cut, just to take the position. I had a couple days to think about it and decided to make the leap-of-faith to a new opportunity, a new career outside of music, and a new business environment I had never experienced before.

I gave my two weeks' notice at the Music Center of Deerfield. Carl and Wanda Bernardi were extremely disappointed because of the friendship and trust that had grown among us since my starting there at age 16. They were a fantastic couple to work for and I still use today (and have used in every music-related position I have since had) everything I ever learned through that music store experience.

I think it only took a couple of weeks shuffling papers at IBM as a sales forecaster to begin feeling that I'd made the biggest mistake of my life. I have no hard feelings toward IBM, but I just felt like a square peg in a round hole. I simply did not fit their corporate model. I felt very out of place in the corporate turf wars, political agendas, and other machinations of corporate ladder-climbing. I felt I would become pigeon-holed for life, waiting for someone to die or retire in order to move up the ranks and regain the significant earnings sacrifice I'd made to accept the position. This was clearly a mistake I made and was no fault of anyone at IBM. Everyone there treated me wonderfully, they appreciated my professionalism, wardrobe, can-do attitude and willingness to try any new assignment the branch office wanted me to take on. But I felt like an employee number (#226946) rather than a person.

The IBM position only required a basic 8:30 am to 5 pm work day. This left me with some time that I felt I needed to keep my sanity- by getting back to music. I had time to continue the orchestral percussion lessons with Bob Tilles at DePaul University in Chicago, and I kept in touch with a select few of the Music Center private instructors. A year into the IBM position it was approaching the branch's once-every-five-year dinner gala designed to recognize people and branch achievements for the past five years. I convinced my Administrative Operations Manager, who was in charge of organizing the event, that they needed a LIVE BAND for this formal sit-down dinner party taking place at the Pyrenees Restaurant in Skokie, Illinois. I assembled a quartet which included three of my regular musicians and used THE FOUR SHARPS as the name.

Branch office Operations Manager Robert Underwood (L). presenting a performance award to Karl Dustman.

I added Bob Dehm from the Music Center teacher roster playing acoustic-electric guitar. I played Vibes, and everyone seemed to enjoy the music and the performance. I believe I requested $300 for the band's 2-set performance, which was approved..

I of course kept working my 40-hour week at the IBM Evanston branch office but felt increasingly frustrated while knowing I had to move on and move out as soon as a suitable position could be found. I knew the word "responsibility" and the costs of having your own apartment and living and providing for yourself. It was not easy- This job-replacement process took took me nearly two and a half years. The MUSIC BUSINESS was calling me back in my mind, but I needed a logical sequence and destination to make another move and wanting to avoid any negative employment track record perspective about "moving around too much".

As I tried to find somewhere else to work, I started sending a resume to Frank Peppler at the Ludwig Drum Company. He was the Vice President of Sales at this time and seemed like the logical person to approach about a position at Ludwig. I followed it up with a letter after a couple of weeks. Another letter six months later, and another follow-up letter.... And six months later another letter. I was persistent, but not to the point of being annoying. Sometimes the letter was simply to congratulate Ludwig on their new catalog or a new ad or product announcement that I considered exciting. I wanted to keep my name coming up in his mail and memory as a "determined young man with a mission, wanting to come to Ludwig".

In June of 1972 I received a call from Frank Peppler's secretary inviting me to come into the Ludwig offices for a meeting with Mr. Peppler. Of course I accepted and we scheduled the appointment. I was MORE than thrilled at the prospect of working for THE LARGEST DRUM COMPANY IN THE WORLD. As it turned out, what created their interest in me and appealed to their present needs at Ludwig was not that I loved drums, or that I could play all of the percussion instruments, but that I had experience in sales forecasting.

SALES FORECASTING was the magic word that appeared in the resume and that's what Ludwig was in need of. I not only knew what sales forecasting was, but how to implement it.... how the sales and manufacturing departments depended on this information, and how it had to be presented. It didn't matter that I was a player, a teacher, or a drummer. It was the idea that I was someone who knew the Ludwig product line, their model numbers, all the different terminology, and could format the information so that it was useful to the company. This was SALES FORCASTING.

As the transition from IBM to Ludwig settled in, my life and mind returned to working in an environment that I took pleasure and pride in. It was a long two and a half year experience at IBM, but without this detour I may have never had the entrance to Ludwig and the many years in the music products industry that followed. I remained in contact with some of the IBM people and was invited to bring the Four Sharps band back for another IBM dinner dance in October of 1972 at the London House-North... Many IBM'ers were cordial, friendly and praised the band's performance once again. MUSIC, continues to unite all past, present and future encounters, friendships and positive business relationships.

Chapter 3

The Ludwig Opportunity of a Lifetime Begins, July, 1972

The thought of working for Ludwig Drum Company was a seed planted in my brain and soul from the very first time I visited the Ludwig factory with my father and took a tour of the complete manufacturing operation. What I would experience in personal accomplishment, percussion industry recognition and true enjoyment of loving something you're working at was never even considered. I just knew Ludwig was where I belonged,....for the rest of my working career in music. I did not ask for anything more.

During my two and a half years at IBM Corporation, I kept in regular written contact with Ludwig about every six months or so just to keep my name, interest, and background on the minds of those within the company who could recognize my interest to work for the company. I got a reply letter back in early June of 1972 from the Executive Vice President, Frank Peppler. While the letter was pleasant, the net result was a "Thanks but no thanks."

Ludwig

LUDWIG INDUSTRIES

DIVISIONS:
LUDWIG DRUM CO
MUSSER
KITCHING EDUCATIONAL
KITCHING SCIENTIFIC
WM SCHUESSLER CO.

June 8, 1972

Mr. Karl Dustman
2131 Walter Avenue
Northbrook, Illinois 60062

Dear Mr. Dustman:

We have your letter of June 1st requesting information on possible employment connection with our Company. At the present time our staff is full and also we have no immediate plans for expanding it so I am afraid that we cannot give you very much encouragement at this time.

However, I will be glad to keep your Resume on file if something should come up in the near future I will be glad to get in touch with you to see if you are still interested.

Sincerely,

F. K. Peppler
Executive Vice President

FKP:mlw

1728 N. DAMEN AVE · CHICAGO ILL. 60647 U.S.A. PHONE 312-276-3360

The ink was barely dry on that letter when two weeks later, I got a surprise telephone call from his secretary asking me if I was available to come in for a meeting/interview with Mr. Peppler. To say I was thrilled would be an understatement.

This was extremely exciting for me at a mere 23 years old. I was confused, however, that I didn't know what changed the company's position from, "There's no opening'" to "Can you come in." My curiosity was killing me.

I went to the factory and first met with Frank Peppler. I learned that this would be a newly created dual position within the firm. The company was looking for a sales forecasting person (who knew the product terminology and Ludwig product line) as well as somebody to help with advertising and trade show displays and exhibits. I learned that with a dual position, you also had dual bosses. One half of my day would be spent on sales forecasting reporting to Frank Peppler, the other half of my day would be working on advertising and trade show displays and anything else in marketing working for a Marketing Vice President, Frank Baxpehler. I met with both Vice Presidents as well as their Advertising Manager, Vern Bush. Everyone was very friendly and courteous with all the standard questions on a first interview meeting.

It became clear that their first interest in me as a potential new employee was to fill the newly created position of Sales Forecaster, and was based upon the appearance of these words appearing somewhere in my resume, outlining with my present position with IBM. I was called back in for a second interview and offered the position. Of course I accepted the position. I had no idea what I was getting into other than it was clear that this was an opportunity of a lifetime, this was a dream-come-true, and I meant to take the opportunity and run with it.

I immediately advised Bob Underwood at the IBM Branch Office in Evanston, giving him a full two week notice. While disappointed in my decision to leave IBM, I believe he ultimately anticipated it at some point in time. The company had a very nice informal going-away after-hours cocktail reception at a nearby restaurant, I left on good terms with everyone and I moved forward.

When I shared the news with my family, my father's recommendation was; "Go in early, stay late, work hard, and you'll be recognized." Back then, that was a basic key to survival. Today? I don't think so.

This was a newly created position within Ludwig. That made it ideal for me, because I was not coming in to fill somebody else's chair, which would have brought certain expectations with it. On the other hand, I had to learn quickly how to avoid getting in the crossfire between the two different vice president bosses I had, each with a different need and expectation from me on their work assignments. Like many manufacturing companies of that time, there were four separate pillars of the "Ludwig management empire" that existed within the organization. These were; finance, sales & marketing, manufacturing, and purchasing. I was in an enviable position in being able to interact with all four management areas, but also vulnerable to the conflicts, turf-wars, and anything else that could have been developing between the departments. My inner voice told me to "make everyone a friend and stay out of the politics, once you find it."

I was given a desk in the advertising department and basically worked for the advertising manager who at that time was Vern Bush. Vern was an experienced advertising pro who had been with Ludwig for many years and had been brought in to the company by Dick Schory. In addition to sitting next to Vern, listening, learning and seeing everything that goes on within the advertising, artist relations and trade show exhibit functions, I was within immediate reach of both vice presidents I technically worked for. We were in one big room that was shared by Jerry Owings who was the graphic designer/art director, and Lorain Levine who was the secretary and handled some of the artist relations along with the trade shows. We four as a quartet handled the advertising/trade show exhibit arm which was Frank Baxpehler's "marketing team".

There were no lines in the sand between all of those areas; there was a great deal of flexibility among the group as we split up the various projects and responsibilities sometimes just based on what was "hot" at the moment or had significant deadlines associated with the project. I did whatever someone told me to do and volunteered for anything that I could see needed doing. I didn't worry about late hours or getting my hands dirty- it was just, "Give me the work, and I will get it done." To my benefit this can-do attitude seemed to be recognized and appreciated by most.

I was quickly immersed in learning that Sales Forecasting is really like a four legged chair. By that I mean that the entire corporation is based upon what marketing was going to sell, and what production was going to manufacture. That involved sales and marketing, planning new products, new colors and finishes, and deleting old products. It also involved guiding production regarding what it had to be able to manufacture based on ever-changing trends, demands and the competition, as well as being able to adjust production requirements to what sales & marketing was "predicting," or "forecasting". The purchasing department needed to know what sales and marketing was going to focus on so they could purchase and schedule the raw materials. The finance area needed to know what sales & marketing was doing in order to pay for this whole pyramid. I was vulnerable because I could have been shot at by any one of the four vice presidents for any number of reasons,...or conflicts among themselves. I realized that I was young and I was disposable so if anyone was going to get shot at or executed, I was at the front of the line.

My introduction to the company, department managers, and V.P.s was smooth and without any real confrontation. I was welcomed quite graciously and fortunately there were no "turf wars" between the vice presidents. Good things were being said about my work directly to me, and as far as I knew, good things were being said (about my work) about me. I got to be known as one of Baxpehler's guys. (All of the junior managers had unofficial titles; "he's a finance guy", or he's a "production guy" or a "purchasing guy". I was clearly one of Baxpehler's guys.)

For those young people reading this section about sales forecasting; it's a great way to learn a corporate manufacturing environment in a family-owned company because you have to interface with all four key areas in the product chain, or legs on the chair. However, what made this unique was that there was also a fifth leg on this chair, and that was called the Ludwig family. What a Ludwig family member said became the final word above any of the vice presidents.

Sales Forecasting is complex. It's a certain amount of historical analysis as well as crystal ball gut-feel for the future. This balanced mix of market demand-production was imperative. For example, the sales and marketing area would need a consensus on how many Model 989 Big Beat outfits we were going to sell for the next fiscal year, in what colors, and with which hardware packs. Every one of these master catalog model numbers could have many different variations that needed to be forecasted and tracked. A lot of this I was pulling this out of the air based on historical data that I had access to in terms of EACH product model number units and dollars sold. I was of course sworn to secrecy on all this proprietary confidential information. Honestly, it's a lot of trust and responsibility to be given to a young new guy that just came with the firm. But I handled it well and took everything very seriously because of the impact my decisions and recommendations would have on the overall company. Yes, there were some checks and balances and I conferred regularly with the sales department and management.

At 23 years of age, I was looking at everything to get a handle on what was selling, what was not selling, what the competition was doing, where the market was heading and so forth. We anticipated changes and were able to adjust and modify production, purchasing, and finance, based upon what the sales-marketing people were seeing for the future. Ludwig could not afford to make some of the same mistakes that the competition was making at this time. We constantly watched the movements, introductions and changes the competition was making.

There was always a certain amount of conflict between Peppler and Baxpehler as to "how is Karl balancing his time and who is getting the majority of Karl's time and project attention?" This was a constant "What are you working on now?" They would come in and look on my desk... "Good- you have all the sales forecasting numbers on the desk- that made Peppler happy. Similarly, Baxpehler would come in seeing that I was proof-reading catalog pages or something,...which pleased him. Everyone was used to the term, "that is your top priority"...and adjust accordingly to how the wind was blowing that day. If you had the wrong thing on your desk at the wrong time for the wrong person, you would have to answer for that. I learned how to tap dance very quickly. I always had a pile of both projects on my desk. That seemed to circumvent many of those type of situations.

Frank Baxpehler had come to Ludwig about 8 or 9 years prior to my arrival and had entered the company as the International Export Manager, a new position back then. That was really his forte and his original full time job. That expanded into being the vice president of marketing as well and the International Export Manager at the same time. The impact that export sales was having on the company was very significant. This grew continuously over the years as basically new business for Ludwig. An international department of three to four people grew to handle the business which called for extensive documentation, scheduling and consolidation of master orders. Frank was an expert at this, and it definitely contributed to the Ludwig's bottom line, market share, and dominance in the world of percussion. He would make one or two four week international business/sales trips a year and bring back a slew of orders which everyone recognized. He traveled Europe, Asia, Far East, Middle East,...as "percussion is the universal language." Sometime these international customers would need a specific type of drum or accessory that Ludwig did not currently manufacture. Engineering and production would work with Frank to develop a special product that could be sold to the international customer in significant qualities...to make it profitable and worthwhile the effort. He was also the driving force in Ludwig's attendance and market dominance at the International Frankfurt, Germany, Messe trade show each year. This remained a "gold star" recognition by the Ludwig family who annually attended this European event.

During this same time, Frank was completing his Masters Degree in marketing on Saturdays at the University of Chicago. That went on for a number of years. Bill Ludwig loved this fact that Frank had the personal determination to improve his already superior skills and that the company would benefit from Frank's ongoing education. Eventually, he completed and received his master's degree. I'm not sure if that meant a raise but I know that Frank enjoyed the learning journey by mentioning this every now and then and Bill Ludwig loved it, so it was a win-win.

International sales and marketing remained a separate arm within the company. Frank led a small team that worked exclusively on building and handling all the growing export business. As this element grew within the company, many of these important global Ludwig distributors would visit the Ludwig company during the year, or in connection with the annual summer NAMM convention at Mc Cormick Place in Chicago. It was like "open house" at the factory after the convention and the entire company was involved in welcoming and hosting their visits to Ludwig.

BEGINNING THE MIDWEST BAND & ORCHESTRA CLINIC-CONVENTION

Growing up, I was aware of the Midwest Band and Orchestra Clinic-Convention in Chicago, but had never attended this event. This is basically a huge music educator's convention focused on anything that has to do with band and orchestral music, teachers, performance, and all instruments of school instrumental music programs. It attracted back then about five thousand music educators from around the country. I am certain it has grown dramatically since then as it now occupies the McCormick Place Convention Center in Chicago. All of the instrument manufacturers have huge display-exhibits for the four days of the convention. The December, 1972, event was held at the Sherman House Hotel on Michigan Avenue in Chicago. This was the final year for the convention there, because they were going to tear down the Sherman House Hotel immediately afterwards. The Midwest was the last conference to be hosted in this landmark hotel of Chicago.

Ludwig always had prominent well-known clini-

A Memorable Moment:

One year the owner of Casale Bauer, the distributor of Ludwig in Italy, allowed his teenage daughter to stay in the US and actually work at a clerical position within Ludwig during the summer months. I believe "Nicki" stayed at the Baxbehler home, as Frank also had a teenage daughter about the same age at that time. Nicki was very gracious, spoke excellent English and understood everything except the American and Chicago slang words or phrases, but quickly caught on to working within Ludwig. She learned a lot and this certainly cemented the working relationship between the Italian distributor and the Ludwig Company. This was an example of Frank's "above and beyond" attitude and commitment to the company. I was impressed by this gracious outreach and connection to "busness"...through family alliances.

A Memorable Moment:

I quickly learned that Ludwig always had a hospitality suite at all of these events; NAMM show, Percussive Arts Society (PASIC), and Midwest Band Clinic. Bill Ludwig always loved an audience and on the final night of the convention and Ludwig open-house suite, he decided to step up on a coffee table and began recounting the history of the Sherman House Hotel and the many years that the convention took place in the Sherman House grand ballroom. The hotel was also known for The College Inn, (a very large live music venue within the hotel) Everyone was cheering and applauding, clinking glasses and celebrating that this was our last time in the Sherman House Hotel. A number of us were scared to death that the coffee table he was standing on would collapse underneath him as it did not look very well-suited as a podium or stage. Surprisingly, It did hold up, and the party continued.

After the hospitality suite closed, Vern Bush and I, along with the rest of the Ludwig advertising team, went to the hotel dining room for a late dinner. We did not realize that the room where we had all placed our winter coats on the bed was actually Bill and Maggie Ludwig's bedroom. By the time we finished dinner and were ready to leave the hotel and go upstairs for our coats, Bill and Maggie had retired for the evening and we had to wake Bill up. (We never heard anything more about this incident, which was probably for the best.)

cians on the Midwest convention program. This year was the masterful Bobby Christian doing a multiple percussion presentation for all the band and orchestra directors in another grand ballroom of the Sherman House Hotel. The clinic was excellent, as Bobby was a gifted percussionist as well as also a showman and stage-character that connected with everyone who packed the ballroom. After his presentation, Baxpehler decided to have a tribute dinner to Bobby and his with Josephine. He invited everyone in his personal inner circle who was sequestered in the Ludwig hospitality suite, announcing, "we're going to go for dinner". I was very pleased to be included, but I was finding out what it meant to be "one of Frank's guys."

We ended up at the rooftop dining room at the Executive House Hotel which offers a stunning view of the dramatically lit-up downtown Chicago skyline from the 30th floor. I'd never been there before so this was a totally new experience. Here we have about 15 people at a wonderful table that Frank had obviously reserved in advance,… and we began thanking and recognizing Bobby for the fantastic clinic presentation he had made at the convention earlier in the day.

That was my introduction to Bobby, who over

the years I became very close to. Bobby became a longtime friend and colleague that I worked very closely with during my Ludwig years. At one point he was the most sought after clinician that Ludwig had on their clinician roster. He surpassed everyone's clinician fee earnings one year by receiving over twenty-five thousand dollars of Ludwig clinician fees. He was a main-stay at all the Ludwig Percussion Symposiums and always had time for me through the years. I was honored to be asked to perform the editing duties for his "Brushing Up on Brush Technique" book available through his publishing company, Malcolm Music. We also featured many of his how-to-play educational articles that were published and included in the Ludwig Percussion Aid Pack.

As the years moved passed, I got more involved

with the Midwest Band & Orchestra Clinic convention. Ludwig continued with even larger and more prominent exhibits, sometimes spanning 50-60 feet long. When the Band and Orchestra Clinic-conference was forced to move from the Sherman House Hotel, the convention moved to the lower-level basement of the Conrad Hilton Hotel which was about a block away but still on Michigan Avenue. Of course the Ludwig Hospitality Suite remained a mainstay. All the convention percussion attendees knew it was there. Bill loved being on the product display speaking with all the directors and percussionists while at the same time inviting everyone up to the hospitality suite. And, everyone (invited or not) came up to the hospitality suite in the evening and the open-house event lasted as along as there were people there drinking. That might be one o'clock in the morning, and of course a few of us "marketing guys" would have to be there to police all of this. After a while I got more comfortable yelling out "Last Round! Twelve O'clock!"

As time moved on, I became more involved in the budgeting for these events as my responsibilities were increasing monthly. By the middle of the 1970s the cost of having hospitality suites at the Midwest Clinic with alcoholic beverages purchased through the Conrad Hilton was astronomical. What I could purchase in a liquor store for ten dollars, would easily cost twenty-five dollars when purchased through the Conrad Hilton hotel when delivered to the suite. We were having real issues with the cost of stocking the bar. I came up with a cost savings solution to the liquor bills that everyone seemed to agree with, but did not want any personal part of. Every morning before I would drive down to the Conrad Hilton Hotel to work the Ludwig exhibit, I took a fiber trap case to the Otis & Lee Liquor store in Northbrook where I lived. With the shopping list I created from the night before, I would buy three hundred dollars or more of various bar-liquor, pay for it with cash, pack it all in the drummer's trap case, load it in the trunk of my car and drive downtown directly to the hotel with all the bottles clinking in the trunk of the car. Upon giving my car to the parking valet at the hotel, I would lift the drummer trap-case out and wheel it up to the hospitality suite. We now had all the expensive alcoholic beverages at a fraction of the price and we only purchased the soft drinks, beer, wine, and cracker-cheese trays through the hotel. I probably enjoyed the "back door liquor caper" more than anyone appreciated the cost-savings I had engineered for the company and my marketing budget.

BEGINNING NEW DREAM-BOOK-CATALOG PRODUCTION

As we entered 1974, we started right in on the production of the new catalog. That was a direct responsibility of the advertising manager, Vern Bush, but he needed all the help he could get in putting together the 103-page full-line catalog that could easily take a year of planning, photography, text-writing, proofing, and printing. Vern was a wonderful "first immediate supervisor," recognizing the dual position I was working for two different vice presidents. He welcomed and recognized my knowledge of the product and my attention to detail. Since I was sitting in the advertising department, I become regularly and constantly utilized.

When I joined Ludwig, the firm did all of the catalog and advertising creation typesetting in-house. We would create the lay-out boards and shoot the product photography through Reed Wallace Photography. Lorain Levine set all the type on the special typesetting equipment. Graphic artist-designer, Jerry Owings would align and strip-in all the headlines and blocks of text for the 103-page catalog. We did catalogs and a lot of the advertising and brochures basically by hand, but it always looked professional. I became one of the principal text-writers and proofreaders. I guess I had enough command of the English language and editorial know-how to contribute a detailed eye to what was going to be printed, sometimes in hundreds of thousands of catalogs. I always jumped at the opportunity to help. We would use all four of us in the Advertising "room" for proofreading, then it went to Baxpehler for the final-final review, then on the printers.

We would put together a mockup that would illustrate the layout; so many pages dedicated to outfits (and which models/finishes), so many pages devoted to the concert percussion, Musser mallet instruments, timpani, marching, all accessories, and so on. Bill would be involved in that to a limited degree. Bill considered himself an advertising expert (and I do not mean that in a negative way) as he had entered his father's original WFL Drum Company as the advertising guy. We respected that and did the politically correct thing; we welcomed his involvement but avoided getting him into the nitty-gritty production elements which would have slowed everything down. Bill's involvement would include "what's going to be on the cover?" and "how are we going to handle the personnel pages?"

I learned a tremendous amount about graphic design, layout, type-setting, product photography and printing. Both Vern Bush and Frank Baxpehler gave me opportunities, and I jumped at every chance to convey my ambition and eagerness to contribute as well as the growing expertise I was acquiring all through this process.

INTRODUCTION TO THE INTERNATIONAL MUSIC EXPO-"NAMM SHOW", CHICAGO

The June, 1973, NAMM show that I attended at McCormick Place was the first show I had attended there. I had experienced smaller conventions in the Palmer House or Conrad Hilton, but had no idea what to expect at a national convention center. (At this point in time there was not a January NAMM Show in California show, often referred-to and named the Winter Market Show.)

Never before in my life had I seen so many musical instruments under one roof. I couldn't believe how massive this was. And Ludwig had one of the largest and most dominant displays there. Every trade show that took place at McCormick place was a major undertaking for the Ludwig Company. Ludwig had the biggest and most dominant floor space in the drum category. It also had to have the largest and best-promoted dealer "by invitation only" event during the convention. Ludwig also had the largest assortment of percussion artists and celebrities visiting and attending the exhibit. The annual NAMM Show took a huge amount of planning, orchestration and money. I got immersed in all of this immediately at the very beginning of my tenure at Ludwig.

"Chicago will belong to Ludwig during the NAMM Show" was the marching order we all worked with. Eventually, this went so far that the company had the newly-hired exhibit manager, Claude Adomaitis, making contact with each of the official Chicago NAMM Show convention hotels to see which bands were playing in the lounges of the six to eight most prominent headquarter hotels during the four to five days of the convention. These prime hotels would become completely booked with the largest music and percussion retailer-dealers that were attending the convention. He would contact the drummer of each band that was performing in each hotel lounge and make certain that drummer was playing a Ludwig set during the four days of the Chicago NAMM show. There was enough friendly and cordial fortitude to convince almost every drummer to "play Ludwig" during the convention, even if they were not already owning a Ludwig set. Bill was clear that the "marketing team" must make certain that Slingerland, Gretsch, Premier and Rogers sets could not be allowed to be in these top hotel lounges during this period of time. Selectively we would either strongly coerce the bandleader or sometimes offer extreme discounts on drum sets to get the mission accomplished. . Whatever was required, we did it because Chicago belonged to Ludwig.

Karl with Claude Adomaitis

By the time that Buddy Rich and Ed Shaughnessy got involved with the company in the mid-1970s, Bill saw the potential for the biggest and greatest Ludwig dealer events during the Chicago NAMM Show. I think Ed came first, with Bill wanting Ed Shaughnessy to bring his entire Energy Force Big Band from California to put on a concert for the Ludwig dealer dinner held at the Hyatt Regency Grand Ballroom. Many hours of planning and thousands of dollars were put into this. Bill wanted the biggest show on earth and it was like a Ringling Brothers Circus! These were by-invitation-only invites; sacred invitations that got mailed to very select Ludwig dealers to bring the owner and his/her spouse to the Ludwig event.

This was followed by Buddy Rich and his entire band being brought to Chicago from wherever they were on tour to put on a concert during the NAMM show. These were huge events. It took a lot of people to help make this happen. From the secretaries filling out invitations, inserting tickets, and licking envelopes to booking hotel rooms, buying airline tickets, and on and on and on. Fortunately, I was immersed in all of this, learning how things got done, how relationships got leveraged, and the protocols of what and how the Ludwig family wanted events to happen.

Eventually as I got older and assumed higher levels of responsibilities in the organization, I took all of that experience and used it with people that worked for me so not as much on-the-job training was required of them as I had experienced. I learned not only how to get things done, but how to show others how to get things done.

Bill Ludwig was an avid and experienced yachtsman. He owned a number of different yachts over the years, parking them at the Chicago Yacht Club. The yachts got bigger as the company grew and became more successful. During one of the summer NAMM Show conventions at McCormick Place, Bill wanted to host a small dinner for the Ludwig dealers at the Chicago Yacht Club and then take all the dealer-guests out on Lake Michigan for a sunset cruise on his yacht. He booked the entire Chicago Yacht Club for the private event, so of course we needed live music. We flew in Dave Samuels and Dave Friedman from New York who were artists for the Musser Division and internationally known as the Friedman-Samuels DOUBLE IMAGE Mallet Duo.

I became responsible for presenting this "performance" to both Davids. Their initial reaction was, "Karl- we don't play cocktail parties!" I responded by saying, "Guys- this is Bill Ludwig's Chicago Yacht Club. Please come to Chicago, I'll have your Vibe and Marimba set up already, and you will play your phenomenal duo music that this audience has never heard before. You're featured." My biggest fear was that the guests would think of this as socializing background music, all walking around with their martinis and their champagne talking and socializing. I warned Samuels and Friedman to not be offended if the guests are not intently listening to you or they are not applauding. "This is live entertainment at a highest level," I said, "remember you are playing Bill Ludwig's instruments and you're going to be paid very well to do it." The DOUBLE IMAGE contribution to this event came off beautifully. The audience was immediately struck by the sound, the music and complexities of the harmonies and blending of the two Musser instruments. Again, this was part of my learning curve- how to suggest, persuade and entice people to do something they don't want to do, so you can create a positive outcome for all. It worked out fine. Dick Richardson from Musser loved it.

In a corporate environment like Ludwig, a lot of the stability of the company would be related to what the national economy was doing. Ludwig had a well-balanced product mix. By that I mean that if drum set sales went down because of consumer economics, the school business (which included marching percussion, concert percussion and timpani,) would consistently be there because those programs were often either state or federally funded. Ludwig could count on those product category sales to always "pay the rent". We realized the drum set sales could be fluctuating from one year to another due to general economic conditions and increasing competition. Recognizing the annual trends that effected sales forcasting called for the consideration of many variables. A major variable that spotlighted the opportunity for growth and new instruments was the new scoring for marching percussion instruments and accessories.

SPOTLIGHT ON MARCHING PERCUSSION

One of Ludwig's leading engineers was also a recognized marching percussion expert, Al LeMert. He worked on many new instrument products while also being an avid drum corps instructor and competition judge who was respected in all those circles. He led the charge for having contacts and relationships with the leading major drum corps. The Blue Devils, The Bridgeman, The Madison Scouts, Phantom Regiment, you name it. At one point almost every one of the top twelve drum corps were all playing Ludwig products on the field. Al was also a member of the North Central States Judges Association which had an annual conference in Chicago. Invariably this was held at the Hyatt Regency Hotel very close O'Hare Airport. Ludwig would have a hospitality suite which was filled with marching percussion snare drums in wood shell, Vistalite, and stainless steel. The company would also use this opportunity to test-market new products with prototypes that were secretly shown to the leading corps instructors. This was as a great connection to the drum corps, their percussion instructors and key corps management.

There was a complete battery of marching percussion instruments brought to this huge Ludwig hospitality suite that would be used as "home base" every evening. Like other educational events, the Ludwig hospitality suite was a center of relationship building and schmoozing with the corps, and it paid off.

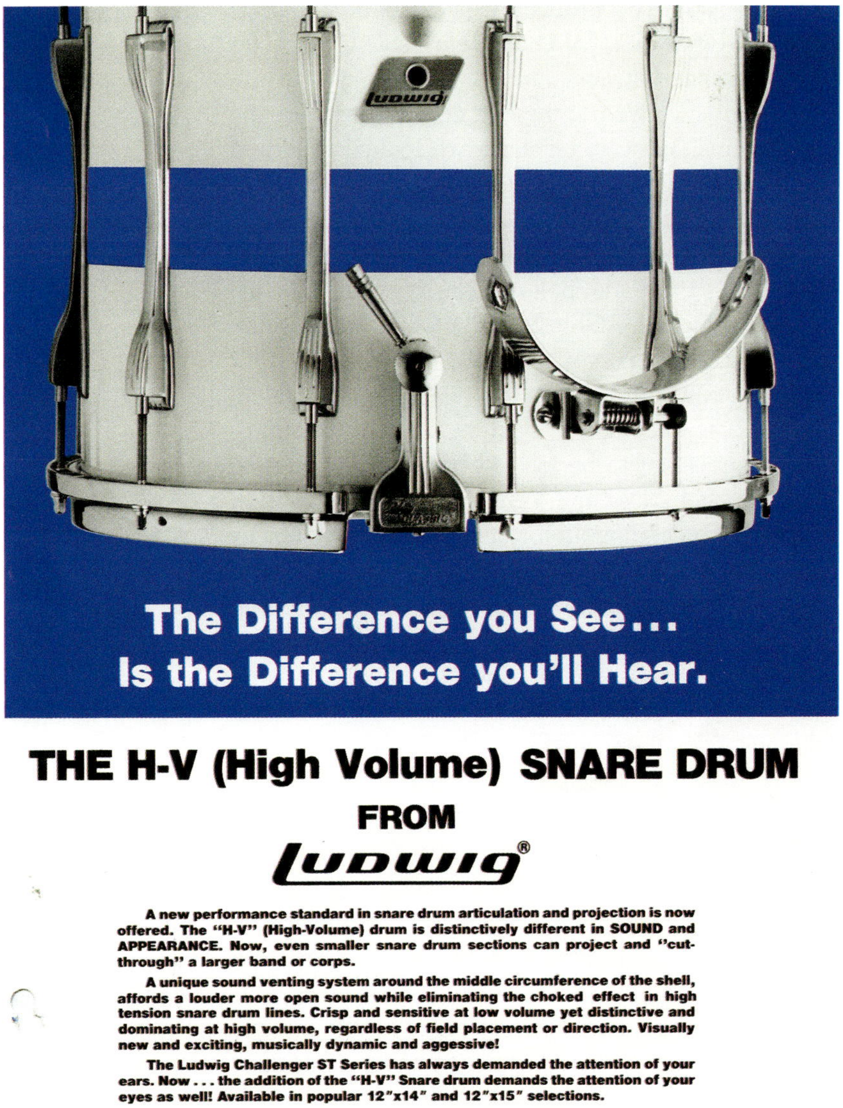

The evolution of the Ludwig HV (High Volume) model marching snare which had a 2 inch horizontal slot opening in the center of the shell was probably researched through these drum corps conferences. A completely new approach to sound projection for marching snare drums, these were an offshoot of the Ludwig Challenger Series and had the center portion of the snare drum shell removed for great projection. Equipped with Ludwig's die cast hoops and top and bottom, the drums were available in both 12x15 and 12x14 shell sizes. This met with a limited market success and appeal, but provided conversation from Harvey Vogel of Lonestar Percussion in Dallas, who thought that this series was named after him. Unfortunately, the HV stood for High Volume.

It was very clear that the brand and model of marching percussion instruments that the leading drum corps were competing and performing with in the highly acclaimed Drum Corps International (DCI) competitions drastically impacted the brand of drums that high schools and colleges would select and purchase for their educational/school applications. DCI corps drive the "brand of choice" for all marching percussion equipment.

The Ludwig marketing team and staff people would work closely with Al in organizing, delivering and setting up the events, display instruments and the product literature that was introduced and coordinated with the annual event.

All of these hospitality suites were heavily carpeted, and the snare drums being tested in this environment were sounding very dead, they just were not resonating. Bill Ludwig pointed out, "Well, that's because you're playing into the carpets, guys!" So he and Al had the Vistalite department make Vistalite (1/4-inch thick Plexiglas) circles about four feet in diameter using pie-shaped triangular pieces of every Vistalite color available. We put these underneath each of the snare drums that were on stands. It looked great and made the drums instantly sound terrific. I thought that was the coolest idea he ever had. Everyone loved the idea, the drums sounded great, and it was a great visual effect. From that point on, every trade show after that included Vistalite Sound Disks on the display merchandise orders.

Larry McCormick was one of the largest dealers of marching percussion instruments in the country and he happened to be located in the Chicago area. McCormick's Marching Percussion created a high school- level competition which became known as Marching Bands of America. This became a highly promoted competition between high school marching bands throughout the U.S.. There were multiple levels of marching bands, based upon the number of band members on the field. This eliminated the unfair competition of smaller bands of 80-90 players competing with high school bands that could have more than 300 performers on the field in competition. This was not a drum corps competition, but a marching band competition between schools that had significant instrumental music programs and had the budgets to be involved in these types of competitions. Participating bands came from all over the United States to the University of Wisconsin in Whitewater. Each year this event would grow in the number of bands competing all week, with twelve selected finalist bands competing at the conclusion of the week-long event on Saturday night under the lights.

In connection with this Marching Bands of America event would be an exhibit hall (usually the university gymnasium) for any participating sponsoring manufacturer to set up exhibits of their musical instrument or marching/parade-type merchandise. This provided a showcase for all the different attending firms to showcase their products, making the complete array of marching products accessible to the competing band's music directors, support staff, and band parents attending. Ludwig always participated and had one of the largest displays, sending a huge truck containing a sampling of everything in marching percussion that Ludwig made. It would take a full day of display set-up just to unpack and assemble all the many different instruments contained in the booth.

These annual MBA competitions were huge events that escalated in band attendance and percussion industry involvement year after year. At the same time Al LeMert was working with all of the major DCI drum corps on products, endorsements and developing a core group of marching percussion clinicians for our growing educational clinic program. Through those efforts and relationships, Ludwig became involved with the Santa Clara Vanguard under the direction of Fred Sanford. Fred was a household name in the drum corps world and was affiliated with Slingerland Drums as their principle marching percussion spokesperson. At the same time, Ludwig was also working with The Bridgeman from Bayonne, New Jersey, under the percussion direction of Dennis Delucia.

Ludwig quickly recognized that Fred Sanford and Santa Clara Van Guards were on the west coast drawing national attention, and Dennis Delucia was on the east coast with the Bayonne Bridgeman drawing equal national attention. However, neither were connected with Ludwig either by brand of equipment or by affiliation with the company. Bill Ludwig wanted this situation corrected and put the decree out through Baxpehler that we needed to get more of these top twelve drum corps marching percussion section leaders affiliated with the company. We first went after Fred Sanford who had a full time position with Santa Clara and we brought him to a full time position with Ludwig as a clinician, a designer, a spokesperson, and an ambassador.

There was also a dedicated recruitment effort with Dennis Delucia. Dennis was a little more apprehensive about the position but he loved the idea of being a clinician and working with the Ludwig Company.

Dick Gerlach, Fred Sanford, and Karl in the conference room circa 1980

He came out with a signature line of Dennis Delucia marching percussion mallets and beaters named POWER-STROKE, which were completely made in the Chicago factory.

The same relationship-building efforts were directed towards the Madison Scouts, then the Phantom Regiment from Rockford Illinois under the direction of Marty Hurley. As a result, Marty became a Ludwig marching percussion clinician and we used the Phantom Regiment percussion section as the grand processional opening for the June NAMM Show at McCormick Place. Ludwig secured the entire convention center main entrance on opening morning to showcase the Phantom Regiment performing both marching and moving cadence performances for about 20 minutes. This was unbelievable and there were thousands of NAMM Show attendees all over the Mc Cormick Place sidewalks, expressway walk-over bridges, all watching this NAMM Show Grand Opening presentation take place, courtesy of Ludwig Industries.

In similar fashion, there were times when the Phantom regiment would be on summer performance competition tour for DCI and were coming through the Chicago area. Al Lemert would ask Marty to bring the percussion section to put on a show at the Ludwig factory for the Ludwig employees. These shows took place during the day and the company's parking lot security cleared the entire parking lot, moving employee cars to surrounding area streets and lawns. Eventually the huge drum corps busses and equipment tractor-trailer trucks would make their way to the company parking lot and assemble for a stationary thirty minute percussion section show in the company parking lot. The employees really loved that, seeing all of the instruments that they carefully manufactured there in the Damen Avenue factory being used by these expert percussionists.

Rick Odello was the percussion instructor for the Blue Devils Drum and Bugle Corps. During the seventies, the Blue Devils were becoming consecutive year unbeatable winners of the annual DCI competition and always took first place in Percussion, regardless of what the final corps placement was. By now the word was pretty much out that Ludwig took care of its drum corps partners with equipment, service and attention to their needs while on the annual DCI competition tour. Ludwig become recognized as quickly responding when any of the top twelve drum corps would need products, parts, and related service. This professional attention was extremely important to any competing drum corps. A lot of this same "taking care of business" attitude and attention stemmed from the very early years of working with the drum set artists and celebrities. This same kind of responsiveness was required for the professional handling of Carmine Appice, Buddy Rich, or Ed Shaughnessy. These artists (and drum corps for that matter) all needed everything yesterday.

As I worked my way up in the company I had more and more people working for me. One key guy was Felix Gureca- a young knowledgeable and dedicated local Latino who was on the production payroll but basically worked for the marketing team. Felix knew how to get things done through the factory production policies and procedures. He knew where everything was manufactured, stocked, and shipped from. He handled all of our educational department demonstration instrument clinic stock inventory. This included all the Ludwig drum sets used by Ludwig artists, all the mallet keyboard instruments from Musser, all the marching percussion instruments, and even the Kitching Educational Orff Instrument clinic stock sets. Felix was the guy everyone in marketing would turn to for getting things done correctly, quickly, and sometimes quietly.

PERCUSSION SYMPOSIUMS ESTABLISH THE CAREER PATH, 1974.

I was still working two positions for two different bosses, Frank Peppler and Frank Baxpehler, doing sales forecasting and a mix of marketing projects. Conflicts were growing, however. I was getting better at dodging more bullets, and I was learning the rhetoric to keep everybody happy. What seemed to be evolving was Frank Baxpehler getting more ear time with Bill on the needs for stronger marketing, sales support, education, clinic programs, and so on. What happened next was sort of being in the right place at the right time.

Jim Sewrey had been brought into the company by Dick Schory years earlier. Jim had been a band director in Iowa and was brought into the company full time to fill the newly created position of Education Director. Jim was doing a marvelous job. He brought a unique combination of commercial marketing aptitude while being able to speak with, and relate to, music educators, and percussion educators. I liked Jim and got to know him well through my attendance at the various nearby state MEA (Music Educators Association) and regional MENC (Music Educators National Conference) conferences. Often this involved state meetings where Ludwig had a significant product exhibit as well as national clinicians on the convention program. I was traveling more each year for the company and by the end of the 1970s I was traveling about twenty-six weeks a year. I was gaining recognition, visibility, and respect from being a consistent volunteer for many different marketing projects. While sometimes the travel was very challenging physically, it also created more of a challenge to keep up with the desk work at the office while being away from the day-to-day activities on Damen Avenue. The travel was both a hindrance and a tremendous asset.

The Ludwig International Percussion Symposiums started out in 1968 as a brainchild of Dick Schory and Jim Sewrey. This summer workshop for anyone and everyone in percussion. Playing, teaching, performing this was attended by everyone from band directors to students to teachers to administrators from around the country. The first symposium in 1968 was for two weeks and was conducted at Northwestern University in Evanston Illinois. At that time I'd been a youngster just out of high school, attending college, working full time, and playing in multiple bands. It was my ambition to attend this two week event but I just couldn't get the time. It grew into a nationally recognized summer event for percussion and eventually was modified to a more affordable one week duration.

By the time that I arrived in July of 1972, the symposium was a major undertaking of Ludwig's Education Department under the direction of Jim Sewrey. He had two assistants, Alice Golinski, and Rochelle Weisman, who helped run the education program. The Symposium events really put the spotlight on Ludwig equipment by bringing in nationally recognized artists and educators to a hosting college or university campus for the one or two week period.

Somehow in the spring of 1973 Jim Sewrey broke his ankle. The two one-week Symposiums were scheduled and planned for July and August, only a couple months away. Jim could not walk and could not come to the Ludwig office. He was working from his home as best as possible, but of course this was before computers, Zoom video conferencing, and related technologies. Frank Baxpehler came to me and said, "We need someone to oversee and run the two percussion symposiums this summer. Karl- are you interested?" Of course I was interested. I looked at the roster of all these national artists that were going to teach. What a great opportunity. Joe Morello, Gary Burton, David Friedman, Al Payson, Mitch Markovitch and many other well know players and teachers. Again, I felt like the opportunity of a lifetime had been presented to me.

The first event was at the University of Miami in Coral Gables, Florida,.and the other was scheduled for two weeks later at the University of Wisconsin in Madison, The Madison event was hosted by percussion instructor/director Jim Latimer, the University of Miami event was hosted by percussion department director Fred Wickstrom. From those experiences, both gentlemen became lifelong friends and our professional paths would cross many times.

I went to Jim Sewrey's home in Glenview two or three days a week so he could coach me on what to expect from all of these artists, and how to prepare for leading these events in his absence. He explained that I would be dealing with attitudes, aptitudes, egos and idiosyncrasies. With his leg in a big cast up on the coffee table, Jim coached and guided me what to do and what not to do while also being flexible, professional and taking charge of the faculty that was teaching at each event for the week.

I managed to survive at both of the events, and they were considered great successes. Each symposium location attracted about 500 students. I felt that it went on record that I excelled at the challenge and showed my inner ability in making these events run smoothly. This internal assessment was not an egotistical thing, but my personal evaluation was, "hey- no one got hurt, no one got arrested, no one got drunk, no one got expelled, and no one died!"

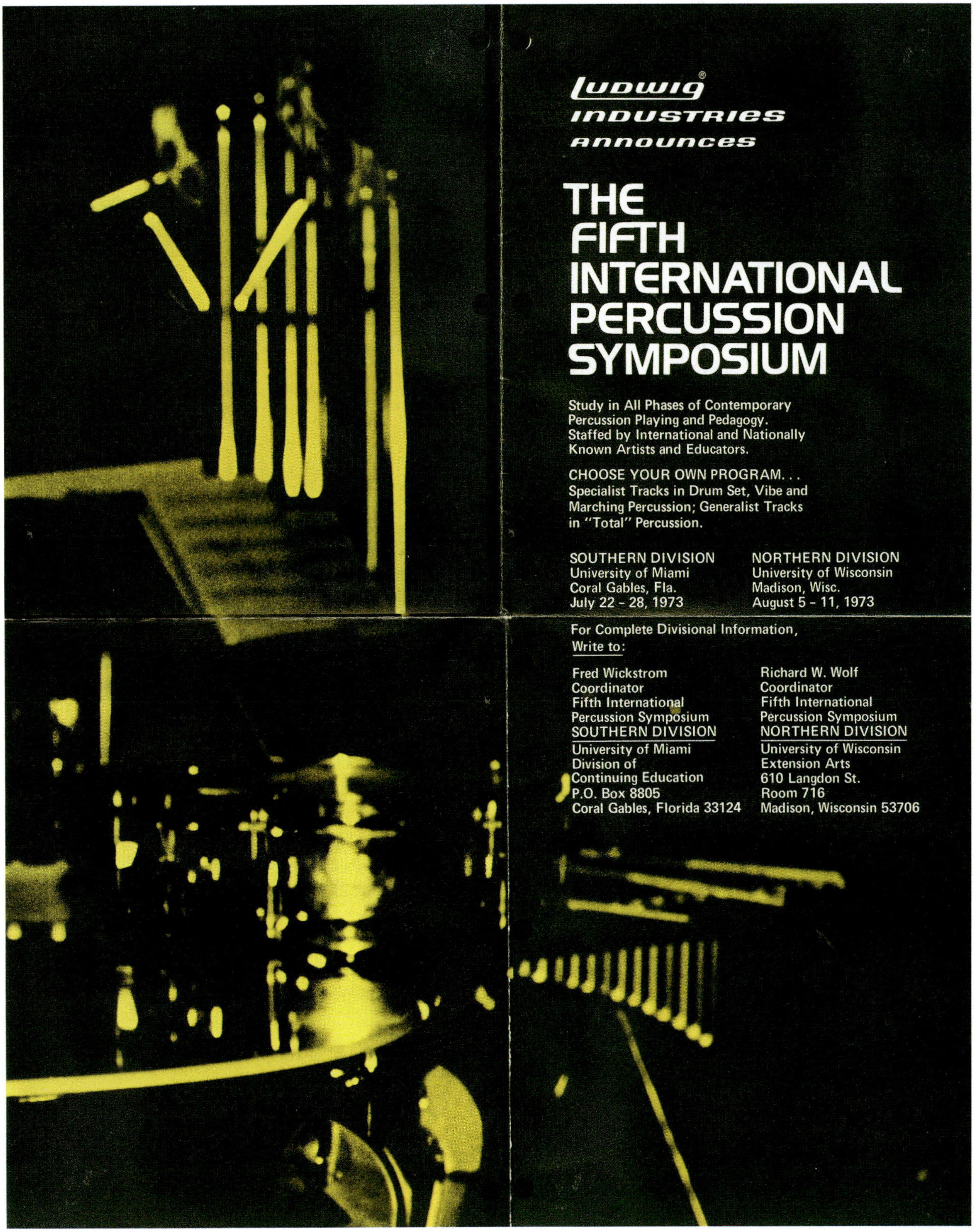

The pair of successful symposiums of 1973 was kind of a feather in my cap, and the Ludwig family was beginning to notice Karl. Bill Ludwig was scheduled to attend the Madison symposium, but his father William F. Ludwig Sr. passed away on July 8th at 94 years of age. This certainly changed his plans and cast a shadow over the entire company at the loss of the founder and Chairman. Bill was devastated but we all knew of Senior's failing health earlier in 1973.

The Wisconsin event included a professional mix of people and organizations dedicated to making the Ludwig symposium a true success. The location host for the event was the University of Wisconsin Extension Arts Division under the direction of Dick Wolf who oversaw all educational outreach for the University of Wisconsin System- he was a very influential person. Jack Pingle was the head of the Wisconsin State Music Association organization. Additionally, there was Rick Young, the forthcoming District Sales Representative for Ludwig, who had the state of Wisconsin in his territory. Bob Southey was a long-time Ludwig sales representative that had the Wisconsin territory and was getting ready to retire, turning the territory over to Rick. All of these people had a chance to see me in action and also learn how a Symposium works, as this was a first time experience for ALL of us. I received lot of the accolades from those symposium partners and leaders which came back to Bill Ludwig and to Frank Baxpehler. Later in the year, Jack Pingle and his wife came to Chicago for a post-event wrap-up meeting about the symposiums and some general schmoozing from the Ludwig organization. It benefited me to have this outside person giving a positive report on my ability and leadership of the symposium. Jack Pingle emphasized to the internal Ludwig team the importance of keeping the symposiums going in the future.

The symposium concept was also supported by the fact that direct product sales were created because of the symposium. At the Wisconsin event, Jim Sewrey convinced Maurie and Jan Lishon from Franks Drum Shop in Chicago to bring a truck load of merchandise (a good amount of Ludwig) and to set up a small goods store in one of the classrooms so they could sell directly to the students and educators in attendance. This "satellite" Franks Drum Shop basically set up a store to sell everything from drum sets to a pair of brushes. Maurie and Jan of course were wonderful to work with. I don't know if they made any money from the event, but they certainly enjoyed the symposium, being away from the Chicago store, and attending all the concerts. Plus they personally knew many of the teaching symposium artists. This was a win for everyone. Many of the student attendees had never seen that amount of percussion gear in one location before because they had never been to Franks Drum Shop.

By the end of 1973 we were approaching another PAS Convention, preparing for another Midwest Band Clinic convention in December, and the 1974 NAMM show in Chicago. I was getting involved in all of this, not because any special treatment, but I got the work done. I was detail-oriented, kept meticulous records, made notes and lists, and was ahead of the curve in terms of when products needed to be ordered and shipped, as well as communicating with the outside sales representatives. It was all about organization.

At the end of 1973, Frank Baxpehler let Jim Sewrey go, to the amazement of pretty much everyone. I didn't know the details behind the decision other than that the position was being eliminated (which is a catch-all phase used in every dismissal). Most people at company were certainly shocked at this announcement and felt terrible for Jim. I think Frank was getting some pressure from Bill that it was not the company's responsibility to teach percussion- "We build and sell instruments, it's not our job to tell them how to play them." A lot of Jim's time had been spent actually teaching percussion and teaching how to teach percussion. This certainly had a positive benefit to Ludwig, as Ludwig was the only company with an Educational Director. However, Pedagogy was a word that began to appear in the Ludwig vocabulary and Bill was kind of like, "What the heck is this pedagogy? Nobody knows what this means! Use words we all understand, Jim!"

Personally, I didn't really see Jim's departure coming but felt very guilty that maybe the things I had done for the summer symposiums and other things I was involved in had contributed to this decision. I remain very respectful of Jim Sewrey and what he did for Ludwig to this day. We remain friends and always speak when we bump into each other at various percussion conferences.

Ludwig Industries announces...
THE SIXTH INTERNATIONAL PERCUSSION SYMP
THE 12th INTERNATIONAL PERCUSSION SYMPOSIUM.
Ludwig
HE NIN
INTERNATION
PERCUSSION
SYMPOSIUM
Eastern Division
at the
University of Tennessee at Knoxvi
for
Music Educators
Students
Professional Performers
July 6-12, 1980
sponsored by
The University of Tennessee/Knoxville Music Depa
and
Ludwig Industries, Chicago, Illinois
Presents...
e Tent
ernatio
rcussi
ymposiu
AUGUST 9-15, 19
THE EIGHTH INTERNATIONAL PERCUSSION SYMPOSIUM
EASTERN DIVISION
THE ELEVENTH INTERNATIONAL PERCUSSION SYMPOSIUM

1975 Ludwig Percussion Symposium hosted by East Carolina University

Leigh Howard Stevens

Photo by Ted Bogsrud

Bobby Christian directing

Photo by Ted Bogsrud

1975 Ludwig Percussion Symposium hosted by East Carolina University

Carmine Appice

L-R: Host Harold Jones, William F Ludwig Jr., Ed Shaughnessy

Photo by Ted Bogsrud

In January of 1974 I was given the education department. That meant that I inherited the clinic program, I inherited all of the Symposium planning, I inherited Alice and Rochelle as well as Educational Representative Frank Arsenault. Frank was a full time employee who traveled 80% of the year doing educational clinics on drumming. Of course he was one of the national champions of rudimental drumming and his LP is still a standard for everyone who ever learned the 26 standard rudiments.

NEWS

DESIGN LAB
1118 West Crescent Avenue
Park Ridge, Illinois 60068
312 825-5551

Release Date: Immediately
For: Ludwig Industries
Subject: LUDWIG ADVANCES THREE

Ludwig Industries enthusiastically announces the promotion of three key personnel to new managerial positions in its Domestic Sales, International Sales and Education Departments.

KARL DUSTMAN moves from the Ludwig Advertising Department to his new position, Manager of Education. The appointment to this position gives Mr. Dustman responsibility for development of instructional techniques and educational materials for both the Ludwig and the Musser-Kitching product lines. All Percussion Education Clinics and Workshops are administered by the Education Department, necessitating the maintenance of close communications with music dealers and music educators at all levels. Mr. Dustman's varied musical and non-musical background includes experience in retail sales, music instruction, advertising, business communications and data processing. Himself a professional drummer and vibist, he continues to actively perform with his own group in the Chicago area.

Contact: Vern Bush, Advertising Manager
Ludwig Industries, 1728 No. Damen Ave.
Chicago, Ill. 60647 Tel: 312-276-3360

INDUSTRIAL DESIGN MARKETING ADVERTISING GRAPHIC DESIGN

I was still involved in the original sales forecasting responsibilities, but my plate of projects and various duties was getting full. Still, I got the green light from Baxpehler to get more involved in a variety of different marketing projects. He had to make this announcement internally without upsetting the Sales Forecasting responsibilities, and my working for Frank Peppler at the same time. I think basically Frank Baxpehler convinced Bill, "I need Karl full time, to lead the educational department activities while contributing to the ever-growing marketing, advertising and trade show elements of the company. We need to find somebody else to do the paper shuffling of the sales forecasting." Eventually, to my complete delight, the position and responsibility of corporate forecaster was turned over more to the production, purchasing, and finance people. At this point Dick Gerlach and Frank Peppler worked together to do some of the forecasting.

LUDWIG INDUSTRIES

DIVISIONS:
LUDWIG DRUM CO.
MUSSER
KITCHING EDUCATIONAL
KITCHING SCIENTIFIC
WM. SCHUESSLER CO.

M E M O R A N D U M

DATE: January 23, 1974

TO: All Salesmen

SUBJECT: New Position of Karl Dustman.

I am very pleased to notify you that Karl Dustman's duties in our corporation have been changed, adding new responsibilities to his job.

First, Karl will no longer be responsible for any matters related to displays. Please direct all of your inquiries and phone calls to Vern Bush, who has filled this position with a talented young man. This man is being broken in right now and Vern will communicate with you on this subject separately.

Karl's position in our company is two-fold. Karl's main duties will be as "Corporate Forecaster" and, in addition, he will also act as Manager of our Educational Department. Since most of Karl's time will be spent in forecasting, which in time will have improving effects on our deliveries, and as such, is in your own very best interest, I very much appreciate your cooperation in dealing with Alice Golinski and Rochelle Waisman on all regular clinic or clinician questions as you have done in the past. Alice and Rochelle will automatically consult with Karl and/or myself in questions which involve spending money. Any projects of great importance, of course, feel free to contact Karl or myself directly.

Let me encourage and assure you that our Educational Department will not only continue to function and promote a self-supporting clinic program, but in addition with this change, I will have the opportunity to concentrate our efforts in areas of product-related educational aids rather than taking over the function of education itself, which was the case so often with Jim Sewrey. Should you have any questions, feel free to contact me direct at anytime.

Cordially,

Frank P. Baxpehler

FPB:bc

1728 N. DAMEN AVE · CHICAGO ILL. 60647 U·S·A· PHONE 312·276·3360

1728 N. DAMEN AVE · CHICAGO ILL. 60647 U·S·A· PHONE 312·276·3360

The clinic program's explosive growth continued every year thereafter. I can't take credit for that. I think that it was simply that everything Ludwig was doing at that point in time turned to gold. The company did not seem to be able to do anything wrong. Ludwig was the largest drum company in the world and was doing everything right to maintain that placement and prestige. In looking back, it was overwhelming- I was all of 24 years old and I was on the upper rungs of the company management ladder. Needless to say, the pressure was on, both perceived and for real.

EDUCATIONAL CLINIC PROGRAM
CLINICIANS FOR CLINIC OR CONCERT APPEARANCE

DRUM SET

Bobby Christian (Chicago, IL) .... Multi-percussionist-performer/Clinician, Stage band-Concert band composer/conductor/adjudicator/performer/clinician, Percussion solo and ensemble clinician

J.C. Combs (Wichita, KS) .... Multi-percussionist-performer/Clinician/adjudicator, Stage band set performer/ Clinician/Adjudicator. Solo and ensemble clinician.adjudicator

Andrew Cyrille (Little Ferry, N.J.) .... Avant Garde Jazz drum performer/clinician - Accompaniment for modern dance ensemble or performing group.

Marvin Dahlgren (Minniapolis, MN) .... Symphony percussionist-performer/clinician/author, Jazz drum and vibe performer/clinician

Alan Dawson (Lexington, Mass) .... Jazz drum set performer/clinician

Charles Dowd (Eugene, OR) .... Jazz/Rock drum performer/clinician, stage band clinician/adjudicator and featured guest soloist. Specialty: small combo to big band and jazz ensembles

Butch Miles (New York City) .... Big band/Jazz ensemble performer, clinician, adjudicator

Max Roach (Conn.) .... Jazz Drum Set performer/clinician

Ron Falter (Goldendale, WA.) .... Jazz rock drum performer/clinician, uses double bass drum outfit. Stage band, concert band and percussion ensemble adjudicator/clinician

Derryl Goes (Greeley, CO.) .... Jazz/Rock drum performer/clinician, stage band-concert-marching band and percussion ensemble clinician/adjudicator

Roy Haynes (Jamaica, N.Y.) ... Avant-garde jazz drum performer/clinician

Ron Keezer (Eau Claire, WI.) .... Combo and stage band drum set clinician/performer/adjudicator

Danny Gottlieb (New York City) .... Jazz/rock drum set performer/clinician. Drummer with Pat Metheny group.

Bob Houston (Commerce, Texas) .... Jazz and big band drum set performer, clinician, adjudicator, high school-college level, percussion instructor at East Texas State University

Al Ipri (Cinnaminson, N.J.) .... Jazz drum set performer.clinician.adjudicator

Joe Morello (Newark, NJ) .... Jazz drum performer.clinician, stage band performer/clinician

Ed Shaughnessy (Los Angeles, CA.) .... Jazz big band performer/clinician, guest artist with concert/stage. marching bands

MALLET PERCUSSION

Tom Brown (Scotia, N.Y.) Jazz.rock vibe performer/clinician, stage band performer/clinician.adjudicator, solo and ensemble clinician.adjudicator.

Bobby Christian (Chicago, IL) .... Multi-percussionist-performer/Clinician, Stage band-Concert band com poser/conductor/adjudicator/performer/clinician, Percussion solo and ensemble clinician

J.C. Combs (Wichita, KS) .... Multi-percussionist-performer/Clinician/adjudicator, Stage band set performer/ Clinician/Adjudicator. Solo and ensemble clinician.adjudicator

Marvin Dahlgren (Minniapolis, MN) .... Symphony percussionist-performer/clinician/author, Jazz drum and vibe performer/clinician

Bill Molenhof (New York City) .... Jazz vibe and marimba performer/clinician small combo or jazz ensemble

Charles Dowd (Eugene, OR.) Jazz/rock vibe performer, clinician, adjudicator, featured guest with small com bo or big band. Multiple mallet instruments for percussion ensemble.

Ted Piltzecker (New York City) Jazz vibe solo performer/clinician. Small combo or jazz ensemble.

David Friedman (New York City) .... Vibe and marimba jazz/rock performer. clinician. Stage band performer - High school and college level

Friedman-Samuels Mallet Duo (New York City) .... Jazz/rock vibe and marimba duo performers/clinicians. Stage band performers.

Karen Ervin (California) .... Multi-percussionists-performer and clinician. Concentration on mallet percussion.
Linda Pimentel (Ohio) .... Multi-percussionist-performer and clinician. Concentration on mallet percussion.
David Samuels (New York City) .... Vibe and marimba jazz/rock performer, clinician. Stage band performer - high school and college level
Leigh Howard Stevens (New York City) .... Classical and contemporary marimba clinician/performer/adjudi cator

MULTIPLE PERCUSSION
Bobby Christian (Chicago, IL) .... Multi-percussionist-performer/Clinician, Stage band-Concert band com poser/conductor/adjudicator/performer/clinician, Percussion solo and ensemble clinician
J.C. Combs (Wichita, KS) .... Multi-percussionist-performer/Clinician/adjudicator, Stage band set performer/ Clinician/Adjudicator. Solo and ensemble clinician.adjudicator
Roger Faulmann (Brookings, S.D.) .... Percussion specialist in the instruction of total percussion through the use of the Musser Junior Percussion Kit. Suitable for music educators and students.
Ron Keezer (Eau Claire, WI.) .... Concert-stage band-[ercussion solo and ensemble adjudicator/clinician. Jazz/rock set drum clinician
Harold Jones (North Carolina) .... Multi-percussionist-performer/clinician/adjudicator. Specialist in mallet percussion.
Jim Moore (Ohio) .... Multi-percussionist-performer/clinician/adjudicator. Percussion ensemble conductor. clinician.adjudicator
Al Payson (Chicago, IL) .... Symphony percussionist-performer/clinician, Solo and ensemble adjudicator/clini cian
Charles Dowd (Eugene, OR) .... Jazz/Rock drum performer/clinician, stage band clinician/adjudicator and featured guest soloist. Specialty: small combo to big band and jazz ensembles

MARCHING PERCUSSION
Bob Houston (Commerce, Texas) .... Corps style marching percussion clinician/adjudicator - high school and college level. Percussion instructor at East Texas State University.
Marty Hurley (New Orleans, LA.) .... Drum corps specialist clinician.adjudicator. Special emphasis on teach ing techniques and application to high school and college marching bands. Scoring and arranging principles for directors, as well as drill exercises will be included. Percussion instructor with the Phan tom Regiment Drum & Bugle Corps
Mitch Markovich (Great Bend, KS) .... Rudimental performer.clinician, author, marching percussion clinician, solo adjudicator/clinician. Corps style teaching and performing techniques
Fred Sanford (Chicago, IL) .... Staff clinician. Drum corps style clinician/performer. Session applicable to complete student percussion sections, band director meetings, and general educator conventions. Consultant to Santa Clara Vanguard Drum & Bugle Corps.
Richard Talbot (Mansfield, PA) .... Teacher/student percussion educator-clinician-adjudicator, concert.march ing/stage band clinician.adjudicator
Chris Theo (Madison, WI) .... Principle percussion instructor for The Madison Scouts Drum & Bugle Corps. Drum corps specialist clinician.adjudicator/arranger/performing techniques
David Vose (Methuen, MA) .... Drum corps style specialist clinician.teacher.arranger.author. Percussion in structor for North Star Drum & Bugle Corps.

TIMPANI
Bobby Christian (Chicago, IL) .... Multi-percussionist-performer/Clinician, Stage band-Concert band com poser/conductor/adjudicator/performer/clinician, Percussion solo and ensemble clinician
Charles Dowd (Eugene, OR) .... Multi-percussionist clinician and performer, solo and ensemble adjudicator. Symphony timpanist performer/clinician
Al Payson (Chicago, IL) .... Symphony percussionist-performer.clinician solo and ensemble adjudicator.clini cian.

As the clinic program grew, we had multiple national clinicians on every PAS convention program, usually in every product category. At the many different state Music Educator's conferences, Ludwig and Musser had multiple clinicians on marching, concert percussion, and drum set, and then I inherited Kitching Educational.

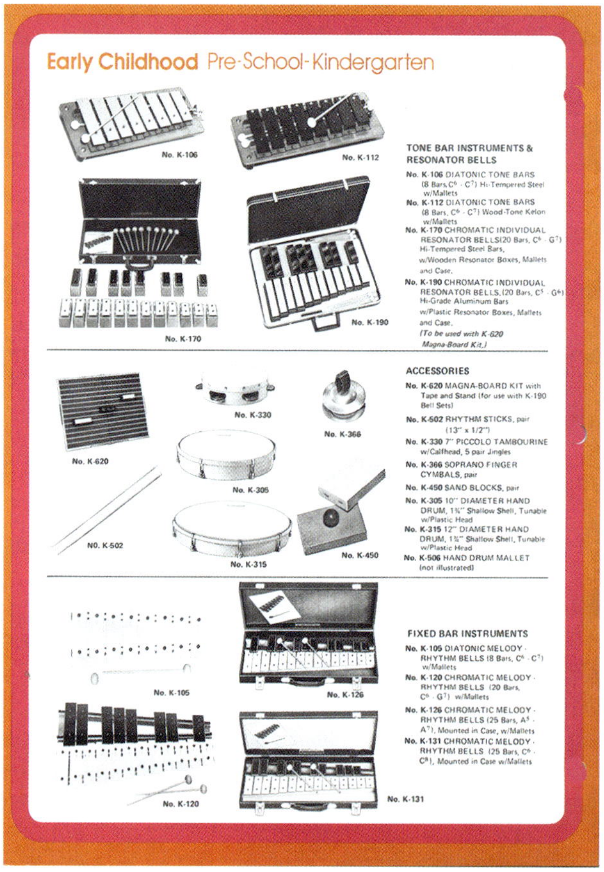

Early Childhood Pre-School-Kindergarten

TONE BAR INSTRUMENTS & RESONATOR BELLS

No. K-106 DIATONIC TONE BARS (8 Bars, C^6 - C^7) Hi-Tempered Steel w/Mallets

No. K-112 DIATONIC TONE BARS (8 Bars, C^6 - C^7) Wood-Tone Kelon w/Mallets

No. K-170 CHROMATIC INDIVIDUAL RESONATOR BELLS (20 Bars, C^6 - G^7) Hi-Tempered Steel Bars, w/Wooden Resonator Boxes, Mallets and Case.

No. K-190 CHROMATIC INDIVIDUAL RESONATOR BELLS (20 Bars, C^5 - G^6) Hi-Grade Aluminum Bars w/Plastic Resonator Boxes, Mallets and Case. *(To be used with K-620 Magna-Board Kit.)*

ACCESSORIES

No. K-620 MAGNA-BOARD KIT with Tape and Stand (for use with K-190 Bell Sets)

No. K-502 RHYTHM STICKS, pair (13" x 1/2")

No. K-330 7" PICCOLO TAMBOURINE w/Calfhead, 5 pair Jingles

No. K-366 SOPRANO FINGER CYMBALS, pair

No. K-450 SAND BLOCKS, pair

No. K-305 10" DIAMETER HAND DRUM, 1¾" Shallow Shell, Tunable w/Plastic Head

No. K-315 12" DIAMETER HAND DRUM, 1¾" Shallow Shell, Tunable w/Plastic Head

No. K-506 HAND DRUM MALLET (not illustrated)

FIXED BAR INSTRUMENTS

No. K-105 DIATONIC MELODY-RHYTHM BELLS (8 Bars, C^6 - C^7) w/Mallets

No. K-120 CHROMATIC MELODY-RHYTHM BELLS (20 Bars, C^6 - G^7) w/Mallets

No. K-126 CHROMATIC MELODY-RHYTHM BELLS (25 Bars, A^5 - A^7), Mounted in Case, w/Mallets

No. K-131 CHROMATIC MELODY-RHYTHM BELLS (25 Bars, C^6 - C^8), Mounted in Case w/Mallets

Lower Elementary Grades 1-3

DIATONIC "ORFF" INSTRUMENTS
with Box Resonators for Floor Placement

METAL BAR INSTRUMENTS

No. K-200 SOPRANO GLOCKENSPIEL (13 Bars, C^6 - A^7) w/Mallets

No. K-208 ALTO GLOCKENSPIEL (13 Bars, C^5 - A^6) w/Mallets

No. K-218 ALTO METALLOPHONE (13 Bars, C^4 - A^5) w/Mallets

WOOD TONE KELON BAR INSTRUMENTS

No. K-230 SOPRANO XYLOPHONE (13 Bars, C^5 - A^6) w/Mallets

No. K-238 ALTO XYLOPHONE (13 Bars, C^4 - A^5) w/Mallets

No. K-247 BASS XYLOPHONE (13 Bars, C^3 - A^4) w/Mallets

MEMBRANIC PERCUSSION

TUNABLE TIMPANI TOMS (Plastic Heads)

No. K-316 13" TIMP-TOM w/Mallets

No. K-317 14" TIMP-TOM w/Mallets

No. K-318 15" TIMP-TOM w/Mallets

No. K-319 16" TIMP-TOM w/Mallets

WIND INSTRUMENT

No. K-700 SOPRANO RECORDER (with Case & Fingering Chart)

No. K-924 RECORDER FOR BEGINNERS (Book)

No. K-950 PLAYING THE RECORDER (Record 33-1/3 L.P.)

ACCESSORIES

No. K-400 SOPRANO CLAVES, pair

No. K-410 SOPRANO WOOD BLOCK w/mallet

No. K-329 8" HEADLESS TAMBOURINE (7 pair Jingles)

No. K-360 6" TRIANGLE w/Beater and Clip Holder

No. K-378 11" HAND CYMBALS w/Straps, pair

No. K-394 SOPRANO COWBELL w/mallet

No. K-402 SOPRANO MARACAS, pair

No. K-406 SOPRANO GUIRO w/Scraper

No. K-452 SOPRANO SLEIGH BELLS ON WEB BAND (not illustrated)

No. K-454 SOPRANO SLEIGH BELLS ON HANDLE (not illustrated)

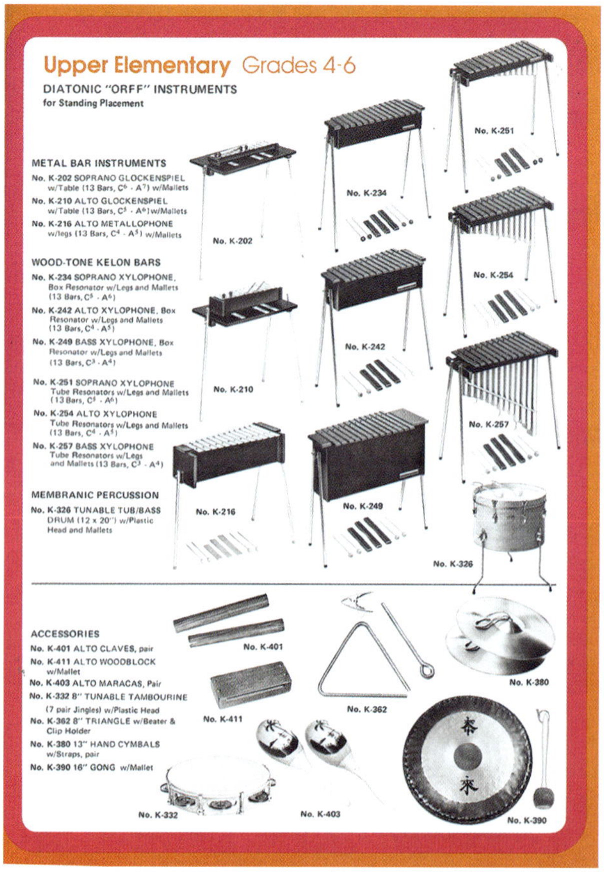

Upper Elementary Grades 4-6

DIATONIC "ORFF" INSTRUMENTS
for Standing Placement

METAL BAR INSTRUMENTS

No. K-202 SOPRANO GLOCKENSPIEL w/Table (13 Bars, C^6 - A^7) w/Mallets

No. K-210 ALTO GLOCKENSPIEL w/Table (13 Bars, C^5 - A^6) w/Mallets

No. K-216 ALTO METALLOPHONE w/legs (13 Bars, C^4 - A^5) w/Mallets

WOOD-TONE KELON BARS

No. K-234 SOPRANO XYLOPHONE, Box Resonator w/Legs and Mallets (13 Bars, C^5 - A^6)

No. K-242 ALTO XYLOPHONE, Box Resonator w/Legs and Mallets (13 Bars, C^4 - A^5)

No. K-249 BASS XYLOPHONE, Box Resonator w/Legs and Mallets (13 Bars, C^3 - A^4)

No. K-251 SOPRANO XYLOPHONE Tube Resonators w/Legs and Mallets (13 Bars, C^5 - A^6)

No. K-254 ALTO XYLOPHONE Tube Resonators w/Legs and Mallets (13 Bars, C^4 - A^5)

No. K-257 BASS XYLOPHONE Tube Resonators w/Legs and Mallets (13 Bars, C^3 - A^4)

MEMBRANIC PERCUSSION

No. K-326 TUNABLE TUB/BASS DRUM (12 x 20") w/Plastic Head and Mallets

ACCESSORIES

No. K-401 ALTO CLAVES, pair

No. K-411 ALTO WOODBLOCK w/Mallet

No. K-403 ALTO MARACAS, Pair

No. K-332 8" TUNABLE TAMBOURINE (7 pair Jingles) w/Plastic Head

No. K-362 8" TRIANGLE w/Beater & Clip Holder

No. K-380 13" HAND CYMBALS w/Straps, pair

No. K-390 16" GONG w/Mallet

Kitching Educational was a separate division within the Musser Company that made early elementary classroom instruments based on the Carl Orff method of music education. All of these instruments were being made in the Musser factory and were being marketed and promoted through the educational department. It was truly an educational department with educational programs, support literature, teaching aids and a nationally recognized clinician staff/roster for Ludwig, Musser, and Kitching Education. The two educational department secretaries worked full time on nothing but orchestrating these clinics. In addition to the scheduling and booking of the actual clinic events between the clinician and the hosting school or organization, there were the hotels, airline tickets, artist logistics, and the scheduling and shipping of clinic stock demonstration loaner instruments shipping to event locations,…and retrieving the instruments immediately afterwards.

Felix remained busy and constantly on-call checking out clinic stock instruments and getting them shipped out. He also had to inspect each return batch of instruments coming back from an artist-used event. The Education Department had a huge amount of equipment at our disposal to support all of these clinics. We were shipping timpani and vibes and chimes and drums all over the country every week- we were conducting 300 clinics a year.

The volume of clinics inspired me to get a huge map of the United States and have it framed and put on the central wall in the education department which by now was located on the fourth floor. That was where Frank Arsenault, Alice, Rochelle, and I clustered together as the education department. I had small color coded flags stick-pinned on the map for every clinic; each flag had the date and the name of the artist. The flags were color coded red for Ludwig, green for Musser, blue was for Kitching. We'd start every January with a blank map and end the year with a full map. Bill Ludwig loved this. Every time Bill would be giving a tour of the factory, he would end the tour up on the fourth floor, marching into the Educational Department office with his guests, and announcing, "Here is the wall of clinics! And this is where all of the booking for 300 clinics a year get arranged!"

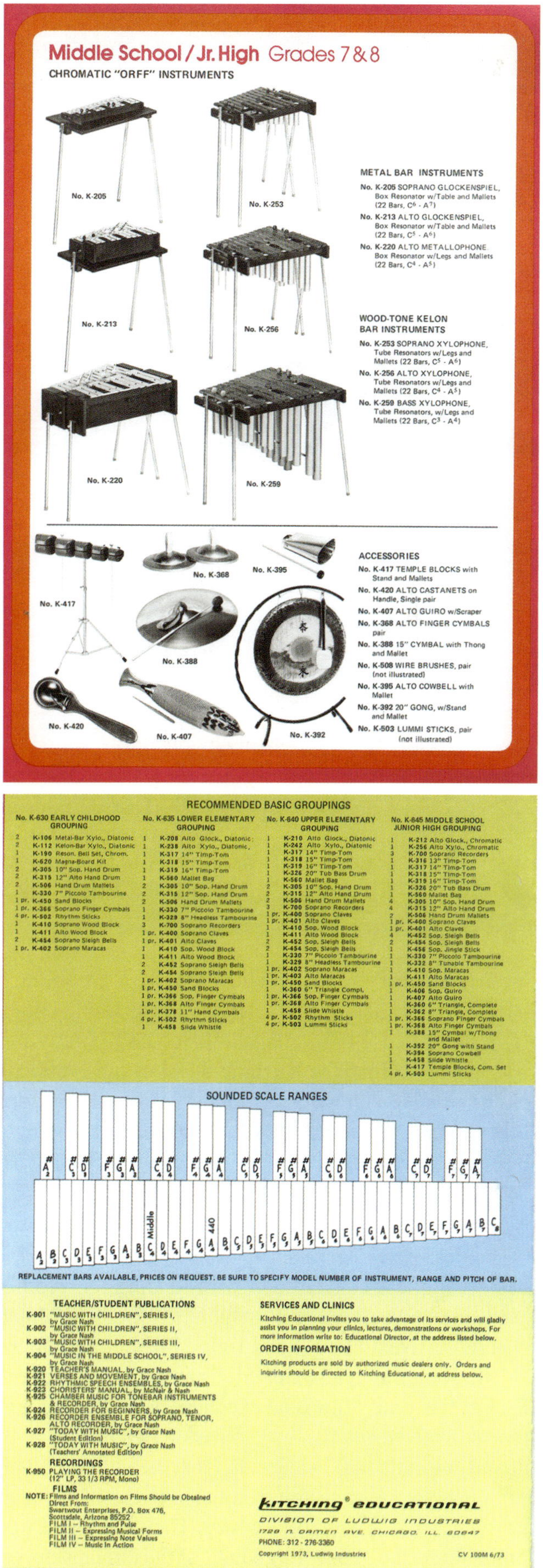

Ludwig Educational Department
Celebrating Karl Dustman's Birthday in 1973
(L-R) Educational Department Administrator Alice Golinski, Educational Director Karl Dustman, Educational Department Secretary Rochelle Waisman

Kitching Educational was growing. Grace Nash was the dominant clinician going all over the country doing these elementary educational clinics. We were selling more and more of the Kitching product and added Barbara Grenoble and Barbara Andress as Kitching clinicians. I was able to hire a product manager, Jim Holton, for Kitching. He did a marvelous job and I pretty much just let him run it. The long term company interest was just not behind the Kitching division and eventually it was gradually scaled down to zero. Bill Ludwig was not infatuated with Kitching. Under his breath he would complain that, "a $20,000. Kitching Educational sale fills a truck!" That did not kill the division, but it certainly placed Kitching further down on our totem pole of priorities. Bill was interested in Ludwig Musser. That's where we had to put the money, and that's where we had to put the time.

SUPPORTING THE VISION & VALUE OF PAS

The Percussive Arts Society grew in size, attendance and importance every year. Ludwig continued to invest heavily in these conventions, with funding for prominent clinicians on the program and elaborate display exhibits covering all product categories of Ludwig Musser. In the early days of the conventions the organization was run by Neal Fleugal and Jackie Meyers, serving as co-executive directors.

PAS went through some serious money management issues; I believe that Jim Petercsak was president of the PAS at this time. Jim is an excellent percussionist, presentation leader and spokesperson for the PAS. He was (and still is) the head of the Percussion Department at Crane School of Music in Potsdam, New York. The Executive Committee of PAS decided that the only way PAS was going to survive was to ask the percussion industry for a one year advance on membership dues. One of the first members they approached with the advance dues payment request was Bill Ludwig. They knew Bill was so committed to Percussive Arts Society that he would probably be the most "forgiving" of the circumstances and would help the organization as best as the company

A Memorable Moment:

By the middle of the 1970s Bill was volunteered to become MENC's Building Fund Chairman, raising donation money for the construction of the new MENC headquarters to be built in Reston, Virginia. The Ludwig Company was actively involved in all the regional and national MENC conferences and national conventions. Whenever he had an opportunity at a clinic or a hospitality suite, he would ask, "Karl! Where is the picture of the building?" He always wanted to show the huge picture of the artist's rendering of what the new MENC headquarters would look like. At the launch of the fundraising and his acceptance as building fund chairman, he donated the seed money of $25,000 on behalf of Ludwig Industries to help them build the building. From that point forward, it became part of his personal mission, which meant that it was my responsibility to be sure that his visual aid (the large picture of the building) was close at hand. To this day, the MENC building in Reston, VA. serves the organization with the same purpose although the name of the organization has since changed to NAfME, National Association for Music Education.

could. The company's PAS communications, membership and promotional focus fell under the Educational Department. Bill instructed me to "Give them our portion of what they need to stay afloat". This started the ball rolling; Ludwig gave them a year's dues in advance, as did Slingerland, Zildjian, and probably Gretsch. Basically the percussion industry bailed out PAS by giving them a huge lump sum representing everyone's membership dues for a year in advance. This fact is not spoken about too much anymore because there are not that many old-timers like me around. The Percussion Industry realized early on that what is good for percussion education is good for the percussion industry and vice-versa. I occasionally remind folks inside PAS that basically it is the percussion industry that has supported the Percussive Arts Society since the early years and quite honestly pays for a large portion of its existence today. The percussion industry partners with the Percussive Arts Society in seeing that the percussion industry survives and percussion education succeeds, survives, and grows. Together, those two entities support each other; neither can survive without the other. My early PAS colleagues John Beck (Eastman), Sandy Feldstein (Alfred Music), Lloyd Mc Causland (Remo), and Lenny DiMuzio (Zildjian) all recognized the mission and value of the PAS in its formative years. [Ed. note: In 1977 PAS President Petercsak appointed Karl to the position of Industry Consultant; he served in that capacity until 1981.]

The Music Products industry was experiencing tremendous growth through the 1970's and 1980's. While the annual June Music Expo in Chicago was considered THE industry's trade show, there was a "Western Market" convention in January, much smaller, that was moving around to different cities, connecting retailers with the industry that did not attend the annual Chicago Mc Cormick Place NAMM convention.

Ludwig watched this emphasis on the west coast market expand. Though the two Coast Wholesale sales and distribution connections in northern and southern California, they were handling the sales and dealer visits for all Ludwig-Musser products. By 1976 Ludwig chose to attend and exhibit at the "Winter Market NAMM Convention" in Anaheim, California. This was a very small convention of only three days and the entire exhibit area fit into the Grand Ballroom of the Disneyland Hotel.

On the success of the double-decker exhibit just launched at the previous Chicago summer convention, Ludwig custom built a smaller double-decker exhibit for the inaugural participation in the Winter Market convention. Bill Ludwig enjoyed the fact that Ludwig was again the only company exhibiting with a double-decker exhibit.

Today, of course these is no longer a June NAMM show convention in Chicago and never will be. The June show has evolved into a smaller Summer Show usually in July and takes place in the expanded Nashville Convention Center.

By 1976, Ludwig was exhibiting at two major NAMM trade shows and there were 40-45 individual state music educator conferences/conventions. In addition, there was the annual Percussive Arts Society convention (PASIC) and the annual Midwest Band and Orchestra Clinic convention in December, always right before the Christmas holidays. And if that was not enough we had at least 300 clinics a year. Were we busy? Unbelievably busy…

As my responsibilities grew, I eventually was given the title of Ludwig Musser Educational Director. I was proud of what was accomplished in a relatively short period of time, and credited the "arrive early, stay late, and work hard" words of wisdom I had received from my father at the very beginning of this Ludwig experience.

I continued to work more and more closely with the territory sales representatives. They knew that Ludwig was continuing to expand the clinician roster to do more clinics. The company knew this educational connection helped market share in every territory. The retailers liked this connection and the salesmen knew this would enhance their connection with all the prominent percussion instructors. Ludwig gave me the budget to recruit and book more clinics that could have direct impact on sales of all product lines. We had found a combination that was successful in selling products through education. Ludwig did not want to become the how-to-play element of the sales equation as they felt that was the responsibility of PAS.

Many of the top territory sales representatives would recommend key top percussion artists that either were already established major influences in percussion education or performance, or soon would be. We recognized up-and-coming gifted virtuoso artists like Leigh Howard Stevens who was graduating from Eastman School of Music under John Beck. Sales rep Leo Palas would contact me, "Karl- we need to get this guy; he is the virtuoso of the world on marimba!" Or West Coast sales representative Hank Larson would contact me, "We need Charles Dowd; he is the head honcho of the percussion department at the University of Oregon in Eugene..." This winning scenario went on and on as we diversified into more clinicians, more artists, and more product and brand visibility.

As the Ludwig educational clinician rosters grew in dominance and international recognition, we expanded the symposium artist teachers at select symposiums. Heinz Von Moisy from Germany attended as a symposium teacher and brought an entirely new dimension to drum set playing, reading and performance, from a European perspective. There were increasing numbers of students and teachers attending. Some participants became recognized for their annual attendance, taking 2-3-4 symposiums and became recognized as "Friends of the Symposium." We recognized them with a special certificates at the final night's evening concerts. It is gratifying that many of those students have become professionals now attending the PASIC conventions and they frequently stop me in the hallways to say hello and remind me of when they attended a specific year and location of a Ludwig International Symposium.

By the late 1970s, Ludwig was including in the symposium line-up the top echelon guys like Ed Shaughnessy, Buddy Rich- and newly recruited Max Roach. Max Roach had his own ensemble called M'Boom Re; Percussion that required a complete assortment of drums from Ludwig and every mallet instrument from Musser. He wanted all of this stuff provided to him at no charge as part of his endorsement of the Ludwig Drum Company. Bill Ludwig approved this cost and endorsement stipulation, knowing that M'Boom Re; Percussion would provide various concerts for the Ludwig company over time.

Ludwig did a photo session with Max Roach and created a two-color artist poster. It seemed like a good move, and I followed it up by featuring Max Roach as the headliner for the Percussion Symposium in the drum set category. We tried to rotate the artists so we were not repeating year after year with the same guys. Max Roach cancelled his appearance at the symposium about three weeks prior to the event. Whatever conflict or situation created the cancellation did not seem justified. There was no physical health issue, no conflict with a world tour or a recording date. Max just said, "Karl, there's a conflict, and I can't make it. I'm very sorry." I immediately advised Frank Baxpehler and Bill Ludwig of the telephone call I'd just received. Bill was livid. I had never seen Bill that angry at an artist.

"What do we do now, Karl? Your headliner cancelled!" All of a sudden, this was MY headliner! I suggested putting Shaughnessy back on the program. Ed had done a marvelous job the year before and was a team player. He knew the symposium ropes; he knew what to expect, and how to handle the teaching routine and students.. We didn't like to use the same headline artist two years in a row, but we had to have a headliner in three weeks. All the Ludwig color symposium ads were done, the brochures were printed, everything was completed for promoting the event and the teaching faculty. I convinced Bill to personally call Ed Shaughnessy from his office with me present and ask if he would be the substitute for Max Roach. Ed understood the situation and circumstances and immediately agreed to do attend the symposium and teach for three of the five days at the symposium. Ed said that he did want us to know that the date of his wedding anniversary fell on one of the symposium days and he was going to have to explain this to his wife, but that was his problem and not ours. At the symposium I personally introduced Ed as a gracious substitute instructor as there was a last minute schedule conflict for Max Roach. Everyone seemed fine with this situation and it was still a complete success. Ed did a fantastic job for Ludwig and the students.

As my position leading the Educational Department grew in title from "Educational Manager"… to the full scale "Educational Director" title previously held by Jim Sewrey, I was being carefully orchestrated out of and away from the sales forecasting elements of my original company-entry position. In early 1975, Executive Vice President Frank Peppler, died unexpectedly of a fatal heart attack in the Detroit airport while on a business trip with Bill Ludwig. This was a huge loss to the company, as "Pep" as he was often referred to, was a longtime member of the Ludwig Company and a personal friend and sailing partner of Bill.

I believe Frank Baxpehler used this change in management to re-align my duties and responsibilities, as my sales forecasting responsibilities eventually evaporated and were turned over to the sales and production areas of the company. Dick Gerlach assumed the position of sales manager and he soon led the company's domestic sales departments both in the field and internal customer service-sales operations.

Although I was no longer doing sales forecasting which meant that I had access to all of sales products records by units and dollars, I still felt that I had a pretty good feel for the financial footing of the company and its trends. I no longer had all of those computer printouts stacked up on my desk. Also gone were the blank sales forecasting forms waiting for me to complete with projections for every model number for the next twelve months. As department managers, none of us were invited to attend the Ludwig Board meetings. But, quite honestly, my "sixth sense" involved listening to conversations going on around me, taking the business-climate temperature of the people around me. I could observe all of the vice presidents from a slight distance and see who was jockeying for which position. Also it was easy to see which department was in the spotlight or hot-seat at the moment. This could change regularly between.... "Is production in the spotlight? Is purchasing in the spotlight? Marketing? Finance?" It changed regularly. It was pretty easy to determine what area within the company was wagging the dog's tail, and that said a lot about what the business climate was. By the early and middle 1970s, a lot was going on within the company and the percussion market. The school business remained the predictable constant for Ludwig during some of the slower drum set sales periods of the seventies. For those economic downturn periods when drum set sales were flat or faltering, the Musser Division and the marching, concert percussion and the timpani product lines were reasonably consistent.

Catalog 75-1, the first to feature Karl's photo with Ludwig personnel

LUDWIG NEW PRODUCT INTRODUCTIONS AND MILESTONES:

A product launch in January of 1973 would provide the greatest impact on the Ludwig company since the "Beatle Boom" of the mid 1960's. VISTALITE. Acrylic transparent shells in five different transparent colors, crystal clear, opaque white and opaque black. While Fibes Drums was recognized as the only company making and selling transparent drums at that time made from quarter-inch thick plexiglass, the idea never really took off until Ludwig starting making drums in different colors. Eventually six different patterns that could employ up to three different colors expanded the market presence. The visual possibilities were endless and the market loved the looks as well as the completely different and extremely loud sound of the drums.

The full color Vistalite brochure was the brainchild of advertising manager Vern Bush.

The "Ludwig 75" catalog was released in December of 1973 with one hundred thousand copies printed. Pages 4 and 5 were always reserved for a two-page spread featuring the newest and greatest Ludwig new products, so in Catalog 75 they featured Vistalite. A twelve-piece Octoplus set using all six available color options was featured on the cover. Eventually this rainbow of color in one set was referred to as a Jelly Bean outfit.

To help the Ludwig outside sales force present and sell the Vistalite products to their dealers, the company produced an 8 ½x11 cardboard window that included 2-inch square color chip-samples of each color held together within a cardboard holder. This sales aid produced a dazzling affect when held up to the light. It really showed the real color of each of the plexiglas samples. These were quite expensive to put together; the process involved cutting the large sheets of quarter-inch plexiglass into hundreds and hundreds of the small 2x2 squares. Then someone in the internal printing and mail-room department assembled these into finished p.o.p. sales aids.

At one point, close to 50% of the Ludwig drum shell production was allocated to Vistalite shells. That ran across the product lines in drum set, snare drums, and eventually marching drums. Vistalite became a real focal point and production priority. Bill, and the entire company for that matter, was enthralled with this additional Vistalite business because there were so many different patterns and configurations available. Every time management would enter the Vistalite department, we would see new sample shells: horizontal

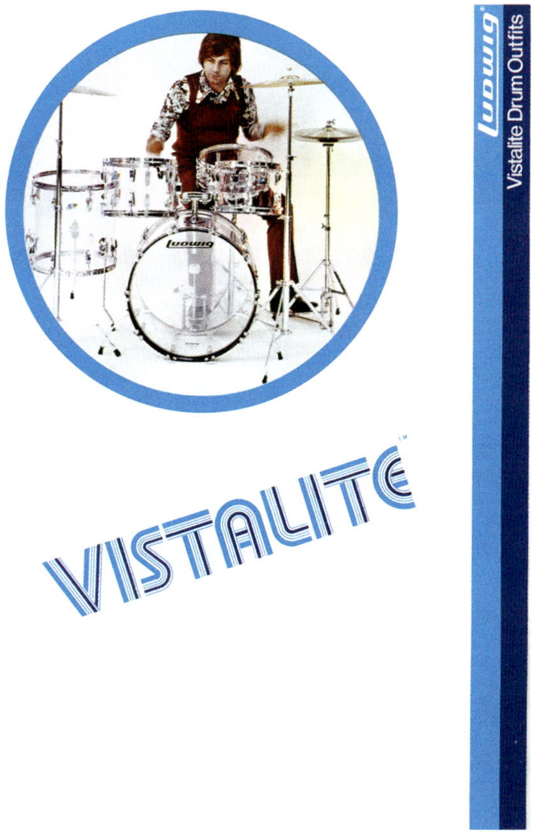

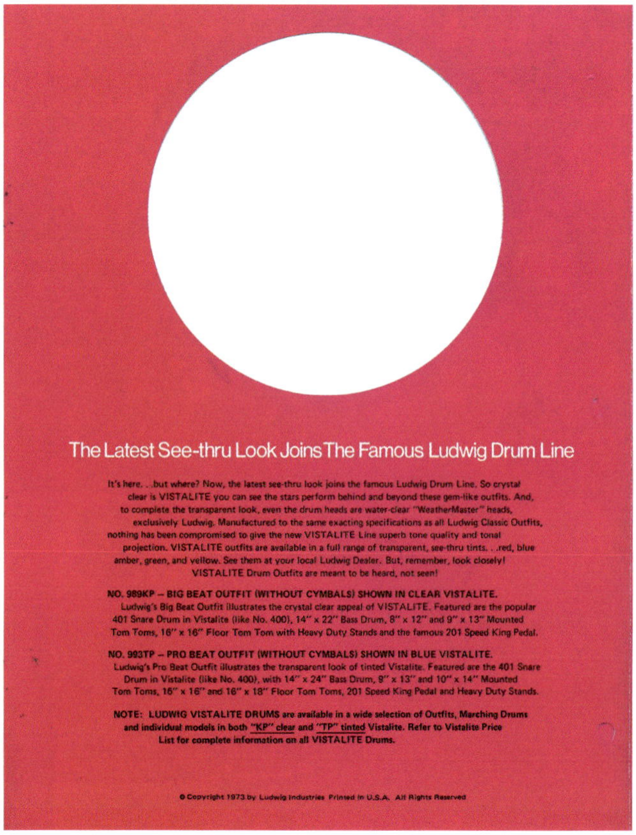

and vertical stripes, barber pole stripes; the patterns seemed endless.

The production department, of course, went crazy. There were too many varieties! Six different colors with six different assembly patterns; it was difficult to turn Vistalite production into a mechanized process and it was very labor intensive. That same versatility, however, gave the Vistalite line a tremendous market share advantage. It meant so much to the Ludwig production line that there was no turning back and it was reasonably profitable product line . As with any new product introduction, there are always "issues" that develop and create quality control concerns. Initially some of the shell seams were coming unglued. The solution to this was to review and refine the heating and gluing process; that was done quickly and it solved the separation problems. The factory of course replaced the problem shells, pre-drilled and free of charge, so those problems went away.

The other concern was that some of the torque on the lugs was so extensive that it created "spider-web" tiny cracks around the lug screw holes. That was eventually solved by drilling the holes a little differently. While I don't quite understand the engineering principle that worked with the revised drilling procedure, the stress was removed from the shell at the edges of those lug-mounting holes.

The next Vistalite development was illuminating the inside of the transparent drums with small Christmas tree lights inside each the drums. That idea evolved into the product named Tivoli. The name came from Bill, who said the small twinkling lights reminded him of the Tivoli gardens in Copenhagen, Denmark.

NO. 2201 CLEAR

NO. 2205 YELLOW

NO. 2216 BLUE

NO. 2241 GREEN

NO. 2209 AMBER

NO. 2236 RED

LUDWIG VISTALITE COLORS

Ludwig VISTALITE Drums are available in all colors illustrated. Be sure to specify color and number on all orders.

VISTALITE Snare Drums are available in the following models for Outfit and Orchestra use.

No. 401KP 5" x 14" Clear Vistalite
No. 401TP 5" x 14" Tinted Vistalite
No. 403KP 6½" x 14" Clear Vistalite
No. 403TP 6½" x 14" Tinted Vistalite
No. 413KP 5" x 14" Clear Vistalite
No. 413TP 5" x 14" Tinted Vistalite
No. 415KP 6½" x 14" Clear Vistalite
No. 415TP 6½" x 14" Tinted Vistalite

NOTE: 401 and 403 feature 10 lugs and are Vistalite versions of the famous Ludwig 400 and 402 Metal Shell Snare Drums. 413 and 415 models also feature 10 lugs and are Vistalite versions of the 410 and 411 Super Sensitive Metal Snare Drums. For additional information refer to Vistalite Price List.

Ludwig DRUM CO.
DIVISION OF LUDWIG INDUSTRIES
1728 N. DAMEN AVE. CHICAGO, ILL. 60647

CV 50M 173

Pattern A, Red/Amber/Yellow Vistalite Illustrated
Pat. No. 4045264

OUTFIT ACCESSORIES

2—1406	Cymbal Stands
1—1131	Hi-Hat
1—1374	Drum Stand
1—781	Dbl. Holder
1—201	Pedal
1 pair	Sticks
1 pair	Brushes

Complete with Tivoli Light system and transformer—ready to use!

LISTED

Ludwig TIVOLI* LIGHTED OUTFIT

This is the newest, boldest, wildest innovation in performance drums from Ludwig. It is the first drum outfit ever designed with built-in miniature lighting!

Tivoli lights turn a song into a show. Bands of tiny lights sparkle through the multi-colored Vistalite* material to produce a unique stage presence.

Years in development, Tivoli lights were perfected and proven in space travel! These same lights are electrifying audiences around the world! Tivoli drums are available in any combination of Vistalite colors! A handy on-off switch is provided. Ludwig's exclusive own-make Silver Dot* heads are mounted on all batter heads except snare.

Drum Outfits with Tivoli* lighting are available only in three band Rainbow Pattern A in the Vistalite "Big Beat" series. Order your favorite color combination of crystal clear, smoke, and transparent tints of blue, red, amber and yellow.

MODEL	TOM TOMS			BASS	SNARE
981	12"	13"	16"	22"	5" x 14" — V-lite
982	12"	13"	16"	24"	5" x 14" — V-lite
1013	13"	14"	16"	22"	5" x 14" — V-lite
1014	13"	14"	18"	24"	5" x 14" — V-lite

No. 981-Outfit with Tivoli lights, Pattern A, Rainbow V-lite. (Cymbals not included.) PATENTS PENDING.

No. 982-Outfit with Tivoli lights, same as above but with 14" x 24" bass drum (Cymbals not included.) PATENTS PENDING.

No. 1013-Outfit with Tivoli lights, 13" and 14" aerial toms, 16" floor tom and 22" bass. (Cymbals not included.) PATENTS PENDING.

No. 1014-Outfit with Tivoli lights, with 13" and 14" aerial toms, 18" floor tom and 24" bass. (Cymbals not included.) PATENTS PENDING.

No. 6950 Set of 4 Molded Cases — for 12", 13" and 16" Tom Toms and 22" or 24" Bass Drum.

Note: Protect your drums! See Ludwig's factory made line of cases on pages 94 & 95.

4 *Licensed under TM. Reg. No. 1,013,476.

Of course none of us had ever traveled it Copenhagen, so we had no idea what he was talking about. The Ludwig engineering team figured out a way to shock-mount the clear lights in all of these drums, and to have the cords come out of each drum and connect to a transformer-box-controller that would be plugged into a standard 110-V outlet. There were some problems with Tivoli without a doubt. Placing small lights inside drums that are constantly vibrating is a real challenge. (To this day I personally feel that drums should not be connected to electricity.)

There was a lot happening and developing during 1973 and 1974. Kitching Educational was a vivid division within Musser. A lot of emphasis was put on Kitching Educational as this also served as an additional/different entrance to the school market business but through the Orff-Kodaly classroom instruments. This expanded into having elementary classroom recorders, a beginner bell instrument, and many different hand-held percussion classroom instruments. At this point the only real competition was Studio 49 and Peripole. Kitching, as a division of Ludwig-Musser, was able to dominate this classroom market because of the muscle of Ludwig and Musser. We had a number of prominent international clinicians; the most notable were Grace Nash, Barbara Grenoble, and Barbara Andres. As part of the educational clinic program under my direction, this grew annually and we ended up with more "Kitching clinic/workshop flags" than ever on the big Educational Department wall-size clinic map. As Kitching Educational increased in time and sales requirements, I hired a Kitching product manager, Jim Holton. This expanded the Educational Department and Kitching remained his sole responsibility as he handled the three huge product demonstration clinic kits that were constantly going out to workshops, and of course returning.

Early on, Ludwig produced a "Junior Percussionist's Kit" that included a 2½ octave keyboard, a practice pad, and a stand that could be used with either instrument. This elementary percussion kit that presented and taught both drum stick instruction (drums) as well as basic melodic note and staff recognition became an essential of the newer beginning percussion education curriculums. It lacked a suitable instruction book that combined both rhythmic and melodic instruction, in one book completely based on the Ludwig Junior Percussionist Kit. Roger Faulmann was the Director of Bands at the University of Illinois and an educator friend of Bill Ludwig. Bill commissioned Roger to write a book on exclusively using and teaching with the Junior Percussionist's Kit. The editing and printing of the entire book became a project for the Educational Department, so now I became the internal Ludwig book editor. Roger would provide me with two or three pages of text and musical exercises at a time, I would review and edit the manuscripts accordingly, then turn both elements over to Cedar Valley Printing for their handling of the original artwork for each of the graphic page "boards".

Throughout 1973 and 1974, there was intense work on the new 103 page full line Ludwig catalog that would carry a cover-date of 1975. There were actually three separate printings of the 1975 catalog. The initial release was a one-hundred thousand copy printing in December 1973. This was followed by revised version labeled 75-1 released in October 1974 with another one hundred thousand copies. The third and final reprint in November, 1975, was seventy-five thousand copies. That totals two hundred and seventy-five thousand 103 page all color catalogs- over 28 million total pages!

I was thrilled to be included in the 75-1 personnel pages of the initial catalog release, being referred to as the Educational Manager. This was a personal accomplishment for me, as I had studied the Ludwig catalog personnel pages for years as a young boy, never thinking I would be part of the Ludwig team at some future point in time. The 1975 catalog was completely under the direction of Advertising Manager Vern Bush and he did a marvelous job. I was fortunate enough to work closely with him on all the elements of catalog production and assist as a member of the proof-reading team.

This was one of the first catalogs that introduced the LUDWIG FAMILY, featured on the inside front cover with a tribute to William F. Ludwig Senior (1879-1973) and page one with photos of Directors, Betty Ludwig Dodson and Mrs.(Maggie) Ludwig and, of course, Bill Jr. This was a clear statement and message to the percussion public; Ludwig was a family owned and operated business. Up until this point the catalogs included only Bill Jr., but by the 1980 catalog it became Bill Jr. and Bill III.

It was becoming apparent that Betty Ludwig-Dodson, Bill's sister, was getting more involved in the company. She was attending all of the board meetings and expressing her thoughts and opinions. Those of us on staff who were non-family members of course recognized that blood is thicker than water and of course showed Betty the appropriate respect. I first got to know Betty Ludwig a little better when she decided to attend one of the percussion symposiums held in Madison or Eau Clarie Wisconsin. It was always great to

William F. Ludwig, Sr.
1879-1973

We dedicate this page to our founder, Wm. F. Ludwig, Sr. who, for 64 years, guided the destiny and development of our company.

Ludwig Industries was founded June 1st 1909, by Mr. Ludwig and his brother Theobold in a humble garage on Chicago's west side. Both were drummers with a mutual interest in improving drum products.

Their first product, a drum pedal, was successful from the start. The success of this venture paved the way for the development of the first all-metal snare drum made on a production basis in this country, pedal tuned timpani and hundreds of new and progressive drummer's instruments and accessories.

We, the associates and employees of Ludwig Industries, salute the Founder of the modern drum industry, Wm. F. Ludwig, Sr., and pledge our allegiance to his lofty ideals in the performance of our duties in this, our chosen work.

©Copyright 1974 by Ludwig Industries Printed in U.S.A. All rights reserved

The Ludwig Family

William F. Ludwig, Jr.
President

Mrs. Maggie Ludwig
Director

Bill Ludwig, III

Bettie Ludwig
Director

The name "Ludwig" designates more than a person, more than a brand of product, and even more than a company. It is a family heritage. . . an inheritance accrued over three generations of total dedication in serving the music profession. The name "Ludwig" has become synonomous with innovation, craftsmanship, product quality, and acknowledged superiority in the field of total percussion. The continuity of what has become to be a family tradition, leadership, is assured by the President of Ludwig Industries- - "The greatest sustaining factor, "says Bill Ludwig, Jr.," is the pride of accomplishment which has been instilled in each member of our corporate family - - our skilled and loyal employees, our highly experienced department heads, our competent executive staff, our energetic company sales force, and the more than 3,500 enthusiastic Ludwig music dealers world wide".

1

have one of the Ludwig family members attending and participating at those events. I knew the importance of seeing that she was treated as a guest of honor; I had her all-access Symposium badge waiting for her in her hotel room, made certain her hotel room was suitable and already "checked-in" upon her arrival, and that her Symposium schedule for the entire event was in an envelope with her name on it sitting on the bed in her hotel room. Betty liked this respectful treatment.

I would speculate that with the passing of WFL Sr. in 1973, Betty started taking on a more active role in the company, probably starting to voice her opinions, questioning her brother's decisions and sometimes this would not sit well. I could get a feel for this immediately after the Ludwig Board of Director's meetings. When that conference room door opened and the officers came out, there was regularly some notable tension among those attendees. My astute awareness picked-up on the conversation tones, the verbal good-byes, or how fast people were walking out of the conference room. Clearly the family board meetings were beginning to get heated. I believe Bill did not like answering to anyone. His father was gone, and my assumption was that he didn't want Betty questioning his decisions. I will not speculate on where or how Mrs. Ludwig expressed her views and opinions, but this must have included sometimes even questioning some of Bill's decisions.

Part of the results for this increasing tension may have been that Betty decided to bring her daughter Pat Dodson into the company. Advertising Manager Vern Bush had been doing artist relations as part of his role in the advertising department, with the support of Advertising Secretary Lorrain Levine. When Lorraine Levine left the firm to move out of state with her husband, the opportunity for Pat Dodson presented itself. Once again, I recognized that this was family, and I made certain to get along very well with both Betty and Pat. Pat was given a very small windowless office on the second floor, immediately next to the elevator. It was pretty much on-the-job training for her, according to "Uncle Bill". Pat was not a drummer, not a percussionist. She needed to learn the product and related vocabulary, she had to learn who the existing Ludwig-Musser artists were, what bands they were in, what tours they were on, and it was a completely new experience. She took on the challenge with serious dedication and worked well with those of us she needed to learn from. Pat learned there were a handful of us who knew most of the answers (or knew how to find the answers) and she was good about seeking us out. At the same time, Bill lll was starting to work within the company assisting in the internal customer service-sales area during the summers and various breaks from his school schedule. This hands-on company experience also included some computer punch-card processing in the new significantly enlarged computer data processing department. With a new IBM 360 one-million dollar computer installed in the company, the Computer Department was a big deal.

More and more projects were developing which required time, money, and people. The mid 1970s were very competitive and we were all being asked to do MORE and diversify the contributions we could make and bring to the company. It was decided to bring in a public relations firm. A number of different firms were interviewed by Vern Bush and Frank Baxpehler. Jack Levy and Associates was selected and they become attendees, participants, and project managers for a number of marketing-advertising-promotion-public relations projects within the company. The country's 1976 Bicentennial year of celebration was approaching and there needed to be some Ludwig-driven big things happening in the percussion market place.

The costs of producing and printing two hundred and seventy-five thousand 103-page full line catalogs were astronomical. The costs were being closely scrutinized, as many new Ludwig drum set related products were immerging on the market and were not included in the 75-1 catalog.

Through the ingenuity of Frank Baxpehler, the first Ludwig Pocket Catalog 76 emerged. We'd found that people were asking for the Ludwig catalog and getting the 103 page full-line catalog when all they were really interested in was the drum set pages. Ludwig was the only drum company and brand that was building and offering maple wood shell, Vistalite, and now stainless steel shell choices for drum set.

The first printing of this "pocket catalog," as it became known, was 150,000. It came out in November of 1975 with the intent of making this a widely distributed consumer drum set focused promotional catalog at a fraction of the cost of a full line 103 page catalog. This was Ludwig's first entrance into providing these pocket catalogs in bulk to authorized Ludwig dealers with a small 3 ½" x 1 1/4" square open box for the dealer to place their own sticker or store identification. The marketing emphasis at this point was concentrated on Ludwig's offering of three different kinds of shells which produced three different kinds of sounding drums. There was the classic traditional wood shell utilizing American maple, the complete array of all the Vistalite drum colors and patterns, and the all new one-piece stainless steel shells available in all the traditional and extended sizes. The pocket catalog served as a merchandising tool as it also included all of the drum set-related stands, pedal, thrones and hardware plus the entire range of related drum set accessories.

A Memorable Moment:

A Memorable Moment: During this time The CARPENTERS were extremely popular with a number of #1 hit recordings supported by national performance tours. Karen Carpenter was a gifted drummer in addition to being a talented vocalist and frontline for The Carpenters along with her brother Richard. The Carpenters were coming to Chicago for a concert performance at the Arie Crown Theater within the McCormick Place Convention Center. This was a huge venue and the one-night-only performance was heavily promoted weeks in advance. Vern Bush asked me if I wanted to go with him to meet with Karen and deliver some Ludwig hardware back stage before the concert. I jumped at the opportunity. I was a huge fan of The Carpenters' harmonic and orchestral arrangement sound, had many of their recordings and meeting Karen would certainly be a wonderful experience. I was right, Karen was a gracious, charming woman who took time to meet with us, did not complain about anything from the Ludwig product or organization, and seemed interested in working with a drum company that manufactured VISTALITE transparent drums.

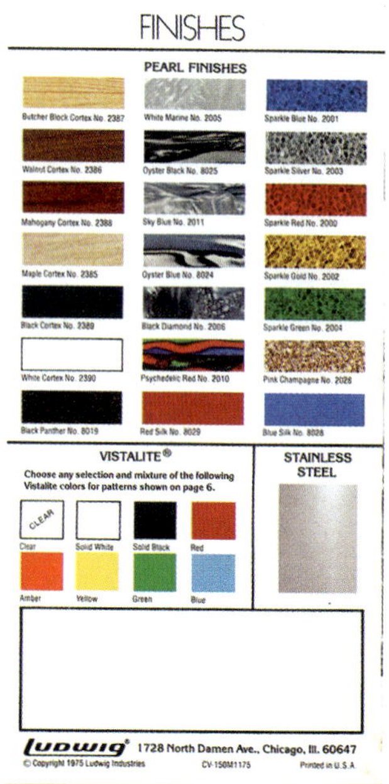

ROY KNAPP

Anyone growing up, working or living in Chicago that anything to do with percussion, knew ROY KNAPP as the premier most colorful drum teacher in town. His reputation for creating many prominent players and teachers was paralleled by his abundant stories about the early days of drumming in Chicago's vaudeville and burlesque theater. Some of his stories were not repeatable, particularly in polite company. Roy was an affable "big man", demanding attention everywhere he went, by size alone. His roots in Chicago drumming, teaching, performing were shared with the vintage drum personalities of Haskell Harr and William F. Ludwig Sr.

Roy's son Donald Knapp created a Roy Knapp Testimonial Day (September 1, 1974) held at the Oakbrook Sheraton Hotel Ballroom. Bill Ludwig became a dominant individual involved in the orchestration of this event. Jerry Owings, the Ludwig internal graphic artist, was given the assignment of creating the full page invitation used to promote the event throughout Chicagoland. Jerry was also instrumental in the artistic rendering for the cover artwork on the Testimonial Day program. This event was well attended by everyone in percussion within Chicago and Northwest Indiana and provided a wonderful "percussion industry tribute" to Roy Knapp. (Roy Knapp would pass away on June 16th, 1979.)

After the Roy Knapp tribute, the decision as to what to do with Roy's original 1920s working drummer drum set became a topic of discussion. Donnie Knapp thought this vintage set should be shared with the percussion world. Bill Ludwig agreed to display the drum set in the front-door lobby of the Ludwig Company for about a year. A special white Plexiglas riser was constructed in the Vistalite department specifically to fit within the size limitations of the lobby. A special tribute information podium was constructed to inform every visitor entering the lobby what the drum set was and who this vintage memorable set belonged to. This attracted some attention in a positive way, but also limited the room for guest seating in the lobby. Eventually this Roy Knapp drum set was returned to Donnie Knapp and he placed it in the Percussive Arts Society's Museum in Indianapolis, Indiana.

Ludwig was one of the very few companies that manufactured all their own drum sticks, wire brushes, and Mylar plastic drum heads. All of this was crammed into a twenty-two page 7 ½" x4" booklet. This was a huge success for the authorized Ludwig dealers and set the precedent for further individual product line catalogs as well as the use of regular dealer imprint and personalization to Ludwig catalogs, promotional pieces, and even drum heads.

At this time the world was experiencing the introduction of vacuum formed cases. Everything from Black & Decker/Skill tools to microphones to delicate testing instruments were being sold in sturdy, transportable, economical vacuum-formed reusable molded cases. Ludwig worked directly with the W.R. Grace Company in developing the double wall UFO snare drum kits and new junior percussionist kits. Both existing products (snare drums and bell kits) were re-packaged in the new vacuum-formed molded cases and were introduced in October, 1975. Getting to this point was a long and challenging process as the tooling costs involved were significant and the components of each kit could not change in the future. There were seven different model number variations on the components of the UFO Kits, based upon the different practice pads and snare models that would kit in the one-size-fits-all case.

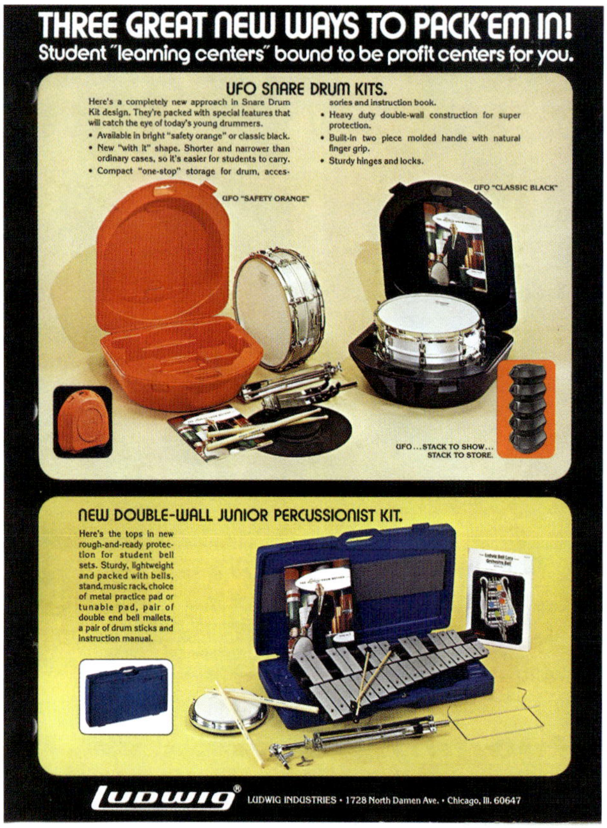

UFO Snare Drum Kits were available in bright bus-stop orange or traditional black and they replaced the heavy traditional accordion-style square cases of the past. As with any new product there were "bugs" in the design. The "living hinge" connecting the top and bottom double-walled sections wore-out after a significant number of openings and closings. The closure "living latches" in the front of the cases also experienced fatigue failure. Eventually both "living hinges and latches" were replaced with metal parts permanently affixed to the molded case. As time wore on, the orange case lost out as sales of the traditional black cases dominated the market. Other drum companies followed the molded-case market development, all learning the same advantages and challenges of the vacuum formed molded case business. These sold by the thousands; the response was tremendous and Ludwig continued to own and dominate a very large portion of the beginner kit market.

The Ringer Timpani project of 1974 was a personal ambition of Bill Ludwig. He had a strong desire to have a professional high-end line of European-style Dresden timpani with his name on them. I think a lot of this started in part through Don Koss, who was the Principle Timpanist with the Chicago Symphony Orchestra. Bill and his wife strongly supported the Chicago Symphony and always had season tickets to the Symphony. On occasion, Bill could not attend an evening concert and would sanction his secretary Kay Holstein to pass these along to select individuals within the management team that would appreciate and enjoy a Chicago Symphony Concert. While this was always a spur-of-the-moment invitation, I accepted on occasion and thoroughly enjoyed the wonderful concert and some of the best seats in Chicago's Orchestra Hall. This was always a treat and I personally would thank Bill and Kay Holstein for thinking of me in passing along the unused Chicago Symphony tickets. Don Koss replaced Ed Metzinger (who always played Ludwig timpani) as Principle Timpanist. Through the early years I remember seeing full page color advertisements for Ludwig Timpani with a picture of Ed Metzinger behind a set of four shiney polished copper timpani. Don Koss refused to play Ludwig balanced-action timpani. They were not European (Berlin, Dresden) style drums. This fact taunted Bill Ludwig and he would become more upset about not seeing or hearing Ludwig timpani at Orchestra Hall every time he attended a Chicago Symphony Concert. It was his decision that purchasing an existing European timpani company would be easier than designing and starting from scratch.

Gunter Ringer's timpani were manufactured in Germany. They were considered top-professional instruments, but were not readily available in the market and certainly not in the United States. While there were other premium timpani in the marketplace; Goodman, Walter Light, Fred Hinger etc, Bill wanted to be in that high-end professional timpani market. The only way Ludwig could see achieving this market was when it became known that Gunter Ringer was looking to sell his company. It was known that each drum was handmade in Germany in a very small unsophisticated manufacturing operation that basically hand fitted each drum together, part-by-part. There were not any real orderly blueprints or specifications, part tolerances etc.

Ringer Timpani became a year and a half to two year project with vast amounts of time, money and effort placed into this potential new product line. Ludwig would send Chief Engineer Dan Mikoz to Germany for two weeks to work on Ringer Timpani manufacturing and specifications. Mikoz would return with all of his notes for three weeks to work on blueprints, manufacturing dies and tooling in order to convert the Gunter Ringer manufacturing process to a Ludwig Chicago-factory production.

The goal was to produce the drums to consistent specifications as opposed to hand-fitting all of the parts on each individual drum like what was happening in Germany. Ludwig was finally able to launch the Ringer "Made by Ludwig" line of timpani in June of 1975. This represented a great personal accomplishment for Bill. It also helped that the line was initially somewhat profitable. Ringer timpani were manufactured in the regular Ludwig timpani department, but to far more exacting standards and requirements on time, labor, parts procurement and assembly. The Ringer timpani produced by Ludwig were a vast improvement to the inconsistencies of the European factory. The engineering expertise at Ludwig made tremendous improvements to some design features, portability, and refinement of parts working and fitting together properly.

The product launch offered standard sets of two, four or five drums in a total of five different traditional individual sizes. I think a standard set of four was selling for about $15,000.00 which included Super Kalfo Irish calfskin heads. In today's economy and market, the Ringer by Ludwig sets of four timpani would probably have to sell close to forty thousand dollars just to make it a profitable venture and product line. Bill was very proud of this Ringer timpani achievement and the placement of his drums in Orchestra Hall in Chicago. This was combined with the widespread feeling in the market that Ludwig was the only United States manufacturer producing professional European-style timpani on a daily basis within a full scale timpani manufacturing factory. A significant achievement for Ludwig and anyone for that matter, at any time in percussion history.

Often United States military bands, colleges, conservatories, and universities would visit the factory to see, hear, and test the Ringer timpani placed in the Timpani Department. Bill got personally involved in hosting some of these guests, escorting them up to the second floor and showing them his drums. He was very proud of the Ringer Timpani, and justifiably so. The six page Ringer Timpani full color brochure released in June of 1975 featured Bill Ludwig with a set of four drums spread across a three page center spread. It's a great pose and all of us at the Reed Wallace Photography photo-session commented on the single diamond stud placed on his tuxedo black bow tie. Twenty-five thousand color brochures were printed and distributed to the global market.

I was personally honored to substitute for Bill on many occasions when he was unable to be in attendance for specific Ringer Timpani guest appointments and visits to the factory. I guess I was selected because of my direct interest in Timpani and orchestral percussion. Everything I learned about the mechanics of Dresden style timpani at that time I learned from Bill Ludwig and through the Ringer Timpani project.

Ringer Timpani was a huge expense and I'm sure John Mahoney, the VP of finance, often verbally questioned the validity of spending the Ludwig time and money on such a niche market product line. How many sets of Ringer timpani can be sold in the world? But Ludwig was Bill's company, and it was what he wanted to do. Personally, I feel that from a marketing standpoint, it made complete sense. Ludwig dominated the timpani market; why not have European-style timpani manufactured here in Chicago?

EXACTING DESIGNS OF THE MASTER CRAFTSMAN GÜNTER RINGER ASSURE YOU OF EXCELLENCE IN HAND-MADE CONSTRUCTION.

EXCLUSIVE SHAPE. The unmistakable "Cambered" shape and hammered pure copper freely-suspended kettle, produces not only the most beautiful timpani, but results in a new dimension of sound.

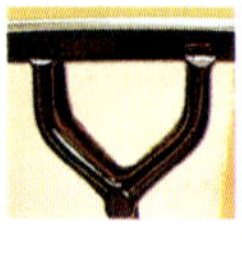

EXCLUSIVE HAND-FITTED CONSTRUCTION. Metal does not touch metal at any suspension point. The kettle, support ring and struts are worked together and fitted by hand. This assures the tympanist a uniformly even rim…a perfectly round sound. And constant pitch, without decay.

EXCLUSIVE FOOT PEDAL AND STIRRUP. With almost unbelievable smoothness, the foot pedal places you in command at the Ringer Timpani. A unique ratchet lock-in gives you quick, positive and reliable tuning. When you set a note… it stays. And when you're ready to change, the response is immediate.

EXCLUSIVE TUNING GAUGE AND ADJUSTABLE LINKAGE. The tuning gauge is directly operated by the movement of the foot pedal. An adjustable linkage also enables you to initially set the pointer during tuning. And because of this a more instant and truer reading is given during play.

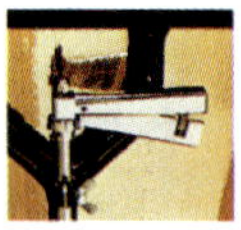

EXCLUSIVE PISTOL GRIP HANDLE FOR EXTRA FINE TUNING. Another advance in quick-response fractional tuning that's concert-quiet. The handle is convenient. The touch is easy. And the result is fingertip control with a detent lock that keeps the master tuning handle exactly where you want it.

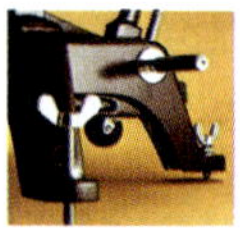

EXCLUSIVE STAGE SCREWS. Large butterfly winged screws offer great versatility. The Ringer Timpani can be anchored to the floor or the screws level the timpani on uneven surfaces. Or the entire kettle can be angled or canted to suite personal preference.

EXCLUSIVE STAGE DOLLY WHEELS. Incorporated in the base is a foot operated lever that engages built-in wheels, giving finger-tip movement about the stage.

The Ringer™ Timpani…in a class by itself. Hand fitted, easy to tune, easy to play, easy control. Easy to understand Ringer's outstanding reputation among the great musicians of our time, top studio artists and leading schools of music.

The Ringer experience begins with decades of recognition by leading professionals as the finest timpani in the world.

A recognition earned by incomparable craftsmanship, unique and exclusive details. All of which result in the most effortless and positive tuning and remarkable projection and resonance.

A recognition maintained by the Ringer sound itself. Matchless! To be heard in performances by the great musical organizations of the world.

Here are but a few of the fine orchestras where the Ringer Timpani is an integral part.

- Chicago Symphony
- Boston Symphony
- Philadelphia Symphony
- Cincinnati Symphony
- San Francisco Symphony
- Minneapolis Symphony
- Milwaukee Symphony
- Honolulu Symphony
- Miami Philharmonic
- Los Angeles Philharmonic
- Berlin Philharmonic
- Bayreuth Festspielhaus
- London Symphony
- Paris Opera
- Vienna Symphony
- La Scala
- Montreal Symphony
- Toronto Symphony
- Peabody Conservatory of Music
- Eastman School of Music
- Curtis Institute of Music
- University of Texas-Austin
- Boston University School of Music
- Indiana University

The Ringer experience. The ultimate in construction, performance and sound.

Soon after The Selmer Company bought out Ludwig Industries, Selmer was very quick to discontinue the Ringer timpani line because they did not feel the line was profitable enough. It is my understanding that even the parts inventory for Ringer timpani has been depleted.

Ludwig® & The Bicentennial

1975 was a year of preparations for America's Bicentennial 200-year celebration in 1976. Ludwig recognized the opportunity to participate in this 200 year celebration as drums were a very significant and visual part of the American Revolution. Bill Ludwig and the company's engineering department designed a series of limited Edition Ludwig Bicentennial drums. The Snare drums were styled after traditional colonial-style, revolutionary-looking drums in sizes 12x15 and 12x14. I believe there were two different 10-inch deep bass drums, and a tenor drum was also included in the product line. Snare drums had the American Eagle-Flag insignia centered on the Maple Cortex-covered wood shell. Simulated Tuning Ropes with authentic leather "ears" for tensioning top and bottom heads were augmented by traditional Silver Parade braids. The snare drums used gut snares and were equipped with the Super Classic strainer throw-off and the Super Sensitive Butt. The complete series looked fantastic and very authentic. While the drums were equipped with Ludwig Weather Master plastic heads on top and bottom, traditional small Classic Lugs were partially disguised under the simulated rope tensioning. Traditional lug tuning with plastic heads and gut snares made the snare drums sound very good.

Karl with his Bicentennial Ludwig parade drum which he uses in his role as a member of the Northcoast Brass. (L-R) Mike McGreen, Karl, James Kunc (see details in chapter 9)

Unfortunately, the Bicentennial series was met with very mild sales response. I'm not sure whether this was because of the price point, or maybe because people figured, after the 1976 celebration, it will be another hundred years before the drums get used and played again. While the Bicentennial Drums and series did not sell well, the drums have become definite collector 's items now. I personally own a 12"x15" Bi-Centennial Snare Drum with all original braids and Weather Master heads in my personal collection. I have used this in professional performance occasionally when appropriate and everyone loves the appearance and sound of the real gut snares.

Another tribute to the country's Bicentennial was the 1976 Ludwig Drummer magazine. This was the first new Ludwig Drummer since the 1972 edition. I was the project manager for this publication because of its educational focus and content. I worked closely alongside Advertising Manager Vern Bush and outside designer/PR firm Jack Levy & Associates. The thirty-nine page Ludwig Drummer 1976, was a major project for me. It called upon my expertise to layout the contents, secure the contributing educational article authors, perform editing duties, and to mix in enough "new Ludwig products" to have a commercial value to the magazine. It was a major accomplishment for the company but was to be the last Ludwig Drummer Magazine to ever be produced.

I believe it was Jack Levy who thought about commissioning an artist to design the wrap-around cover for the publication that created a visual drumming timeline, "drums through the ages," the original painting that became the cover for the magazine. I have a personal connection to the graphic design of the cover artwork, as I have the original commissioned artwork framed and on display in my personal office.

It also became a separate Ludwig promotional piece which included the signatures of all 500 Ludwig employees on the inside. Everyone employed by Ludwig, Musser, Kitching Educational had their signature included celebrating the nation's Bicentennial. Truly a magnificent recognition of every American employee who was working to build drums at the largest drum factory in the world.

That Ludwig Drummer commissioned cover artwork became the centerpiece for the next Chicago NAMM show Ludwig exhibit. For 1976, the Ludwig exhibit was the biggest and best that Ludwig had ever enjoyed. It was a double-decker with a spiral staircase in the middle leading up to the second level. There were a total of eight order-writing offices for the sales-team, four on each level.

Of course the upper-level was the most popular as it had a crow's-nest viewpoint of the entire NAMM Show exhibit display floor stretching across the main level of Mc Cormick Place.

That mural was 40 to 50 feet long of the total sixty-foot outside back wall of the Ludwig exhibit. Guests were enthralled with the "history of drums" mural and would line up to have their picture taken standing in front of the mural. It was very impressive.

We, the people of Ludwig, wish to express ourselves at this moment in history. We come from every walk of American life. We are black and white and red and yellow; young and old; men and women. We represent just about every creed, and dozens of nations of origin. We are 500 strong.

And we have come together to continue Ludwig's part in American drum history.. We are proud of our past. We are proud of our craftsmanship. We look forward to the wonderful years ahead... always grateful for the opportunities we share. And we all promise our dedication to the cause of "good, old American know-how" and quality. So...Here's to America's Drummers...from all of us at Ludwig.

Walter A. Myszewski?
Al LeMert
Marianne Kulnig
Donald Mackowick?
Carmen Burrel
Melvin Adamczyk
Bill Phelus?
George Schweda
H. Larson
Billy Lowe?
Lorraine Young
[illegible] Waters
Albert Thompson
Edward J. Hough Jr.?
James K. Larsen?
Rafael Gonzalez
DJ Figura
Vernon Johnson
Herminio Muniz
Benny Fiorito
Mary Carpenter
Daryl Losee
Larry Brown
Richard Szyttspik?
Pete Lozano
Henry Cellak
Jim Holton
Joseph Vasko
Frank Mocarski?
George S. Rodriguez
[illegible]
Angel Luis Cruz
Lisa K. Mitchell
Oscar Andrade
Norma Fletcher
George E. Davies?
Edward Johnson
John A. Mahoney?
Ray Mi[illegible]
Luis A. Tran?
José Marurio?
Luis De Leon
Juan Rivera
Francisco Alloyo
Hector Nigaglioni
José R. Delgado
Ronnie Yates
Ethan Cox?
Antonia Vega
Evelyn Neris
Justiniano Murray Jr.?

Ronald Taylor
Saundra Frare?
Juan Feares?
L. Fletcher
[illegible]
Sol Hicks
Sidney Norwood
Brad Radakovitz?
J.R. Patterson
Mary Kolo
Ruth Updike
Helen Kuzniar
Celia Estrada?
Pat Kowalski
Kay Holstein
Ralph McCoy
Zacharias Hoeams?
Mary B. Campbell
Rajanbabu T. Mistry
[illegible]
Linda Sppalatto?
Juan A. Roman?
Bob Hill
Honorata Jaworowski
Francisco Rivera
Luis A. Rodriguez
Jerry Owings?
Joe Rodriguez
Elizabeth Simmons
Helen Surman?
Martha Martin
Corinne Bleifuss
David Amehee?
Edythe Leonhardt
Sophie Balik?
E.J. Zeschke?
Louise M. Romin?
Patrick Brownlow
Miriam Rios
Hector Ayala
Alejandro Vazquez
[illegible]
Adolph Bednar
Jesus Ramon Jaramillo
Celso Fratelli?
Darcy D. Guyton?
Alberto Galindo
Brad Racan?
George Sahanitic?
James Bohl
Willet Langelo?
Victor E. Camp

Margarita Lebrón
Wallace Nolan
Ann Chillamantha?
R. Hall
Guy R. Wolf?
Thomas J. Wegrzyn
Luther Lee Walker?
Jim Komzinski?
Jack Guenther
José Torres
Juan Rodelo?
Duane E. Martin
Lawrence Korona
Bob Kawalski?
Willie Lewis
Pat Hanniff?
Dennis Scott
Maxine L. Prine?
L. Jacek
Stan McMurry
Fred Lurech?
Joan H. Hetcher
Don Rigney?
Lupe Ramirez
Shirley Tate
Lillie Dieret?
Frank O. Saxpehl?
Dolores Lange
Angie Hill
Carol Carson
Marie Fenaga?
Sarah Sibbs?
Corine Johnson
Leona Uyling?
Deanne Rogo?
Virginia Kubory?
Roda Chlanowski?
Lillian Riggie
Craig Alan Taylor
Haldon V. Holt
Carl E. Lopsell?
Erwin J. Hadasa?
R. J. Southey
Donald H. McKenzie
Rafael Figueroa
Jerry Maly
Ray Mark?
M. Manning
Robert L. Hunt
Stefan Faller
Chester Grzesiewicz?
Edward Paul
[illegible]

Elizabeth B. Lowerand?
Brooke Crowden
D. Tolfree
Otis B. Jones Sr.
Robert S. Busso?
Ciro Justus?
Erik Richardson?
George Stadler?
W.H. Ford
Boonruang Chobchai
Charles Pruett Broomfield
David Miranda
Gene Jorany?
Robert Andre?
Michael J. Majka
Wayne Rodgers
Mildred Cezowska?
Arthur Bradford
Diane Wakefield
Stella Zablocki
Wm. F. Ludwig Jr.
Marilyn Calaranan?
Jessie Koglowski?
Mildred Bone
Lynette M. Dettoff
Annette Buzek?
Karolynn Schulz
Rose Cascio
Ken Bush?
Dick Gerlach
Mary Lou Cerwenka?
Fred Allsbrook?
Lorraine Levine
Dorothy O'Brien
[illegible]
Helen Sornik?
Janet Meyer
Beverly Wade
George Hamm?
Earl Wagstaff
Willie Grimes
J. B. Frazier Jr.
William Pyke
Frank C. Zuhradnik?
Oscar R. Johnson
Donald J. McLain
Vilma Landman
Frank Kolumbar?
Steve T. Crolik?
John Cummings
R. Urban
A. Sieloff?
L. Van Rooyen

Manuel Castillo
James C. Stratton?
Hector M. Torres
Gary M. Kiedick?
Leonard Lombardy?
José Reyes Olivares
Gladys Grazulis
Jim Krause
Maggie Ludwig
Clinton Brooks
Fred Fox
Virel C. Marry?
John Bundelik?
Earl Heard
Eddie J. Dixon?
Charlie Hooker?
Arlene Gallo
Hayward Grimmett?
George Carr
Terri Langowski
Carl McKinney
Sharon Hardrick
W. L. Smith
R. Little Jr.
Bill Ludwig III
Johnny L. Trimble
Victor Matos
Marlene Partyka
Rick A. [illegible]
Cleveland L. Walker?
Kenny Brown
Chuck Cemany?
Earl C. Mortimer?
James Lee?
John G. Moretto
Green H. Moore
R. Rupert
James Elkins?
Robert Trumble?
Mike Hogan
Don Green
S. McComb
Iris Windross?
Leroy Outlaw
Evelyn Puschek?
E. Cornejo
N. Ravine
E. Rowey?
Angie Burrell
D. Dickman
Jerry Strasburg
[illegible] Hodson
Bettie Ludwig
T. Pendleton

3

The Musser division also was creative in joining the Bicentennial band by creating a red, white, and blue two-octave aluminum-bar marching bell lyra. There were not a lot of people still marching with these bell lyra instruments, which went all the way back to the John Phillip Sousa era. Most marching bands and drum corps were currently using horizontal framed instruments intended for either field movement or placement in the sideline "pit section" of the ensemble.

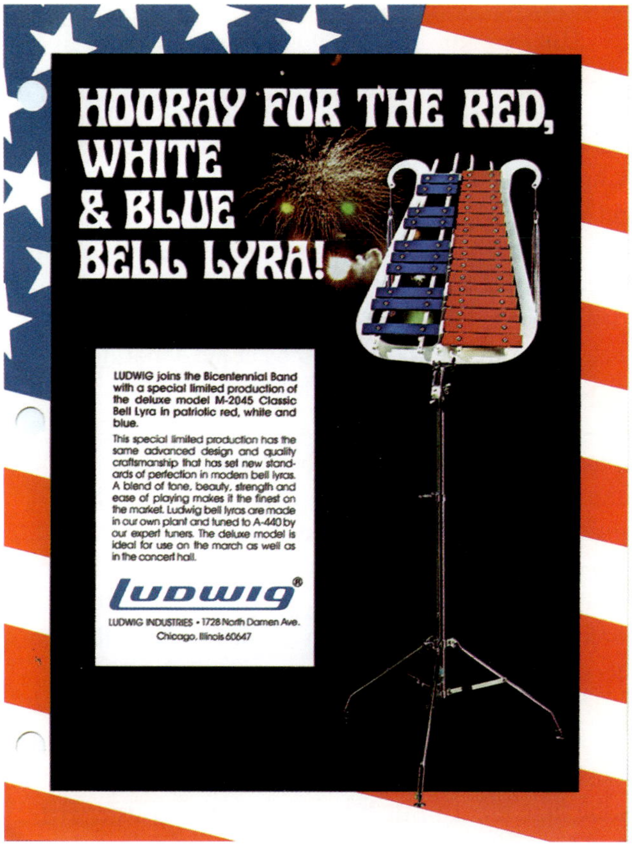

The 1976 Ludwig double-decker exhibit was a major project with an enormous cost associated with the design, construction, and setup with the McCormick Place Convention Center. Llewellyn & Best Displays designed and built the complete exhibit. The company was located just a couple blocks from the Ludwig factory. The Ludwig marketing team could walk over and see the exhibit under construction. The exhibit was constructed in sections and the marketing team would be called by Ed Best to come by and see the section by section setup in process and approve the various elements. This was an engineering marvel, as the upper level of the exhibit had to withstand the weight of potentially twenty-or more people standing on the second level floor. Failure by any definition was NOT an option. Bill and Maggie Ludwig loved it. They loved going up on the upper level and looking across the NAMM exhibit area from a vantage point higher than anyone else.

1976 also marked the beginning of the two month silver anniversary and first reunion of the Dave Brubeck Quartet, coinciding with the country's Bicentennial. Ludwig got involved in the two month performance tour in a big way, as drummer Joe Morello had been associated with Ludwig for decades. Morello was featured prominently in many Ludwig percussion symposiums, ads, and campaigns. Ludwig created and placed a special "Morello and Ludwig" advertisement in the concert tour program book, conveying the longstanding relationship. As an avid youngster I had listened to and collected all of the Dave Brubeck Quartet albums, so I jumped at the opportunity to get involved in any facet of this event. By now I had already worked with Joe at the symposiums, so the friendship and relationship was already in place by the time the tour started at Orchestra Hall in Chicago. Of course all of the Ludwig family attended the concert, as did many of the Ludwig managers and significant dealers. The collectable silver anniversary program book remains framed and on display in my office to this day.

By early 1977, Betty Ludwig Dodson seemed to have quietly left the company, and soon after Pat was absent as well. I never knew the details, but I assumed at the time that Bill Ludwig bought out his sister Betty's share of the company as part of a "family agreement." We never really saw Betty or Pat around the company again.

This was the same year that Ludwig revived the legendary Black Beauty Snare Drums, recognized as some of the most coveted snare drums in existence dating back to it's origin in the early 1920's. The May 1977 product flier offered four different Black Beauty models all using one-piece black-plated spun brass shells. In 1979 the line was expanded to offer engraved six-leaf, four pedal design on the same four model configurations. These were beautiful looking and sounding drums and I have a 5x14" Engraved Super Sensitive model in my personal collection. Unfortunately, this was the last advertising project that was directed by Advertising Manager, Vern Bush. (See Page 70 for complete Black Beauty Series, Snare Drums for the 80's brochure)

Bill lll was already quite active in the company and fully assumed the artist relations position immediately upon Pat Dodson's departure. He had already been attending numerous pop and rock concerts as a representative of the company, as Pat Dodson had seemed more comfortable with the orchestral percussion and Musser side of the artist relations responsibilities. The artist relations position required full time attention by an individual like Bill lll who could speak the language of the products, the band's music and recordings, as well as deal with various artist's drum techs that handled their Ludwig drums and related gear. Bill was perfect for this position and assignment.

Bill III had always been gravitating toward the artist relations area which was of course a natural fit; he was young and energetic, he knew who the drummers were, and he knew how to talk the language. If any drummer got a call and heard, "This is Bill Ludwig," they took that call. He developed an artist program that was unsurpassed in the drum business. Anybody and everybody that Bill lll approached about using, playing and endorsing Ludwig, eventually became a Ludwig artist.

In August of 1977 Bill III developed a remarkable series of five posters featuring a tremendous array of the Ludwig artists gathered all together for one large group poster-photograph. The first of the series was headlined, "Ludwig's Stable of Stars Doesn't Horse Around". This meant Bill lll had to get all these separate artists to agree to a unanimous photoshoot date, each artist agreed to pay their own airfare to Chicago, and Bill orchestrated all the logistics for moving twenty-plus artists in and out of hotels, Chicago airports and a celebration dinner party for everyone. Back in the 1970s there was no digital photography, no Photoshopping missing artists into the photo. The drummer was either there and included in the one-time photo-shoot, or left out. The success of this mass gathering of artists for a Chicago photoshoot developed even further over the years to come as more artists got involved and participated as part of the Ludwig family photo-gathering. I don't think anyone else in the company, or the percussion industry, for that matter, could have pulled this off as successfully as Bill lll.

Bill Jr. wanted his son (Bill lll) even more involved in the company. I believe he wanted Bill lll to start in advertising, just as Bill Jr. had done himself when he first joined the family business. Longtime Ludwig employee and Advertising Manager Vern Bush was an overnight departure. That was unfortunate for Vern, who had been Frank Baxpehler's right-hand man. Vern had also taken me under his "wing of guidance' for my early years in the company so there was a friendship and working relationship with all the marketing and advertising department people. The change was very abrupt. There was no transition period, so there were some hurt feelings and disappointment. I believe this transition could have been created and implemented differently which would have made it much easier for Bill III. But, we all learn to move on, adapt to change, and do the very best we can every day within an increasingly competitive market place.

Frank Baxpehler and I knew we had a situation involving on-the-job training for Bill lll, so we all did everything we could to help Bill III get completely immersed in every element of his new advertising director position.

This significant change in "Frank's Team" brought significant changes in how various marketing support departments would operate and who they reported to. While Vern Bush had worn many different hats during his many years of contributions to the Ludwig Company, (Advertising, trade shows/ conventions, Artist Relations etc.) it was becoming apparent that the marketing work was needing to be spread out to a diversified team.

Ludwig delivers.

Ludwig delivers the sound these stars want.

1. Bill Ludwig, III – **Artists Relations**
2. Tim Gehrt – **Streets**
3. Myron Grombacher – **Pat Benatar**
4. Rick Downey – **Blue Oyster Cult**
5. J.I. Allison – **The Crickets/Waylon Jennings**
6. Sandy Gennaro – **Independent**
7. Roger Earl – **Foghat**
8. Steve Thomas – **Shooting Star**
9. Clay Caire – **Nashville Now – T.V. Show**
10. Bobby "T" Torello – **Michael Bolton**
11. Tom Compton – **Alvin Lee**
12. Cliff Davies – **Independent**
13. Barry Connors – **Toronto**
14. Aynsley Dunbar – **Independent**
15. Bobby Blotzer – **Ratt**
16. Steve Palmer – **John Kay & Steppenwolf**
17. Mike Arturi – **Jade**
18. Phil LoMedico – **Clipse**
19. Alan Gratzer – **R.E.O. Speedwagon**
20. Steven George – **Ministry**
21. Paul Quinn – **Joe Kelly**
22. Richard Allen – **Def Leppard**
23. John Bee – **The Rockets**
24. John Beke – **Crossfyre**
25. Jim Marshall – **Freelance/Studio Drummer**
26. Gunner Ross – **Almighty Strut**
27. Larry Tolfree – **Joe Jackson**
28. Alan White – **Yes**
29. Danny Gottlieb – **Elements/Freelance**
30. John Stacey – **Nashville Studio**
31. Gary Smith – **Freelance Studio**
32. Vince Dee – **Jump 'n the Saddle**
33. Michael Derosier – **Formerly w/Heart**
34. Don Brewer – **Grand Funk Railroad**
35. Kevin Valentine – **Donnie Iris**
36. Vern Wennerstrom – **Studio Musician**
37. John Shearer – **Iron Butterfly**
38. Robin Steele – **Studio Musician**

Not pictured due to schedule conflicts:

Bun E. Carlos – **Cheap Trick**
Eric Carr – **KISS**
Bobby Chouinard – **Billy Squier**
Lee Crystal – **Joan Jett**
Jimmy Marinos – **Romantics**
Steve Negus – **Saga**
Darrell Sweet – **Nazareth**
Ginger Baker – **Independent**
Bob Benberg – **Supertramp**
Steve Brooking – **.38 Special**
Jack Grondin – **.38 Special**
Fred Edwards – **Charlie Daniels**
Nigel Glockler – **Saxon**
Dave Lauser – **Sammy Hagar**
Matt Frenette – **Loverboy**
Nick Mason – **Pink Floyd**
Joey Kramer – **Aerosmith**
Roger Taylor – **Queen**
Herman Rarebell – **Scorpions**

For a poster-size copy of this ad, send $1.00 to: The Selmer Company, P.O. Box 310, Elkhart, IN 46515

Ludwig
A SELMER COMPANY
1728 North Damen Avenue
Chicago, Il 60647

Photography by Robert Keeling. Special thanks to the Barclay Hotel, Chicago
Peterbilt supplied by Summerfield GMC Truck Company, Inc. Ravens Trailer supplied by Area Truck and Trailer

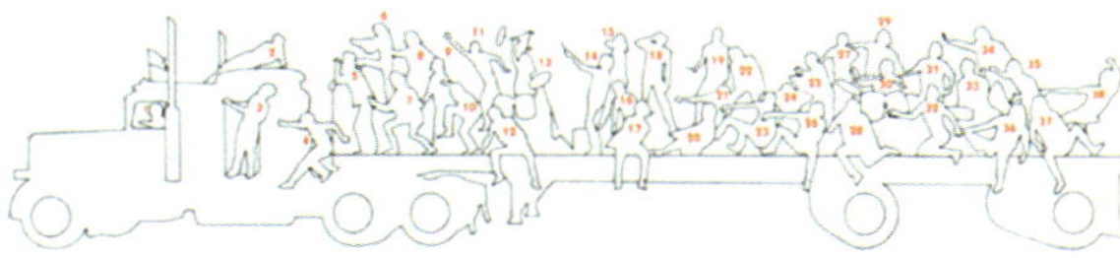

Class Act!

The Most Famous Drummers In The World... Toast The Most Famous Name On Drums!
Ludwig

On August 26, 1984 these top name drummers arrived in Chicago to celebrate seventy-five years of business. Three quarters of a century of hardwork and dedication, something they all know and relate to. That's why they believe in Ludwig, that's why you should too! Visit your local Ludwig dealer soon, and join the celebration.

1. **Johnny "Bee" Badanjek** – *Mitch Ryder & The Detroit Wheels*
2. **Vincent Dee** – *Jump 'N The Saddle*
3. **Chuck Turk** – *Independent*
4. **Hirsh Gardner** – *Independent*
5. **Tony Brock** – *Rod Stewart*
6. **Bill Ludwig, III**
7. **William F. Ludwig, Jr.**
8. **Gunner Ross** – *Almighty Strut*
9. **Joe Morello** – *Joe Morello Quintet*
10. **Terral Santiel** – *L.A. Studio, Touring with Patrice Rushen*
11. **Graham Ward** – *Studio, Touring with Haircut 100*
12. **Tim Gehrt** – *Streets*
13. **Don Brewer** – *Formerly, Grand Funk Railroad*
14. **Herman Rarebell** – *Scorpions*
15. **Roger Earl** – *Foghat*
16. **Bobby "T" Torello** – *Jim Dandy's Black Oak Arkansas*
17. **Jerry Shirley** – *Fastway*
18. **Eli Konikoff** – *Eli Konikoff's Tour De Force (Formerly with Spyro Gyra)*
19. **Stephen George** – *Ministry*
20. **Tony Cerniglia** – *Boys in White*
21. **Luis Cardenas** – *Renegade*
22. **Steve Thomas** – *Shooting Star*
23. **Leigh Howard Stevens** – *Marimba Virtuoso*
24. **Fred Edwards** – *Charlie Daniels Band*
25. **Gary Smith** – *Chicago Studio*
26. **Steve Palmer** – *John Kay & Steppenwolf*
27. **Aynsley Dunbar** – *Independent*
28. **John Shearer** – *Hurricane*
29. **Don Powell** – *Slade*
30. **Phil Rowland** – *John Eleface Band*
31. **Vic Mastrianni** – *Shelly West*
32. **Tom Compton** – *Johnny Winter*
33. **Scott Rockenfield** – *Queensryche*
34. **Mike Arturi** – *Big Twist & The Mellow Fellows*
35. **John Stacey** – *Nashville Studio*
36. **Paul Quinn** – *Joe Kelly*
37. **John Beke** – *Crossfyre*
38. **Cliff Davies** – *Ted Nugent*
39. **Alan White** – *Yes*
40. **Bobby Blotzer** – *Ratt*
41. **Barry Connors** – *Coney Hatch*
42. **Robin Steele** – *Independent*
43. **J. I. Allison** – *The Crickets*
44. **Kevin Valentine** – *Donnie Iris*
45. **Bobby Chouinard** – *Billy Squier*
46. **Roger Pope**
47. **Jerry Pickett** – *Ghalib Ghallab*
48. **Bruce Crump** – *Molly Hatchet*
49. **Jim Marshall**
50. **Vern Wennerstrom** – *Independent*
51. **Khurt Maier** – *Max Havoc*
52. **Rick Downey** – *Blue Oyster Cult*
53. **Steve Negus** – *Saga*
54. **Michael Derosier** – *Orion The Hunter*
55. **Bun E. Carlos** – *Cheap Trick*

PHOTOGRAPHY BY ROBERT KEELING
SPECIAL THANKS TO THE BARCLAY CHICAGO HOTEL

LUDWIG ENDORSERS NOT PRESENT DUE TO SCHEDULE CONFLICTS

Willie Ackerman – *Hee Haw Show*
Nigel Glockler – *Saxon*
Sandy Gennaro – *Cyndi Lauper*
Leonard Haze – *Y & T*
Ralph Molina – *Neil Young & Crazy Horse*
Dan Mustoe – *Waylon Jennings*
Jimmy Marinos – *The Romantics*
Gina Schock – *The Go Go's*
A. J. Pero – *Twisted Sister*
Bob Benberg – *Supertramp*
Richard Allen – *Def Leppard*
Lee Crystal – *Joan Jett & The Blackhearts*
Alan Gratzer – *REO Speedwagon*
Joey Kramer – *Aerosmith*
Darrell Sweet – *Nazareth*
Myron Grombacher – *Pat Benatar*
Roger Taylor – *Queen*
Eric Carr – **KISS**
Jason Bonham – *Airrace*
Ken Janson – *Tammy Wynette*
Randy Hardison – *John Conlee*
Nick Mason – *Pink Floyd*
Roy Haynes
Alan Dawson
Ginger Baker
David Lauser – *Sammy Hagar*
Clay Caire
Danny Gottlieb

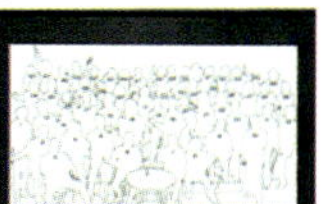

Ludwig
A SELMER COMPANY

Ludwig had its own internal printing department that also included the mail room operations. I believe it was during the Dick Schory era that Ludwig purchased their own two color printing press, collating equipment, basic binding, paper-cutting, and stocking equipment. This provided support to the enitre company, as well as cost-effective marketing support. The company used a vast assortment of internal forms and documents in all of the production, manufacturing, data processing, purchasing, and accounting functions. These forms were all printed and padded internally and used throughout the company. The marketing needs were constantly increasing as more new products were being introduced. We were able to produce low cost two color announcement fliers that could be printed in reasonable quantities and immediately mailed to the dealers and salesmen.

The department consisted of Bill Phebus as the full time pressman who was assisted by Emma Price and Maggie Kellner. Gary Kaiduk handled the mail and all the mailroom functions. This was a great internal support operation that was of value to all departments and functions within the Ludwig company. This support service was also provided to the Musser operations in LaGrange.

It was this printing department that helped me accelerate the content and popularity of the internationally recognized "Percussion Aid Pack". Created early on by Jim Sewrey, this educational/promotional tool contained a vast assortment of one-color educational articles about everything in percussion performance, education, care and maintenance, and adapting new Ludwig products into the growing marching percussion arenas. This was widely sought after by band directors and educators at every level, was in constant demand at the many conventions that Ludwig participated in, and became a huge success element of educating every facet of the market- courtesy of the Ludwig Drum Company. Upon taking over the education department I immediately jumped on the opportunity to expand and diversify this "Percussion Aid Pack," recruiting new informative articles from the clinician staff as well as those "friends of Ludwig" that I was developing relationships with. Contributing authors did not receive compensation for their educational article contributions, knowing that their contributions, which included their photos, name and bio would be printed by the thousands and distributed throughout the world. Recruiting qualified authors and contributions was never a problem.

While this printing department operation always reported to Vern Bush under the marketing support umbrella, Frank Baxpehler turned this department, responsibility, and personnel over to me, effective immediately. My plate of duties and responsibilities was growing and my time was getting more and more precious as to what I worked on the most. My personal involvement and reach into all the marketing functions and operations was expanding rapidly and I accepted the challenges.

As advertising manager and artist relations director, Bill III continued to work with art director Jerry Owings, the most gifted art director that I had ever met at that point. He also hired a new secretary/artist relations assistant, Elizabeth Allen. By now, the overall office space on the first floor was getting very crowded for advertising and artist relations. The solution put in place was to expand the first floor office space by taking some of the manufacturing area and converting it to office space.

At the same time, the Education Department moved from the fourth floor office in the new warehouse down to the newly expanded first floor office area with the advertising functions. We now had advertising, artist relations, trade show exhibits, and the education department all connected in one large area. Bill III had his Plexiglas cubical office next to my similar cubical. We worked pretty closely together, as there was a lot of overlap in duties, responsibilities, and various functions all of these people. Things really started to jell quite nicely. I worked closely with Bill, and tried to pass on all the advertising and graphic arts/layout experience and knowledge I had learned from Vern Bush. This helped Bill III quickly get a grasp on everything he was becoming "responsible for". We made it work, because we were all very busy and the working space was close.

Competition in the percussion marketplace was growing. We were all watching and becoming aware of this as more and more Asian products and brands surfaced in the global market. More than once we would purchase a competitive Asian-branded drum set and physically take the entire product apart on the conference table, screw-by-screw, just to see how poorly and cheaply the products were being manufactured to flood the market with cheap drums. Without a doubt, Ludwig's market share and dominance in the percussion industry was being challenged by many. Bill Ludwig would occasionally mention "It is more difficult to stay on top of the market than to claw your way up to the top of the market." These words stuck with me in the tough times ahead for the company, and for many years later throughout my career path.

It was realized that if Ludwig was going to sell more drums, we had to create more drummers. In 1977, Frank Baxpehler came up with a brilliant concept for a very grass-roots way of doing that by target marketing and going after a very non-music segment of the population to create more beginning drummers. Ludwig started running 1/3 column coupon ads in boys and girls clubs, scouting magazines, any youth market magazine that was non-musical. By mailing in the consumer coupon to Ludwig with just $2.00, the person would receive a pair of drumsticks and a beginning drummer book. The book was a little 8-page publication that the Art Director Jerry Owings put together in-house.

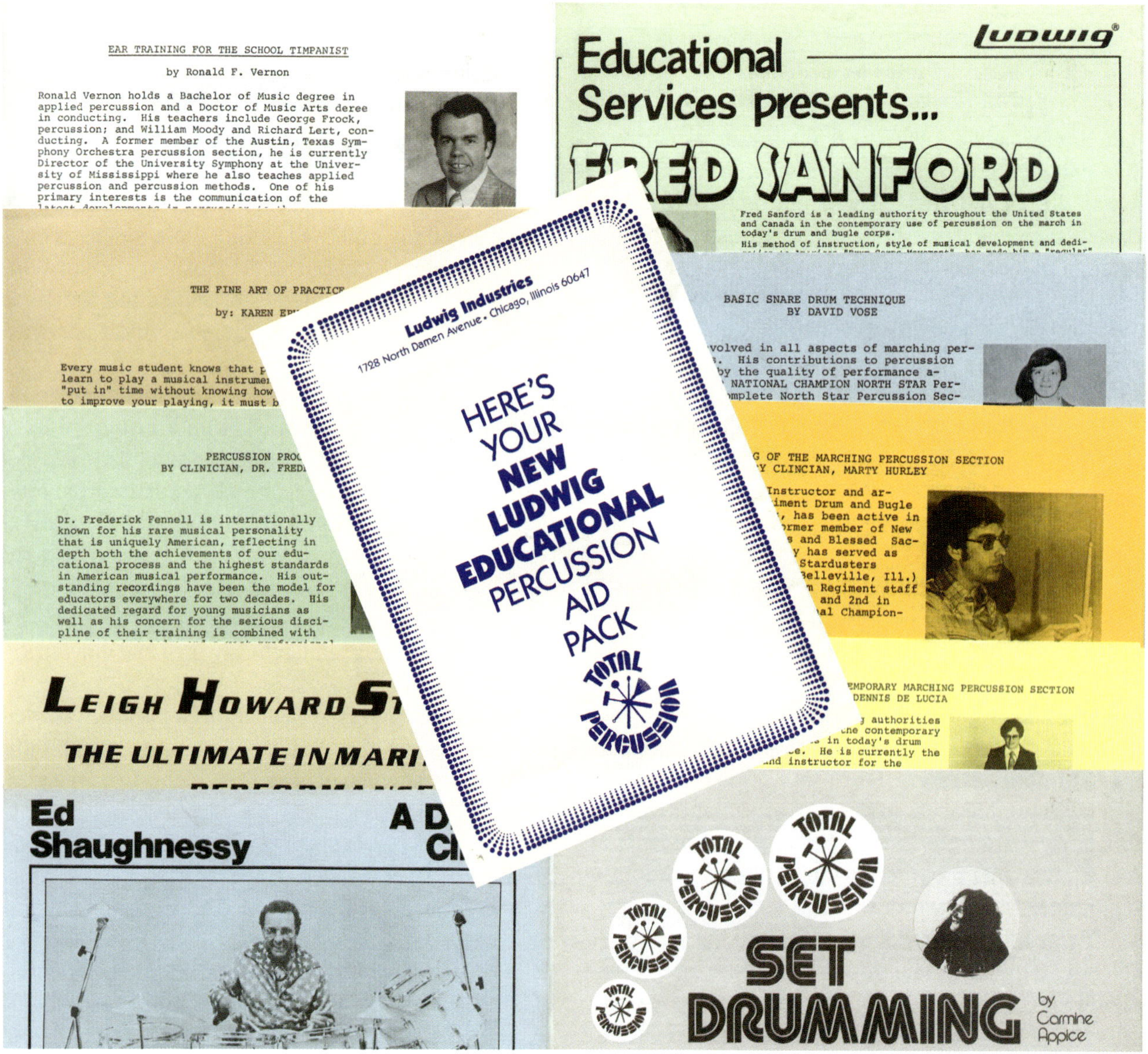

The response to the "Beginning Drummer" coupon ad was huge. The mail room started getting so many of these envelopes with $2.00 in cash or $2.00 checks that we had to hire a temp secretary to come in and do nothing but open the envelopes, handle the money, stuff the envelope with the sticks and books, type the label, and deliver the completed packets to the mail room for handling. That was all she did three days a week for months. It was labor intensive, but it was very successful in getting Ludwig drumsticks into the hands of people who would not have done this had they not seen this coupon. Ludwig could not wait for potential new drummers to walk into a music store or drum shop. It needed new customers who wanted to learn and play drums. Ludwig provided them their first pair of sticks and starter book. That program was in place for over a year.

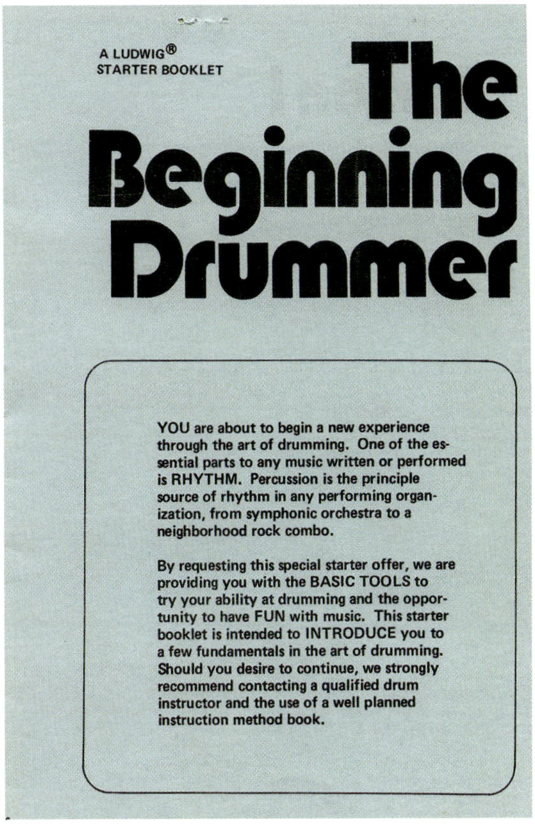

1977 and 1978 brought further growth and opportunities for new products, market penetration and diversification. Ludwig was always considered a market leader with new products, promotions and superior brands. Vacuum forming was a growing technology, as it offered tremendous production opportunities by turning flat sheets of plastic into an array of different shapes and sizes of cases and objects. While Ludwig purchased the Schuessler Case Company back in 1967 and moved it to a building within a few blocks of the Damen Avenue factory, the market was changing for fiber drum cases. The company embarked on a long hard journey of making vacuum formed drum cases in a vast array of different sizes. This required two different molds for every size case as one case telescoped into the other. This was an expensive and challenging project that required time, money and patience. I believe it paid off in sales, but I don't know.

Occasionally, already existing products were brought to the company's attention by Ludwig or Musser artists. Some of these products had high recommendation and Ludwig was seeing and feeling the competition from these very small niche products. Good Vibes Mallets were high quality rattan mallets being built by a very small operation. The success of their products was making the brand a household name with vibe and marimba players everywhere. Good Vibe Mallets were endorsed by David Friedman and David Samuels. Musser already had an extensive mallet line and manufacturing operation in the LaGrange, Illinois, factory for both rattan and the less expensive white plastic handle mallet line. The David's (Friedman and Samuels) convinced Musser Vice President Dick Richardson to explore the purchase of the Good Vibe Mallets brand and tooling. Bill bought the Good Vibes operation and brand out. Musser made this a vibrant part of the Musser operation over time. And Musser marketed the twelve models of Good Vibes on a global basis. These are still handled today by Ludwig and included in the Musser division catalogs.

The Ghost Pedal was another example of Ludwig's continuing efforts to expand and improve the product line. It seemed like everyone was using the Ghost pedal. Bill Ludwig was hearing more and more about the superlative feel and performance of the Ghost Pedal. Obviously, this started cutting into the demand and sales for the original Speed King bass drum pedal that helped found the Ludwig company years earlier. Again, this became a "fight-them, join-them, or buy-them" decision. The decision was made to buy out the Ghost Bass Drum Pedal and build them in the existing Ludwig pedal department. The Ghost Pedal was significantly improved when it became part of Ludwig's manufacturing process.

The seventies continued with more and more emphasis on marching percussion. Al LeMert was making tremendous inroads with the newly improved marching carrier holder assemblies. The units became adaptable to a multitude of instruments and were interchangeable between the various different marching percussion instruments. Power toms became enhanced with the new vacuum formed Sound Projectors attached to the bot-

tom of trios and quads. Sound Projectors looked like space suit helmets coming out of the molds, cut in half, and spray painted to match the drum shell colors. These units were cost effective, easy to mount or remove with company-supplied Velcro strips, and could be used even with competitive brands of marching toms.

Musser was developing creative ways to have mallet keyboard instruments "walking around on the field". For the first time, a complete melodic percussion section could be mobile, connecting with the marching band or drum corps. While these instruments were heavy, bands seemed to find super heavy duty strong players for these instruments. Chimes, bells, xylophones, and even marimbas marched on the field.

By late 1977 the need for a completely new Total Percussion full line catalog was felt. With Bill lll in the advertising manager position, this would be a huge project that required extensive new product photography, a complete new cover design and focus, along with many internal updates to the products and specifications that had changed since the release of the last 1975 cover-date catalog released in late 1973. The catalog would be cover-dated "Percussion 80" and became available in July of 1978. Bill lll and Frank Baxpeher worked extensively on this project. I provided some assistance in the art board proof reading elements.

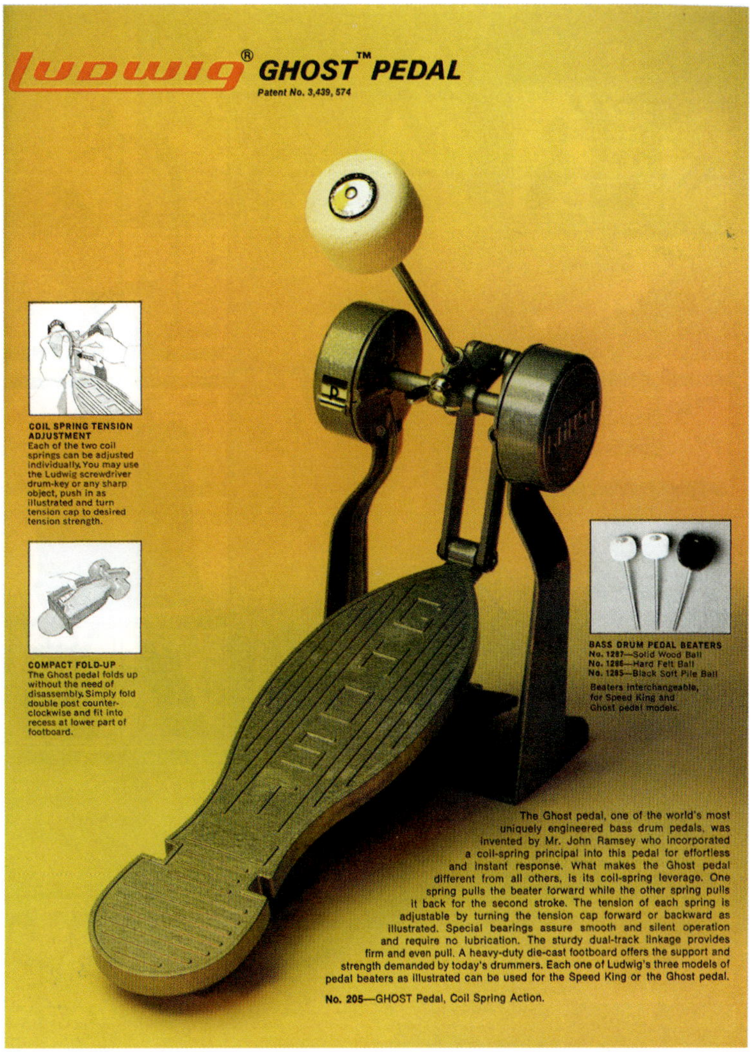

No. 684Y White Cortex illustrated with optional die-cast hoops at extra cost.

No. 675Y Red Cortex illustrated with optional die-cast hoops at extra cost.

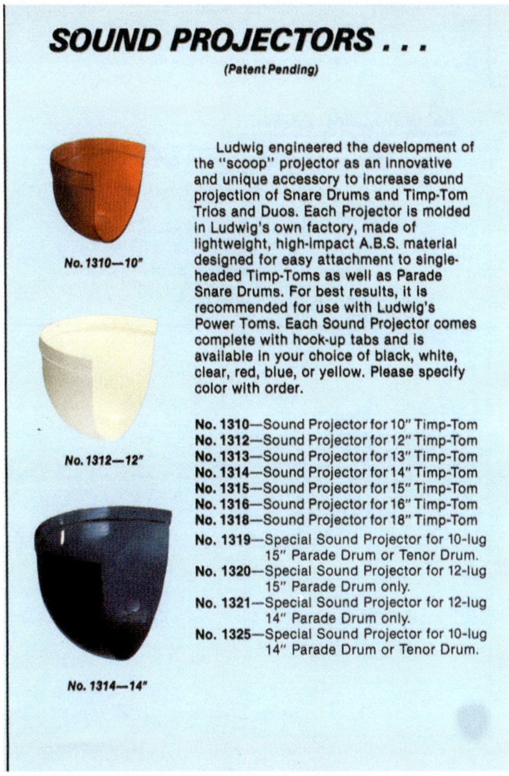

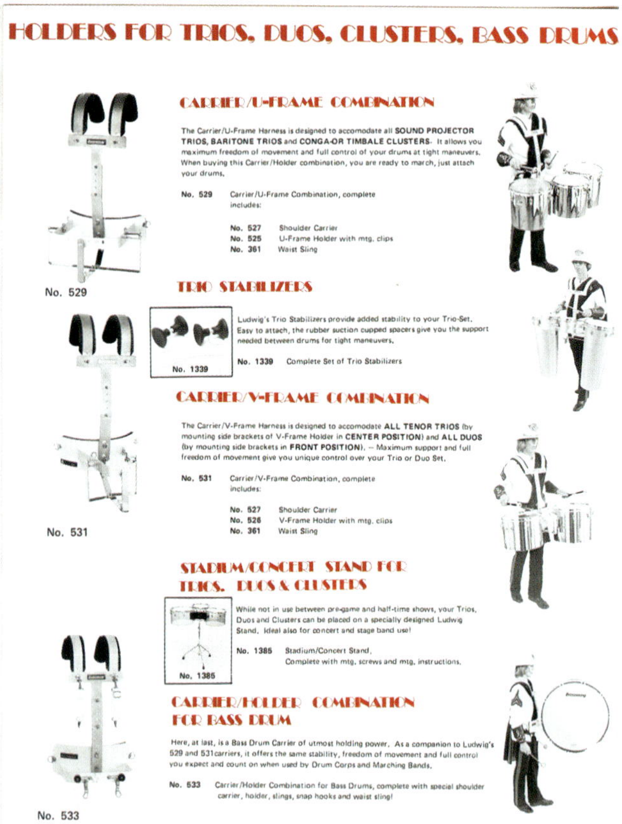

HOLDERS FOR TRIOS, DUOS, CLUSTERS, BASS DRUMS

CARRIER/U-FRAME COMBINATION

The Carrier/U-Frame Harness is designed to accomodate all **SOUND PROJECTOR TRIOS, BARITONE TRIOS** and **CONGA-OR TIMBALE CLUSTERS**. It allows you maximum freedom of movement and full control of your drums at tight maneuvers. When buying this Carrier/Holder combination, you are ready to march, just attach your drums.

No. 529 Carrier/U-Frame Combination, complete includes:

- **No. 527** Shoulder Carrier
- **No. 525** U-Frame Holder with mtg. clips
- **No. 361** Waist Sling

No. 529

TRIO STABILIZERS

No. 1339

Ludwig's Trio Stabilizers provide added stability to your Trio-Set. Easy to attach, the rubber suction cupped spacers give you the support needed between drums for tight maneuvers.

No. 1339 Complete Set of Trio Stabilizers

CARRIER/V-FRAME COMBINATION

The Carrier/V-Frame Harness is designed to accomodate **ALL TENOR TRIOS** (by mounting side brackets of V-Frame Holder in **CENTER POSITION**) and **ALL DUOS** (by mounting side brackets in **FRONT POSITION**). – Maximum support and full freedom of movement give you unique control over your Trio or Duo Set.

No. 531 Carrier/V-Frame Combination, complete includes:

- **No. 527** Shoulder Carrier
- **No. 526** V-Frame Holder with mtg. clips
- **No. 361** Waist Sling

No. 531

STADIUM/CONCERT STAND FOR TRIOS, DUOS & CLUSTERS

No. 1385

While not in use between pre-game and half-time shows, your Trios, Duos and Clusters can be placed on a specially designed Ludwig Stand. Ideal also for concert and stage band use!

No. 1385 Stadium/Concert Stand, Complete with mtg. screws and mtg. instructions.

CARRIER/HOLDER COMBINATION FOR BASS DRUM

Here, at last, is a Bass Drum Carrier of utmost holding power. As a companion to Ludwig's 529 and 531 carriers, it offers the same stability, freedom of movement and full control you expect and count on when used by Drum Corps and Marching Bands.

No. 533 Carrier/Holder Combination for Bass Drums, complete with special shoulder carrier, holder, slings, snap hooks and waist sling!

No. 533

MARCHING BELLS, XYLOS AND MARIMBAS

Ludwig's new Carrier/Holder family extends into the Marching Mallet Instrument field, offering the same exclusive advantages as in the drum line. This light-weight carrier with its many adjustable features not only gives you a most comfortable and natural fit but provides the stability, firm support and unhampered freedom of movement so necessary in tight maneuvers.

It is made available in two models, one for Steel and Aluminum Bells and one for Xylophones and Marimbas.

M-480 CARRIER/HOLDER COMBINATION FOR BELLS

No. M-480 Carrier/Holder Combination for Steel and Aluminum Bells, complete. Includes:

- **No. 527** Shoulder Carrier
- **No. M-483** Holder
- **No. M-484** Set of 2 Brackets w/mtg. attachments
- **No. 361** Waist Sling

No. M-481 CARRIER/HOLDER COMBINATION FOR XYLOS AND MARIMBAS

No. M-481 Carrier/Holder Combination for Xylophones and Marimbas, complete.

Includes:

- **No. 527** Shoulder Carrier
- **No. M-483** Holder
- **No. M-485** Set of 2 Brackets w/mtg. attachments
- **No. 361** Waist Sling

MARCHING ALUMINUM BELLS

Marching Bells — — a true natural for today's concept of melodic marching percussion. Featuring lightweight aluminum bars in satin finish tuned to A-440, range of 2½ octaves from G^5 to C^8, bars 1¼" wide and 3/8" thick. Weight 18 lbs. exclusive of holder. Two pairs of suitable mallets are included.

No. M-65 Aluminum Marching Bells, complete with shoulder carrier, holder, brackets, waist sling and mallets.

MARCHING STEEL BELLS

Superb projection and the special brilliance of high-carbon tempered steel bars assure that your Steel Bells will be heard. Tuned to A-440, range of 2½ octaves from G^5 to C^8, bars 1¼" wide and 5/16" thick. Weight 25 lbs. exclusive of holder. Two pairs of suitable mallets are included.

No. M-69 Steel Marching Bells, complete with shoulder carrier, holder, brackets, waist sling and mallets.

MARCHING XYLOPHONE

Utilizing Musser's exclusive Kelon® Bars brought a more recent addition to the melodic marching percussion field: the Marching Xylophone with resonators. Featuring bars made of Kelon which keep their pitch regardless of outdoor weather condition, are extremely durable and have that greater tonal projection and sound power you are looking for in the field. Tuned to A-440. Range of 2½ octaves from C^5 to G^7. Bars 1½" wide and 5/8" thick. Weight 28 lbs exclusive of holder. Two pairs of suitable mallets are included.

No. M-67 Marching Xylophone, complete with resonators, shoulder carrier, holder, brackets, waist sling and mallets.

No. M-66 Marching Xylophone as above but without resonators.

No. M-34 Xylophone Conversion Kit, including 2 sets of resonators with mtg. attachments.

MARCHING MARIMBA

At last, a marimba you can carry! Ideal for your Latin arrangements. Featuring Musser's exclusive Kelon bars with resonators, tuned to A-440. Range of 2½ octaves from C^4 to F^6. Bars 1½" wide and 5/8" thick. Weight 27 lbs. exclusive of holder. Two pairs of suitable mallets are included.

No. M-68 Marching Marimba, complete with resonators, shoulder carrier, holder, brackets, waist sling and mallets.

STADIUM/CONCERT STAND FOR BELLS, XYLOS AND MARIMBAS

These unique "U" frames are newly designed to snap on the frame of Bells, Xylos or Marimbas so your marching mallet instrument may be used indoors or on the field when not marching.

No. M-132 Set of 2 "U" frame legs for marching Xylos, Bells or Marimbas.

The 1980 catalog which came out in July of 1978, was the first time we showed a Buddy Rich model drum set. Where in the catalog that model and page got positioned was a decision-making process that Bill was actively involved in. He did not want Buddy's set on the cover, he did not want that as the first drum set in the drum set section of the catalog. "That is *one* of our drum sets, and we will devote *one* page to it." Those kinds of decrees we of course honored, and he always seemed pleased by what we came out with. The Ludwig Family inside front cover page was exclusively devoted to Bill Jr. and Bill lll leading the "Largest Drum Company in the World". Bill lll was titled Advertising Manager/Artist Relations Director. The traditional personnel page-one was updated significantly and I was included once again, but with the title of Educational Director.

The up-front emphasis was clearly on the three available Ludwig shells; Stainless Steel, Vistalite, and the new die-electric molded 6-ply maple shells. A beautiful five piece Tivoli Vistalite set launched the drum set section. It's interesting to note that the new Buddy Rich Signature Set did not appear until page 14.

There is still much speculation as to why Buddy's set was placed so far back in the book. There was a two-page catalog center-spread (pages 48-49) devoted to Ringer Timpani with Bill Jr.'s photo. There was a complete absence of any mention-of, or photograph of, any artists in the catalog with the exception of Buddy Rich's set.

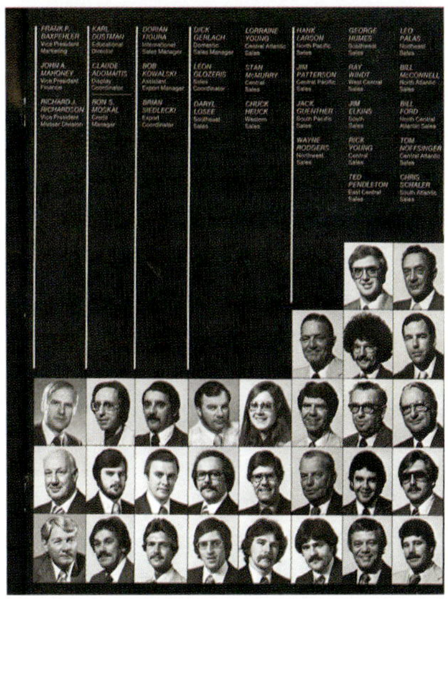

TOTAL PERCUSSION EDUCATION

Ludwig — leader in educational services for over 50 years!

THE LUDWIG DRUMMER® MAGAZINE—

The Ludwig Drummer presents the latest percussion trends and specific percussion techniques in all areas of outfit, Latin drums, marching, timpani and mallet keyboard. Articles are written by leading performing artists and educators and are treasured by students and teachers alike. A most valuable learning tool for anyone interested in percussion. — Available through your local Ludwig dealer or write to Ludwig's Educational Department.

THE PERCUSSION AID PACK—

Ludwig provides a highly informative packet of educational aid articles, music examples and educational outlines contributed by well-known authorities in all fields of percussion. Constantly being up-dated with new material, the Percussion Aid Pack covers the whole range from simple to most complex topics and instruction pointers. To find answers for your many questions in percussion, look for the answer FIRST in the Percussion Aid Pack! Available through your local Ludwig dealer — Free of charge.

PERCUSSION SYMPOSIUM—

Imagine going to school "For Percussionists Only." A full week of specialized intense instructions, covering every aspect of percussion, taught by internationally know artists and educators. Class scheduling includes five tracks of study: drum set, mallet keyboard, marching percussion, total percussion and general percussion. Details of dates and location are available through Ludwig's Educational Department.

INFORMATION EXCHANGE—

Ludwig welcomes questions "from the field." Questions from teachers and band directors about improving or modernizing the percussion section of their bands, for example. Questions about percussion in general. And when we don't know the answers, we ask the experts! Ludwig has a full time Educational Department which will help and service you and — speak your language.

CLINIC PROGRAM—

Percussion clinics — one of Ludwig's oldest educational services and efforts — bring high level talent right into your own backyard. Arrangements can be made by Ludwig's dealers, schools, universities and music educator associations with the experienced staff of Ludwig's Educational Department to book clinics or workshops of top name artists. Learn first hand from the PROS!

I was extremely pleased to write the text and select the photography for a full page presentation of Ludwig's Percussion Education Department. With two hundred thousand copies printed, this would be the last Ludwig full line catalog with the company under Ludwig family ownership.

I view the period from 1978 to 1981 as one of Ludwig's most creative and competitive eras.

By 1979 Ludwig had Buddy Rich, Ed Shaughnessy, Carmine Appice, and Max Roach as endorsers. Add to that quartet of headliners all of the rock and pop artists that Bill III was bringing on to play Ludwig. Signature Series Drum Sticks were becoming ever more popular, and Ludwig was one of the very few companies still making all of its own hickory model drum sticks within the Damen Avenue factory. The same was true of the marching mallets and beaters, timpani sticks, wire brushes and related items. It was time to really promote the snare drum sticks by creating Buddy Rich

and Ed Shaughnessy model drum sticks. Full page ads supported these new items but sales proved to be somewhat disappointing.

As Ludwig was basking in the limelight of having so many significant drummers (including Buddy Rich) coming on-board playing Ludwig, the idea of a DRUM-A-THON evolved between Ludwig and Sam Ash Music stores. The idea grew from discussions during the 1978 NAMM convention with Jerry Ash, and developed into a huge percussion collaboration on September 14th 1979 which attracted over 1500 people to the Calderone Concert Hall in Hempstead New York. This was larger than just an educational event, but I became the Ludwig ring-leader for all the artists and logistics. Ludwig provided and organized top artists Joe Morello, Carmine Appice and Buddy Rich on the program. The grand finale for the event was the concert-style performance of Buddy and his complete band. Amazingly, everything went according to plan. This became a headline promotional, educational, and sales creation event, solidifying the business relationship that was on-going for years between Sam Ash Music Stores and the Ludwig Company. The post-event editorial coverage was extremely positive and set the tone for future events and dealer collaborations which I would use and carry forwards in my career path.

With Ludwig dominating the timpani market, a personal project for Bill was the development of a professional organized "Ludwig Timpani Owner's Manual". Up to this point, the care, tuning, and adjustment to the Balanced Action Timpani Pedal mechanism was a simple two page instruction sheet, attached to the fiber head protector which accompanied every timpani. Over the years I saw Bill always captivating an audience of band directors and music educators at a Ludwig exhibit booth. He would turn a kettle drum over and explain in detail the internal mechanics of how the balanced action worked, and how to properly adjust the pedal and head tension so the pedal would not slip in any pitch position. Years of these explanations must have encouraged him to create a formal owner's manual for all Balanced Action Timpani. Bill created the content, layout and text, working on it with the help of art director Jerry Owings. While this was not a revenue-producing project or product, it was a consumer-satisfaction element that had tremendous value in helping music educators properly use, tune and appreciate the sound of in-tune Ludwig timpani. This Timpani Owner's Manual was released in January of 1980 and it covered everything you need to know about Ludwig timpani It is still used and supplied with every Ludwig timpani under the Selmer ownership of Ludwig.

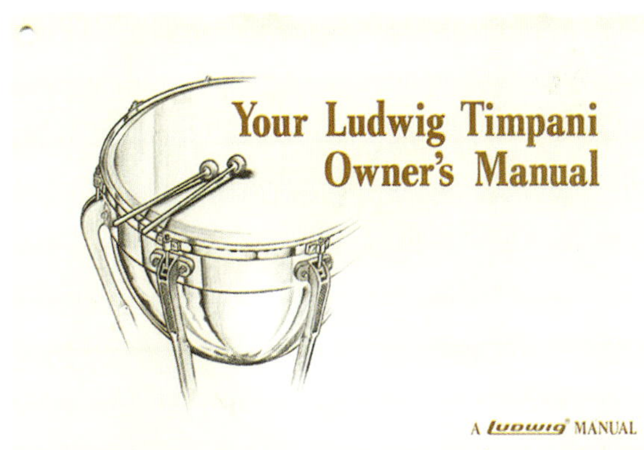

The name LUDWIG is synonymous with snare drums. While the world is full of all kinds of drums, every drummer seems to own and cherish at least one Ludwig snare drum in their arsenal of drums. This fact was beautifully presented and promoted through the 1979 release of the "Snare Drums For The 80s" all-color snare drum brochure. This featured a wide array of drums and the diverse group of professional drummers and percussionists that used and played them. The cover photography was lavish and conveyed a touch of the "old world hand-made craftsmanship" theme to a wood-shell snare drum being assembled on an old-fashioned work bench.

The artists included in this line-up were the company's greatest testament of snare drums and drummers. If there was ever a promotional piece that created a demand to own one more snare drum, this was it, from Ludwig. Ludwig embarked on a tremendous engineering project that consumed enormous amounts of tooling costs. There was a need for counter hoops that could handle the extreme (and still increasing) tensions that drums were being tuned to, both on drum sets and on marching percussion drums. The solution was to explore and develop a line of die cast steel counter hoops that would not bend, crack, or go out of round. These hoops initially were an option when ordering any Ludwig drum. That required a separate catalog number to designate when die cast hoops were required in the order. This presented a huge production project and cataloging issue.

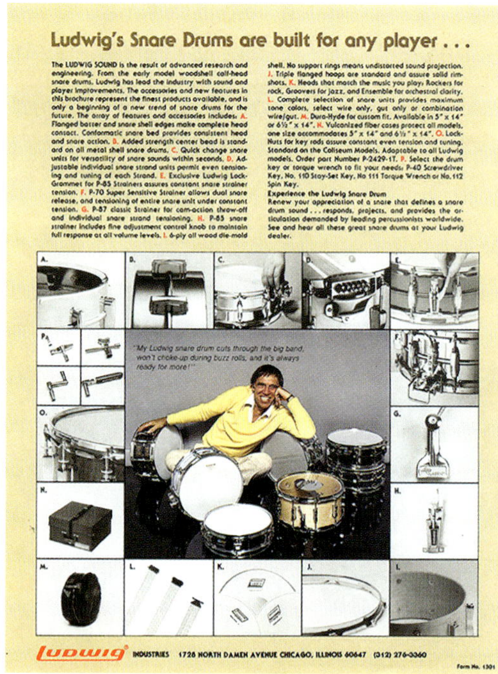

Ludwig's die cast hoops began to appear on competitive brands of drums, so it made sense to market the hoops as more than just an option on the Ludwig branded drums. The tooling was a monumental project, but it was a very profitable product line. The size options included 6" all the way through 18". Snare drum bottom hoops required separate tooling and cataloging to allow for the required snare gate attachments of snares to the drum shells.

Cost-effective measures were starting to be included in all discussions and everything the marketing-advertising and educational departments did was being carefully watched for costs and R.O.I. (return-on-investment). Budgets began getting tight, as there was increasing competition from "The Rising Sun in Asia". The company began to see more Yamaha, Pearl, and Tama; all encroaching on the global and domestic drum set market. This was also slowly evolving and beginning to appear in the educational and school market product categories. A cost-effective alternative to creating and investing in another 103 page full line catalog was to develop individual product line catalogs.

Ludwig's old traditional tom holder was being outdone by the new Asian drum brands entering the market. More Ludwig drum sets were being ordered without holder, which became a source for considerable discussion, decision making, and another huge investment of capital in tooling and new product promotion. The market pressure to compete with a better tom holder system prompted us to come up with hardware innovations that would surpass anything that was currently available in the market with increased flexibility for "building and designing your own drum set, exclusively, with all Ludwig hardware. Frank Baxpehler spearheaded the engineering department's new hardware project, named Modular Drum Grouping Support System. This was an engineering marvel that took a lot of effort to pull together. This carried the drum set market through some very difficult times because it was so far ahead of its time. This product launch was supported by a beautiful wall size poster catalog which featured all the various tom holder options, from a single tom to six individual toms all mounted on one master holder, attached to the six ply all maple bass drums, capable of handling the weight and vibration. It also provided an opportunity to showcase eight beautifully featured different drum set configurations, new finishes, and complete versatility for the drummer to have as many tom-placement and sound options as desired.

This completely new modular holder system of 1980 brought about the immediate need for a supporting parts catalog devoted exclusively to providing detailed drawings and part numbers for all the various components and adjustments. The full size, six-page tri-fold brochure was dramatically illustrated through artistic line drawings created by the talented Jerry Owings, working for Bill lll in the advertising department. His ability to artistically compliment engineering renderings and mechanical drawings was unsurpassed in my opinion.

TRIO MODULAR OUTFIT

Ludwig's new Triple Modular Tom Holder allows three power toms to be grouped either in a horizontal spread, side by side, or in a triangular pyramid configuration. The deep power bass drum with a double set of extra heavy duty spurs provides the foundation for this powerful triple tom outfit.

No. 3105—Trio Modular Outfit in your choice of finishes. (Cymbals not included.)

No. 3106—Trio Modular Outfit in your choice of finishes. (Cymbals not included.)

OUTFIT ACCESSORIES

1-1131	Hi-Hat
1-1374	Drum Stand
2-1411	Cymbal Booms
1-3003	Modular Trio Holder
1-201	Pedal
1 pair	Sticks & Brushes

MODEL	TOM TOMS Dbl. Hd.	TOM TOMS Floor T.	BASS	SNARE No. 402
3105	11" x 12" 12" x 13" 13" x 14"	16" x 16"	16" x 22"	6½" x 14"
3106	11" x 12" 12" x 13" 13" x 14"	16" x 16"	16" x 24"	6½" x 14"

CHROME-O-WOOD ILLUSTRATED

OUTRIGGER—TRIO OUTFIT

Through innovative design and research, Ludwig created a combination of the space-saving Outrigger stand concept with the Triple Modular Holder, featuring a powerful quintet of double-headed power toms. A power bass drum with two sets of heavy duty spurs supports this remarkable Set-Up!

No. 3130—Outrigger—Trio Outfit in your choice of finishes. (Cymbals not included.)

No. 3131—Outrigger—Trio Outfit in your choice of finishes. (Cymbals not included.)

OUTFIT ACCESSORIES

1-1131	Hi-Hat
1-1374	Drum Stand
2-1411	Cymbal Booms
1-3016	Outrigger T. Stand
1-3003	Modular Triple Holder
1-201	Pedal
1 pair	Sticks & Brushes

MODEL	TOM TOMS Dbl. Hd.	TOM TOMS Floor T.	BASS	SNARE No. 402
3130	9" x 8" 9" x 10" 11" x 12" 12" x 13" 13" x 14"	16" x 16"	16" x 22"	6½" x 14"
3131	9" x 8" 9" x 10" 11" x 12" 12" x 13" 13" x 14"	16" x 16"	16" x 24"	6½" x 14"

SPARKLING SILVER PEARL ILLUSTRATED

This became a tool for everyone handling the Ludwig product line internally as well as salesmen, customer service, and certainly all the percussion retailers selling and servicing Ludwig drums and the new Modular Holder and Support System.

Soon after, the new Modular Drum Grouping and Support System needed a consumer-friendly merchandising tool to help the drummer dream and build their own drum set to their personal specifications. All the Modular options got a little complex for salesmen to present all of the various options. Dealers needed guidance and consumers needed to know exactly what to order to get exactly what they wanted.

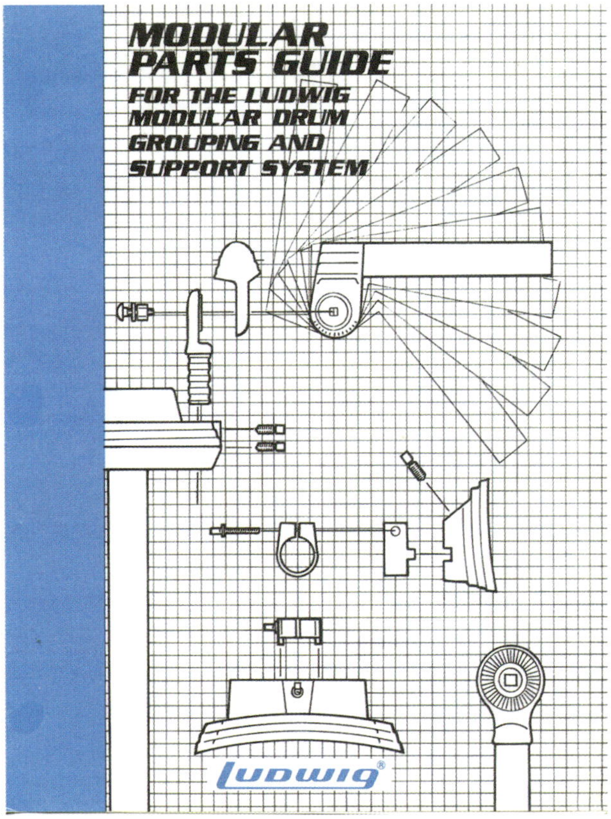

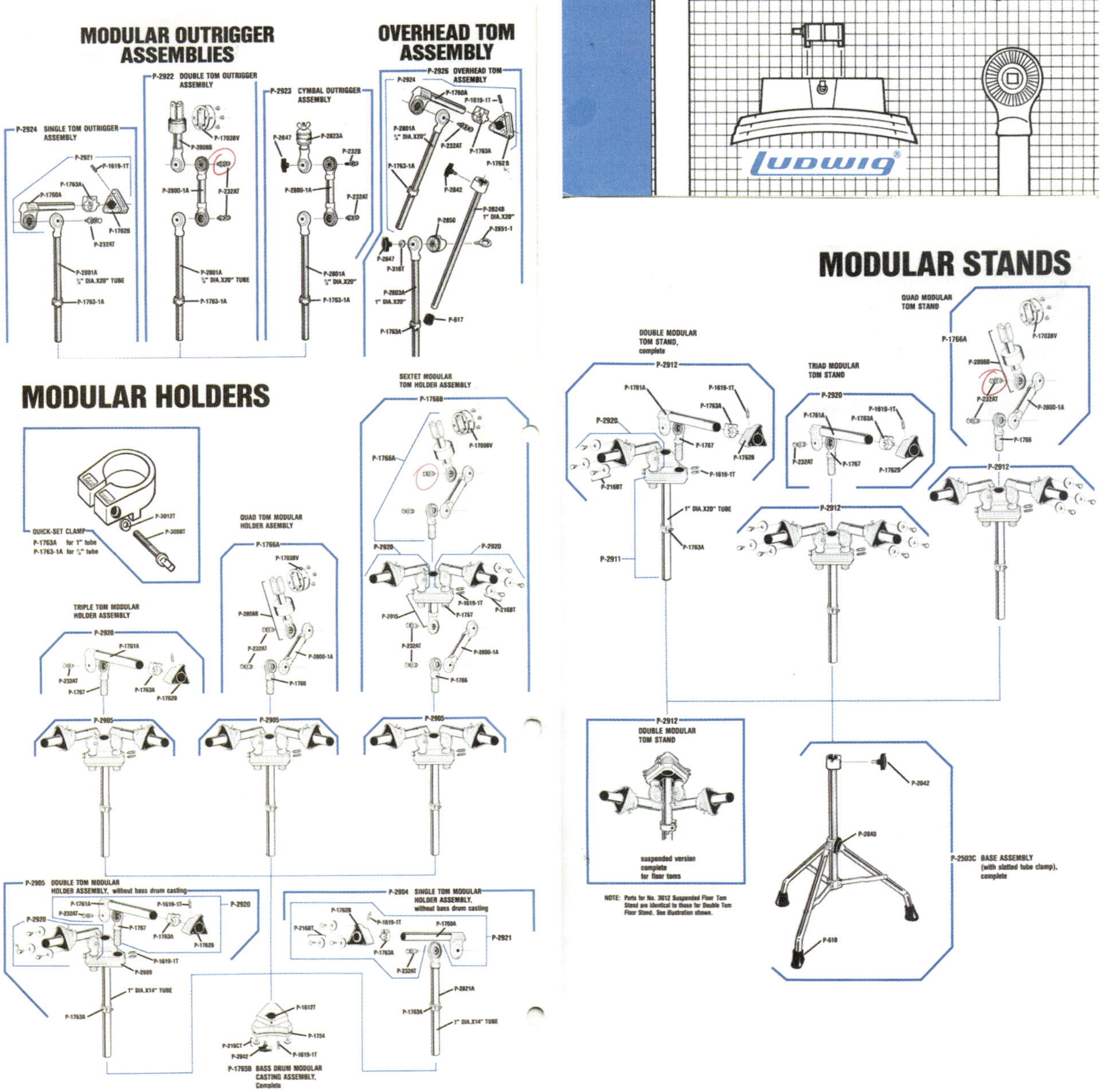

Frank Baxpehler and Jerry Owings collaborated on the creation of the Ludwig Do-It-Yourself Guide to Building The Set of Your Dreams two-color brochure. A magnificent idea and clearly illustrating all the options in drums and holders. Extension-arms and groupings could be added to existing sets or could be built totally from the bass drum up. Once again, the line drawing illustrations were magnificent and combined well with black & white photos of the product line for toms, bass drums, snare drums and all the holder options. This was well received and seemed to accelerate the Modular Holder System sales and placement in the market.

Musser's December, 1980, catalog, "Galaxy of Sound" The Trend Setter for the Eighties," was the first time in decades that Musser had its own full-color 16-page catalog that included all the instruments, mallets and accessories. While many of the color photos were picked up from the previous full line Ludwig-Musser catalogs, this Musser product expose' conveyed the market leadership that Musser had experienced for many years.

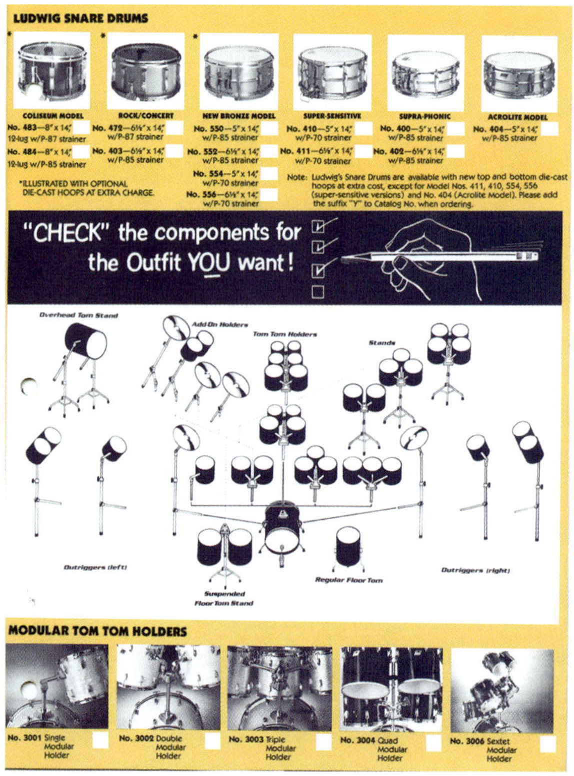

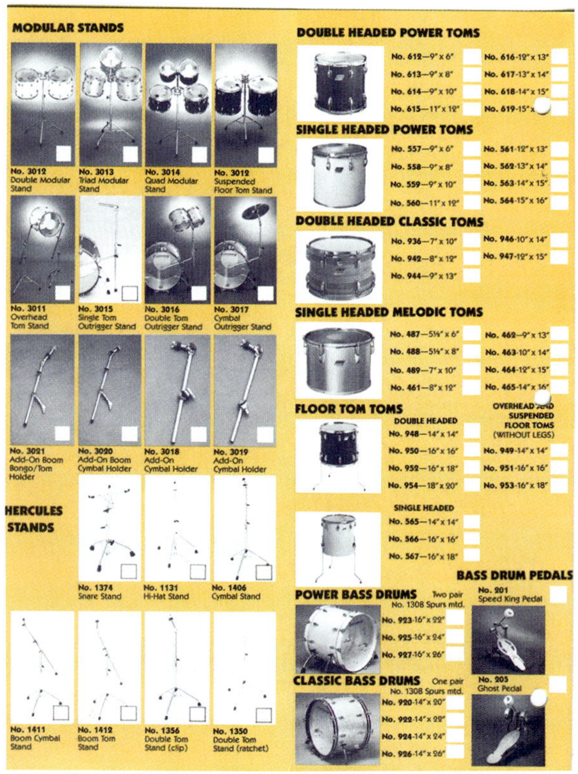

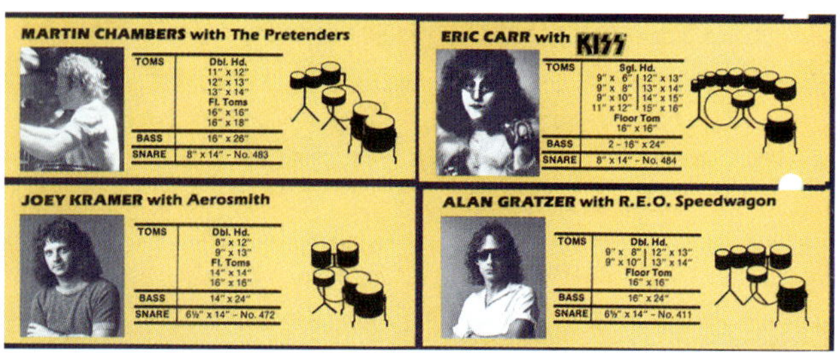

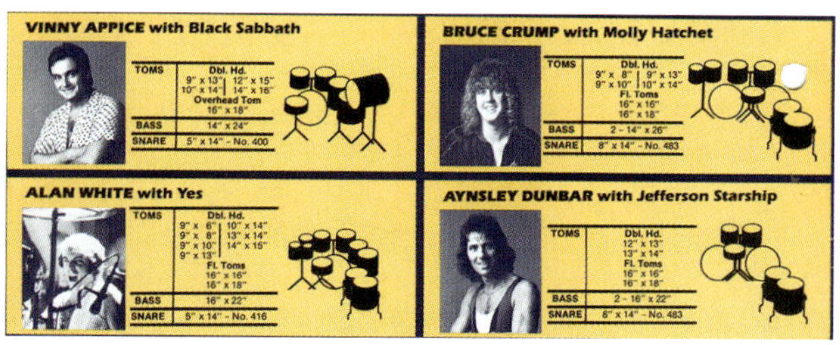

This was completely focused on orchestral mallet percussion, leaving out the vast assortment of marching percussion Musser instruments to be handled separately. The dramatic catalog cover color photograph was exceptional, contemporary, and became a signature Musser illustration for other promotional pieces in the future. The fact that Musser was known for the versatile bar material choices of Rosewood, Metal (steel/aluminum), and Kelon synthetic materials amplified the breadth and scope of the Musser product line.

By 1981, the complete Ludwig-Musser Marching Percussion product line had expanded and outgrown the product line as originally portrayed on the 1978 Total Percussion full line catalog (released as Catalog 80). I immediately got involved in the cover design element, as this was going to have a similar graphic artist rendering appearance as I had presented for the cover of the 1976 Ludwig Drummer magazine. I called upon the same graphic artist to commission original art, based upon the various drum corps uniforms that were using and playing Ludwig products on the field. I provided detailed drum corps photography for authentic uniform portrayal as well as "people with product" photographs that could dictate the shapes and sizes of the images that would also wrap around the front and back catalog outside covers.

"Ludwig 81 Total Marching Percussion, The Trend Setters for the 80's" carried forward the common cover headline theme. The cover was artistically beautiful; everyone recognized the various drum corps by the uniforms; Blue Devils, Casper Troopers, Phantom Regiment, Madison Scouts, and Bayonne Bridgeman, they were all represented in the artistic rendering. I have the original artwork framed and in my office as a remembrance of this tribute to so many wonderful drums corps using and playing Ludwig.

Ludwig returned to its roots in making wood shell drums. Stainless steel had become far too expensive to continue manufacturing. Vistalite was no longer the trend-setter it was when introduced in 1973. Much of the product line had changed, and there was an immediate need for a compact cost-effective Ludwig drum set catalog. A new outfit catalog was developed and released in March of 1981. Bill Jr. and Bill III appeared on the inside front cover. Neither had appeared in any marketing literature since 1978's Catalog 80.

The thirty-six page all color catalog was dominated by twelve continuous pages of beautiful Ludwig sets, featured in a massive array of colors, finishes, and various configurations. Ludwig wanted to reinstate its presence and standing in the professional drum set market and this exclusive drum set catalog made its mark. For the first time, Ludwig placed a $1.00 price tag on the cover of the catalog, appealing to the thought that catalogs had to have a perceived value. I don't believe any dollars ever changed hands as a result of having this printed on the front cover. This catalog had the 2"x4" dealer imprint box on the outside back cover and one hundred thousand copies were initially printed.

With the emphasis completely on Ludwig's 6-ply maple shells, referred to as "The Star Maker," the entire book represented everything that was new, different, and exciting about owning and playing Ludwig. This was a Bill lll project and he injected twenty-five individual photos of his various artists on the fold-out back cover.

All the related accessories were included with special emphasis on the new Ludwig Weather Master drum head packaging and merchandising program designed by Frank Baxpehler. Rockers, Striders, Ensemble, and Jazz were four distinctly different marketing and packaging images, even though the drum heads themselves may have been the same material or thickness. The four colorful logo identifications on the packages and the black images on the actual heads created a perception of what heads were intended for each type of music be played.

I never felt this drum head packaging campaign had the hoped-for momentum it needed. Plus, the factory inventory issues in production were getting cumbersome in terms of which heads would go on what drums. They could not be be mixed on the same drum set or concert tom assortment. Ludwig was feeling the competition on drum head sales and this was one of a few attempts to re-capture market share.

By the end of 1979 or beginning of 1980, I believe Bill Ludwig was being approached about the idea of transitioning out of the ownership position at Ludwig and this was beginning to take root in Bill's mind. The Asian presence in the marketplace was continuing to be felt more and more. It seemed like the Chinese were photographing and copy-manufacturing everything new that Ludwig would be launching and showing at the annual music industry trade shows. The Chineese were exceptional at copying anything, even our mistakes. 1980 brought continued labor union problems to Ludwig. Union negotiations had gotten extremely difficult and Bill did not handle this well with negotiations. At the same time, the federal government's OSHA was

For every kind of music, there's a different kind of drummer. And now, a different kind of drum head.

Rockers are drum heads designed especially for rock. They're tough, fast action heads that match rock power with head power.

Ensemble heads are designed especially for jazz, concert and ensemble percussion. Each head is highly responsive and specially designed to help produce a clean, rich, musical sound.

Striders are drum heads designed especially for marching percussion. They're durable and strong enough to take the torque that's necessary to project sound across a marching field.

Ludwig drum heads feature Headlock® — the most reliable head locking system.

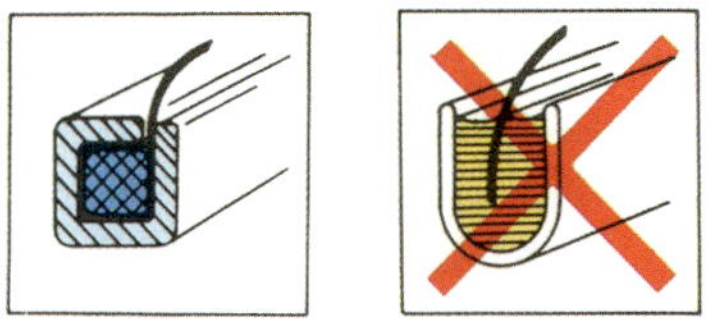

Ludwig head with Headlock® system. **Competition's head with epoxy method.**

One reason why Ludwig is a drummer's favorite is the mechanical interlock system called **Headlock.®** Designed by Ludwig's own engineers, this system permanently locks the drum head in place. While temperatures and other weather conditions may affect other heads, Ludwig drum heads resist change in pitch and loss of strength.

Other drum heads are set into a reservoir of epoxy, making them susceptible to cracking or loosening under pressure. Instead, Ludwig's select head material is first wrapped around a metal bar. Then, the bar is encased and compressed in a metal outer hoop, producing counter-leverage that permanently self-locks the head in place. The more pressure, the tighter it locks. This stops the head from pulling out. And practically eliminates customer returns.

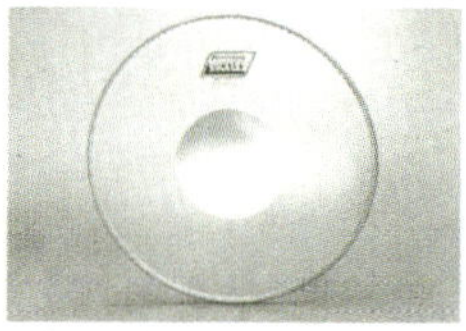

Ludwig's finest head: Silver Dots.

When you play heads with Silver Dots, playing is easier. Sound is brighter, and crisper. Tone is full and rich. A special air column movement increases volume at all dynamic levels. Sound projects farther with less overtone. And Silver Dots last longer because of lower center fatigue.

		INCH SIZES	6"	8"	10"	12"	13"	14"	15"	16"	17"	18"	20"	22"	23"	24"	25"	26"
	HEAD WEIGHT & TYPE	Approximate METRIC SIZES (cm)	15	20	25	30	33	36	38	41	43	46	51	56	59	61	64	66
ROCKERS® Ludwig®	SILVER DOT (HEAVY)	CLEAR	RO 6106	RO 6108	RO 6110	RO 6112	RO 6113	RO 6114	RO 6115	RO 6116		RO 6118	RO 6120	RO 6122		RO 6124		RO 6126
	HEAVY	CLEAR	RO 4106	RO 4108	RO 4110	RO 4112	RO 4113	RO 4114	RO 4115	RO 4116		RO 4118	RO 4120	RO 4122		RO 4124		RO 4126
Ensemble® Ludwig®	MEDIUM	CLEAR	EN 3106	EN 3108	EN 3110	EN 3112	EN 3113	EN 3114	EN 3115	EN 3116		EN 3118	EN 3120					
		WHITE	EN 3206	EN 3208	EN 3210	EN 3212	EN 3213	EN 3214	EN 3215	EN 3216		EN 3218	EN 3220					
		COATED	EN 3306	EN 3308	EN 3310	EN 3312	EN 3313	EN 3314	EN 3315	EN 3316		EN 3318	EN 3320					
	HEAVY	CLEAR										EN 4118	EN 4120	EN 4122		EN 4124		EN 4126
		WHITE	EN 4206	EN 4208	EN 4210	EN 4212	EN 4213	EN 4214	EN 4215	EN 4216		EN 4218	EN 4220	EN 4222		EN 4224		EN 4226
		COATED	EN 4306	EN 4308	EN 4310	EN 4312	EN 4313	EN 4314	EN 4315	EN 4316		EN 4318	EN 4320	EN 4322		EN 4324		EN 4326
special heads	RESONANT SNARE X-THIN	CLEAR					CC 1113	CC 1114	CC 1115									
	TIMBALE MEDIUM	COATED					CC 12313	CC 12314										
	TAMBOURINE PRACTICE PAD MEDIUM	COATED		CC 10308	CC 10310													
	BONGO/CONGA HEAVY	WHITE	CC 11206	CC 11208		CC 11212												

(31)

intensifying it's presence and increased its visits to the Ludwig factory. In addition, there were increasing federal mandates about the health issues connected with plating, painting, and ventilation.

I could see that there was a deliberate effort to conceal the fact that money and budgets were getting tight. I had been at Ludwig long enough to recognize the difference between the easy-come/easy go times and the periods when every dollar is measured. I had lived through and survived various economic peaks and valleys within the company before. But this time the feeling, my senses told me, was different.

The end of 1979 saw further measures being taken to remain competitive and profitable, to sustain market share, and to present an image of "all is well". But the realities of increased competition and the fixed overhead were not only converging, but bringing change and heartache. Every department was being financially reviewed as to where costs could be cut, where savings could be made, and how each could become more integrated and efficient in everything that Ludwig was doing. Combined with the forthcoming Labor Union negotiations in the very near future, changes were mandatory.

The cost of operating the internal printing department seemed to be a contentious topic between Frank Baxpehler and VP of Finance John Mahoney. Discourse regarding the feasibility of continuing to operate the printing department grew to a stand-off by the middle of December. The Finance Department and John Mahoney won this battle and the decision was made to close and eliminate the complete in-house print operations. I was give the task of hand delivering the small annual Christmas bonuses, final payroll checks, and a two week severance check to my four printing department people on the last day before the Christmas holiday break. I informed the team that the printing department was being eliminated and all were being discharged from the company effective immediately. "Go home, try to have a Merry Christmas and don't come back to work". I was devastated having to do this to these hard working team members right before Christmas, but it was my job. This unfortunate duty and responsibility ruined my Christmas. I had a good idea what was ahead, without the people and the print-shop operations.

As a result of this change, Cedar Valley Printing assumed an even greater role in printing and producing materials for Ludwig. All the internal production-accounting-purchasing forms, the Ludwig Percussion Aid Pack contents, and countless other day-to-day items were now outsourced. I wondered about the costs of all this printing and whether there was an actual savings.

MORE CHANGE IS COMING, as expected.

In the early part of the summer, 1980, Bill contacted me to indicate that Selmer had interest in the Ludwig Company and that they would like to send one of their representatives from Elkhart, Indiana, Rollie Bunn, to attend the percussion symposium as a percussion spectator. The symposium was approaching very quickly and I had a lot on my plate, but now had to also handle the "Guest" that would be attending. I knew he was there to watch every move and decision I would make for this week-long educational event. I was told this in need-to-know confidence, and directed to be very careful in how we represented the Ludwig Company. At the same time, it was my responsibility to basically create and lead the same symposium that Ludwig and I had always organized.

Rollie Bunn attended that summer's Percussion Symposium as planned. Neither Bill Ludwig nor anyone from the Ludwig company attended, as they wanted to stay out of the way of any attending Selmer Guest. Rollie was a gracious, very laid-back person who really welcomed the opportunity to see what a Ludwig Symposium was. I believe he was very impressed with what Ludwig was doing and the impact this had on young percussionists, music educators and percussion instructors all in attendance for the week-long event. I got the feeling afterwards that his report to Selmer (and Ludwig for that matter) was very positive about the event and the leadership I displayed. Rollie was also quick to try and place me at ease in knowing he was there strictly to observe, not to critique and evaluate. This ease of conversation continued during the entire week. (Its interesting to note that I would deal with Rollie Bunn again many years later after he was out of Selmer, as he started his own import distribution company which included Ajax Timpani.)

At the same time, we were getting ready for the PAS convention to be held in November of 1980 in Indianapolis, Indiana with Paul Burns as the convention host. I suspected that Ludwig would be visited and watched by "guests from Selmer". Again, Bill told me, "Karl- do everything that you have always done with PAS. We will have a huge exhibit and we'll have a hospitality suite." I followed his directives and implemented the usual very prominent and dominant presence at the Indiana Convention Center. Ludwig-Musser had artists in every product category. By now I was seeing signs of making the company as strong and valuable as possible for the benefit of "potential company buyers". Everything we did had an underlying element of making the company profitable, viable and worthy of a change in ownership. The elements of change were evolving, one month at a time. We saw the sale of the company coming before the end of the year. Meanwhile the Labor Union negotiations were ongoing and getting more difficult. Bill did not handle this well.

A DAY TO REMEMBER

I call November 4, 1981, the day that the percussion world stood still. That was the day that the contracts were signed and the Selmer Company took ownership of Ludwig Industries. There was an uncertainty about what was next, how this would impact the company and each Ludwig employee. I saw Selmer's VP of Finance, John Mussleman, signing payroll checks and knew instantly; the change had taken place, forever.

Bill Jr. wanted to become my best friend at that point. He saw that I have survived the transition thus far, at least on a daily basis. The first immediate change was the release of all of the Ludwig-Musser vice-presidents. The three vice-presidents from Selmer came to the Ludwig Company on a weekly basis to interact with all of the managers. They would typically come in on a Tuesday and leave Thursday afternoon. The challenging part for me was that for 8 hours a day while they were there, I would be interacting with them all day. Bob Kane wanted to learn everything about the marketing and education departments of Ludwig. At the same time I had to get my "regular" daily work completed that required at least 8 to 10 hours a day of my time.

Frank Baxpehler was offered an international sales position, but chose to leave the company. His secretary, Brooke Crowden (Bill Ludwig's daughter) also departed the company immediately. The other VP Ludwig personnel who were eliminated included John Mahoney (finance), Bob Andre (purchasing), and Ed Ebel (Production). Dick Richardson immediately left the Musser company and went over to become the new President of the Slingerland Drum Company in their Niles, Illinois factory. He accepted this position under new Slingerland owner Danny Henkin.

The Ludwig "internal understudies" took over the VP duties without the VP titles or pay. I was very disappointed at the very abrupt changes that were taking place. I became the Ludwig Marketing Manager and moved into Frank's office on the Executive Office side of the first floor offices. Throughout my time at Ludwig, Alice Golinski had been with me as Educational Department Secretary. And she was with Jim Sewrey before that. She had seen and experienced a lot at Ludwig and I considered her one of my loyal right arms. She moved over to the desk right outside my office. Despite Selmer's continued re-assurance that everyone would remain employed and an active participant in the future, I saw changes occurring faster than I could keep up with them. Plans were also developing for Selmer to sell off its ownership portion of Premier Percussion which they quickly and quietly accomplished without much fanfare.

The three Selmer vice-presidents, (or as I called them, the three musketeers) were Bob Kane, Pete Ryan, and John Mussleman. Occasionally Selmer President Bill Petersen would also visit Ludwig for a day or two of meetings and observation. Selmer's advertising and marketing manager Carl Bovard also began coming to Ludwig to interact with us.

Selmer figured out a way to utilize Bill Ludwig Junior; allowing him to travel the United States presenting his History of Percussion lecture to over three-hundred colleges, universities and other venues that recognized the value and opportunity to have Bill Ludwig Jr. visit their school. He created a presentation about 90 minutes in length with a slide show, samples of sound effects and historic drums. He would arrange his bookings himself and travel around the country. This was partially funded by Selmer as a PR connection. They were keeping the Ludwig family involved with the company, but certainly not its operation. Bill was happy doing this. He no longer had the day-to-day worries of union negotiations, meeting payroll and the family-company leader. I would imagine this was a huge burden off his shoulders at this point in his life.

In spite of the staff assurances, efforts to purge the two separate outside sales forces (Ludwig and Selmer) came quickly.

Bob Kane would meet with the various outside sales representatives of Ludwig to determine how to establish the best territory coverage. This usually resulted in assigning the Ludwig sales rep a much smaller and less revenue-producing territory. The Ludwig sales force disintegrated quickly, as one-by-one the Ludwig salesmen left the company. I firmly believe this was the internal intent of Selmer all along. The easiest and fastest way to integrate a newly acquired company as a Division of the Selmer Company was to continue to use the very same (Selmer) sales force, modifying the territories as needed. I witnessed this when Selmer salesman Ted May was appointed as the Chicago area salesman. Ted was great guy, a team player, and a wonderful Selmer Salesman, but had learned very little about percussion through his Premier percussion experience.. He certainly did not have any relationship with the percussion stores or department heads in the Illinois-Wisconsin territory like Ludwig's Bob Southey or Rick Young. (Bill Ludwig would occasionally remind us that band instrument salesmen are not percussion and drum salesmen. He learned this hard way when sharing a sales force with Holton Band Instrument Company in the 50's or 60's.)

Ludwig, was being dismantled month-by-month, person-by-person, from the inside-out, and being made to conform to becoming just a Division of the Selmer Company.

Bill lll was still on board under the new ownership, (I can only speculate this was a stipulation in the Ludwig sale agreement) interacting with Selmer on advertising and continuing the artist relations elements. But it was clear Selmer wanted to bring the complete Ludwig-Musser advertising decision-making and creative aspects to Elkhart. Bill continued to run the artist relations department, but the budget clamp-downs were soon put on all marketing department line-items. Selmer perceived the Artist Relations program to basically be a product-giveaway program in exchange for an artist's endorsement. It was clearly not in the Selmer mindset why you had to give away this amount of equipment to secure endorsements. I believe this became a major bone of contention. Bill stayed on and we worked closely together on trying to stay ahead of the Selmer mindset on everything. We did not have a crystal ball but our gut feeling prevailed and we were correct in most anticipated changes. I believe Bill lll saw the handwriting on the wall early on.

Selmer's Bob Kane wanted me to work closely with Bill lll during the transition, which was perfectly OK with me, as we worked well together on everything. Bill III continued attending a lot of the various major venue concerts when any of his Ludwig artists came to Chicago or anywhere close. That of course led to the backstage socializing after the concert as well as the occasional delivering of parts or products to the artist's drum tech. Those after-concert "duties" could go on until two o'clock in the morning. This resulted in the fact that he would occasionally not be at his Advertising Manager's desk at 8:30 a.m. the next morning. This started to become an issue, but we worked around it the best that we could. Selmer did not understand this part of the "artist relationship".

Shortly after the sale of the company, Bill went on a vacation trip to Europe. He took his wife, his Daughter Brooke, and her husband Bill Crowden. They took a wonderful trip through Europe on the Orient Express Railroad. Somehow Bill Jr. knew and remembered that I am an avid model railroad enthusiast. Bill brought back a gift for me of an Orient Express railroad car with a book about the history of the Orient Express. I don't even know how he knew that I was interested in model trains, but I was touched. This special railroad gift is treasured and is still on display in my office.

Upon his return to the office from the European vacation trip, Bill of course wanted to know what was new and what was happening within the company. I think I was the only person that survived the first two months of new ownership who would tell him anything and confide in him what I could. He of course knew never to ask me questions that would put me in the uncomfortable position of saying, "Bill- I cannot tell you that."

The sale of the company was completed, Bill had returned from vacation, and the Midwest Band & Orchestra convention in the Conrad Hilton Hotel was coming quickly.

December brought multiple command appearances that are memorable. Selmer had its traditional company Christmas party at the Elcona Country Club in Bristol Indiana, near Elkhart. Dick Gerlach, Bill Ludwig and I were invited to attend this event, representing the "newly acquired Ludwig Division of Selmer". We were honored guests and Bill made a wonderful spirited speech presentation during the event. He is never at a loss for words and loves an audience. He was perfect in this setting. It was interesting that each of us were assigned seats at different tables; there was to be no Ludwig congregating at one Ludwig table. We all stayed overnight at the local hotel after the event, realizing "we had survived our first Selmer social event".

During traditional normal times, Bill and Maggie Ludwig would host a by-invitation-only catered Christmas party at Bill's home immediately following the Midwest Band Clinic in December. Everyone knew that this took place, but it was a very limited number of people who were invited to attend. Up to this point in time and my Ludwig career, I had never been personally invited and didn't feel hurt by that. I just was not in that inner circle, yet. In December of 1981 I was invited to the Ludwig Christmas party at their beautiful Oak Brook home. I was honored by the invitation and to be finally included, for whatever reason.

As the newly united companies moved forwards together into 1982, the day-to-day stress, challenging situations and continuous explanations to Selmer and its Vice Presidents continued. I was experiencing, what I would refer to later as a 13 month brain-drain which basically was an extended opportunity for Selmer to learn anything/everything I could provide them about marketing and the educational department, functions and operations. In the meantime Selmer tried to keep the momentum of the Ludwig company going forward. Many new products and marketing pieces were launched in record time.

By 1982 Ludwig was becoming known for it's increasingly delayed delivery. The back order situation had become desperate by the time the company changed ownership. This was a major concern for the Ludwig dealerships, the territory salesmen, and of course the end-user-customers who were waiting for their specially ordered instruments. Determined to fix this situation, Selmer delivered a decree to dealers that Ludwig would ship any Ludwig or Musser product within 14 business days of the order date, or they would pay the freight charges. Of course the fastest way to fix the back-order problem would have been with an infusion of cash. Cash to buy more materials, to build more products, to stock more finished goods.

DIVISIONS
LUDWIG DRUM CO
MUSSER

LUDWIG INDUSTRIES

July 30, 1982

TO ALL LUDWIG DEALERS

FULFILLING THE LUDWIG - SELMER COMMITMENT

This photograph was taken on November 5, 1981, on the occasion of the signing of the agreement joining Ludwig Industries with The Selmer Company.

At the time this photograph was taken I restated my pledge to Bill Petersen, President of The Selmer Company, that our first move under the new management would be to expand our production capacity and improve our delivery picture. I am pleased to report to you now that this has been accomplished.

This effort could not have been accomplished without the encouragement of Bill Petersen and Pete Ryan, and the complete cooperation of all Ludwig people in our Chicago and LaGrange factories and offices. It demonstrates once more how American free enterprise can accomplish big jobs efficiently and quickly.

> The result of the effort is that now we can promise, with very few exceptions, to ship your orders for all of the instruments, hardware and accessories manufactured by our Company within fourteen working days after we receive your order in Chicago.
>
> In the event that, for some unforeseen reason, we cannot keep that promise, we'll pay the freight on any item we can't ship within the stated period.

We call our new program the ASSURED PROMPT DELIVERY PLAN. We hope you will make good use of it. Tell your customers about it. Everybody benefits. It places you in a highly favorable competitive position, and lets you assure your customers they can get the superior quality American-made percussion instruments they need – quicker.

All the details are explained in the attached flyer.

Cordially,

W. F. Ludwig, Jr.:mgb

1728 N. DAMEN AVE. CHICAGO ILL 60647 U.S.A. PHONE 312-276-3360

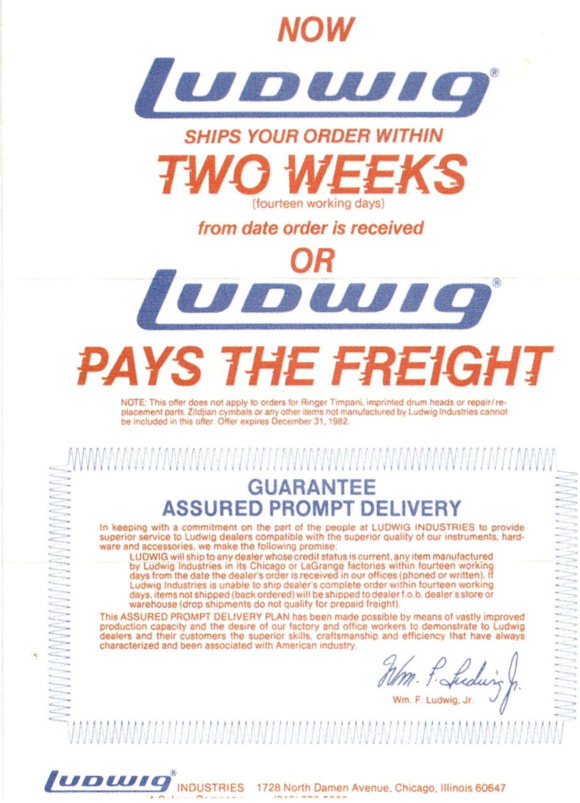

NOW
LUDWIG®
SHIPS YOUR ORDER WITHIN
TWO WEEKS
(fourteen working days)
from date order is received
OR
LUDWIG®
PAYS THE FREIGHT

NOTE: This offer does not apply to orders for Ringer Timpani, imprinted drum heads or repair/replacement parts. Zildjian cymbals or any other items not manufactured by Ludwig Industries cannot be included in this offer. Offer expires December 31, 1982.

GUARANTEE
ASSURED PROMPT DELIVERY

In keeping with a commitment on the part of the people at LUDWIG INDUSTRIES to provide superior service to Ludwig dealers compatible with the superior quality of our instruments, hardware and accessories, we make the following promise:

> LUDWIG will ship to any dealer whose credit status is current, any item manufactured by Ludwig Industries in its Chicago or LaGrange factories within fourteen working days from the date the dealer's order is received in our offices (phoned or written). If Ludwig Industries is unable to ship dealer's complete order within fourteen working days, items not shipped (back ordered) will be shipped to dealer f.o.b. dealer's store or warehouse (drop shipments do not qualify for prepaid freight).

This ASSURED PROMPT DELIVERY PLAN has been made possible by means of vastly improved production capacity and the desire of our factory and office workers to demonstrate to Ludwig dealers and their customers the superior skills, craftsmanship and efficiency that have always characterized and been associated with American industry.

Wm. F. Ludwig, Jr.

LUDWIG® INDUSTRIES 1728 North Damen Avenue, Chicago, Illinois 60647

On July 30, 1982, Bill sent an announcement to all authorized Ludwig Dealers, announcing the new LUDWIG-SELMER COMMITMENT and promotion for on-time shipment of Ludwig-Musser products. The mailing included a picture of Bill Ludwig and Bill Petersen, and a commitment of Selmer's immediate steps to correct the back-order situation.

Ludwig Total Concert Percussion was one of the dominant and lasting strengths of the Ludwig Company and brand. The need for an updated and complete new Concert Percussion Catalog became an overnight priority in preparation for the June NAMM Convention. This underlined the cost effectiveness of having Concert Percussion separated from drum sets and marching percussion. The thinking was that concert percussion customers may not necessarily be interested in catalogued outfits and vice versa. The forty-four page catalog was released in May 1982 with a printing of thirty thousand copies. Concert Percussion was the most closely aligned product line of Ludwig that connected to and enhanced Selmer's band instrument market, sales, mentality and budget priority.

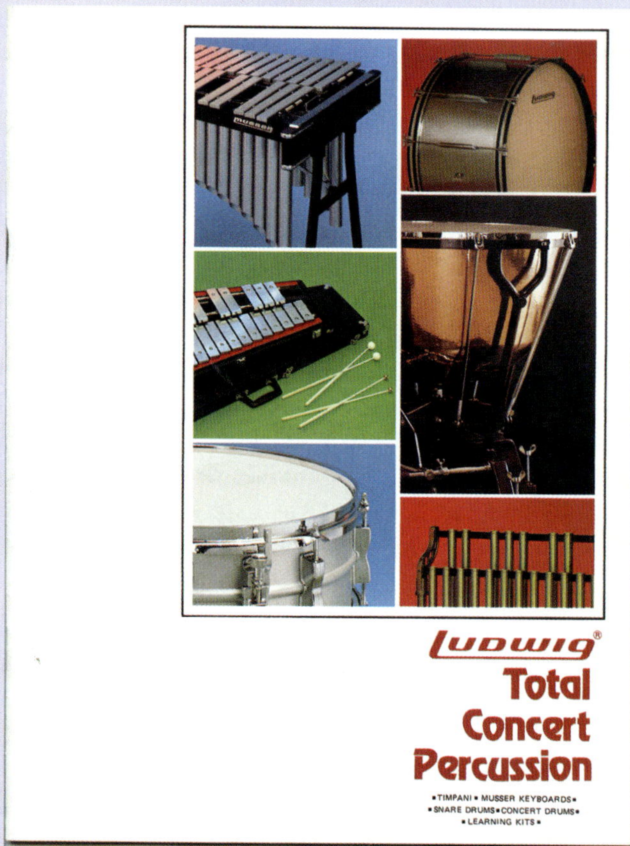

Powerline Marching Mallets and Beaters designed by Dennis Delucia entered the market with a significant positive acceptance. These were all manufactured at the Ludwig factory and included a sturdier product that combined a patented Mallet-Head-Lock, laminated all-wood handle-shafts and plastic Sure-Grip Handles on every model. By now Dennis was a leading clinician/instructor at Ludwig's Percussion Symposiums and a highly respected DCI Adjudicator and director of the Bayonne, NJ, Bridgmen Drum & Bugle Corps. Powerline DeLucia signature mallets helped draw attention to his formal relationship with Ludwig.

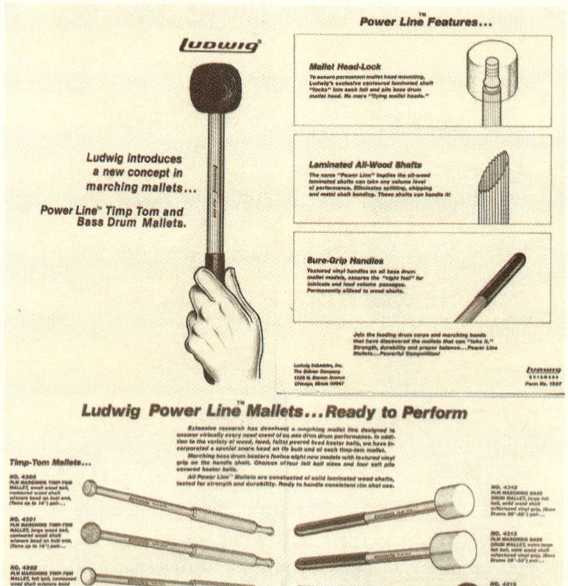

NAMM SHOW Preparations:

The June, 1982, NAMM show was held in Atlanta and Ludwig would become an integrated product within the The Selmer Company display and market profile. As Ludwig Marketing Manager, I was responsible for creating a large internal "NAMM SHOW showbook" that was to include all new products, NAMM Show specials and incentives and details for the attending combined sales force to work with during and after the convention. At this point Bill III was still helping me put these things together. Bill did some of it, I did some it, all with Selmer's Carl Bovard and Bob Kane keeping an eye on the process.

For the first time in my life I had to room with someone, and I was assigned Dick Gerlach. I had no problem sharing a room with Dick, but he always had a story he wanted to tell. It was sometimes a bit of a challenge to stay focused while the stories continued at the booth, in the hotel room, and in between. Dick and I worked well together and as two guys from German families based in Milwaukee, we probably had more in common than we thought.

Fortunately, I was able to continue to using Cedar Valley Printing in Chicago to produce the Ludwig and Musser sales literature. Ludwig's previous in-house printing department and presses at the L&L building were sitting still and dormant.

New Silk and Gloss Finishes for drum sets were featured at the Atlanta convention which led way to a completely new 12 page all-color Ludwig Outfit and Accessory Catalog. There were no artists; the spotlight was really on the Silk Finishes and the new STANDARD line drum sets. This provided an updated appearance under the Selmer banner and became the DRUM OUTFIT catalog for the moment. Thirty thousand copies were released in August. A photo of William F. Ludwig Jr. and an opening statement was included on the inside front cover.

A History of Tradition and Quality...

William F. Ludwig, Jr.

From the very beginning back in 1909, the Ludwig brothers, William F. Ludwig, Sr. and his younger brother, Theobald, earned the excellent reputation among percussionists in the Chicago area for providing innovative products and designs, while also working any percussion performance assignment in the area. Their original floor model bass drum pedal created an instant demand and quickly led to the invention of the first throw-off snare unit.

Today with nearly 75 years of heritage and dedication, the Ludwig name represents the finest American technology and craftsmanship. All aspects of drum and accessory production are under demanding quality requirements while hundreds of employees strive to provide you with the "latest in sound and design" in the percussion world.

The Ludwig family dedication goes on with the unveiling of many new products illustrated in this new Outfit Catalog. We welcome all of our drummer friends and customers to visit our manufacturing facility to witness "history and tradition" being made.

Wm. F. Ludwig Jr.

RE-introduction of STANDARD LINE:

Selmer decided it wanted to re-introduce the Standard Line that had originally been brought to market by Dick Schory in the mid 1960's. The products were created, priced, catalog and photographed for launching at the Atlanta 1982 NAMM show. I don't believe the line ever saw tremendous market acceptance as there were better looking and performing sets proliferating in the entry-level drum market, coming from Asia. Those consumers were looking for price, not made-in America brands or quality.

Ludwig Standard USA

Ludwig sets a new standard for a low priced drum set

That Great Ludwig Sound . . . it's here, now more affordable than ever! Ludwig recalls the Standard Line™ as an era in a class by itself. In style and construction, Ludwig leads the competitive edge over imported equipment, in a product you can buy with confidence and continued dealer service and dependability. Better still, it's made in America by the company that's been setting standards in the percussion world for decades.

Exclusive Standard Line™ features include regular Ludwig line hardware and holder . . . famous Speed King bass drum pedal and tough, fast action Ludwig Rocker™ plastic heads through-out. Available in four popular finishes . . . Red, Blue, Black and White Cortex.

The Ludwig Standard Line™. . . . famous features and quality at an affordable price!

Ludwig®

Ludwig Industries, Inc.
The Selmer Company
1728 N. Damen Ave.
Chicago, Illinois 60647

See Standard Line™ at your Ludwig Dealer soon!

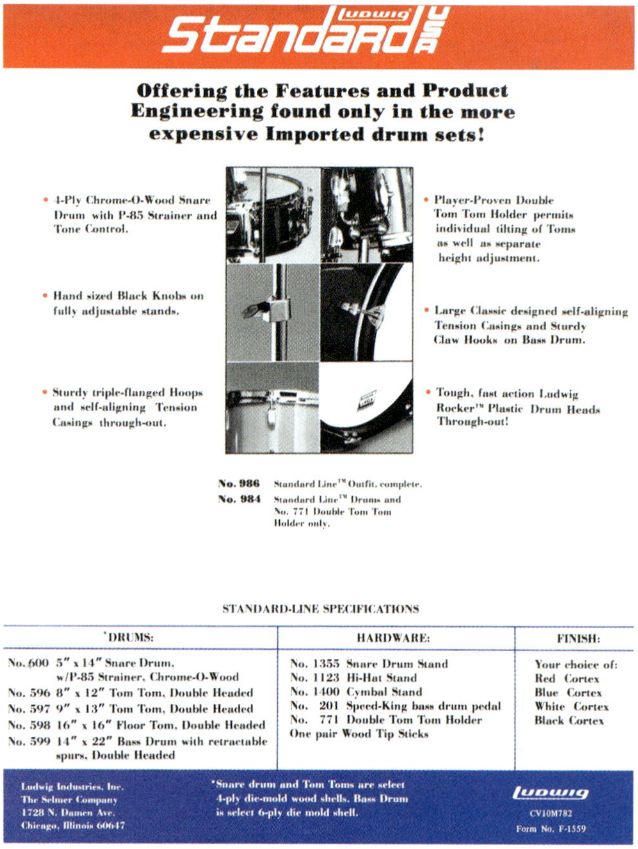

Ludwig Standard USA

Offering the Features and Product Engineering found only in the more expensive Imported drum sets!

- 4-Ply Chrome-O-Wood Snare Drum with P-85 Strainer and Tone Control.
- Hand sized Black Knobs on fully adjustable stands.
- Sturdy triple-flanged Hoops and self-aligning Tension Casings through-out.
- Player-Proven Double Tom Tom Holder permits individual tilting of Toms as well as separate height adjustment.
- Large Classic designed self-aligning Tension Casings and Sturdy Claw Hooks on Bass Drum.
- Tough, fast action Ludwig Rocker™ Plastic Drum Heads Through-out!

No. 986 Standard Line™ Outfit, complete.
No. 984 Standard Line™ Drums and No. 771 Double Tom Tom Holder only.

STANDARD-LINE SPECIFICATIONS

*DRUMS:	HARDWARE:	FINISH:
No. 600 5" x 14" Snare Drum, w/P-85 Strainer, Chrome-O-Wood No. 596 8" x 12" Tom Tom, Double Headed No. 597 9" x 13" Tom Tom, Double Headed No. 598 16" x 16" Floor Tom, Double Headed No. 599 14" x 22" Bass Drum with retractable spurs, Double Headed	No. 1355 Snare Drum Stand No. 1123 Hi-Hat Stand No. 1400 Cymbal Stand No. 201 Speed-King bass drum pedal No. 771 Double Tom Tom Holder One pair Wood Tip Sticks	Your choice of: Red Cortex Blue Cortex White Cortex Black Cortex

Ludwig Industries, Inc.
The Selmer Company
1728 N. Damen Ave.
Chicago, Illinois 60647

*Snare drum and Tom Toms are select 4-ply die-mold wood shells. Bass Drum is select 6-ply die mold shell.

Ludwig
CV10M782
Form No. F-1559

Customized Ludwig Drum Head-Dealer logos:

There was a concerted effort to get back some of the drum head business with a dealer personalized imprint program. With the purchase of certain minimum quantities of Ludwig heads packed in master cartons, the dealer's name and logo was imprinted on each head. The concept was unique and a first for Ludwig.

It also provided the opportunity to restate the patented HEADLOCK design of how Ludwig heads do NOT pull out of the aluminum flesh hoop. The dealer imprint was available on all heads and the customer's artwork was retained for re-orders in the Ludwig head manufacturing department. This met with some initial success, but the momentum was not maintained through the years. Graphic Artist Jerry Owings did a marvelous in-house artist rending of all the illustrations. While the brochure used the "Start Heads Rolling" in the headline, I was overly sensitive to the term heads rolling. (I wonder why?)

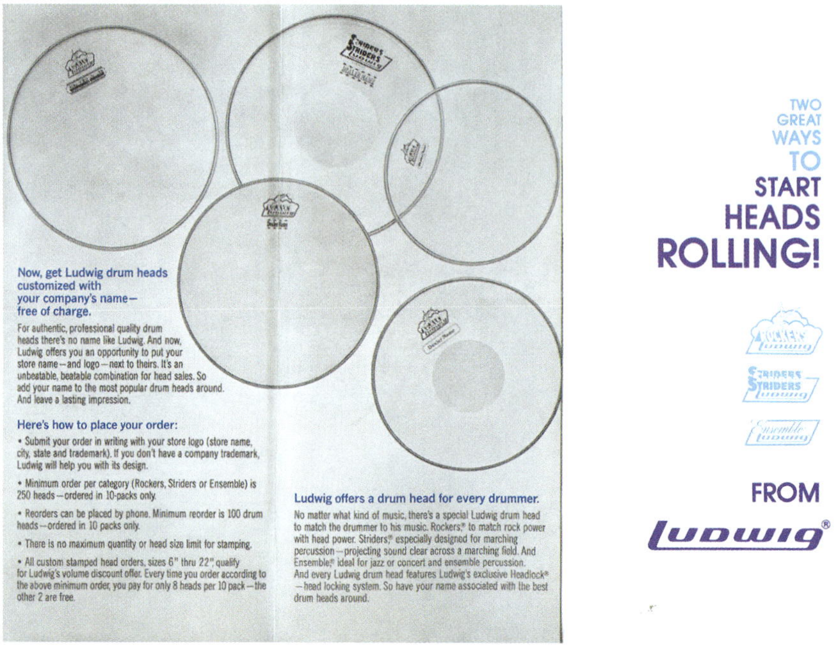

Now, get Ludwig drum heads customized with your company's name—free of charge.

For authentic, professional quality drum heads there's no name like Ludwig. And now, Ludwig offers you an opportunity to put your store name—and logo—next to theirs. It's an unbeatable, beatable combination for head sales. So add your name to the most popular drum heads around. And leave a lasting impression.

Here's how to place your order:

- Submit your order in writing with your store logo (store name, city, state and trademark). If you don't have a company trademark, Ludwig will help you with its design.
- Minimum order per category (Rockers, Striders or Ensemble) is 250 heads—ordered in 10-packs only.
- Reorders can be placed by phone. Minimum reorder is 100 drum heads—ordered in 10 packs only.
- There is no maximum quantity or head size limit for stamping.
- All custom stamped head orders, sizes 6" thru 22", qualify for Ludwig's volume discount offer. Every time you order according to the above minimum order, you pay for only 8 heads per 10 pack—the other 2 are free.

Ludwig offers a drum head for every drummer.

No matter what kind of music, there's a special Ludwig drum head to match the drummer to his music. Rockers,® to match rock power with head power. Striders,® especially designed for marching percussion—projecting sound clear across a marching field. And Ensemble,® ideal for jazz or concert and ensemble percussion. And every Ludwig drum head features Ludwig's exclusive Headlock®—head locking system. So have your name associated with the best drum heads around.

TWO GREAT WAYS TO START HEADS ROLLING!

FROM Ludwig®

Ed Shaughnessy created a drum clinic video cassette that Ludwig helped merchandise through all Ludwig dealers. A special mailing to all dealers was launched in October calling attention to the video and advising everyone that they could order this directly from Ed Shaughnessy.

TAKE ADVANTAGE OF THIS SPECIAL CHRISTMAS INTRODUCTORY OFFER!

Ed Shaughnessy Drum Clinic VIDEO CASSETTE!

Holiday Special

Americas most in demand drum set clinician is now offering this outstanding One Hour Video Cassette for home study by all levels of drummers.

- HELPFUL TO TEACHERS
- AID TO MUSIC EDUCATORS
- SCHOOL PROGRAMMING

Subjects Covered Include:

Analysis of good rhythm playing
Warm - ups
Building of weaker hand
Cross - sticking
Reading on the set
Improvisation

CLIP AND MAIL TO:
ED SHAUGHNESSY ENTERPRISES INC.
P.O. BOX 53222
OKLAHOMA CITY, OKLAHOMA 73152

Please send me the Video Cassette(s) checked below:

	LIST	DEALER NET
☐ ½" VHS Format	$65	$49.95
☐ ½" BETA Format	$65	$49.95
☐ ¾" U-MATIC Format	$80	$65.00

Dealer Name __________
Address __________
City ______ State ______ Zip ______

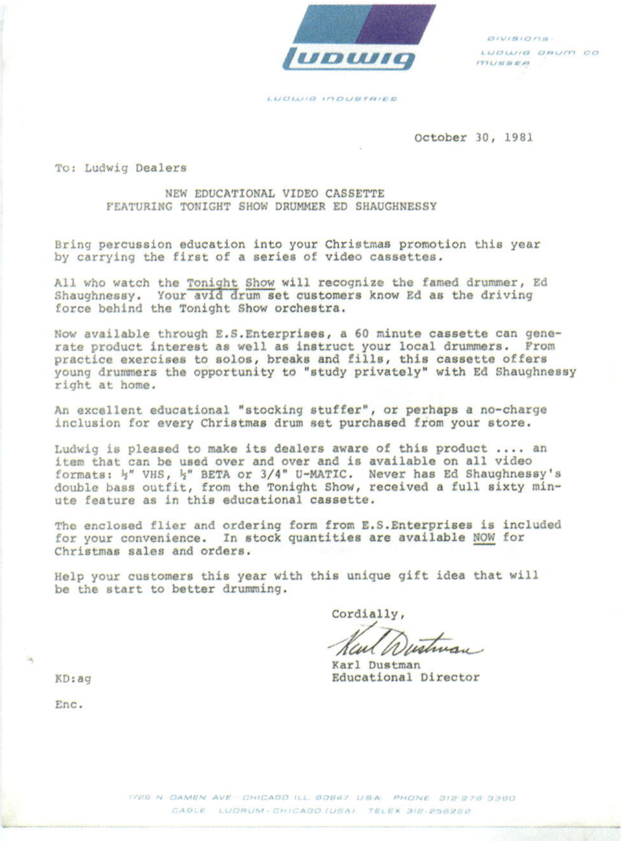

LUDWIG

DIVISIONS:
LUDWIG DRUM CO
MUSSER

LUDWIG INDUSTRIES

October 30, 1981

To: Ludwig Dealers

NEW EDUCATIONAL VIDEO CASSETTE
FEATURING TONIGHT SHOW DRUMMER ED SHAUGHNESSY

Bring percussion education into your Christmas promotion this year by carrying the first of a series of video cassettes.

All who watch the Tonight Show will recognize the famed drummer, Ed Shaughnessy. Your avid drum set customers know Ed as the driving force behind the Tonight Show orchestra.

Now available through E.S.Enterprises, a 60 minute cassette can generate product interest as well as instruct your local drummers. From practice exercises to solos, breaks and fills, this cassette offers young drummers the opportunity to "study privately" with Ed Shaughnessy right at home.

An excellent educational "stocking stuffer", or perhaps a no-charge inclusion for every Christmas drum set purchased from your store.

Ludwig is pleased to make its dealers aware of this product .... an item that can be used over and over and is available on all video formats: ½" VHS, ½" BETA or 3/4" U-MATIC. Never has Ed Shaughnessy's double bass outfit, from the Tonight Show, received a full sixty minute feature as in this educational cassette.

The enclosed flier and ordering form from E.S.Enterprises is included for your convenience. In stock quantities are available NOW for Christmas sales and orders.

Help your customers this year with this unique gift idea that will be the start to better drumming.

Cordially,

Karl Dustman
Educational Director

KD:ag

Enc.

1728 N. DAMEN AVE · CHICAGO ILL. 60647 USA · PHONE 312-276-3360
CABLE LUDRUM-CHICAGO (USA) TELEX 312-256292

Using Selmer's new format for advertising, Ludwig was instructed to create and design a "Fall Specials" brochure. This two-color piece looked very much like a Selmer band instrument piece. One of the more market-noticed changes was that Ludwig was identified as "Ludwig Industries, Inc , a Selmer Company".

Ludwig tried to maintain momentum in the marching percussion market by recognizing seven of the top drum corps in the recently completed 1982 DCI competition. Those seven DCI champions who were using Ludwig products exclusively and the seven other drum corps with long-standing Ludwig relations had not yet begun to feel the influence of Selmer. We tried to channel all communications with the corps through Ludwig to avoid any corp's perspective of Ludwig that it might now be feeling more like a band instrument company than a drum company.

All These Corps had the final word about who placed in the 1982 DCI Finals.
Their percussion equipment?...Ludwig, of course!
That's why Ludwig salutes these corps.
They represent Seven of the Twelve Finalist Corps competing.
Congratulations!

LUDWIG IS READY FOR THE HIGH TORQUE CHALLENGE!

Ludwig®
LUDWIG INDUSTRIES, INC.
A SELMER COMPANY
1728 North Damen Avenue, Chicago, IL 60647

In the fall of 1982, I got a call from Bob Radock of Disney World in Orlando, Florida, regarding the Grand Opening of the Epcot Center scheduled for October of 1982. Bob Radock was the person in charge of the Grand Opening ceremony portion that featured the 450-student All American High School Marching Band. The students came from all across the country. Bob asked me if Ludwig would be interested in providing all the drums for this event. This involved percussion instruments for 45 percussionists performing on roof tops as well as marching in formation through the Grand Opening ceremonies of Epcot Center. I thought this was a fantastic opportunity for Ludwig product visibility as this was a major media campaign that would be covered on a national basis. I received authorization from Selmer to accept the invitation and to commit Ludwig to providing all percussion instruments for this event. I organized all product orders in Ludwig production so that a trailer load of equipment would be ready to ship to Orlando to the designated hotel for the band's rehearsals, commencing right before the Grand Opening date of Sunday, October 24, 1982. A tractor-trailer full of Ludwig white cortex marching percussion; quads, trios, bass drums, snare drums, cymbals, all the mallets, all the beaters- everything, was organized for this significant event. A huge project!

In return, Ludwig had a chance to really promote this. A coordinated effort with Ludwig and Selmer advertising developed and ran full page color ads announcing that, "Ludwig Drums Are The Drums Of Choice at Epcot Center/Walt Disney World Grand Opening". A personal perk was being able to take my family to the event, paid for by Disney. This was a once-in-a-lifetime event that I treasure to this day. The band's performance and sound was breathtaking. The Friday evening Spaceship Earth Gala provided live performances on all different stages set-up around Epcot Center. The performers included Count Basie and his Orchestra featuring Vocalist Joe Williams, Lionel Hampton and his Big Band, Woody Herman and The Young Thundering Herd, Harry James and his Big Band, The Glenn Miller Orchestra, Bob Crosby and The Bobcats, and Pete Fountain and his New Orleans Jazz Band. No where on earth had I ever seen or heard this assortment of wonderful music all performed in one location outdoors on one beautiful evening.

The Tops in their Classes.

Ludwig drums are marching toward the future. Together with the world's finest entertainment organization and the highest achieving college musicians in the country, Ludwig is playing an instrumental role in a history-making event. An event that calls for nothing but the best.

EPCOT Center, Walt Disney's living showcase for the technologies and dreams of tomorrow, opened in October at Walt Disney World with the most publicized recognition ever given a project of private enterprise. And Ludwig is there, represented in the EPCOT Center All-American College 450-piece Marching Band. The tops in their classes of 148 American Colleges, these talented musicians are the professional performers and educators of tomorrow. And the 56-piece percussion unit played the top of the class instruments, Ludwig.

Walt Disney's greatest dream has come true with the reality of EPCOT Center. We at Ludwig are proud to be a part of it.

Ludwig®
1728 North Damen Avenue, Chicago, Illinois 60647 (312) 276-3360
A Selmer Company

In late 1982, Carl Bovard, who had been promoted to Selmer Group Marketing Manager in 1980, started to become more active in Ludwig's advertising. He began coming to Ludwig on Damen Ave on a weekly basis. Carl took over all of the advertising creative design and placement for all of the ad schedules starting in 1983. I knew there would soon be conflicts and challenges.

In the summer of 1982, I went with Carl Bovard to Selmer's advertising agency in Kalamazoo, Michigan, the Wm. R. Biggs Agency to review what they had come up with since being given the assignment of preparing for Ludwig's change in advertising focus and leadership. It was an eye-opening experience to see for the first time the strategy and graphic layout "comps" that they envisioned for all of the Ludwig products. Clearly they did not understand the drum business. I could see that this was going to look like a band-instrument owned drum company. I am not being egotistical or condescending when I say that Selmer simply didn't "get it".

I got the sense that I was being evaluated (by everyone in the room) at this point. Was I a team player, or not? For me to tell Bovard and the Biggs Agency that the full page color advertisements they were designing and planning to implement were not even close to what the percussion market was used to seeing from Ludwig would be my suicide. I was beyond a rock and a hard place.

Another Selmer change was to gradually eliminate all of the printing being done at Cedar Valley Printing of Glenview, Illinois. All printing for Ludwig would be done through Selmer's resources. I was instructed to gather up all of the plates and the original art and ship it all to Elkhart- that was the end of using Cedar Valley. Although this was a blow to the relationship and the friendship, I somehow felt that we would be working together again down the road.

Friction was developing and increasing between what had been Ludwig's marketing and education departments and Selmer. Clearly it was not quite what Selmer had in mind for marketing and education. They wanted everything to conform to a Selmer perspective and persona, which would lose the true flavor of the brand and the authenticity of the market. I could see that Selmer was becoming frustrated and I certainly was becoming frustrated that this was not going in the direction that it should for the good of the Ludwig brand.

By the end of the year, Carl Bovard had sprinkled enough negativity in the ear of Selmer marketing head Bob Kane that Kane felt motivated to make a change. On December 22 of 1982, Bob called me into my office to say that things were not working out; today was my last day. He said I would get a severance check that would be mailed to my home. I was asked to empty my office immediately of all personal items so I could be escorted to the door for loading this into my automobile.

For one last time, my longtime helpmate Felix Gureca helped me. We boxed up all of my personal stuff and carried it out to my car which I backed up to the loading dock. I thanked Felix and drove away from Ludwig for the last time.

A RETROSPECT

I knew of course that there would be life after Ludwig, but my concept of "come early, work hard, and stay late" was shattered. I was still in my 30s. I knew I had many years of a career ahead of me.

The Ludwig ten and a half year career provided me an opportunity to learn more about the music products industry, people, myself, and relationships than I could have ever imagined. I am grateful for that opportunity probably now more than ever as I realize that everything I may have accomplished after Ludwig is a result of what I leaned and worked on at Ludwig. I valued the people, the friendships, the encouragement, and whatever recognition I may have achieved as a result of my time at Ludwig Industries.

Over the years that followed, I remained in contact with some of the Ludwig people and the Ludwig family. Some of these contacts and relationships will be rekindled in different settings, circumstances and companies that I will work for someday. I still own and play exclusively all Ludwig-Musser percussion instruments.

In 2002 I was contacted by the Percussive Arts Society to provide assistance in helping with their planned "LUDWIG A Retrospective Celebration" running July 2002 through May of 2003. I was thrilled to help and offered my assistance to head PAS Museum Curator Otice Sircy. I provided the requested products as well as something they did not know I had, but recommended be included in the Ludwig exhibit being constructed at the Lawton, Oklahoma PAS headquarter location. I provided the 1976 Bicentennial 12x15 Rope-Rod snare drum illustrated in the photograph with Bill Ludwig Jr. as well as a personal 5x14 Engraved Black Beauty Snare drum and some supporting product literature. This event was covered by the local Lawton media and included in the large Percussive Notes cover story about the Ludwig Company. I am proud to have been a part of the Retrospective Celebration.

Ludwig: A Retrospective Celebration

July 2002–May 2003

The Percussive Arts Society is pleased to announce the opening of an exhibit honoring the many contributions of Ludwig Industries to the development of percussion since the company's founding in 1909.

Ludwig: A Retrospective Celebration features historically significant percussion instruments, as well as journals, catalogs, and methods books published by the company. This collection is supported by the generosity of individuals across the United States whose loans have supplemented the exhibit.

The centerpiece of the exhibit is a portrait of William F. Ludwig, Sr. formerly displayed in the corporate headquarters. The portrait is currently on loan from the Chicago Historical Society.

James Campbell, left, president of the Percussive Arts Society, looks over Karl Dustman's 1976 Bicentenniel snare drum while William F. Ludwig II looks on.

Harry Ekman '73
Percussive Notes
The ... sive Arts Society • Vol. 40, No. 3 • June 2002
LUDWIG:
A RETROSPECTIVE
CELEBRATION

LUDWIG: A RETROSPECTIVE CELEBRATION

A 1960s Ludwig ad promoting the "Total Percussion" concept

A CELEBRATION OF LUDWIG INDUSTRIES' CONTRIBUTION TO THE DEVELOPMENT OF PERCUSSION DURING THE TWENTIETH CENTURY

Beginning in July and running for a full year, the Percussive Arts Society Museum in Lawton, Oklahoma will feature an extensive display documenting the contributions of the Ludwig Drum Company to the invention and manufacture of instruments, as well as the company's contributions to percussion education.

The exhibit will also include the original portrait of company founder William F. Ludwig Sr. that is reproduced on the cover of this issue. The oil-on-canvas painting, which is 49 inches tall and 42 inches wide, was completed by artist Harry Eckman in 1975 and given to the Chicago Historical Society by William F. Ludwig II in 1985. The portrait will be on loan to the PAS Museum throughout the year-long exhibit.

Several of the instruments and publications that will be featured in the exhibit are pictured on the following pages, along with a history of the Ludwig company written by William F. Ludwig Sr.

My Life at the Drums

By Wm. F. Ludwig

The following is excerpted from the 1965 edition of My Life at the Drums *by William F. Ludwig.*

My life at the drums encompasses years of playing and building drums.

I was born in 1879 near the Rhine River in Germany and came to America with my parents at the age of eight. We chose Chicago and a small home on the west side to live in.

At the age of eight, my boyish curiosity led me to a political rally in a huge tent erected for the occasion in a neighborhood lot. The torchlight parade was just rounding the corner headed by a drum corps of the First Regiment Illinois National Guard. Twelve drummers, one bass drummer and a drum major wearing a huge shako presented a magnificent spectacle on this warm summer night in 1887. The impression this corps made on me decided my future career then and there!

My Dad was a professional musician who played trombone and baritone. At times I had overheard discussions at home as to what instrument I was to take up. I lost no time in telling my Dad of my decision to study drums, but he objected on the grounds that drumming did not require classical musicianship. We finally compromised. I could start on the drum but only if I took up violin as a major instrument. That fall, my Dad took me to John Catlin, one of Chicago's foremost drummers, for my first drum lesson.

John Catlin, an expert rudimental drummer, prescribed the Bruce and Emmet book as the introduction method, a very heavy practice pad, and an exceptionally heavy pair of black ebony sticks. I say heavy because I carried pad, sticks, and my book two and a half miles to my weekly lessons at 25¢ each. Teacher Catlin was rather strict and insisted that certain rudiments be mastered before I played on a drum. My progress must have been slow, because it took three years for that drum to arrive!

It was a brass shell, four inches deep and 14 inches in diameter, purchased from Norman Henshel, a drummer in the Park Theatre, for $3.00. It was an old drum but in fair condition. It added new life to my dreary pad and I soon paraded all over the neighborhood.

One of our neighbors was nominated for alderman of the 10th ward. I became the official one-man drum corps to rally up the torchlight brigade. At 50¢ per parade I was able to help pay for that drum in a few weeks.

I now began to broaden my field of operations to include amateur band rehearsals, occasional local picnics and small dances in the winter. Two drummers were used. One on bass drum and one on snare drum in the ten and twelve piece orchestras. The foot pedal had not been invented. A few theatre drummers played double drums overhand. The bass drum was placed to the right of the player with the cymbal on the top. They would strike the bass drum and cymbal with the snare stick, then quickly pass to the snare drum for the afterbeat with an occasional roll squeezed in. This seemed too complicated for the dance drummer, so two men were always used.

Then came the Chicago World's Fair in 1893. Musicians were much in demand and my Dad found no trouble in getting a good trombone job with a twelve piece orchestra for one of the attractions on the Midway. In this group there was a drummer vacancy so I tramped down for a tryout. When I arrived at the appointed time with my trusty $3.00 drum and my only pair of sticks, I found to my surprise that I was to play double drums. My Dad had borrowed a bass drum and a cymbal which he had set up on the platform ready for my debut into professional circles. I was a fair reader at the time but scared stiff. I gave one look at the march placed on the stand, and it seemed to move away into the distance. I don't think I played one bar correctly. When the end finally came, I was not surprised when the director told me to pack up and go home for further practice. Believe me, this was a bitter disappointment. But it did fire me with greater ambition and I practiced harder than ever.

I now realized the importance of proper equipment and preparedness. The following winter, I met Fred Zietz, who played double drums at Hooley's Theatre and had just started to use a pedal. Fred Zietz sent me to Mr. Stone—a bass player in Sam T. Jacks burlesque house who was also a wood worker and had made a few pedals. I purchased one of his pedals for $2.00. It was made entirely of wood with a wood knob as the beater ball. This was a heel-pedal, as were all the first models because it was assumed that the toe pedals would not have enough force for accents.

That winter, I also bought a bass drum, tripod wood snare drum stand, and a few other necessary accessories and set out to do some real trap drum practice. The younger drummers began using pedals while the old timers refused to use the "bloomin' contraptions."

In the Spring of 1895, Dad and I joined the Wood Brothers Circus. After this circus experience I felt qualified to turn professional. I joined the Chicago

Federation of Musicians, Local No. 10, which was just organizing, for the small sum of $1.00.

The balance of the winter was taken up by playing occasional dance jobs. The Wood Brothers Circus opened in Chicago for a second season. Dad and I joined again, but left in mid-season to join an Uncle Tom's Cabin show. Then I struck out with a minstrel show that fall.

I made up my mind to try for a Chicago theatre job. Additional coaching seemed necessary, so I sought the assistance of Joseph Schumacher, one of Chicago's best theatre drummers. Bells were used sparingly, but I wanted to be modern and invested in a set of bells made of blue steel bars mounted in a case. I also bought a three octave xylophone make by Mr. Schumacher of maple bars mounted on straw instead of felt and without spacer pegs. Resonators were unknown as far as bells or xylophones were concerned. An occasional gallop or polka played on this maple bar xylophone between the acts was a novelty. This feature alone secured my first Chicago theatre engagement at the Criterion on the North side.

After ten weeks of the Criterion job, there was an opportunity to substitute two weeks for the regular drummer at Sam T. Jacks burlesque. I took the opportunity and that led to a steady vaudeville engagement at the Olympic. I was the youngest drummer (17) in a downtown theatre and felt that I was gaining both in prestige and experience. But remembering the fine advice of my teacher, Joseph Schumacher, to always prepare for a better job, I accepted an opportunity to join the Salisbury Concert Orchestra.

The summer of 1898 I played at the Omaha Exposition. This engagement afforded me an excellent opportunity to hear many of the great bands of that day who played at the Exposition. Most important of all was the Washington Marine Band led by John Phillip Sousa, which permitted me to hear and see the finest drummers in the country, Sims and Johnson, who were drumming for Sousa at that time. They proved to me conclusively the value and flexibility of the rudiments which my first teacher, John Catlin, stressed so forcefully.

Returning to Chicago, I added a set of tympani and a suitable band drum to my outfit and took tympani lessons from Joseph Zettleman, the great tympanist of the famous Theodore Thomas Symphony Orchestra, which later became the Chicago Symphony Orchestra. The help and advice of this great artist proved extremely valuable and led to a few concerts that winter with the Chicago Marine Band.

One of these engagements at the Buffalo Exposition proved to be a turning point in my career. We augmented the band for the Exposition and drew on some of the Sousa Band men. Among them was Tom Mills, who John Sousa acclaimed the best drummers he had ever

Ludwig Black Beauty Snare Drum
(2001)
On Loan from Dick Gerlach Loan 1-2002

Ludwig & Ludwig first used the name Black Beauty in their 1932 catalog to describe the snare drum that had been called the Inspiration and later the DeLuxe model in earlier publications. In making this change, Ludwig was simply following the lead of drummers of the era who had popularized the name by calling all engraved black drums "black beauties."

The name Black Beauty is now generally reserved for engraved or un-engraved black nickel-plated, brass-shell snare drums. First manufactured in 1919, the drum that came to be called the Black Beauty was produced originally with six, then eight, and finally ten tube lugs, before eight Imperial lugs became standard in 1935. With World War II, the production of Black Beauties—along with every other all-metal drum—came to an immediate halt. The Black Beauty was not produced again for nearly forty years.

This special 5 x14 Ludwig Black Beauty with die-cast hoops, brass-plated hardware, and the new Millennium strainer is part of a limited edition of ninety drums commemorating Ludwig's 90th Anniversary. It is the first drum to be assembled using a new hardware configuration recently designed for the Black Beauty. The shell is constructed of a single sheet of machine-drawn brass that is spun into a seamless unit and then given a Black Nickel finish.

This unique instrument was hand engraved by John Aldridge, following a traditional scroll design used in the early decades of the last century. It was presented to Dick Gerlach on the occasion of his retirement from Ludwig Industries in 2001 after 41 years of service beginning in 1960.

Sources: John Aldridge, *Guide to Vintage Drums* (1994) and Paul Schmidt, *History of the Ludwig Drum Company* (1991).

had. Tom used an all-metal drum of European make. It was separate tension and the first all-metal separate tension drum I had ever seen. I marveled at its tone and power. I saw immediately that, as crude and clumsy as it was, the principle was there, so I tried to buy it from Mills. It took a year of pestering but I finally got it from him and, from this drum, the seed was sown in my mind which later grew into my first all-metal separate tension drum which I was to build in later years.

[Ludwig spent four years with the Chicago Marine Band, and then spent the next five years (1904–1909) playing timpani with the Henry W. Savage English Grand Opera Company. In the fall of 1909 he began playing musicals in the Chicago theaters, beginning with the Ziegfield Follies.]

The show in New York had used two drummers— one for bass drum and the other for snare drum and bells. But in Chicago I was to play double drums. I used a 14" X 30" bass drum, my 6 1/2" X 14" all-metal snare drum and a pedal which swung from the top of the bass drum hoop to the center of the head. A leather strap connected the foot pedal with the overhanging beater rod. Many of the old timers will remember the swing pedal.

This pedal was not powerful or fast enough for the fast ragtime tempos and our leader, Morris Levy, called for faster tempos and stronger accents. In vain I tired to supply what he wanted, but it was useless with that slow overhanging pedal. Then I secretly set to work on an idea which had long been tossing through my mind. Why not have a shorter beater rod connected close to the beating spot? Several rough experimental models were cobbled together and I took one down to a rehearsal for a practical test. Crude as it was, it worked and satisfied the director. Word quickly spread about town that a new pedal had been born. Soon I was deluged with requests to make the same pedal for other drummers. Under much pressure, I decided to do this.

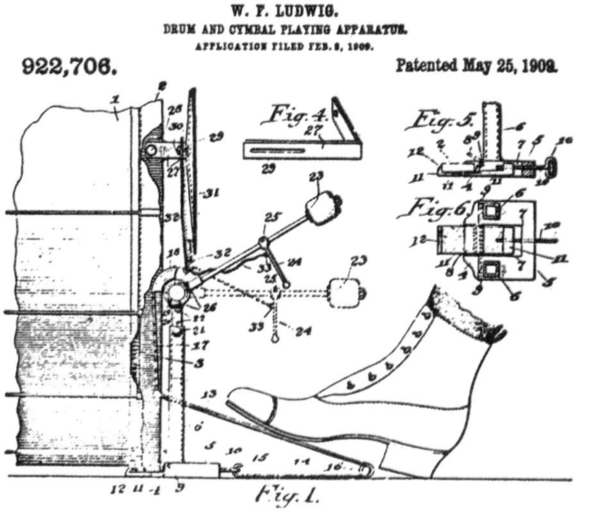

The Ludwig Drum and Cymbal Beater was the first floor pedal ever made, replacing the old-fashioned "swing" pedal that hung from the top of the bass drum hoop to the center of the head. Ludwig catalogs through the 1920s point with pride to the pedal's direct lever action, natural "arm stroke" tone, and a long, powerful stroke whose balance is so perfect that speed is unlimited. The cymbal striker is attached to the beater rod with a clamp that is "universally adjustable" and can be regulated to emphasize or subdue the sound of the cymbal.

My brother, Theobald, then 20 years old, was also a drummer and had just returned from a summer's employment with Innes' Band. Together we decided to open a small drum shop in the old Omaha building, calling it Ludwig & Ludwig. Between shows, Theo and I made pedals, and as fast as we made them, drummers bought them. We took out patents and this first crude floor model pedal became the famous Ludwig Pedal which in later years was used universally from coast to coast.

With the success of this new business venture assured, both Theo and I determined to devote all our spare time to building pedals. Theo played the Hof-Brau Cafe while I accepted the long awaited opportunity to play tympani in a symphony orchestra. The famous Pittsburgh Symphony Orchestra under Emil Paur offered me the position as tympanist, which I immediately took. To me this seemed the climax of my career. The tympani parts were very interesting, yet extremely difficult on the three hand tympani I had to work on.

After months of work on the hand tympani in the Pittsburgh orchestra, an idea crept into my mind that all tympanists should possess the advantages of pedal-tuned tympani. Gradually, my plan to build a practical pedal-tuned tympani in America took shape. The demand was there—I was determined to fill that demand. At this time all pedal-tuned tympani came from Europe.

While thus engaged in the Pittsburgh orchestra throughout the season of 1910–1911, my sister entered our small business in Chicago to take care of the books while Theo made the pedals and I helped sell them in Pittsburgh and other eastern cities in which the orchestra happened to play. At the close of my first season in the spring of 1911, I hurried back to Chicago and found our business beginning to show signs of increasing. Together, Theo and I worked on our first all-metal separate tension snare drum, which was patterned after Tom Mills' old drum. The size was 6 1/2" deep by 14" in diameter. It proved a valuable contribution to the drum world and enjoyed immediate and wide use throughout the middle west.

In the meantime, my sister married Mr. R. C. Danly, a man of tremendous mechanical ability, who was employed as a tool designer in the International Harvester Company. Mr. Danly decided to help us. We rented a 50 X 50 foot barn, installed a gas engine for power with some tools to make Ludwig pedals for the general trade, and to develop a new line of percussion instruments, and he undertook immediately the task of building the first pedal-tuned tympani in America. This was also the first collapsible-type tympani in the world. This new type of tuning mechanism did eventually revolutionize present methods of tuning kettle drums. Before the tympani were finally completed, which took two years, Mr. Danly redesigned the foot pedal, improved the all-metal drum, and patented the first complete throw-off strainer. He also added many small accessories to the line which Theo and I conceived. Mr. Danly carried on all experimental and development work in his own private machine shop while Theo and I continued to sell the first products and hold down drum jobs as well, to add to our meager capital.

In the fall of 1911 I joined the Chicago Grand Opera Company as snare drummer. At the end of my second year in the Chicago Grand Opera Company, we brought out our first set of pedal-tuned tympani. This set operated on a hydraulic principle. An expanding flexible tube ran under the head around the rim of the kettles. Water was pumped in from a small compression foot pedal by moving the pedal up and down. As the hose expanded the pitch was raised, and as the hose deflated, the pitch was lowered. This first set was shipped to St. Paul for trial in the St. Paul Symphony Orchestra by Lawrence Manzer, the tympanist. Needless to say, it received considerable notice and even was featured in a half-page notice with pictures in the music section of the local newspapers.

The mechanism worked perfectly, but the rubber tubing would petrify after about six months of use, and it was impossible to get tubing which would not petrify. Mr. Danly and I then decided to replace this mechanism with a cable principle. After another four years of experimentation, we produced the first cable set of tympani. This worked well and was the first successful pedal tympani made in this country. Many of these original cable-tuned tympani are still in use today and in excellent condition.

The Ludwig Bass Drum Pedal Chicago
Originally Patented in 1909
On Loan from Bob Bloom Loan 2-2002

In the spring of 1916 I accepted the position of bass drummer in the Chicago Symphony Orchestra. Things went along smoothly and I was able to devote much time to our prosperous little business. A real blow to all of us was the sudden death of my brother, Theobald, on October 28, 1918 at the age of 29. Theo fell victim of the great flu epidemic which swept the nation at that time. His death made it necessary for me to leave the orchestra and Mr. Danly to leave his business in order to concentrate our united efforts and attention on the drum company, which was growing by leaps and bounds.

Musical shows were in full swing, running long seasons in New York City and then going on the road. The Follies of 1917 with Will Rogers, Tom Brown and the Six Brown Brothers, and Irene and Vernon Castle played the McVickers Theatre in Chicago during the fall of 1917, with Max Manne as trap drummer. Vernon Castle, in appreciation of Manne's excellent playing of his act, had our firm make a gold drum to be presented to Manne. This was the first genuine gold-plated drum that had ever been made to my knowledge. The fad then turned to not only improved mechanical equipment but to fancy drum finishes such as gold-plated snare drums and pearl finishes on the entire outfits.

With America's entry into World War I, the Government placed material restrictions on all non-essential industries, which included us. However, we were able to secure some drum business from the Government, having one order consisting of 400 drums. These were 12 X 15" rope tensioned drums with iron hooks and we made thousands of them for the doughboys.

When the war was over, musicians went to work in larger numbers. Modern motion picture palaces with large orchestras sprang up in all of the land, and

Ludwig & Ludwig Snare Drum
(c. 1917-18)
Donated by Florence "Flip" Manne.
1995-02-16.

The first gold-plated snare drum made by Ludwig & Ludwig was purchased by dancer Vernon Castle, who presented this 6-lug, 6 1/2 x 14 instrument to Max Manne, Chicago trap drummer for the New York touring company of the *Follies of 1917* (and father of jazz drummer Shelly Manne). The drum is inscribed to Manne "with sincere appreciation" for his contribution to the success of Vernon and Irene Castle's popular ballroom dancing exhibition. (The original strainer was replaced with a later W.F.L. model.)

larger houses began to use stage bands as well. In 1921, Paul Whiteman came to New York City and opened at the Palace Royal inaugurating a wave of cafe dance bands.

To meet this new demand, constant improvements were made on our drums. The most important of these were the balanced action fast tuning pedal tympani, the super-speed ball-bearing two-post pedal, the supersensitive snare drum for radio work and many other modern devices and accessories.

I joined the Columbia Commandery Band in 1919 and later undertook to teach various drum corps which the American Legion was then forming. There was a scarcity of suitable drum corps music and instruction material. I wrote two numbers—"The Legion Drummer" and "Here They Come." These two marches became so popular that we thought it advisable to write a book of marches for drum corps with elementary instructions for the drum and bugle. This book, *The Ludwig Drum and Bugle Manual*, enjoyed a larger circulation than any other book every written on the subject.

In my teaching of corps, I observed that the players had great difficulty in alternating correctly, and to facilitate this, I designed and patented the horizontal-valve piston bugle. In 1930 we added the baritone bugle to the corps, which gave a solid foundation to the melody and harmony.

At about the same time I began designing the chromatic bell lyra. In Europe, crude forms of the bell lyra were in use in the Army bands, but they were made of steel and had only one row of bars pitched in the diatonic scale. The player carried extra bars in a special pocket to change a B-flat or E-flat bar when the composition required it. It seemed quite logical to me that this, as well as all other instruments, should be chromatic, but adding more bars meant increasing the weight. The natural step, then, was to make the frame and bars of aluminum alloy. I had the honor to play the first chromatic bell lyra ever built with the Medinah Band at the Shrine Convention in Toronto, Canada, June 3–7, 1930.

In the professional field, drummers were taking the drum rudiments seriously enough to argue about them, where previous to 1918, they had been slighted. In fact, some of the influential drum teachers definitely advised against the use of rudiments in the so-called "Art of Drumming." There were those, however, who took issue on that theory rather seriously. One of these, and the first to enter the battle for the revival of the rudiments in all drum fields was Sanford A. (Gus) Moeller. At the time, Mr. Moeller was on the road with a musical show that had covered the continent several times and had contacted drummers in all parts of the country.

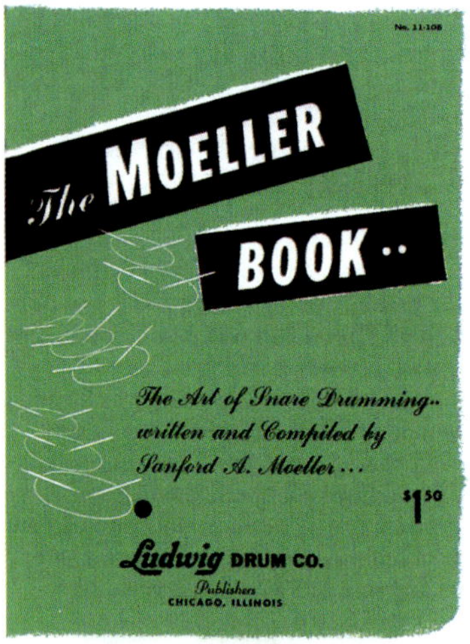

The demand for better drummers everywhere and in all fields inspired Mr. Moeller to write a more comprehensive book on rudiments than any on the market at the time. Our firm decided to publish the book, which is now known as *The Moeller Book*.

A new addition to our factory was built in 1923, adding 10,000 square feet to the plant and requiring additional equipment and personnel. We employed 240 workers and ours was the largest drum factory in the world.

In 1929, as the well-remembered depression drew near, some of us became concerned about the future. The Stock Market collapse choked business and we owed money on our new building.

After considerable deliberation, it was decided that the best way for Ludwig & Ludwig to ride out the storm would be to merge with the C.G. Conn Co. of Elkhart, Ind. Thus Ludwig & Ludwig was moved from Chicago to Elkhart. The Conn Co. also took over the Leedy Drum Co. of Indianapolis, Ind. The two firms were consolidated into Leedy and Ludwig, a division of the C.G. Conn Co. which it remained for the next 25 years. I was no longer able to control major decisions affecting design and construction of drums and tympani. I, therefore, in 1936 left the employ of the Conn Co. on amicable terms.

In 1937 at age 58 I decided to start all over again in the drum manufacturing business and bought the factory building at 1728 N. Damen Ave. in Chicago where we are now located, only three blocks from the original plant. The new firm was named the Wm. F. Ludwig Drum Co. That first year was hard, but in the

W.F.L. Snare Drum
(c. 1937)
Donated by James L. Knapp.
PAS 17 [1993-12-17].

This snare drum, which was part of Roy Knapp's drumkit, carries an original W.F.L. badge that includes the trademark words "WFL Line" inscribed within a music lyre above the vent hole, and "Wm. F. Ludwig Drum Co. / Chicago, ILL" below.

This 6 1/2 x14 drum has an unvarnished wooden shell, eight double-tension lugs, and a Ludwig Whitecalf calfskin batter head. (The strainer and snares are not original.)

The Ludwig Drummer

Before there were such publications as *Percussive Notes* or *Modern Drummer*, percussive journalism was pioneered by *The Ludwig Drummer.* The first series was published from 1926 through 1948, and a second series ran from 1962 through 1976. Along with announcements about new Ludwig products, the magazine contained articles on virtually every facet of percussion, written by such notable performers as Vida Chenoweth, Al Payson, Gary Burton, Dick Schory, Mitch Markovich, Bob Tilles, Gordon Peters, Joe Morello and other prominent players who were associated with Ludwig. The PAS Ludwig exhibit includes original copies of most issues of this influential publication.

spring of 1938 a New York dealer placed several large orders with us. This gave us a good push and by the first anniversary we were rolling along in pretty good shape.

My son, Bill Jr., joined the firm in the spring of 1938 and took over the duties of Sales and Advertising manager.

The first product in this new firm, as in the original drum plant, was a pedal—the Speed King. Many name drummers started using the Speed King pedal right away.

In 1939 we decided to change the name of our new fast-growing little drum company to W.F.L. Drum Co. in order to eliminate confusion with the parent firm, which was now our competitor as a division of the C.G. Conn Co. Our factory at the time boasted 78 employees. Our 64-page catalog of modern drums and drummers' equipment was producing an excellent volume of business in spite of the war talk that was buzzing about us. The picture changed on December 7, 1941. We were at war.

Among the first official documents affecting our industry were the restrictive measures limiting the use of critical materials to 10% by weight of the instrument and prohibiting the use of all copper-base alloys in the manufacture of musical instruments. Tympani production came to a halt.

It looked as if these restrictions would spell the end of drum production. But our engineer, Cecil H. Strupe, redesigned our line of drums in remarkably short time. He used wood lugs and counterhoops, with a method of inner-tensioning that employed flexible bows actuated by only a few tension rods. Thus we were within the Limitation Orders, using less than 10% of metal, but drastically restricted in total volume.

We submitted to military authorities a sample of a screw tension drum, together with a rope drum in which the hooks were eliminated, the cord being run through the counterhoops. These were within the limitations and resulted in the largest contract for field drums that had ever been placed with a single manufacturer.

Production of all traps, foot pedals, high sock drum stands and catalog drums was suspended. Later, however, we developed a high sock pedal using steel cymbals of a special gauge. We also made all-wood drum stands.

The factory, now working on government contracts of screw machine products, also made trap drum outfits for government dance band units. These were sent to practically all parts of the globe to army camps, hospitals, etc.

After the war ended, our first big job was to switch our outfit production over from Government outfits in drab mahogany finishes to the colorful dance finishes of today. Second, we tackled the problem of replacing worn-out machinery and getting our accessory line back into production. Third, we started work on a new tympani—the Symphony model with a new balanced action spring tension which made the pedal operate more freely.

In 1947, our first post-war catalog was ready. It featured our new Classic line of tension casings and had a marvelous picture of Buddy Rich on the cover. This catalog was written and designed by Bill Jr. Our business gradually returned to normal.

The year 1948 saw us introduce the Symphony model tympani at the New York Trade Show. We also had enlarged our complete line of pearl outfits and brought out new models of drum sticks and wire brushes. In 1953 we erected a sizable factory addition consisting of 15,000 square feet.

Our greatest and best catalog came out in 1955 and the line was larger. But an even greater event occurred, for in March of that year I was able to repurchase back from the C.G. Conn Co. the Ludwig Division of Leedy & Ludwig and thus the old firm of Ludwig & Ludwig was returned to me in Chicago and incorporated into the W.F.L. Drum Co. After 25 years, I "owned" my own name once more!

We changed our company name to Ludwig Drum Co. Bill, Jr. got busy changing over all the company's stationery, advertising, logos, art work, books, and mailing pieces to the new name. Along with the name and machines we repurchased the original patents, copyrights and instruction books. Many of the

The W.F.L. Victorious Field Drum
(c. 1943)
Donated by George Boberg 2001-01-01

During World War II, the American government set limitations on the type and amount of materials used by all non-defense manufacturing. Drum companies were permitted only 10% metal (by weight) in their instruments.

Cecil H. Strupe redesigned the W.F.L. line of drums with Manila mahogany shells, maple lugs and counterhoops, and an innovative method of inner-tensioning by using expandable wooden bows. The *Victorious* design was granted a patent in October 1943.

This 7 x 15 drum has black lacquer finish, inlayed stripes of pearl-finish Proxalin on the counterhoops, and gut snares. "U.S.N." is painted on the shell, identifying the drum as having been manufactured for the U.S. Navy.

Joe Morello's Supra-Phonic 400
On loan from Rick Mattingly
Loan 3-2001

This mid-'60s Ludwig 5 x 14 Supra-Phonic 400 snare drum belonged to Joe Morello and was used on several recordings and tours with the Dave Brubeck Quartet during the 1960s. The only modification Morello made to the drum was to remove the internal muffler. (The drum has since been fitted with new heads and snares.)

In the 1965 Ludwig catalog, the drum carries a list price of $88.00. It boasted a "one-piece Acousti-Perfect seamless shell...beaded in the center and flanged in at the edges for triple strength." This was one of the few snare drums of its day to feature ten lugs per head instead of eight, and the shell is chrome plated.

In his book *The Making of a Drum Company*, William Ludwig II recalls meeting Joe Morello when Marion McPartland asked him to come to the Down Beat club to meet her new drummer. Morello was having trouble with his Speed King pedal, which Ludwig repaired on the spot. Praising his "fast wit and sunny disposition," Ludwig says, "That was the beginning of one of the greatest friendships I have ever had. It continues to this day."

Morello joined the Dave Brubeck Quartet when he left the Marion McPartland Trio, and the Brubeck Quartet quickly became one of the top jazz groups in the world, topping the pop charts with "Take Five." Morello became Ludwig's leading endorser during the mid-'60s, appearing in full-page Ludwig ads.

Morello also became an active clinician, and his three instructional books, *Rudimental Jazz*, *Off the Record* and *New Directions in Rhythm*, which were exclusively distributed by Ludwig, were big sellers.

"He was a great clinician," Ludwig said, "and he was just a natural teacher, even though severely handicapped since birth with near blindness. He memorized every arrangement and never missed a beat. He was born to drum! And his technique was almighty."

original items have since been incorporated into the line, such as the original Ludwig & Ludwig balance action tympani, which is now the "Universal" model with wheels. The original rubber-covered wire brushes are back, as well as the concert drum stand, Imperial die cast drum lug used on concert bass drums, the original Super Ludwig all-metal snare drum with 10 rods per side, the original *Ludwig Tympani Instruction* book, *America's N.A.R.D. Drum Solos*, the *Ludwig Drum and Bugle Manual*, and the *Ludwig Drum Major's Manual*. All of these fine old standard instruction books have been revised, rewritten, brought up-to-date and republished.

Design-wise we invented the first "upbeat pedal" for our reversible Compacto

drum outfit, which could be played either way. The first single-screw tunable bongos with metal shells, expandable conga drums, and the first Cocktail Lounge Drums were added to the line.

Finally came the greatest drum development of them all—plastic weatherproof drum heads. Mr. Joe Grolimund brought this idea to our attention. Joe had been our first advertising manager and had moved up to his present position as Chairman of the Board of the H. & A. Selmer Corporation. Joe had noticed how marvelously water-repellent plastic clarinet and sax pads were and now decided to try this new material on drums. This started us on an extensive experimental program, first as to durability, then as to tone. Both were very satisfactory. Then followed a real problem, that of proper mounting of this new tough hard fibre on flesh hoops. After two years we developed and patented a double metal hoop method clinching this slippery new material mechanically in such a way that it will hold any tension requirements it may be subjected to. Coating of the heads for brush response and finding the proper thickness were the next problems.

Today, the use of plastic heads is universal with school, jazz, and symphonic musicians. Plastic tympani heads have proven very successful and are widely used.

The years 1964, 1965 and 1966 are the years of the rock 'n' roll boom. To serve it we designed many new and enticing outfits for the teenagers to enjoy.

Our research and development continues in every aspect of the drum making art. We at Ludwig Drum Company are drummers. We work and design for drummers. We have you in mind when we design.

I am now 87 years of age and at work every day. I appreciate the many opportunities I have had in my lifetime to serve my fellow drummers. As I enter each year it is with renewed optimism and enthusiasm that I face the future growing ever brighter each passing day. Thank you for your interest.

Sincerely,

Wm. F. Ludwig

Wm. F. Ludwig

Wm. F. Ludwig Jr. presented a custom made gold plated Super-Sensitive snare drum to RINGO STARR and the BEATLES at a special press conference prior to their recent Chicago concert appearance.

In making the presentation, Mr. Ludwig stated, "I have never known of a drummer that is more widely acclaimed and publicized as you, Ringo Starr. Your millions of fans throughout the world have honored you and the other members of the famous BEATLES group by their overwhelming acceptance of your many recordings, movies and concert appearances. On behalf of the management and employees of the Ludwig Drum Co. I would like to express our appreciation to you for choosing our instruments and for the major role you are playing in the music world today."

—From *The Ludwig Drummer*, Fall 1964

Wm. F. Ludwig Jr., Vice President/ General Manager of the Ludwig Drum Co. presents gold plated Super-Sensitive snare drum to RINGO STARR as Dick Schory, Advertising-Education Director for the Ludwig Company looks on.

Chapter 4

THE GREAT GRETSCH SOUND,…a New Career Chapter Ignites From the Ludwig Ashes (May 1983-December 31, 1984)

The thought of rebuilding my life and career after Ludwig was overwhelming, as I had not even thought about applying for a new job, creating a resume or cover letter for over eleven years. I was not prepared to start a job search, not ready to be home during the weekday instead of at "work". Everything was upside down as I resist change as a personal characteristic. My whole identity was tied up into what I DID, (used to do) at Ludwig. I didn't have a business card with my name on it and I was afraid I never would again.

For the very first time in my life, I found myself in a line filing for Illinois unemployment. It called for a quick ego adjustment to stand in line at the Cook County Board of Unemployment. I had responsibilities, obligations and needed to get working and earning in a timely manner. I knew I would burn through the Selmer pay-off severance and unused vacation compensation in no time. Taking a rest after Ludwig was not an option.

I assembled my thoughts with my strategy and priority geared to staying in the music products industry and remaining in the Chicago area if at all possible. I started sending letters of introduction out to a variety of companies I knew something about or people within those organizations throughout the country. Time and winter in Chicago marched on and I realized that I was going to have to adjust my thinking. I would be willing to relocate if the right opportunity presented itself. I did not limit my search to the percussion industry, but obviously I felt that I had significant momentum in the music industry in general and percussion in particular. I was wary of stepping outside of the industry and making the same mistake that I'd made when I left the music industry and went to work at IBM. I didn't want to put myself through that again. I stuck with approaching and contacting known recognized companies that I knew of, hoping they were aware of my previous accomplishments and reputation with Ludwig for almost eleven years.

On March 3rd of 1983, one of my letters went to Charlie Roy who was President of Kustom-Gretsch in Gallatin, Tennessee. (Actually it was a cover letter and a packet of materials that illustrated my work experience.) Charlie responded shortly after receiving the packet. We had a good telephone conversation about what he was doing with the company, where the Gretsch Company was going, what their needs were, and so forth. Charlie explained they were getting ready for the Gretsch Company 100-year Centennial of 1983 and they were in the middle of preparing for the summer NAMM show at McCormick Place. That conversation left us both with some things to think further about.

On April 27th I sent a follow-up letter to Charlie, basically explaining that I was interested in a position there with Gretsch and was prepared to move into the next stage of discussions. Never at a loss for words, I included with the letter a "Gretsch Percussion in the School Market" document explaining what I felt was a unique opportunity for Gretsch Drums to eventually enter the school drum market, how I envisioned this happening and how I could help facilitate this growth and product line expansion. The discussions up to this point sounded like Kustom-Gretsch was doing reasonably well in the drum set market and they were getting ready to launch the highly desirable Gretsch guitar line in the near future. I knew from my Ludwig experience that when the drum set market goes down because of the economy, the educational school business and market could have sales stability and profits during challenging times. Charlie liked the idea of product and market diversification even though I don't think he really understood the school drum and percussion market. He was intrigued by my overview commentary document which was unsolicited. I created and used this "school market topic" to illustrate

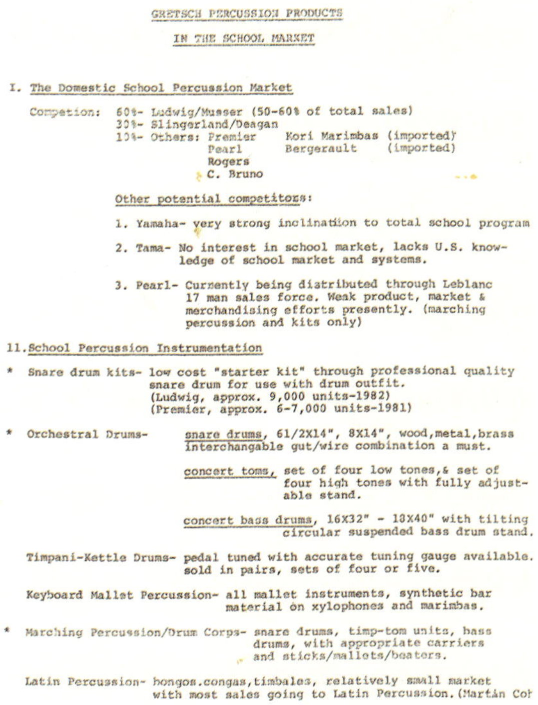
GRETSCH PERCUSSION PRODUCTS

IN THE SCHOOL MARKET

I. The Domestic School Percussion Market

Competion: 60%- Ludwig/Musser (50-60% of total sales)
30%- Slingerland/Deagan
10%- Others: Premier, Pearl, Rogers, C. Bruno; Kori Marimbas (imported), Bergerault (imported)

Other potential competitors:

1. Yamaha- very strong inclinatiion to total school program
2. Tama- No interest in school market, lacks U.S. knowledge of school market and systems.
3. Pearl- Currently being distributed through Leblanc 17 man sales force. Weak product, market & merchandising efforts presently. (marching percussion and kits only)

11. School Percussion Instrumentation

* Snare drum kits- low cost "starter kit" through professional quality snare drum for use with drum outfit. (Ludwig, approx. 9,000 units-1982) (Premier, approx. 6-7,000 units-1981)

* Orchestral Drums- snare drums, 61/2X14", 8X14", wood,metal,brass interchangable gut/wire combination a must.

concert toms, set of four low tones,& set of four high tones with fully adjustable stand.

concert bass drums, 16X32" - 18X40" with tilting circular suspended bass drum stand.

Timpani-Kettle Drums- pedal tuned with accurate tuning gauge available. sold in pairs, sets of four or five.

Keyboard Mallet Percussion- all mallet instruments, synthetic bar material on xylophones and marimbas.

* Marching Percussion/Drum Corps- snare drums, timp-tom units, bass drums, with appropriate carriers and sticks/mallets/beaters.

Latin Percussion- bongos.congas,timbales, relatively small market with most sales going to Latin Percussion.(Martin Co my thought process and grasp of the market while conveying how I felt I could be productive.

In early May, Charlie called to say he was coming to Chicago to visit the display company that was building their NAMM convention exhibit for use in McCormick Place. He wanted to meet face-to-face and we agreed to meet in the lobby of the Hilton Hotel at O'Hare airport. It was a cordial meeting over a drink in the hotel bar. In the short time we were together, Charlie explained the nature and culture of the company that I could be stepping into. This company was a lot different than the corporate structure that I had been a part of at Ludwig. Kustom-Gretsch was a fraction of the size of Ludwig, the marketing budget was a tiny fraction of the $2.5 million marketing-advertising-educational budget I'd had at Ludwig. In spite of those comparisons, Charlie wanted to be clear that I should not consider this a step backward in terms of career advancement and he wanted to offer me the position. He offered to fly me down to Nashville to meet the people, see the operation, and experience the southern hospitality of a small town like Gallatin. I accepted his kind invitation. We agreed on a three-day time period and moved forward quickly. He picked me up at the Nashville airport and we drove the 30 miles or so out to Gallatin, which is a Northeast suburb of Nashville.

As we arrived at the Gretsch offices, I found myself looking at a small stand-alone single story office building in the center of downtown Gallatin. I said to Charlie, " where is the factory?" I had been expecting a large building with smokestacks, the smell of lacquer and sawdust.... "Karl,There is no factory here. The factory is in Dequeen, Arkansas, in an old Baldwin piano factory building. All the drums are made down there- this is strictly the corporate headquarters. We work here and communicate with the factory on a daily basis. " This was something of a jolt to me because my marketing background was so closely aligned with being able to go out the back door of the office and walk out into the drum factory to work with the production people. I was used to a direct communication with production as to what marketing and education departments needed for displays, clinics, artists, promotions and photo-shoots, and when we needed it. This separation of headquarters and factory production was going to be a very different working procedure but I had to remain open minded. The factory in Dequeen was also producing the Kustom amplifiers and the Sho-Bud steel guitars.

This visit to Kustom-Gretsch was a preliminary introduction to his team; who the people were, what everybody did, and how the company functioned. It was clear Charlie had notified the managers and staff before I arrived regarding who I was, where I came from, and that we were in discussions about a newly created position of Percussion Marketing Manager. The entire group in Gallatin was cordial, friendly and welcomed my possible assistance and contribution to the company in the future. This was an important element in understanding that this was a *new* position and that I was not walking in someone's previous footsteps and expectations. The impression I got was that everyone there was doing a little bit of everything. There did not seem to be a lot of departmentalization. I think that was largely because most of the staff in Gallatin had moved there recently from Chanute, Kansas, as a group when the Kustom-Gretsch company relocated from Chanute to Gallatin in the spring of 1982. Everything had been moved lock, stock, and barrel. Charlie and the management team all had bought houses in Gallatin, they all had children in school, and were pretty-well settled-in to the area and life of this small Nashville suburb.

The company was faced with preparing for the 1983 Centennial celebration which involved many different marketing-sales-promotion-public relations needs. There was a new catalog, a new trade show exhibit, new product press releases, new endorsing artists, the launching of Centennial limited-edition drum sets, new artist posters, and new sales-development campaigns for dealer expansion. There was far more work to do than there were hours in the day and knowledgeable people to get everything done. This was an obvious to me from the very first visit to Gretsch.

I accepted the position as Marketing Manager and arrived in Gallatin in early May filled with hope, hesitation, and the desire to get constructive and productive in a working environment that could use everything I knew and could contribute to the company. For the next three months or so, I would call Shoney's Motel and Restaurant my home.

I got to know and work with the entire staff quickly. I was learning and contributing at the same time. Anything I was asked about, I had an opinion to share; an idea or recommendation, all based upon what I had learned at Ludwig and the retail dealer's perspective in having worked music retail in the 1960's. I was more than busy, but it felt good after close to four months of waiting for an opportunity to get back to work. Everything else related to relocating; selling my Northbrook home, moving all my "stuff", etc. would have to be dealt with later in the year after the rapidly approaching NAMM convention in Chicago.

I drafted a press release announcing my joining Gretsch, for immediate placement in all the music industry trade journals. Charlie agreed to my suggestion that he send out an announcement card to my percussion industry contact list, announcing that Karl Dustman had joined the Gretsch team. This was not ego-centered but I felt it was important to let the percussion industry know that Gretsch now had an established drum guy on their team. I had 300 "Charlie Roy is pleased to announce" cards printed up and sent them out all over the music industry.

In short order, the congratulatory letters and cards started arriving in the mail from many industry friends, contacts, associates and well-wishers. This of course made me feel good. The press releases appeared in all June issues of the trade magazines that were hitting the streets just before the NAMM show.

From the very beginning, I began contributing projects that needed to get done by the pending NAMM convention and the launch of the Centennial drum sets. In many cases I was left to go ahead with projects and decisions on my own. It was twice as fast to get things done when there was not a committee approach. What helped immediately was being able to utilize resources I'd had in Chicago that had not been used by Ludwig since Selmer became involved and took ownership. I called on and brought in the Chicago photographers for product shoots and Chicago printers for catalog price lists, Techware cartons, full color poster printing, and various promotional pieces. Every professional resource and supplier connection that I had been working with while at Ludwig had

Charlie Roy
President of

The Gretsch® Company

Is Pleased to Announce the
Appointment of

KARL DUSTMAN

as
PERCUSSION MARKETING MANAGER

KUSTOM-GRETSCH
P.O. BOX 1250 GALLATIN, TENNESSEE 37066
(615) 452-0083

KUSTOM GRETSCH
P.O. Box 1250, Gallatin, Tennessee 37066
615/452-0083 TELEX: 786571 [Gretsch] Gatn

June 2, 1983

TO: All Trade Publications
FROM: Kustom Gretsch
SUBJECT: Immediate Press Release

KARL DUSTMAN JOINS GRETSCH

CHARLIE ROY, PRESIDENT OF KUSTOM GRETSCH, HEADQUARTERED IN GALLATIN, TENNESSEE, ANNOUNCED THE RECENT APPOINTMENT OF KARL DUSTMAN AS PERCUSSION MARKETING MANAGER FOR GRETSCH.

DUSTMAN HAS BEEN RECOGNIZED IN THE PERCUSSION INDUSTRY FOR OVER ELEVEN YEARS IN A VARIETY OF MARKETING AND EDUCATIONAL POSITIONS WITH LUDWIG INDUSTRIES. PRIOR TO JOINING GRETSCH, DUSTMAN WAS MARKETING DIRECTOR FOR LUDWIG-MUSSER, IMPLEMENTING AN INTENSE EDUCATIONAL CLINIC AND SYMPOSIUM PROGRAM THAT HAS GAINED INTERNATIONAL ACCLAIM. HIS RESPONSIBILITIES INCLUDED THE ENTIRE ADVERTISING FUNCTION, COLLATERAL MATERIAL PREPARATION AND ARTIST RELATIONS AND DEVELOPMENT.

ROY COMMENTED, "KARL BRINGS TO GRETSCH A WEALTH OF EXPERIENCE IN ALL FACETS OF THE PERCUSSION MARKET. HIS ADDITION TO OUR MARKETING EFFORT IS INDICATIVE OF GRETSCH'S NEW AGGRESSIVE APPROACH TO THE DRUM BUSINESS, NOW CELEBRATING ITS 100TH YEAR OF OPERATION. KARL WILL BE INVALUABLE IN THE OVERALL MARKETING OF OUR PERCUSSION PRODUCTS WITH INITIAL EMPHASIS ON EDUCATIONAL CLINIC PROGRAMS, NEW PRODUCT DEVELOPMENT AND ADVERTISING-ARTIST PROMOTIONS. HIS RESPECT BY MUSIC EDUCATORS, ARTISTS AND THE MUSIC INDUSTRY WILL BLEND VERY WELL WITH OUR OVER-ALL GROWTH AND DEVELOPMENT GOALS FOR THE FUTURE.

DUSTMAN, A LONG TIME RESIDENT OF CHICAGO, RECEIVED MOST OF HIS PERCUSSION TRAINING THROUGH LOCAL INSTRUCTORS, MOST NOTABLY THE LATE BOB TILLES. HE AND HIS FAMILY WILL RELOCATE IN THE GALLATIN AREA.

been phased out by Selmer. These contacts were all enthusiastic about working with Gretsch because they were no longer working with Ludwig. Eventually I brought in supplier contacts for snare drum kit cases and for quality drum stick manufacturing. This was a "win-win" for everyone, but Selmer.

A big priority as we all prepared for the NAMM trade show was the creation of a new Gretsch Drums catalog. It was already under construction (and nearing completion) when I joined the team. As "the new guy" and the Percussion Marketing Manager, I knew enough not to come in and start changing what everybody else, as a team, had already created. I knew from experience that consensus is key to how things should be done. There were things I disagreed with, including the format of the catalog. It actually was a huge fold-out two-sided wall-poster. It really did not constitute what I would call a "dream drum catalog". This was a beautifully orchestrated promotional piece with excellent photography, imagery and a variety of new configured drum sets.

Recalling past days at Ludwig and earlier generations, there was the Ludwig "dream book". I felt that Gretsch had lots of outstanding new and traditional products along with a hundred years of history which could be leveraged. Gretsch was also one of the oldest drum companies in the world, and founded in the United States. I really felt that there needed to be a "Gretsch dream catalog." Consensus moved ahead with the poster format and I convinced myself that this poster-catalog format could still become a Gretsch collector's keepsake. People to this day still cherish that Centennial poster but it did not do what a catalog is truly meant to do, and that is sell product.

[ed. note: even the *next* Gretsch catalog would eventually become a keepsake, as it was basically a reworked version of said poster, with updated ownership graphics.]

My immediate solution to the "poster-catalog" and everything I felt it was missing could be accomplished in a completely new well-illustrated price list. It became my responsibility almost overnight to create a new price list, something that had not been done in over a year. I called upon my graphics and printing people in Chicago (Cedar Valley Printing) to help me create a price list that would include imaginative drum set component icons representing all the drum and hardware configurations of current Gretsch model numbers and names that were being marketed. This provided instant clarity to the customer and dealer conveying exactly what the sizes of the drums were or what the hardware pack consisted of. The price list was a true companion piece to the big fold-up oversized poster.

I personally feel that the most dramatic thing about that poster was the design of the outside back image photograph which was the "When You're Hot" drum set on fire image. This was a fantastic photograph that the current advertising agency in Kansas took great pains in creating. In my opinion this was an award-winning photograph that included drum heads covered in flames and massive amounts of smoke from fogger machines. The adjoining panel next to this image included seventeen Polaroid-framed snapshots of the most prominent Gretsch artists.

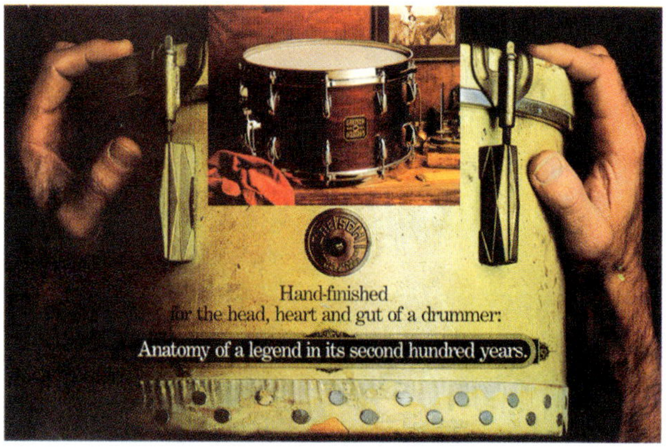

The key to the upcoming NAMM show was the completely all new exhibit. This was a design that Charlie had worked on with his chosen display company in Chicago. I would estimate that it was about a $50,000 exhibit. Back then; this was a heck of a lot of money, particularly for a smaller company or what could be referred to as a "starting out, or restarting of a branded" company. This exhibit was truly spectacular in appearance and was of the status and prominence

of a Ludwig exhibit prior to the Selmer era. If I can recall correctly this was 50 feet by 40 feet, and it dominated the drum section part of the exhibit hall. I still don't know how Charlie somehow wrangled the prime location in McCormick Place.

The Kustom amplifier and Sho-Bud pedal steel guitar lines were represented in a smaller exhibit booth directly across the aisle from the massive drum booth, allowing sales reps and management team to easily move back and forth between divisions and exhibit areas.

Charlie Roy was a visionary and I appreciated everything he was trying to accomplish knowing there were some limitations on the time, money and personnel resources he had to work with. The 1983 Centennial Gretsch exhibit booth was something that Gretsch would never experience again (except for the final 1984 NAMM show) under any change in company ownership or distribution. Charlie fully appreciated the significance of the 100-year anniversary, and wanted to really capitalize on it. He knew another opportunity like this would not come along for another 100 years. He simply said, "Karl- Just do it. And make it big! But be cautious of costs."

Remember that my start date was in early May, the trade show was in the latter-half of June, and we had a very limited number of people working from the Gallatin headquarter offices . Because I was living in the Shoney's Motel and Restaurant about two blocks from the Gretsch offices, I was only commuting back to my family in Northbrook, Illinois, once every couple weeks. As a result of this interim transition circumstance, there was nothing to keep me from working 12-hour days as well as Saturdays and Sundays. There was so much to get done before the convention, and there was nothing else to do! I just worked constantly on everything that needed to be done and was happy to be a part of something that I could contribute to and be appreciated for. There was positive industry recognition for Gretsch that would compliment my personal reputation and achievements.

I didn't really know whether Charlie was making a big gamble on this trade show to generate a wave of cash to pay for all of this, or whether perhaps Charlie simply had very deep pockets. I guess I felt it was a combination of both. I respect Charlie for his ambition and drive-for-success to this day. He knew what he had in Gretsch, he knew what the potential was, and he knew what the company and products could be. I don't think that he had the financial backing, or personal capital to dump millions of dollars into this company that he was still buying from Baldwin Piano & Organ Company on a monthly payment basis. We all knew the things that Charlie Roy wanted to do, and he entrusted me with a tremendous amount of responsibility in terms of how to spend whatever money he authorized me to use. I focused on getting the biggest bang for the bucks that we had available. If I would have had a bottom drawer of my desk full of a million dollars in cash for my marketing budget, it would of course have been five times bigger than what we accomplished. We were all capable of dreaming bigger than our pockets could provide for. Every expense and investment could be a complicated situation in that we were running short on all three resources; time, money, and the people. All were required to get everything done.

The Press Release announcing the 100 Centennial Celebration received significant press and media coverage. The Music Trades Magazine covered the celebration and we orchestrated a by-invitation reception for the media and related percussion industry partners. Everything was well received and came off as planned including the massive centerpiece "Birthday Cake" prop surrounded by freely flowing campaign.

CELEBRATING THE 100th ANNIVERSARY of the Gretsch Co., Kustom/Gretsch staged a reception, complete with massive birthday cake, at the recent NAMM show. Flanking the Gretsch Cake are (l-r) Wayne Summers, sales manager; Karl Dustman, newly appointed Gretsch marketing manager; Charlie Roy, owner and president; Randy Houck, international sales manager.

Gretsch Celebrates 100th Anniversary

America's Oldest Drum Maker Poised For Future Growth

With one hundred years of being "The Standard Of The World," Gretsch enters its second century of leadership in the percussion market place. Gretsch products have acclaimed worldwide recognition and acceptance for their hand-made craftmanship. "We're combining today's technology with the quality reputation established by Friedrich Gretsch one hundred years ago," commented Charlie Roy, owner and president of the Kustom Gretsch Company.

A History Of Innovation

The history of Gretsch is an admirable one. A closely owned company since 1883, it became a subsidiary of Baldwin Piano & Organ Company in 1968. Last year it returned to private ownership with Charlie Roy purchasing the Kustom Company. Prior to the sale, Roy directed the move of plant operations from Bonneville, Arkansas, to DeQueen, Arkansas, to accommodate the increased demand for Gretsch products. Corporate offices have been established in Gallatin, Tennessee, a community adjacent to Nashville. Roy added, "The importance of artist relations, promotional opportunities, and product testing necessitated being closer to the major music and recording mecca. Our role in visibly making Gretsch drums the leader in the domestic manufactured drum market will be concentrated through clinics, endorsements, and increased trade advertising."

Gretsch is recognized for many innovative "firsts" in product design and features. Roy has dedicated himself to seeing the product, its reputation, and the Gretsch name achieve new standards in all aspects of the percussion field. Some leadership firsts include: disappearing bass drum spurs, internal shell tone controls, die-cast hoops on snares and toms, and shell mounted cymbal and tom holders. Its recent addition of deep shell power toms to its product line has created a worldwide following among artists looking for the acclaimed "Great Gretsch Power Sound."

Commitment To Quality

"Our dealers and artists will play a more important part in our company than ever before. The first concern of each of our employees is directed towards quality and being the best product on the market. I will not allow our long enduring reputation to become diluted in our second hundred years," commented Roy.

Gretsch percussion products have retained many of the hand-finishing production processes established by Friedrich Gretsch in the early years of the company. Each 6-ply maple shell has staggered butt-jointed laminations for added strength and truer head "seating" around the edge circumference. The ten day shell manufacturing process involves trimming, machining, and white wood sanding . . . washing the shells in a special solution . . . the shells are then stained, sealed, and sanded. Six coats of lacquer are applied with sanding between the coats to give the finish depth and purity of color. The finished drums are hand-rubbed and waxed, the insides coated with a special formula silver sealant. Each drum is then hand tuned and carefully packed.

CHARLIE ROY cuts the Gretsch birthday cake as Toomas Paiste, president of Paiste Cymbals, Switzerland, looks on. Gretsch is a major U.S. distributor of Paiste cymbals.

The Gretsch centennial year brings with it the introduction of exciting new lines, colors, and finishes. A limited edition "Centennial Series" will be offered with only one hundred outfits being produced. Available in three custom wood finishes, each drum will be numbered on a commemorative brass plaque with the signature of Charlie Roy after his personal inspection of each drum.

Celebrations, special promotions, and artist advertising will spotlight the new Gretsch ownership and centennial product introductions. Roy added, "The legacy of the Gretsch sound and craftsmanship will evolve to setting new standards for the percussion industry in its second century."

THE MUSIC TRADES, JULY, 1983

In addition to the new catalog-poster, completely new price list format, and the massive NAMM convention exhibit, there was the creation of the limited edition (100 sets) Centennial Collector Edition custom-made signature series drum sets. These were introduced at the June, 1983, NAMM show in three exotic finishes; Birds-Eye Maple, Carpathian Elm, and Burled Walnut. The drum-mounted hardware, hoops, and tom holders were offered in either gold-plated finish with matching Evans gold drum heads or traditional chrome plating.

GRETSCH 1983 CENTENNIAL DRUM SETS, BY AUTHORIZED DEALER

SET NO.	DEALER NAME	Date	Order Number	SPECIFICATIONS	
27	Guitar Center	8.12.83	112509	Carpathian Elm/Brass	12,13,14,16,22, + snare (6)
5	Phil Collins/Artist	1.31.94	120213	Carpathian Elm/Brass	12,14,18,20 +snare (5)
28*	Leo's Drum Shop	11.16.83	117593	Carpathian Elm/Brass	12,13,16,20, + snare (5)
2	Paul Jamison	4.6.84	122601	Carpathian Elm/Brass	14,15,16,18 , + snare (5)
?	Mac Stewart	6.28.83	110599	Carpathian Elm/Brass	10,12,13,14,,18, 24X2 +snare (8)
?	Dales Drum Shop	8.29.83	113318	Birds Eye Maple/Brass	12,13,14,15,16, 22 (6)
?	Romero Music Co.	6.23.83	110341	Birds Eye Maple/Brass	13,14,16,18,24 +snare (6)
25	Modern Music	11.14.83	117501	Carpathian Elm/Brass	10,12,13,14,16,18,24 + snare (8)
?	West Coast Drum	6.28.83	110566	Carpathian Elm/Brass	10,12,13,14,16,20,24 +snare (8)
?	Music Workshop	12.12.83	111525	Birds Eye Maple/Brass	13,14,16,18,24 +snare (6)
?	Modern Music	11.14.83	117502	Carpathian Elm/Brass	10,12,13,16,22 +snare (6)
?	Sodja Music	11.15.83	117547	Burled Walnut/Brass	8,10,12,13,16,22 +snare (7)
?	Griffin Music	11.1.83	116968	Carpathian Elm/Brass	10,12,13,16,22 +snare (6)
?	Lier's Drum Shop	8.23.83	110813	Carpathian Elm/Brass	13,`14,18,24 +snare (5)
?	West Coast Drums	8.19.83	112953	Carpathian Elm/Brass	10,12,13,14,16,18,24 +snare (8)
?	Apple Music	10.7.83	115927	Burled Walnut/Brass	12,13,14,15,16,18,24x2 +snare (9)
?	Reliable Music	9.21.83	114365	Carpathian Elm/Brass	13,18,24 +snare (4)
?	Metro Music	8.26.83	113208	Carpathian Elm/Brass	13,14,18,24 +snare (5)
?	D'Amico Music	8.23.83	113086	Carpathian Elm/Brass	12,14,20 +snare (4)
53	Andress Music	8.18.83	112320	Carpathian Elm/Brass	12,13,14, 16,22 +snare (6)
?	Fantasy Music	8.18.83	112816	Carpathian Elm/Brass	13,14,18,22 +snare (5)
?	Dow's Music	8.18.83	112815	Carpathian Elm/Brass	13,14,18,24 +snare (5)
?	Atlanta Pro Perc,	8.17.83	111216	Carpathian Elm/Brass	10,12,13,14,16,18,22,24 +snare (9)
52*	Bill's Country Music	?	112739	Carpathian Elm/Brass	12,13,14,16,22 +snare (6)
?	Music Workshop	7.19.83	111525	Birds Eye Maple/Brass	13,14,16,18,24 +snare (6)
?	Drums!	7.19.83	111499	Burled Walnut/Brass	13,14,16,18,24 +snare (6)
?	Gary Ferguson/Artist	7.13.83	111226	Carpathian Elm/Brass	10,12,14,16,22 +snare (6)
30*	Action Drum & Guitar	7.7.83	111037	Carpathian Elm/Brass	12,13,16,22 +snare (5)
?	ABK Drums	6.30.83	110762	Carpathian Elm/Brass	10,12,13,14,16,24 +snare (7)
20	Sampson Music	6.30.83	110742	Carpathian Elm/Brass	12,13,14,16,24 +snare (6)
?	Good Vibrations	6.29.83	110670	Carpathian Elm/Brass	13,14,18,24 +snare (5)
?	Music World/Hanich	3.9.84	121665	Carpathian Elm/Brass	8,10,13,14,16,22 +snare (6)
14*	Paragon Music	9.21.83	114371	Carpathian Elm/Brass	10,12,13,16,22 +snare (6)
15	Haley's Music/Europe	9.22.83	114432	Carpathian Elm/Brass	13,14,18,22 +snare (5)
24	Professional Drum Shop	6.28.83	110573	Carpathian Elm/Brass	12,13,16,22 +snare (5)
25*	Modern Music	11.14.83	117503	Carpathian Elm/Brass	8,10,12,13,16,22 +snare (7)
?	Leo's Music	11/14/83	117472	Carpathian Elm/Brass	10,12,14, 18BD +snare (5)
?	Leo's Music	10.13.83	116110	Carpathian Elm/Brass	8,10,12,14,16,18,22 +snare (8)
3	Jamie Oldacker			Carpathian Elm/Brass	(no information in production schedule)
2	Jeff Porcarro				(no information in production schedule)
98*	Tommy's Drum Shop	?	126051		(No information in production schedule)

Drum sales at that NAMM show were good. It did not overwhelm, but a lot of business was written; it was a successful show. Of course a lot of what goes on at a trade show over four days does not get put on an order pad immediately. It's the repeated follow-up that happens for months afterwards. The Centennial sets were well received, even as expensive as they were. Gretsch aficionados knew that this was a once in a lifetime opportunity to own a Centennial set and they better order while they were available.

I was assigned to create the Centennial drum set Certificate of Ownership that President Charlie Roy would sign. There were special sequential-numbered name plates that would go on each drum in the ordered set. These Gretsch name plates were signed by Charlie Roy in gold ink. All of these components and details became time consuming and a challenge to complete on time. Walt Jordan was the only personnel carryover from the Baldwin era that became part of Kustom Gretsch in Chanute and then made the move from Chanute, Kansas, to Gallatin, Tennessee with the company. He was basically the purchasing agent/office manager and became the person responsible for getting all of the parts and the plating together for these Centennial sets. The project was huge. This was a full time job just in itself. He had to source the 14-Karat gold plating on all of the drum and holder parts. While this special plating did not involve the actual floor-mounted stands, all of the tom-holders, lugs, die-cast hoops, and tom mounts were available in gold plating.

The progress on this Centennial project was not going well and in a couple of our internal closed-door manager meetings, Charlie was getting frustrated. He basically told us as a group, "You will get this completed or heads will roll." Rarely had he ever used those terms before, and we all got the message. Probably no one got the message more strongly than Walt did, and the Centennial drum project became all that he worked on from that point.

As the fall of 1983 started, I was looking to Charlie to give some directive or direction. I wanted to exercise some caution about just doing things and not communicating with him on everything. I was still finding the "lines in the sand" that defined our communications. Sales Manager Wayne Summers became my best resource for information and interpretation of Charlie along with bouncing ideas off of him on a daily basis. Wayne also became a close friend through this process and we worked closely together for the duration of my time at Gretsch.

I purchased a home in Gallatin and moved my family down to Tennessee before school started in September. Acquiring this beautiful home was a "fringe benefit" of the decision to move into this region. Home values were significantly lower and my investment bought more of a home there than it would have in the Chicago area. This was also my first (and last) experience of owning and paying for two homes at the same time, Northbrook and Gallatin. Upon the arrival of the United Van Lines truck in the circular driveway of the new home, we had a great anticipation that we could find peace, stability and a southern way of living in a less stressful area than the cosmopolitan Chicago suburbs.

The drum market was starting to see exciting things happening from Gretsch with the full page color ads in Modern Drummer that matched the images appearing in a series of six corresponding full size wall posters. This high visibility consumer awareness was started before I arrived at the company, but I quickly got further involved as I became the "drum guy" to the public. People were noticing what Gretsch was doing with their products and with their ads.

GRETSCH
KUSTOM
P.O. Box 1250, Gallatin, Tennessee 37066
615/452-0083 TELEX: 786571 [Gretsch] Gatn

August 1, 1983

MEMO TO: All Trade Publications
FROM: The Gretsch Company
SUBJECT: Immediate Press Release

ROY BURNS JOINS GRETSCH ENDORSEE-CLINIC STAFF

Gretsch Percussion Products announced the recent addition of Roy Burns to its educational clinic staff. As a product endorsee, Burns will be available for guest clinic and concert appearances through Gretsch's educational operations.

Karl Dustman, Gretsch's Percussion Marketing Manager commented; "The addition of Roy Burns to our clinic staff opens new opportunities in the outfit market place within the educational community. Roy will participate in product development as well as printed educational pieces as part of our drummer's "Educational Aids" series now in development."

Burns is widly recognized in the U.S. and abroad for his wide experience as a performer, clinician, manufacturer and method book author. Clinic tours have taken him to over ten European countries, the Far East, Australia and Canada. He has given a clinic and/or performed at all leading music educator conferences throughout the U.S.

His past performances with greats like Woody Herman and Benny Goodman as well as Urbie Green, Doc Severinson, Gerry Mulligan and Dizzy Gillespie make Burns "at home" with any given performance situation. Often referred to as "the drummer's drummer" for his approach to the Percussive Arts, he has developed

Press Release
ROY BURNS JOINS GRETSCH
Page two

a following among players, educators and non-percussionists for his easy-going, warm personality both on and off the stage.

Roy Burns shares his expertise regularly through a feature column in Modern Drummer magazine, entitled "Concepts". This column is followed by drummers of all ages and abilities in over fifty countries. His percussion accessory manufacturing company, Aquarian Accessories, has gained international prominence for inventive, unique drummer's products and essentials.

Complete details on scheduling, fees and sponsorship of a Roy Burns clinic for in-store or local concert use with high school/college bands can be obtained by contacting Gretsch Percussion Marketing Services: P.O. Box 1250, Gallatin, Tennessee, 37066, Telephone (615)452-0083. A clinician press kit is immediately available for review.

END

Drum makers since 1883

GRETSCH

P.O. Box 1250
Gallatin, Tennessee 37066

(615) 452-0083
TELEX 786571 Gretsch Gatn

GRETSCH EDUCATIONAL CLINICIAN ROSTER

DRUM SET ARTISTS

BARBARA BORDEN: San Francisco, California

Guest clinician/featured soloist with combo or big band. Current drummer with all-women jazz quintet, "Alive", three albums, percussion studies under Roland Koloff, San Francisco State University.

CLYDE BROOKS: Nashville, Tennessee

Clinician appearances, top Nashville recording studio drummer, author of "The Recording Drummer", Award Music Company, contributing author to Percussive Notes Magazine.

GERRY BROWN: Los Angeles, California

Clinic appearances for in-store promotion, festivals, drummers workshops. Featured drummer recording artist with international performing group, Lionel Richie.

ROY BURNS: Los Angeles, California

Guest clinician or featured soloist with combo or big band. Musical arrangements available for performance with high-school or college organizations. Author of instruction books, column "Concepts" for Modern Drummer Magazine, and sought after back-up for leading acts.

CHARLIE PERRY: Hempstead, New York

Reknown teacher/clinician/author - suitable for in-store, school, clinics, educator's conventions, master classes. Concert appearances with highschool/college combo or jazz ensembles. Faculty member, Five Towns College, Long Island, New York.

MARK SANDERS: Los Angeles, California

Clinic appearances for in-store clinics/festivals/workshops, suitable for mixed audience relating to contemporary music. Primarily known for extensive touring/recording with Tower Of Power.

RICK SHLOSSER: Los Angeles, California

Guest clinic appearances for in-store promotions, workshops, and guest concerts with highschool/college performing groups. A complete background as a multi-percussionist, previously known for his past association with Van Morrison, and presently with James Taylor.

KENNY SOULE: Raleigh, North Carolina

Guest clinician for in-store/workshop appearances, a multi-percussionist with formal training in tympany, mallets and orchestral percussion. Known for his nine-year association with Nantucket, presently developing new group, P.K.M.

TONY WILLIAMS: San Francisco, California

Featured clinician for in-store appearances, summer workshops, and guest soloist with highschool/college level jazz combo. Musical arrangements available for performance. Reknown jazz artist having played with every leading jazz great including Miles Davis. Presently performing with V.S.O.P.

MARK CRANEY: Los Angeles, California

Clinic appearances for in-store promotions, festivals, drummer workshops, featured drummer and recording artist with super star Gino Vannelli. Tremendous appeal to rock drawing audience.

BRUCE GARY: Los Angeles, California

Clinic appearances appealing to the rock audience, for in-store promotion/festivals and workshops. Now touring with a variety of top acts, known primarily for association with The Knack.

RICHARD GATES: Raleigh, North Carolina

Clinic promotions, in-store clinics/workshops, known for his appearances with the group Nantucket, recording, video and extensive touring.

JEFF HAMILTON: Los Angeles, California

Guest clinician/featured solo artist with educational expertise in musical structure and on-stage communication, appropriate for highschool/college level combo/stage band adjudication and critique. Known for present touring and recording with L.A. Four.

GRAHAM LEAR: Los Angeles, California

Guest clinician for in-store or school appearances. Reknown artist for years with Gino Vannelli and presently jazz-latin flavor of Carlos Santana. Vast touring and recording background.

HARVEY MASON: Los Angeles, California

Featured guest clinician/soloist for retail store promotion, highschool/college combo or jazz ensemble concert. Internationally known for extensive studio and clinic work.

Drum makers since 1883

GRETSCH

P.O. Box 1250
Gallatin, Tennessee 37066

(615) 452-0083
TELEX 786571 Gretsch Gatn

GRETSCH EDUCATIONAL CLINIC PROGRAM

LISTING OF CLINICIAN FEES

	1½ - 2 Hour Clinic	Concert With Student Ensemble
BARBARA BORDEN	$ 400.00	$ 550.00
CLYDE BROOKS	400.00	550.00
GERRY BROWN	500.00	--
ROY BURNS	400.00	550.00
MARK CRANEY	500.00	--
BRUCE GARY	400.00	--
RICHARD GATES	400.00	--
JEFF HAMILTON	400.00	550.00
GRAHAM LEAR	500.00	--
HARVEY MASON	750.00	900.00
CHARLIE PERRY	300.00	450.00
MARK SANDERS	400.00	--
RICK SHLOSSER	400.00	550.00
KENNY SOULE	400.00	550.00
TONY WILLIAMS	1,200.00	--

* All clinician fees are established by individual artists and are subject to change without notice.

* Dealer, school/college, convention and seminar appearances of Gretsch clinicians are co-sponsored by The Gretsch Company, conditions and amounts of financial support details available upon request by contacting Marketing Services of the Gretsch drum company.

* Availability of artist for guest clinic and concert appearances subject to schedule of clinician. Sponsor to provide three choices of clinic dates.

* Formal clinic agreement contract prepared by The Gretsch Company for each scheduled clinic appearance.

* Gretsch clinicians are exclusively booked for clinic appearances through The Gretsch Company.

A Memorable Moment:

While the moving van delivery was completed two days ago, there were boxes everywhere in the new home. The unpacking had begun but we were barely functioning, trying to find silverware, dishes, the coffee maker etc. A team of Gretsch management and employees decided to have a surprise welcoming party at the Dustman new residence and showed up unexpectedly with beer and a bottle of Champaign. This was a very kind and warm welcoming gesture from a group of people that barely knew me and certainly didn't know my family. Somehow we found some paper cups in a moving box and sat around on boxes drinking beer and wine. This form of open welcoming was so wonderful as I embarked on this completely new venture in a completely strange and different region of the country. I remember this wonderful Gretsch welcome to this day.

While Charlie was generally a very approachable person, I still was the new guy, learning the culture of the company. "Does he want to be involved in all of this? Should I only bother him if it involves larger amounts of money?" At one point Charlie basically said, "Karl- Do for Gretsch what you did for Ludwig." That made it perfectly clear that he wanted a lot of noise and positive market attention to the fact that Gretsch was made in America, and making drums for all drummers. This was no longer just a jazz-drummer's drum company. This company was about rock and roll, country, pop, to jazz, to heavy metal. We were building drums for every drummer that was out there. Those pretty much became my marching orders; I was to do whatever I did at Ludwig to make the drum world take notice.

Meanwhile, the Gretsch Guitar project was on the back burner. It was a project and vision of hope matched with a cloud of "some day". Again, there was a great potential for reintroducing all of the great Gretsch guitars; the White Falcon, Country Gentleman, Tennessean, world-famous models and so forth. These were probably going to be made in Asia as I started seeing prototype samples arriving in the usual rice paper cartons. Walt Jordan was again responsible for sourcing those guitars and getting samples made and air-shipped to the United States so they could be inspected and evaluated by Gretsch guitar aficionados. From those samples and qualified product evaluations, Charlie would know whether to proceed with the project or to develop further samples and continue to evaluate the potentials for a separate Gretsch guitar division. But for now, it was all about drums. Even the Kustom amplifiers were on the back burner. Sho-Bud Pedal Steel Guitars was moving forward with some limited production at the Dequeen factory and some instruments were selling through within the expanding Nashville market for these types of instruments.

I saw an opportunity in my marching orders from Charlie to create a professional artist relations program. Gretsch already had many internationally recognized great drummer-artists, but they were not being nurtured and communicated with to build lasting relationships. Some of the better known artists were already working with the Gallatin team upon Charlie's purchase of the company and moving it to the Nashville market in 1982. But Gretsch needed to convey and demonstrate to the existing long-time artists like Tony Williams, Mark Herndon (of the group Alabama), and so forth that there was now a full time, experienced "drum guy" at Gretsch Drums in Nashville. Gretsch artists needed to be treated like artists, knowing a name and contact telephone number in the Gallatin operation for a person they could reach to make-things-happen as promised. (Remember we did not have e-mail or texting back then). It became my responsibility to make that connection with the current artists but also to grow the family of top artists-of-influence in the market.

As we got into the second half of 1983, we were recruiting more and more artists. Gerry Brown (Lionel Richie) was with Yamaha and looking to make a change. Harvey Mason with Tama was looking for a change.

My longtime friend Roy Burns contacted Gretsch late in the summer to inquire about working together as a Gretsch artist. I knew Roy would be a perfect complement to the Gretsch artists and clinician roster. He was a well-respected educational clinician with years of experience and many percussion retailers already knew of his professional presentation. Having Roy associated with the Gretsch product and brand would bring many opportunities and benefits as we were developing and promoting the new Gretsch Educational Clinic program.

The Gretsch artist roster began to grow at a fairly aggressive rate. There were full-page color magazine ads being run when I came on board but now there were professionally written press releases announcing

products, artists, and Gretsch events, all building the momentum and visibility. At the same time, Selmer was starting to gear down the Ludwig artist program. Bill Ludwig III remained at the company and started juggling the percussion symposiums and struggling to keep Selmer in tune with the artists in the program he had marvelously developed and nurtured.

Bill was doing his best with Ludwig artists, however some saw the changes in Selmer's methods for Ludwig's artist relations program and started looking around for an alternative American drum company to become aligned with. Some knew I had moved on to Gretsch in Nashville and began to contact me about becoming part of the Gretsch family. I was of course more than happy to talk to them. Gretsch was not in the business of giving away drum sets or other equipment, as we just didn't have the budget to do that. Unlike Ludwig, there was no budget for large quantities of free no-charge product. That give-away provision didn't exist at Gretsch. I tried developing an internal effort to sell very limited products to select artists at our manufacturing cost and that was successful in many cases to build a relationship while nurtuting the artist's vested interest in the products he or she was playing.

For the first time, Gretsch had a formal endorsement contract, it had a clinic program with contracts and an artist clinic price sheet that listed every clinician. The whole artist and clinic program was run like a professional business rather than an unpredictable response to an inquiry call from an artist, a Gretsch dealer, or possible promotional opportunity for further brand recognition. I was happy to provide this element of organized process and procedure, as it helped everyone in the office become more productive and focused.

In the past these "PR-Promotional topics" would be passed on to Wayne Summers. Now, however, he was responsible for and overseeing the entire inside telemarketing sales people as well as the outside district sales managers that were making sales calls on the dealers nationwide. All of that sales management was a full time job in itself. Wayne did not need to become involved in all these other marketing activities. He had a wonderful sales team under his direction. Inside sale representatives included Alan Bechler, Tommy Day, Rob Goldsmith and Mark Richards. Outside sales representatives included Scott Fish, Arnie McLerran, Mike Pritchard and John Alfiers. The international sales side of the company was managed by Randy Houck. Before my arrival, Randy had inherited some of the marketing-artist-advertising projects. His focus was on selling the complete Kustom-Gretsch product line on an international platform. He'd be traveling throughout the world developing sales for the entire

Gretsch Frankfurt exhibit,

product line and managing the complete Gretsch exhibit-presence at the Frankfurt Messe each spring. Again- that was a full time job in itself. He did a fine job and was well liked and respected by all the international distributors.

I was dealing with drum hardware issues; floorstands pedals, thrones etc. By this time, almost every drum company was going to Asia to get their stands and pedals produced. I felt that Gretsch was missing an opportunity to sell Gretsch branded hardware with the drum sets which could add to the profitability of the complete order. It would also place Gretsch in the position of having their own separate brand of hardware. Techware, was the name that was researched and decided upon. Every floor stand had the new Gretsch patented QUICK-LOK memory-lock with male/female locking mechanisms, and the Gretsch name molded into the tooling. Gretsch paid for and owned the tooling to make these multiple-sized memory-lock devices and the corresponding height adjustment mechanisms that matched the memory lock tooling.

At this time, most of the hardware was coming from Asia packed in bulk and arriving at the Gretsch Dequeen, Arkansas factory for consolidated shipment with drum orders. I convinced Charlie that we needed to put every one of these Techware stands into American-made sturdy heavy-duty white cardboard boxes with the words "Techware by Gretsch" on each box. I called upon my previous Ludwig friends and resources at Cedar River Printing again. With logo artwork completed, they produced and printed a series of different sized white quality boxes that were shipped flat in bulk to the factory in Arkansas. Plant Manager Ben Johnson would have his team discard the Asian lightweight rice-paper type cardboard wrappings we received the Taiwan stands in and repackage the stands in the new white USA boxes. It really helped Gretsch look like it was seriously into the hardware business as a separate entity. New patented memory lock height adjustment, new sturdy white cartons with Techware logo, all produced a positive image to the Gretsch drum customer. It also helped us sell additional stand and pedal hardware as add-ons.

The June, 1983, NAMM convention provided the opportunity to test-market an affordable entry-level drum set that could be merchandised within the Gretsch brand, but not distract from the Made-in-USA Gretsch products and quality image. The "BLACKHAWK By Gretsch" basic seven piece set was shown at the NAMM convention with a positive response. Five-piece sets had a retail price of just $899. Seven piece sets retailed for $1099. By the end of the summer Gretsch was thoroughly immersed in the competitive entry-level drum set market. Industry-wide product introductions increased as more and more low-end budget drum sets entered the playing field. To combat the growing market penetration of low-end starter sets, Gretsch took the position of "join the race:...rather than ignore the opportunity". Using the brand name of Blackhawk, Gretsch researched the market and came up with affordable Asian-manufactured sets sold through authorized Gretsch dealers. These sold-through and met reasonable sales expectations for 1983 and 1984.

KUSTOM GRETSCH
P.O. Box 1250, Gallatin, Tennessee 37066
615/452-0083 TELEX: 786571 [Gretsch] Gatn

August 1, 1983

MEMO TO: All Trade Publications
FROM: Kustom Gretsch
SUBJECT: Immediate Press Release

GRETSCH INTRODUCES NO. P-560 BLACKHAWK POWER OUTFIT

Gretsch's economy Blackhawk outfits have taken on power shell dimensions in a normal five piece set-up. This imported line distributed exclusively by Gretsch includes heavy-duty wide angle double braced floor stands and versatile tom holder. Wood shell sizes include; 16x22" bass drum, 10x12", 11x13" mounted toms, 16x16" floor tom and 6½x14" metal shell snare drum. Available in choice of black, silver or dark blue metallic finishes, suggested list price, $899.00. Dealer quantity discounts are available.

Also introduced for the expanding Blackhawk line is the No. P-561 add-on tom pack consisting of an 8x8" and 8x10" double headed power toms with wide angle double braced floor stand. Suggested list price is $199.00, available in three Blackhawk metallic finishes. Dealer quantity discounts are also available.

For complete details contact: Gretsch Marketing Services, P.O. Box 1250, Gallatin, Tennessee, 37066.

GRETSCH
P. O. Box 1250 • Gallatin, Tennessee 37066 • (615) 452-0083 • TELEX 786571 Gretsch Gatn

August 21, 1984

Dear Journal Editor:

Enclosed are three new press releases and photographs of new products and developments for Gretsch drums.

* New Gretsch Blackhawk Electronic Drum Set.
* New Hickory Drumstick Line
* New Finishes Available

We would appreciate your inclusion of these items in a future edition of your journal, as I know the readership will be most interested in this news from Gretsch. Our research indicates through buyer and educator surveys that percussion products and peoply in "news from the industry" sections receive broader and quicker market response.

Thank you in advance for your interest and cooperation in sharing this information with your readers.

Sincerely,

THE GRETSCH COMPANY

Karl Dustman
Percussion Marketing Manager

KD/km

Enc: Three press releases.

1983 ended with a significant achievement in recruiting PHIL COLLINS to a formal Gretsch endorsement agreement that would bring tremendous impact to the Gretsch brand, product and endorsement development program within the company. Inside sales representative Mark Richards knew from his contacts and his dealings with tour production experts Showco that Phil Collins was searching for a drum company relationship and he was already playing and favoring Gretsch Made-in-USA drums.

A Memorable Moment:

Charlie Roy immediately supported this opportunity to align Gretsch with one of the hottest names in pop music. Phil Collins had global recognition as a drummer-band leader. A date and time was established for me to meet directly with Phil Collins at the Four Seasons Hotel in Dallas where he was staying. With a firm date and time for the meeting established, I flew to Dallas filled with hope, anticipation and some anxiety. Phil come into the hotel lounge with Robert Plant, I introduced myself and Phil sat down at my table. Plant went on to another table, away from the conversation. Phil Collins was a very normal, gracious and approachable person that enjoyed conversation about drums and drumming and did not pose any real exorbitant demands for signing a formal Endorsement Agreement with Gretsch. For the use of his name, autograph and photograph, Gretsch would provide two complete complimentary left-handed White Nitron drum sets complete with an assortment of the new Techware hardware. Once completed and thoroughly inspected at the Gretsch factory, each set would be shipped to his designated locations in the United States. It was simple, quick, and painless and I was thrilled that this went so smoothly. Immediately following was Collins' complete cooperation on providing photography with the new white Gretsch sets. I recall this meeting with fondness as Phil Collins was one of the most down to earth "super-drummers" I would meet and know through the rest of my career.

The start of 1984 brought the planning for another significant exhibit at the January NAMM Winter Market convention in Anaheim, California. This was a slightly easier production because the Kustom-Gretsch entire exhibit was stored within the Drum Workshop warehouse under the direction of Don Lombardi. Gretsch was purchasing all the Gretsch bass drum pedals from Drum Workshop, so Charlie already had the relationship in place. I just stepped in to make the connections, establish booth number location assigned by NAMM, and engage the same set-up crew that did DW to set-up the Gretsch exhibit. The focus of the convention was an array of new exciting natural wood-stained finishes and colors which included Lucerne Green and Caribbean Blue. By now we also had professionally thought-through dealer NAMM Show Specials for existing dealers and invitations for the many new dealers that were becoming interested in Gretsc drums. Once again. Gretsch was starting to make a lot of noise in the market and it was being noticed.

Further emphasis and development was placed on increasing the importance of artists, in-store clinics, and growing the roster of top artists that could influence the Gretsch brand and customer selection. Dealers now had access to a Gretsch-organized professionally run clinic program. We established the first "Gretsch Day" event in March of 1984, hosted by Paragon Music in Tampa Florida. Using the West Tampa Convention Center for the noon-to 5:00 p.m. event, leading Gretsch artists Harvey Mason, Graham Lear and Roy Burns each provided individual educational clinics with the day concluding as an "open forum" of all three artists performing and answering questions from the audience. Close to 500 enthusiastic people attended the event. Door prize drawings, artist autographs and audience photography with the Celebrity

GRETSCH
Drum makers since 1883
P.O. Box 1250
Gallatin, Tennessee 37066
(615) 452-0083
TELEX 786571 Gretsch Gatn

For Immediate Release

"GRETSCH DAYS" PROMOTION BEGINS WITH PARAGON MUSIC CLINIC

Gretsch recently announced the creation of an educational clinic program whereby Gretsch dealers will now have access to in-store clinics, workshops and promotions, utilizing international and regional drum clinicians. As part of Gretsch's intensified educational promotion efforts, a concept of multiple "star" clinicians combining for a dealer event has been implemented under the "Gretsch Day" publicity name.

Paragon Music of Tampa, Florida will be the first of a series of sponsors for "Gretsch Day" promotions beginning on Sunday, March 25th, 1984. Gretsch artists HARVEY MASON, GRAHAM LEAR and ROY BURNS will be on hand for this event with individual clinics and an "open forum" with all three artists concluding the day's activities. The event will be conducted at the West Tampa Convention Center beginning at 12 Noon through 5PM. Anticipated attendance for all clinics is between 500-700 drummers of all ages drawing from all areas of central and southern Florida, including Orlando and Miami.

Special door prize drawings will add to the festivities which will include a Gretsch tour jacket.

Time allotments for autographing and photography will be provided for the expected record attendance to see these three internationally known "drum stars".

New Gretsch natural wood outfit colors of Lucern Greene and Carribbean Blue will be introduced to the area at this event, having just been displayed at the NAMM Winter Market.

Future "Gretsch Day" dates and locations will be announced within the next few weeks according to Gretsch Marketing Manager Karl Dustman.

Direct all inquiries on the Paragon Gretsch Day to Tracy Hoeft, at Paragon, (813)879-1580. Other dealers requesting information on hosting a Gretsch Day in their area should contact Gretsch Marketing Services, (615)452-0083.

Artists made the event a memorable educational, promotional and a complete success for Paragon Music and Gretsch. This was a planned template for further development of more "Gretsch Days" educational events in the future.

SABIAN ENTRY & EXIT WITH GRETSCH

Bob Zildjian had already entered the cymbal market with his creation of Sabian LTD before I arrived at Gretsch. There had been several years of litigation between Bob and his brother Armand as they parted ways at the Zildjian company. The court decree and settlement resulted in Armand Zildjian retaining the complete Zildjian company and name, while Bob Zildjian acquired the Zildjian manufacturing facility in New Brunswick, Canada, where he started the Sabian cymbal company. (The company was named after his three children Sally, Billy, and Andy.) Early on, Sabian had arranged principal distribution through three companies in the U.S.; Pearl (in Nashville), Charles Alden (in Walpole, MA), and Gretsch (Gallatin, TN). Gretsch established a significant Sabian cymbal inventory at the Dequeen, Arkansas, manufacturing/distribution facility.

The Gretsch inside sales force and the field salespeople were all now selling Sabian Cymbals and related products. It was assumed that all three of the designated US distributors had some retail accounts in common, while other retail accounts were set up to do business with only one or two of the distributors. Bob Zildjian's four lieutenants were Dave McAllister (a Canadian who had come from the food produce industry), Dan Barker (a former Zildjian production executive), Craig Gardner (the chief financial officer who passed away about four years into the company), and Roy Edmunds (artist relations, marketing, sales, etc., formerly with Selmer-Canada).

I got along well with the entire Sabian team, although I did feel that there was a lot of high pressure placed on Gretsch to move as many cymbals as was humanly possible. I suppose that was the natural outcome of having two companies now attempting to dominate the cymbal marketplace that had been the domain of a single company. The situation and competition among the three USA Sabian distributors was intensifying and Charlie began feeling that Gretsch was at the bottom of the distribution "totem pole". Bob Zildjian had a long-time friendship relationship with Pearl USA President, Walt Johnston, and an even longer personal friendship with Charles Alden. It became apparent that Charlie somewhat resented the "in and out" short visits Bob Zildjian would make to the Gallatin offices before running over to Pearl to have meetings and dinner with Walt Johnson. It just didn't feel like a level playing field among the three Sabian distributors all competing for the same dealer purchases.

Early in 1984, it all "hit the fan" when someone on the Gretsch-Gallatin inside sales desk told Charlie that he had learned Charles Alden Music was selling below everyone else's Sabian prices because Alden was getting a better discount by 5%. Charlie was absolutely furious, and decided he wanted to get out of the Sabian distribution business altogether. He immediately started a "price war" on all in stock Sabian products, blowing out all of the Sabian cymbals that he had bought, paid for, and was stocking in Dequeen. Knowing Charlie's boiling point, he probably blew out the remaining Sabian inventory at cost or even in some cases below cost. Part of his motivation was simply to create some chaos in the Sabian marketplace and to sever the relationship with Sabian while sticking it to Charles Alden Music.

There had been a relationship between Gretsch and the Italian Ufip cymbal company for years, though the relationship was not very well defined. Charlie felt that he could resurrect Ufip and that the Sabian relationship was not essential. Ufip cymbals re-appeared in the April, 1984, Gretsch price list with the hope of developing the Ufip brand and relationship. In the end, Gretsch had more important issues and priorities than wholesaling somebody else's cymbals. Despite the internal efforts at Gallatin, we were unable to cultivate market interest to establish Ufip in the manner he envisioned.

By that point Modern Drummer Magazine was receiving regular monthly advertising insertion orders from Gretsch along with a regular Press Releases on products, programs, campaigns and people. Rick Mattingly contacted me to inquire about doing a feature story about the "New Gretsch" that would include a visit by him to the Gallatin Gretsch offices as well as a trip to the Gretsch factory in Dequeen Arkansas. This visit from Modern Drummer was scheduled for May of 1984 and signaled to everyone within Gretsch that what we were collectively doing for Gretsch Drums as a company was definitely being recognized in the market. I was assigned to oversee and host Rick's visit and see to everything connected with this once-in-a lifetime opportunity for Gretsch.

I picked up Rick at the Nashville airport and we immediately started working together on the Gretsch story that would combine some early company history from one hundred years ago, but more importantly what was going on in Gretsch now. Rick was a gracious guest, wanting to meet everyone, wanting to photograph the Gallatin team and at the same time placing a certain spotlight on myself and everything I was working on within the company. (Rick and I still speak about this project over thirty years later.) As soon as we completed the interviewing and story development in Gallatin, we jumped on a commercial flight to the Gretsch factory in Arkansas.

Dequeen is not an easy place to get to. We picked up a rental car at the Fayetteville airport and made the two hour drive to Dequeen in the dark. Dequeen is a very small town of about 600 people. There were three principle employers in Dequeen; the Gretsch factory, the chicken slaughter-processing factory and a gym-shoe company. This was my first trip to the Gretsch factory as well so I learned quickly to adapt, while recognizing that the work force at Gretsch brought a vast amount of expertise from the quality furniture manufacturing skill-set. Furniture manufacturing was a big business in Arkansas but had moved on and out. Gretsch benefited tremendously from this furniture production expertise in its drum-shell finishing operations, quality of people and workmanship, and attention to details.

Rick worked directly with factory manager Ben Johnson who provided a detailed guided tour and explanation of every manufacturing process for the Gretsch drum building. Rick absorbed all of this, photographed all of the processes, and created a wonderful feature story titled "INSIDE GRETSCH, 100 Years of Gretsch" that appeared in the May edition of Modern Drummer. The visit to the Gretsch factory encompassed the most complete and accurate editorial and photographic record of the Gretsch Drum brand and product that was ever produced. I immediately seized the opportunity to create a sixteen page reprint which included two prominent Gretsch advertisements including the "When You're Hot" ad (drums on fire) featuring Phil Collins, Harvey Mason, Gerry Brown and Mark Herndon. Each provided their own individual quotes on topics ranging from wood shells, finishes, and snare drums to the new Techware hardware. This was a brilliant piece of educational merchandising that brought the Gretsch dealer and consumer closer to Gretsch and inside the American-made factory production.

DeQueen, Arkansas Gretsch drum factory

Inside Gretsch

100 Years of Gretsch

A Visit To The Gretsch Factory

Inside Gret

100 Years of Gretsch

There's a certain mystique about Gretsch. Mention the name to a group of drummers and you'll start hearing about such things as "round badge" kits from the '50s; Gretsch/Gladstone drums; Gretsch Drum Nights at Birdland; jazz drummers such as Max, Art, Philly, Tony, etc.; various distinctive colors and finishes; K. Zildjian cymbals; and most of all, that *sound*. You would be surprised by the number of drummers who, although they endorse other brands, have confided to *MD* that their favorite set is "this Gretsch kit that I've had since . . . "

Why are drummers so sentimental about these old drums? Surely, with all of the technological advances of the last ten years, drums must be better than ever. A lot of people don't seem to think so, however. In the same way that guitar players talk about Fender equipment that was made before CBS bought the company, drummers seek out Gretsch drums made before Baldwin took over. But did the drums actually change? Were the same people still making them? Why did their address keep changing? And now that Gretsch is no longer owned by Baldwin, what's going to happen? To put all of this in perspective, we're going to take a look at the 100-year history of Gretsch. The story involves both drums and people, starting with the man who put his family name on the drum.

Jo Jones (center) and Phil Grant (right) at the Gretsch factory in Brooklyn. (The snare drum to the upper right of Grant is a Gretsch/Gladstone.)

Photo Courtesy of Manny's, NYC

Friedrich Gretsch was born in Mannheim, Germany, in 1856, the son of a middle-class grocer. At the age of 16, not wishing to be drafted into the military, he immigrated to America, and settled in Brooklyn with his uncle, who had a prosperous wine business. But rather than work for his uncle, he took a job with the Albert Houdlett & Son company, who made drums and banjos.

Following the example of his father and uncle, who had their own businesses, Friedrich opened his own shop in 1883, at the age of 27. He was soon turning out drums, banjos, tambourines and toy drums for various wholesalers. The firm only employed a dozen workers, and was located in a small wooden shanty on South 4th Street, in Brooklyn. At the time he began his company, he had a three-year-old son, Fred Gretsch, Sr.

By 1895, the business was doing well, and 15-year-old Fred was attending Wright's Business College, so Friedrich decided to pay a visit to his native Germany. But after arriving in his homeland, Friedrich suddenly died. His teenaged son—who was still wearing knickers—

A Gretsch separate-tension snare drum from 1906, as pictured in an early catalog.

An early sock cymbal as built by Gretsch in the '20s.

A 1930s Gretsch tom, with the old-style lugs.

sch

by Richard Egart

took over the Gretsch company.

Despite his young age, Fred showed remarkable business sense. Within five years, he had moved the company from the small shanty he inherited from his father to a three-story plant at 104 Middleton St., and he'd expanded the business to include mandolin making, and the importing of a full line of accessories and string instruments. As energetic as he was enterprising, Fred did not confine himself only to working at his desk in the plant. He also went on the road to sell, and could even be found up on the roof of the building tanning hides. (In those days, Gretsch bought skins from a New York slaughterhouse, and made their own drum and banjo heads.) Fred also brought his younger brothers, Walter and Louis, into the company after they finished school around the turn of the century. Walter stayed until 1921, and then opened a wholesaling firm. Louis only stayed a year, and then went into real estate.

Duke Kramer

Fred Gretsch, Sr.

Fred Gretsch, Jr.

In 1916 the business moved to a ten-story building at 60 Broadway, in Brooklyn, and that is where the company remained until the early '70s. That building, with the Gretsch name at the top, still stands today, and can be seen as one crosses the Williamsburg Bridge from Manhattan to Brooklyn.

In 1928, Gretsch opened a branch in Chicago, which was headed by Phil Nash. According to Duke Kramer, who joined Gretsch in 1935, and took over the Chicago office in 1948, "Gretsch was broken up into two distinct units. One was the factory and the eastern sales office in Brooklyn; the other was the western sales office in Chicago, which handled everything from Ohio to the West Coast. New York had the factory operation, sales on the eastern seaboard, and exports. We each had an independent sales force, and our own payrolls, inventories and accounting. Our only involvement with the New York office was that we bought the factory merchandise from them, like a regular customer, and we sent Fred Gretsch a monthly statement."

It should be noted that, in those days, Gretsch's main concern was *not* the manufacture of instruments under their own name. The drums that they made (as well as the banjos and guitars) were primarily for other distributors, who would put their names on them. Gretsch was more a merchandiser than a major-line company.

One of the people Gretsch made drums for was Billy Gladstone, who was known as much for his inventions as for his incredible drum technique. Back when all drumheads were calfskin, the biggest problem drummers had was keeping the heads tuned during a performance, because temperature and humidity changes in a room would immediately affect the heads. Gladstone devised a three-way tuning key: One section of the key tuned the top head; another section tuned the bottom head; the third section tuned both heads together. And what was really nice was that all of these tunings could be done with the drum mounted on a stand. Gretsch built these drums for Gladstone, and after Gladstone later began making drums himself, he still used Gretsch shells.

Fred Gretsch, Sr., remained president of Gretsch until 1942, when he retired to become president of Lincoln Savings Bank, and a director of Manufacturer's Trust Co. After Fred, Sr., retired, he appointed

"Rocket" snare drum, built by Gretsch.

World War II Gretsch tom, with wooden lugs.

his son, Fred Gretsch, Jr., president of the company. Fred, Jr., had started working at the factory when he was ten years old, coming in on Saturdays to pack phonograph needles. He became treasurer of Gretsch in 1931. (Like his father, he was interested in finance, and served as a vice president of the Lincoln Savings Bank, and a director of the Suffolk County Trust Co.) Shortly after becoming president in '42, however, he left the company to serve in the navy during World War II. His brother, William Walter Gretsch, had been running the Chicago Gretsch office, so he moved back to New York and became president of Gretsch. When Fred, Jr., returned to the company after the war, William remained president, but soon became ill and subsequently died in 1948, at which time Fred, Jr., assumed the presidency again.

During World War II, the Gretsch company had been somewhat inactive. In addition to Fred, Jr., other key personnel had also left for military service, including Duke Kramer. Because of government regulations and the shortages of materials, drums had to be made with wooden hoops and lugs. For a while, Gretsch even stopped making musical instruments, and the plant was used for the manufacture of war products.

After everyone returned from the war, Fred, Jr., called a meeting, which Duke Kramer remembers well. "We all met in New York to decide where the company was headed. We all decided that we wanted to develop Gretsch as a major line. After the meeting we split up into two-man teams. We covered every major nightspot in New York that we could find, and asked the drummers what they wanted in a drum. We were going to attack drums first, and guitars later. From that survey, we found that there was a need for smaller drums, because the New York drummers were always carrying drums around from gig to gig, and to recording sessions, and the large drums didn't fit into cabs. Plus, because of the way hardware was designed, it took them forever to set up and break down. These drummers wanted something that they could set up quickly, and that they could cart around easily. So from that, and working with Davey Tough, we developed the 20" bass drum, the shell-mounted tom-tom holder and cymbal arm, and the disappearing spurs. All of those things came out of that meeting, and they were all firsts. The hardware was all developed in conjunction with the Walberg Company, in Massachusetts."

Louie Bellson with one of his first Gretsch double bass drum setups.

One of the people at that meeting was a new employee named Phil Grant, who had just come out of the navy. Grant had been a drummer with the Pittsburgh Symphony, and with the famous Edwin Franko Goldman band. Phil was also an avid jazz fan who frequented the New York nightclubs, where he got to know the drummers personally. After the two-man teams had completed their survey, Phil Grant continued the direct contact with the drummers, which was important, as Fred Gretsch, Jr., was not particularly knowledgeable about drums. Louie Bellson remembers going to the Gretsch factory in those days. "Fred was a very nice man, but he was not a musician. He was a businessman—a very smart one and a very good one. Whenever I went to Brooklyn, I would always stop in to see Fred. He would always ask, 'How's everything going? Do you have any problems?' If he didn't understand something, he would always turn to Phil Grant and say, 'Well Phil, this is your department. If you think this is right, go ahead and do it.'"

Phil joined the company as a salesman, and went on the road to sell and promote Gretsch drums. During a trip to Buffalo, he presented a clinic at East High School. One of the students at that school was particularly impressed—a young drummer named Mel Lewis. "Phil put on a fantastic clinic," Mel recalls. "He had a set of Gretsch *Broadkasters,* a Gretsch/Gladstone snare drum, bass drums, cymbals and timpani. He was a superb percussionist and he demonstrated all of the instruments well. In those days, Gretsch was really an ugly drum. They were mostly nickel plate and the rims still didn't have a flange on top. But when I heard the sound I said 'Wow!' And I liked the way he explained the shell. So a couple of weeks later I ordered a set of Gretsch drums in gold sparkle, and I took those drums on the road after I got out of school."

Mel Lewis wasn't the only drummer to be impressed by Phil Grant. In 1947, Louie Bellson showed Phil an idea he had for a double bass drum kit—an idea that had already been turned down by other drum companies. "Phil looked at my design and said, 'That's pretty wild, but I don't see why it can't work,'" Bellson remembers. "So they built the first one for me. I was criticized at first by a lot of people, but

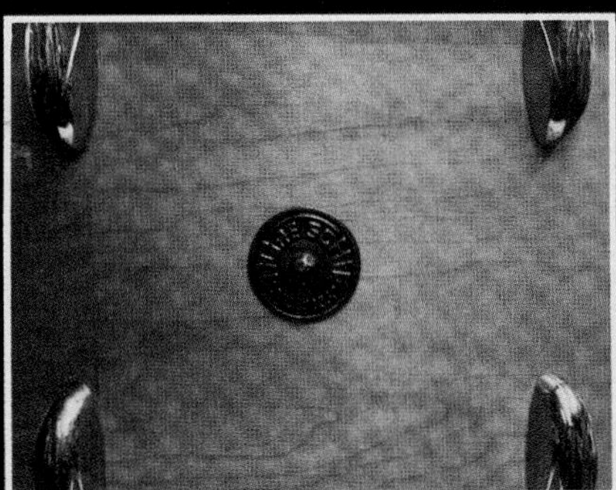

Originally, toms did not have vent holes and the badge was tacked on.

An early '60s snare drum, with Micro-Sensitive *strainer.*

Gretsch saw the possibilities and I always respected them for that."

Phil Grant recalled another idea, that came from a drummer named Jimmie Pratt. "A lot of drummers used a piece of felt across the bass drum head to muffle the sound, but there was no way to regulate it. So the Jimmie Pratt tone control was developed, which allowed you to control the amount of tension on the felt." Another drummer with an idea was Chico Hamilton, who wanted tom-toms with no bottom heads. So Gretsch made single-headed toms for him back in the '50s, long before rock drummers started removing their bottom heads.

In addition to the innovations suggested by the drummers, the Gretsch company itself was constantly refining and improving the way drums were made, starting with the shell itself. Originally, Gretsch made shells the way most other companies did. They bought three-ply wood, and molded it into a circle. Shells of that type required reinforcement rings at the top and bottom to keep the shell in round. But then, while Fred Gretsch, Sr., was president, Gretsch began laminating the wood themselves, as they molded the shell. By joining the plys in three different places, the shell no longer required the reinforcement rings. Those shells were made right there in the Brooklyn factory. Then, in the early '50s, they changed to the six-ply shell, which is still being used today. Despite the increase in plys, the shell did not get noticeably thicker, as the plys themselves were thinner. But the shells could now be joined in six different places instead of just three, and that added to the overall strength. Duke Kramer feels that the absence of reinforcement rings in the drums was what gave Gretsch its distinctive sound—"That Great Gretsch Sound."

Gretsch started using die-cast hoops on their 14" snare drums prior to World War

A Gretsch ad from the '50s.

II, and after the war, they started using those hoops on the standard tom-tom sizes. The shell-mount tom holders that were developed after the war were also die-cast. Another simple but practical idea was their patented snap-in drumkey holder, which remains a popular feature of Gretsch drums today.

Also in the '50s, Gretsch was the first company to stop using nickel plating, going to chrome exclusively. Most companies offered a choice of the two, but according to Grant, "We said that the only way to make a drum was with chrome plating. It gave a little dignity to the drums, and was also a good selling point."

One of Gretsch's most famous products over the years has been their *Floating Action* bass drum pedal. Interestingly enough, that was not originally a Gretsch product. Briefly, it started out as the Martin Fleetfoot pedal, and was then sold to Camco. Gretsch liked the pedal and made a deal whereby Camco made the same pedal for Gretsch, with Gretsch's name on it. Nevertheless, drummers would argue about which was the better pedal.

As mentioned earlier, Gretsch was also in the business of importing instruments, and one of the companies they imported was Zildjian cymbals from Istanbul. Originally, Gretsch owned the trademarks *K. Zildjian, A. Zildjian,* and *Zildjian.* In order to keep a trademark, a company has to demonstrate continuous use of a product with that name on it. The Gretsch company soon gave up the *A. Zildjian* trademark, because of confusion with the Avedis Zildjian cymbals made in America. Later they lost the *Zildjian* trademark also. But until the '70s, when the Avedis Zildjian company finally made a deal with Baldwin (who then owned Gretsch) to get the *K. Zildjian* trademark back, the Gretsch company was the exclusive supplier of K. Zildjian cymbals.

The cymbals were warehoused in the Brooklyn factory, and drummers could go there personally to pick out cymbals. But a lot of drummers preferred to let Phil Grant choose their cymbals for them. As Mel Lewis remembers: "Phil knew K. Zildjians. He picked out a few for me that I still have to this day. He always knew where the good ones were. I'd start to look through a pile of cymbals and Phil would say, 'I think you'll find what you like right on top,' or 'There isn't a good one in the lot; don't even bother with this pile.' When Art Blakey was working at Birdland, Phil might walk in with a 20 or 22 under his arm and say, 'Here Art, I think you'll like this one.' It would be a typical Art Blakey-type cymbal."

Phil Grant recognized the importance of having respected drummers associated with the company, and as jazz was becoming the prominent music of the '50s, Phil sought out all of the prominent players.

Mid-'60s concert snare with original Lightning Throwoff.

The Lightning Throwoff *was redesigned in the early '70s.*

Gretsch called their engraved, gold-plated snare drum "the most beautiful drum in the world."

Thanks to Ken Mezines, Charlie Donnelly and Glenn Weber for their help in tracking down vintage Gretsch drums.

The 1954 Gretsch catalog featured such jazz artists as Louie Bellson, Denzil Best, Art Blakey, Jo Jones, Don Lamond, Mel Lewis, Shelly Manne, Charlie Perry, Max Roach and George Wettling. Mel Lewis recalled what it meant to be a Gretsch endorser: "They gave you drums and cymbals, and you could always stop by the factory if you needed sticks or brushes. But they didn't give you unlimited equipment. In fact, when you got a new drumset you had to turn in your old one. Gretsch never, ever paid anybody to play their drum. They even preferred that you already owned a set of Gretsch before they offered you an advertising deal. Fred wanted to know that you played the drums because you liked them. The only contract you had with Gretsch was that, in return for a set of drums, they were allowed to use your name and picture in their advertising, and that contract could be broken anytime. But all of these drummers wanted to play Gretsch drums.

"We were all close to each other through that company," Lewis continued. "We all loved Gretsch; there was a common feeling there. When one of us played somewhere, Phil Grant would come around to hear us, and he might bring some of the other drummers with him. It was like a fraternity."

That fraternal spirit was manifest in the Gretsch Drum Nights, which, of course, were Phil Grant's idea. "I think that was the best idea I ever came up with," Phil states. "I was a fan of Birdland. I would go there frequently, and most of the drummers were playing Gretsch. I got to know the manager, and one night I suggested that we make a special set of drums that could be used as the house set for anyone who played there. We came up with a set made of solid green shells, and I had all of the metal gold plated. I was able to do that because we had gold-plating facilities for our Gretsch guitars. So that set became quite a showpiece at the club.

"Then one night I suggested having a Gretsch Drum Night, with three of our drummers. The first one broke all attendance records at Birdland, so we continued it for several years." The second one, in 1960, was recorded and released on Roulette Records. It featured Art Blakey, Elvin Jones, Charli Persip and Philly Joe Jones, who were all Gretsch artists at that time.

Mel Lewis participated in a couple of Gretsch Drum Nights, and recalled what they were like. "Those were fun. We had a rhythm section and a horn player, and we would each take a turn playing with the group. Then all the drummers would get out in front—we had four drumsets—and we'd work our way through trading choruses, then sixteens, then eights, down to fours, and then swing out together. We always agreed that nobody was going to try to overshadow anybody else. The idea was to keep the continuity going. It worked out just great, and it was wonderful for Gretsch, because nobody else could boast that many top drummers."

The 1966 Gretsch catalog contained photos of Elvin Jones, Tony Williams, Max Roach, Art Blakey, Don Lamond, Sonny Payne, Chico Hamilton and Mel Lewis. The featured drumset was the *Progressive Jazz* kit, which was made up of a 5 × 14 snare, 14 × 20 bass, 8 × 12 mounted tom and 14 × 14 floor tom. In many ways, this catalog documents the reason Gretsch lost its position of supremacy in the '60s. In 1964, the Beatles had arrived in America, and started the "rock revolution." Suddenly, a lot of people started playing instruments and forming rock bands, but the drum that became associated with rock was Ludwig, largely because that's what Ringo Starr played. When jazz had become the dominant musical style in the '50s, Gretsch was right there. But when tastes changed suddenly in the '60s, Gretsch quite simply did not keep up with the times. Duke Kramer agrees: "We were always a jazz-oriented company, and when the rock thing came along, we really missed it. Yet, in the long run, not counting all of the dollars we could have made, it was probably the best thing to do, because during that time we developed the wood-finished drums, while everybody else stayed with the plastic and pearl finishes. When drummers eventually started going to wood finishes, Gretsch had a position of dominance."

In 1967, Phil Grant and Duke Kramer made their annual trip to the Frankfurt Music Fair in Germany. When they returned, Fred Gretsch, Jr., met them at the airport and invited them out for dinner. While they were eating, he informed them that he had sold the Gretsch company to Baldwin, who manufactured pianos and organs. The announcement came as a total surprise to both of them. Duke Kramer explained: "Fred was very excited about it because he was 60 years old and didn't have a son to leave the business to, so he wanted to sell it, which was probably a smart thing for him to do. So Baldwin bought it, Fred was put on the board of directors of the Baldwin company, and Phil and I [who were both vice presidents of Gretsch by this time] were given long-term contracts, which Fred saw to. Then it was a matter of trying to fit into a corporate scene, after coming from a small, family-held company."

And what did Baldwin want with Gretsch? Like everyone else, Baldwin wanted to cash in on the music craze that had been going on since 1964. Their intention was to get into a full line of band instruments, so they began buying other companies. They bought such names as Burns guitars (from England) which were renamed Baldwin guitars; they bought Ode banjos; they bought Sho-Bud pedal steel guitars; they had a line of band instruments under the name Baldwin. But despite all of these things, they still were not getting their combo division off the ground. Buying Gretsch gave them a successful line of drums (and guitars) and an already established merchandising operation.

As Kramer recalls, "The first thing they wanted to do was to close the New York factory, which was probably a good thing because we had outgrown it terribly." The factory operation was moved to Booneville, Arkansas, and despite all of the good reasons for making that move, there was also the negative side, which Phil Grant remembers with sadness. "They moved all of the machinery out, and they took the plant manager, but what they forgot to take with them was the knowledge of the people who had been making Gretsch drums. Some of those people had been there for years, and we had to tell them they didn't have a job anymore. Baldwin offered them severance pay, but they didn't want pay; they wanted their jobs." Baldwin eventually closed the New York sales office altogether, and moved it to Chicago. A couple of years later, the Chicago office was closed too, and everything was moved to Baldwin's main office in Cincinnati, Ohio. In the midst of all these moves, there were two major fires at the Booneville factory (in '72 and '73) which resulted in major setbacks for the company.

Phil Grant never made any of those moves. When the New York office was closed, Phil decided that he'd had enough, and moved to Vermont. Upon his departure, a lot of drummers felt that they had lost their best friend, and several years later it was common to hear them say, "Gretsch was never the same after Phil left."

The people at Baldwin had good intentions, though, and wanted Gretsch to be a success, but there are certain things inherent in a corporate structure which are not always in the best interests of the product itself. Perhaps the biggest single problem during the Baldwin years was that no one actually had the title of president of Gretsch. Duke Kramer was still an official in the company, but as he recalled, "I went through so many titles that I can't remember them all." A lot of different people had the authority to make decisions in different areas, and some of those decisions were based on the piano & organ business, rather than the band instrument business, which involves a different set of criteria. One very visible indication of this situation was the fact that, between 1979 and 1981, the logo badge on the drums changed four times. It was not uncommon for a single drumset to be made up of drums with two different logos, and you can see three different ones on the back of the '81 catalog.

Baldwin sincerely wanted Gretsch to be

big, so they were looking for things to add to the company. They decided that a major amplifier line would complement the Gretsch guitars, so in 1979 they purchased the Kustom amplifier company and merged it with Gretsch, forming the Kustom/Gretsch company. Along with the amplifiers, the company had some real estate in Chanute, Kansas, which became the headquarters for Kustom/Gretsch. Kustom also had Charlie Roy, who was put in charge of Gretsch.

Roy described what shape Gretsch was in when he became involved in '79. "The drums were the mainstay of the company, but there were a lot of problems with them. The hardware had not been changed for years. There hadn't even been a new catalog for seven years. The average delivery time was six months. There was a problem with the colors; we might have five different shades of a single color. There were other business problems that had nothing to do with the quality of the drums themselves. There were a lot of things that needed to be straightened out. We had to organize the company from a business standpoint and try to create some semblance of order. We also needed to get the quality of the product up to what it was supposed to be."

Charlie Roy was doing everything he could to improve the drums—such as junking a lot of old hardware—and finally, during a meeting at which the quality was being discussed, the Baldwin people asked Roy if he would like to buy Kustom/Gretsch. His answer was, "Yes, I would."

Roy officially bought Gretsch in the spring of 1982, and moved the corporate offices to Gallatin, Tennessee, which is just outside of Nashville. A year before that, the factory operation had been moved from Booneville to DeQueen, Arkansas. In 15 years, Gretsch had gone full circle from private ownership, to being part of a corporation, back to private ownership. And for the first time in 15 years, Gretsch had an actual president.

It's easy to look back at all of the problems of the Baldwin years, and wonder why a small company would ever want to be part of a large corporation, but there are a few reasons, which Charlie Roy explained. "In order to keep up with improvements and changes in the industry, a drum company must have a lot of tooling, which is very expensive. You could open an amplifier company tomorrow with parts from Radio Shack, but you couldn't open a drum company because of the amount of equipment involved. So one of the advantages of being with a large corporation is that they can give you the necessary backing to purchase equipment. Also, from a business standpoint, they can often provide better distribution, and can offer financing for the dealers. Plus, you can benefit from other people in the corporation who have business experience.

"The advantage of private ownership is that if you see something that needs to be done, you do it. You don't have to wait a month for somebody to check it with 15 other departments. You *do it*. That's a terrific advantage, because it helps you bend to the marketplace quickly. Also, if we were part of a large corporation, and the drum business suddenly went under, the corporation would still go on. But with a small company, everyone is directly affected, so that gives us a sense of urgency, and a sense of pride. That's an intangible asset that I value highly."

Over the past two years, Charlie Roy has proceeded to do it, addressing every problem from how the business is run to how the drums are made. And he's very proud of those drums. "The truth is," he states matter-of-factly, "the best drums Gretsch ever made are the ones we are making now. Everyone who works at the factory is proud of the product, and we are constantly walking through and talking to them, asking, 'What can we do to make this product better?' We also get feedback from our artists; in fact, if we don't get feedback from someone, then there's little reason for that person to be with us. The reason we hired Karl Dustman was so that we would have someone totally dedicated to working with the artists—someone who would always be here if they called in with a question or a comment, although they are also free to call in and talk to me, or to anybody here for that matter. I think the way for a company to stay on top is through the artists, because they set the trends. One of the reasons I wanted the office near Nashville is because that gives us access to a lot of artists. We all catch a lot of acts, and spend time talking to the drummers. New York or L.A. can be so hectic that the drummers don't always have time to sit down and talk, but this is out of the way enough that often they're looking for someone to talk to."

Despite the various improvements that are being made, Gretsch is determined to maintain the tradition of the company. As Charlie Roy explained, "We don't improve things to the point that they end up like the ancient cathedral which is renovated to the point that it loses its warmth and becomes a monument to modern architecture. We like to improve things that aid the function of the drums, without interfering with the sound, because if there's anything Gretsch is known for, it's 'That Great Gretsch Sound.' We'll never change that."

A Visit To The Gretsch Factory

It's funny how things can change. Not too many years ago, products that were made in America were considered to be the absolute best, while "Made in Japan" was considered a joke. And yet, today, many people seem to hold the opposite view. For all of the reasons given as to why American products have lost their former position, the reason that seems to be quoted the most often is that the American workers have lost their personal pride in the products they produce. That's probably true in some cases, but it's not true everywhere, as a visit to the Gretsch factory will attest.

DeQueen, Arkansas, is made up of a variety of industries, ranging from rubber, to paper, to a major chicken-processing plant. Because of all this industry, the labor market is strong. And Gretsch, because of the nature of its product, attracts the best. As plant manager Ben Johnson explained, "Our people are very proud of the product, and we have 500 applications on file of people who want to work here. We have no trouble getting the best of the crop when we want it. This is the finest labor market I've come across in a long time." As our tour of the factory progressed, the pride and skill of the workers was very much in evidence, and I was reminded of a comment Charlie Roy had made: "You'll be able to judge my commitment to quality control when you meet the people who actually build the drums. All I can do is let them hear my thoughts. They are the ones who have to emulate those thoughts."

We began our tour of the factory at the loading dock, which, of course, is actually the final step in the total process. But the very beginning of the process is reflected here also, in the form of a label that is attached to each box.

"This is our control tag," Ben explained. "It carries the model number and color, the serial number, the order number, and the customer's name. The drum is tagged once it comes out of finishing, and the tag stays right with it all the way to the customer. That's how we control our orders, so we can find out where a customer's drum is in the process and come fairly close to delivery dates. We have three loading docks, and every order is rechecked prior to shipping."

I asked Ben how much time elapsed between the time the tag was written, and the box appeared on the loading dock. "Normally we complete the entire manufacturing process in about four weeks. With the equipment we have and with the way the layout is now, I don't feel we have any capacity problem here—none whatsoever."

The next stop was the machine shop, where Gretsch has the facilities to develop their own fixtures, patterns, and hardware, as well as research and development of prototyes. "We can do everything but make castings," Ben boasted. "And I have the talented people to do it—pattern makers, machinists. So we feel we have a lot of

The Gretsch main office in Gallatin, Tennessee.

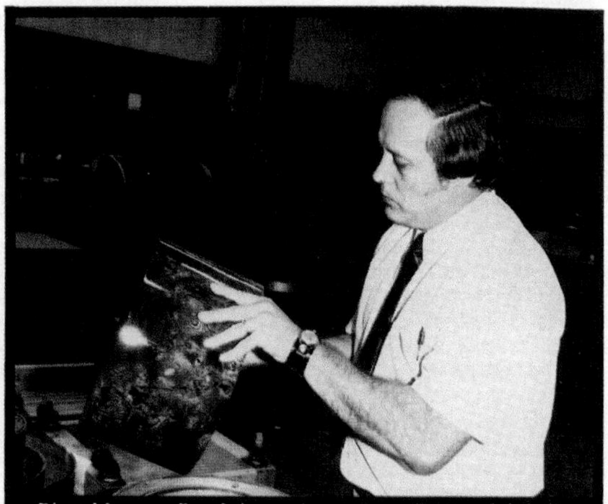

Plant Manager Ben Johnson inspecting a Centennial shell.

The round badge, which was used until 1971.

The octagon-shape badge was first used in 1971.

Around 1979, the wording on the badge was changed slightly.

In 1980, due to the popularity of multiple-tom outfits, the badge was changed to a squarer shape, which would look the same no matter which way a tom was mounted.

(left to right) National Sales Manager Wayne Summers, International Sales Manager Randy Houck, Operations Manager Walt Jordan, President Charlie Roy, and Marketing Manager Karl Dustman.

flexibility."

Passing into the woodworking shop, the first thing we encountered was a huge stack of raw drumshells. These shells are manufactured at a separate facility, which Gretsch was reluctant to have photographed, as the shells are, after all, the core of the Gretsch sound. The people at Gretsch are no more willing to talk about the exact process by which their shells are made than the people at Zildjian are willing to reveal how they blend their metals. But this much can be said: The shells are still being made by the same process and people that have been used since Gretsch changed from the three-ply to the six-ply shell. And the shells are *definitely* made in America.

The shells are manufactured in 13 different diameters, and, except for large bass drums, a number of drums are cut from a single shell. A 14" diameter shell which is 32" long could produce two 14 × 14 floor toms, or up to six 5 × 14 snare drums. The cuts are planned carefully, to avoid waste.

The shells are divided according to the visual beauty of the grain. The better looking shells are used for the natural-wood lacquer finishes; the shells of poorer visual quality are used for the drums with pearl finishes. Gretsch emphasized that this is *only* a visual separation, based on the grain pattern. Coverings are not used to hide defects in the wood. If a structural defect turns up, the shell is destroyed.

In early '81, a redesigned octagon appeared.

By late '81, the square badge had returned, and is still being used today.

This is the special Centennial badge, which only appears on 100 drumsets. Each badge was numbered and personally signed by Gretsch president Charlie Roy.

After being cut, the shell is given a rough sanding on a belt sander. This removes any glue that may be on the outside of the shell from the manufacturing stage. It also opens up any cracks. Gretsch wants to find defects as soon as possible, so that time is not wasted on a shell which will not be used.

After being belt sanded, the shell is placed on a turntable which trues the rim. This compensates for the tendency of a saw not to end up in exactly the same place it started.

After truing, the shell is put on a special machine that cuts the bearing edge, which is so critical to the tuning of a drum. "We shape our bevels on a single-spindle shaper," Ben explained. "The bevel is not controlled by the employee; it's controlled by the configuration of the cutting tool. We purchase the cutting tools to meet our exacting specifications. What we're doing is getting the head of the drum to tune on the outer ply. That's really the only surface that the head comes in contact with." Both ends of the shell are beveled, making it possible for any shell to become either a single- or double-headed drum.

As we watched shells being cut, trued, beveled and sanded, Ben commented on the touch of the worker. "In woodworking and in musical instruments, there's a lot of feel. If you watch Merle closely while he performs these operations, you'll see that he's not really looking. He's feeling it. That's really what it's all about."

The final sanding is done by hand, with the shell spinning on a turntable. This is the last step before the shell is either finished or covered. This step is especially important for those shells which will be given a natural-wood finish, because, as Ben explained, "There's a fallacy that the finish will hide and cover everything. The truth is, the finish will highlight every mistake we make. If the drum is not properly prepared, we're going to have a product of inferior quality at the end of the line. That's all there is to it. So the woodworking is critical.

"Everybody makes such a big deal out of sanding, and they go out and get digital readout computers to analyze how much sanding should be done. The real trick is the detailed attention that the employee pays to it. Merle can tell how much he's going to have to sand it by the grain structure."

Ben re-emphasized the importance of catching defects early. "Everybody in the system is looking for the defect. We want to stop it before we have all our money in it. We normally don't have a high scrap rate. That's the whole name of the game and everybody in this building is an inspector. That's a part of everyone's job. All employees inspect their own work, as well as the work of whoever is feeding them, and if they see a flaw anywhere on the line as they're walking by, they'll point it out."

After the sanding is completed, the shells are loaded onto a dolly, and taken either to the covering area or the finishing area. We stopped first at the covering area and watched a bass drum shell receiving a pearl covering. "This is a straightforward, simple operation," Ben commented. "I'm sure that everybody does it about the same. Both the shell and the covering material are coated with contact adhesive and allowed to dry. I know that some companies use double-face tape, but we have not found that to be adequate. We start it by hand on the top just enough to hold it, and we put it through the pinch roller."

After the covering has been applied by machine, the overlap on the ends of the shell is trimmed by hand.

To get from the woodworking shop to the finishing department, we walked down a long corridor and through a heavy door, which is always kept closed. Ben explained the reasons for the separation of these departments. "If you're going to have a class finish, you're going to have to keep the dirt out of it, and the woodworking generates a lot of dust. That's why we've isolated the dust and dirt of woodworking. It adds clarity to our finishing. The booths are cleaned and the floors are mopped daily."

The finishing area seemed warmer than the area we had just left, and I commented on that. Ben replied, "We have to control humidity in this room. Right now the humidity is a little high, so we're forcing heat in here. If it's 85° outside and the humidity is too high, we still force heat in here to drive the humidity out. Likewise, we have a static problem in finishing if the humidity gets too low. So at that point we pump moisture back in. We like to maintain about 42% humidity in here. There are days when we can't do that. Mother Nature just does not cooperate at all and equipment can't overcome it. We will not sacrifice the quality of our production just to keep the line going. Therefore, it is possible that we may have to shut down the finishing area completely for a day or two."

The first step in the finishing process is the application of a wash coat, which is merely a colored tint. As Ben explained, "This will show up defects that we have not been able to see in sanding. If there's any glue there, it will jump right out. If there are any cracks, they will show up. We can either block sand them by hand to get the glue off or send them back to woodworking to be started all over again."

After being wash coated, the shells are stained. Depending on the grain structure, a shell may be given from one to three coats of stain. Ben described the process: "In staining, it's a real talent to be able to blend these colors and make them match the control chip. We have to know when to stop. Otherwise we're into a rework situation. We let the coating dry and then recheck it. If it's just a shade light, we put on another coat to make it darker. If it happened to be too dark, we would wash it back with alcohol."

Throughout these operations, the skill of the workers was evident, and Ben commented again on their touch. "In our staining operation, our people can actually tell which one of the woodworking operators finished the shell by the feel of the wood and the way it takes stains. The quality isn't different; it just has a different feel.

"Our next operation is sealing. We wash coat; we stain; we seal. That's it on the first day. Then we shoot one coat of lacquer per day. We sand the second coat, put two more coats on, sand the fourth coat, and then apply the final two coats. It takes seven days to put lacquers on because we allow two days' drying after the sixth coat before we go to buffing. That allows the solvents to get out. Most companies are laying two coats a day. We're putting on one coat, letting the solvents dissipate, and it reduces the shrink. Lacquer will shrink into grain. Sometimes, as on guitars, you can see where the lacquer has shrunk into the grain, and it looks like it's checked. That's what we're trying to eliminate."

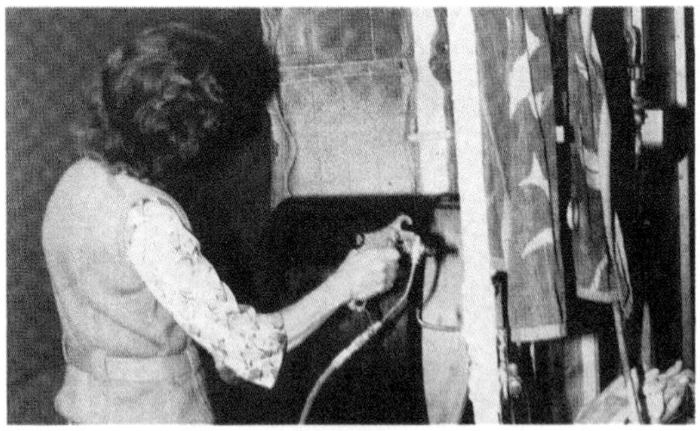

After the final coat of lacquer has been allowed to dry for two days, the shell is wet sanded. "We use just soap and sandpaper for this process of removing the lacquer buildup."

The next step is the application of the "magic coating"—the silver-colored sealer on the inside of every Gretsch shell. Again, this process is important to the Gretsch sound, so the company was reluctant to discuss the chemical structure of the sealer, or to have the application process photographed. However, I witnessed the process and can verify that the coating is *not* used to cover up inferior wood. Scratch it away and you'll find high-quality maple. I questioned Ben about the reason for putting anything on the inside of a drumshell. "It seals the wood. In finishing, if you only finish one side of the wood, the wood is not stabilized. Moisture will affect the other side and work one side of the surface against the other. You want a protective covering so that the moistures are not attacking the interior. As far as the specific covering that we use, all I can say is that it's 'That Great Gretsch Sound.' The sealant that we use gives more of a resonator effect to the shell, so that the shell carries the vibration of sound without absorbing it."

The next step is to buff the shell. Ben explained why the wet sanding which was done after the lacquering operation is important. "That makes it easier on the buffer, because the buffing wheel generates so much heat that you can scorch lacquer. We could go directly from the final lacquer to the buffing wheel, but it heats up the lacquer so much that we would have a lot of rejects. So we put that extra sanding in to cut down on the buffing time.

"We have a wet wheel and a dry wheel. The wet wheel has an abrasive, and that takes the wet sanding even further to smooth out the lacquer. Then it's washed off with naptha and goes to the dry wheel. There's no compound at all. You can actually see the lacquer moving and you have to know when you're applying too much pressure so you don't scorch or cut through it. Here again, it's the craftsman's feel that makes it controllable. I have not found a machine that could do it without someone directing it.

"What we do better than anybody is wood finishing, because we start it out properly and we finish properly. We're woodworkers and finishing people. We just do it better than anybody. Nobody can touch us without rushing the process. We could put them out a lot faster, but not any better."

The next step is the drilling, and that is where a shell becomes a specific drum, for a specific customer. "We're really a custom shop," Ben commented. "I believe we have 56 different models depending on the combination of heads and hardware. So once a shell hits that drill, it's really identified. There are always some drummers who want a muffler only on the bottom head, some want it on the batter side, some want both, and some don't want one at all. It's just impossible to warehouse them all, so that customer is really getting individual treatment on every order that comes through here.

"The drilling is done with a multiple-spindle head that we set up per model. We can either drill single- or double-headed drums. We've chosen to limit our drilling to one lug station at a time, because that results in better alignment."

At this point, the shell moves down an assembly line. The Gretsch nameplate is installed, lugs are mounted along with whatever holders and mufflers are required, heads and rims are added, the finished drum is inspected, given a thorough cleaning, put into a plastic bag, and then into a carton. From there it's only a few steps away to the loading dock, where our tour began.

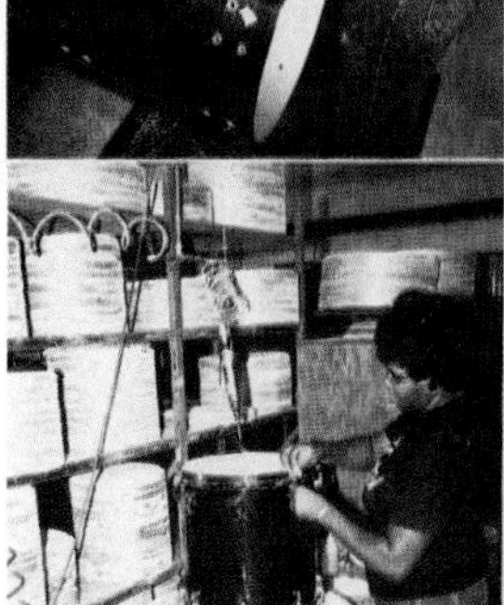

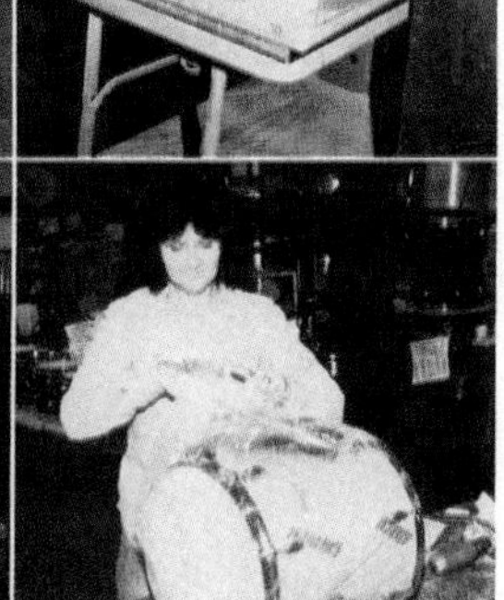

Before leaving, though, we stopped off to see some of the other jobs that are done at the factory. We saw mufflers being made, snare strainers being assembled, and the Gretsch logo being silk-screened onto bass drum heads.

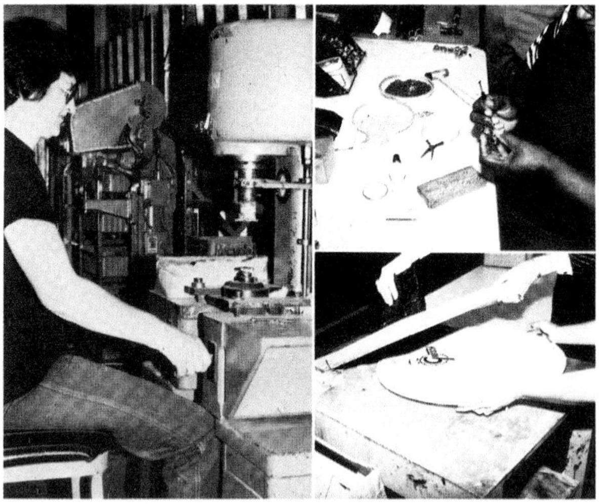

I remember someone once telling me: "Too many companies make drums like furniture. Furniture is made by machines; musical instruments should be made by people." I spent several hours at the Gretsch factory, but I don't really remember the machines. What I do remember are the people, and the obvious respect they have for the drums they are making. We all know how much drummers love their drums. I venture to say that the people who make Gretsch love the drums just as much.

In anticipation of the forthcoming June NAMM convention once again in Chicago, we started looking further at logical drum accessory categories that would complement the current and growing Gretsch product mix. This might be thought of as the early definition of "bundling," having related branded products that could be sold and delivered with the usual Gretsch marketing strategy and could increase brand awareness. We looked at a completely revised and enlarged drum stick line for development. Gretsch was known for making drum sticks and having a diverse assortment of models and designs. Gretsch, however, never really owned lathes to manufacture their own drum sticks. Gretsch sticks had to be made to Gretsch specifications by an existing outside resource drum stick manufacturer. There were certain stick model numbers that were distinctively Gretsch. At this time there were a number of existing and new Gretsch artists who were willing to give the company a signature-stick model to support and enhance the formal endorsement agreement that existed. Gretsch developed Phil Collins, Harvey Mason, and Mark Herndon drum stick models. The artists helped us promote their sticks. With a well-established stick manufacturer we were assured of a quality stick and consistent delivery of every model. The announcement in time for the June 1984 NAMM convention included new stick labeling and packaging. The line sold reasonably well but it would take time to have Gretsch brand drum sticks back into the market, having ignored this product category for many years.

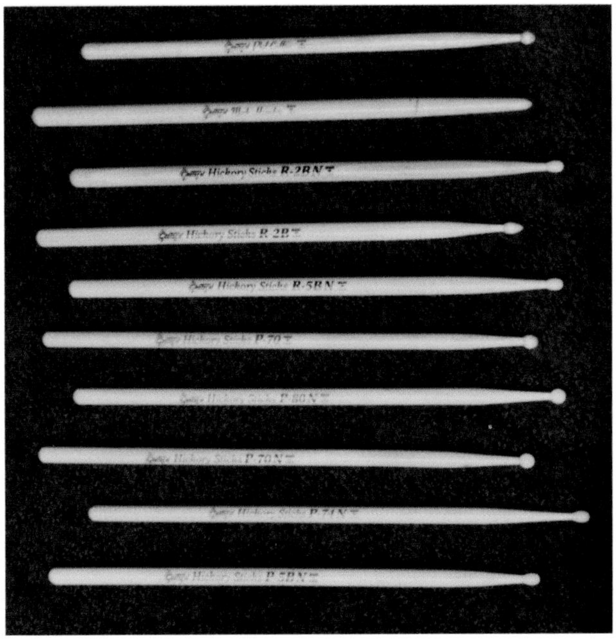

GRETSCH

P. O. Box 1250 • Gallatin, Tennessee 37066 • (615) 452-0083 • TELEX 786571 Gretsch Gatn

GRETSCH INTRODUCES NEW ALL HICKORY DRUM STICKS

Twelve of the most popular sizes and shapes of all-hickory drums sticks is plain and wood tip are now available from Gretsch in three distinct catagories. Each model carries the Gretsch identification, your assurance of precise consistent model selection with every pair.

NEW GRETSCH HICKORY STICK IMPROVEMENT:

Select dense close-grain hickory used.
Sure fitting nylon tips secure to shank with special adhesive.

Precision finished bead and and butt ends.
Medium lacquered finish provides solid grip of stick when hands become moist.

*Competitive prices/Exceptional dealer incentives.

NEW MODELS & SPECIFICATIONS:

Pro Series:

P-80 wood } 16" X 9/16" diameter
P-80 nylon } small ball bead

P-70 wood } 16-3/8" X 9/16 diameter
P-70 nylon } small ball bead

P-74 wood } 16-1/8" X 9/16" diameter
P-74 nylon } medium olive bead

P-5A wood } 16" X 9/16" diameter
P-5A nylon } medium olive bead

P-5B wood } 15-7/8" X 9/16" diameter
P-5B nylon } medium olive bead

P-2B wood } 16-1/8" X 5/8" diameter
P-2B nylon } medium acorn bead

Royal Series:

R-5A } wood 15-3/4" X 1/2"
R-5A } nylon medium olive bead

R-5B } wood 16" X 9/16"
R-5B } nylon medium acorn bead

R-2B } wood 16" X 5/8"
R-2B } nylon medium acorn bead

Artist Series:

Tony Williams/wood } 16" X 7/8" medium acorn
Tony Williams/nylon } bead

Mark Herndon/wood only - 16 3/8" X 5/8" tipless

Phil Collins/wood } 14 3/4" X 1/2" small ball
Phil Collins/nylon } bead

All wood tip hickory Gretsch sticks..........$ 6.80 per pair
All nylon tip hickory Gretsch sticks.........$ 7.00 per pair
Use suffix "N" after model number for nylon tip selection.

June '84

The June, 1984, NAMM convention allowed me to make certain the appeal of Gretsch to the percussion retailer was solid and professional to entice dealers to place orders and for non-dealers to open Gretsch accounts. I created the first NAMM Music Expo "Show Specials" which Wayne Summers and I worked on together. It included package deals to include UFIP Cymbals and Gretsch brand T-Shirts/Muscle shirts as part of the multiple drum set buy-in. The new drum stick line available in both wood or nylon tip was included with more than competitive discounts beyond any current competitive discount schedule.

The focal point of the NAMM Convention exhibit was a series of new colors that launched at the show. There was "Kool Green" named after the Kool Jazz festivals, Candy Red, and Ice Blue. These were opaque lacquered high gloss finishes that offered bright exciting new colors that would stand out on any stage. Plus, it gave the sales representative something new to speak about with their dealers and we provided color photos of popular set configurations to share with the music and percussion stores while supporting a media press release campaign.

GRETSCH

P. O. Box 1250 • Gallatin, Tennessee 37066 • (615) 452-0083 • TELEX 786571 Gretsch Gatn

August 20, 1984

TO: ALL TRADE JOURNALS
FROM: THE GRETSCH COMPANY
RE: IMMEDIATE PRESS RELEASE

NEW DRUM FINISHES AVAILABLE FROM GRETSCH

Gretsch recently displayed their new finishes; CANDY RED, ICE BLUE, and KOOL GREEN which are being introduced as a simulated "covered shell". These three finishes are solid colors with Gretsch's normal high gloss lacuqer finish, without a wood grain appearance.

The acoustical advantage to these finishes allows the shells to "breathe" and resonate like natural wood finishes, however gives the appearance of a solid color seamless "covered shell".

A metallic effect adds dimension to the brillant Candy Red, while the Ice Blue has a rich "deep" refreshing appearance. Kool Green matches the official color for the 1984 Kool Jazz Festivals, which Gretsch was the official drum supplier for.

A dramatic addition to Gretsch's already brillant offering of drum finishes, the solid color appearance in high gloss lacquer will undoubtedly head the list of popularity for new 84 colors.

Dealers are already taking delivery on all three New colors. Retailers are advised to contact their Gretsch representatives to inspect the New samples and color photography available to present these New colors.

Further details may be obtained by contacting: Gretsch Marketing Services, P.O. Box 1250, Gallatin, Tennessee 37066.

The KOOL GREEN color evolved from a promotional opportunity that I was approached with in having Gretsch provide two complete loaner drum sets for the forthcoming KOOL Jazz Festivals throughout 1984. This was in the era when there were numerous jazz festivals like the Playboy, Newport, Montreal, Nice, France etc. Many of these festivals were tied to brands of alcohol, cigarettes, credit cards or other commercial consumer branded products. With Charlie's approval, I responded to the festival management proposing that Gretsch provide two complete loaner Kool Jazz Festival five-piece drum sets The drum shell finish would be matching KOOL GREEN lacquer high gloss finish that matched the Kool cigarette brand packaging shade of green. Each set was equipped with a custom gold reflective Evans front bass drum head that had matching green lettering "Kool Jazz Festival". It was a great opportunity and every stage within the six major-city venue site would be equipped with a 5-piece Gretsch set in Kool Green. These sets were later sold off to dealers that recognized the special significance of the sets and their widely recognized stage visibility. These were sold as "Kool Jazz Festival" sets.

That success and reality of the free publicity that Gretsch received from this festival production led to similar opportunities like the Pacific Jazz Festival. Festival management was realizing the staging logistical delays and conflicts that were arising when personal drum sets needed to be removed and replaced for every different performing band that was featured on the festival program. Moving equipment and musicians on and off stages was imperative to keeping their festival program running on time and moving forwards. While not every headlining artist's drummer would agree with playing the "stage provided drums", the festival organizers loved having drums already set up so that the drummers could simply walk on stage, make minor height and angle adjustments, and be ready to perform. Gretsch was certainly a name-brand American drum manufacturer that was synonymous with Jazz. Playing a brand new set of Gretsch drums that looked fantastic under the stage lighting seemed to be a success for all concerned.

This Gretsch loaner-stage-set program expanded into the annual National Jazz Educator's Conference. I knew Matt Betton, Executive Director of NAJE quite well through the Ludwig connection and he seemed to support the promotional and educational contributions I sought to bring to the annual Jazz Educators Conferences scheduled around the country. The visibility afforded by these venues created the impression that Gretsch was the brand of choice, while actually it was simply "stacking the deck" by offering free use of these professional five or seven piece Gretsch drum sets. These sets were not given for the event management or promoters to keep, as they were instructed and agreed to retaining all master shipping cartons and Gretsch prepaid return shipping labels were provided. Sometimes we had area dealers that were willing to pick up the sets at the festivals immediately afterwards. Gretsch would give authorized dealeers extremely deep discounts on the used sets along with some extended payment terms to motivate the dealer to purchase and sell-through these "demo sets". This direct relationship building-block with the dealer created huge amounts of good will, and eliminated the concern about the packing and shipping of used products back to the factory. It also avoided the return freight costs for any returned equipment. All of this promotional strategy of course, came from the lessons I learned from Bill Ludwig during the days that he insisted on having Ludwig drums being used at all of the most visible Chicago NAMM convention hotel lounges.

J.C. Combs, the percussion instructor at Wichita State University, was one of the instructors at the percussion symposiums I directed for Ludwig. He followed me to Gretsch, saying, "I see all these Gretsch drums at festivals- Karl, you must be behind this." Now he wanted drums for the Wichita Jazz Festival. I flew out there and met with the festival management and we again stacked the deck, as Gretsch provided six drum sets to be used exclusively for the performance stages during the festival. Some came back afterwards, some got sold, but it was a winning scenario for everyone involved.

As a result of this positive experience once again working with J.C Combs at the University, I began to consider how Gretsch could leverage this momentum by using Charlie's marching orders of "do for Gretsch what you did for Ludwig." I was recognized for the success and development of the many International Percussion Symposiums conducted over my eleven- year tenure with Ludwig, so I approached Charlie about doing a Gretsch Percussion Symposium. I showed him the framework; how the hosting organization pays for fees, the drum company pays for the hotel, food, and transportation, and that there is a mutual co-sponsorship of the entire event, which attracted 400-500 young impressionable drummers. A key was to have a hosting organization like Wichita State University that had the necessary money and vision for wanting this educational outreach and inaugural event at their school. Combs agreed to get approval from his music department chairman to host such an event planned for 1986. The people on the proposed Celebrity Artist-Instructor Roster were Gerry Brown, Roy Burns, Bobby Christian, Phil Collins, Mark Craney, Jeff Hamilton, Graham Lear, and Harvey Mason. An amazing line-up of Gretsch artists sharing their drumming talents.

As 1984 moved forwards, J.C and I continued to put out "market response/interest" feelers by making announcements such as, "Watch for news about the First International Drummer's Workshop, sponsored by Gretsch and Wichita State University, coming soon," as we tried to figure out whether this drum set-based event could become as successful as Ludwig's Total Percussion Symposium had been. All indications were that this could be a spectacularly successful program if Gretsch supported it financially and if an appropriate hosting university like Wichita State university could be enlisted. The marketing expense for Gretsch was going to be in the neighborhood of $15,000, which for Gretsch presented a much higher hurtle than it had been for Ludwig. Charlie saw the vision; to get 500 young drum set students as a captive audience for a week long intensive instruction with internationally known drummers at an event that promised to grow in stature and size over time. Gretsch could pull this off with time, money and cooperation between the university and the company.

Another set of my "Ludwig footprints" that I felt I could follow as we explored opening up other revenue streams was the concept of a beginner's snare drum kit. I remembered becoming brand sensitive and brand loyal as a result of having my first Ludwig beginner's snare drum kit. I convinced Charlie to let me explore, assemble and propose a Gretsch student snare drum kit to determine what might be feasible for entering this market product category.

The Banks Arrive, Charlie Disappears

In about April of 1984 we began to see visitors we did not recognize coming into the Gretsch offices for meetings with Charlie. These well-dressed men were not introduced to any of us, but they looked to us like serious business people, perhaps bankers. I could smell "bean counters". These guys looked like either bankers or corporate leaders, and I knew that this generally spelled trouble. The handwriting on the wall became clearer. Charlie was getting very uncomfortable and very anxious. This unrest spread through the organization. Who were these people? Was Charlie in trouble? Was the company being sold, or taken over? While I did not have access to the company's financial statements, I could sense money issues.

Sales Manager Wayne Summers was Charlie's longtime friend and right-hand man from the original Chanute, Kansas, team and he did not like what he saw either. Neither of us understood what was going on day-to-day. In early May we came to work one day and Charlie was gone. There was no discussion. Charlie was no longer with the company. Baldwin Piano and Organ Company put out a press release saying that they had re-acquired Kustom-Gretsch. Those of us in the management positions were asking ourselves, "What is happening with Charlie Roy and the change in ownership?"

Duke Kramer suddenly appeared in our offices and announced himself as the new General Manager for Kustom-Gretsch and that we would all be reporting to him. I had met Duke Kramer about fifteen years earlier when he was the sales manager for a Chicago-based branch of the Gretsch Company, also then a division of Baldwin. I felt a strong sense of Deja-Vu; it felt very much like it felt at Ludwig when Bob Kane from Selmer arrived. And like Bob Kane had done, Duke Kramer spent hour after hour with me asking detailed questions about our operations; marketing, promotion and each of the employees.

Gretsch Enters Electronic Drum Market

Simmons electronic drums were now in the marketplace and we recognized that this was creating a lot of turmoil and uncertainty about the acoustic drum market. Would electronic drums replace acoustic drums? This had every drum company worried, including Gretsch. We looked at it as a "fight 'em or join 'em" option. Wayne Summers, Charlie Roy and I had chosen to join the fight. Significant time and effort had already been invested in the early part of the year to find a suitable high quality electronic drum kit that could be branded "Blackhawk by Gretsch" and be available for the June NAMM convention product launch.

We sourced from Asia an electronic kit with five pads, a controller, and all the connection cables and related electronics. Blackhawk was a trademark owned by the Gretsch Company and at the time was being used on the imported Asian entry-level five and seven piece acoustic kits, complete with hardware. The new electronic kits were shown at the 1984 NAMM convention in Chicago and the forthcoming PAS convention later in the same year. Simmons immediately jumped on Gretsch about the shape of the pads that Gretsch had chosen to use, claiming that it was infringement of their design patent to have a six-sided pad. By the time we regrouped and decided to go to round-shaped-pads like pretty much everyone else was using, the wind had gone out of the sails and we were questioning whether we really wanted to be in the electronic drum market.

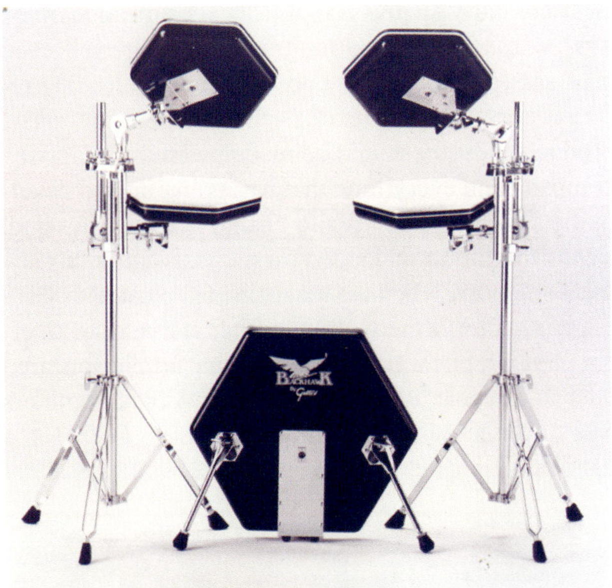

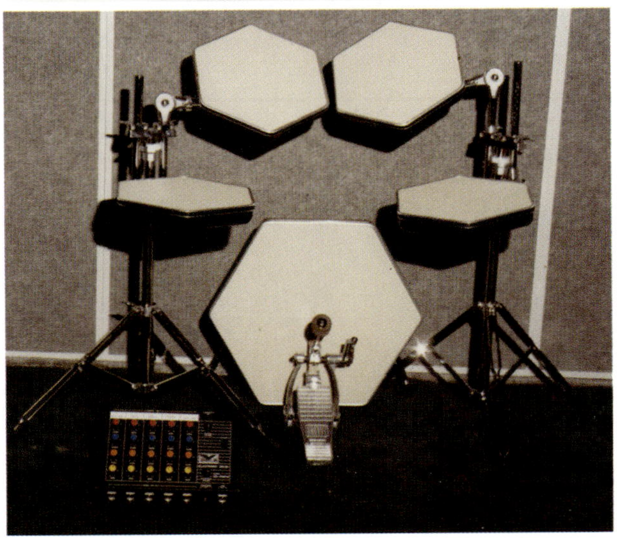

There were some obvious problems with the Asian source and there were some quality problems, By the end of the year it seemed that everyone was getting into this electronic drum market with look-alike, sound-alike, and priced-alike products. Our management consensus was to question why we should bother with this electronic drum product when we should be concentrating on what we did best, which was building American-made high quality acoustic drums in Dequeen, Arkansas. So instead of getting into round pads, we decided to get out. The electronic "Blackhawk by Gretsch" sets were launched at the 1984 June NAMM convention to moderate acceptance. The press releases ran through the remainder of the calendar year.

Shortly after the June NAMM convention, Wayne Summers was next to be removed from the company, a real loss to the company and leadership team. As a result of this unfortunate decision, Duke basically told me that I was going to run Gretsch and that I would be reporting directly to him. He would be coming to Gallatin for a week each month so we could sit down and review how things were going. The Baldwin bean counters continued to come in and visit unannounced. They would simply show up, and clearly were really digging into the financials of the company. It was of course a natural thing for them to be there, but the manner in which they were handling the situation created a lot of uncertainty and apprehension. We had no idea what they were really doing. I had seen all of this before, and I was getting very uncomfortable with what I was seeing and hearing. I got the impression that although the factory personnel knew that Charlie was gone and that Duke was in charge, they were similarly "out of the loop" on what was happening and why. I don't think Duke ever bothered to visit the factory.

Walt Jordan continued with the purchasing responsibility for all the drum-building materials from the Gallatin office and Plant Manager Ben Johnson in Dequeen built the drums and shipped them. Duke was not involved with the Gretsch dealers, the outside or inside sales reps, or with customer service. He was more interested in the credit department, specifically the accounts receivables to track what money was coming in, and what money was supposed to be coming in but was not arriving in a timely manner. Although we were all confused at the time about the situation, in retrospect it made perfect sense. Duke Kramer was sent in to the Gretsch-Gallatin headquarters to do exactly what he was supposed to be doing; positioning the company on paper for the company to be sold-off from Baldwin. While this may have not been discussed or even alluded to, it certainly was becoming obvious to those of us now running the company.

Regardless of the changes in ownership and personnel, the June, 1984, NAMM convention in Chicago was around the corner. We basically did the same exhibit booth arrangement as the prior year for the Centennial celebration. We had a good show, sold a lot of product, hosted lots of artists, had appointments with lots of dealers, and spent a lot of money that the company probably did not have. What I probably remember most from this period of time is that Duke Kramer told all of us in the Gallatin offices that there would not be any changes. However this was being declared as he was terminating Wayne Summers. No one believed Duke, for all the obvious reasons.

I could see that Baldwin's Smith and Harrison did not understand the drum business, and what was even more discouraging, I didn't get the feeling that they wanted to learn anything about the drum business. That gave me nightmares. I would wake with the clear premonition that there was an agenda in place that I was not seeing. With little else to do in terms of solidifying the long-term footing of the business, I worked up a document titled "The Reorganization Of The Gretsch Drum Company". I felt it would be helpful to give the new owners a clear vision of what needed to be done immediately to sustain the company. I made it clear that the Gretsch staff needed to remain in place and we needed to continue to grow and diversify the product line while not burning any bridges simply because Charlie Roy was no longer the figurehead of the company. I presented this document, for which I never received any acknowledgement. It went nowhere.

Duke Kramer continued to come into Gallatin one week per month, and I continued to do everything that I possibly could to keep all of the projects, programs and sales going forward in the face of increasing uncertainty and speculation.

Following the success of the summer NAMM convention I was contacted by Musical Merchandise Review magazine; they wanted to do a story about Gretsch and visit the Gallatin location headquarters. This was a great opportunity to bring Gretsch even greater exposure, as this publication was a leading resource for all music retailers. Everyone in the music products industry would be reading about the Gretsch company and everything that was going on and developing for the future. While change was in the wind, it was my job to make certain the visit and interview went smoothly when the magazine team came to visit. I spent a lot of time with the writer and a lot of internal photographs were taken. The final article appeared later in the year, unfortunately after Wayne Summers was no longer with the company.

Wayne Summers, John Crawford, Karl Dustman, Alan Bechler, Mark Richards

A Memorable Moment:

I already knew of the current Baldwin Piano and Organ owners, who were at this point Harold Smith and Dick Harrison. They wanted a confidential one-on–one meeting with me during the NAMM convention. They explained that Duke was monitoring the situation for them, and basically they wanted me to be the leader of the Gretsch Company for the long term. They said Baldwin had bought the company back (really repossessed it) from Charlie Roy, Baldwin would continue to own Kustom-Gretsch and I would continue to run it. They further explained that once the present ownership transition settled down, Duke Kramer's involvement and appearance in Gallatin would not continue. I didn't buy this. I knew I was being lied to-my-face and it sounded like the same lies I was told from Selmer taking over Ludwig. I didn't have a choice in the matter other than to accept it at face value. I could see through this lie, but did not know the time frame for anything further to develop.

September of 1984 was an attempt at "business as usual" even though things were not as-usual. Charlie Roy was missing and thc future of the company (and all of its people) was in question, yet I needed to portray a leadership of continuous efforts to move Gretsch *forward*.

Charlie had moved Kustom-Gretsch from Kansas to Nashville in 1982 with the intent of owning the Nashville music market for Gretsch drums, Kustom amplifiers, and ShoBud steel guitars. That intent always was and remained a directive that I was working toward. Not being immersed in Country Music before arriving in Nashville or knowing the various leading drummers in the Country Music scene, I needed inside guidance. The internal Gretsch sales staff in Gallatin, were for the most part active players, primarily guitarists. They knew the country music market and they knew who the top drummers in the top bands were who lived in Nashville. It was easy for me to just walk down the hall and ask, "Who do we need to get playing Gretsch Drums in Country Music here in Nashville? Who are the drummers or bands that are household names to drummers and all country musicians?" The inside sales team gave me three "must have" names; Clyde Brooks, (Studio Ace) Jerry Carrigan (John Denver), and Clay Caire with the nationally televised show *Nashville Now.* I went after those three artists and eventually Gretsch signed artist agreements with all of these leading Nashville drummers.

GRETSCH

page 1

P. O. Box 1250 • Gallatin, Tennessee 37066 • (615) 452-0083 • TELEX 786571 Gretsch Gatn

September 6, 1984

MEMO TO: ALL TRADE PUBLICATIONS
FROM: THE GRETSCH COMPANY
SUBJECT: IMMEDIATE PRESS RELEASE

"GRETSCH SECURES LEADING RECORDING ARTIST ENDORSEMENTS IN NASHVILLE"

The Gretsch Company recently announced the addition of two leading percussion recording artist in Nashville, Clyde Brooks, and Jerry Carrigan. According to Gretsch, these two additions to their endorsement roster "secures" Nashville recording activity. Gretsch drums will be utilized on most leading artist and jingle work.

CLYDE BROOKS is considered one of the busiest studio drummers for most of the major Pop and Country acts recording in Nashville. He has also involved himself as a producer in new projects and is gaining additional recognition in "drummers circles" because of his vast array of studio experience and following in all studio markets.

A native of Milwaukee, Wisconsin, Brooks went through the normal local performing opportunities. He continued his avid percussion interest commuting to Chicago for mallet instruction under the late Bob Tilles. Then, on the New York for work with Henry Adler. Now ready for college, he attended Berkley School of Music where he studied under well known instructors Alan Dawson for drum set and Fred Buda, timpani and mallets.

Clyde has extensive experience in all phases of recording, including radio and TV commercials. He has performed over 2,000 commercials for most major market and regional advertisers, such as Kraft, McDonalds, Toyota, Mattel, Kelloggs, and many more. However, this does not begin to unveil his talents as an artist.

His list of recording performances would include such performers as Barbara Mandrell, Dolly Parton, Loretta Lynn, Kenny Rogers, Conway Twitty, and The Oak Ridge Boys only to name a few. His talent is not only in a studio, but also on television. Brooks has shown his great ability as a drummer on such shows as Dolly Parton Show, Tonight Show, Pop Goes the Country, Nashville Music, and Nashville Network Shows.

Brooks articles have appeared in past issues of Percussive Notes Magazine of the Percussive Arts Society and will be a contributor to Gretsch's Educational "Drummers Aid Pack" scheduled for release in 1985.

JERRY CARRIGAN is often refered to as "the drummer most in demand" by Nashville producers. From sound tracks, radio, jingles, or top hit recording artists, you have heard the "Carrigan Sound."

A native of Florence, Alabama, Carrigan's first recording session was at age thirteen. Since then, the recording studio has been his "home" except for the occational tours that he travels with John Denver. Carrigan was immersed in the early R & B movement from the very beginning. This lead to the musical explosion for country music and the growth of Nashville into the nation's major recording center during the seventies. He played on hits for some of the biggest country stars of that era; Charlie Rich, Tammy Wynette, Johnny Paycheck, Elvis Presley, and Johnny Cash.

As musical styles and popularity changed, so did Carrigan to continue his "dominance" in Nashville with more contemporary sounds of Waylon Jennings, Willie Nelson, Dolly Parton, Jerry Reed, and Kenny Rogers. By 1977, he was playing approximately twelve three-hour sessions per week. Billboards top 100 country single and album charts could be matched to Carrigan's contribution, and therefore being on 15% of those hits every week.

An innovator of sound, Jerry Carrigan is largely responsible for establishing the "big fat drum sound" associated with Nashville recordings, and was the first to bring single headed concert toms to the Nashville studio.

His present association with John Denver since 1981 has made a complete mixture of musical enviornment. Traveling with Denver about eighteen weeks a year allows for intense concentration on the studio in Nashville. He avoids being a "distant drummer" as he defines many studio players try to do it all; videos, jingles, tours, records, and TV. Thus, not building consistancy in sound or artist association.

As Carrigan expands his already impressive four page listing of recording credits, his ambitions include educational clinic work as well. With his concentration on SOUND, Jerry prides himself with his experimenting for different unique sounds to add in a conventional recording situation.

Complete details on Clyde Brooks or Jerry Carrigan clinic availability can be obtained by contacting Gretsch Marketing Services, P.O. Box 1250 Gallatin, Tennessee 37066. (615) 452-0083.

Jerry Carrigan

Clyde Brooks

Fall, 1984

Duke recognized that the next big event on the Gretsch calendar was the annual Percussive Arts Society conference. The event was set to take place at the University of Michigan School of Music building in Ann Arbor, Michigan. Duke instructed me to do whatever I needed to do in order to continue to build the Gretsch image within the industry. He wanted Gretsch to be perceived as the leader, the emerging giant of the drum industry. He said Baldwin would allocate the money necessary to achieve what needed to be done. He said, "Make it big, Karl!"

I booked a huge exhibit booth space for Gretsch, I arranged to have high visibility artists at the event, and I purchased full-page ads in the official conference program book. I made sure that Gretsch was involved in all kinds of activities at the PAS conference event. I spent a lot of money implementing the "Make it Big" directive. Although we had an excellent convention, I was becoming even more nervous about the future of the company.

When I got back to the Gallatin office, Duke told me that Fred Gretsch wanted me to come to Savannah (actually Ridgeland, South Carolina) to see the operations of Fred Gretsch Enterprises and discuss moving to South Carolina to run the Gretsch Drum Company. During the first week of December, I flew to Savannah and Fred picked me up at the airport. Fred and his wife Dinah were very gracious in welcoming me to the area and their beautiful home which was all decorated for the Christmas holiday. I toured his huge warehouse

A Memorable Moment:

During the PAS convention, I received a hand-delivered message at the booth (this was of course long before cell phones) that I was to telephone Duke Kramer immediately in the Gallatin office. I had a district sales manager working the booth with me who could watch the exhibit, so I excused myself and made my way to a pay phone booth. I called Duke, who promptly informed me that the Gretsch Drum part the existing company had been sold to Fred Gretsch. Fred Gretsch will take ownership of the entire Gallatin operation on January 1, 1985, and that Fred planned to close the entire Gallatin operation. Everyone there would be eliminated eventually except for me. Duke said that I needed to know this information right away because the deal had already been signed between Baldwin and Fred Gretsch. WOW,…now I had to fight off the shock of that phone call as I returned to the exhibit booth and tried to conduct business for the Gretsch Drum Company while not letting anyone else know what I had just learned about the future of the company.

that served as his company headquarters. I quickly realized that there would not be any problem fitting all operations of Gretsch Drum manufacturing and warehousing within this existing facility.

We had various meetings, targeted discussions, and a wonderful dinner in Savannah with Fred and his wife. He also made a company vehicle available for me to tour the Ridgeland and Beaufort area on my own. By the end of the three day period Fred conveyed that both he and Dinah hoped I would consider moving there for the long term and taking on the leadership of the Gretsch Drum Division within Fred Gretsch Enterprises.

I thoroughly enjoyed my visit, but had to consider all elements that the relocation would entail. I soon learned that the cost-of- living in what was basically the surrounding areas of Hilton Head, SC, would be at least 30% higher than in Gallatin, Tennessee. I could see that it was very unlikely that I would be able to duplicate the beautiful home that I had in Tennessee if I moved to the Ridgeland, SC, area. At the conclusion of the South Carolina visit, Fred and I agreed to both consider all the elements of this employment relationship and he asked me to work up a written proposal as to what I would need in terms of moving accommodations, compensation, job description and related issues and concerns in order to make the move to Ridgeland. I promptly created a realistic written proposal that addressed and included all the basic elements of going through another family move only twenty months after arriving in Gallatin. In the end, Fred and I were not able to come to a mutually acceptable agreement and I prepared to turn in my company-office keys on December 31, 1984 as the ownership of the company transferred to Fred W. Gretsch. I also prepared letters-of-advisement to all contacts in the percussion community, the Gretsch Sales Representatives, and those potential Gretsch Endorsement individuals that were "in-process" at the end of the year before my departure.

Duke Kramer remained in Gallatin on January 1st and took care of letting the Gallatin staff know that their positions were being terminated. Shortly after the first of the year, all employees were released from the company and the complete contents of the Gallatin offices were auctioned in the parking lot on January 24th, 1985. This included Kustom Amplifiers, Gretsch guitars, miscellaneous banjos, violins, and any other musical instrument samples that were stored in the Gallatin office.

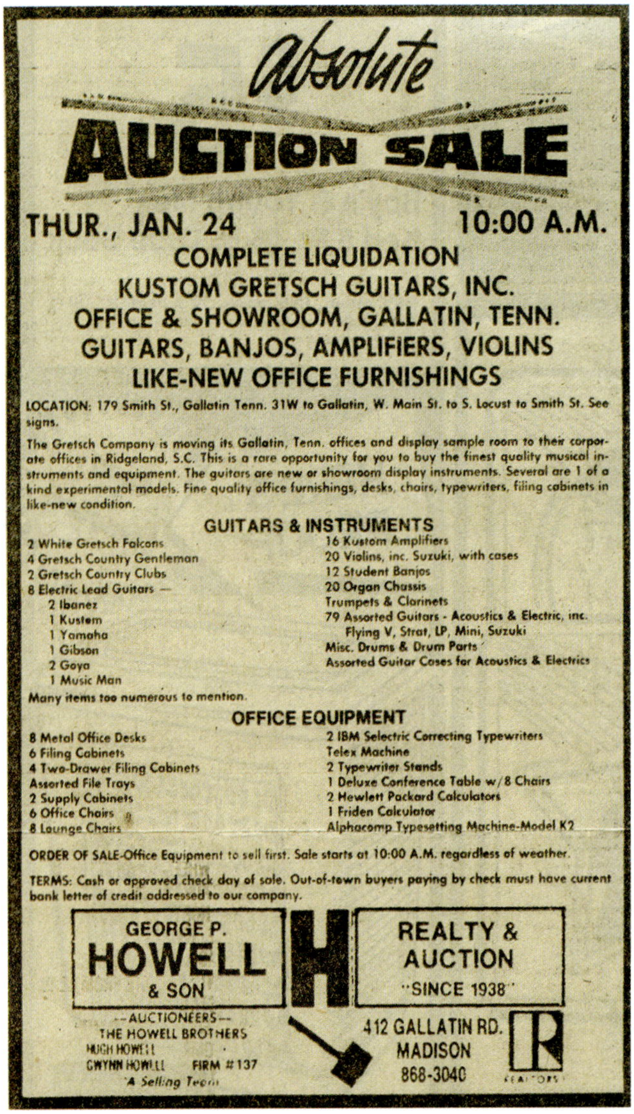
Absolute
AUCTION SALE
THUR., JAN. 24 10:00 A.M.
COMPLETE LIQUIDATION
KUSTOM GRETSCH GUITARS, INC.
OFFICE & SHOWROOM, GALLATIN, TENN.
GUITARS, BANJOS, AMPLIFIERS, VIOLINS
LIKE-NEW OFFICE FURNISHINGS

LOCATION: 179 Smith St., Gallatin Tenn. 31W to Gallatin, W. Main St. to S. Locust to Smith St. See signs.

The Gretsch Company is moving its Gallatin, Tenn. offices and display sample room to their corporate offices in Ridgeland, S.C. This is a rare opportunity for you to buy the finest quality musical instruments and equipment. The guitars are new or showroom display instruments. Several are 1 of a kind experimental models. Fine quality office furnishings, desks, chairs, typewriters, filing cabinets in like-new condition.

GUITARS & INSTRUMENTS
2 White Gretsch Falcons
4 Gretsch Country Gentleman
2 Gretsch Country Clubs
8 Electric Lead Guitars —
2 Ibanez
1 Kustem
1 Yamaha
1 Gibson
2 Goya
1 Music Man
16 Kustom Amplifiers
20 Violins, inc. Suzuki, with cases
12 Student Banjos
20 Organ Chassis
Trumpets & Clarinets
79 Assorted Guitars - Acoustics & Electric, inc. Flying V, Strat, LP, Mini, Suzuki
Misc. Drums & Drum Parts
Assorted Guitar Cases for Acoustics & Electrics
Many items too numerous to mention.

OFFICE EQUIPMENT
8 Metal Office Desks
6 Filing Cabinets
4 Two-Drawer Filing Cabinets
Assorted File Trays
2 Supply Cabinets
6 Office Chairs
8 Lounge Chairs
2 IBM Selectric Correcting Typewriters
Telex Machine
2 Typewriter Stands
1 Deluxe Conference Table w/8 Chairs
2 Hewlett Packard Calculators
1 Friden Calculator
Alphacomp Typesetting Machine-Model K2

ORDER OF SALE-Office Equipment to sell first. Sale starts at 10:00 A.M. regardless of weather.

TERMS: Cash or approved check day of sale. Out-of-town buyers paying by check must have current bank letter of credit addressed to our company.

GEORGE P. HOWELL & SON
REALTY & AUCTION "SINCE 1938"
--AUCTIONEERS--
THE HOWELL BROTHERS
HUGH HOWELL
GWYNN HOWELL FIRM #137
"A Selling Team"
412 GALLATIN RD.
MADISON
868-3040

Gretsch headquarters
179 Smith, Gallatin, Tennessee

Immediately after the end of the employment relationship I started seeking contact with Baldwin concerning the money I was still owed. I'd had some concerns about this matter long before the end of the year. I was surprised to find that Baldwin was reluctant to settle up with me when it came to the compensation that I was owed per my employment contract with them. I still had a bonus coming, as well as unused sick days and vacation days. As we got into January, no one had made it clear to me whether it would be Baldwin or the new owner Fred Gretsch who would be legally responsible for this settlement. I could understand Baldwin's reluctance to pay for the debts of a company they no longer owned, but I could also understand why Fred Gretsch Enterprises would be reluctant to assume responsibility for the obligations of the previous owners.

In the end, I employed my family lawyer in Chicago to get involved in getting this matter professionally resolved and obtaining a full scale settlement for *all* the money I was owed. Fortunately, I kept excellent company records on Gretsch sales, profits, all the details of the company buy-out from Baldwin, and related information. This was all extremely helpful by my attorney and used in calculating and *receiving* the final employment bonus I had earned and was entitled to.

IN RETROSPECT

It was disappointing to have gone through all the time and effort to make such progress in bringing Gretsch drums to a level of professional respect, awareness, and market growth- only to have another American drum company sold to an uncertain future. I learned a great deal through this experience, I received many compliments on the progress that Gretsch had achieved.

Drummers at all levels around the world recognized what Gretsch was doing as an American drum company. This was because of the efforts of a dedicated team of professionals that worked for Gretsch, the retail music dealers, and Gretsch artists,

I knew I could grow professionally through this twenty-month relationship, despite the hardship and uncertainty of the future.

As time and the future of Gretsch marched forward, it became clear what was ahead and in store for all those Gretsch dealers, artists and dedicated drummers. What bothers me most to this day is the blatant efforts to completely erase, destroy, and ignore the 1982 through 1985 period of time in the history of Gretsch drums. This time period, spearheaded by the visionary leadership of Charlie Roy, created unprecedented Gretsch global market presence, leadership and prestige in the brand and product. This product and marketing leadership has not been matched or surpassed by anyone since the end of 1984.

I mention this not to spotlight what time or talent I may have brought to the company, but to unequivocally challenge anyone who feels differently. Anyone who truly knows Gretsch drums knows that the best drums, the most innovative marketing, the greatest new product development and brand awareness, all came during the time Gretsch was headquartered in Gallatin, Tennessee.

THE GALLATIN "CODA" for 1985-
Helping a friend in need

January of 1985 brought a southern winter and time on my hands, trying to figure out, *what next?*

The 1983 Gretsch catalog poster featured an antique Gretsch drum that was loaned to Gretsch for the cover photography by my long-time friend Tommy Winkler of Nashville. We remained in communication throughout the time I was in Nashville and the news of the Gretsch demise traveled quickly in early 1985.

Near the end of the Gretsch-Gallatin era, Tommy had run into a troublesome situation with his Winkler Drum Company. This was based upon an agreement he had with Hartley Peavey about entering the drum market with Peavey drums that was not going according to plan. The agreement called for Tommy Winkler to exclusively manufacture Peavey branded drum sets in Hendersonville, Tennessee. Tommy had created the factory to make these drums. He bought all the tooling and set up a complete drum manufacturing production line by leveraging every dollar that he had.

I believe the prototype Peavey Drums were shown for the first time at the June, 1984, NAMM convention in Chicago. From what I recall the drums were well-received and orders were taken for standard five and seven piece acoustic drum sets. But now, Hartley Peavey had changed his mind and decided to not enter the drum business at all.

When Tommy first was faced with this situation, he presented his dilemma to us (Gretsch) in Gallatin, suggesting that he use his ready and available drum production facility to manufacture a new and separate line of drums for Gretsch. Gretsch had no interest in having another line of drums built, and was not in need of another manufacturing facility. Unknown to Tommy at that time, the future of the Gretsch Company was already in question and Charlie Roy would soon be gone.

Tommy approached me in January of 1985 hoping that there was some way that I could help him with his worsening dilemma; he was desperately trying to save his manufacturing facility. He explained that the banks were coming after him and they were foreclosing on his home used as collateral. Tommy had a signed purchase order from Peavey for drums, but Peavey was declaring the purchase order null and void.

Tommy had a close relationship with country music star Conway Twitty who had an entertainment theme park in Hendersonville called Twitty City. Twitty had money invested in the Winkler/Peavey plan. I was asked to meet with Tommy and Conway Twitty's business manager Hugh Cardin to discuss ways that we might be able to salvage the agreement between Tommy Winkler and Peavey. Conway Twitty was an endorser of Peavey amplifiers and knew Hartley Peavey personally.

It was decided that we all (Tommy Winkler, Conway Twitty, Hugh Cardin and myself) would meet with Hartley in an attempt to work this out. We boarded Conway Twitty's personal Lear jet and flew to Meridian, Mississippi, where the Peavey headquarters are located. We met with Hartley Peavey who picked us up at the airport. We went right to Peavey headquarters and met in the company conference room. Hartley remained adamant that he did not want to move forward with the drum project at that time. He clearly felt no obligation or commitment, no financial or legal responsibility to Tommy or the Winkler Drum Company. While the drums had been test-marketed at the most recent NAMM show in June of 1984, Hartley Peavey wanted out. The drums had reportedly met with great success at the product launch and dealers placed orders for the drums and hardware with Peavey. Despite Conway Twitty's leveraging his friendship with Peavey to help re-unite the business agreement and relationship, Peavey stood firm that he had simply decided not to go forward at that time. If I recall correctly, Twitty even offered to invest additional funds into the drum company if Hartley Peavey would keep-his word and honor the purchase order to the Winkler Drum Company.

The four of us got back on Twitty's private plane and flew back to Nashville. End of story. It did not appear that there was anything that could be done legally to induce or require Peavey to buy the drums that Tommy was completely prepared to professionally produce. At that point, I believe the bank repossessed everything from the Winkler Drum Company and Tommy personally. Everything began to be auctioned off, the tooling and hardware, the office equipment, the bookshelves, etc. at a large auction site. I attended the auction. That was the end of the Winkler Drum Company.

As 1985 moved forwards, Tommy asked me to help create and assemble a professional business plan in an attempt to help him find outside investors. Unfortunately this did not meet with success.

While the Winkler Drum Company may no longer exist, I still remain friends with Tommy Winkler and respect his talents, skills and abilities in the drum-building business.

Chapter Five Hohner-Sonor-Sabian

Another Transition, Another Move, Another Opportunity?

Anytime you're not thoroughly engaged in working, learning and contributing to a project, time slows and the definition of "in-between" seems like forever. And 1985 was no exception. Watching the complete demise and disassembling of the Gretsch Company was difficult. However what laid ahead was a complete new learning experience and realizing the vast differences between MUSIC WHOLESALE…and MUSIC DISTRIBUTION. At the same time I would learn more about human character, integrity, professionalism and honesty, .than ever before.

The job search strategy once again was to select prominent musical product brands and companies that had a certain long-term standing in the music products industry. While trying to remain in Nashville and avoiding another relocation was a priority, I was also realistic that opportunities do not always come from the first choice regions of the country that we prefer to live and work in.

I prepared and sent a letter of introduction and resume to Horst Mucha, President of Hohner-USA. in Richmond, Virginia. While the company had nothing to do with percussion, my musical abilities and experiences covered a broad spectrum of musical instrument categories. This was a "nothing ventured, nothing gained" approach to getting my name and credentials out to as many qualified people and companies as possible. I was not aware at the time that Hohner was looking to expand and create a separate entity that would become HSS. I wrote the company to both introduce myself as well as inquire about any career opportunities that could be developing in Nashville, or Richmond, Virginia, where Hohner, Inc's headquarters were located. Horst responded personally that he had an interest in speaking to me about how I might fit in with their planned growth. He was going to be in Nashville on other business and wanted to meet at the Marriott Hotel near the Nashville airport. A meeting date and time was established according to his travel plans.

The preliminary meeting and discussion went well with most of the discussion focused around what I had been doing at Ludwig and Gretsch previously. There was not a lot disclosed about Hohner's expansion plans or a separate division or entity being created in the near future. Music wholesale was a completely different entity within the music products industry and I was not sure how I could contribute to the Hohner business model.

HSS (Hohner Sonor Sabian) represented my first experience in working within the wholesale-distribution segment of the music industry. While there were many similarities to my experiences in manufacturing with Ludwig and Gretsch and the retail connection with the Music Center of Deerfield, I found that wholesale is a completely different environment and mentality.

UNDERSTANDING THE BACKGROUND

A note of background about music industry product distribution in the 1980s: there were "new school" and "old school" methods of wholesale. The "old school" method that was in place back in the 1960's and 70's consisted of longtime entities like Midco, Harris-Teller, Coast Wholesale, David Wexler, Targ & Dinner (the new name of what was formerly the 20th Century Music), Jack Westheimer, and Henry Grossman Music. Those were all wholesalers who founded the MDA, the Music Distributor Association.

The marketplace was changing in the mid 1980s. Historically, these wholesalers had been selling a limited amount of recognized branded instrumental accessories and a lot of private-branded low-cost/lower quality products that were made in Asia. The focus of this music wholesaling was not really the marketing and promoting of name-brand internationally recognized products like Sonor Drums made in Germany or Sabian Cymbals made in Canada. The 1980s was seeing a significant change in the business model, making a distinct difference between wholesale and distribution. The old school accessory music wholesalers were being pushed out into obsolescence; many of them were trying to join the emerging mindset and product profile for getting involved in name brand quality product distribution.

Hohner-Germany was seeking a broader and more successful base of distribution for their own manufactured products (primarily harmonicas, accordions, and melodicas) in the USA market. Hohner-Germany was trying to diversify its product offering into private-label Hohner-branded amplifiers, guitars, drum sets and even portable keyboards- none of which were manufactured by Hohner in Germany. The misconception that Hohner can place its name on any product and expect it to sell like hotcakes, was completely wishful thinking. The name Hohner is recognized for Harmonicas, Melodicas and Accordions. Period! This superiority thinking from Hohner-Germany would ultimately lead the demise of Hohner as a significant musical instrument company.

Out of this change emerged two forces that ultimately converged. Hohner-USA owned approximately 40% of the old-school Chicago wholesaler Targ & Dinner, which was losing money. The second force was basically the expansion of Robert Zildjian's operations. In the early 1980s, Bob Zildjian had created Sabian cymbal manufacturing and had also bought out Charles Alden Music, a distribution firm in Massachusetts which was also the long-time United States distributor for Sonor Drums. Bob Zildjian and Charlie Alden were longtime friends and business partners. To my understanding, Charles Alden became terminally ill, prompting Bob Zildjian to buy Alden out completely. The largest product line for Alden at the time was Sonor drums. Another factor that probably played into Bob Zildjian's decision to purchase Alden was to help with the distribution of Sabian product in the United States. (The Sabian factory was located in Canada.)

Probably more to the heart of the matter, Bob Zildjian was looking at the same situation that Hohner Inc. in the U.S. was seeing with Targ & Dinner. Charles Alden Distribution was also losing money by the carload and teetering on going out. Bob bought Alden and pumped in enough money to salvage it. Eventually Bob Zildjian and Horst Mucha got together to discuss the feasibility of a joint venture that would be called Hohner-Sonor-Sabian, HSS, recognizing the premier brands featured by the new entity. Sonor-Germany was the key to the prestige of a new entity, and Hohner-Germany owned somewhere between 40 and 50% of the Sonor company which was founded by the Link family.

Early discussions between Bob Zildjian and Horst Mucha centered on where such a new operation would be located, who would run it, who would be the operational decision makers, and what sales force would be combined or utilized. The question for me was, how could or would I be able to lead this new distribution company?

Targ & Dinner had grown out of the era of the "music jobbers". Music jobbers were individuals who basically sold all kinds of accessories out of their cars. They were self-employed individuals who simply

Horst Mucha

Robert Zildjian

drove their cars or vans around to the mom & pop brick and mortar music stores to sell everything from guitar strings to picks to cables, concertinas, harmonicas, and so forth. The role of jobbers was fading at the same time that the old school method of wholesaling was changing. It became crystal clear to me early on that while Hohner needed Sonor and Sabian, Sonor and Sabian didn't really need Hohner.

Horst Mucha of Hohner-USA and Bob Zildjian did have a common ground in that Hohner-USA needed to get out of the Targ & Dinner arrangement and it's losing money-situation, while Bob Zildjian needed to get out of the Charles Alden losing-money situation. There were so many losses at Targ & Dinner that there was about a $330,000 tax credit sitting on the books from accrued losses that could be transferred to Hohner-USA if it shut down Targ & Dinner successfully and basically ended its existence. The world didn't need to know that it was restarting under a different name called HSS Inc.

One problem realized with the potential restructuring was that the Targ & Dinner wholesale customer base was primarily the very small music stores scattered across the country who were buying small accessories. The product mix did not contain any name-brand, professional-level instruments that demanded specialized sales expertise or feature-benefit training. The existing Targ & Dinner customer base was not qualified to sell and promote Sonor Drums and Sabian Cymbals. Plus, these small brick & mortal general music stores were typically running 60 to 90 days past due dates on their invoice payments.

I examined and explored this further, learning that the Targ & Dinner sales force consisted of four or five at-home telemarketing sales people who occasionally did some regional or long distance traveling but basically conducted as telemarketing operation. This was probably effective for selling the typical Targ & Dinner products to the average corner music store owner, but they did not have the special skills or detailed product knowledge to present more sophisticated products. I am not being critical of the Targ & Dinner salespeople or dealers. These people were for most part honest, hard-working folks who simply did not have the training or background to effectively market these professional level products and brands. Sonor drums were very high quality, made in Europe, and probably the most expensive drums in the world. Sabian was a derivative of the Zildjian cymbal brand, and needed to be properly presented to accelerate its on-going growth into the very competitive cymbal market.

My entry into the development of HSS started early, initially as a consultant, as both Mucha and Zildjian were still planning how and where to establish HSS as a completely new entity. I of course suggested Nashville, not simply because I lived there, but primarily because Nashville was a cost-effective place to do business and was centrally located. Nashville is located within five hundred miles of sixty percent of the U.S. population. The Tennessee State tax structure was also conducive to this kind of operation as there is no State income tax.

Bob Zildjian and Horst Mucha flew into Nashville, I picked them up at the airport, and we started looking at real estate around Nashville that could be a potential headquarters for HSS. This initial search indicated that the newly created company would have to either build a new building or "build out" an existing facility. Bob Zildjian and Horst Mucha even entertained both personally putting money into the joint venture as real estate partners, thus purchasing a building and renting this to HSS. However both potential building partners were surprised at how much up-front money it would require- all hinging on the potential success of HSS.

Another option under consideration was Hanover, Massachusetts, using the facility that was in use by the Alden operation. I flew to Boston to look at the Alden facility. As a suburb of Boston this was a very expensive region to operate. (Actually the entire state of Massachusetts was very expensive to do business in.) The cost of living was much higher there as well. I pointed out to Bob and Horst that it was going to cost me twice as much just to live in the Boston area as opposed to Nashville.

The next location under consideration was Richmond, Virginia, operating within the existing Hohner-USA structure. While this would require an 8000 square-foot warehouse addition to the existing building, the vacant land already existed and was owned by Hohner Inc. However, while all this "search and rescue" effort was going on for Targ & Dinner and Charles Alden, I was *not* working for anyone.

Initially, I started working for HHS as a consultant not by choice, but by definition. Gil Fernandez was the president of Targ & Dinner and was waiting for my arrival at the Chicago office-warehouse facility. On September 2, 1985, I was handed a four page contract with a job description for Karl Dustman and a list of duties. I did not realize it then, but this document was written by Horst Mucha for Gil Fernandez on Targ & Dinner letterhead and included overly one-sided provisions for me to begin working within the structure of Targ & Dinner. This arrangement, called for me to be partly a Targ & Dinner employee and partly a Hohner-USA employee. This would last for about four months getting a handle on the Targ & Dinner operations and establishing the best possible solution for the present state the company was in.

By October, the decision to *liquidate and shut down* Targ & Dinner came from Hohner-USA. I would be concentrating my time and efforts at the Chicago Targ & Dinner operation until all of the merchandise was liquidated, all of the furniture and fixtures were liquidated, the company-owned automobiles were sold, and all the warehouse-operations people were termi-

Up Beat

News

Hohner, Sabian form marketing division

RICHMOND, VA—Hohner, Inc., and Sabian, Inc., Meductic, Canada, announced the formation of a division, through a joint venture, to market and distribute Hohner, Sonor and Sabian Professional Lines of musical instruments in the United States.

Horst Mucha, President of Hohner, and Robert Zildjian, President of Sabian, stated that the new company will be named H.S.S., Inc. (Hohner, Sonor, Sabian) and will be headquartered in Richmond. The company will be under the direction of Karl Dustman, executive vice president and general manager. The company's shipping points will be Ashland, VA, and San Jose, CA.

Hohner, Inc. will continue to supply music distributors with its regular product line of musical instruments such as Harmonicas, Melodicas and Accordions.

The professional instruments to be marketed by H.S.S., Inc. will consist of a new generation of Hohner Electronic Keyboards, Digital Reverb Units, Guitar and Keyboard Amplifiers, Headless Series of Guitars licensed by Steinberger, Standard Series Electric Guitars and Basses and Acoustic Guitars. The drum category will include Sonor Acoustic and Electronic Drums, Pro I drum sets and hardware and Sabian Cymbals. In addition, the company will carry Remo heads, Firth and ProMark drum sticks and Calato products.

Karl Dustman

H.S.S., Inc. will also be responsible for the distribution of Sonor/Orff Educational Instruments, a division to be headed by Robert Cotton.

The new venture brings together three of the most respected names in the music industry. This marketing strategy, in which three companies join forces, has been successful in Europe and is now being applied to the U.S. market.

H.S.S., Inc. will take over the distribution functions formerly performed by Targ & Dinner for Hohner and Sabian/Alden for Sabian Professional Products.

nated. That was a full time job for me for three to four months, which required regular commuting between my home in Nashville and Targ & Dinner in Chicago.

This ran through the end of the year. By the beginning of 1986, the newly formed joint venture (HSS) was announced by Bob Zildjian and Horst Mucha, with Karl Dustman as the executive vice president. As mentioned earlier, the new HSS would be in Virginia, but I had been working primarily in Chicago shutting down Targ & Dinner while my home was still in Nashville. It became something of a triangular life; commuting, driving, flying back and forth between Richmond, Nashville, and Chicago. I had some growing concerns as to when I would visit the Hohner facility in Richmond, particularly if I was going to be working and living there.

The "working-employment arrangement for the future" was getting very cloudy and drawn-out without clear discussions and decisions about a compensation package, relocation cost provisions and the usual new employee entitlements, as well as moving and living provisions for actually moving to Richmond. I was growing concerned because there were decisions being made about HSS structure, operations, and inventory purchases that I was not being involved in, yet I knew I would face responsibility for in the future. I was willing, however, to see how the startup of HSS could work in Richmond. On December 18th I received a one-page fax containing the basic outline of Hohner's relocation assistance policy and program which at least indicated that Hohner was moving forwards in thought and planning for my relocation and arrival in Richmond during 1986.

In February of 1986, I was sent to my first Frankfurt fair. It was the only Frankfurt fair I ever attended. I went with Hohner-USA's advertising manager Jack Kavoukian. It was a tremendous experience and I appreciated the opportunity. What really impressed me was that Hohner in Germany was a big, big deal. In the USA, Hohner-USA was a very small fish in a very big pond. The mentality of what was going on in Germany and what was going on in the USA was totally different.

In retrospect, by the end of this annual European music industry event I had a feeling that I was really sent to the Frankfurt Messe to be "introduced and paraded-around" to the Hohner-Germany top management leaders for evaluation. They seemed to be interested in who Mucha had recruited to run his new organization in the United States, named HSS.

In Germany, Hohner Inc. was like the God of handmade, old-world, traditional German-made musical instruments all manufactured in Trossingen, Germany. To draw a parallel, I would compare Hohner Inc. in Germany to the Catholic church. By that, I mean that every branch that Hohner Inc. had around the world had to send money back to Hohner Inc. in Germany. The "Pope" was Dr. Schmidt, the Chairman of Hohner Inc., while Trossingen, Germany, was sort of like the "Vatican". So Hohner-USA, under Horst Mucha, was driven to generate profits and send them back to Trossingen, the fatherland. This arrangement drove every decision that Hohner-USA made, including how could they take some of the planned profits from HSS and send that money back to Hohner Inc. in Germany. Those profits from HSS never developed, or at least not fast enough. The losses that Hohner-USA incurred during the startup of an unplanned and loosely structured HSS were into the hundreds of thousands of dollars. Obviously the flow of cash was going in the wrong direction from Hohner-Germany's perspective. Upon my return to the U.S., I forced an invitation to visit Richmond with my wife and arranged for the rental of an apartment and furnishings at Copper Mill apartments. Hohner refused to sign any apartment or furniture lease provision; this was strictly and completely at my own expense. I listed my home in Gallatin with a Nashville real-estate firm. I officially arrived in Richmond, Virginia, for full time employment and leadership of the Hohner-Sonor-Sabian company on March 18, 1986.

The initial meetings in Richmond were very friendly, with everyone excited about the potentials for a growth opportunity in the creation of HSS. I was graciously welcomed by everyone and many of them provided insights on learning the best regions of the area to live, best restaurants and related newcomer information. I found very quickly that that there were basically two inner-circles within the Hohner-USA organization. Hohner-USA had moved to Richmond from Hicksville, New York, in 1982 under the direction of a previous Hohner-USA president. A core group of seven or eight people moved from Hicksville to Richmond, the company built a new building, and continued the operations of Hohner-USA under the direction of President Horst Mucha. That core group was "circle" number one.

Circle number two was comprised of Richmond, Virginia, residents who had been hired by Hohner-USA to fill all the other positions in administration, middle-management, shipping and receiving, finance-accounting and internal computer systems. I showed up as the guy new to both circles of people and as the guy that was supposed to be spearheading the new company called HSS. The excitement about the newly created HSS seemed to fade quickly because it looked like HSS was going to simply mean more work for them in their existing positions. It felt like there was already something of a cloud hovering over the new HSS.

From the very first day of my arrival, I was told to turn my focus on Targ & Dinner. But, I wondered, what about the creation and start-up of the newly formed HSS? Another element of that Targ & Dinner dismantling was to oversee and manage the hundreds of thousands of dollars worth of payables that Targ & Dinner owed to its suppliers. These suppliers included Zildjian, Vic Firth, Calato, Remo, you name it. Targ & Dinner was into all of these companies for a lot of money. It was Hohner's directive for me to approach each of those creditors with an offer to settle the outstanding debt for ten to forty cents on the dollar. If they would agree, I was authorized to have a Hohner-USA settlement check issued immediately to clear the account and outstanding Targ & Dinner debt. I felt more like an auctioneer or bank foreclosure representative than the executive vice president of a new entity named HSS. My professionalism prevailed as expected, but I was now trading on personal relationships with some of the percussion company suppliers that I knew and dealt with over the preceding years. My personal friendships and relationships were being leveraged, by Hohner-USA.

I encountered every imaginable reaction as I contacted each of the Targ & Dinner supplier-creditors. I guess the factor that led to my success, as it was called, was sincerity and tone of voice that was sympathetic to the situation that each creditor/supplier was facing. I rehearsed a telephone script that explained, "Look. Targ and Dinner owes Hohner-USA a lot of money. It would be my personal recommendation to encourage you to accept something now directly from Hohner, while you can get it. Eventually, when Targ & Dinner goes down, you will not see anything. If it files for bankruptcy, you will not see a dime on a forty or fifty thousand dollar outstanding payable." So people started responding, "Hell, yes. Send me the Hohner check and I will send you a "paid in full" receipt." This illusive cover I created and provided for Hohner is something that I am *not* proud of and still regret today.

I basically washed away all of the sins of Targ & Dinner's accounts payables. I didn't like doing it, because I was dealing with friendships in many of these circumstances. I was saying to old friends like Jerry Donnegan and Craigie Zildjian, "take forty cents on the dollar right now today and I will mail you a check tomorrow." And they said, "Ok. If that's how you see it going, Karl, we appreciate you giving us the heads-up, we'll bail out and take the hit now." In the meantime, the remaining Targ and Dinner salespeople were blowing out all inventory that was not bolted down to the floor, to anyone. That is how Hohner washed its hands of Targ & Dinner and removed that entity from the music products industry.

I think another thing that needs to be explained in this music-wholesale context is that for many years Targ & Dinner had become something of a dumping ground for Hohner-USA products and inventory. Any dead, distressed or obsolete inventory in the Richmond Hohner-USA warehouse got dumped on Targ & Dinner whether they wanted it or not. Naturally Hohner-USA was concerned about no longer having a dumping ground because of the elimination of Targ & Dinner. Horst Mucha knew that the long-time Targ & Dinner telemarketing salesmen would be staying on in the new HSS structure. This assured Hohner of an on-going solution so HSS became the considered readily available possible solution. Inspite of my continual reminders to everyone within both Hohner and HSS that you cannot mix "junk" with name brand merchandise like Sonor drums and Sabian cymbals, my cautions fell on deaf ears.

Bob Zildjian was looking for a way to close down and get out from underneath the financial burden of the Charles Alden Company he completely owned. This included selling all of the dead Charles Alden inventory through HSS while eliminating the Alden warehouse operation and fixed costs completely. On paper, this all sounded practical. In reality, we were mixing in two globally known name-brand products (Sonor and Sabian) with merchandise (Hohner) that never really fit together.

Part of the learning curve for me, and for anyone reading this, is knowing the end of HSS is really the first part of the story and that the demise of HSS was pre-cast from the beginning. I attribute this to the arrogance and incompetence of the President of Hohner-USA, despite his good intentions for the company. The more I saw and heard, the more that I realized what was taking place. The mixing of oil and water product lines, (Hohner with Sonor-Sabian) created an inevitable outcome.

The foundation for HSS was built on quick-sand. A true high quality professional sales force did not exist and it was not reasonable to expect the inherited Targ and Dinner "wholesaler- jobber" sales force mentality would be successful in selling high-end sophisticated products and brands like Sonor and Sabian.

This lack of product-line compatibility was also seen at the NAMM shows, as Hohner and HSS combined all of the product into one large exhibit area. Professional drum shops and music store owners who were attracted to the Sonor and Sabian product were not much interested in seeing, learning about, or being distracted by all of the Hohner family of products. There would be a wall of accordions, and a wall of harmonicas, POP (Point of Purchase) displays featuring Marine Band Harmonicas; this was all a distraction to the two leading brands (Sonor-Sabian) of a "three legged chair". It made Hohner-HSS look more like a conglomerate than a high end specialty brand "distributor".

But Hohner-USA was pretty much in-charge and calling the shots for everything at this point, so that is the way Hohner-HSS was presented at NAMM shows. There were Hohner keyboards on display, and Hohner amplifiers, Hohner headless guitars made by Steinberger, a whole collage of merchandise not directly related to percussion, and this was a serious distraction. It reminded me of the mindset that was demonstrated by Selmer when it took over Ludwig/Musser. The Selmer product emphasis was on band instruments, string instruments, wind instruments, and now Selmer would blend-in percussion as well.

By April, I was basically finished with the Targ & Dinner liquidations and settlements. Hohner-Germany was wanting to know where were the HSS profits that were supposed to be going back to Germany. I knew the start-up of HSS would create "red ink" (losses) for months until the salesmen were trained and qualified to be selling Sonor and Sabian products. They were harmonica salesmen. I called it the "Harmonicat mentality". We just did not have the infrastructure to sell, promote, and advertise the internationally branded names that were being misaligned with harmonicas. This would take time, money and some compounding losses before everyone would realize that the basic foundation for the creation of HSS was flawed and doomed from the very beginning.

The other red flare that went up for me personally at this point was not being able to receive or review the monthly HSS financial statements that were supposedly showing the accumulating losses. As the executive vice president of the company I was ultimately responsible for (HSS), I should have been able to see the profit and loss statements. I was refused access to them and this was becoming a monthly problem.

Meanwhile, the startup of the permanent HSS physical location as an expanded warehouse of the existing Hohner building started. There was a groundbreaking on the 8000 square foot warehouse addition that would become filled with HSS inventory. The deadline for the completion of this structure was December of 1986, after which it would be immediately filled with Sonor drums, Sabian cymbals, and additional Hohner merchandise. Further lack of planning and organization became apparent when I saw that there was no office space for me. Since my arrival, I had been seated and working out of a Hohner-USA conference room right next to Horst Mucha's office. I would remain there until new designated HSS offices could be constructed in the Hohner warehouse conversion.

By the time that HSS was operational, a lot of the start-up decisions and implementations had been made while I was focused exclusively on the Targ and Dinner liquidation, debt resolutions and closure of the company. I had a feeling of being invisible as this arrangement was being set up. I was out of the loop on many decisions being made that I felt were errors in judgment and demonstrated a lack of qualified expertise. I was there because of what I knew, my accomplishments, and my experienced background, but I was not being utilized. Another red flag went up.

Eventually the new HSS warehouse was finished and more containers of Sonor drums started arriving while Hohner-USA merchandise was filling in. More Sabian cymbals began to arrive. While this was a good sign of having adequate warehouse space for a growing and diverse inventory, there were inherent flaws in this plan as well.

The new HSS full page color advertisement was starting to appear in the respective music industry publications, illustrating the vast product lines that included drums, cymbals Hohner keyboards, amps, guitars, processors, all in one color ad. Again, the mentality here was "advertise and sell everything" from Hohner, all supported by quality brands of Sonor and Sabian. I had very little input on the creation of this advertisement, as this was directed by Hohner Advertising Manager Jack Kavoukian.

Everyone seemed surprised that the original Hohner warehouse and new HSS warehouse additions were on two different floor elevations. The concrete ramp connecting the two warehouses was at too steep of a grade for the forklifts to navigate. (Horst Mucha had selected the architect and approved all building plans.) Because of this incorrect grade between the two warehouses, the entire ramp had to be jack hammered-out and replaced with a longer, smaller-grade ramp.

And still, there were no offices for HSS. It was decided to partition off part of the existing Hohner warehouse to create some HSS office space for Bob Cotton, myself, and the inside sales telemarketing team . These offices did not have doors and ceilings, but were open air cubicles with sliding patio-type glass doors. It was like trying to conduct business in a train station- it was very noisy. The glass doors offered no conversation or telephone-call privacy or noise abatement. Everything echoed like an guitar amplifier. Another problem was that there were no windows. The "train station" (aka HSS office area) was a dark environment even with the dropped lighting from the ceiling. Mucha made another decision, to add a skylight. At a cost of probably around $40,000, a huge hole was cut in the roof to install a skylight over the "office" area. The immediate effect was to compound the already poor acoustics with the addition of the highly reflective glass-bubble that also served as a sound baffle to every conversation. The next problem was sunlight. There was no way to shield the seated staff from the sunlight below, which moved according to the movement of the sun over the building. During the intense summer, all of us began to feel the direct sunlight in one position or another. Lauren, Carol, Susan, and Mindy were the four staff women assigned to HSS and they continued to vocalize, "It was hot".

This required the installation of an expensive ceiling drape that could be drawn to provide shade from the direct sunlight pouring in from the newly installed skylight. I point this out because it just seemed to be one error multiplying on another. I was not involved in any of this engineered planning of decision-making.

Here Comes The Beginning of The End- already?

In August I was called to a one on one dinner meeting with Horst Mucha and was told that the six months of temporary housing was now up and I was on my own. I was being told, "If you're planning on staying, you will be paying your own rent and expenses". To that, he added, "in my opinion you would have been better off joining a company that really needed you". I thought to myself, "Well, isn't why you hired me, because I have an expertise that you needed?" The red lights were flashing in my mind. I was told that I needed to get out of the office and spend 40 to 50% of my time traveling with the sales reps to different parts of the country to earn my keep by generating sales for HSS. Hohner would not be responsible for any hardships or losses encountered from selling my Nashville house which was at the time listed for sale. It sounded to me like Hohner was sharpening the guillotine or making the relationship so threatening and uncomfortable that I would leave on my own.

I should note that at this time the very same attorney that had represented me when dealing with the legal issues surrounding the final payments due me upon departing from Gretsch now advised me to keep meticulous notes and records about everything that was taking place at HSS. It is these detailed week-by-week personal notes to myself that helped reconstruct this chapter and the memory of this time period. (Something of a recommendation to those reading this chapter)

With this hostile atmosphere and my future in question, I decided to cut my losses and protect myself. I immediately moved out of the Richmond apartment, had the rental furniture picked up and loaded a rental cargo van to drive home with everything I had brought to Virginia. I sent everything, and my family, back to Nashville. This was a time to take care of myself and my future regardless of the direction HSS was headed.

I remained in Ashland (a suburb of Richmond where Hohner-USA was headquartered), and negotiated a deal at the Hanover House Motel which was basically a purple-door no-tell motel fleabag for about $20.00 a night. I then tried to arrange my schedule so I would spend the least amount of time in Hohner offices and the least amount of time living in the motel. I spent more and more time out of the office and on the road. When I was traveling on business with the territory salesmen my expenses were paid by the company.

Part of the problem was that the HSS sales force was inherited from Targ & Dinner. These were good people. They were hard workers, they were dedicated, they had been with Targ & Dinner for years and they had been successful selling the products that Targ & Dinner had, which included a lot of Hohner products.

Rick Kylan, Gary Porter, Neil Paskvan; they were wonderful guys, but they did not have the expertise or the background or product knowledge/professionalism to sell Sonor and Sabian products. I began to build an independent rep sales force of people who were experienced at selling high end percussion instruments.

The Sonor factory in Germany was having some challenges on a global basis because their product was more expensive than most of their competitors. All of the various Sonor distributors were voicing their concerns about not having an inexpensive Sonor series to market and sell as a true entry level drum set. Sonor caved in by creating Panther, Performer, and Performer-Plus Series drums targeted to specific price points. The full page color "template advertisement" was created by Sonor but allowed each distributor to place their own suggested retail selling price in the advertisement. Certain elements like the tom holder and other hardware were original Sonor-Germany manufactured components, yet the shells were Asian imports and not close to the quality that was expected of the Sonor brand. Time marched on.

I started recruiting people like Bob Lynch (from Kaman), Gary Curry (from Slingerland), Al Martel and Les Butts (from Paiste), John Clark (from Zildjian/ Slingerland) and these people became independent reps.

The result was that we began to see some balancing with Sonor and Sabian. These guys basically forgot about the Hohner products and concentrated on percussion. The HSS product lines and salesmen commissioned earning potential was expanded further by bringing in Remo, Calato, and Vic Firth percussion accessory brands. These were compatible and non-competitive with Sonor and Sabian but aligned with percussion merchandising.

Sabian had their own sales manager that they had recruited from Kaman, Dick Mann. Dick had been with Kaman for decades, was very well respected and very knowledgeable when it came to the Sabian product line and to some degree Sonor. Sabian wanted HSS to absorb Dick Mann into the HSS sales operations and payroll. Dick and I got along well, I respected his knowledge, professionalism and the fact that he was a true salesman/sales manager. He did a great job and everyone could learn something from him just by being around him. But he also was quick to ascertain that the sales force was not in many cases qualified to sell Sabian cymbals. Sabian was his alliance and he concentrated most of his time and energy on Sabian Cymbal market development and sales. He would also travel with the sales force in an effort to educate them on how to sell Sabian cymbals. It certainly helped.

I continued to hear about HSS losing money, but still was not given any access to financial statements. I had no idea where money was being lost or where profits were being made.

By the middle of 1986, I sensed that Hohner and Horst Mucha were being put in vise grips by Hohner headquarters in Germany as it sought and demanded profitability. The challenges that were facing Hohner-USA were also happening around the world. The Hohner subsidiaries were not sending the expected profits back to Hohner Germany, the "Vatican". The pressure was mounting, and the message was clear; there had to be a way to send money back to Hohner-Germany. One way was to lower the employee head count so there would be less fixed overhead which would automatically increase profitability. A detailed organization chart with incomes of all employees was prepared and provided to Dr. Schmidt, detailing those Hohner versus HSS employees and those that were shared between the two companies.

A July, 1986, telephone conversation between Horst Mucha and Dr. Schmidt, addressed many topics and laid the groundwork for forthcoming significant changes and implementations:

-The former Targ & Dinner warehouse in San Jose, California was going to be moved to a smaller and less expensive location.

-The Hohner-Canada operation, facility and people would be eliminated, and the servicing of that Canadian business and market would become a responsibility channeled to Hohner-Richmond.

I also learned that Horst Mucha sought the legal guidance of Attorney David Dorset in Richmond regarding the discussions about "Reductions in Employment". There were concerns that the Age Discrimination and Employment Act would have some restrictions and obligations concerning certain employees aged forty and over. Horst Mucha was given in writing specific advice and precautions dated July 31, 1986 regarding certain employees that were the target of the company's employee reduction/elimination list.

SABIAN ATTACKS HSS

Converging forces were closing in on Hohner and Horst Mucha as Sabian launched an attack during the closed-door meeting in the Hohner-Richmond conference room on September 4, 1986. The focus was on Sabian's unhappiness with HSS, with Hohner-USA, with HSS people, and the entire relationship.

The specific points of discord included:

-Sabian was spending close to a million dollars a year in promoting Sabian product nationally and felt that HSS was doing very little to support the alliance with Sabian in terms of selling and promoting.

-Hohner-USA was busy cleaning up its Targ and Dinner mess while Bob Zildjian was busy cleaning up his Charles Alden situation and HSS was suffering fromlack of attention.

-Nothing was being done in the HSS San Jose, California, warehouse to support Sabian in the west coast marketplace.

-Hohner-USA and HSS were concentrating on selling Westheimer guitars (junk) and sacrificing time and attention from Sabian products.

-No importance was being given to the midwest region where Sabian dealers existed in significant numbers.

-Sales manager Bob Cotton and Dustman are basically hand-tied, not able to make any decision unless it involves Mucha approval.

-Sabian is the most profitable line for HSS, but it is ignored the most.

-HSS has exclusive distribution for all Sabian products but is cutting back on purchase orders just one year into the new relationship and is now asking for extended terms beyond the normal "net 90 days".
-HSS had been dragging its feet in the midwest, southwest, and southeast until they introduced independent sales rep John Clark.
-No one is traveling with the sales reps to train on Sabian; Sabian is doing all the work to train the sales reps.
-The HSS credit department is slow, the computer is all screwed up, deliveries of Sabian are slow going out the door, and Sabian was better off dealing with Alden. They were starting to rethink the HSS arrangement.
-Should Sabian start selling direct and go with additional distributors like Calato, Kaman, Yamaha, and Tama?
-Should Sabian start it's own sales force and let the customer decide who to buy Sabian from?

Of course there was a September 4th written rebuttal by Horst Mucha to Sabian, explaining how much HSS had done, and would do in the future, and that Sabian was incorrect in its assessment. I am still amazed at this document..

Part of the solution Sabian decided on, and and implemented on its own, was to have Andy Zildjian move to Richmond, Virginia, to become the southeast sales representative and to work a territory. Bob Zildjian bought Andy a home and Andy started working a designated sales territory along the East coast. This would provide Sabian with an inside spectator into what was going on within, Hohner Inc. and HSS.

By November, I was informed that HSS had finally reached a break-even financial statement. I never received or saw either the monthly statement nor the accumulating year-to-date financials. 1986 was drawing to a close and a very difficult year was about to end. I continued to have hope and faith that HSS could survive, that I could work further into the future of the company and there would be some satisfaction in this new relationship at some point in time.

I was not aware that Hohner Inc. gave bonuses out at the end of the calendar year. While this was not public knowledge, it is the sort of information you learn about from coworkers. Employees expected these year-end bonuses, and many considered it part of their compensation package. When bonus envelopes were handed out right before the Christmas break, everyone got one except for me. These were significant bonuses at this time; on the order of $3,500 to $5,000 per person for the managers. I took this as a clear message that said, "Karl, Leave on your own." By this time, however, I was becoming so obstinate, for lack of a better term, that I was determined to force Hohner's hand on HSS and let the future play out to see what developed.

The January, 1987, NAMM Winter Market convention in Anaheim was far better than the previous summer convention in McCormick Place-Chicago. There was a plan, a strategy, trade show specials for dealers, and reasonable sales of most HSS products were achieved. By then we also had a number of independent sale representatives that were working the booth with advance appointments made with dealers and new accounts being opened. I never heard anything about the improvement in HSS sales, exhibit-display presence or the traction that the company was just-starting to experience.

The first shoe dropped January 27th, 1987, when I was informed that Hohner-USA would not be responsible for anything that would happen if my Nashville home was sold. Bob Zildjian and Horst Link from Sonor were unhappy with HSS performance and therefore unhappy with me. The question mark in my mind was, "What about me makes them unhappy?" For the first time in my life, I was called incompetent to my face, by Horst Mucha, who said he would be seeking financial assistance from Horst Link and Sonor to subsidize my compensation in the future and that this would be discussed further during a forthcoming meeting in Germany.

Upon Mucha's first day back in the office from international travel (February 10th)), he informed me that the position I held, executive vice-president, would be eliminated, and they would create a new title. My income would be cut 29% and basically I needed to sign the new employment document or we would be parting ways. My new duties would be concentrating on artist relations for Sonor, there would be no commuting cost reimbursement, and all insurance would become self-paid. This February 18th document also stipulated that I return the company car that had been provided. (I had been paying one third of the expense, and was glad I hadn't signed the lease agreement.) Bob Cotton, the vice-president of marketing, would become my boss. He use to work for me, now I would work for him. It was clear to me that Mucha was using this process to show Dr. Schmidt (the Hohner "Pope") in Germany that he was acting (at my expense) to improve the disappointing profits situation and take any necessary action to create profits, at any cost.

It's important to know that on the very same day, Mucha created a Memorandum for the files, documenting and covering himself concerning the specified Hohner and HSS changes that were discussed and promised while he was in Germany. The tone and context of the document conveyed that I was the chosen sacrificial lamb for the abundant errors, blunders and miscalculations that Horst Mucha made in the creation and development of HSS. The last line of his memorandum illustrates some of his personal admittance, "*Ultimately, however, it is Horst Mucha who is responsible for the bottom line of HSS as it should be, because after all, the creation of HSS was his idea*".

Sonor had really been my primary focus in all of this, so I focused my energy in that direction. Sonor needed all the help and attention it could get in the US market. I basically ignored anything with the Hohner name on it, let Sabian take care of itself, and focused on Sonor drums. Using my positive experiences and achievements with Ludwig and Gretsch, for the first time Sonor began a professional clinic program, an artist roster, a co-sponsorship clinic program with dealers, a clinic program agreement, an artist relations agreement, and a cost analysis of every event that Sonor sponsored and HSS hosted. Never during the previous Charles Alden distribution period did Sonor receive this concentrated attention and professional guidance as it was now experiencing.

Sonor now had an artist relations development plan seeking outside artists and worked with existing Sonor artists like Jack DeJohnette and Steve Smith. For the first time, Sonor artists had someone to talk to in the United States about Sonor products, programs, product support and coordinated promotions. Sonor now had a Celebrity Artist Program for regional artists recommended and supported by local Sonor dealers that founded and built these relationships for the brand.

Through HSS I worked at supplying drums for various prominent music festivals. One example was the City of Chicago Summer Music Festival. There were stages all over the city during the summer and I figured out a way to loan the City of Chicago three Performer Series Sonor drum sets that would be rotated around to all the different stages. This was close to the identical relationship to what I had done at Ludwig and at Gretsch to gain visibility. However, HSS chose to loan the cheap Performer Series sets for this purpose instead of a real professional level drum set for the guest drummers to experience. I was still fighting the Harmonicat Mentality!

HSS Inc.
HOHNER • SONOR • SABIAN
PROFESSIONAL MUSICAL INSTRUMENTS

1987 SONOR EDUCATIONAL CLINICIAN ROSTER

Gerry Brown - International drummer most noted for recording and touring with Lionel Richie. A sought-after clinician for appearances in retail drum shops, performances with high school and college ensembles, featured lectures at percussion association meetings and special multiple-day work shops. Relates to audiences of all ages and player abilities. An excellent promotional opportunity to combine percussion education with a realistic approach to organized study techniques, presented by a "master".

Jack Dejohnette - Recognized veteran of percussion and popular music. Respected in all music circles as an innovative drummer, keyboard specialist, band leader, composer and record producer. Accomplished clinician, adjudication and master class speaker in high school and college levels. Performance with school group acceptable on same day of clinic. Musical arrangements available for instructional school use.

Bernard Purdie - Reknown artist with a list of performance and recording credits matched by very few. One of the most respected and in demand percussion personalities in the business. Studio accomplishments include Rolling Stones, Beatles, Roberta Flack, Tom Jones, Aretha Franklin and many other notables. Clinic presentations focus on musical awareness for all musicians, suitable for all levels and age groups. Performance musical arrangements available for use with school ensembles at high school and college level.

Bobby Rock - The newest generation of heavy metal rock drummers, now experiencing national recognition after the first tour with Vinnie Vincent (formerly of Kiss) and success with their first album, Vinnie Vincent Invasion. This showman "attacks" the huge Sonor kit with an energy level that becomes a sound and musical encounter never experienced before. National publicity of the group in heavy metal circles and periodicals is planned.

Clinic presentations run the gammit of endurance body building, four-way independence, musical awareness in a rock setting, and "shop building" in a high volume - high energy performance.

Steve Smith - Recognized for his achievements during his tenure with "Journey", this Sonor veteran has more accomplishments to his list of credentials than many of his percussion colleagues. Now completely involved in his new jazz-oriented group Vital Information, he returns to the road for extensive touring and drum clinics. A master of communication with students and music, his clinics are truly an educational experience. Will work with a local rhythm section or rehearsal band.

Jeff Watts - The creative rhythmic backbone of famed trumpeter Wynton Marsalis, Watts is attracting national attention for his dynamic role in forming this group's sound, recording success and international acclaim. A "schooled musician", he is adept in mixed settings of retail store presentations or in-school workshops at high school and college levels. Suitable musical arrangements for performance with school ensembles are available at both high school and college levels.

Lakeridge Park • Sycamore Drive, Ashland, Virginia 23005
P.O. Box 9167, Richmond, Virginia 23227 (804) 798-4500
446 Nelo Street, Santa Clara, California 95050 (408) 727-7005 (800) 532-7900 in California (800) 852-0100 West Of The Rockies

July 17, 1987: Sonor, Germany attacks HSS.

By now I was realizing the very opposing comments and views as to the development of HSS and Sonor Percussion. Horst Mucha was always portraying a doom and gloom picture of unhappiness, unpleasant and threatening actions. Knowing the significant progress that was being made for Sonor, I could *not* believe that Sonor President Horst Link was as disappointed and negative as Mucha wanted everyone to believe. I made it a personal mission to find out the real truth and discussions between the two individuals. Hohner and HSS had just completed another combined trade show exhibit for the NAMM Convention in McCormick Place-Chicago, and a follow-up fax that arrived at our shared office caught my attention. The focus of this fax was a request for a meeting in Richmond, Virginia, with Horst Mucha and Bob Cotton to discuss the internal Sonor-Germany Horst Link recap-report on the June, 1987, NAMM convention at McCormick Place in Chicago. Among the topics of conversation that Horst Link felt warranted immediate discussion and improvement:

-What can be done to make Sonor of greater attention to the HSS salesmen, should the commission structure be changed?

-What can be done to improve Sonor presentation in Anaheim at the upcoming January, 1988, NAMM?

-What can be done to better educate the salesmen about Sonor drums in terms of features, benefits, related product designs, and how to professionally sell Sonor?

-It is difficult to locate and access Sonor products when they are mixed in with Hohner guitars, keyboards, amplifiers, and Sabian cymbals. There was an absence of any kind of Sonor banner at the booth.

-The booth lighting was insufficient; it made the drums on display appear dark and uninviting.

-There had been an absence of any Sonor artists at the booth for discussion and autographs.

-There needs to be a soundproof booth so guests could hear and experience Sonor sound. The sound of the drums is extremely important to appreciating the Sonor quality and reason for product higher costs than other brands.

-Sonor, in contrast to Sabian, did not have as much activity, presentation, or artist presence and excitement… why?

-While Sonor sales at the booth were not entirely unsatisfactory, they were not outstanding.

-The new Sonor Performer Series drums did not receive much attention or interest. Why?

-Most of the interest was centered on the new HLD-500 8x14 brass shell snare drum, priced at $2,000. Considered the most expensive snare drum in the world, Americans love these superlatives and this drum should be displayed at all international Sonor exhibits from now on.

-Sabian sales were considered to be "phenomenal" while Sonor sales were not.

-Bob Cotton and Karl Dustman as leaders of HSS are two persons of outstanding capabilities and character "leading the charge".

-Buz King, product manager for Sonor, and Lauren Hergenrader, inside sales rep for Sonor, need further education in selling Sonor and perhaps should attend the Frankfurt Messe at Sonor, Germany's expense.

-Mucha and Cotton needed to have a meeting to discuss the necessary improvements to the Sonor presence in the USA.

-Sonor Performer Series products could carry a lesser salesman's commission of 5% while Sonor-Germany products should pay 8%.

-Sonor literature was not clearly available for guests to find and take with them. Visitors had to ask for it or simply try to find it.

-There was customer interest in an orchestral bass drum and in concert drums which seemed to be increasing. HSS should try to obtain a Yamaha sample model for observation.

I of course found this communication from Horst Link to be extremely interesting. First, it clarified to me how many obscure and fictional negative comments Hohner-USA was communicating to me about Horst Link's feelings concerning *my* work on Sonor. Secondly, it made clear how unhappy Horst Link was with HSS, (not Karl Dustman) over issues that were beyond my control and were clearly decisions made by Hohner-USA and not myself.

Now I felt motivated to begin taking matters more into my own hands. Buz King and I were quietly in agreement about everything that was wrong with Hohner and their handling of Sonor Drums within HSS. Elisabeth Link was attending the American Orff Schelwerk Association convention somewhere in the U.S. earlier in November which supported the Sonor Orff instruments being displayed by Hohner Inc. and Bob Cotton. She would be visiting Hohner in Richmond immediately after the AOSA conference.

Feeling that I really had nothing to lose, I created a letter to Elizabeth and Horst Link dated November 21, 1987. It was basically a follow-up to the meeting I'd had with Elisabeth Link when she visited HSS. During that time I explained to her in depth, the problems with the Hohner "Harmonicat mentality" that was not paying appropriate attention to Sonor product in the United States. My letter outlined and reiterated what I felt needed to be done with Sonor Drums in order to properly market Sonor in the US market. The proposal outlined the needed for Sonor to create its own marketing-promotion and artist entity in the USA that is owned and operated by Sonor, Germany and managed by Buz King and myself. If HSS were to remain a Sonor distributor, so be it. But Sonor-Germany needed to have a USA-based managing director to run Sonor Percussion marketing; support that would direct and professionally manage Sonor's clinic program, artist program, and to professionally develop an advertising program. It allowed HSS to just ship and distribute Sonor Drums to a growing retail-dealer network.

By the end of 1987 I was beginning to be recognized as "the Sonor guy" in the USA market and was starting to field suggestions like the request from Hargrove Percussion for Sonor to get into the marching percussion market. I again wrote to Elisabeth and Horst Link with specific suggestions for Sonor market penetration in the USA. Buz King was aware of these letters I sent and their contents. I knew that if I was successful in leading Sonor to an autonomous USA Marketing Support position, I would need to include Buz in the new organization. That was the goal.

Another NAMM Winter Market convention took place in January at the Anaheim Convention Center, attended by both Horst and Elisabeth Link.

Karl Dustman and Buz King, 1988 NAMM show

Karl Dustman, Bob Cotton, Jerry Brown, Towana Brown

Buz King, Karl Dustman

My letter to Horst and Elisabeth dated January 29th reiterated the concerns I had about HSS, Hohner, and how Sonor drums were being positioned and handled in the United States market. I had the hope that these personally written letters to Germany would convey the sincere interest I had in seeing Sonor Drums succeed and expand in the US market. It was becoming very obvious that Sonor would never receive the attention it deserved with HSS and eventually would be negatively affected by the pending demise of HSS.

In the meantime the Sonor clinic program was growing and receiving noticeable exposure and recognition in the percussion world. Newly recruited Gerry Brown provided a Master Class at Berklee School of Music in Boston. This created the template for other high visibility educational connections of Sonor artists and the brand of their drums.

Berklee
COLLEGE OF MUSIC

April 21, 1988

Mr. Karl Dustman
HSS, Inc. Sonor
P.O. Box 9167
Richmond, VA 23227

Dear Karl:

I want to thank you again for helping the students and faculty of Berklee College of Music experience both Gerry Brown's clinic and the the Sonor Drums that you have provided us with.

I have enclosed a catalog of the college as you requested. Please let me know if you need more.

I will probably be in contact with you over the summer regarding the possibility of a Fall or Spring clinic by one of your endorsers (Omar, perhaps?). Until then, thanks once again for all of your support.

Sincerely,

Dean Anderson
Chairman, Percussion Department
Berklee College of Music

Hohner-Germany owned a large stock portion of the Sonor Company in Bad Berleburg-Aue, Germany. I believe this was between 40 and 50%. Sonor in Germany needed a cash infusion that it could not get from Hohner, which led to Hohner deciding to sell their share of Sonor to an outside company called Skane-Gripen in July, 1988. Skane-Gripen was a long-time distributor of Hohner products in Europe. They were a multi-corporation enterprise that had the capital to expand Sonor. I took this announcement of July 1, 1988, as possible good news along with questionable news. Did this mean that Sonor in Germany now had some cash to create a United States partnership marketing-support alliance as I proposed? Or did this mean more interference from an outside entity that knows nothing about the drum business? I didn't know.

The press release announcing the changes in Sonor's alignment with Skane Gripen was released in June to the music industry and internally to HSS in July. There were the usual disclaimers in the announcements to the effect of, "This will not disrupt or change the established distribution of Sonor by Hohner affiliates," but that was standard boiler-plate copy. There was enough going on with all of this to give me the feeling that this was not going to be a long term thing.

I began to consider my options. I had a strong notion that the best thing for me personally was to get out of HSS (and the Hohner agenda) and now return to Nashville where my home and family were while I still had my sanity intact. I had to carefully and quietly create a strategy that allowed me to determine the timing and terms for my resignation and departure from HSS.

HSS Inc.
HOHNER · SONOR · SABIAN
PROFESSIONAL MUSICAL INSTRUMENTS

MEMORANDUM

TO: All H.S.S. Personnel — July 1, 1988

FROM: Robert W. Cotton

RE: Sonor/U.M.I. (United Musical Inst. Co.)

Enclosed is a copy of a press release outlining the recent change of ownership of one of our long term important suppliers, Sonor. Until recently, Hohner AG owned a large portion of the stock in the Sonor Company. Since Hohner could not give Sonor the much needed capital to help in the expansion of Sonor, it was decided to sell their shares to Skane-Gripen, a long-time distributor of Hohner products in Europe. Skane-Gripen, a multi-corporation enterprise, has the much needed capital to help in the expansion of Sonor.

We all view the recent change with much anticipation of an expanded and more powerful Sonor Company. In full agreement with Skane-Gripen, there will be no change in the distribution of Sonor products through Hohner affiliates.

A copy of this press release is also being sent to all Sonor product accounts throughout the U.S. in order to settle any rumors affecting distribution.

Robert W. Cotton
Vice President - Sales & Marketing

/kn

Encl.

akeridge Park · Sycamore Drive,
shland, Virginia 23005

O. Box 9167,
ichmond, Virginia 23227
104) 798-4500

46 Nelo Street,
anta Clara, California 95050
08) 727-7005
00) 532-7900 In California
00) 852-0100
est Of The Rockies

My plan was to start making contact with Pearl in Nashville. This was about a five month process starting with a letter of introduction, a resume, some samples of my work, all sent to the executive vice president of Pearl, Ralph Miller. This was of course done quietly and confidentially as I did not want HSS realizing that I was orchestrating a move.

Remember, this was a time before there were cell phones. In order to make a personal telephone call to Pearl during the work day I would use my lunch hour to drive one exit ramp down Interstate-95 where the Holiday Inn had pay phones in the lobby. There, I could make confidential calls to Ralph Miller to remain in contact and to nurture the potentials for joining the Pearl organization. I followed this process for about five months.

In early July I was invited to have a meeting with Ralph Miller and Pearl President Tak Isomi, for a Saturday whenever I was commuting back home to Nashville. We established a date and time on a Saturday morning and met in the breakfast dining room of the Holiday Inn Hotel near the Nashville airport. The three of us chatted casually about my background and experiences to just the break the ice and get the conversation going. Ralph excused himself and departed allowing Tak Isomi and I to discuss the pending changes within the Pearl headquarter operations that were being contemplated.

This first and only meeting with Pearl proved successful in receiving an offer to join Pearl International in Nashville as soon as possible. With confirmation (a start date, compensation agreement, etc.) that I had the position at Pearl to immediately move forwards to, I was ready to resign from HSS.

Unfortunately Horst Mucha was out of town in July either on business or vacation so I called together Rosemary Harrington, Mucha's personal secretary, and Percy Pickeral, the Hohner Controller, for a brief closed-door meeting in Percy's office. I explained my planned departure from HSS, provided a letter of resignation accompanied by my two week notice indicating my last day to be July 22nd.

I immediately made preparations for a smooth departure and exit from the Hohner-HSS operations. I mailed out a carefully worded communication to all of my related business associates, contacts and sales representative that I'd been working with letting them know that I was voluntarily leaving HSS and would soon be announcing where I was going. Bob Cotton put out an internal memo announcing my departure to the internal Hohner-HSS staff.

Although I did not announce where I was going, I received at my home a nice letter dated August 18th from Bob Zildjian, recognizing my departure from HSS and stating that he certainly understood why I was leaving. He was looking forward to working together again as he was aware that I would be joining Pearl.

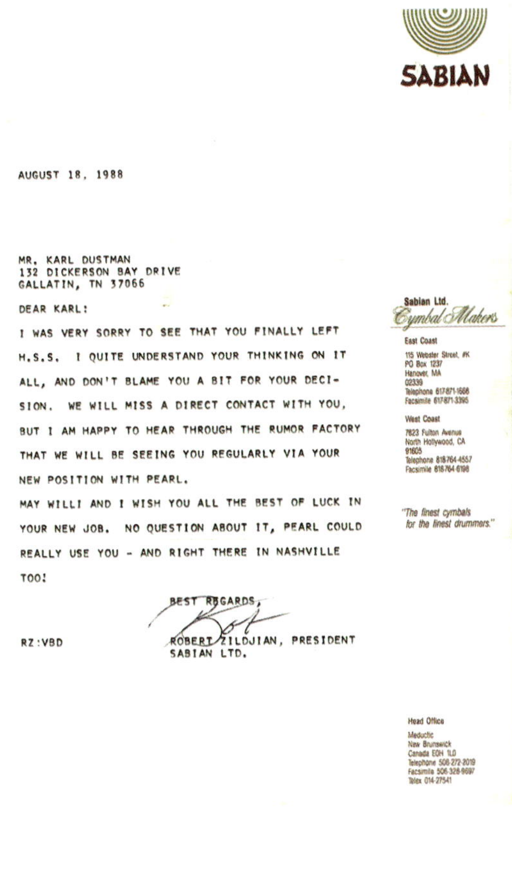

SABIAN

AUGUST 18, 1988

MR. KARL DUSTMAN
132 DICKERSON BAY DRIVE
GALLATIN, TN 37066

DEAR KARL:

I WAS VERY SORRY TO SEE THAT YOU FINALLY LEFT H.S.S. I QUITE UNDERSTAND YOUR THINKING ON IT ALL, AND DON'T BLAME YOU A BIT FOR YOUR DECISION. WE WILL MISS A DIRECT CONTACT WITH YOU, BUT I AM HAPPY TO HEAR THROUGH THE RUMOR FACTORY THAT WE WILL BE SEEING YOU REGULARLY VIA YOUR NEW POSITION WITH PEARL.

MAY WILLI AND I WISH YOU ALL THE BEST OF LUCK IN YOUR NEW JOB. NO QUESTION ABOUT IT, PEARL COULD REALLY USE YOU - AND RIGHT THERE IN NASHVILLE TOO!

BEST REGARDS,

ROBERT ZILDJIAN, PRESIDENT
SABIAN LTD.

RZ:VBD

Sabian Ltd.
Cymbal Makers

East Coast
115 Webster Street, #K
PO Box 1237
Hanover, MA
02339
Telephone 617-871-1666
Facsimile 617-871-3395

West Coast
7823 Fulton Avenue
North Hollywood, CA
91605
Telephone 818-764-4557
Facsimile 818-764-6198

"The finest cymbals for the finest drummers."

Head Office
Meductic
New Brunswick
Canada E0H 1L0
Telephone 506-272-2019
Facsimile 506-328-9697
Telex 014-27541

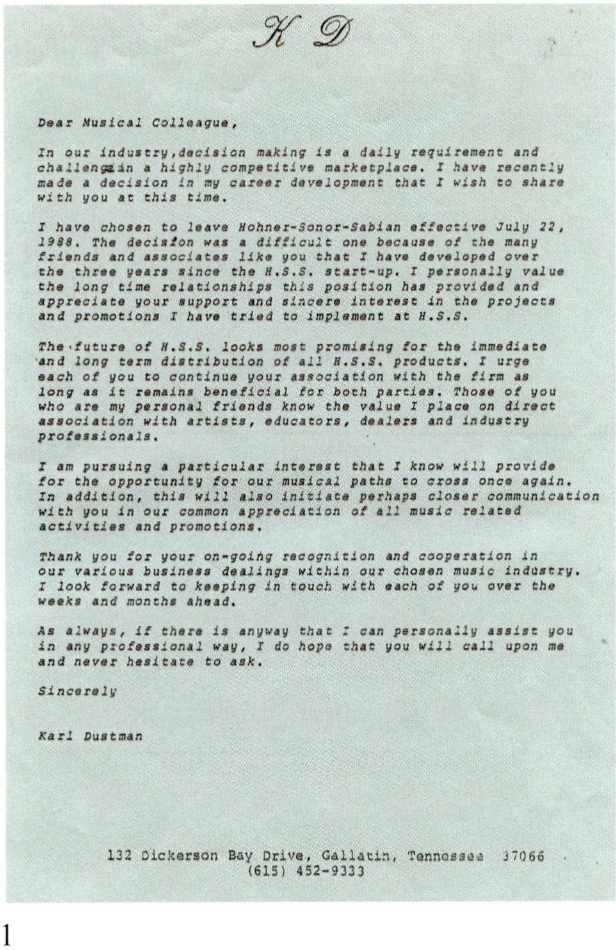

K D

Dear Musical Colleague,

In our industry,decision making is a daily requirement and challenge in a highly competitive marketplace. I have recently made a decision in my career development that I wish to share with you at this time.

I have chosen to leave Hohner-Sonor-Sabian effective July 22, 1988. The decision was a difficult one because of the many friends and associates like you that I have developed over the three years since the H.S.S. start-up. I personally value the long time relationships this position has provided and appreciate your support and sincere interest in the projects and promotions I have tried to implement at H.S.S.

The future of H.S.S. looks most promising for the immediate and long term distribution of all H.S.S. products. I urge each of you to continue your association with the firm as long as it remains beneficial for both parties. Those of you who are my personal friends know the value I place on direct association with artists, educators, dealers and industry professionals.

I am pursuing a particular interest that I know will provide for the opportunity for our musical paths to cross once again. In addition, this will also initiate perhaps closer communication with you in our common appreciation of all music related activities and promotions.

Thank you for your on-going recognition and cooperation in our various business dealings within our chosen music industry. I look forward to keeping in touch with each of you over the weeks and months ahead.

As always, if there is anyway that I can personally assist you in any professional way, I do hope that you will call upon me and never hesitate to ask.

Sincerely

Karl Dustman

132 Dickerson Bay Drive, Gallatin, Tennessee 37066
(615) 452-9333

IN RETROSPECT:

Early in this chapter I stated that knowing the sequential end of HSS was essential to understanding the reasons for the complete dismantling of the company and the eventual collapse of HSS entirely. The very same lack of market understanding, product marketing and top management errors and decision-making I encountered continued long after my departure from the company.

The people at Hohner and HSS were basically nice people, dedicated and hard working at their positions and all had good intentions for the company. It was the personal lacking in top Hohner leadership caused by arrogant intimidation and a demeaning personality that clouded the real management needs of the company and the real potential for the success of HSS.

As the years moved forward quickly, Horst Link of Sonor-Germany lost further interest and respect in Hohner-HSS of Richmond and moved the US Sonor Drums distribution to Korg USA. This created an opportunity for HSS to replace Sonor with Slingerland which Fred Gretsch would suddenly sell off, further crippling HSS. Sabian grew tired of the Hohner Harmonica mentality and added Kaman Music as a dual distribution outlet for all Sabian products. Kaman immediately overshadowed the in-ability of HSS. Eventually HSS lost the Sabian distribution all together and HSS would go out of business completely. Hohner-Richmond, would be left with the same harmonicas, melodicas and accordions that it started with when liquidating Targ and Dinner in 1985.

When the Asian based musical instrument conglomerate KHS International based in Nashville purchased the complete Hohner global operation and organization in 1995, Hohner became just another division of KHS International.

Personally I learned a great deal about the music wholesale versus music distribution process and doing profitable business. At thirty-nine years of age the primary experience I have taken with me from this encounter centers on the importance of always having mutual respect, honesty and openness with everyone I work with and who works for me. It's ironic that sometimes we learn what real rewarding working relationships are by seeing, experiencing and witnessing this complete lacking in others.

Chapter 6 Pearl International

Coming Home to Nashville with my first Japanese Experience

I was optimistic about the prospects for a long term relationship with Pearl. What I was about to experience was a completely different employment and working relationship in that this was my first encounter with an Asian company. Up to this point in time I had dealt with American and German manufacturers so I was moving forwards with the Pearl experience with an open mind knowing that there were going to be some similarities but probably some vast differences.

During the early part of the preliminary conversations with Pearl leading up to my start date, I was not aware of the internal people problems that were going on. By that I mean the shared sales force that Pearl Nashville had with the Gibson Guitar company which was at this point owned exclusively by Henry Juszkiewicz.

This was a major obstacle to any Pearl marketing person in this environment. The Gibson sales force was a highly professional group of experienced sales representatives, but they had their priorities and their income directly tied to Gibson products. Pearl was an "add-on" to the product and brand offering they had to present to the entire United States.

The other element that I was not aware of was the revolving door of people coming in and out of the Pearl Company in Nashville. The various marketing directors were averaging twelve to eighteen months, to two years maximum, in the marketing leadership position. I didn't know this before embarking on this experience with Pearl.

Karl Dustman, Tak Isomi

Background with Pearl

It's 1988; the end of my tenure at Ludwig had been in 1982, so six years have gone by already. I now found myself working for one of the Asian companies that had basically infiltrated the United States marketplace and totally turned Ludwig upside down in the late 1970s and early 1980s. I referred to this as "sleeping with the enemy" and knew I needed to get beyond that mentality. I told myself, "This is a new ball game with a new company and a new opportunity. What was in the past I have learned from, but I cannot hold Pearl responsible for what took place when Ludwig ignoring the red flags which were Pearl, Tama, and Yamaha threatening Ludwig as the king of the percussion-market-mountain.

My first Pearl experience was in late 1984 after the closure of the Gallatin Gretsch operations. I asked for a meeting with Pearl President Walt Johnson who had been with Pearl since the CMI (Chicago Musical Instrument) days. Walt had been with Pearl for 20 to 22 years at this point in time and had established himself as the lead Pearl figure in the U.S. market. I had known Walt through the years as friendly competition and now I was looking for a new career opportunity that could allow me to stay in the Nashville area. Walt was receptive to having me visit Pearl for a complete tour of the Nashville Pearl facility. Pearl was manufacturing drums in Nashville at this time, which I had not even been aware of up to this point. They had a complete assembly line, a spray booth for lacquering, and they were making some marching drums, as well as some high-end drum sets. In addition to being a U.S. distribution point for everything that Pearl was manufacturing in Japan and Taiwan, they were also stocking, manufacturing and shipping their own "made in the USA" Pearl drums. That was an eye-opening experience.

In July of 1987, Walt Johnson was let go from Pearl International in Nashville after 20 plus years of developing the company, brand and product in the United States and North American market. Tak Isomi had been in the USA and working for Pearl-Nashville for probably a total of 5 years at that point. He had been running the east coast warehouse for a while, then running the west coast warehouse for a while. This seemed like he was essentially was being groomed by Pearl headquarters in Japan, to take over the United States operation headquartered in Nashville. Seeing the direction and inevitable path my relationship with HSS was heading towards at this time, in July of 1987 I initiated a confidential dialog with a letter of introduction directed to the Tak Isomi. I introduced myself by explaining my qualifications from my experiences at Ludwig, Gretsch, and HSS. (I was still at HSS in Richmond, Virginia when I wrote this letter. This is about a year before the end of my relationship with HSS, so I was careful that this communication and contact effort was carefully worded and confidential in nature.

Through the years in the percussion industry I had a friendly relationship with Al Duffy who evolved into the figurehead of Pearl in the United States after Walt Johnson had been let go. Al attended all the trade shows, he attended all the PAS meetings, he was an active in R&D and served on the Board, he was also a recognized and respected product designer, avid player, teacher, and he worked for Pearl at the same time.

George Humes was a former Ludwig sales representative in Texas for many years and he had moved over to PearI for the same sales territory after the complete dismantling of the original professional Ludwig-Musser sales force by Selmer. George recommended that I contact Al Duffy in confidence about my interest in Pearl and any potential for joining the company. That would become my strategy.

I approached Al Duffy and indicated that I was interested in joining the Pearl organization in Nashville. I told Al that I was not getting any response positive or negative (or even an acknowledgement) from Tak Isomi. Al basically said, "I'm not surprised. This is just not the way the Japanese do business. No answer means no interest, Karl." Al became interested in me and could see some potential matches for my experience and reputation while knowing the internal turmoil that was going on within Pearl management at that time. That early discussion resulted in Al Duffy's offer to share some internal Pearl International report documents which he had created for some select marketing-condition reports to Pearl headquarters in Japan and to Pearl, USA. His personal reports were focused on various activities and events which he was attending as a representative of the Pearl Company. I greatly appreciated this gesture and friendship, allowing me to look at the inside of the company, from the outside.

Getting an Inside Insight…. in Advance

The first of those Duffy reports that I found most interesting was relative to Pearl's intent to keep at arm's length away from the Percussive Arts Society by continuing a boycott of the annual convention display arena. While Pearl was a Sustaining Member of PAS, they were showing their displeasure with the PAS organization. According to Al Duffy, Pearl had the feeling that PAS just wanted to "milk the cow," meaning "PAS would gladly use and take Pearl clinicians and artists for the convention program at Pearl's expense, and that the PAS organization would gladly accept Pearl's purchased advertisement placement in the convention program books. Pearl saw the escalating exhibit fees as further extension of PAS's revenue priorities without any recognition for all the positive financial and artist support Pearl was contributing to the PAS organization." Pearl's answer to that perceived imbalance and non-existence of a reciprocating two-way street, was to boycott the convention and not exhibit.

At the same time, Pearl was really recognizing the push, strength, and determination of Yamaha as being the largest threat to Pearl's market share, existence, and growth potential. An example of that was the November, 1987 PASIC convention where Yamaha had six booths. Pearl had no exhibit, yet Gretsch had only one booth, manned by one salesman named Dave Patrick. (Duffy's report also contained significant examples of the current fumbling of Gretsch, alienating dealers, artists and relationships in all directions following the closure of the Gallatin, Tennessee operation at the end of 1984.)

This was also a time when Pearl was trying to take over the position of the Total Percussion marquee, previously created and sustained for decades by Ludwig-Musser. Pearl wanted to become the next Total Percussion company. Pearl's first effort to expand into mallet keyboard instruments within the Pearl organization was a potential buyout of Ross Mallet Instrument manufactured in Chipawa Falls, Wisconsin. This manufacturing facility was a start-up created by Don Green, the former Musser Division Plant Manager from La Grange, Illinois. Yamaha wanted to become the Total Percussion Leader, and was on a high speed course for achieving this in the United States and global percussion market. (Today, Yamaha builds their own mallet keyboard instruments, their own complete line of marching and concert percussion, builds their own timpani, and bought Deagan to expand into traditional orchestra chime manufacturing under the former now-extinct Deagan brand name.)

Much to Pearl's aggravation, Yamaha was approaching a Total Percussion marketing perspective and product array much the way Ludwig-Musser had, and basically trademarked it. Tama was not approaching the school market at all. Tama remained a vibrant division of Hoshino USA, focused completely on being a drum set rock and roll company. Because of this, Tama was not regarded as a threat to the Total Percussion marketing ambition.

The issue of Pearl and it's arms-length-distance relationship to PAS was brought up at the SMAC (Sustaining Members Advisory Council) committee meeting(Chaired by PAS President John Beck of Eastman School of Music) which met that November to plan the following year 1988 PASIC to be held in San Antonio, Texas. The SMAC committee recognized that PAS needed another financial bailout. (You will recall that in the Ludwig chapter, there was a bailout arranged in the 1970s where PAS went back to all the sustaining members and asked for a year's worth of membership dues in advance)

Duffy reported that for the current 1987 PAS operations the same thing was happening again. Pearl saw this as an inner weakness of the organization and its leadership. Part of the financial shortfall of the PAS operating budget as it was defined at the SMAC meeting was from the PAS publication Percussive Notes spending up to forty thousand dollars more per issue in production costs than it was bringing in from advertising revenues. This was becoming very lopsided and bleeding the PAS organization as a whole.

In the same meeting, the SMAC committee voiced concerns about Yamaha starting to dominate in the same manner that Ludwig had dominated the PAS conventions in the 70's and early 80's, with large visible exhibit booths and placing a prominent clinician on the convention program in every category. (Refer back to the Ludwig chapter for specifics on the company's support and participation at PASIC conventions) PAS and Pearl saw Yamaha becoming the same kind of dominating company. Pearl was applying pressure on PAS to try to keep Yamaha in check.

(There were also rumors circulating that there was an association between Yamaha and Zildjian that they had become somehow strategically and monetarily connected. This of course turned out to be false.)

Al Duffy ended his report indicating that Pearl boycotted PAS in 1988 and basically sent the message that Pearl did not have the deep pockets to support PAS if they were going to be continually asking its sustaining members to bail out the organization. It was *his* recommendation that Pearl must be a full scale participant at the planned 1989 PASIC convention 1989.

The second report that Al Duffy provided me included his insights from the DCI Rules Congress meeting which was held every year in Chicago. The rules committee was seeing the same market dominance of Yamaha, and Pearl was feeling this. Yamaha of course had an interest in every aspect of drum corps not only for percussion but because of their brass instruments. It's recalled that previously Ludwig had monopolized this Rules Congress in the past. Between Al LeMert, Fred Sanford, and Dennis Delucia, the deck was stacked for the company's pursuit of all the drum corps to be playing Ludwig. Duffy cautioned the Pearl management that Yamaha influence was growing and that Pearl would need to ramp up DCI presence and visibility and remain aggressively positive to claim a portion of this DCI "spotlight" for Pearl DCI percussion sections and work closely with the percussion section captains.

In January of 1988 Al Duffy and I had an off-the-record meeting during the NAMM winter market convention in Anaheim. We discussed at length my interest in Pearl and the lack of response from Tak Isomi. I decided to mail Al Duffy copies of all of my previous communications to the Pearl company that were not being answered or acknowledged so he could see these materials and cover letters. Duffy basically provided copies of all of his documents in exchange for all of my documents.

Unfortunately what followed that meeting and exchange was the sudden death of Al Duffy in February 1988. Al Duffy was my one and only connection to a person inside the Pearl-Nashville organization. Even though Duffy was recommended for approaching within Pearl by district salesman George Humes, there was no one else really at Pearl who knew of my interest up to this point in time. Presently, there was no longer a Walt Johnson, now there was no Al Duffy and I now I was faced with continuing my Pearl pursuit and approach by trying to communicate with the brand new President, Tak Isomi.

In Feb of 1988 a press release was put out, announcing that Pearl Nashville had new people and positions in place within the organization. The new president was Tak Isomi who was following the longtime president Walt Johnson. Tak was also the former VP of Marketing, he had served as the warehouse operations manager for New York and California. Ken Austin was moved from artist relations manager to marketing manager. Ken Mills was moved from the east coast distribution center to serve as general operations manager in Nashville. Seeing this internal change, George

Humes suggested that I contact Vice President and Controller Ralph Miller.

In March of 1988 I began the dialogue as previously mentioned and outlined at the end of the HSS chapter. I presented a complete reintroduction of all of the communications and dialogue I'd shared with Al Duffy which had been resent in confidence to Ralph Miller. Seeing the cloud of uncertainty within HSS expanding rapidly, I took the attitude that nothing could be lost in making a ramped-up communication with Pearl through this new contact. By March 10, there was a phone call from Ralph Miller thanking me for all of the materials and by April 8 I received my first letter from Tak Isomi (now president of Pearl Nashville) who was back in Japan. Isomi explained that he had a whole new team in place, he had no openings, there were no changes, so thank you but we do not have a need for your services. On April 15 I sent a letter back to Tak Isomi in Japan providing an overview perspective that there was a need in his new organization for the qualifications and the expertise that I could bring to his management team. I stood everything to gain and nothing to lose in doing this without insulting him. I sent another letter, this one to him in Nashville, indicating the high-visibility and brand success that was taking place with the Music Fest USA in using the Bob Stone Big Band in Orlando, Florida. This was an event center stage using Sonor drums that I placed there through HSS. It was obvious that this was something lacking at Pearl; not knowing who to contact to make these high visibility connections. Again, I felt nothing ventured, nothing gained. This Music Fest featured performance was an alliance that I had put together between Sonor and the LeBlanc band instrument company of Kenosha, Wisconsin because many of the Bob Stone Big Band played LeBlanc brass and woodwind instruments.

I continued my organized pursuit. I sent another letter on June 23rd to Tak Isomi as a prelude to the forthcoming NAMM summer convention in Atlanta. I said I was looking forward to meeting him in person for the first time and chatting with him further. I would seek him out at the Pearl display during the convention. It never happened. I went back to the Pearl display numerous times, Tak was never at the exhibit. Finally I asked where he was and was told he had already left the convention and returned to Nashville.

In early July, much to my surprise, Ralph Miller invited me to have a meeting with him and Pearl President, Tak Isomi, for a Saturday whenever I was commuting back home to Nashville. We established a date and time on a Saturday morning and we all met in the breakfast dining room of the Holiday Inn Hotel near the Nashville airport. The three of us chatted casually about my background and experiences to just get the dialog started and conversation going. Ralph excused himself and departed allowing Tak Isomi and I to discuss the pending changes within the Pearl headquarter operations that were being contemplated.

This first and only meeting with Pearl proved successful in that it led to an offer to join Pearl International in Nashville as soon as possible. With confirmation (a start date, compensation agreement, etc.) that I had a firm position and offer at Pearl, I immediately submitted my written notice of departure from HSS, as outlined in the previous chapter.

There was an established start date at Pearl of Monday July 25. The first day immediately started with introductions to the Nashville staff in sales-support, marketing, credit, and artist relations. Artist relations was led by Ken Austin and supported further by Pam Haynie. There were additional full time artist relations people on each coast; Ray Tregellis and Eric Hall. In all, there were four full time people working on artist relations. At this point I also got my first taste of what a shared sales force with Gibson Guitars was all about.

I was escorted over to Gibson to meet with Gibson President, Henry Juskiewicz. I also met with Ben Rhodes, the Gibson sales manager who was a personal appointee of Henry. Both Gibson leaders were cordial and friendly at our first meeting and seemed receptive to my arrival at Pearl. Again, I was somewhat reminded that I stepped into a revolving door situation of Pearl marketing directors, marketing managers, and whatever titles given to them. The Gibson perspective was that the marketing guys at Pearl kept coming and going, and this concerned them. (Documents I later acquired clearly indicated a lot of bantering back and forth with Pearl headquarters in Japan related to who was, should be, and would be the marketing person for the immediate future. This became a micro-management issue that went on for years before I arrived and obviously created the perceived revolving-door of Pearl marketing directors.)

The Pearl relationship with Gibson was a shared District Manager Salesman (DSM) Force only. Pearl did all of its own accounting, order-entry, accounts receivable, shipping, billing and so forth. Gibson was only used for combining an outside traveling sales force that would visit existing Pearl dealers and review potential new accounts within the respective sales territories. This shared sales force was for Drum Set/ Combo Percussion only and did not include any of the developing Marching or Concert Percussion product lines.

Once a month Pearl would send Gibson a commission check payable to the company for the entire Pearl Combo product that had been shipped that month. Gibson would then manage and distribute those commission-funds within their individual sales force by territories. I learned that this shared sales force arrangement had been in place for a considerable length of time, regardless of the mutual frustrations between the two companies.

I was discovering in the first weeks at Pearl where exactly the minefields were. The first big one was learning about the Gibson-Pearl shared sales force contract. Pearl headquarters in Japan was very clear that Pearl Nashville was to work with Gibson and do nothing to antagonize Gibson management, disrupt or irritate this relationship. Basically I was told, "Play nice, regardless of how screwed up this is."

Nothing in the contract between Gibson and Pearl spelled out how much Pearl sales volume Gibson was required to create for Pearl product sales. There was no sales quota placed on the total sales initiative nor the individual sales territories. This clearly indicated that Pearl could not claim that the Gibson sales force was not keep their end of the agreement. There was nothing in the agreement to advise Pearl regarding where the Gibson DSM's (district sales managers) were traveling or when. Pearl did not know where each of the Gibson salesmen were on any given week or day or who they were calling on. There were no DSM call sheets for Pearl to review and provide follow-through support. There was no coordination for Pearl to know when any Pearl authorized dealer was being visited by the assigned Gibson sales representative. While each account was assigned a specific geographic territory number and sales rep, Pearl had very little input on the development and management of each account.

Shortly before I arrived, Pearl Nashville decided to create and establish its own internal customer service department to provide direct assistance to dealers and sales representatives Monday through Friday. This was done completely at Pearl's internal expense to insure that Pearl Nashville would survive. Pearl was then at least able to establish direct lines of communication with the dealers that were buying and stocking Pearl product. Pearl could not rely on Gibson's sales force to create the volume of sales required to meet the Pearl Nashville sales goals. I was, therefore, the Pearl marketing person charged with establishing sales goals, but with no say in how the sales would occur through a sales force that we had no control over or voice in. This all was explained to me in detail after I had begun in the position that I was hired to fill.

For opening a new Pearl dealer, Gibson was responsible for all of the paperwork to establish the account. The credit application, the dealer application, and so on was all controlled by the Gibson salesman. A potential new drum shop that might be a great candidate to be a Pearl drum dealer was evaluated exclusively by the territory sales representative. That Gibson DSM

PEARL EXPANDS MARKETING DIVISION

(Left to right): Pam Haynie, Ken Austin, Tak Isomi (President, Pearl International), Karl Dustman, Bob Morrison, Terry West. (Not shown: Ray Tregellas and Eric Hall.)

Pearl International recently announced the arrival of Karl Dustman as new Director of Sales and Marketing. Dustman is well-known and respected within the percussion industry, having previously held management posts with Ludwig, Gretsch, and most recently HSS, Inc.

Ken Austin will undertake the responsibilities of Marketing and Public Relations Manager, which includes direction of the Pearl Artist Relations program. The Regional Artist Relations management team will now consist of Pam Haynie (corporate headquarters, Nashville), Ray Tregellas (Pearl East Coast, Fairfield, New Jersey), and Eric Hall (Pearl West Coast, North Hollywood, California). Terry West is Advertising and Art Director, while Bob Morrison will handle marketing for Marching and Educational Percussion. Both are based in Nashville.

would either approve or decline the application. What was occurring was that perhaps the drum shop *down* the street would be perceived as a competitor to the music store *up* the street that was selling Gibson and perhaps another brand of drums. The Gibson DSM would obviously have as his first priority a desire to keep his Gibson account happy, even if Pearl sales were perhaps impacted in a negative way.

This was all laid on the table in the first 30 days that I was at Pearl.

Shortly after my arrival, the press release announcing my arrival at Pearl appeared in Modern Drummer and most of the percussion and industry trade magazines. A letter from the past president of PAS, Jim Peterscsak, was sent to Tak Isomi, congratulating him on this hire and observing that this appointment would have a positive impact on the public perception of Pearl-USA. Tak Isomi never let me know about that kind letter of congratulations to Pearl- I received a copy from Ralph Miller.

POTSDAM COLLEGE
of the State University of New York

THE CRANE SCHOOL OF MUSIC
(315) 267-2413

August 23, 1988

Mr. Tak Isomi, President
Pearl International
408 Harding Industrial Drive
Nashville, TN 37211

Dear Mr. Isomi:

I would like to congratulate you and the Pearl Co. on the appointment of Mr. Karl Dustman to your administration. Karl has been an important person to the percussion industry for some 18 years. He has been very supportive of the Percussive Arts Society and to the ideals for which we in the educational world stand for. To that end alone, his contribution to the Pearl Company will be enormous and greatly accepted throughout the U.S.A.

As past president of P.A.S. and executive director of its International conventions, we have always desired the input and participation of the Pearl Co. However, a positive framework and contact person has never materialized. Now that has all changed with the addition of Karl to your staff. He will most certainly contribute to the percussive arts as he has in the past only with his Pearl association. I feel this will be a new era for everyone concerned. I know Mr. Dustman will be highly visible in a field where he has always commanded great respect and achieved many fine accomplishments. I also look forward to working closely with Karl over the next few years to create a positive association for the enrichment of the Percussive Arts Society in the USA and throughout the world.

Sincerely yours,

Jim Petercsak
Professor of Music

JP/jm

I needed to find a trustworthy confidante within the organization. It was quickly becoming obvious that there were two circles of people within the Pearl-Nashville organization. There was the Tak Isomi fan-club circle, and there was the old-school circle which was Ralph Miller (VP and controller) and myself. We were basically the two old guys. I was about ten years younger than Ralph but we shared communication skills and saw eye-to-eye on decisions being made as well as evaluating personalities. Ralph immediately began feeding me information, recommendations and survival techniques, knowing this would be a bumpy ride regardless of my abilities or experience. His support and friendship became more important as the months rolled on. I had a tremendous respect for Ralph from the very first telephone conversation I received from him in 1988.

It became very obvious that my first challenge was to figure out how Pearl Nashville could work better and in tandem with the Gibson sales force. Pearl had to become more involved with the existing Pearl dealers and especially the major key accounts, all without circumventing those regional territory DSMs. This was a fine line of balance, as any leadership traits I could convey would be construed as a threat and interference to Gibson, yet Pearl was looking for someone to "fix their existing problem with Gibson," which I of course did not create in the first-place.

I inherited a lot at Pearl, existing people being shuffled around to different positions, problems with sales-force, interference from Pearl Japan and an undermining element that *no one* would ever satisfy the Japanese Pearl mentality in the marketing and sales position that I now held.

I was tasked with preparing a presentation for the annual Pearl Musical Instrument corporate meeting in Japan, which was scheduled for October 11-13, 1988 at Pearl headquarters in Chiba, Japan. This would be my first trip to Asia and I was looking forward to meeting the parent company management and owners, touring the factory and experiencing some of the inner working of these Pearl headquarter operations. I attended the meeting along with Ralph Miller and Bob Morrison, who was overseeing the Marching and Concert Percussion product lines. We were there for four days of intense nonstop meetings that would continue on into the evening social dinner hours with lots of Saki which I did not participate in. My Marketing-Sales presentation was scheduled for the very first day of the meetings. The spotlight was on "the new guy".

The key elements of my presentation were:

***US Market Perception.** Pearl was looking for some insights from the new guy, evaluating the status of the company. I pointed out that the company was basically in some serious marketing disarray following the release of the former President and twenty-plus year Pearl veteran Walt Johnson 18 months earlier. The company did not have anyone to bring that leadership perspective to the market. Al Duffy had partially stepped up temporarily, but then he died. The United States market was looking for a "Mr. Pearl" visibility, but at that time there simply was no person in that role. I compared the situation to other US and foreign drum companies who had visible leaders within the market. Pearl did not. These leaders had longevity with brands and companies and had become household names in the percussion industry. This was a lacking which I hoped and planned to correct by having myself involved in all the percussion industry activities with a focus on Pearl representation.

* **Pearl Singular Strength:** From the outside looking in, the Pearl Export Series appeared to be the sole strength of the Pearl company. The market perception was that Pearl Export was the singular focus target of the Pearl brand. This perception in the consumer and dealer market needed to diversify quickly. It was imperative to change this perception because Pearl Export sold itself in the market based on price point and superior consistent quality. Gibson salesmen were basically order takers to Pearl Export. They were not presenting the total company line which included, high-end birch, high-end maple, marching percussion, concert percussion, even electronics and Pearl Cymbals.

***A 13.3% sales shortfall was predicted for calendar year 1988.** This was not as bad as we had expected and the projections for year-end 1988 would not be as severe as earlier estimates.

* **The marketing department currently had no direction, no supervision, and no leadership.** That was not to criticize the earlier personnel, it was to criticize the revolving door. It was my perception that the cause for this revolving door was that Pearl USA and Pearl Japan would never be satisfied with any marketing director that worked in the company, and that could include me. Personnel stability must become a character trait of Pearl in the US and North American markets.

***The issues and problems related to Pearl USA sales would in part be solved by the hiring of a Pearl National Sales Manager.** This person would go on the road full time and work with the Gibson DSMs and the authorized Pearl dealers on how to sell Pearl prod-

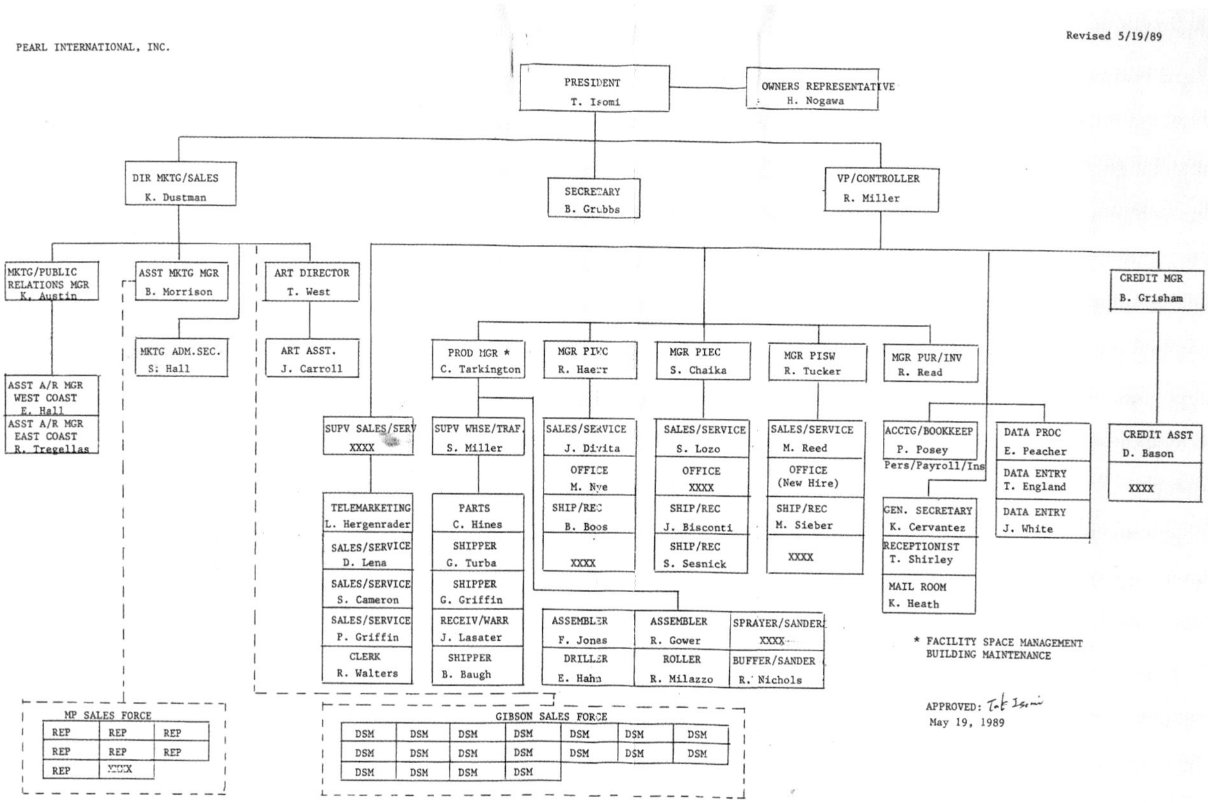

ucts in *all* the product categories, including those that were currently being ignored. (This topic also surfaced in the earlier confidential fax documents I acquired)

* **There was a potential for possible Sabian cymbal distribution as HSS distribution was faltering.** I obviously knew of and saw this developing. The exclusive sales agreement between HSS and Sabian was destined to evaporate. Should Pearl be looking at an exclusive Sabian distribution? The multiple Pearl warehouses strategically located in NJ, TX and CA, would have aligned with this plan.

***Long-time Sonor artists like Steve Smith and Jack DeJohnette might be looking to explore possible endorsement alignment changes, as HSS was stumbling with its Sonor artist relations.** This could become an opportunity for Pearl. Conversely, I also advised that Chester Thompson, a current Pearl endorser, was on his way moving over to Sonor for a product endorsement deal. There was some "coming and going" between Pearl and Sonor. With four full-time artist relations people within Pearl-USA, there was an obvious heavy emphasis on artists to promote and sell Pearl drums on the professional level. We needed to address these issues and priorities within Pearl USA through our artist relations team, currently led by Ken Austin.

***Pearl did not have a formal artist relations agreement contract that was used throughout its A/R program.** This amazed me. At this time there was no uniformity in how artists were being recruited and services were provided according to the needs of artist representation. I did not understand why this vulnerability existed and there was a need for a written consignment/loan agreement as well as a full endorsement promotional donation to an artist. It was a giveaway program. We were just giving stuff away based upon what day it was and who was asking for it and how much it was worth. There needed to be a formal program.

***There had to be a stronger Pearl product floor plan inventory monitoring by the Gibson sales force.** There was a need for weekly salesman call reports, although the current Gibson-Pearl contract did not require that kind of monitoring or reporting back to Pearl.

***There was an immediate need for a formalized clinic program structure;** documents spelling out the terms of each clinic situation. I was offering to provide a set of documents that could be used as templates; all Pam Haynie would need to do was go through and change the company and artist names. Standardization of printed program elements, policy and procedures were paramount in this area.

***The customer service and telemarketing needed to be revitalized.** There were only two men at present answering the phone, Paul Griffin and Dave Lena, dealing with all the Pearl dealers and Gibson salesmen. Both inside sales/customer service representatives were well versed and knowledgeable about Pearl products and policy, but were overwhelmed with calls and requests for assistance. There were simply not enough people to handle the influx of calls. I recommended the hiring of a full time telemarketing/customer service person, Lauren Hergenrader whom I had hired at HSS. I suggested recruiting her away from HSS and moving her to Nashville as she was a known quantity and a great asset. This was approved at this meeting. There was also some faltering with the northeast territory Gibson rep and I also recommended the recruiting of the top HSS salesman, Bob Lynch, and bringing him into Gibson and Pearl. He knew how to sell drums and he was selling Hohner guitars, so certainly he could sell Gibson guitars. That was approved by Gibson and they brought in Bob Lynch. Basically we were cherry picking the best people assets of the HSS company.

***We were preparing for the Pearl Orient Express dealer incentive trip that was scheduled for April of 1989.** We were working on the decision and selection process to qualify the winning Pearl dealers and who would participate in the actual trip, and so forth. We were organizing a champagne press conference to take place at the Pearl exhibit booth during the January 1989 NAMM convention. I felt this was a tremendous Pearl and Dealer photo-op to bring major attention to the dealer recognition that Pearl was giving to these valuable dealers, all while occupying prime visibility space in all the leading trade publications. Unfortunately, I would have to orchestrate this event myself, as no one really knew how to, or understood the significance of, what this involved on a convention booth in the middle of the Anaheim Convention Center. All winning dealers would have to be present for the meet and greet with Pearl President Tak Isomi. The trip was going to be a 10-day event in April of 1989.

***The concept of closing or consolidation of three other warehouse locations in California, Texas, and New Jersey.** This was another key topic of discussion at that meeting. It was estimated that the cost of these closures due to broken leases and employee severance packages would be $300,000.00, so it was decided not to do this at the time.

The net result of the trip was that for the first time, Pearl-Japan had an opportunity to hear the marketing director whom Tak Isomi and Ralph Miller had brought in to the company in July. I never heard anything from Tak after the meeting about my presentation or comments from the Japan management team. I received some positive feedback comments from Ralph Miller that Pearl Japanese management had been highly impressed and complimentary of me and the presentation I had brought. I was glad for the positive commentary even though it seemed no one within Pearl-Nashville wanted me to know about it.

Trying to understanding the Japanese mentality was an immediate new challenge for me which I remember to this day. There had been a table full of people staring at me throughout this presentation, absolutely expressionless. There was no facial expressions to indicate whether they were agreeing with my points, disagreeing, or even understanding what I was speaking about. I did know that all of them understood English; I had heard them speak in English. But if they wanted to speak among themselves and not be understood by all of us, (Ralph, Bob and I) they would immediately revert to speaking Japanese so we could not understand them. It was a stacked deck. I had been in these types of corporate-board meetings at American companies such as Ludwig, Gretsch and even HSS. I was used to being able to read the audience and gather immediate feedback. I was accustomed to the participants interacting through raised eyebrows, asking questions, agreeing or disagreeing, making suggestions, or even making jokes- before there was even a period at the end of my sentence. This Pearl headquarters audience was a very different business environment.

Fall of 1988 was coming- We were identifying the 20 Pearl dealers that had the highest percentage of increase from their previous year's sales; 1987 vs. 1988. It was my job to make contact with the winning dealers and organize the official PR recognition during the winter NAMM convention coming up in January.

At the same time, part of the change created with the passing of Al Duffy (who was Pearl's primary marching percussion specialist) was to implement a replacement for him. Bob Morrison had started in California at the warehouse doing a little bit of everything. Prior to my arrival at Pearl, Bob was moved to Nashville to oversee and directly manage the marching percussion/concert percussion elements of Pearl Nashville.

Ken Austin (Artist Relations) and Karl Dustman

P-950 Pedal

Pearl's new P-950 double chain drive bass drum pedal represents the ultimate in functional heavy duty pedal engineering. Never before have so many technological advancements in design been incorporated into one pedal.

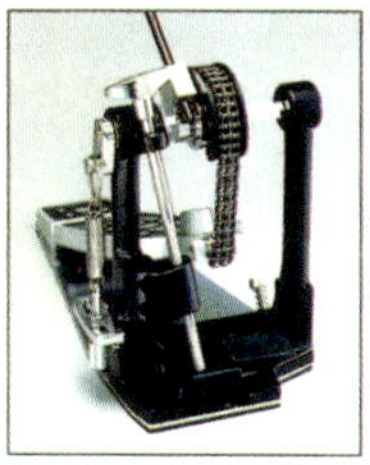

Utilizing a double width, small link chain drive system, the P-950 offers greater flexibility and is more stable than large single chain drive units. Pearl's patented felt lined chain channel guide system offers quieter, faster action than from sprocket type chain pedals.

The P-950 features Pearl's new easily accessible top mounted, spring loaded counter hoop clamping system for effortless set up and tear down.

The P-950 tensioning system allows you the ability to fully adjust both footboard tension and beater angle independent of one another.

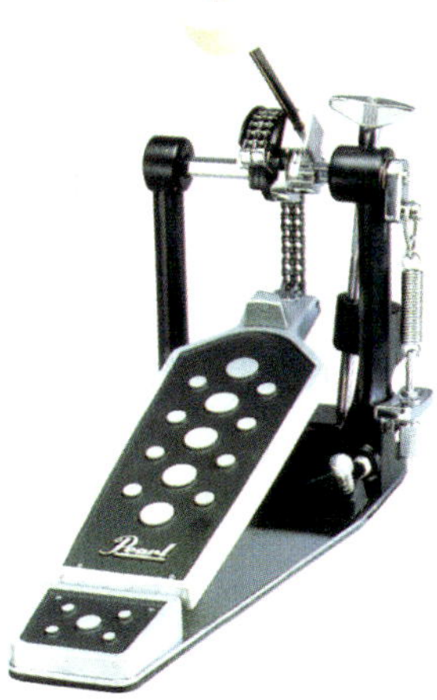

EXPORT
THE
BEST SELLING DRUM KIT
IN THE WORLD.
FOR ALL THE RIGHT REASONS.
Today's Pearl Export Series Drum outfits are the hottest selling drums ever. No one else but Pearl can offer the professional quality, great features, the most popular colors and the outstanding value that has kept the Export number one. And now more than ever dealers across the country are pricing the Export to make it an even greater value. For a limited time only (until Jan. 15, 1989) when you purchase any size Export kit, from the basic five piece kit, to the double bass seven piece Hard Rocker kit shown here, or even the large double bass nine piece kit with all the options, you'll receive Pearl's new Meltdown Kit . . . absolutely free.
The Meltdown Kit contains Pearl's most wanted drummer accessories. Included in the kit are a pair of leather drummers gloves, a Pearl headband and a pair of arm bands, a Pearl gig towel, a new Pearl K-025 tuning key with leather key chain strap and Pearl's black nylon Meltdown Kit bag. Everything you need for those hot workouts at rehearsal or on stage are included, and it's all free and available only with the purchase of any Export kit.
Pearl
Pearl
Pearl
Pearl's EX-22DW-7 "Hard Rocker" is illustrated above in #71 Ferrari Red. Cymbals not included.
THE Meltdown KIT
Free
WITH ANY EXPORT SET
To receive your free Meltdown kit, simply send your dated sales receipt (or a copy) before 1-15-89, to: Pearl International, Dept. EX. Promo, P.O. Box 111240, Nashville, TN 37222-1240.
Please provide your return address, name, age and phone number.
Pearl.
For a full-color catalog, please send $2.00 for postage and handling to: In U.S.A.: Pearl International, Inc., Dept. EX2P, P.O. Box 111240, Nashville, TN 37222-1240; In Canada, Dept. T2, 378 Rue Isabey, St. Laurent, Quebec, Canada H4T 1W1; In United Kingdom: Pearl Music Ltd., Dept. EX2P, 11 Garamonde Drive, Wymbush Milton Keynes, England MK8 8DF.

Pearl
LATIN PERCUSSION
Our standard Timbales consist of 13" and 14" chrome plated solid steel shells. Each set comes with Pearl coated WA heads and features our high quality adjustable double braced timbale stand with cowbell holder. Cowbell sold separately.
TM-150 Timbales
Our professional CG-300 Series Congas feature carefully selected seasoned Redwood, chrome plated hardware and steel counterhoop and highly responsive natural hide head. Three available sizes include the 10" quinta, 11" conga and 12" tumba in both Natural or Wine Red finish. Conga stands sold separately.
CG-300 Series Redwood Congas
BG-209R, BG-30RW Bongos
Pearl Bongos are available in either the Redwood or Rubberwood Series. With chrome plated hardware and natural hide heads as standard, these high quality professional bongos will long outlast the most determined of musicians.
The Pearl CG-200 Series Congas retain all of the top Professional features of our Redwood Congas but are constructed from more moderately priced Rubberwood. The professionally styled hardware and natural heads give this series the same outstanding style at an easily affordable price. Sizes are 10", 11", and 12" and are available in Natural or Wine Red. Free standing collapsible tripod stands are sold separately.
CB-5, CB-6, CB-8 Cowbells
Pearl's top quality Professional Series Cowbells are crafted of steel to compliment our full line of Latin Percussion. Three sizes are available 5", 6" and 8".
CG-200 Series Rubberwood Congas
The Pearl Professional Conga Stands are the essential compliment to the Redwood and Rubberwood Series Congas. Each stand features three fully collapsable rubber tipped legs that makes sure your conga set-up stays firmly in it's place. Available in three sizes to accommodate a 10" Quinta, 11" Conga or 12" Tumba.
CSS1-M Conga Stand
U.S.A. January 1989

According to the constantly-changing Pearl organization charts, he did not work under me, but I believe they gave him the title of marketing manager for marching & concert percussion. Bob was a young ambitious young man with many fine attributes which time and greater-longer experience would polish and hopefully benefit Pearl's positive image and product offerings.

December came, which was a big opportunity for Pearl to participate in the Midwest Band Clinic at the Conrad Hilton Hotel. Obviously I was very familiar with the Midwest Clinic as I had attended for many years and knew the importance of having the brand and product in front of all those music educators attending this annual event, right before Christmas. I believe this was Bob Morrison's first Midwest Band Clinic and he seemed well prepared to jump into this marketing opportunity. He had a complete display of Pearl's marching percussion and concert percussion.

Bob also had done a brilliant job of assembling a brand new marching and concert percussion catalog. Another achievement that I give Bob full credit for was the creation of a Pearl Percussion Education Resource Kit; basically the same thing as the Ludwig Percussion Aid Pack I had assembled over a decade before. Pearl International-Nashville had a complete series of educational articles written by Pearl artists involved in marching percussion that were directly associated with drum corps or marching programs that all used Pearl marching percussion instruments. This Pearl Resource Kit was received very well and expanded the brand recognition over time.

IMPROVING YOUR "QUALITY OF SOUND": THREE KEYS
By Thom Hannum

PEARL PERCUSSION EDUCATIONAL RESOURCE

A goal of every musician is to produce the best possible sound from their instrument. Although tuning and implement selection are always important, the method of playing is paramount. For the percussionist there are three guidelines which I've found to be essential to improving the "quality of sound".

1. Establishing and maintaining a proper grip.
2. Playing from the wrist.
3. Using the natural rebound.

Before discussing these guidelines I want to comment on the "quality of sound". Although important, the quality of any sound is not something that is measured by the lack of error (execution) in a performance. From an individual standpoint, it is the ability to produce the best fundamental tone from an instrument. A pure tone which is not clouded by unwanted overtones, or partials.

For tympani, keyboards, multi-tenors, and bass drums the result is a full, resonant sound: a focused tone. For the snare drum, when tuned adequately, it is the brightest, most articulate sound; the result of the highest degree of snare response. Eventually these characteristics separate the very best percussion ensembles from those that are very good.

Recommended Percussion Instrumentation
By Dr. Ben F. Miller

PEARL PERCUSSION EDUCATIONAL RESOURCE

At first glance it might seem as if the following suggestions for your school's percussion inventory might be excessive. However, please remember that a complete string section must have more than just violins, a complete brass section must have more than trumpets alone. The percussion of your band or orchestra provides the color to your ensemble. A composer will decide which woodwind or brass instrument should be used to play a specific passage. Unfortunately, this is rarely done in the percussion section. Usually a part will only be marked "snare drum" or "tom-tom." Your audience deserves to hear all of the colors of your ensemble.

It is advised that the conductor and the percussionist work together to decide which instrument should be used in a particular piece of music. Also, it is suggested that you experiment with changing the tension of the drum head and/or the stick or mallet being used to strike the drum or accessory instrument to alter the timbre.

Your school's percussion instruments are used for *every* musical rehearsal and performance on and off campus. That includes marching band competitions, solo and ensemble festivals, concert band contest, Broadway musical productions, recruiting demonstrations at elementary schools, basketball pep band, jazz ensemble, show choir, combined concerts with choral ensembles, etc.

Suggested Instrumentation For A Junior High School Percussion Section

Snare Drum*	5-½ metal shell with stand S850L (usually supplied by students from their beginning drum kits - SK600).
Concert Bass Drum	14" x 28" (PCB1428) with Fiberskyn heads or 16" x 32" (PCB1632) with Fiberskyn head with folding concert bass drum stand (CBS10) or tilting concert bass drum stand (CBS30)
Timpani	Set of aluminum bowl (pitch indicators included) 26" (7026) 29" (7029)
Crash Cymbals	1 pair of 16" or 18"
Suspended Cymbals	18" medium thin with stand
Orchestra Bells	2-½ octave with stand
Xylophone	3-½ octave (synthetic bars)
Concert Tom Toms	10", 12", 13", 14" (PCT0234) with 2 T850 tom stands
Gong	28" gong with stand*

* Students should be required to have a percussion kit (PK500) or a snare kit (SK600) depending upon the teaching method of the school.

Some Thoughts on Scoring and Arranging for the Marching Percussion Ensemble
By Ralph Hardimon and Robert Morrison

PEARL PERCUSSION EDUCATIONAL RESOURCE

The Percussion Ensemble as an Educational Experience
By Bill Rice

PEARL PERCUSSION EDUCATIONAL RESOURCE

The Five Secrets of Teaching and Learning New Music
By Matt Savage

PEARL PERCUSSION EDUCATIONAL RESOURCE

The Evolution Of Competitive Drum Corps Percussion
By Marty Hurley

PEARL PERCUSSION EDUCATIONAL RESOURCE

It became clear that additional personnel was needed specifically to handle customer service issues for the marching and concert percussion product lines. Scott Cameron was brought on as a marching percussion customer service specialist.

The newly enlarged and upgraded customer service and telemarketing team was an achievement, both for me and the Pearl-Nashville organization. I pushed for a press release and photo shoot of this internal team so the percussion world could see the development and investment that Pearl was making to service the dealers, now accessible on all Pearl products.

What was evolving, which was not the intent, was a second company within the Pearl company. I do not mean in a negative sense, but the marching and concert product lines were becoming, by Morrison's directions, a hands-off sacred cow rather than a significant product line within the company structure. I do not know whether this was ego, inexperience, or by directive from Japan, but it was becoming a problem. All marketing efforts, identity, and individuals *should* have been working together and communicating towards the common goal of positive sales and brand development. Ralph Miller and I both saw the red flags occurring on a daily basis as alienation with other co-workers was developing.

Tak Isomi seemed to ignore this situation , or just did not want to deal with it. Not very many people at Pearl really understood marching and concert percussion. I was probably the only person who knew the value of having a complete professional marching and concert percussion products line as I experienced through the Ludwig years. Plus, I knew from Al Duffy that Pearl Japan had an agenda to become the next global Total Percussion Drum Company, overshadowing everything Ludwig-Musser had ever achieved.

This conflicting personality and characteristic that was created became somewhat of an weak spot for the company. Bob needed to work with anyone and everyone within the Pearl organization. Marching and concert percussion were his product lines to manage, but it was not his company. This friction was realized and seen by Ralph Miller and I. There was no apparent solution that Tak Isomi would acknowledge or support. This problem was left unchecked.

The success of these product lines was dependent upon the independent sales force Morrison had assembled being able to work within the Pearl organization as a company. Competent sales reps for marching and concert Percussion consisted of Jack Hartranft, L.A. Brown, Joe Guth, George Humes, Len Minix and Ted May.

L to R: Dave Lena, Lauren Hergenrader, Paul Griffin, center-seated, Scott Cameron)

At the end of 1988 I got my first employee review, (something they do in corporate mentality organizations like Pearl) from executive vice-president Ralph Miller. I was given congratulations and a $5,000 Christmas bonus. I knew I must have done something right from July through December to warrant that kind of recognition. This was the highest bonus I had ever received and I felt good about it.

We were drawing closer to the Pearl Orient Express trip scheduled for April of 1989. The top twenty Pearl accounts (by calendar year increase in sales) had been identified and two individuals from each dealer were scheduled to go on the trip. In addition, Ken Austin, Tak Isomi, and I were included, representing Pearl. Gibson sent sales manager Ben Rhodes and his top three field reps David Pastore, Lyndle Volz, and Brian Wood. The trip to Japan, Taiwan, and Hong Kong was from April 3 to April 13th. There were a total of 46 people at a cost of approximately $3,600 per person for food, transportation, and hotels. If you do the math on that, it's $165,000. There were also a few people from Pearl Japan who joined us on part of the trip, so I'd estimate that the total cost was about $180,000.

The real underlying mission or purpose was to visit the Pearl Musical Instrument Company headquartered in Chiba, Japan. There was an at-length and in-depth tour of that facility and we saw all of the Pearl products from top to bottom as they were being manufactured. What I found interesting was that many of the dealer trip winners brought their spouses on these factory tours, which made for a mixed bag of attendees as we toured the factory. It was great to see the interest and enthusiasm for these factory tour experiences.

We also visited the Pearl Musical Instrument Company headquarters in Taichung, Taiwan. That was an even larger production facility. We spent an entire day going through that facility. There were of course days in between the factory visits that allowed for rest and relaxation, including various tourism activities in each of these countries. There was socializing, there were dinners, and it made for a good mix of activities.

Pearl Dealers at the Heian Shrine, April 7, 1989

DEALER PARTICIPANTS

Bringe Music Center
Robert Gooden
Henrietta Gooden

Lone Star Percussion
Joan Vogel
Nancy Vogel

Drum World
Donald Sfarzo
Connie Manis

Woodwind Brasswind
David Mester
Marjorie Mestor

Veneman Music
Joseph Kane
Mary Ann Kane

Guitar Center
Raymond Scherr
Janet Scherr

Thoroughbred Music
A.J. Altieri
Susan Altieri

Daddy's Junky Music
Addison Minott
Paul Rindone

Hermes Music
Albert Kreimerman
Carmen Kreimerman

Cascio Music
Michael Cascio
Patricia Cascio

Rhythm City
Gary Ferguson
Glenda Ferguson

Sam Ash
Steve Bender
Patricia Bender

Drum Keyboard Guitar
Kathleen Simmons
Michael Henry

Resurrection Drums
John A Becker
John G Becker

Rit Drums
James Rittenour
Lynn Ritenour

ABK Drum & Guitar
Bob Kasha
Linda Kasha

Brook Mays Music
Tom Nuckols
Deena Nuckols

At the Taiwan factory: Karl Dustman, Masani Yanigasawa, Tommy Nuckols (Brook Mayes Music), and Tak Isomi

Karl explaining the Pearl brand of cymbals warehoused in the Pearl factory

Karl explaining shell production of the Pearl Export series

The only consistent issue or complaint with the large and diverse group of dealers that were participating that I remember was that there were smokers who wanted to be able to smoke on their bus, much to the dislike of the many non-smokers that were part of the group. So one of the two busses became designated as a smoking bus, while the other was non-smoking.

The third element of the trip was a visit to Hong Kong where we spent a day and a half on strictly a tourism visit. Overall, I felt positive about the trip, the investment Pearl had made in these longtime Pearl dealers, and the potential for long term further development of relationships and Pearl sales resulting through these selected trip-winning accounts. As with any group this large, I felt like a clipboard camp director, always looking for the late or lost member of the group, in search of and tracking lost luggage, or separating dealers that were not getting along etc. I was on-call, all day, all night- every day of the trip.

After the event, I heard nothing from Tak Isomi about the success or the failure of the trip in his opinion or perspective. There was absolutely nothing mentioned or discussed about my contribution or what I would consider my shared trip-leadership of Ken Austin and me. By now, I was starting to recognize this was normal-no-comment Tak Isomi and eventually I would hear his thoughts and opinions through someone else, second hand.

Shortly after the safe return from the Pearl trip, I received two very nice personalized letters from participating retailers who took the time to say, "Thank You" to me. One was from Woodwind-Brasswind of South

Bend, Indiana, the other from Bringe Music of St Petersburg, Florida. I appreciated the comments these individuals made concerning the trip, my efforts in making it comfortable and enjoyable, as well as the impact it had on their impression of Pearl as a company.

Immediately after the trip I recall both Ken Austin and I felt disappointed at the isolation Tak Isomi made of himself during the trip. He would go off and sit somewhere away from everyone by himself or he would remain on the bus alone. Tak's withdrawal and isolation was almost like he didn't want to be there on the trip. This was definitely being noticed by all of the dealers and they would comment about the un-sociable attitude, "What's with Tak?" they would ask us. No one really knew what Tak was all about. Personally I felt that this kind of isolation, attitude and demeanor of Tak definitely overshadowed the whole trip, as Tak's character as a company president was brought into question.

In May of 1989 I was seeing, hearing, and feeling the "storm clouds coming". Part of this was the awareness that Pearl Japan was considering the purchase of Ludwig/Musser. It became well known through the various trade journals that Ludwig was up for sale, again, by The Selmer Company. The finance company conglomerate that owned Steinway, Conn, Selmer, and Ludwig/Musser was looking to dump the entire music division and sell it off piece by piece. The investment banking firm of Bowles, Hollowell, Connor & Co. in Charlotte, North Carolina was in charge of brokering the Ludwig-Musser sale deal.

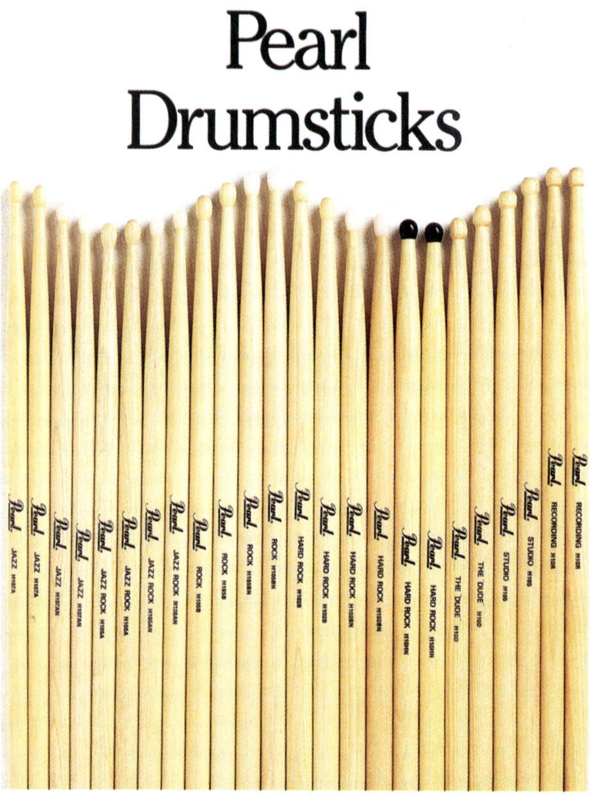

There were confidential communications that I had access to which indicated that Tak Isomi and Ralph Miller would visit Ludwig and Musser factories incognito on Monday June 12th and Tuesday June 13th to tour both factories with the brokerage company. These communications had handwritten notes from Tak indicating that special care was to be taken to avoid Pearl Nashville marketing personnel from learning of this visit or the investigation into a potential Ludwig/Musser purchase. I was completely baffled by Pearl's insistence to keep this possible acquisition and investigation invisible to me. If anyone knew those Ludwig/Musser factories intimately, that person was already in Pearl's management team. Why they would not utilize my knowledge, experience and insider insights was totally beyond any reason I could find. Another red light about the future lit up.

By now the feeling of increased and complete isolation from Tak Isomi had reached a near boiling point. I was not being included in anything that a Marketing Sales Director *should* have been discussing with the president of the company. (Ken Austin and Ralph Miller expressed their concerns about to how TAK was *not* communicating with his marketing director.) I felt like something was going to give, soon. I knew that the Pearl Nashville company was doing well financially, but not as well as it should be because of the binding contract with Gibson on the shared sales force. Pearl Japan was aware that we had one arm tied behind our back so we were not being held totally responsible and it did not appear that Pearl would separate from Gibson in the very near future.

On May 22 I addressed a letter to Pearl management in Japan expressing my growing and documented concerns. This was sent to the third generation owner of Pearl, Masani Yanagisawa, now completely in charge of the global Pearl organization. The concerns I highlighted were:

*Tak had been sidestepping communication regarding my work by communicating only with Ken Austin and Ralph Miller. This was undermining a cohesive team effort in working together.

*Changes in personnel and functions affecting marketing were not being discussed; they were simply posted on a bulletin board.

*I had been eliminated from the internal discussions about the possible purchase of Ludwig/ Musser by Pearl and was not invited to tour either the Ludwig/ Monroe NC or Musser/LaGrange, IL. manufacturing facilities. How could they ignore the assistance and insights I could provide?

*A Tak Isomi Clique Club had been created that Ralph Miller and myself were *not* a part of. Tak had created an exclusionary inner circle of people, excluding the majority of the management team.

*Tak continued to question my creativity, there was a need for joint discussions of priorities and solutions on a multitude of sales and marketing topics and issues. Tak was not approachable.

*Tak had established "pet" accounts and salesmen and was now surveying dealers and salesmen about the new marketing director, (me).

*There were issues with the Pearl Nashville staff working with and developing relationships with the Gibson sales force. This was in spite of the fact that Gibson sales manager Ben Rhodes was saying that "Karl is better than anyone Pearl has had holding the Marketing position in the past."

*Tak was continuing to air strengths and weaknesses with company outsiders which was unprofessional, inappropriate, and irresponsible.

*Tak was not involving me in decision making that was effecting my job duties and would not discuss much of anything with me, even though I was the third ranking individual on the company organization chart of authority.

*A new price increase had taken effect in June of 1989 that I had not been made aware of. Apparently the prices had already been set, factored, and turned over to the Pearl art department for the new price list- unbeknown to me. This would affect all the budget work I was preparing for the fiscal 1990 operating budget.

*Marketing needed an alliance with Marching/Concert Percussion product categories. Tak was operating that division as a separate company-within-a-company, allowing Bob Morrison to create a mental empire of his own. This extended into a personnel issue as Morrison isolated his division from the customer service and telemarketing departments. This was alienating everyone else on the marketing team.

*There was no advisement or discussion of the potential closing of the East Coast warehouse-artist relations facility which would impact the service of key accounts. We needed to be prepared for the changes to our 48th street NYC marketing strategy as well as artist relations in the very important NY/Boston/DC market. This was on the heels of the very recent dismissal of the number two person in Pearl's artist relations department, Pam Haynie.

*Tak was making decisions and discussions on ad-

A Memorable Moment:

Long Island Drum Center opened a new branch at the beginning of 1989. Ken Austin and I flew out to New York City to be there for the grand opening event and to thank Long Island Drum Center for their Pearl support at all of their multiple locations. We took shirts, hats, sweatshirts, and other giveaways, there were a variety of top national artists present along with the owners Dennis and Jerry Ricci who I remain friends with to this day.

The trip also gave me the opportunity to attend the Bruce Hornsby And The Range concert at Jones Beach in Long Island and meet his drummer, Pearl artist John Mollo. The Hornsby group was on the top of the charts at the time. We met John Mollo backstage and it gave me a chance to see Ken Austin in action; he did a marvelous job working with the artists. I saw a lot of Bill Ludwig III in Ken. It takes a certain temperament, an understanding of their music, the band, the recordings, who was hot; all of those things are part of artist relations. (It kind of reaffirmed my thought that I was glad I was not responsible!) Something that came out of that event was an interview that Ken did with John Mollo which appeared in the Pearl News in the fall of 1989.

vertising and new catalog develop with Advertising Manager Terry West which was fine, but there was no communication or discussion directly with myself and the marketing function connection. Advertising and Marketing had to be related.

*According to Gibson sales manager Ben Rhodes and the DSM's, the attitude of credit manager Bill Grisham was costing Pearl 2 million dollars per year in sales volume.

*The newly expanded and improved customer service and telemarketing functions and people had been placed under operations and finance. They should have remained a part of Sales and Marketing functions to create seamless communication to DSMs, dealers, and Gibson management.

On May 23rd I received a fax reply from Masani Yanagisawa in Chiba, Japan. He indicated that he did not grasp the reason for my "desperate effort to force Tak Isomi to respect and use his appointed Director of Sales and Marketing". He basically was scolding me for bothering him with these internal communication problems that I should have solved directly with Tak. Copies of his message were sent to Tak Isomi, Ralph Miller, and Nogawa (A Pearl Japan representative who was occupying an office in the Pearl Nashville facility).

On Friday, June 2nd, I received a written notice from Tak and Ralph Miller advising me that because of unsatisfactory work performance I was being immediately terminated with 2 weeks of severance pay and an additional two weeks of vacation pay if I would sign a one-year Security non-disclosure agreement, which I did.

After a cooling off period during the month of July, I'd had a chance to think further about the Pearl-Nashville experience and really wanted to express my personal disappointment in Tak Isomi and the Japan Pearl management team for allowing Isomi to conduct such unprofessional practices in Nashville. I created and mailed a three page letter to Masani Yanagisawa made up of post-employment observations and making the point that I did not feel that any marketing director would ever have the respect of Tak Isomi, the Nashville management team, with the exception of Ralph Miller. There was no leadership at Pearl Nashville as long as Tak Isomi was there. There was no response from Pearl headquarters in Japan..

I prepared a general statement letter to all percussion industry associates and colleagues explaining my abrupt departure from Pearl International.

If I knew then what I know now….

By the time of my departure from Pearl, I had become aware that from 1985 onward there had been tremendous indecision regarding who and what a marketing director should be for Pearl. There were constant fax messages between Nashville and Japan related to the potential decisions about marketing leadership. It was clear that the removal of marketing manager Todd Mauer and the elimination of long time Pearl ambassador/President Walt Johnson, both in 1987, led to tremendous internal strife, conflict, and turf wars for years to come.

It also became known through documents I acquired that the conflicts and challenges were present between Ralph Miller and Tak Isomi going back to August 1987 and again in February of 1988 whereby Ralph Miller became so disillusioned with Tak that he sought to resign from the company and requested a fair severance package.

And the years roll on…

Life went forwards without any contact with anyone from Pearl. In 1995 I was a candidate for a college position (Director of Contemporary Music Center) in Cleveland and asked Ralph Miller for a letter of reference/recommendation, as he had direct knowledge of my experience, knowledge and professionalism. Ralph politely obliged and provided an extremely positive letter to the director of Staffing, regarding my candidacy. Ralph Miller eventually became the President of Pearl International in Nashville, replacing Tak Isomi.

Pearl

KARL DUSTMAN
DIRECTOR OF MARKETING / SALES

PEARL INTERNATIONAL
CORPORATE DIVISION
408 HARDING INDUSTRIAL DRIVE
NASHVILLE, TENNESSEE 37211
FAX - 1-615-833-6242

(615) 833-4477

Chapter 7 Sonor Becomes Part Of Korg USA

June 1989 - April 1991

By March of 1989, word was starting to leak out into the industry that Sonor was about to make some changes in distribution within the USA market and would soon be severing the relationship with HSS. Horst link called Horst Mucha at HSS on March 20th advising him that the United States distribution for Sonor Drums would be changing at the end of May. Mucha immediately shot back a two-page memo to Link in Germany expressing his disappointment with the decision and the way this change in distribution was being handled. He also outlined the many advance paid deposits in place for Sonor-related activities as well as the June NAMM convention exhibit space in Chicago. The "friendship" between the "Horsts" was obviously strained but Horst Link pressed onwards with implementing this change for Sonor Drums.

Korg USA was already openly speaking about the forthcoming change of Sonor Drums becoming part of the Korg-Marshall family of distribution. The word was out in the market, so HSS immediately implemented a damage-control press release to eliminate the rumors that HSS was disbanding. Sabian got into the act and demanded a press release to dispel any negative speculation. This was all done before Sonor Germany could review and contribute to the tone and character of the announcement. Elisabeth Link sent Bob Cotton a scathing fax message expressing how disappointed the Link family was in not having a chance to review in advance any press release that mentioned future Sonor distribution. When I learned of this change for Sonor Drum distribution, I immediately (March 30th) sent a congratulatory letter to Mike Kovins at Korg, planting the "seed of discussion" about Sonor leaving HSS and going to Korg. I included copies of some of my 1988 confidential letters to the Links in Germany about necessary changes for Sonor in the US market and HSS operations that needed immediate attention during my time at HSS in Richmond, Virginia. By May, all the trade publications were publishing the press release announcing the separation of Sonor from HSS and Sonor drums going to Korg USA for distribution.

The Beginning

My association with Korg goes back to my friendship and various conversations with Mike Kovins, executive vice president of Korg USA, over a number of years, without any real discussion of the drum business. He was a former Hohner USA employee when the company was headquartered on Long Island, in Hicksville, New York. We shared a common knowledge of and distrust for Horst Mucha and the basic "harmonicat mentality". While Kovins never worked for Hohner during the Richmond, Virginia regime, he sympathized with what I had experienced in Hohner-Richmond. Through previous letters of introduction, Kovins knew who I was and was familiar with my reputation in the music products industry.

Michael Kovins

Sonor Drums Exits HSS; Korg To Distribute

HSS (Hohner Sonor Sabian) Inc. has announced the departure of Sonor drums from its U.S. distribution partnership. Effective June 1, the German-made drums will be distributed here by Korg, USA Inc.

According to HSS Vice President of Sales & Marketing Robert Cotton, the high price of Sonor's products denied them a major market penetration in the United States. "Although we regret the departure of Sonor," Cotton stated, "this will allow our sales people to concentrate more on products with high volume, good margin and excellent growth potential, like Sabian cymbals and Hohner Professional guitars." Sonor had been with HSS since the Richmond, VA-based division was formed in 1986.

Dave McAllister, vice president of marketing for Sabian Ltd., Meductic, New Brunswick, Canada, stated that his company will continue its international affiliation with Sonor AG as its distributor in Germany and the United Kingdom. HSS Inc. also will continue to have a connection with Sonor as the U.S. distributor of Sonor-Orff educational instruments.

In mid-1988, United Musical Instrument Corp. (UMI), parent of C.G. Conn, King and Armstrong, acquired Hohner's interest in Sonor Percussion. Thus, UMI became partners in Sonor with its director, Horst Link, grandson of the founder of the 115-year-old West German company. Sonor drums are distributed worldwide and enjoy a high reputation for quality of sound and workmanship.

In a December, 1988, *MMR* interview, Korg Vice President Mike Kovins stated Korg would be interested in a new line "that fit in with our product lines as they are now." In Sonor, Korg has taken on a line with a prestige aura. However, as was the case with HSS, the task remains to overcome consumer resistance to Sonor's hefty price tags, a situation which has been aggravated in recent years by the weak position of the U.S. dollar with respect to the German mark.

Musical Merchandise Review
May, 1989

In May of 1989, I was at Pearl and the whole relationship was unraveling quickly. I saw the handwriting on the wall that I was going to experience another career upset very soon. I got a call from Mike Kovins and Korg's brand new sales manager Pat Mazie informing me that Korg would be taking over the distribution of Sonor Drums from Germany as of June 1, 1989. They were looking for a marketing manager/ sales director to head up the new Sonor Drum division to become part of the Korg and Marshall distribution headquarters in Westbury, New York.

Originally, Korg USA was a division of Gulf & Western when they were diversifying into the music products industry. Now separated from that connection, Korg was plotting it's own course and direction for the North American market. Expanding into percussion seemed logical to blend and align with already prominent brand names in electronic keyboards and amplification. At this point, Korg USA consisted of Korg (which was made in Japan), and Marshall amplifiers (which were made in the UK). Sonor would be the third division to be exclusively handled through the Korg-USA Westbury, NY operation. I was interested in this possibility, the position they outlined, and the potential opportunity to once again be associated with Sonor Drums made in Germany. I accepted their invitation to fly me out to Westbury on May 18th to visit the Korg company and the executives for the day and then take an evening return flight Nashville. I met with many of the company leaders including newly hired National Sales Manager Pat Mazie, (who I would directly report to in the beginning) Mike Kovins, and Korg USA President, Don England.

Patrick Mazie

Don England

There was a lot of discussion and planning in development for the forthcoming Summer NAMM convention in Chicago the next month. I knew that Long Island was one of the most expensive places in the country to live- far more expensive than what I was experiencing in Nashville. I really was not interested in relocating, selling my Nashville home and moving my family once again. However, I discussed this possible relocation and Korg offered to fly my wife and I out to Long Island for a three day investigation into where to live, the possible costs of housing rentals on Long Island, and related issues to a decision-making process. We flew to Islip airport on Long Island on-May 26 and worked with a realtor who would help make the relocation from Nashville to New York. Following the trip and touring of Nassau County around the Korg headquarters, I evaluated the real costs of this move and decided that relocation package was just not adequate to accept the offer. I respectfully declined the offer from Mike Kovins. As described in the previous chapter, I was terminated from Pearl on the morning of Friday, June 2. I was given my separation papers, my final checks and my personal possessions, ending the Pearl chapter. By that afternoon, I was back on the telephone calling Mike Kovins, explaining the situation, and asking him if the offer to run the Sonor division of Korg USA was still open. He said it was. We had already talked about moving and compensation, insurance, and benefits during the interview, so I pretty much knew what was at stake. It was either acceptable or it was not.

Dustman Named Sonor's Director Of Sales

Sonor Drums, exclusively distributed in the U.S. by Korg USA, has announced the appointment of Karl Dustman as the new director of Sales and Marketing of the prestigious percussion company. An industry veteran who is well known and respected, Dustman has served in management positions with Pearl, Ludwig, Gretsch, and HSS and has now been called upon by Korg's senior vice president, Mike Kovins, to turn the Sonor line for the rapidly-growing firm.

"Karl was the obvious choice for the position," states Kovins, "because of his experience in the music business and particularly because of his expertise in the percussion market. We are very pleased that Karl is able to join us in launching Sonor into a new era."

As Sonor director of Marketing and Sales, Dustman will be based in Korg's Long Island, NY headquarters and will be responsible for all of Sonor's operations. "I am pleased and excited to have the opportunity to help guide Sonor into a new phase of development," Dustman asserts. "Now that Sonor has a stable and growth-oriented company like Korg behind it in the U.S., I believe we will be able to meet and exceed all of the challenges presented to us in the coming decade."

I accepted the invitation, which was dependent upon my ability and agreement to immediately come to Korg USA the following Monday, June 6th, as a start date. The summer NAMM show at McCormick Place in Chicago was coming up in June and there was going to be a huge launch of Sonor drums as a new division of Korg USA. Since my visit to the Korg headquarters, the company had hired a Sonor product manager, Gary Carnivalli, who was a former drum department manager from either Sam Ash or Manny's on 48th Street. There was, however, no one to really lead and run the Sonor Division, no one to introduce it to the dealers and salesman, no one to write the Sonor deals and incentives for the NAMM convention, and so forth. Korg needed a recognized percussion industry expert immediately. I jumped on a plane that Monday morning and basically lived on Long Island in a hotel for that month, going directly to the NAMM show in Chicago, then directly back to Korg USA on Long Island after the convention. I arrived at Korg and jumped in immediately. Everything that needed to be done had to be accomplished with lightening speed. I was given a small open cubicle office which was a little challenging in itself. I was used to having an office with a door and a window; now I had a cubicle that was open-air to the entire organization.

I was seated across from the Korg credit department, listening to them wrangle all day on the telephone trying to get dealers to pay past due invoices. Gary Carnivalli had just been hired about a week or two before my arrival, beginning his basic Product Manager duties. The start-up inventory was already arriving from HSS-Richmond at the Korg warehouse. On Friday morning of my first week in getting acclimated with Gary, he did not arrive for work. I called him at home. He said "this is not the position I was looking for and therefore will not be coming back to Korg". Being the "new guy" that I was, everything was a challenge and learning experience. Eventually I would bring my own personal automobile to New York which forced some confrontation and discussion about getting a parking space in the executive parking lot. At this point in my career and life I had learned how and with whom to get things done. The main thing was that we got started proactively in handling the Sonor product, marketing, sales and promotion all within the framework of the existing Korg organization. I had to work with *everyone* from the very beginning in helping Sonor get up to speed within the company. I made everyone a "friend". Korg got a press release going immediately which was well written by Larry DeMarco and was released to the music industry trade publications. There appeared to be tremendous potential for Sonor. It was only eleven to twelve months from when I'd departed HSS to when Sonor became part of Korg. Upon departing HSS, I had of course taken with me everything that I had worked on during HSS; all the Sonor product and parts information binders, all of the Sonor-HSS dealer lists, all of the various product discount schedules, Sonor clinic programs, and so forth. I brought a wealth of information to Korg about Sonor that dramatically helped during the transition. I also had a certain amount pride and satisfaction in knowing that I was reconstructing Sonor for Korg USA and that the product line was "being removed from HSS". I felt this abrupt change in distribution was based upon the unhappiness that Horst Link had about all the things I already knew regarding HSS not developing the mar-

KORG SALES NETWORK

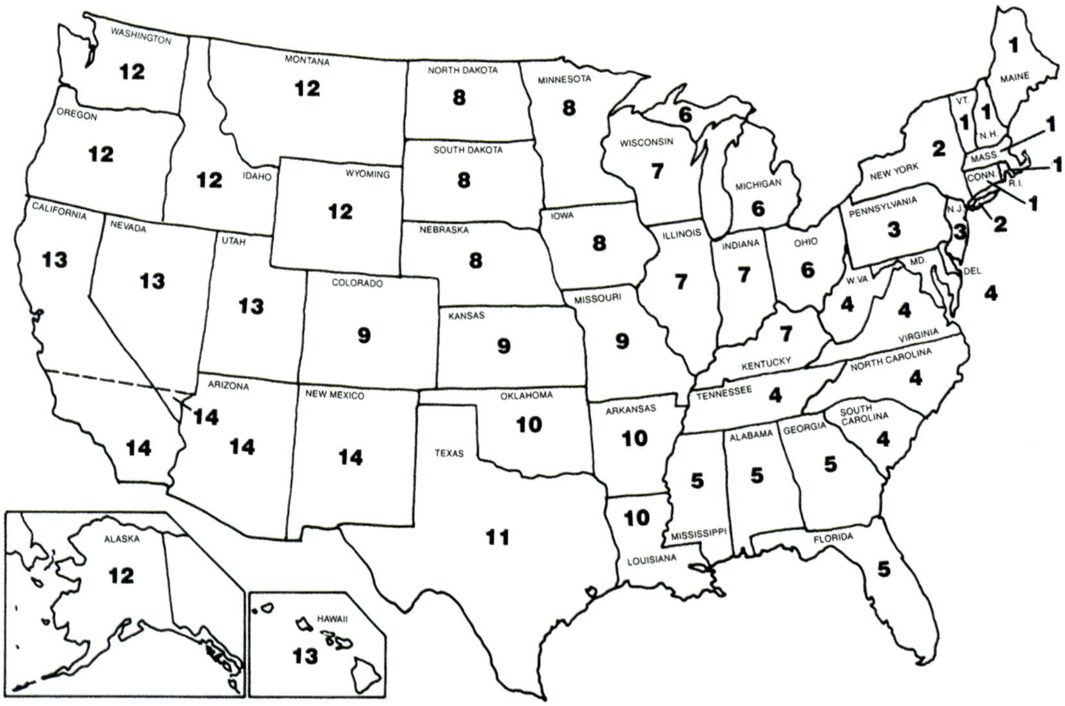

REGIONAL SALES REPRESENTATIVES

TERRITORY NUMBER	DISTRICT SALES MANAGER	CUSTOMER SALES REPRESENTATIVE	TERRITORY NUMBER	DISTRICT SALES MANAGER	CUSTOMER SALES REPRESENTATIVE
1	Marcel Lessard	Debbie Kallansrude	11	Ron Taylor	Maria Kalaj
2	Allan Pearlman	Ronnie Beck	12	Fred Gillis (Korg & Marshall) Doug Martin (Concert Series)	Teresa Breen Gaye Zangara
3	Ken Cilione	Ronnie Beck			
4	Pete Acree	Gaye Zangara	13	Peter Markovich (Korg only, except Utah–Korg & Marshall) Mike Doyle (Marshall only) Doug Martin (Concert Series)	Rich Koestner Teresa Breen Gaye Zangara
5	Charlie Lytle	Rich Koestner			
6	Jeff Dunmire	Debbie Kallansrude			
7	Ken Zemanek	Gaye Zangara	14	Ken Peveler (Korg only) Mike Doyle (Marshall only) Doug Martin (Concert Series)	Teresa Breen Teresa Breen Gaye Zangara
8	*To Be Announced	Debbie Kallansrude			
9	Larry Manzi	Maria Kalaj			
10	Vince Smith	Maria Kalaj			

ket for Sonor Drums. This change was inevitable but seeing the distribution going to Korg USA was unexpected.

The Korg management and mentality was perfect to take on Sonor distribution. Korg is a combo oriented company. Even while Korg USA was owned by a Japanese company, they had the financial resources to do whatever it would take to place Korg, Marshall, and Sonor on a high-visibility platform. This fact made it a lot easier for me to convince Korg management, "This is what we need to do… This is how we're going to do it…and this is what it's going to cost…." Korg had the financial backing for me to use the word "patience", meaning "this is not going to happen overnight." This was totally unlike Hohner's completely unrealistic thinking that HSS was going to turn an immediate profit in the first months of its existence, no less the first year. Korg knew that the newly created Sonor Drum Division was going to create red ink (losses) for quite a while but those start-up losses would be earned back eventually. If Korg could do for Sonor what they had done for decades with Korg and Marshall, the template for success and profit was in place, and that certainly helped me.

Time went by extremely fast in June as I was immersed in learning about a new company and their people while trying to train and educate everyone about drums, drum dealer thinking and the finer points of Sonor made in Germany quality and price justification. As we got into the June summer show. Sonor was introduced as part of the Korg family handling the North American marketplace for Sonor Drums. The show was attended by both Horst Link and his wife Elisabeth.

Korg made a tremendous effort and investment in making certain Sonor looked excellent and was well presented in all aspects of product and fixture display, booth lighting, signage/overhead banner, guest artists and support literature. Everything that HSS should have done when handling the Sonor distribution.

The NAMM convention provided a unique opportunity for me to get to know Seiki Kato, who was the son of the founder of Korg in Japan. He was positioned at Korg USA in Westbury and was learning his way in every facet of Korg USA operations in the US market while also providing liaison assistance with the Korg headquarters in Japan. It was quietly known but never spoken that Kato would succeed Don England as President. Seiki was a very kind and soft-spoken individual and he spoke excellent English. Upon my arrival at the Korg exhibit in McCormick Place in Chicago for the booth set-up process, he saw me contemplating this huge mountain of Sonor product boxes in the designated Sonor area. These were piled high all

Karl Dustman, Horst Link, Jack Dejohnette

waiting to be unpacked and set up for the exhibit. The Sonor company in Germany had selected the products for the display and we really did not know what they had decided to exhibit and ship to Korg for this display. Seiki came over to me and said, "Karl-son! You look like you need some help with all of these Sonor boxes!" I graciously accepted his offer to help. He and I unpacked and set up the Sonor display single handedly. He did not know anything about drums, but was able to sort the boxes for me by model number creating smaller mountains of boxes that could then be unpacked and the product set-up. I really needed and appreciated this physical assistance from him. Quite honestly, Sonor never looked so good. The lighting, signage, and overhead banners looked great.

The Drum Business: Karl and Mike Kovins

Karl and Roy Burns reconnect

There were key Sonor artists on-hand, there were plenty of Sonor literature bins, and Korg basically did everything that HSS didn't do and that Horst Link complained to Horst Mucha about that HSS were not doing. I looked at this situation in having been re-united with Sonor as possibly fate, good fortune or a second chance to really accomplish something with the Sonor products and brand. This was a new "game" in really bringing Sonor to a competitive forefront where it had never been before. I found satisfaction and joy in having this opportunity after some of the struggles and conquests with HSS and Pearl Inc. The NAMM show was completed and was viewed as a complete success for all three divisions and it was time for me to officially move to New York. I rented a condominium and temporary furniture in Haughpaugh, NY which is quite a distance out in Suffolk County. This was a much less expensive area but I also soon learned that the traffic on Long Island is a killer. I could spend an hour or more just traveling to the Korg office in Westbury using the Long Island Expressway or the Northern State Parkway. Hello, New York!

The next real priority was to get the inside customer service people, who were very competent and knowledgeable on Korg and Marshall, totally immersed and wrapped up in Sonor Drums. They knew nothing about drums other than they knew the names of the rock and roll artists that played them. The same immediate education and training was necessary for the highly trained and skilled Korg and Marshall corporate sales force. The Korg Sales Force were mostly a dedicated long time and highly paid sales force that had been associated with Korg and Marshall for years. Now the salesman had a third division and product line called Sonor that they were expected to learn and know how to sell to all the existing Sonor dealers across the country. It was my job to provide that guidance and information on percussion products that were far more technical than the salesmen were accustomed to dealing with. The sales team were mostly experts at selling Korg or Marshall products but now they had sales quotas by territory for Sonor as well.

This position at Korg enabled me to rekindle my relationships and friendships with the traditional Sonor artists. Steve Smith, Jack DeJohnette, Jeff Watts, and Bobby Rock were all happy to see knowledgeable leadership back in the Sonor brand supporting the Sonor product and artists. This seemed like a conclusion for the eleven to twelve months of desperate uncertainty as to what HSS was going to do and how this would impact Sonor. The future of HSS was unknown and for many of the artists they were relieved to see Korg take over the distribution and continue the relationship I had developed with many of the long-time Sonor artists. As time moved forwards quickly, it became clear that there was much more work to be done with Sonor than I could handle myself in a timely manner. Korg was patient, but I realized after Carnivalli's abrupt departure in early June that I could still use a right-hand Sonor Product Manager. If we had twice the people we could ramp up Sonor sales twice as fast. Kovins instructed, "We will hire a product manager for Karl who will be under him and will do whatever Karl needs him to do for Sonor." Mike Kovins and I started looking for a full time product manager. We connected with Bob Saydlowski who at the time was a freelance writer for *Modern Drummer* magazine and did all of the monthly new product close-up product reviews and editorial writing. Bob did that work for Modern Drummer from his home in Massachusetts. I knew who Bob was, though I'd never really dealt directly with him. Over the years I probably sent him various products for *Modern Drummer* product review close-up and feature in the publication. He was already known and recognized to a degree in the percussion industry. His work for Modern Drummer seemed to always be well respected.

Kovins and I moved quickly. After I chatted with Bob on the telephone we flew Bob down to Long Island for an interview. We came to an agreement and Korg authorized me to pay his moving and living expenses to relocate to Long Island. We placed him in the same small cubicle with me, sort of like birds of a feather in a very small nest. Bob is very much a "gear guy" which is exactly what Sonor within Korg needed right now. He got into all of the technical information, exact model numbers, part numbers, hardware compatibility and drum finish codes. Bob would handle all of the technical product aspects far better than someone with my temperament could. We had what I believed was an excellent combination of personalities and expertise supporting the Sonor products within Korg's corporate environment. It was decided that Bob and I should visit the Sonor factory in Germany in August of 1989. We were picked up at the Frankfurt airport and greeted by Karl Heinz Menzel who was the right hand man for Horst Link , responsible for international sales to the United States. Part of his responsibility was based of his excellent personality; his ability to deal with international distributors, he related well with the Sonor artists on a global basis, and he spoke fluent English.

Bob and I spent an entire week, August 13-18th , going through the factory in detail. This was fantastic, as we basically saw and learned everything that was manufactured and fabricated in the Sonor factory.

We learned who ran what department, and how to deal with any issue on product, special orders and customer needs in the USA market. Up until this time and trip, all of the Sonor-Korg questions we had were faxed almost exclusively to Karl Heinz Menzel and he would be distributing them out through the Sonor organization. There were other people within the Sonor-Germany organization who could speak and read English, so we were put in direct contact with a wider group.

Oliver Link, Karl Dustman, Bob Saydlowski

The time we were together at the Sonor factory was extremely productive and encompassed a very intense and diverse list of topics, people and discussion on establishing amicable work relationships, trying to understand the complexities of the USA market, and the manufacturing issues at the Sonor factory.

L-R: Karl Heinz Menzel (Sonor-Germany), Karl Dustman, Bob Saydlowski

Monday started with a tour of the new "Sonor Museum" that displayed decades of different Sonor products that were produced throughout different time periods of the company's history. This segued directly into intense discussions on how Korg could enter the marching percussion market in the US with Sonor made-in-Germany drums and related accessories. Details on snare drums, bass drums, timp-toms units carriers ensued, developing two different product line definitions; Exclusive Series for college and drum corps competitive level, Professional Series for junior high school marching band applications. Immediately following this meeting we moved into serious discussions and review of the prototype FORCE 2000 series drum sets. Eleven key recommendations were established in providing direction and clarity on how the new product line needed to be presented, marketed, labeled, branded, and manufactured. An enjoyable dinner followed, hosted by Karl Heinz Menzel.

Tuesday started with a compete factory tour conducted by Karl Heinz, bringing special attention to the specific areas of manufacturing improvement, growth and the establishment of a finished "shell bank inventory" This would definitely assist with better product delivery and container shipments to the US. The increased market demand for lacquered shell finishes versus covered shells prompted Sonor to create a flawless finish area within the factory as well as entering the metallic fleck finish market by creating special spray "operating room" environment. This was very impressive. In the afternoon we moved into direct discussions with Oliver Link who oversaw Sonor's advertising, promotional catalog-materials, artist relations, and new product introductions. This included communicating the intentions of the Korg USA marketing strategy for the "First Dollar campaign" that was in development before our departure to Germany. The handling of international artists, recruitment of competitive brand artists and the forthcoming Sonor artist advertising and poster campaign to launch the FORCE 2000 were thoroughly reviewed. Further discussions included the Sonor-Korg plans for the Modern Drummer Festival Weekend, the Percussive Arts Society convention, the Natl. Association of Jazz Educators Convention, and the prospect for further opportunity in working with the Disney World Epcot Center music program. An enjoyable dinner followed, hosted by Oliver Link.

Wednesday started with further discussions with Oliver Link targeting the forthcoming Sonor-Korg "DETAILS BOOKLET" and supporting wall-size poster in development. We moved into the next segment focused on export order development and scheduling with the factory. Details on handling special orders, shell-drilling requests, order consolidation, catalog numbering of new products and open communication in working with the Sonor factory and production. This was a lengthy discussion, bringing to the forefront how to best work together in manufacturing and order development. The day ended on a positive note of "better communication" and resolution on the complete gamut of principles, production problems and priorities. Dinner followed, with Siegfried Acker and Karl Heinz Menzel.

Thursday and Friday concentrated on detailed discussions and requests Bob and I made for Sonor support;

-Salesman training kits and dealer-call product discussion samples

-Berklee School of Music request for an additional Hi-Lite loaner kit to augment their 3-Sonor kit teaching facility.

- New product development, Piccolo and Side-Drum…snare drums

- New Double-Pedal introduction for PASIC convention

- Pricing for potential Marching Percussion product lines, definition of Exclusive and Professional Series

- Beginner Snare Drum product development, pricing and competitive features.

- Market introduction of the 1988 Sonor Protec hardware line, available in silver satin finish and black gloss.

This time spent in the Sonor factory was extremely beneficial to all and considered a complete success.

This laid the groundwork for further trips to Sonor

and even more memorable experiences.

Korg had Steven Ross & Associates in New York City on a retainer as their advertising agency and public relations firm. They were in charge of anything and everything related to print, media, advertising, logo design, and anything artistic with brand management and promotion. Obviously this was before the age of social media or the internet, so the electronic connection was not part of the equation. The primary Sonor challenge and hurdle was the ongoing resistance of the United States buying public to Sonor products because of the high prices of the products. The continuing changes in the currency rates between the German Mark and the US dollar made the situation even worse. There was no question Sonor was *the* highest quality product, no question that it was made in Germany, but not everybody could afford a "Mercedes Benz-type" percussion musical instrument. This was the same market challenge previously encountered for Charles Alden as well as HSS.

It was the recommendation of Steven Ross and Robbie Cline that the initial PR focus for Sonor as a brand and product was to create a campaign that focused on justifying why Sonor products were more expensive. This became a consumer educational and awareness podium as to why the drum customer needed to invest a little more to own drums and related products that were so much better. The Ross Agency outlined a campaign that launched October 1st through January 31st 1990, basically for brand recognition and trying to eliminate the high-cost purchase barrier. In September, the ad campaign launched with a full page ad, "You're A Dollar Closer To Perfection." What this basically did was create the consumer incentive and desire for visiting an authorized Sonor Drum Dealer to check out the Sonor products on display. At the same time it immediately created a corresponding two-page spread advertisement that listed all Sonor dealers by state. It identified who were the Sonor dealers across the country.

Sonor-Korg wanted drummers to visit those Sonor dealers and test/evaluate Sonor products that are on display, pick up and complete the "Compare Sonor Drums" questionnaire, and send this to Sonor at Korg. They would then receive the twelve-page GET SERIOUS, LOOK AT THE DETAILS Booklet. Included in the inside front cover of the booklet was a real one-dollar bill as a "start to saving and purchasing your Sonor set". You would also get a wall poster that illustrated specific points of product quality and features. The emphasis was to explain why the customer should invest and why the Sonor product was worth the extra costs.

Korg realized that Sonor needed a broader diversification of the consumer price point at the entry level. Looking at the global drum set market, it is pyramid shaped. The bulk of the sales are in entry-level lower

priced sets, or the base of the pyramid. The pinnacle of the pyramid was the Sonor Signature Series averaging about $8,500 Retail. There was not enough volume at the top of the pyramid to support any company or to build market share recognition. It was obvious that Sonor needed to become "entry-level friendly" for the dealers and the drummer-consumers. This was a constant topic of discussion and many hours were spent outlining the basic product requirement during the August trip to the Sonor factory. Recalling from the HSS era and experience, Sonor previously attempted "low cost drum sets by importing them from Asia". This failed miserably on quality through the introduction of the International Series, Performer Series and the Panther Series, all manufactured in Asia. This needed another answer and further investigation with input from recognized USA percussion retailers.

Sonor decided to send the eldest Link son, Joerg Link, to the United States for a week in September. He was going on tour around the country with me for a week calling on Sonor dealers and non-Sonor dealers. I would personally select the dealers that I wanted him to visit. We established a time table for this trip, I set up the schedule with dealers, cities, dates and times so that Joerg Link could see, hear, and experience a vast assortment of US percussion retailers. We questioned the dealers about Sonor products, what was selling, what was not, what price points were selling best. Joerg did this in a very methodical manner based upon his "doctorate of business" type background. I set everything up in advance with the flights, the hotels, the car rentals, and so forth. We basically went on a one week tour around the country. I knew up front this would be a challenge, but it was also an opportunity to have a Link family member see and experience my ability to organize and conduct the tour. More importantly, he could experience my relationship with the leading percussion retailers we would visit. I was on a first name basis with many of the dealers because of the Pearl Orient Express tour. Tommy Nuckols ran the drum department at Brook Mayes Music in Dallas, Texas, and was one of the first dealers we visited with a predetermined confirmed appointment date and time. I don't think Brook Mays was a Sonor dealer at that time, but Tommy would certainly take the time to meet, knowing that one of the Link family members had flown over from Germany to visit with him. Dealers were generally impressed by this personal visit and desire for their input. This personal contact helped open the door in the future for Sonor sales in many cases. While Jeorg got confronted directly by these dealers, they were honest in telling him what Sonor needed to do to gain a broader acceptance and market share in the US market. He also heard why they would never stock and sell the Sonor product line until this and that happened. Jeorg took all of these notes back to Germany and basically unloaded this on the factory as to what he heard, saw and experienced during this cross country trip with me. Sonor Germany at this time was introducing an unprecedented quantity of new products entering the global market. Many of these products were now starting to arrive at Korg USA. There was a whole new series of drums called the Hi-Lite Series. These were beautiful, with brass-plated hardware, special lacquered metallic finishes, and quite expensive. The line of anodized, brush-coated hardware called Protec introduced in 1988 continued to expand and now be offered in matching brass finish stands to compliment the HiLite series. The Protec stands were beautiful, very slick in designed, no scratching, no denting, no slipping, and also quite expensive.

At the same time, the factory came out with a whole new series of snare drums; featuring different sizes, different materials, different shell-thicknesses, etc. Sonor was really doing exciting new things in Germany to bring the brand and product to even more global

attention and desirability. Unfortunately this also supported the perception that Sonor makes the most expensive drum equipment in the world.

Sonor also developed their own drum head manufacturing capability in the factory. Oliver Link designed a breathtaking Sonor Drum Head-Made in Germany Catalog that was truly a "work of art". The company manufactured its own heads for every drum the factory manufactured. The only product line they did not make their own heads for was timpani. The line included all drum set heads, marching and concert percussion heads and were all being made at the Sonor factory in Germany. A huge investment of time, factory space and engineering development.

In November of 1989, Sonor participated in the annual Modern Drummer Festival in New Jersey.

As the new 1989 Sonor drum head catalog pointed out, Sonor had a history of manufacturing drum heads that went back over a century, to 1875! Of course all drum heads up until the 1950s were made of calfskin and drum head production was a skilled trade.

The large bass drum head in the photo shown in the historical photo included in the 1989 catalog was one of the world's largest, produced in an era when drums could be made no larger than the largest steer hide that could be processed.

The Modern Drummer Festival was an annual event run by the magazine and Rick Van Horn did a masterful job in orchestrating this very complex event. The Festival was a two day event conducted in a performance auditorium near the MD publication headquarters. Both festival days were nonstop, showcasing a diverse assortment of US and international artists giving drum clinics and demonstrations for two full days. Sonor had never participated in this event in the past, so this Festival became a priority for market visibility and consumer awareness. It was a natural event to participate and support as it was right across the Hudson River from New York. Bob Saydlowski and I rented a truck and took an entire assortment of Sonor products to display in the auditorium lobby of the theater. And to contribute to the top level artist line of performers, Sonor sponsored Jack DeJohnette to be featured on the program. He did a marvelous job as a player and Sonor representative.

Jack DeJohnette

Karl Dustman, Jack DeJohnette, Aldo Mazza

Bob Saydlowski, Karl Dustman, Jack DeJohnette, and Robert Zildjian

I continued to pursue and keep the topic of school percussion business on the front burner of discussion, both with Korg and the Sonor factory. I originally approached Mike Kovins with school percussion products early on in our discussions and basically got a green light from him to go ahead and investigate this with Sonor Germany as well as my domestic resources. I stressed the concept that the development of school orchestral and concert percussion instruments from Sonor-Germany was a measure to protect both Korg and Sonor Germany from the vulnerability of the drum set market. The topic of Marching Drums specifically was discussed at length during the August meetings in Germany at the factory. I also pursued an introduction of a beginner snare drum kit very similar to what was being sold by all USA domestic companies. You will recall from the Ludwig Chapter my commentary concerning that any time there is a blip in the United States economy, drum set sales are going to falter. This consumer-spending economic stagnation will instantly slow the demand for and production of drum sets. The only way of surviving that period financially and in terms of market brand awareness, is to have school business instruments available in the market. During the regular economic down-turns of the seventies, Ludwig survived on school business and snare drum kit business alone.

By the end of the year, I continued regular communications on snare drum development and the requested samples of marching percussion instruments. This met with a receptive response. Early discussions focused on developing a complete line of marching drums in both the "drum corps level" and "high school-junior high level" series. This called for a great deal of market research, and I was going out and buying competitive samples from Ludwig, Pearl, and Yamaha, to send to the factory in Germany where they took them apart and studied them. We had as a goal to come up with some product to show at the Texas Music Educators Association convention in February of 1990 and the Midwest Band and Orchestra Clinic convention in December.I picked up where I left off with some of the same people I'd spoken to about the Gretsch molded snare drum kit cases. Sonor already had a complete marching line including mallet instruments, so it was not like they didn't know anything about marching instruments and carriers, but it was made for the European market. I felt the line could be modified to fit the American market without reinventing the wheel.

Progress was being made in communicating the product needs and adaptations necessary for the US marching band and drum corps markets.

I started getting marching snare drum samples from the Sonor factory and called upon my friend and the former chief engineer and marching specialist at Ludwig, Al Lemert. Al had started his own drumstick company, Silver Fox, when he departed Ludwig in 1981. I knew he was still very active in the marching percussion market and competition circles. I asked Al to take a look at these marching snare drum samples, 12x15, 12x14, and give me his engineering-vision and terminology as to what needed to be improved or modified for use and sales in the U.S. market. Al graciously did this out of friendship and gave me pages of detailed recommendations which I immediately shared with the German factory. Fortunately, Sonor was very appreciative of getting this in engineering style technical text details.

Al Lemert analysis of Sonor marching snare drum prototype

Silver Fox Percussion

Innovative Percussion Products

April 27, 1990

Karl Dustman
Korg, USA
89 Frost St.
Westbury, N.Y. 11590

This is a report on my test and evaluation of the Sonor Exclusive 12 X 14 marching snare drum.

Instrument as received:

Appearance: over-all, excellent.
Chrome detail: very good, however, some pre-chrome sanding/polishing marks evident on hoops and snare mounting brakets.
Shell: long scratch on white finish, next to carrier mounting bracket.

Functional aspects:

1. Snare hoop stands (3), not needed. (2) would suffice, as on returned sample. (Cost factor) The part could be longer to match the drop-gate hoop, but not of necessity, if at all.

2. Bearing edges (2) are too sharp, blend (lite sand) to a smooth radius. The profile and edge location is fine just as it is. The use of the outer ply as the bearing edge adds strength, to prevent shell collapse under high tension. All of the bearing edges should be lubricated and polished. (Parafin) Lubrication stops the head from binding on the shell edge during tensioning.

3. Snare bed depth and span:

   The depth of the bed, at center is approximately .100 (decimal) thousands. The span, (spread side to side) is 46°/52° depending on which end is checked. The ideal span for this snare bed depth (.100) would be 75° to 80°.
   A short span, plus depth, causes head distortion at the bed area. The plastic must be tensioned more at the cut area to make it conform to the deep-short bed. This also causes the hoop to distort in the same area. This bed design works well wih a non-extended snare like the Ludwig (400). That is, the snare plates are resting on the head itself, not extended beyond the shell edge. Extended snares work best with the wider snare bed.

4. Shell diameter/concentricity:

   Measured, across snare beds: 13-13/16".
   Measured, at 90° to snare bed" 13-3/4".
   No problem with concentricity.

   The shell diameter should be at 13-7/8" for minimal head channel inside diameter, to shell outside diameter clearance. This prevents the head channel from rolling excessively and deforming. (Pull-out.)

cont'd.

P.O. Box 06884 Fort Myers, Fl. 33906-6884 (813) 332-4141

Al Lemert analysis of Sonor marching snare drum prototype

5. Hoop inside diameter:

The excess clearance between the inside of the hoop and the out-side of the head channel, adds to the rolling/deforming of the head channel, (pull-out). As the head is tensioned, (usually non-uniformly), it can and will move within the hoop, until it (head channel) contacts one side of the hoop inside diameter. This then increases the clearance on the side-opposite, thus putting the hoop pressure point at the outer edge of the head channel, resulting in channel roll and head pull-out. This also causes excessive radial pressure on the shell edge. This in turn can cause shell collapse.
To avoid re-tooling for the hoop I.D., head centering pads (rubber/plastic) could be added to the head channel O.D., or to the hoop ~~out~~ IN-side diameter.

6. Tension casings:

The (2) screw fastening system is totally inadequate to prevent casing distortion. Upon removal of several casings from the shell, imprinting of the shell finish was quite evident. The drum, as delivered, had only a minimum amount of head tension, and showed moderate imprinting on the finish. Under high tension, the finish would develope wrinkles at each end of the casing. Eventually, due to stress, the casing would fail and break.
A second mounting boss could be added at the location of the **ejector** pin pads inside of each end of the casing. This would prevent casing distortion. Prevention of imprinting can also be helped by increasing the area (thickening) of the end section of the casing. (At the tee-nut web.)

7. Drum weight:

19.5 lbs. is far too much for the average high school band drummer to carry. Not to mention the additional weight of the carrier.
Aluminum castings, (High grade alloy) would reduce the total weight of the casings by 28%, which would reduce the drum weight by 1 lb. 2 oz. (527 gm.) Aluminum (high grade alloy) hoops would greatly reduce total drum weight, without sacrificing reliability and strength.

8. Snare mechanism:

The Signature unit is too expensive, too complicated and too heavy. (4.5 lbs.) Adaptibility, through modification would be too costly and not solve the problem.
The existing throw-off unit is basically, temporarily, acceptable, if the following items are considered.

a. Replace the string suspension with synthetic belting. The snare plates have existing slots.
b. Develope an adjustable snare strand unit.
c. The existing throw-off unit can be converted to an extended, one end drop-off unit. Eliminate the roller unit at the throw-off end. Fasten the butt end of the snare plate over the butt roller using a synthetic belt attached to the snare tension unit. Fasten the (NEW) adjustable snare plate to the throw-off assembly. (Some tooling here.) Raise the throw-off unit up towards the shell edge. This system would allow vertical movement of the snares at the throw-off end and allow horizontal movement at the butt end. (TENSION)

Best regards;

AL.

Sonor Expands Product Line With Competitively Priced Force 2000

Sonor Percussion of Aue, West Germany, has long been recognized as a leader in the manufacture of high-end professional drum kits. At the January NAMM show, however, the company announced plans to aggressively pursue the entry-level drum market with the introduction of its new Force 2000 drum series. With a five-piece kit set to retail for under $1,600, the Force 2000 represents an entirely new price point for Sonor.

"We are attempting to make Sonor quality accessible to virtually every drummer," explains Karl Dustman, director of marketing for Sonor at Korg USA. "The challenge in making the product was to maintain the quality and performance Sonor is known for, while achieving a more affordable price. Rather than just go to Taiwan and purchase a non-descript product, Horst Link and his engineers developed a completely new drum line from the ground up."

The new Force 2000 offers a entirely new hardware line that is produced at the Sonor plant. Like all other Sonor hardware, it is triple chrome plated for a brilliant and durable finish. The nine-ply cross-laminated poplar combines light weight with exceptional strength. Shells will be available in three covered finishes (white, red, and black), and the line will consist of standard five- and seven-piece kits.

The Force 2000 offers a number of features that are generally associated with products costing far more. A newly designed bass drum spur boasts a patented memory device that enables the drummer to set the spur to the same angle every time. The line also includes a newly designed chain-operated drum pedal, similar to the renowned Sonor Pro-Tec pedal.

SONOR PRESIDENT HORST LINK and U.S. Marketing Director Karl Dustman (left) unveil the new competitively priced Force 2000 drum line. Manufactured entirely in West Germany, the new line will retail below $1,600 for a five-piece set.

The Force 2000 will be fully described in a lavish new full-color catalogue that will be available at the NAMM show. In addition, ads featuring Chester Thompson, Steve Smith, and Nicko McBrain will begin running in the second quarter of 1990. Dustman indicated that Korg will begin shipping the Force 2000 in late February.

"With the addition of this new product line, we can now offer our retailers Sonor quality at every price point," explained Dustman. "The new Force 2000 is a great value for novice percussionists and a great profit opportunity for retailers. It is a high-quality, distinctive set that reflects Sonor's unmatched heritage of quality."

1989 ended with a feeling of optimism and anticipation of the coming year of 1990. We had accomplished a tremendous amount in a very short period of time and there was starting to be a feeling of Korg and Sonor working together. Communicating and responding to faxes improved, and everyone was beginning to see the vision of what Sonor could become. The end of the year also marked the retirement of Korg President, Don England. Seiki Kato became president, and Mike Kovins continued as the executive vice president. My real inside-person and ally really remained Mike Kovins because he saw and knew what I was accomplishing and recognized what it was going to require in terms of time, money, effort, and people to make Sonor distribution work. The Sonor operation was basically functioning. Customer service and the outside salesmen had a basic understanding of the Sonor product line. Even though they were constantly asking Bob and I questions, they were learning. The integration of Sonor into Korg was truly on-the-job training. We were able to secure the part-time secretarial assistance of Claudine Reynolds to help with the huge amount of reports, artist communication, faxes and letter preparations. We had a Sonor team in place.

The New Year Of Sonor Growth And Opportunity

We were all eagerly anticipating the new lower-cost Sonor drum series which was in development for almost the entire second half of the previous year. This developed and was launched as the Force 2000 series and was revealed in early 1990 with a press release of Horst Link and I photographed at the Sonor factory. The new Force 2000 was referred to as the answer to the need for an affordable, made in Germany drum set as required by the market, the consumer, and by Korg. I got the feeling that the Korg-Sonor distribution agreement was contingent upon Sonor agreeing in advance that they would create a more affordable line of German-made drums geared specifically for the U.S. market. Sonor was keeping their word in doing that. This Force 2000 replaced the previous attempts through the Asian-made 1986-1987 Performer and Panther series' which had poor acceptance and poor quality coming from a foreign factory.

The first shipment of Force 2000 sets arrived, we unpacked them, and there were problems from the very beginning. These would be resolved, but we needed to find the resolution quickly. Part of the initial problem was how the drums were packed and nested. The drums arrived with sawdust and fingerprints on them, and the black covering was so thin that it was showing bubbles of dust filaments that were underneath the shell-wrap material. The biggest problem for Korg, however, was that we had started shipping these preliminary Force 2000 sets in limited quantities without knowing how bad the drums looked coming out of the cartons. We soon learned that there were further problems. Most of the height adjustment castings on the floor-stand hardware were coming loose. The castings were swiveling on the cymbal stands, the hi-hat stands, and the snare drum stands. Every time the drummer made a height adjustment, that height-adjustment casting was supposed to remain stationary on the lower tube. It wasn't. The casting was now rotating- on every stand. This was a huge problem for everyone involved. This was so serious as a manufacturing defect that Sonor Germany immediately flew over one of their technicians to Korg USA to remedy the problem on every stand in every hardware pack Korg received. Korg set up the German Sonor technician in a corner of the warehouse with a workbench. He spoke excellent English, and understood the problem and the sensitivity of the situation. He was a very nice and knowledgeable factory worker who became caught up in the middle of a Sonor factory quality control nightmare. The technician unpacked and took apart every Force 2000 drum set hardware pack to inspect and modify every floor stand in the entire shipment. He was able to punch a security-pin into a newly drilled side-casting hole to keep it from swiveling. This saved us from having to ship back the first 86 drum sets' hardware boxes to Germany. He also unpacked and inspected each drum shell in the shell pack, cleaning the dust and fingerprints from the shells.

There was of course no way to fix the pimples underneath the shell covering. Korg sold the drums as they were, with a huge cry to Sonor that this was unacceptable and certainly not the made-in-Germany quality Korg and the United States market expected.

After the technician modified and repaired thehardware and thoroughly cleaned the drum shells, he repacked all of the drums. We needed to start shipping Force 2000 sets, immediately. There was also a packing issue that needed to be addressed. The components for each five-piece drum set were shipped in two large master cartons. One carton for just drum shells and snare drum, and the other carton for all the stands, tom holder and pedal. Sonor Germany, however, was not aware of UPS-Ground size and weight restrictions for the most economical shipping rates in the U.S. market. One of the cartons exceeded the UPS shipping specifications, which then increased the shipping cost to the dealer. Korg purchased some alternative hardware shipping cartons so that it could be shipped by UPS with the most economic size and weight requirements.

Carton bar-coding was being introduced nationally at this time to expedite warehouse material handling. Korg had already mandated bar-coding on all of the keyboard cartons coming out of Japan and all of the Marshall amplifier cartons coming out of England. Korg needed to get the very same inventory control bar-coding on all of the drums coming in from Sonor. This became a little bit of an "issue", as it would require Sonor to reprint all of the Model-Color labels for the various product boxes. Eventually Sonor complied with the bar coding requirement, but it had become a Korg warehousing issue. Korg was on top of the new inventory control technology in terms of how the warehouse personnel was unloading Sonor containers full of product. All that the Korg warehouse team did all day long was unload 40-foot containers of Korg, Marshall, and Sonor, and they did it all using the new technologies of carton bar codes.

January of 1990 marked the anticipation and frenzy of preparing for the NAMM Winter Market convention in Anaheim. This was a "big deal" for Korg and now with Sonor in the mix it was even bigger.

Sonor was thoroughly integrated into the company and the dominating branding established by Mike Kovins. Korg published their regular January issue of "Korg Dealer News" which contained the first "Sonor Corner" that I was asked to write. I was thrilled to be asked to contribute to this prestigious Korg Dealer News and have Sonor featured on the inside front cover.

SONOR CORNER

by Karl Dustman

Heading into the 1990s, Sonor has already begun aggressive programs to capture a larger share of the drum market. With the introduction of many new products, new advertising campaigns and increased player/artist promotions, Sonor will create new consumer demands in the retail store, ranging from the serious beginner to the discriminating professional. Many of the successful strategies employed by Korg and Marshall have been expanded to include Sonor as part of the exclusive distribution agreement with Korg that began in June 1989.

FORCE 2000

Sonor has decided to capture the imagination of the economical drum kit market by introducing the Force 2000 Series. Made in the same Sonor Factory in Germany with the same materials and craftsmanship, Force 2000 becomes the final link to Sonor's higher visibility in the coming decade: a competitively priced kit that provides superior sound, while introducing a new look and features not previously found on "far east" sets in this price range. An extensive advertising campaign will instantly unveil this set to your customers as the new standard for affordable, serious drums. Force 2000 is being introduced in both catalogued five-piece and seven-piece configurations with an assortment of colors.

Force 2000 is not the only introduction in Sonor's aggressive new plan. Among many other products, Sonor is introducing the new Protec Z 9392 Double Bass Pedal, an accessory that has become a necessity to the "happening" drummer who wants double bass sound, while only carrying one bass drum. Fashioned after the Z9390 chain drive model, Sonor will offer this product complete as a double unit, or as an add-on "slave" to the existing Protec pedal players.

The new 4" x 14" maple shell and 4" x 14" birch shell piccolo snare drums expand Sonor's offerings in one of the hottest segments in retail right now. This addition complements the HLD593 cast bronze shell and D-420 Ferro-Manganese metal shell.

Back on the hardware side, the multi-purpose Sch27 pedal beater eliminates the need for four different bass drum pedal beaters by offering a four-in-one model. Wood, felt, acrylic and rubber impact surfaces provide four different bass drum sounds, while reducing the pedal drag of larger, bulky beaters. This is an accessory that will work on every brand of pedal.

Sonor's "Dollar Closer to Perfection" advertising campaign has been hailed as a huge success by leading dealers. This program brought unprecedented numbers of potential Sonor customers into the retail stores. The campaign rewarded each customer who completed the test drummer comparison in the store, and sent it to Korg, with a complete "Look at the Details" book and one crisp new $1.00 bill to be used towards their first Sonor purchase. A record number of consumer responses were processed.

With seven months completed in Korg's distribution of Sonor products, full scale parts and service is up and running at Sonor headquarters in Korg's Westbury, NY establishment. An updated replacement parts price list is near completion. Included will be recently introduced service parts for the new HiLite Series drums and Protec hardware. A dealer mailing is planned immediately after printing. Recently added to Sonor's endorsers are John Tempesta (Exodus), Glen Evans (Nuclear Assault), Brad "Tricky" Lane (Sweet F.A.), Steve West (Danger Danger), Michael Shapiro (Sergio Mendez), Clay Caire (Nashville Now Television) and John Hartman (Doobie Brothers).

More drummers than ever before are turning to Sonor drums to consistently provide the sound, durability and appearance they demand in their professional performance. Look who's playing Sonor now! High product visibility in concerts, MTV and recording means more product demand in the retail store. Watch For It!

Karl Dustman is the Sales and Marketing Director of the Sonor Division, Korg USA.

A Memorable Moment:

Over time the Sonor containers coming from Germany became the most anticipated and openly discussed truck loads of inventory by the Korg warehouse workers to arrive at the back warehouse docks. The front office never really knew why this was (including myself). Claudine's brother, Donnie Remolds, worked in the warehouse and usually assisted in the unloading of the Sonor containers from Germany, he quietly indicated that the Sonor factory regularly included a case of premium German beer carefully packed and hidden in the middle of the 40 foot container of Sonor merchandise boxes. About twenty feet into the container a "gift-pack of beer" was searched for by the warehouse. The gift was positioned half way into the container as it would not be notice by any United States Federal Customs Agents perhaps opening and inspecting the cargo arriving and going through New York customs. I shared this enthusiasm that the Korg warehouse had for the Sonor shipments arriving with the Sonor factory in Germany with much appreciation. This resulted in the beer continuing to be secretly arriving on a regular basis. This certainly helped Bob Saydlowski and I get the containers unloaded quickly by the Korg warehouse workers, at least to the middle of the Sonor cargo container!

Sonor Germany created the first Force 2000 catalog which was beautifully done; it was very attractive and had a space for the dealer to personalize the catalog. They provided the catalog to Korg in massive quantities. The second Link son, Oliver, is a graphic arts designer and was creating all of the Sonor Germany literature; the photography, the text authoring, and overseeing the printing in Germany. I would interact with Oliver regularly; he would write and ask for the best translation of a phrase, and so forth.

This was the first convention for which we actually had time to create and prepare for a concentrated professional marketing campaign and trade show presence. The stakes were high this year, as FORCE 2000 was here in the U.S. marketplace and the usual "Sonor's too expensive" excuse by the dealers for not buying, stocking, and selling Sonor profitably was now eliminated. The need for organization and professional leadership for the coming trade show was drawing on my experience at Ludwig and Gretsch.

I had created many trade show specials, campaigns, and incentives over the years. My primary focus was on getting the salesmen trained on how to present and sell the Sonor trade show specials to the dealers. Korg had an annual day-long sales meeting in our headquarter hotel, the day before the show started. All of us were locked up with the sales force (district sales managers as well as the inside customer service staff) and each product-division had an hour and a half to deliver our presentation on how to present, sell, and promote Korg, Marshall, and Sonor. I had all the new Sonor product there for show and tell, there was all the new product handout literature, and new Force 2000 catalogs. I created a slide presentation using Sonor photography from Oliver Link and I asked Bob Saydlowski to videotape the entire presentation for my personal review afterwards. I heard later-on during the convention that this Sonor presentation was well received by everyone.

SONOR® 516-333-9100 ext. 245

Exclusively Distributed in the U.S. by Korg USA, Inc.

89 Frost Street, Westbury, NY 11590-5007

KARL DUSTMAN

Director of Sales & Marketing

FAX: 516-333-9108

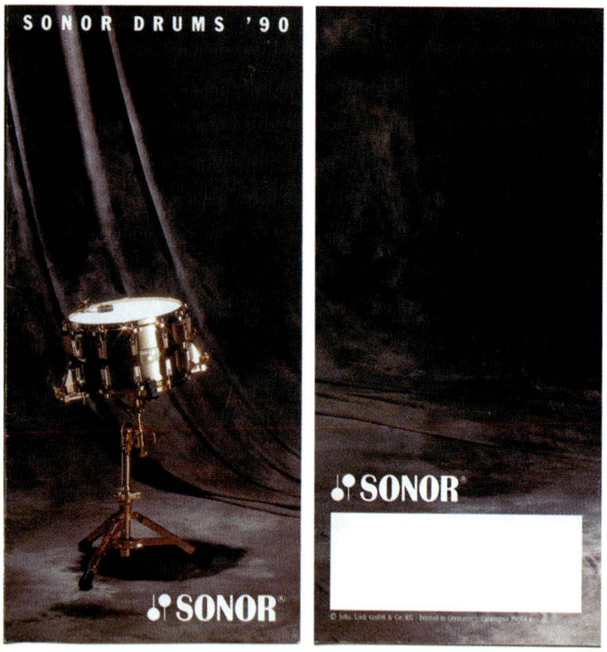

Note the creative evolution of the "pocket catalog" concept that had been introduced by Ludwig ten years earlier, now also including the dealer imprint box on the outside back cover.

Sonor was now considered a full member of the Korg family. The Korg Dealer News emphasized Sonor in every issue with new product news, the new advertising campaign, and artist development. The interest in playing Sonor increased drastically. I could see this within the percussion market because Ludwig was faltering and Gretsch was faltering even further, leaving Tama, Yamaha, and Pearl (all Asian companies) as the alternative. Sonor had the vision at that time of being the highest quality and most expensive drum on the market. Everyone wanted to play Sonor but could not afford to buy it.

The artist relations program exploded. Bob Saydlowski deserves much of the credit for this because he related extremely well to the artists. He spoke their language, he knew and followed the bands that the drummers were playing in, and he knew what tours and albums they were making. He related to these drummers much better than I did. I was the older guy always with the suit and tie on. My role was to create an artist relations program for him that would keep him between the yellow lines, meaning Korg cannot just give away $80,000 worth of Sonor product every year to recruit and develop key artist personalities to play and use Sonor exclusively. Now Sonor had a formal artist questionnaire and we required a media pack from each artist that was approaching Sonor wanting to endorse the product and brand. This was all pre- internet, and all of artist promotional bio-pack materials were mailed to us. We were receiving boxes and bags of media packs from all sorts of artists; top level, intermediate, entry level; all wanting to play Sonor and feeling that they wanted to endorse the product.

Sonor Endorser Roster 1990

Jack DeJohnette - Special Edition
Steve Smith - Vital Information, Steps Ahead
Chester Thompson - Genesis/Phil Collins
Bobby Rock - Vinnie Vincent, Nitro
Nicko Mc Brain - Iron Maiden
Gerry Brown - George Benson
Simon Wright - AC/DC, Dio
Jeff Watts - Wynton Marsalis
John Hartmann - Doobie Brothers
Bernard Purdie - Studio
Steve West - Danger Danger
Adam Nussbaum - Brecker Bros.
Clay Caire - Nashville Now TV
Ron Wikso - Cher
Tom Rivelli - Randy Travis
Glenn Evans - Nuclear Assault
John Tempesta - Exodus
Charlie Quintana - Havalinas
Mike Shapiro - Sergio Mendes, Airto
Michael Lean - Tuff
Peter Clemente - Diving for Pearls
Mike Boyko - Scatterbrain
Louie Perez - Los Lobos
Terl Bryant - Peter Murphy
Jussi Tegelman - Havana Black
Pat Tomek - Rainmakers
Tricky Lane - Sweet F.A.
Rick Lonow - Bellamy Bros.
Ian Froman - Independent
Steiner Krokstad - Stage Dolls
Liam Jason - Rhino Bucket
Michael Gage - Messano
Joel Spencer - Independent
Pete Lee - Magnificent Seven
Steve Missal - Studio
Randi Scott - Risque
Mark Edwards - Criss Angel

What is an endorsement?

Often an artist had the impression that Sonor was endorsing them. That's not how it works. They were endorsing Sonor. The company is the endorsee, the artist is the endorser. For example, when you endorse Nike, you are the "sport-talent" holding up the Nike product and brand as gear that you favor. It's the same in the music world. When a musical artist has an endorsement agreement with a musical instrument manufacturer or distributor, they are agreeing to communicate to the public that the product and brand is so superior it warrants the artist's favored "endorsement". It does *not* mean that the *company* is endorsing the *artist*. The goal of the artist relations staff is to say: "Look at this high-profile artist who favors our product!" They are *not* saying, "Look at who this company favors above other artists!" This is an important distinction that is often misunderstood or misstated by endorsers.

Bob Saydlowski
Steve West
Karl Dustman

Tal Bergman

Bobby Rock

Gerry Brown

Steve Smith

Michael Lean

John
Tempesta
SONOR
SONOR
SONOR
Jack DeJohnette
Bernard
Purdie
Jeff
Watts
Chester Thompson
SONOR
SONOR
SONOR

The artist program and criteria was in place. I was able to stand back and gladly turn the mechanics of the program over to Bob. We had to figure out a way to keep potential selected artists interested, yet keep the financial budget for Sonor as a division to keep Korg happy that we were not giving away product. If there was an internal consensus to have a particular artist formally associated with Sonor, the first step was to figure out what the artist wanted. Did they simply want equipment? Did they want to do clinics? Were they willing to be featured in advertisements? Did they require touring equipment support? If so, were they willing to participate in meet & greet events while on the road? For the most part, drummers approaching us wanted specific Sonor drums and a collection of Sonor hardware. We evaluated the situation by figuring out the net landed cost of the drums requested, and the net landed cost of the hardware. We often agreed to provide the drums to the approved artist, and *sell* them the hardware at a reduced price. That reduced price of the hardware was equal to the net landed cost of both the drums *and* the net landed cost of the hardware. (In other words, we were breaking event on the transaction from a cash standpoint. All of this was "in exchange" for the global endorsement from the artist. The approved artist felt he was getting the drums for free, and the cost of goods sold covered the complete cost of the drums and selected hardware. This seemed to work well within the limitations of the Sonor artist relations budget. It worked because it filled the ego of the artist thinking he was getting something for free. Bob was able to "sell" this concept to the artists he was approaching. Korg liked it, everybody was happy. The momentum and visibility was developing fast and opportunities continued to present themselves for further Sonor market awareness and showcasing. My relationships with various national music festivals carried forwards from HSS. I was contacted by Dr. Lynn Skinner, the executive director for the annual Lionel Hampton Jazz Festival, hosted by the University of Idaho. I had worked closely with him previously on having a Sonor Performer Series drum kit with throne to be donated for one of the grand prizes awarded to one of the participating high school jazz ensembles. Now I had an opportunity to "own" all *nine* performance stages at the February, 1990, festival event by providing nine complete Sonor Performer five-piece sets with thrones. Participating schools would not be allowed to bring or use their own drum sets, as the purpose was to have permanent on-stage equipment for each band to use for rehearsal and performance. The Grand Stage was equipped with a dazzling Sonor HiLite Kit, used by all headliner drummers on this platform. A wonderful presentation of product, brand and sound. This form of visibility and promotion has been proven to be a tremendous success and market impact. Even without a nearby Sonor percussion retail store, Korg authorized the sale of the used Performer kits at half-off to schools, dealers and even students (through dealers), just to get the sets liquidated immediately following the event. As the Brandon Marsalis Band was a featured festival performing band, Sonor artist Jeff Watts was scheduled to attend this event. I immediately established a special drum set clinic for Jeff Watts during the event. In addition, he did his clinic on a loaned Sonor Performer Series kit and made it sound fantastic. For me, this Festival was a true joy to attend. I had the opportunity to hear the Lionel Hampton Band for the very first time and to chat directly with Lionel Hampton. He was a Musser vibraphone artist and I built my communication and friendship with this legendary Vibraphone artist on the basis of the wonderful Musser relationship years we had established with him before the sale of Ludwig-Musser to the Selmer Company. This event was attended by over nine thousand people, drawing attention throughout the United States and globally. This set the stage for me to expand this relationship and Festival presence through the use and staging of the FORCE 2000 Series kits for February of 1991.

By now Seiki Kato was President, and moved into Don England's presidential office. I was successful in securing Seiki Kato's old office, and Bob eventually got his own office as part of the expanded office build-out in the warehouse. This also included a large air-conditioned sound-proof demonstration sound room for Korg, Marshall, and Sonor products. Many artists came to visit the Korg operation in Westbury and wanted to test and evaluate the new instruments. This became a showcase for all the new product introductions along with the research and development input from some of the visitors. The main entrance foyer to the building added the Sonor name to the Korg and Marshall identification on the entrance wall.

I felt things were going well enough by now that I needed to relocate my residence to be closer to the Korg building. I moved to Mineola, New York, in Nassau County. I found a two-bedroom condo near Winthrop Hospital and the Long Island Railroad. I asked the furniture rental company to move my furniture to the new Mineola address. Long term decisions about completely relocating to New York were still undecided, so I kept the home in Nashville and it remained idle indefinitely.

By now all the new full page and double-page spread advertisements were being seen in percussion and industry trade magazines. Awareness about Sonor's FORCE 2000 was increasing monthly. The Steven Ross Public Relations partner orchestrated a photo shoot in California for the Force 2000 using a silhouette figure that was back-lit, representing "everyone could be a Sonor drummer" now with the affordability of the Force 2000 series.

The clout that Korg had with all the trade media publications was vast because Korg bought so much advertising space for Korg and Marshall. The buying power Korg had was tremendous in placement of the ads and special recognition and favors. The magazines would *give* Korg basically anything they wanted for Sonor. Sonor benefitted tremendously from the advertising buying power that Korg provided. Sonor would have never been able to create this much buying power influence on its own without the alliance and positioning with the Korg and Marshall brands.

As monthly full page Sonor ads were now appearing in *Modern Drummer* and *DRUM!* magazines, I contacted the folks at *Modern Drummer* and told them I wanted to send them a Force 2000 kit. Modern Drummer did a product review in April of 1990 and gave it a five star rating as one of the best products on the market for the price. Again, it was the best advertising we could ask for.

Sonor entered the arena of publication-sponsored "Free Gear" drawings. These became popular immediately and remain a component of publication promotion and visibility. Everyone likes to win free stuff, particularly drummers. *DRUM!* magazine created a $12,000 winning-package collaboration of Sonor, Paiste, Promark, and Beyer Dynamic microphones. The new Sonor HiLite Series was the dominant image and centerpiece for the promotion running through September of 1990. *Modern Drummer* Magazine established the same type of giveaway promotion by offering Sonor Soprano and Sonor Piccolo snare drums running through February 1, 1991.

Mike Kovins was a close friend of the Majeski family that owned and operated *The Music Trades* magazine. Kovins wanted national recognition of Sonor and the factory in Germany through a special editorial feature article. Mike told me he wanted Brian Majeski and I to go to the Sonor factory in early March so *The Music Trades* could prepare a story on the Sonor Percussion's Legacy of Excellence. This moved forwards very quickly and Brian and I both flew over to Germany for in-depth conversation and photography of the Sonor manufacturing operations. The April edition of *The Music Trades* came out with a four page feature article on Sonor Percussion's Legacy of Excellence. It included the history of the company, emphasis on the new Force 2000 product line launch, and everything that Korg USA was doing to market and distribute the brands in North America. We couldn't have asked for a better free advertising piece at any price.

The year was moving extremely fast and in May I was sent back to Sonor Germany to discuss at length the initial start-up problems with the Force 2000 entering the United States market. I went for a week, May 3-8, and I went prepared to sit down with Horst Link and all of his product managers to discuss all of Korg's issues with the Force 2000. These meetings included detailed discussions about improvements, product expansion, color options and the actual quality control issues Korg first experienced from the first shipment of Force 2000 product. At the same time, we wanted to discuss the Force 3000 development and introduction. The Force 3000 was the outgrowth of Jeorg Link's visit to the USA the previous year when he visited dealers with me touring throughout the U.S.. Jeorg felt that a whole new generation of product was needed to expand the FORCE Series. We discussed the evolution and introduction of the new line and the introduction of lacquer finishes for the Force 3000. It was believed that the Sonor Force series warranted serious development as a permanent part of the Sonor traditional product offering. A completely new catalog, brilliantly created by Oliver Link, was presented,

once again. This was scheduled for global release in the fall of 1990.

I continued to press hard for a suitable marching percussion product line based upon the favorable product introduction and test-market launch at the February Texas Music Educators Convention in San Antonio Texas. I also continued to push for exploration into a suitable Sonor snare drum kit using the molded case concepts I initiated for Gretsch years ago. My time in Bad Berleburg, Germany, at the factory included an assembly of all the marching percussion product people in Sonor. Lengthy discussions included the product but also the competitive price points needed to be able to compete with the Ludwig, Pearl, and Yamaha market leaders. We dissected all of the critical improvement points that Al Lemert had given me for incorporation into a new series of product that could be introduced later in the year at the PAS convention in Philadelphia, PA, or at the December Midwest Band Clinic convention in Chicago.

A Memorable Moment:

It was during this week long trip that Karl Heinz Menzel was assigned to look after me during my time at the Factory. He was gracious and very easy to be with. Because of his kind and thoughtful consideration, the time out of the Sonor office during a layover weekend was most memorable. Karl Heinz orchestrated three separate outings which I remember to this day:

-Somewhere near the Sonor factory was a deer sanctuary that attracted about 150 different size deer for a nightly feeding ground assembly. Visitors would assemble in this small completely dark log cabin heated only by a fireplace, with windows on all four sides of the building to watch all the deer cautiously come out of the woods to eat the food that the local community would put out every evening. This was truly a beautiful sight to see these wonderful creatures emerge from the woods and congregate for the nightly feeding.

-On a beautiful Saturday afternoon, Karl Heinz arranged for a touring aircraft to fly us over the dense forests of the regions to see the many different tree lines and forestation throughout the region. Another breathtaking experience from high above the trees.

-Finally on Sunday, we made the automobile trip to Cologne, Germany, to visit and tour the Cologne Cathedral. This is a tremendous structure dating back to 1248. With its two magical spires each towering 157 meters in height, I had never seen or experienced anything like this before. I made the trip up one of the spires which included over five hundred stairs in the circular staircase.

This time and these experiences have stayed with me through time and career developments as some of the most enjoyable elements of my musical journey through life.

The Sonor marching percussion equipment was well received at the market research-entry in Texas. The most significant problem with the marching product line was the price. I chose *not* to inform the Texas MEA convention audience of the price points at this early stage, as there would have been an instant disqualification mindset when hearing what the "possible selling price would be". The product quality was excellent, but the product was heavy for marching. I felt the bands and corps considering the Sonor products line would concentrate more on the durability and quality of sound and would get over the heaviness factor if they could afford it. Based upon my pricing analysis I had completed in March, Sonor was not yet, in May of 1990, priced competitively enough with Pearl, Yamaha, and Ludwig to really enter the market. The seven- page detailed report on the trip to Sonor-Germany I prepared for Mike Kovins immediately following my return, addressed many topics and issues concerning present quality control issues on the Force 2000, and the relationship with Korg and the Sonor factory. I dispelled the presumption by Sonor-Germany management team that "Korg is too picky about everything". A good amount of my time and effort was in explaining the United States market. Sonor Germany had not really ever heard or learned this information from Charles Alden or Hohner-HSS. The mere-fact that the rest of the global distributors for Sonor were *not* complaining about Force 2000 quality was irrelevant in my (our) opinion.

The United States market leads the global market. The U.S. dealers and consumer will not accept inferior Asian- looking quality from the highest quality and most-expensive drum maker in the world. Nor will Korg. I believed that all the Sonor managers understood what was at stake in having flawless superior products entering the U.S. market. It was a requirement for an ongoing positive relationship with Korg.

Mid-Year Reset

By mid-year a new Korg National Sales Manager, Joe Bredeau, had arrived, replacing the short-term Pat Mazie whom I originally interviewed with. Bradeau was another former Hohner USA employee at the same time Mike Kovins was there. That previous working relationship was the foundation for their mutual friendship. Joe also considered himself a frustrated drummer, which could be very dangerous to have around. We now had three people within the Korg USA management team that knew of and shared a common denominator of knowledge and identical opinion of Hohner USA and it's Hicksville leadership-management team now located in Richmond, Virginia. The internal stories about Hohner USA-Hicksville occasionally coming out into the open were unbelievable and very humorous. June must have been the predetermined "Employee Performance Evaluation" time period or it was my one- year anniversary date for joining Korg. In either case, this was the sit down with Mike Kovins to discuss "how is Karl performing within the Korg USA structure and organization". This obviously was a corporate protocol for all employees and Kovins had me on his list. While this was very straightforward and positive in receiving a "superior" summary rating, I did question some of the comments indicated in the hand written report. I questioned far more the irrelevant later-added comments from sales manager Joe Bredeau, scratched into the report margins. For fear of not wanting to be construed as "touchy", I did not press the issue. However I created an August 21 two page commentary internal memo to Mike Kovins, addressing some of the issues discussed while conveying my continued dedication to the Sonor Division leadership within Korg. In looking back and reviewing this document now, there must have been discussion issues concerning my apparent intentional delay in officially moving to New York for the long term, and my choosing to continue a dual residence in Nashville until the future of the Sonor Division was known further. Little did I know then what would occur in 1991.

June, 1990, Summer NAMM Chicago: "The Wake On The Lake"

We entered the annual NAMM convention in Chicago with full preparation and another outstanding product display and presentation for Sonor. This event was to become widely known as the "Wake on the Lake" because it was the very last year there was a NAMM convention in Chicago. There was extremely poor dealer attendance and the cost of exhibiting was exorbinately expensive. The Chicago trade unions that operate everything in the conventions centers made the cost of exhibiting ridiculous. If you needed an extension cord, you needed to get it from the union electrician at $25.00. If you needed a light bulb for your booth, you needed to get it from a Union electrician at $40.00. The industry finally said, "no more. We will never go back to Chicago." The Korg, Marshall, and Sonor presence dominated the convention floor with brand new displays, products, and organized sales incentive strategies.

SUMMER NAMM CONVENTION CHICAGO, ILLINOIS 1990

Apparently the entire percussion industry had time on their hands during this final McCormick Place convention and someone assembled the Percussion Industry personalities together for a group photo. I obtained a copy of the photo from Bob Saydlowski. Unfortunately, many of these people are no longer with us.

back row L-R:

Dave Patrick (Kaman), Karl Dustman (Sonor-Korg USA), Larry DeMarco (Korg), Mike Kovins (Korg Executive Vice-President), unknown, unknown, Steven Ross (Steven Ross & Associates-KORG PR Firm), unknown, unknown, Bob Gatzen (Noble & Cooley), unknown, Bob Zildjian (Sabian)

middle row L-R:

Mike Morse (Zildjian), Jerry Andreas (Yamaha), unknown, Rich Mangicaro (Paiste), John Good (DW), Bob Beals (Evans), Jim Catalano (Ludwig), Lennie DiMuzio (Zildjian)

front row L-R:

David McAllister (Sabian), Robbie Klein (Steven Ross & Associates KORG USA PR Firm) Bob Saydlowski (Sonor-KORG USA), Wayne Blanchard (Sabian)

1990 PASIC Convention

The Sonor exhibit for the 1990 PASIC convention held in Philadelphia was huge. Mike Kovins agreed with Horst Link that in order to sell Sonor drums you needed to be able to hear Sonor drums. There were sound restrictions in the PAS exhibit halls which prevented any visitor to really hear the sound of the drums, and the differences in Sonor drum heads. Kovins gave me the authority to go out and rent an air-conditioned soundproof booth that would accommodate four to five drum sets and make it part of the Sonor exhibit at PASIC. The rental for that soundproof booth alone was $3,000.00. Almost all constructed of thick plexiglas and soundproof material, it had a structural room capable of handling a roof-top air conditioning unit. The Sonor booth had a huge exhibit floor footprint, so the visibility of Sonor at that gathering was unprecedented.

Another first for Sonor was a by-invitation-only evening open house courtesy of the Sonor division of Korg USA. This was previously never considered or even thought about by any previous USA distributors like Charles Alden or HSS. I provided Sonor's Administrative Assistant, Claudine, the invitation list in advance and she handled the creation and mailing of all the invitations to the select individuals and companies on "The KD List". The guest list included some of the friendly competitors, all of the media, the PAS President and all of the officers.... all schmoozing together in the Sonor private hospitality ballroom of the convention's headquarters hotel.

Korg USA was basically providing Sonor Germany every professional element, including the soundproof demonstration room that Horst Link had demanded in writing to Horst Mucha of Hohner-HSS in order to attain the market visibility and domination that Sonor wanted and needed. Bravo! to Korg USA who did everything that Horst Link desired. This tremendous market orchestration took time, money, and expertise of people to do all of this correctly. The impact was being made and recognized in the market.

A Memorable Moment:

In planning the Sonor open house during the PASIC convention, I was dealing with the hotel's banquet manager who assisted in selecting a suitable event room in the hotel for the Sonor function. With a decision made and the event booked, I was then advised that the hotel's house band regularly performs in this room and leaves their instruments on the circular riser/stage in the middle of the open room. I asked what brand of drums was on the stage. When I learned that these were Gretsch, I asked the hotel to ask if the house band drummer would mind removing the drums from the stage for the one evening and was told " No!" I did not want a confrontation, but I could not have Gretsch drums on a spotlight display in the Sonor open-house room. I asked the hotel for a bed sheet, and quickly removed the drums placing them in the corner of the room and covered them with the white bed sheet. I believe that there are times when it is better to "ask for forgiveness rather than permission" "NO!" was definitely not in my vocabulary.

Sonor as a division of Korg USA was certainly making its presence felt. I believe the industry recognized that I had the full support of Korg in funding all of this Sonor presence at the PASIC convention. This was more than a "brand coming out", this was a marketing threat to all the other drum companies in the industry. The German Giant had started its strategy to take over a significant part of the percussion industry market. Mike Kovins' directive was to "just make it big and impressive." And that's what we were doing .Sonor was noticed for real, for the first time.

By the end of the year, I needed to do something for the internal Sonor staff and team at Korg to recognize and thank them for the efforts made for Sonor during 1990. I thanked the Korg support team with custom-edition Sonor jackets. This was a Christmas present to anyone who had anything to do with Sonor. I personally paid for these expensive leather embroidered Sonor jackets for everyone. My gratitude for all the help the Sonor Division received from within Korg that year was very much appreciated.

As fall approached we were building momentum week after week. We now had solid Sonor exhibits and displays at all the significant percussion and industry-wide events and conventions. We had extensive marketing and sales tools for the salesmen, discount schedules, and quantity buy-ins with incentives. Korg had made it possible to formulate these programs by telling me, "Do what you need to do to sell this stuff. We can't lose money, we're in this to make a profit, but we need market share and visibility. If we have to give away 5% to do it, just do it. Make the stuff sell through." By now there was a complete Sonor "swag product offering" that included many very cool items that also appeared in the corresponding Korg and Marshall branded product lines. Steven Ross and Associates designed the three separate product sell sheets for the three brands, and handled the photography, layout and contents for the line. The sourcing of all three swag brands was handled by Larry DeMarco as part of his marketing support responsibility. Sonor received the benefits of this corporate structure in launching all three brand swag product offerings at once.

Force 2000 was at the front and center of the Sonor movement within Korg. There were small advances in market penetration, but the success and sell-through was not happening as fast as everyone had expected. The full page ads and the product reviews were all great, but the R.O.I was being scrutinized by Korg. I could feel it. It was decided to "spice up the incentive to consumers" late in the fall with the "$500 Worth of Sonor Quality Free!" advertising campaign designed by Steven Ross & Associates. The premise of the headline and text meant to convey that the superior quality of the Sonor hardware would cost you five hundred dollars more if purchased separately. In-store counter cards were sent to all authorized Sonor dealers. Consumers who completed the questionnaire would receive a free Sonor T-shirt. If a Force 2000 set was purchased, Korg would send the consumer five *free* Sonor replacement batter heads for the set. (A $95.00 value). Mild response prompted us to extend the offer to February 28, 1991.

1991 NAMM

SONOR
SONOR
SONOR
SONOR
SONOR
SONOR

SONOR
SONOR
SONOR
SONOR

As we entered 1991 we were very absorbed and focused on the forthcoming January NAMM show in Anaheim. Everything was looking good; we had improved quality Force 2000 sets in stock, and we were planning to introduce the Force 3000 sets which were a step up in both price (about 20%) and quality. There were lacquer finishes instead of just wraps. There were also improvements to the hardware, tom holder, foot pedal, snare stand, and the shell materials. We had a complete line of Sonor branded wearables. Sonor was as prepared for a successful and industry impactful NAMM show as it ever had been or could be. Within the Anaheim Convention Center, Korg had a separate display-exhibit room, presented to the attending dealers as an exclusive closed-door Korg-Marshall-Sonor exhibit area in the convention center. This meant we were not out on the display floor mixing and mingling with the crowds, the noise, and the distractions of a trade show. When dealers arrived and entered the big double doors, they were immediately immersed in a huge room full of all of this Korg, Marshall, and Sonor products. There were lots of order-writing tables & chairs, abundant coffee and soft drinks, and some good-looking Korg USA customer service girls running around working the room. It was fantastic. Bob Saydlowski did the complete Sonor exhibit merchandise ordering, and the product looked outstanding and mesmerizing. Sonor never looked so good, so complete, and well presented.

As the NAMM convention rolled on, I gradually became aware of some quiet rumor discussion about Sonor being purchased. Quite honestly, I didn't know it was for sale! The word being circulated was that Zildjian was going to buy Sonor. What disturbed me the most was that Horst Link was having a lot of "corner conversations" with Mike Kovins that I was not involved in. I was concerned that perhaps this meant Horst had issues with something that I was doing or not doing, or that Korg was not doing. How could Horst Link be displeased with any element of what Korg USA was doing to present, promote and sell Sonor products? Maybe that was a little paranoia on my part as I have seen similar "earmarks of potential change" before. As the convention continued, I was uncomfortable with more of these quiet conversations taking place. Over the four days of the convention, the rumors continued to grow about Sonor changing hands (and probably distributors) very soon, on March 31st. So here we were... after just two years Sonor distribution was going back to HSS, the company that defaulted by handling it terribly just prior to the Korg distribution agreement. I was told that my employment would end on March 31st , 1991. I was devastated again. Bob Saydlowski would be staying on at Korg a little longer to help liquidate the entire Sonor inventory that Korg had bought and paid for. Bob eventually accepted a position with HSS and relocated to Richmond, Virginia, working for Bob Cotton and Horst Mucha. The March issue of The Music Trades magazine ran an editorial on this change and development of Sonor distribution, "Hohner Acquires 100% of Sonor Percussion"

Once again I prepared a suitable announcement letter to all my industry contacts and associates informing them of the changes at Sonor and my departure at the end of March 1991. This clarity was essential so the industry would fully understand what happened to Sonor and me. Of course all Korg USA marketing and promotion of Sonor stopped abruptly. Horst Link was quoted in the Frankfurt (Messe) Daily 4.3.91 as saying, "I made up my mind very quickly. I have no family heir and the opportunity of finding a potential partner doesn't happen every day. We have worked closely with Hohner over many years and work well together; two German companies with product range that does not overlap."

That statement was not true. There were three adult Horst Link children who could have taken over the company and its leadership, and become fourth-generation owners of the family company. Horst Link decided to take the five million dollars cash, and cash out.

So in March of 1991, I was again faced with the question of, "What is next?" This was the third company that had been sold out from underneath me in less than ten years. The national unemployment at this time was at 13% nationwide. It was not a good time to be looking for work. I was living on Long Island, one of the most expensive parts of the country to live, and I was on a year-to-year lease. I signed up for New York state unemployment insurance but knew that the $1,200 per month from the state would not take me very far.

IN RETROSPECT

The Sonor experience through Korg USA was altogether different than anything HSS could or would be able to do with the products or brand, even with the 1991 “second chance”. Mike Kovins (Korg’s Executive Vice President) had the vision and Korg had the financial resources to make Sonor a huge success over time. The company had the patience and determination to bring Sonor to footing and success equal to what it had achieved with Korg and Marshall. The Horst Link interview in the Frankfurt Fair Daily indicated, “I have no family heir”.....which was untrue. I was hurt and offended personally that Horst Link chose to cash-out of the family-company ownership and would never discuss or tell me this information directly to my face. I never saw Horst Link again. Cash (five million dollars) conquerors all I guess. Sonor North American distribution returned to Hohner, Inc. HSS in Richmond Virginia only to have a “weak and short re-start”. Very soon after the 1991 change for Sonor, the entire global Hohner Inc organization, including Sonor, was purchased by an Asian musical conglomerate, KHS International. I remained in contact with Mike Kovins over the years. Korg never entered the drum business market again until 2019 when it purchased the Sakae Drum Company. The music products industry lost Kovins to a terminal medical condition and I lost a personal friend who seemed to appreciate everything I did and tried to do for Sonor within the Korg-USA organization.

Hohner Acquires 100% Of Sonor Percussion

No Statement Made On Future Of U.S. Distribution of Sonor And Orff; $5 Million (US) Bid Tops Zildjian Offer

THE SONOR FACTORY IN AUE occupies approximately 125,000 sq. ft. and employs over 300. The company's $20 million in sales are evenly divided between Orff instruments and Sonor drums.

On February 4, 1991, Matt. Hohner AG of Trossingen, West Germany, reached a definitive agreement to acquire 100% of Johannes Link Percussion GmbH, manufacturers of the world renowned Sonor percussion line. The agreement was jointly announced by representatives from Hohner, Horst Link, managing director of Johannes Link GmbH, and Bernhard Muskantor, chairman of United Musical Instruments and a majority shareholder in Link GmbH. Horst Link and his wife Elisabeth will remain active in the management of the firm.

Hohner's announcement ended months of speculation as to the future ownership of the German percussion maker. The Zildjian Company had made a serious offer for the company and was involved in negotiations up until three days before Hohner closed the deal. Muskantor was also rumored to have considered making a bid. Chris Noblet of Zildjian commented, "We wish Hohner and the Link family continued success and hope that the transaction is beneficial for all parties."

While details of the purchase agreement were not disclosed, informed individuals revealed that Hohner paid slightly more than $5.0 million (US) for the Link Company. For the most recent fiscal year, Link had worldwide sales of slightly over $20.0 million (US). In the U.S., Sonor drums are distributed by Korg USA and the company's line of Orff Percussion instruments is handled by Hohner USA. As of this writing, Hohner had not made any statement about its future plans for distribution in the U.S.

Located in the Aue, a small mountain village in Northern Germany, Link GmbH employs over 300 and operates a 125,000-sq.-ft. manufacturing facility. The company's output is evenly divided between Sonor drums and Orff percussion instruments. In addition, Link distributes guitars, sound re-inforcement equipment, and a variety of other music products in Germany.

THE LINK FAMILY'S involvement in percussion dates bact to 1875. (l-r) Oliver Link; Horst Link, managing director; his wife, Elisabeth Link; Georg Link.

Hohner's acquisition of Link GmbH unites two of Germany's most respected companies and represents the culmination of a longstanding relationship. The founding of Link percussion dates back to 1875 when Johannes Link, a tanner by trade, began making drums in Weissenfals, Germany. By 1900, Link had registered the Sonor trademark and employed over 60 people in his factory. He died in 1914 and was succeeded by his son Otto, who successfully guided the company through the Great Depression and World War II.

With the Russian occupation of East Germany following World War II, the Link family's percussion business was nationalized in 1950, and Otto and his son Horst had to flee to West Germany. They settled in Aue, where they began drumhead production in an abandoned British Airforce barracks. Financing for the fledgling business initially came from the Princess of Sayn Wittgenstein, a local noblewoman with a longstanding personal ties to the Link family. In the late fifties, Hohner helped finance Sonor's expansion by purchasing a substantial equity position in the company. Robert Zildjian also made an equity investment. In the fifties and sixties, the Sonor line of drums established an international reputation for quality. A strong Deutsche Mark and increased production costs in Germany recently made Sonor products extremely costly, yet they are still regarded as the pinnacle of quality.

In 1982, Robert Zildjian sold his shares in Link GmbH to Hohner to help finance his then fledgling Sabian Cymbal Company. Five years later, Hohner sold its 51% stake to Bernhard Muskantor.

Chapter Eight

Going On Your Own... Can you survive, Can you create a future at the same time?

This juncture in my career and life turned into a learning experience that has no ending. The decision to start my own business was made for me, based upon the time and circumstances I faced. I was about to learn the value of my years in this industry as well as what I DID know, and what I did NOT. I never looked back for the status of being employed, I was about to work for myself, forever.

It was April of 1991, my tenure at Korg USA was completed as a result of the complete Sonor Drum Company being sold to Hohner, Inc. Korg would no longer be distributing Sonor and the entire division within the company was eliminated. I needed to analyze what I was going to be doing next. The economy of the country at this time was equivalent to what the entire music products industry would be going through in 2008-2009 when the real estate market melted down. Unemployment was at about 13 or 14%, inflation was rising every month, I was living in the most expensive part of the country, and I had to create a plan and make some decisions. I felt that the best plan was to immediately analyze my own qualifications and experience assets to determine what expertise I had that could be of value to music products industry companies. A skill-set would become the center of my self-marketing.

I had never thought of myself as a consultant, normally that word has a connotation that you are unemployed, or self-employed, or looking for anything to do in creating income. I thought back in time to the Winkler Drum Company project. Basically I had been a paid consultant for a number of months to work for the Winkler Drum Company Board of Directors to oversee the chapter 11 reorganization for the small manufacturing facility, working with the SBA, the Tennessee Valley Administration and creating a five year business plan to use in seeking investment offerings. I was a consultant without realizing that I was a consultant. In creating that 30-page "Proposed Business Plan and Company Introduction" I was consulting. In addition, I created a number of advertising rendering comps that conveyed the presentation of the products, brand, and made-in-USA platform to a) support the Business Plan book, and b) convey the expertise and qualifications I bring to the project and potential reorganization of the company.

I needed to leverage my contacts within the industry. I needed to recognize my strengths and weaknesses, and come up with a strategy or a business model that would appeal to businesses both in and out of the music industry. I was basically creating an entity called *Dustman & Associates, Creative Marketing with Imagination.* I also needed to create some documents to clearly convey to any potential client that I was an expert in certain fields. Also I needed to identify who could benefit from my expertise, what, precisely, services I could provide, and how I worked and completed assignments.

CREATIVE MARKETING WITH IMAGINATION
KD & Associates

SPECIAL CREATIVE, MARKETING, COMMUNICATIONS, ADVERTISING, PROMOTIONAL SERVICES AVAILABLE:

Marketing
New Product Launch & Development
Brand Identity Programs
Customer Strategic Marketing
Market Testing & Analysis
Trade Show Theme Development
Exhibit Booth Design/Graphics
Point of Purchase Displays/Campaigns

Communications
Media Relations, Schedules, Budgets
Event Organization/Sponsorship
Trade Show Identity & Presence
Speech Writing
Press Media Kits
Sales Meeting-Theme & Planning

Public Relations
Internal Story/Article Development
Community/Corporate Events
Customer Satisfaction Identity
Special Recognition Programs
Sales Achievement/Award Presentation
Gift-Award-Travel Recognition
Media Story Pitch & Promotion
Press Releases
Newsletters, External-Internal

Sales Promotions
Sales Force Training/Manuals
How to Work A Trade Show Exhibit
Key Account Recognition
Price List/Discount Materials
New Account Intro Packets
Cross Selling Products/Services
Professional Development

Research
Competitive Analysis
Product Testing
Product Endorsements
Selling Through Research
Market Share Analysis

Advertising
Trade & Consumer Graphic Design
Product Support-Silent Salesperson
New Product/Logo Development
Direct Marketing Creation
Catalog Design, Print, Layout
Showroom/Retail Promotional Design
Art & Photography Direction

Trade Show/Convention Exhibit
Exhibit Design, Construction Supervision
Exhibit Site Coordination
Graphic Theme/Advertising Message
Pre-Show Publicity/Press Conference
Special Event-Trade Show Coordination

I began my client search by looking in the New York area to see if I could find some potential clients in need of my expertise. I knew John D'Addario (the second generation of the well-known music industry family) quite well over the years and the D'Addario company was located on Long Island, not far from the Westbury Korg headquarters. I contacted John and he invited me to visit him at his company. He was extremely kind and gracious in giving me his time and a complete tour of D'Addario, which was at that time primarily a string manufacturing company. I believe D'Addario was also distributing Vandoren reeds for woodwind instruments. This visit and factory tour was long before the company took ownership of ProMark Sticks from Herb Brochstein or Evans Drum Heads from Bob Beals. We had a nice conversation, but nothing came out of it in the way of a client project.

I had also visited Steinway Hall located very close to Carnegie Hall in midtown Manhattan. I was so impressed with the magnificent showroom and presentation of all the Steinway pianos that I sent a letter to Bruce Stevens, President of Steinway, at the Steinway USA factory located in Astoria, New York. Steinway was at the time introducing the Boston line of pianos "by Steinway" to the market place. There was lots of publication and media coverage of this new division within the Steinway organization. The Boston Piano series was a new level of less expensive pianos that were to be manufactured to specific and exclusive Steinway specifications by Kawai Pianos in Japan. Once again the communications were cordial and friendly. I received a copy of the wonderful book, *Steinway*, with a personal letter from Mr. Stevens thanking me for my visit and enthusiastic remarks about the Steinway Hall visit. There were some phone calls, letters, and a couple of meetings, but again, nothing positive came from my efforts to create a relationship with Steinway.

I realized that if I was such an expert at marketing music products successfully, I needed to be able to market myself. The reality was that it was going to take longer than I had expected because of the poor economy and the high national unemployment at that time. In many cases, the economic cut-backs that were taking place were altogether eliminating the positions of marketing director, advertising manager, and related titles. While this created a discouraging cloud for these types of positions, it did open the door for consulting. Invariably within a large organization, when the marketing director was eliminated, much of their responsibilities fell into the hands of the company's financial officer, who knew nothing about marketing. I learned that most financial officers were interested in farming out anything and everything related to marketing, advertising , promotion and sales, to qualified affordable consultants. The priority was just to get those marketing duties and responsibilities off their desks. I looked at my newfound "consultant status" as more of a search for companies with non-advertised "help needed" issues rather than non-existent "help wanted" situations.

I had the advantage of being able to market myself in three different cities at the same time; New York City, Cleveland, and Chicago. I came up with three sets of letterhead, three different client services listings, and I had the ability to have three different telephone numbers, so I worked at marketing myself in three different markets. Potential clients would never know what city I was really in at any given time of telephone conversation. Face-to-face meetings could be set for whenever I was scheduled to be in that particular city.

Client No. 1
Baldwin Piano & Organ, Chicago, IL.

In studying and researching the client potentials in and around Chicago, I learned that the Baldwin Piano & Organ company owned five of its own retail stores in the Chicago area. Baldwin indicated they were looking for some marketing expertise. I contacted Steve Marcus, the regional manager for all five Baldwin corporately-owned retail stores in the Chicago area. My percussion expertise did not come into play, but my experience in the music products industry and apparent reputation seemed to create some interest in how I could contribute to this acoustic and digital piano retail operation. Steve recognized that I knew retail and wholesale, I also knew about product distribution and clearly my skill set could be used to develop a marketing plan for all five retail stores. I spent some

Baldwin Piano store, Golf Mill Shopping Center, Niles

time learning and training at the headquarters Baldwin store on the west side of Chicago. This was an ambitious task, learning their current marketing campaign, sorting out the weaknesses and strengths, learning what some of the retail problems were, and what some of the personnel problems were.

I thought of it as starting out by dusting off pianos; I would stand in the showroom and listen to the sales presentation pitches that their present sales force was using with showroom customers who came in looking for an electronic or acoustic piano. There were things that I liked, some that I disliked and some things I did not understand. I was not a piano expert, but I knew I could make some improvements. Then I started traveling to all five area branches, which included their "glamour" store located at street level of Wacker Drive in the Civic Opera House in downtown Chicago. This was the most elegant of the five stores. I started spending more time at the mall store in the Golf Mill Shopping Mall in Niles. That was the store that was faltering the most in sales, promotion, interior design and stability of sales personnel. I started with some store interior layout changes, decorations, and tried to give the store an improved appearance. Unfortunately the store was not located on the main concourse, and shopper foot traffic was weak. The local buying population did not recognize or appreciate elegance in a piano store, as the local clientele were working class families of foreign descent seeking to give their children an affordable musical educational experience. Eventually I addressed some of the quality and professionalism of the sales people and forced some changes to make improvements. It also helped having a Spanish speaking floor sales lady as she could communicate comfortably with a large Spanish speaking buying public. That helped the store achieve some positive sales numbers. Over time, the Golf Mill Mall store location was no longer the weakest of the five stores.

I commuted from Cleveland to Chicago every two weeks either by car or by jumping on a flight from O'Hare airport to Cleveland. The flights were only about $81 round trip if you purchased the tickets 30 days in advance. I was operating under a consulting contract, though most of the Baldwin people working around me did not know that. Baldwin wanted my true identity as a contract consultant to remain unknown. I would also learn over time that most of my clients preferred this incognito identity. I was to remain with invisible status, as this would add some perceived team symmetry and I would not be thought-of as a hired-gun or visiting hatchet man who would be firing everyone and then leave.

Baldwin was my introduction to piano sales and I soon learned what an armory sale was. An armory sale was basically taking inventory from all five stores, renting a large armory hall over a two-day weekend and putting the entire inventory on display. The entire event was promoted as as a liquidation sale. The buying public thought that they were getting a better price than if they were visiting an official Baldwin retail store. The bottom line was that customers were really *not* getting a better deal on their piano selection or purchase. (As with any large expensive item like automobiles and appliances, there are two to three discount price columns available to the commissioned sales person) The Armory sale was presented as a once-in-a-lifetime savings opportunity. I never knew that such a thing as an armory piano sale existed. The event I attended and participated in was during a typical Chicago winter; the armory hall was freezing cold and I caught a terrible cold immediately after.

I then started reading about University Piano Sales at Northwestern University. These pianos had nothing to do with pianos that Northwestern University owned or were selling off. The impression created for the buying public was that the university was liquidating their extra slightly used pianos. In reality, this was warehouse inventory from Baldwin being taken to the university concert hall and being sold off. Baldwin was renting concert hall and stage space to provide a perspective to the consumer that, "these are being liquidated at unbelievable once-in-a-lifetime prices- *buy now*!" While there is nothing wrong or unethical with this practice it was a complete learning experience for me.

Another new term in my vocabulary became "front pumping." Front-pumping basically means taking a piano out in front of the store in a mall environment and playing the piano for the public walking past the entrance. I did not play the piano. I knew the keyboard, but I was not a pianist. With a digital piano, I could push the "demo" button and have it play itself. People in the mall were drawn to the source of the "live music". Every day we would be rolling a new piano out into the store's front entrance area to draw attention to the Baldwin store. Many of the sales people Baldwin employed were very fine pianists who played very well. They would just go out there and start playing either from memory or with sheet music. If I was ever left alone in the store and had to do some of the front pumping, I just rolled out a digital piano.

I quickly learned the difference between American and Chinese-made pianos. I paid particular attention to

A Memorable Moment:

The Baldwin removal and pick-up of the competitive-sample Samick piano remains a continuous memory. As the very heavy acoustic Samick piano was being carried down the front steps of the Northbrook home, one of the Baldwin delivery-team workers started to lose his balance and looked like he was going to drop the piano down the concrete steps. I immediately jumped in to help the worker and avoid the dropping of the brand new Samick piano, only to have the piano fall on my left ankle at the bottom of the front steps. This ankle immediately swelled up to the size of a basketball, became extremely bruised and black and I could not walk on it. I went to the doctor who indicated nothing was broken, but the bruising would last for a month. Baldwin paid all the related medical expenses and life went on. Today, whenever I stand on an uneven hill or slanted pavement, I feel the soreness of the "Baldwin Ankle" acting up again.

this, as I was intending to purchase a grand piano for my home in Cleveland. Chinese pianos were entering the American market as fast as they could unload the containers from the ships. This prompted Baldwin to seek a source for purchasing a competitive branded piano that could be used to show the superior mechanics, components and sound of the Baldwin acoustic piano versus the Chinese instruments and brands. Baldwin chose the Samick brand made in China for this comparison. I became Baldwin's "silent shopper," going to nearby Naylor's Music and purchasing an upright Samick piano without letting on that I was really with Baldwin. I had the instrument delivered to my home in Northbrook during the work-day. Within a day or two after the delivery, the Baldwin piano mover team picked up the Samick piano at my home in Northbrook and took it to their showroom where the Samick piano was exclusively used for comparison purposes. Baldwin sales people became trained in presenting to customers the many significant differences in quality of parts, manufacturing-assembly, appearance, playability and sound between the American Baldwin and Chinese-made Samick instruments.

The best outcome of this very first client experience (a nine month project) was that I was able to purchase a beautiful Baldwin made-in-America seven-foot black ebony grand piano which had a retail value of around $18,000. I purchased this for $5,000. and had it delivered to Cleveland by one of the Baldwin cross-country piano delivery trucks.

It was not really my job to sell pianos. I concentrated on store design, sales training, and so forth. I did manage to sell one piano and by coincidence it was to my very first private drum teacher's sister. I had studied with Bill Olive/Drum Specialist back in the late 1950's. His sister came in to the Golf Mill Mall store looking to purchase a piano for her home. and I was thrilled to help her select and buy one.

Client No. 2
GENEVA INTERNATIONAL, Wheeling, Il.

Geneva International was a growing family-owned musical business whose ownership learned of my longstanding relationships in the industry, and association with guitars in particular, through my experiences at Hohner, Gretsch, and Gibson. Earl and Elaine Matzkin founded the firm in the 1980's and its success was based on their success as the exclusive U.S. distributor of Petrof and Weinbach pianos manufactured in the Czech Republic. This was expanded to other musical instruments which also included band instruments and string instruments coming from the Czech Republic.

The company had recently introduced five different sizes of Czech-made nylon-string classical guitars under the name Amada. This was a unique product line and offering. The market was wide open for retail-

ers to show, demonstrate, and sell the newly available smaller guitars, perfect for younger students and beginners. While the beginner violin market had multiple size instruments, Amada was the first quality brand and product to offer multiple size guitar instruments.

I met with Earl Matzkin multiple times to discuss and explore how Amada Guitars could enter the U.S. guitar market and how they could be marketed and sold to music retailers across the country. At this point in time there was no Amada guitar product literature, photography, or sales promotion with new-dealer incentives. Amada was a product that existed without any sales or marketing strategy, or even a business-model to work from. Starting from "scratch" would be the definition. Earl liked the consulting contract idea which had me working incognito with the rest of the full time employee team members. Geneva International had a beautiful office and showroom location that was a pleasure to work in and invite retailers to visit to see, hear and play all the various instruments beautifully displayed.

Georg Seger was the national sales manager for all the non-piano musical instruments, Greg Schonneck (a former Selmer/Ludwig salesman) was the single sales representative for all band and orchestral instruments on a national basis. Vince Grantano was handling the sales and marketing for the very beautiful decorative imported glass that the Czech Republic was internationally known for. The Amada classical guitars would be my complete responsibility.

Geneva In'tl Corp.: Vince Grantano, Karl Dustman, Earl Matzkin. Company debuted fractional-size acoustic guitars from Czech Republic.

While there was never a mention or definition as to what "success" was, I took care of creating, designing, and doing all of the photography and product literature to get the complete Guitar and mandolin line together. Some of the Amada guitars sizes were already in-stock,. Other sizes were forthcoming from Europe. I was already at a disadvantage because everything from photography to brochure size specifications was to be marketed as a complete "family" of five different sizes. We could not begin anything untill I had all five sizes of guitars in my office.

It was late April of 1993 and there was no support literature, no discount schedules, and no marketing dealer incentives . The annual Summer NAMM show in Nashville was quickly approaching. It was my responsibility to establish a presence for Amada Classical Guitars at the 1993 summer NAMM convention. Because this annual event was primarily a guitar show this was a very significant opportunity to bring immediate market identification and presence to the product, brand and uniqueness of the Amada product line. Guitar retailers from across the country would be in attendance. Fortunately, all the elements for presenting the product came together just before I arrived in Nashville to set up and direct the Amada Classical Guitar exhibit. This was pretty much a one man, one booth exhibit located near the center of the guitar section on the exhibit floor.

I did some research on identifying the national guitar retailers and started some telemarketing to some of them. Earl also wanted me to start traveling with the guitars, calling on Midwest retailers. I wasn't real

thrilled with the prospects of this element of the project, as I didn't see myself as a traveling guitar salesman. This is not to sound "above" selling guitars to retailers, I had just never done it before and I knew there were seasoned guitar sales people who could sell guitars far better than myself. I felt my skills and talents were better suited to national marketing, campaigns and incentives to make the product line and brand appealing on a national scope. However, since I was the one man in charge of Amada Classical Guitars, I was to be the one-man sales force to create and achieve orders for the instruments.

Previously unknown quality issues with some of the guitars soon came to light. We became aware that some of the bridges on certain guitars were coming "unglued" from the guitar body. Retailers were not happy, and the guitars were immediately picked up and replaced with inspected and approved guitars without any quality issues. There were already hundreds of guitars of all five sizes in the Wheeling, IL. warehouse, waiting to be used for filling orders. Up to this point, guitars coming in as container loads from the Czech Republic were not being inspected, set –up or tuned by anyone from Geneva International prior to being sent out to the retailer. I was immediately directed to "drop everything and go out into the warehouse to unpack and inspect every Amada guitar in the inventory". I definitely did not like the element of going out into the mid-summer heat in the warehouse to become the quality control inspector on instruments coming in from the Czech Republic. This was further troubling as my time, attention, and efforts needed to be focused on marketing and selling the guitars in North America, not becoming a product inspector. Eventually I was able to complete the inventory inspection locating any guitar model that had a defective bridge, warped neck or questionable fingerboard quality. Those guitars were shipped back to the factory in Europe and replaced with new instruments which must have received a more complete quality control effort before leaving the manufacturing facility. Quality control issues were solved, and it was time to get back to the real reason I was brought into the company, which was to create and develop a market for the Amada Guitar line.

This was an uphill climb, sales traveling while still trying to create and implement marketing campaigns and strategies from the Geneva International office. I would schedule my sales trips for a week here and there, always by establishing a predetermined date and time appointment with a store's individual who would be expecting my visit to their store. Cold calling would always be a waste of time, money and effort.

By the fall of the year, Amada sales and brand identity was starting to happen. I was getting some nice six-piece orders. Some orders were concentrated on a specific instrument size, others would experiment with 3-4 different sized instruments. Amada was developing and progressing according to the plan, but it was not happening fast enough for Earl. I feel that I had successfully started the flame for Amada Classical Guitars but never really reaped the recognition or benefit of launching this brand and product in a highly competitive market.

Eventually Geneva International continued without me when my contract did not get renewed. The discontinuation of a "contracted consultant" was easy and quiet; it was that transition which appealed to many

Reprinted courtesy of Musical Merchandise Review (July, 1995)

'Students Of All Sizes' Learn on Amada Guitars

Amada classical guitars are the most popular student instrument in Marshall Music's impressive lesson program in Lansing, Michigan. Approximately 60 percent of the aspiring guitarists who buy their first instrument when they enroll in the 350-student program are selecting from the lineup of European-made Amada models. This comes as no surprise to Marshall's senior guitar teacher, Roger Humphrey.

Roger Humphrey, senior guitar teacher at Marshall Music, Lansing, MI, with several of the dealership's 350 guitar students.

"It's easy to see why they're so popular," said Humphrey. "The guitar comes in fractional sizes, so there's an instrument that fits everyone, even our four- and five-year-old students. And the quality of the guitar makes it easier for students to develop on the instrument."

However, Humphrey admits when he first learned of the Amada line, he had his doubts the guitars would ever be accepted by Marshall's customers. "Chris Wood [the store's guitar manager] told me about this new line of fractional nylon-string student guitars, and then he told me their price was a little higher than the brands we had in stock," recalled Humphrey. "This concerned me, because at the time our fractional and student guitar business was strictly price-driven, because there was no quality to be found in any of the models that were available. Parents just went ahead and bought the cheapest guitar they could find — we couldn't get them to spend $25 more, or even $10 more, on an instrument. Everything was price, price, price."

This was before Humphrey took a closer look at the Amada instrument. "Chris took me over and said, 'Just play it.' I did, and I was totally amazed — this was a real instrument, not a toy," related Humphrey. "I couldn't believe anyone would make a guitar of such high quality for that kind of money. I'd thought Amada was just another student guitar, but it was a true instrument, even at the fractional sizes."

According to Humphrey, who also teaches guitar at several area colleges and has written a method book, the superiority of Amada over other entry-level lines is readily apparent. The guitar's tonal characteristics, construction, wood quality, finish, tunability, and ease of play are comparable to that of an instrument three times its price, he estimates.

of my clients. I mentally was getting acclimated to the fact that none of the client projects I would work on would last forever. Functioning as a consultant rather than an employee, there were no benefits to sort out, no sick days, no hiring or firing procedures. Contracts had built-in starting and ending clauses. The renewal of a consulting contract is never taken for granted.

Eventually the Czech Republic owner of Petrof and Weinbach Pianos severed the piano distribution agreement with Geneva International. The pianos had pretty much been the umbrella that paid for everything else that Earl and Elaine Matzkin were doing as a company and eventually the company closed.

CLIENT No. 3
THE CHICAGO MUSIC MART
DePaul Center, Chicago, Il.
Karl goes back to DePaul University

I learned that DePaul University was working on a project called "The Chicago Music Mart at DePaul Center." They were intending to recreate, at the corner of State St. and Jackson Blvd, the musical center of downtown Chicago. Once known as Music Row. Wabash Avenue had been *the* musical heartbeat or destination for everything in music through much of the 20th century. Originally the area was best known for musical manufacturing; by 1910 50% of the pianos sold in the USA were made in Chicago. By the 1950s, the area was a Mecca of musical retailing that rivaled New York's 48th Street area. Franks Drum Shop, Bill Crowden's Drums Limited, Lyon & Healy, Carl Fischer, all helped to create the music retailing zone. DePaul University had purchased the vacant 11 story Goldblatts department store building from the city of Chicago for one million dollars. The building had been dormant for over a decade and was considered a prime piece of real-estate. By forfeiture, the City of Chicago took over ownership and wanted to get out from owning a vacant piece of real-estate that should be paying taxes to the city. In transferring ownership, the city required DePaul to do something creative for the city on the first two concourse levels. The rest of the building and floors could be used by DePaul to do with whatever they wanted.

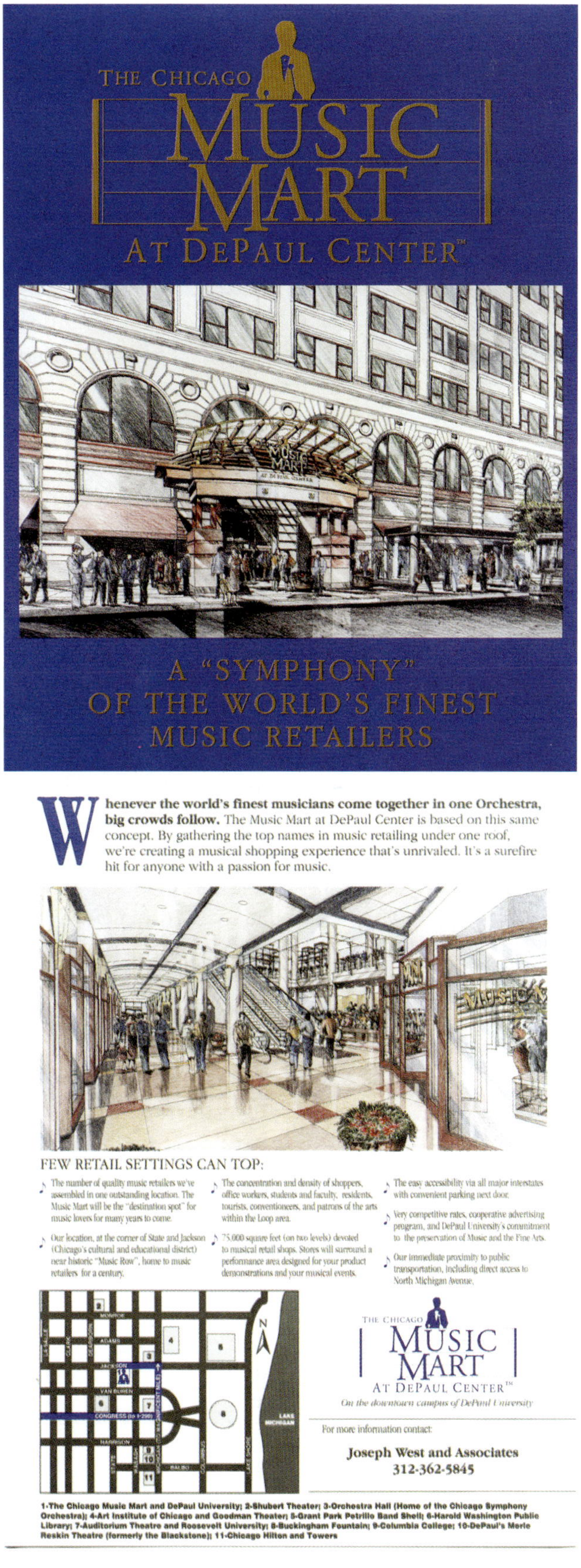

The music industry trade publications started covering this creation of the Chicago Music Mart and I saw this as an opportunity. I could find no mention of any person with music experience working with DePaul University, the City of Chicago or the commercial real-estate broker. Could De Paul be embarking on this massive project without any music products industry expertise involved? I contacted the University's Executive Vice President, Ken McHugh, with a cover letter and packet of materials presenting my experience and qualifications. McHugh turned my packet over to the university's real-estate consultant, Greg Davey. Davey called and invited me to come into the city to meet with him about the Chicago Music Mart project and discuss their present and future needs. Based on that meeting and Davey's personal recommendation to the University, I was quickly brought into the project as a Music Marketing Consultant which I viewed as the opportunity of a lifetime.

DePaul loved the idea of a consulting contract because it established our relationship over a defined term. This meant that they would not be subjected to entanglements that conventional employment contracts can bring; we could cleanly part ways by simply not renewing the consulting contract. (I was more "disposable" than a "regular" employee.) I was able to work with the university, the city of Chicago, the mayor's office, and was qualified to work with all the various PR firms that the university would hire. It was inconceivable to me that the largest Catholic university in the United States would embark on this very specialized type of retail merchandising project without having anyone on board who knew anything about music, the original Wabash Avenue Music Row or who the major musical instrument companies or brands were in the music products industry. This was not just diverse downtown general population retail rental space, this had to be a complex assortment of music retailing that would create a musical destination with a balanced product and service offering to compliment each tenant. There was no one connected with the music industry to guide the development of 75,000 square feet of retail space on the main first floor and lower concourse levels for the university's planned $11 million renovation.

The contract was assigned and it basically outlined what I would be doing. I needed to wear multiple hats with multiple missions to cover the needs of the musical elements of the project. This meant cultivating music products industry awareness as well as working with the various Chicago-based public relations firms on how to develop exposure and publicity in the city. The downside of that was that DePaul changed PR firms about every six months. This constant change was simply because the University was unhappy with what the P.R. firms were doing and what the University thought they should be doing. The local media was certainly covering the evolving Chicago Music Mart with the Chicago Tribune and the Chicago Sun Times both covering the developing destination point in Chicago. The music products industry publications were also paying attention to this unique and unprecedented retail mall approach to music retailing.

Every time there was a change of a PR firm, it took me three weeks to bring the new PR firm up to speed. I had to work with them to define the project while also helping them to understand the music industry. I also had to work with the Mayor's office on

Chicago has a strong and diverse musical legacy – both in terms of education and entertainment. Historic "music row" along South Wabash Avenue long embodied that connection between education and the arts throughout most of the 1900s.

The spirit and vibrancy that made South Wabash Avenue a special place ... a destination point ... is still alive and stronger than ever at Chicago's new "music row," The Chicago Music Mart at DePaul Center.

With the University's own historic roots in music and music education, it was only natural that DePaul University should be a part of this new, and exciting retail concept. It represents a highly visible display of DePaul's long-standing support of cultural diversity, and commitment to quality education and the music industry in the broadest sense.

For the practicing musician, professional or anyone who appreciates music ... for the Rachmaninoff aficionado and the Rolling Stones fan ... The Chicago Music Mart provides a common attraction and appeal for everyone – namely, music.

Kenneth A. McHugh
Executive Vice President/ Operations

The New Heart of Chicago's

Throughout most of the early- and mid-1900s, Chicago's "music row" along South Wabash Avenue was home to a variety of music manufacturers and retailers, attracting musicians and music lovers from all over the Midwest. Renowned piano, harp and organ makers, as well as printed music sellers, offered the greatest assortment in musical instruments and accessories in the Midwest.

It was here on "music row" that the first American-made harp was produced by Lyon-Healy, and several other firsts were introduced ... the upright piano, player piano, spinet piano, electric organ and Thomas Edison's gramophone. Unfortunately, the hustle and bustle along "music row" dissipated with the growth of the suburbs, and the attraction of the enclosed shopping mall.

Today, The Chicago Music Mart at DePaul Center has recaptured the innovative spirit and excitement associated with a strong concentration of music industry leaders and merchandise set within the vibrancy and activity of a central business district. It is the new heart of Chicago's historic "music row."

The Chicago Music Mart is a truly unique retail center. It's the only self-contained shopping emporium in the country dedicated exclusively to music, musical instruments, and related gifts and accessories.

With approximately 75,000 square feet, The Chicago Music Mart encompasses two entire levels of an historic landmark building. For nearly 50 years this building was the flagship store of a prominent Chicago area department store chain. Following an extensive, $65 million interior and exterior renovation,

city-wide promotions so that they would get behind the project through the City of Chicago Tourism aspects of it. I worked early-on with each of the prospective tenants to help generate interest in the Music Mart and the desire to become a retail tenant within the Music Mart. This challenge called upon my experiences as a music retailer and an understanding of the workings of DePaul University while coping with the paranoia of the commercial real-estate broker, Joe West and Associates.

Ken McHugh worked closely with myself, Greg Davey, and the licensed commercial real estate broker on various different rent abatement packages. This meant signing a ten year lease but at only a fraction of what the real downtown Chicago rent values would have been. This rent-abatement made coming in the Music Mart almost "risk free". Various incentives were created, including offering a start-up *rent free* enticement for three to four years without any rent. I started to create four-month marketing plans, coordinating this with the Music Mart's Tenant Coordinator Janice Javors, and the commercial real-estate broker Joe West, The real-estate broker was basically a small husband and wife team that had somehow found a way to work with DePaul University on their commercial real-estate contracts. Joe West was very uncomfortable having Greg Davey as a real-estate consultant to Ken Mc Hugh, as well as having me as the music industry consultant reporting to both Ken McHugh and Greg Davey. For some reason West felt very threatened by having a music consultant involved in this project working on recruiting tenants. I don't understand this to this day.

Histotoric "Music Row"

DePaul Center, as it is now dedicated, is an 11-story mixed-use building that combines retail, university operations and office space.

From its legendary State Street address, DePaul Center is located in the middle of Chicago's downtown cultural district – across the street from the new, world-class Harold Washington Public Library and only blocks away from the Art Institute, the Auditorium Theater, and Orchestra Hall (home of the Chicago Symphony Orchestra). The Michigan Avenue retail area, as well as Chicago's financial and central business districts, are also key ingredients supporting the economic synergy of The Chicago Music Mart.

For everything musical, there is no experience like The Chicago Music Mart at DePaul Center.

Instrument Try-out Rooms

Comparing different brands and models of an instrument is vital to a musician's purchase selection. At The Chicago Music Mart, sound-proof test rooms are designed to allow discriminating players to "test -drive" any band or orchestra instrument in private before making a final selection.

Performance Stage

Located on the Concourse level of The Chicago Music Mart is a performance stage area where live performances by professional and amateur music-makers invite visitors to sing and/or swing to the beat. The performance stage is available for guest clinic appearances, lecturer presentations and showcases of all kinds of musical talent. Seating is available for up to 250 guests.

The ways in which music is changing and th rapidity of that change ar inevitably reflected in music education. This change is also mirrored by the diverse group of retailers and products tha comprise The Chicago Music Mart.

Music education mus be connected to the past even as it reaches towar the future. Teaching students how to interpre the music of Brahms for example, is not essentiall different than it was 100 years ago when Brahms was living. At the same time, technological advances have had a great impact on all aspects of music – from sound synthesis and "sampling" techniques to a wide variety of computer applications.

As a result, career choices in music are no longer limited to just performance or teaching. Today's music student could be preparing for professions in recording technology and sound design as well as retailin publishing, marketing an even arts management.

The Chicago Music Mart is a reflection of what we are doing in music education, connecting the past to th future with today's technology.

Frederick Miller
Dean, School of Music

I worked with the various tenants' architectural firms to provide symmetry and compatibility with all of the musical instruments and public interest platforms. I also started working with a lot of the local area schools, inviting them to visit the Music Mart as part of a downtown Chicago field trip as well as inviting them to perform on the open atrium stage in the center of the grand concourse. I knew that many schools also had various summer tours where student groups would come through Chicago taking tours of the Ludwig factory, and the LeBlanc woodwind factory up in Kenosha. This had to be marketed as a musical destination not to be missed.

The open-air center atrium was a remarkable feat in itself. We started marketing the daily live performances as a "Tunes at Noon" series with an actual calendar of performances. We worked with parents, the teachers, the bus drivers, the students-whatever it took to get them to converge on the Music Mart. I found the DePaul School of Music to be a gold-mine of opportunity to bring further attention to the Music Mart. I was introduced to the Dean of the School of Music, Fred Miller, and we got along well from the very beginning. While he had a School of Music to run, he wanted to support the downtown campus and the Music Mart's mission. We worked on the development of the new four-page color brochure, which provided a conduit for both Ken McHugh and Fred Miller to combine their messages about "The New Heart of Chicago's Historic Music Row".

I was using and creating every form of diplomatic relations and contacts I possessed, to attract attention for the Music Mart while leveraging the uniqueness of what De Paul University was creating. Larry Linken, the president and CEO of NAMM, was personal friends with Fred Miller and very supportive of the "rebuilding of the Wabash Avenue Music Row" story for downtown Chicago.

With the Summer NAMM convention approaching, we discussed ways to promote the Music Mart at the summer NAMM show and the following winter market convention in Anaheim in January. Bob Larkin was the director of the DePaul Jazz Education program and a strong supporter of the Music Mart. It was decided that we would use the DePaul University jazz ensemble as kind of a showpiece live musical ambassador for the Music Mart. Using live music as a magnet to draw people's attention and the media coverage seemed to spark a positive chord with everyone. All partners considered this a win for DePaul, the School of Music Jazz program, and the Music Mart.

I convinced DePaul University to invest in flying the entire jazz ensemble down to the summer NAMM show in Nashville for a featured convention opening-night live performance with the assistance of NAMM President and CEO Larry Linkin. NAMM provided complimentary exhibit space in the convention center for the Music Mart to have a "meet and greet".

Chicago Music Mart NAMM Exhibit

The DePaul University Jazz Band under the direction of Bob Larkin

The success that this NAMM convention presence had in the eyes of Ken McHugh and DePaul opened the door for me to escalate music industry presence by having DePaul fly the entire jazz ensemble out to the International Jazz Educator's Convention in January of 1994 in Anaheim, California. Working with my previous IAJE contacts from previous years I was able to get the Music Mart ambassadors to be a featured opening night performance. By now we were creating national visibility and making some very strong contacts. The Music Mart was being spotlighted even before the grand opening would take place in the Fall of 1994.

Fred Miller, Larry Linken, and I talked about different ways we could leverage this national publicity into further music industry support, participation and tenantcy for the Music Mart. It was decided to have a by-invitation music products industry breakfast in Anaheim hosted by the Chicago Music Mart, DePaul University, and NAMM. This special invitation was made for all the major musical instrument brands in all the product categories to come and learn about how the Chicago Music Mart was evolving. Ken Mc Hugh was the featured guest speaker, addressing the group and providing detailed information about the Music Mart and why it was important for the music products industry to support this partnership venture.

We were successful in getting Baldwin, Yamaha, LeBlanc, and most major brands to be tenants and participants in the Music Mart through these combined efforts with NAMM. By now the Chicago media was constantly providing regular update stories and coverage of the Music Mart. The music industry publications were also gracious to providing regular stories and press releases about the project's development, new tenants coming on board, and the various educational and guest performances that were taking place on the stage within the center of the Music Mart. Things were going, almost according to plan.

The second half of 1994 proved to be very positive in bringing in new and potential tenants. Baldwin and Yamaha Piano companies invested thousands of dollars in their custom interior build-outs. Band and combo instruments were also included in the mix along with Carl Fischer Music as a cornerstone of support and participation in everything the Music Mart embarked on. September included the 13th Annual President's Club Dinner, focused around the success of the Music Mart, located on the roof-top level of the

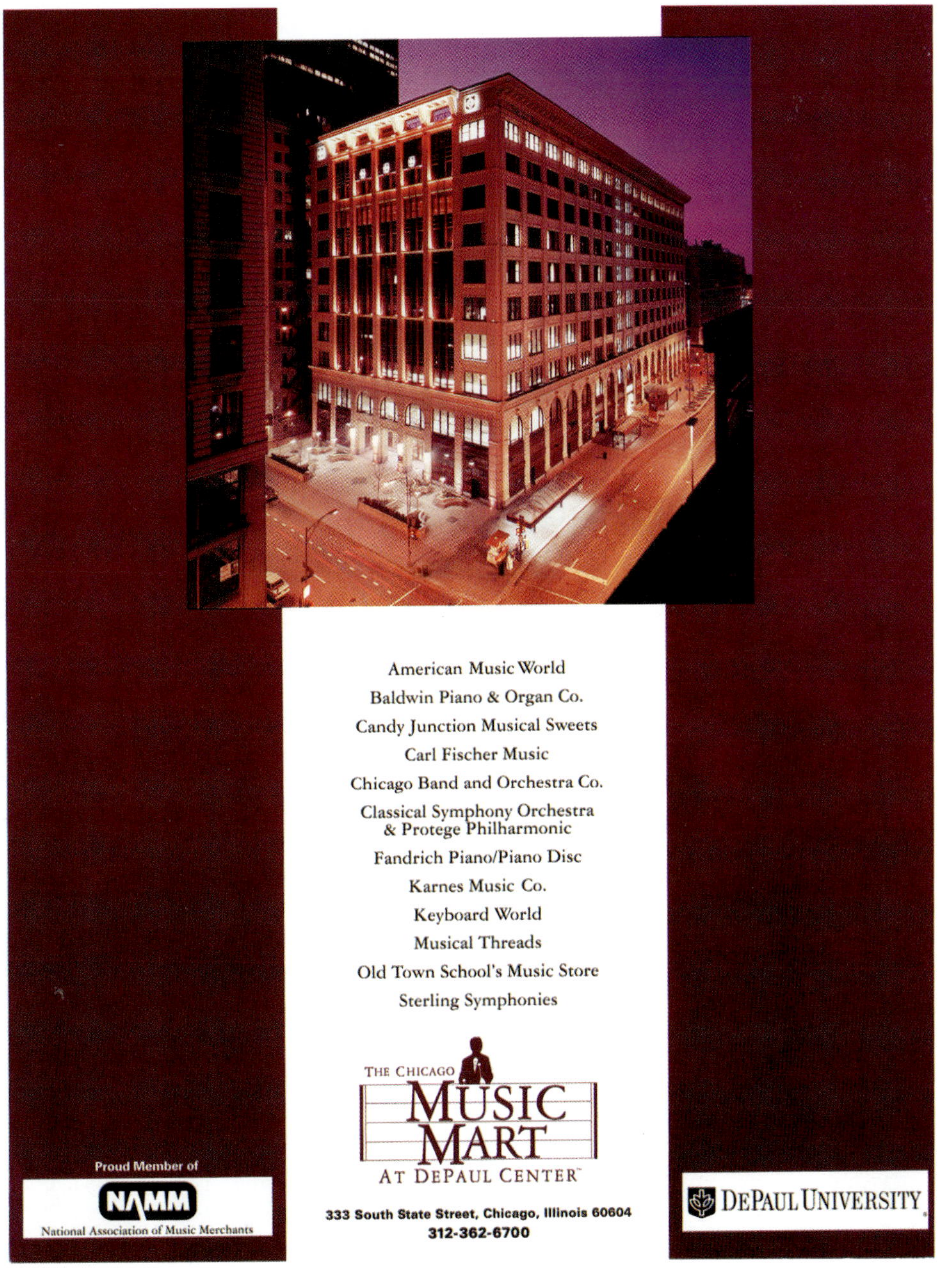

Baldwin
SILVER HOUSE & CO.
presents

Karl and DePaul Music Mart Tenant Coordinator Janice Javors at the Presidents Club dinner

building with lavish food and beverage accommodations, speeches and recognition for the success of the Music Mart project. A black-tie event, I was thrilled to be included (as an outside consultant) while also having the ability to connect socially with many of the wonderful DePaul University people who assisted me in getting the job done.

The official Grand Opening celebration of the Chicago Music Mart took place in September with tremendous live coverage of the ribbon cutting outdoors on a September morning. The commuter pedestrians passing the high visibility corner of State and Jackson were caught up in the extravaganza that included guest speakers, live music and "an EVENT" which DePaul University was so adept at orchestrating and conducting in downtown Chicago. The culmination of the media recognition and support was the MUSIC INC. December 1994 cover story on the Chicago Music Mart. Eight pages were devoted to the Mart's development, opening, tenant committments to be part of this large scale retail operation.

Music Inc. representatives, David Jaworski and John Janowiak did a marvelous job interviewing University officials, tenants and myself. I was thrilled that this project received cover-story placement and the entire music products industry would be reading about this project that I was deeply involved in.

October brought the first drum clinic presentation into the main performance stage of the Music Mart, featuring Kenny Aronoff as part of the International Drum Month national campaign. Widespread media

Kenny Aronoff

attention by the current P.R. firm, Debra Gordon Public Relations, resulted in a better than average Chicago area press coverage and attendance.

1994 ended on a positive note with momentum that everyone felt positive about. I was encouraged that the university was supporting my efforts, ideas and recommendations. While I was often reminded to "not take everything so personal" coming from anyone involved in this project,. I was committed to seeing this extremely unique and national-in-scope project succeed and grow as the years would follow. By April of 1995 the music products industry became even more aware of the Music Mart, as new name-brand tenants came on board with rent abatement incentives and provisions and brought into the start-up equation by the university's executive vice president, Ken McHugh. The April edition of *Musical Merchandise Review* featured three pages of editorial and photos of the up and running Music Mart. This was further encouraging that the Music Mart was becoming a destination with a world-class musical retailing experience few had seen in Chicago for decades.

Part of the problem for a consultant in doing your work too well is that a client may "no longer feel they need your professional services". This was the case with the Music Mart. The Music Mart was open, it was functioning, attracting new tenants and the work of a music consultant was complete. My contract did not get renewed and many people were sorry to see me eliminated from the further and ongoing work that really needed to be done.

Reprinted courtesy of Music Inc. magazine, December, 1994

THE CHICAGO MUSIC MART AT DEPAUL CENTER

CAN IT WORK?

1

It began with an unprecedented idea: Revive the spirit of Chicago's legendary Music Row with a downtown theme mall. Now that the Chicago Music Mart at DePaul Center is a reality, tenants and administrators respond to the challenge of making it a success.

BY DAVID ZAWORSKI & JOHN JANOWIAK

3

Reprinted courtesy of Music Inc. magazine, December, 1994

2

4

KARNES PHOTO: LINK/FREEMAN ADVERTISING

1) Music Mart outside. 2) Mart associates from left: Frank Mares, DePaul University; John Berger, Karnes Music; Eliza Jin, Sterling Symphonies; Ralph Cox, Baldwin; singer Ginger Tam; Ken McHugh, DePaul; Jim Rubino, Rubino's Music & Sound; Bob Black, Chicago Band & Orchestra; Fred Miller, DePaul; Ed Richards, Fandrich Piano. 3) Interior of Karnes by design consultant Robert L. Link. 4) Tam and pianist Jeremy Kahn.

Reprinted courtesy of Music Inc. magazine, December, 1994

IT'S SHOWTIME IN CHICAGO. HOUSE-lights have dimmed, and the curtain has gone up for the debut of The Chicago Music Mart at DePaul Center.

The music-products industry has never witnessed a production like this before. Designed, created and funded by DePaul University, the Music Mart brings together piano, combo, band instrument, percussion and print music retailers under one roof in a one-stop shopping mall for music consumers. It's a risky venture. While many retailers have fled downtown locations in recent years, these retailers defy the trend. The question remains: Can they succeed here?

Mart retailers agree that DePaul's help has eased the task of launching their new businesses. To help them flourish, DePaul invested $65 million to renovate the building and provided design services, leasing incentives and advertising funds. It's a large-scale experiment that could offer new dimensions to music-product retailing. Although their outlooks range from wide-eyed enthusiasm to only-time-can-tell realism, most retailers have taken the stage confident in their mission.

Inside the mart: *From top to bottom, mart retailers Bob Black (left) and Steve Baughman of Chicago Band & Orchestra; Jim Rubino (center) and Diana Moss Rubino with staff members; Barbara Fandrich and Ed Richards of Fandrich Piano.*

DePaul's Vision

By funding retailers' startups in the Music Mart, DePaul steps beyond the role of traditional landlord and enters into a partnership with retailers. DePaul has leased space to corporations like McDonald's before, but it has never embarked on a business partnership like this. Karl Dustman, a 25-year music industry veteran who is serving as a project consultant for DePaul, concedes that the university is new to the music business. However, the university's overall effort is long-term and goes beyond business knowledge and funding.

"What [DePaul] does have is a vision of trying to recreate an environment for a music industry that is on questionable pillars in terms of where it's going," he said. "Numbers are going down, stores are closing, schools are in trouble. They have put their money into it to make certain that [the mart succeeds]. There isn't any other entity that could pull this off."

DePaul's vision harkens to Music Row, an area on Chicago's Wabash Avenue where music manufacturers and retailers like Story & Clark, Lyon & Healy, Baldwin and Kimball thrived during the 1950s and '60s until a suburban exodus forced many of the businesses to move or close.

'Our focused goal is to be 100 percent occupied by May 1, 1995.'

—Ken McHugh

Ken McHugh, executive vice president of operations for DePaul, has seen the vision take shape since it was first suggested by Gary Sigurdson, general manager of print retailer Carl Fischer Music (see story, Page 38). The vision has proceeded as McHugh expected but with one exception. "It has taken us a lot longer than I had hoped," he said. Construction delays and store vacancies blocked plans for a March grand opening. Officials then postponed a summer grand opening to give retailers extra build-up time and to promote fourth-quarter sales, Dustman said.

Despite these obstacles, approximately 90 percent of the mart's lower level concourse was filled as of the grand opening in late September. It houses four piano retailers, a combo retailer, a print-music retailer, a band-and-orchestra instrument dealer, a percussion shop, a folk-oriented music store, plus a musically themed candy shop, a music-related clothing-and-gift store and a music-related sterling silver shop.

Taking Tenants' Temperatures

If enthusiasm is all the Music Mart needs to succeed, Jim Rubino could provide enough of it to keep the mart going. The owner of Rubino's Music and Sound Center, the mart's primary combo retailer, gushed about the visitors who stopped by his store even as he prepared it for the grand opening. "I had 50 to 100 people a day and I wasn't even open," he said. "We sold quite a few items."

One customer from Japan liked a guitar so much that he pulled out a Visa Gold card and bought it at list price, Rubino noted. Tourists may be unlikely piano customers, but half of Rubino's customers have been foreigners wanting "a piece of America to take back to their countries," he said. In 1993, 933,000 tourists visited Chicago, according to the Chicago Office of Tourism.

Compared to his Merrillville, Ind., shop, twice as many people visit his Chicago store daily, Rubino estimated. It reaffirms his long-standing belief in the strength of numbers. Several years ago, he sent a petition signed by 416 of his customers to Johnny Carson requesting a solo by the Tonight Show band's bassist. Carson aired the bit, and Rubino plays the videotape to show that cooperative effort can make the Music Mart survive. "With powers in numbers, you can accomplish anything," he said.

John Berger, president of Karnes Music, has adopted a wait-and-see attitude. As one of four piano retailers in the mart, Berger expresses a cautious realism about the concept's success. "The proof is still in the pudding," he said. "If it can be successful, we'll have evidence in the next 90 days."

The piano stores take up one wing of the concourse level and are all within 100 feet of each other. According to Berger, one of the original concepts for the mart was to have several piano retailers carrying various brands so customers can choose among them. It's a one-stop shopping zone akin to Boston's Piano Row on Boylston Street, where several piano retailers operate within a short distance of each other. "The concept seems to be working in Boston," Berger said. "There was a fear [there] that the businesses would impact each other's business and everybody would get hurt. It has been completely the opposite."

Ray Fajmon, owner of American Music World and one of Berger's competitors, is certain that customers will shop at the mart once they realize the concept's advantages. "The problem consumers have is they are never satisfied in just seeing one piano," Fajmon said. "They are more comfortable looking at two or three. Now they can just come to one place and make a decision."

One of Dustman's functions is to make sure the retailer mix is varied enough to prevent product overlap and price wars. "We don't want to turn this into a bargain approach where customers can go to six different stores for the same product and hammer them," he said. "Because at that point, you're almost creating an on-site mail-order proposition."

A youngster performs inside the mart.

Cutthroat competition like that won't happen because retailers must be neighborly to survive, said Ed Richards, Fandrich Piano vice president. "The real strength of the Music Mart has to do with diversity of selection. It's the real reason why people come here to shop. If we start trying to become predatory with pricing, that's just going to hurt."

That doesn't mean competition will be nonexistent. Fajmon remembers the days on Music Row when piano retailers would give quarts of ice cream to customers on hot days. The reason: It forced them to go directly home to put the ice cream in their freezers rather than visit the next store. That same competitive spirit will prevail among the retailers, he said. "Some customers who have been loyal to us may wander and see what the other guy's got, but the same thing will happen with their customers. Everybody will very likely get their share. It happens in shopping malls, too."

Targeting City Customers

If selection and prices at the mart prove to be appealing, where will the consumers come from? Not necessarily from the suburbs, according to Dustman. "If the vision of it was to attract only suburbanites and thrive off of that, there would be a big question mark," he said. "The success of this is not tied to the suburban shopper." Rather, he said, the plan is to target the nearly half-million people who live and

BIRTH OF A MUSIC MALL

The Chicago Music Mart at DePaul Center grew out of Gary Sigurdson's desire to fill a void left by music retailing's exodus to the suburbs from Music Row, a concentrated area of music merchants and manufacturers that served consumers for decades on the city's Wabash Ave. Sigurdson, general manager of Carl Fischer Music, proposed the idea of a music-themed shopping mart to Ken McHugh, executive vice president of operations for DePaul University. "I was aware that [DePaul] had made some overtures for retail activity in the building when they took it over from the city," Sigurdson said. "They were in need of an idea; I had a plan."

'They were in need of an idea; I had a plan.'

—Gary Sigurdson

DePaul had purchased the old Goldblatt's building from the city of Chicago in 1991 and, as part of a redevelopment plan for the structure, decided to include two floors of retail space to help the revitalization of the south Loop area of downtown Chicago, McHugh said. DePaul officials considered various theme alternatives for the retail space, including a bookseller's row, a quality discount mart and a high-tech mall, before hearing Sigurdson's suggestion.

"That caught our imagination, so we sent a team of people to look at this concept and check the reality of it," McHugh said. The team researched similar retailing areas like Boston's Piano Row on Boylston St. DePaul also flew the team to Anaheim for the 1993 Winter NAMM International Music Market, where they studied the music industry with the help of Larry Linkin, NAMM president. Based on the team's findings, DePaul decided to make the retail space into a music mall.

"It was something that blended well with the university," McHugh said. "It had definite synergies in that our school of music enjoys a strong reputation. It had unique possibilities of something that would capture the imagination of the city of Chicago and had the potential of becoming a tourist attraction."

work within a three-mile radius of DePaul Center. Research of demographics, per capita income, per household income, and work- and leisure-time profiles cemented DePaul's belief that there was enough of a downtown shopping market to pursue, Dustman said.

That's good news for Bob Black, owner of Chicago Band and Orchestra and Chicago Percussion Center. Since he already has a store in suburban Evanston, his expansion into the mart helps him seize an untapped urban market. "It seemed like the right opportunity," he said. "There was no major band instrument or percussion store in downtown Chicago."

Other retailers in the mart have maintained a downtown customer base for years. Fajmon moved from Wabash Avenue after the Chicago Symphony Orchestra bought the building where he leased space. Baldwin Pianos left a space in Chicago's Lyric Opera building because the mart offers more exposure and a lower leasing agreement, said Marty Hahnfeld, Baldwin's division manager for Chicago retail. He wasn't the only retailer who found the rent affordable.

"I thought the rent would be more expensive than it was for downtown Chicago," Richards said.

Onlookers at the mart's Opening Act

Leasing for Less

To make leasing spaces cost-effective, DePaul consulted the National Association of Music Merchants' (NAMM) Cost of Doing Business Survey to learn about retail profit margins and operating costs.

The research showed DePaul that music retailers couldn't afford the $50-per-square-foot rents for ground-level stores. Lower- level spaces were more conducive to retailers' budgets, so DePaul restructured its leasing game plan to develop the lower level first. In exchange for reasonable leases, the retailers gave up ground-level accessibility and window presence. That presents a retailing challenge, said Eric Maletsky, president of Malet Realty Ltd., a real estate firm that manages and operates the former Lytton's department store building across the street from the Music Mart. He has been active in downtown Chicago real estate for nearly 15 years and has participated in other conversions of building space to retail and office use.

"When you're retailing out of a lower

MUSIC MART MERCHANTS

Company name: American Music World/ Keyboard World.
Type of store: Acoustic and digital pianos, electronic keyboards, organs.
Principals: Ray Fajmon, president; Judy Crago, treasurer; Jacqueline Fajmon, secretary; Richard Fajmon, Loop manager.
Lines: Hammond, Hyundai, Ibach, Korg, Roland, Story & Clark, Technics, Young Chang, Zimmerman.

Company name: Baldwin Piano & Organ Co.
Type of store: Piano and organ.
Principals: Marty Hahnfeld, division manager of Chicago retail; Brian Seydlitz, store manager; Ralph Cox, Debut manager.
Lines: Baldwin.

Company name: Carl Fischer Music.
Type of store: Print music.
Principals: Gary Sigurdson, general manager; Jeff Hansel, store manager.
Lines: All publishers.

Company name: Chicago Band & Orchestra and Chicago Percussion Center.
Type of store: Band & orchestra instruments, percussion and accessories.
Principals: Bob Black, owner; Channing Philbrick, general manager; Steve Baughman, general manager; Paul Jacki, manager of Chicago Percussion Center.
Lines: Armstrong, Artley, Bach, Benge, Besson, Boosey & Hawkes/Buffet Crampon, Conn, Dave Guardala, Deagan, Gemeinhardt, Keilwerth, King, L.A. Sax, Leblanc, Ludwig, Mike Balter, Musser, Paiste, Pro Mark, Selmer, Tama, Vic Firth, Yamaha, Zildjian.

Company name: Fandrich Piano.
Type of store: Piano.
Principals: Barbara Fandrich, president; Ed Richards, vice president.
Lines: Fandrich, Grotrian, PianoDisc, Weber.

Company name: Karnes Music.
Type of store: Piano and organ.
Principals: John Berger, owner/president; Roger Eaton, director of retail sales; Mark Heuer, store manager; Steve Gulley, store manager.
Lines: Disklavier, Lowrey, Yamaha.

Company name: The Old Town School's Music Store.
Type of store: Folk-related musical instruments, recordings and accessories.
Principals: Ted Parrish, manager.
Lines: Dobro, Enriquez, Flatiron, Gibson, Kentucky, Martin, Oscar Schmidt, Reiter, Washburn, Yamaha.

Company name: Rubino's Music & Sound Center.
Type of store: Combo/MI and home entertainment.
Principals: Jim Rubino, CEO; Diana Moss Rubino, secretary/treasurer/manager; Todd Poznanski, manager; Denise Moss, manager; Michelle Green, bookkeeper.
Lines: Alvarez, American DJ, Ampeg, Boss, Cerwin-Vega, Crest, Digitech, Ensoniq, Epiphone, ESP, Fostex, Gibson, Harmon Kardon, Martin, Meteor DJ Lighting, Numark, Peavey, Raw, Renkus-Heinz, Sound Advanced, Technics.

Other Tenants: Musical Threads, a clothing and gift shop; Sterling Symphonies, a silver jewelry store; Candy Junction Musical Sweets; Classical Symphony Orchestra & Protege Philharmonic, a non-retail organization that provides orchestral training and experience for young musicians.

level, you've got a lot of obstacles and hurdles to overcome," Maletsky said. "You've got to draw people down to where you're retailing."

DePaul plans to attract people downstairs by filling the ground-level spaces with traffic-building tenants like a CD/tape store and a restaurant with musical-themed menu items. "As we move into the first floor space, we'll be dealing with tenants who will be in a position to pay more of a market rent," McHugh said. "We'll be able to use that rent to subsidize what we are able to do downstairs." Sterling Symphonies, a silver shop, was the only store on the ground floor at press time. "Our focused goal is to be 100 percent occupied by May 1, 1995," McHugh added.

A 200-seat performance stage in the lower-level atrium provides another way to attract customers. Jazz, rock, country and classical musicians played there during the grand-opening festivities and throughout the preceding summer. The Classical Symphony Orchestra and Protegé Philharmonic, which rents space in the concourse level, has an open rehearsal there each Saturday. Lunch-time performances are held daily to attract the office workers and university students in the building. Sigurdson said these concerts are a surefire way to boost the interest of consumers who are not already musically oriented.

'The success of this is not tied to the suburban shopper.'

—Karl Dustman

"That is significant because it is raising the level of musical consciousness in general," he said. "[People] hear music, it becomes important to them and now, instead of buying that video game, they may think, 'I'll get the kid a guitar.'"

Cooperation is the Key

If the Music Mart becomes the place for consumers to buy musical items, retailers can take partial credit for keeping a cooperative spirit alive. Retailers contribute to an advertising fund that is used for the mart's radio and newspaper promotions. And because the stores are specialized, they often refer customers to each other.

"I don't have to sell sheet music anymore," Rubino said. "People want sheet music and I say, 'Go to Carl Fischer, they're over there.' They must have sent us at least a dozen guitar students already. The concept is everybody should feed off of everybody."

According to McHugh, the cooperative feeling at the Music Mart is in line with DePaul's urban mission to create partnerships and work within the community. The university is nurturing the Music Mart as it takes its first steps on stage. But Hahnfeld pointed out that retailers can't wait for DePaul to make the concept successful. To get rave reviews from the audience, the players will soon have to act without the director's assistance. That means each retailer must take responsibility to create interest in the Music Mart. "If each store does that," Hahnfeld said, "it should become a real success."

As a consultant, this was probably the most interesting project that I had worked on to date. Quite honestly, it used everything I had ever learned about music, about musical instruments, and about people and really understanding the diplomatic relations one must have when you are a consultant. I was wearing the hat of representative for the City of Chicago, for DePaul University, for the School of Music, and for the Chicago Music Mart. This was one of my most favorite projects ever. Unfortunately, as time marched on, the Chicago Music Mart did not survive, for reasons unknown to me. Eventually the Music Mart closed and the retail space on the two concourse levels now has diversified into all sorts of retail products and services.

GOING BACK IN TIME, A Sidebar of History and Perspective:

In 1990, Bill Crowden was preparing to sell his business, Drums Limited. This was a longstanding dominant percussion retail pillar founded in downtown Chicago and had survived the test of time. I had met Bill during my years at Ludwig and had gotten to know him quite well through my many different affiliations. He was always a constant trusted friend, mentor and supporter of everything I was ever working on or towards. I served on the Board for the Illinois Chapter of the Percussive Arts Society with Bill when he was President. Our paths and associations crossed many times over the years and a true friendship developed which I still value to this day.

Bill found a buyer for his business in a partnership between Terry Horler and Jack Cox. Bill was taking Terry and Jack around the Anaheim NAMM show introducing the new owners of Drums Limited to all of his various suppliers and contacts. This transition of ownership really started while I was with Sonor and Korg. Once the sale was complete, Terry and Jack started out with Drums Limited when it was located on Jefferson Avenue. The first signed tenant agreement at the Music Mart in early 1993 was Drums Limited. This had taken place before I become involved with the Music Mart as a consultant later that year.

The new owners of Drums Limited signed an extended lease for a huge footprint of space on the main first floor concourse. However even before that store's move and relocation into the Music Mart in early 1994, Drums Limited was faltering. The new owners were two percussionists who were not necessarily businessmen knowing how to run a highly specialized retail operation or knowing how to work with so many different product suppliers. By the time I arrived at the Music Mart, Drums Limited had moved in, faltered, and collapsed. There was all kinds of random product inventory scattered around in this corner retail-space. At one point I was asked by the university to help figure out what merchandise was left behind by the owners and what to do with it. This was an internal "black cloud' within the university in realizing that the first tenant did not survive much past the relocation and moving into the Music Mart. While this was no fault of the Music Mart, it got things off to a sour start.

Because the owners of Drum Limited defaulted on the lease and went out of business, the name Bill Crowden's Drums Limited (which also owned the name Franks Drum Shop) transferred to the university as an asset of the foreclosure on the store. At one point the university explored the thought of taking over the Drums Limited business and having it run quietly as a separate entity of the Music Mart. Having the first tenant come into the Music Mart and fail was not the publicity and fact that DePaul University wanted to publicize. Continuing Drums Limited as a separate operation of the Music Mart was considered, and I was also consulted on how this could start, develop and potentially succeed. Eventually the university felt the best path was to "move on with other tenants" and let someone else bring drums and percussion into the Music Mart as a future tenant.

For those who have visited and toured the original Ludwig factory before the takeover by The Selmer Company in November of 1981, you will recall the massive 72-inch diameter Paiste gong on the steel custom suspension stand that was in the Ludwig lobby at 1728 N. Damen Avenue. This was a visual focal point when walking through the offices. Whenever this gong was played, the massive sound and volume was heard and felt through the entire building. All telephone calls would have to be placed on hold for twenty-seconds. The only person really allowed to "play the gong" was Bill Ludwig when hosting his guests or conducting a factory tour.

When the complete Ludwig Company was sold, Bill Ludwig gave that gong to Bill Crowden. The massive instrument was not part of the company asset sale to Selmer. So Bill Crowden's Drums Limited displayed this gong in his store for years, with the custom made special stand that could support that amount of weight. Upon the sale of Drums Limited, that Paiste gong transferred to the new owners, Terry Horler and Jack Cox. When the new owners moved the entire Drums Limited into the Music Mart in early 1993 the Paiste Gong moved into the new location as well, becoming a visual focal point of anyone entering the store. By early 1994 the new owners defaulted on the Music Mart lease with DePaul University and went out of business. The 72 inch gong was a monster to move anywhere and was just left behind in the vacant abandoned storefront that Drums Limited had occupied for a very brief period of time.

Eventually, DePaul University purchased the Blackstone Theater located a very short distance away from their main downtown campus. It was decided that the gong would be moved to the Blackstone Theater for dramatic productions by the Theater Department of DePaul. (Imagine The Mikado Opera with that gong reverberating!) To this day, that gong is part of the DePaul University Theater Department and to my knowledge remains at the Blackstone Theater of DePaul University.

Before selling Drums Limited, Bill Crowden bought the name Franks Drum Shop when it went out of business. Bill chose never to use the name, he just wanted to put it to rest forever. Bill was very disappointed when Bill Crowden's Drums Limited failed under the new ownership and new location in the Music Mart. The trade names of Bill Crowden's Drums Limited and Franks Drum Shop technically became assets of DePaul University as part of the businesses' default and closing.

In 2003 Bill Crowden contacted me asking how and if I could help him get his name back from DePaul University. He didn't know anyone within the university structure, the Music Mart was already dismantled, and Bill was in need of guidance in trying to obtain both company names from DePaul in a legal manner. I reviewed my contacts at DePaul, and eventually worked with the DePaul University Staff Attorney, Rick Raguse to secure an assurance that DePaul did not claim any exclusive right to the two trade names in question. I was very happy to help Bill to bring some legal closure in this matter. It is my understanding that the names Bill Crowden's Drums Ltd and Franks Drum Shop are now both owned by the Crowden family.

CLIENT No. 4
Comdisco, A Technologies Services Company

I learned of an agency in the Chicago area that was kind of like a "rent an expert," specializing in marketing, advertising, promotion and sales management. Whether it was a marketing director, a graphic arts person, creative writer or exhibit-display manager or whatever, they had connections to market private consultants to projects in the area that needed designated expertise of a project or specific duration. I signed up with this agency for them to be aware of my consulting business and the experience and qualifications I had to offer clients they might be working with. While I did not have extremely high expectations from this experience, I tried to get the word out of my availability and the experience I could provide as a consultant. Within a week or two the agency had a client who was looking for a marketing expert with specific experience and knowledge of trade show exhibit design, signage, and marketing messaging. I was called and immediately contracted to start with the client.

This was a project and opportunity entirely outside of my comfort zone in the music product industry, but I looked at the assignment with the attitude that "marketing is marketing". There is a lot of truth to that statement, but I probably learned more in this project than I would have ever expected.

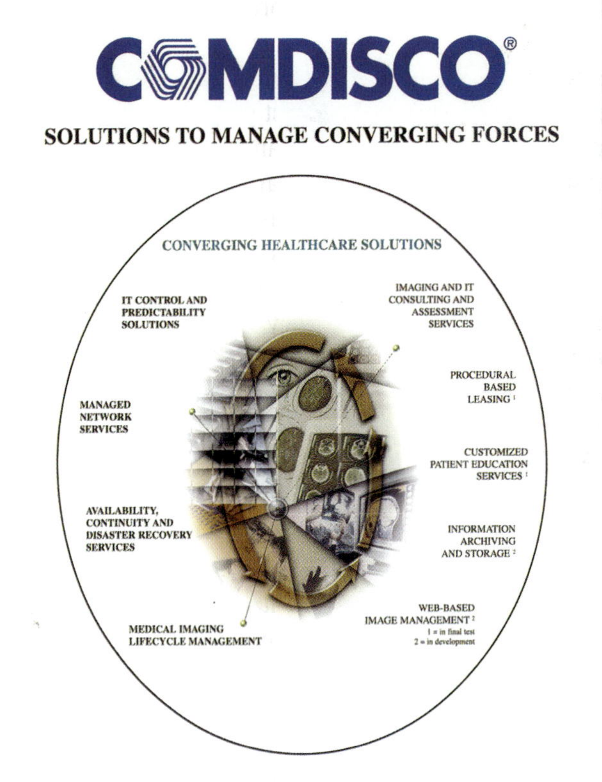

I knew I could help the company and achieve the desired results the company was seeking. My concern was, "What do I know about medical equipment and leasing?" The reality was that I would be dealing with medical radiology equipment and related medical terminology. In both areas I did not have any background or experience. There was a complete disconnect with the product, but the project was very interesting. I was assured that there was a group of medical doctors and specialists involved who would take care of all of that medical terminology. Comdisco needed an expert to coordinate the massive trade show exhibit

COMDISCO
DELIVERING THE PROMISE OF TECHNOLOGY DELIVERING THE PROMISE OF TECHNOLOGY

COMDISCO
DELIVERING THE PROMISE OF TECHNOLOGY
RSNA

SOLUTIONS TO MANAGE CONVERGING FORCES
TECHNOLOGY
FINANCIAL
WEB TECHNOLOGY
LEGAL
HUMAN RESOURCES
SOLUTIONS

THE PROMISE OF TECHNOLOGY

with the marketing message, their print message, and with the display elements for the company's participation in the annual radiology convention at Chicago's McCormick Place. This event would be attended by 60,000 health care professionals.

They needed a marketing professional to establish the connecting-audience-message, the theme of the booth and services offered, the completely new graphics, all tied with the print brochure, advertising and message for the convention. Comdisco had already contracted for an expensive rented double decker exhibit that was basically a two story "white box" with stairs. Now it was up to Comdisco to turn the booth into a custom-made looking exhibit. While they didn't have a clue on how to do this themselves, I was brought in to coordinate the exhibit development. I worked with the exhibit company extensively on the graphics, budget and the timeline leading up to the November 1995 trade show and conference at McCormick Place. Comdisco was primarily a medical professional organization that was not accustomed to working trade shows. They did not have the trade show mentality or experience to anticipate the challenges, costs and decisions that were needed to make all the elements come together. There had to be a cohesive connection of all marketing elements, centered around the trade show exhibit. I was the person assigned to make this happen.

Realizing the inexperience of the company professionals and individuals that would be working the exhibit" I felt it was necessary to create nine very specific convention trade show Marketing Aids. These were basically a fast-course training guide to inform and educate the medical personnel how to work a trade show exhibit booth. For the most part, this conference and exhibit was a first time experience for the people working the company's trade show exhibit. I knew that they would be able to communicate the medical elements of the company and services provided, but they didn't understand some of the basic principles of professional trade show exhibit staffing. These basics included: -you do not stand around in the exhibit booth sipping a Coca-Cola, You do not stand in the exhibit smoking a cigarette, you do not congregate with your company buddies as this makes you unapproachable by a visitor, guest or media representative. The basics of being at a convention and working a trade show exhibit were totally new to this group of people.

The training, the coaching, the guidance and cohesive marketing message I created and provided must have been successful, as Comdisco seemed very pleased and communicated this to the marketing-services agency I was contracted with for this five month assignment. I considered this a win from all perspectives while also proving to myself, "marketing is marketing".

Once the convention was over, the contract was up. They were well pleased and I've used them as a reference ever since. Comdisco was just a totally different kind of project which reconfirmed to me that I was able to adapt and apply what I knew from the music products industry to a completely unrelated industry. The bottom-line, whether it's musical instruments, or medical equipment, if you coordinate and market the exhibit, connect the visuals and message of the collateral with the media advertising, the complete message will be consistent in all the essential marketing areas.

ABOUT COMDISCO

Comdisco provides global technology services to help its customers maximize technology, availability, predictability and functionality, while freeing them from the complexity of managing their technology. The Rosemont, (IL) company offers a complete suite of information technology services including business continuity, managed network services, IT control and predictability solutions and certain industry specific technology lifecycle management services. Through its subsidiary, Prism Communication Services Inc., Comdisco is developing a high-speed, always-on digital network, which will provide customers with leading-edge connectivity. Comdisco also offers equipment acquisition services through its electronics, communications, healthcare, laboratory and scientific, and computer-integrated manufacturing businesses, and through its ventures group.

FOR MORE INFORMATION ABOUT COMDISCO, PLEASE VISIT THE COMDISCO WEBSITE AT www.comdisco.com OR CALL 800-272-9792

Client No. 5
Clevelander Drum Company, Cleveland, Ohio

By the end of 1995 I was happy to be able to bring an end to the regular commuting between Chicago and Cleveland. The living in two cities was a challenge, expensive, and exhausting.

I had been watching the evolution of the Clevelander Drum Company, seeing their ads in *Percussive Notes* magazine of the Percussive Arts Society. I knew that the company had been founded by the long-time Principal Timpanist of the Cleveland Orchestra, Paul Yancich. From a distance, the products looked exceptional, the brand was starting to make an impact and I thought Paul could use some help building and operating Clevelander Drum Co. In my mind, I was wondering how anyone with a demanding performance and teaching schedule like Yancich could own and operate a drum company. Running a business, even a very small business, is a full time job in itself.

I mailed Paul Yancich a complete introductory packet about who I was and the services that my Dustman & Associates Marketing Communications company could provide to Clevelander Drum. Paul contacted me and wanted to explore how we could work together to bring Clevelander to the next level of sales, visibility and brand recognition. Again, the idea of a consultant under contract was appealing to Paul, as he was not interested in employing people. He needed expertise, a knowledgeable professional that was connected and respected in the percussion business. Paul envisioned that he could become a smaller version of Vic Firth, a rare and unique combination of professional timpanist and percussion industry business founder-owner. He realized that he needed someone to help him achieve that.

The company was manufacturing in Cleveland a professional line of Dresden style timpani, a complete line of hand-sewn timpani sticks in both bamboo and cherry handle models, and a complete line of orchestra snare drums of different sizes, shell materials all equipped with a revolutionary new triple snare mechanism.

My first assignment was to do something that would move the mentality of Clevelander from a dining-room table operation in his home to a professional percussion product line with center stage presence. The mentality of owning and operating a profitable business is totally different than that of a symphonic musician. My job was to create a bridge Paul would understand and agree to on how to move forwards with the products, the brand, and the image of the company. Clevelander had outstanding products that were selling and were well respected, but the company needed marketing expertise and guidance. It needed a full time business management person who was already familiar with the protocols of running a business. While Paul had limited experience with the business world, he was receptive to learning and doing what needed to be done. Paul was (and still is) one of the top five professional timpanists in the United States. That fact needed to be leveraged in helping the Clevelander Company and its products be accepted and purchased by a larger audience.

The Clevelander operation was local and small. Clevelander had a professional machine shop that worked on the hand-made manufacturing of all the timpani. Paul personally tested, played and evaluated every timpani that was manufactured. While he had two students building timpani sticks for him and assembling snare drums, Paul was intimately involved in the quality control of the assembly and the procurement of the parts and materials used in each product. At the same time, Clevelander had created a very impressive listing of orchestral percussionists who were using, playing and promoting the Clevelander products, all made in the U.S.

Paul needed product exposure and brand recognition. I started working on a marketing plan that would involve new color product literature, orchestral target market advertising and getting the brand more recognized by colleges, universities and conservatories on an international basis. An impending priority was having a Clevelander Drum Company exhibit at the Percussive Arts Society convention in San Antonio, Texas, and the Midwest Band and Orchestra Clinic in Chicago. I designed all of the orchestral graphics, the product fliers, arranged the photo sessions with a professional photographer.

Clevelander Drum Company
Artist-Clinician Affiliations

Tim Adams
Indianapolis Symphony Orchestra
percussion

James Babor
Los Angeles Philharmonic
percussion

Raynor Carroll
Los Angeles Philharmonic
percussion

Patricia Dash
Chicago Symphony Orchestra
percussion

Perry Dreiman
Los Angeles Philharmonic
percussion

Frank Epstein
Boston Symphony Orchestra
percussion

Peter Flam
San Antonio Symphony
timpanist

Tom Freer
Cleveland Orchestra
percussion

Donald Miller
Cleveland Orchestra
percussion

Mitch Peters
Los Angeles Philharmonic
timpanist

The image and market presence was starting to look "as good as the true product really was".

Business management and development 101 through 104 were being experienced at lightning speed. I learned that Clevelander did not even have a bill of materials for the various products which meant that the cost-of-goods-sold was unknown and therefore the profit margins were unknown. This could become financial suicide if product costs are not known, controlled, and evaluated on a regular basis. I took it upon myself to create a bill of materials and a cost analysis for every product that he was selling. Fortunately for Paul, the margins were healthy. He was not losing money on any product but your company can't control anything if you don't know what it's costing to build a $37,000 set of timpani.

Time moved forward quickly and there was always something happening, going on, preparations for and just the normal market development initiatives that were neverending. I handled incoming calls and inquiries from prospective buyers of Clevelander timpani, individuals and schools inquiring about snare drums, and the many consumers. Progress was being made and money was being spent, to make money.

Eventually, the business had to be moved out of the sun room within Paul's residence and relocated to a small office and manufacturing area near his home. Unfortunately, I became too expensive for Paul to continue renewing the consulting contract and we parted ways on a positive note. Paul attempted to continue doing everything that I had set up and established, but on his own. Over time this became a step backwards and started once again consuming more time and effort than he was able to commit to for running a business. Over time, Paul wanted to sell the company. He asked me to help him with locating logical companies or individuals who would be candidates for him to approach. I suggested that he contact Richard Berger who was the second generation of Grover-Trophy Music, located for decades here in Cleveland. Grover Trophy was both a distributor and manufacturer and a highly respected profitable company. This company had grown out of the original Grossman Music Company, one of the original old-school music wholesalers. I knew Richard Berger quite well and always respected his business acumen and kindness. Paul worked directly with Richard Berger in designing a change in ownership and Paul helped with the manufacturing transition for a time after the sale. Paul sold the entire Clevelander product line and brand name to Richard Berger as part of Grover-Trophy Music.

Clevelander went through many changes over the years, adding and discontinuing various products. While they did not necessarily understand the timpani business, the brand and quality of remaining products continues positive for the future. There are dedicated people at Grover-Trophy Music who are committed to keeping this brand and select products available to the market. Through my personal start-up orchestral percussion showroom, Professional Percussion Products, I stocked, displayed and sold a significant quantity of all Clevelander products over the years. (See Chapter nine for more complete details) Today, we continue to service with parts and expertise the complete line of original Clevelander timpani, snare drums, and timpani sticks.

THE CLEVELANDER DRUM COMPANY

- CUSTOM PROFESSIONAL SNARE DRUMS
- CUSTOM PROFESSIONAL FIELD DRUMS
- STANDARD PROFESSIONAL SNARE DRUMS

The Clevelander Drum Company utilizes the experience, creativity and knowledge of today's leading performers in the design and fabrication of custom instruments.

CLEVELANDER SNARE DRUMS

World-class instruments, built by and for professionals

Client No. 5 Clevelander Drum Company

"Prized for their beauty of appearance and sound, Clevelander Custom Professional Snare Drums have become the instrument of choice for professionals world-wide because they produce the right sound, performance after performance. Rock, orchestral, jazz, concert band, alternative ... since you select the shell and snare system, you'll always get the customized snare drum sound you need for the music you perform. Every instrument has been designed, fine tuned and tested by professional percussionists. World-class instruments built by and for professionals."

Paul Yancich, Founder, The Clevelander Drum Company
Timpanist, The Cleveland Orchestra

CUSTOM PROFESSIONAL MODELS

These world-renowned snare drums produce a clear, focused, projecting sound with maximum snare response and articulation throughout the entire dynamic range. They are equipped with Clevelander designed shells, strainer, butt, tubular lugs, the patented snare clamping system and die cast hoops.

SOLID BRASS
One-piece construction.
Polished laquer or chrome plated.

CDC-614 PB

6 ½"x 14"

Brilliant, cutting, dynamic sound. Rock, Orchestral, Concert Band, Alternative, Military, Studio.

CDC-514 PB

5"x 14"

Lighter, brilliant, cutting, dynamic sound. Orchestral, Rock, Concert Band, Military, Studio.

CDC-514 PBH *(shown in chrome)*

5"x 14"

Brilliant, powerful and sensitive. Incredible "crack" on rim shot. The loudest snare drum ever built. One-half inch shell thickness. Rock, Orchestral, Alternative.

NORTH AMERICAN BIRCH
Handmade construction.
Laquered finish, mahogany stain.

CDC-614 PW

6 ½"x 14"

Mellow, rich, blending sound. Orchestral, Concert Band, Rock, Country.

CDC-514 PW

5"x 14"

Lighter, mellow, rich, blending sound. Jazz, Orchestral, Studio, Concert Band.

CDC-1215 PW
CDC-1416 PW *(not shown)*

12"x 15"
14"x 16"

Authentic field drum sound. Rich, dark, coarse, dynamic. Orchestral, Marching, Military.

STANDARD PROFESSIONAL MODELS

A world-class snare drum designed to fit all budgets. The Standard Professional Snare Drum utilizes the same shell, strainer, butt, and patented snare clamping system as our Custom models and is equipped with die cast lugs and steel hoops. Great sound and response.

CDC-614 SW

6 ½"x 14"

North American Birch. Mellow, rich, blending sound. Orchestral, Concert Band, Rock.

5"x 14"

North American Birch. Lighter, mellow, rich, blending sound. Orchestral, Concert Band, Jazz.

(Available with Wire or Blue Cable-Wire only)

CDC-514 SW

THE CLEVELANDER SNARE SYSTEM

Choose from five different sounding snare systems to customize the snare drum sound you need. The patented snare clamping system allows the simultaneous use of several individually tensionable snare materials, resulting in incredible snare response and clarity throughout the entire dynamic range. Snare systems are interchangable so your Clevelander can easily be adapted for any performance situation.

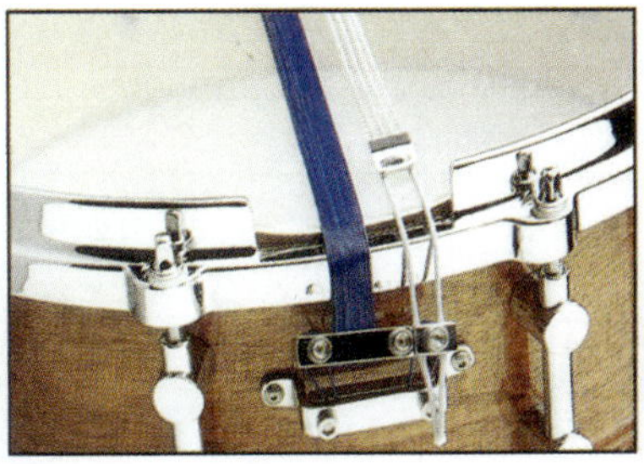

BLUE CABLE-WIRE

A slightly dry sound. Clarity, projection and sensitivity from *ppp* to *fff*. Orchestral, Studio, Concert Band.

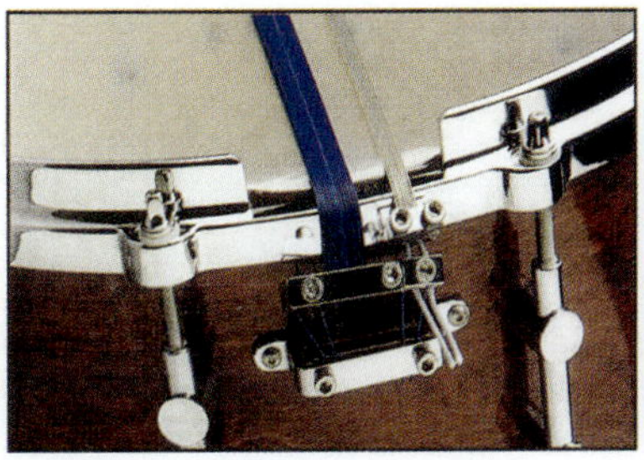

BLUE CABLE-BARE CABLE

A dry, distinct, projecting sound throughout the entire dynamic range. Orchestral and Studio.

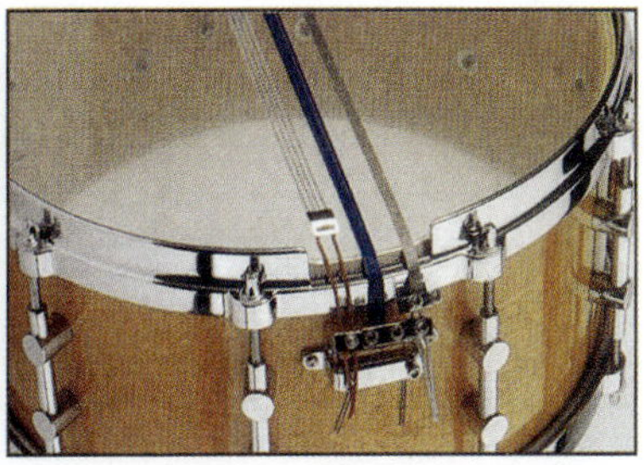

BLUE CABLE-BARE CABLE-WIRE

The Ultimate blend. Full-bodied, projecting sound. Orchestral, Concert Band, Rock, Jazz, Studio.

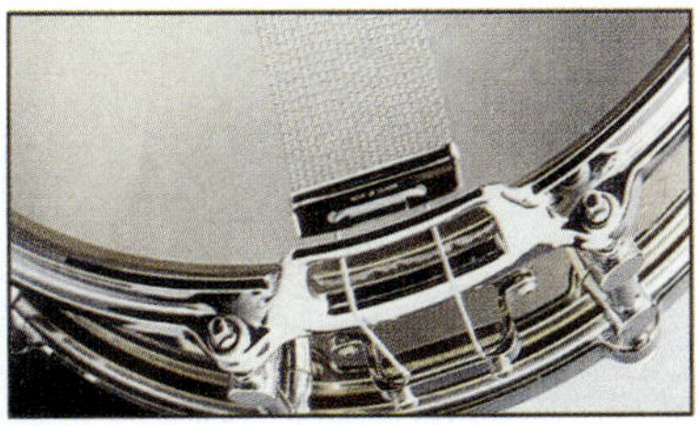

WIRE

Powerful and sensitive. The traditional drum kit sound. Rock, Jazz, Alternative, Country.

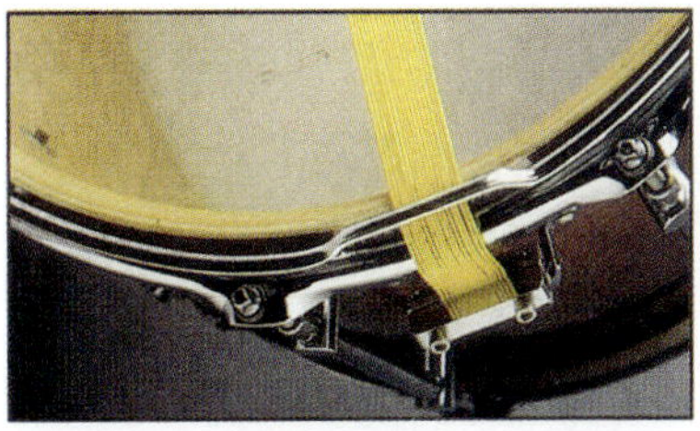

YELLOW CABLE

A dry, coarse, cutting, dynamic sound. Military, Orchestral, Studio.

FEATURES:

STRAINER: Positive action, silent throw-off guaranteed not to accidentally disengage. Thumb screw for instant snare adjustment. Exclusive Clevelander design.

DIE CAST HOOPS and STEEL TUBULAR LUGS: Solid response, even tuning and durability.

CUSTOM ENGRAVING.

Client No. 5 Clevelander Drum Company

THE CHOICE OF PROFESSIONALS WORLD-WIDE

"THE CUSTOM PRO BRASS MODELS ARE THE FINEST SNARE DRUMS I HAVE EVER PLAYED. THEIR RESPONSE AND TONE THROUGHOUT THE ENTIRE DYNAMIC RANGE IS TRULY OUTSTANDING."

FRANK EPSTEIN — Boston Symphony Orchestra
5x14, 6½x14 Custom Pro Brass

"THE DRUM IS BLAZING!"

WILLIAM CALHOUN — Living Color
5x14 Custom Pro Brass

"I AM ECSTATIC OVER THE SOUND AND QUALITY OF THE STANDARD PRO MODEL. ALL CLEVELANDER SNARE DRUMS ARE BY FAR THE BEST INSTRUMENTS AVAILABLE."

MITCHELL PETERS — Los Angeles Philharmonic
6½x14 Standard Pro Wood

"OUTSTANDING WORKMANSHIP, GREAT FEEL AND SUPERIOR SOUND. THAT'S WHY I PLAY A CLEVELANDER."

RICHARD WEINER — Cleveland Orchestra
6½x14, 12x15, Custom Pro Wood

"THE LOUDEST SNARE DRUM IN EXISTENCE. TRULY UNBELIEVABLE."

CHRIS VRENNA — Nine Inch Nails
5x14 Custom Pro Brass

"FROM BRUSHES TO STICKS, FROM THE SMALLEST TO THE BIGGEST ARENA, THE DRUM IS UNBELIEVABLE."

ANDY KUBISZEWSKI — Stabbing Westward
5x14 Custom Pro Brass

"MAXIMUM SNARE RESPONSE AND ARTICULATION IN ALL DYNAMICS. THE ULTIMATE IN BEAUTY OF SOUND AND APPEARANCE, LOOK NO FURTHER."

JIM ROSS & PATSY DASH — Chicago Symphony Orchestra
5x14, 6½x14, 12x15 Custom Pro Wood

"THE DRUM IS INCREDIBLE!"

NDUGU CHANCELOR — L.A. Artist
5x14 Custom Pro Brass

"CLARITY, PROJECTION AND RESPONSIVENESS. SIMPLY THE BEST ORCHESTRAL SNARE DRUM MADE."

PERRY DREIMAN — Los Angeles Philharmonic
5x14 Custom Pro Brass

"MY CLEVELANDER WOOD MODELS ARE CLEAR, DELICATE AND SENSITIVE. THE BRASS MODEL IS DOMINATING. THEY'RE BEAUTIFUL INSTRUMENTS."

CHRISTOPHER LAMB — New York Philharmonic
5x14, 6½x14, 14x16 Custom Pro Wood
6½x14 Custom Pro Brass

THE CLEVELANDER DRUM COMPANY
1371 OAKRIDGE DRIVE
CLEVELAND HEIGHTS, OH 44121
(216) 691-9152

Client No. 6
Washburn International, Vernon Hills, Illinois

Understanding the background of Washburn and its market placement in the mid 1990's
from Wikipedia

The remarkable story of Washburn and its Owner-President, Rudy Schlacher, goes back to the early 1960s.

The Chicago Guitar Gallery (located in the same South Wabash building as Franks Drum Shop) hired Rudolf "Rudy" Schlacher, a young German violin builder, as a repair technician. A few years later, Schlacher opened The Sound Post in Evanston, Illinois, to focus on guitars. He soon realized the sales potential for lower-cost quality instruments.

Tom Beckmen and his wife Judy Fink Beckmen in 1972 left careers as music salesman and teacher (respectively) to launch a wholesale music business in Los Angeles, Beckmen Musical Instruments. It was Beckmen Music that resurrected the Washburn name, and beginning in 1974 applied it to a series of quality imported acoustic guitars, made in Japan by Terada, as well as a selection of mandolins and banjos.

Fritz Tasch, Rudy Schlacher, and Rick Johnstone, as Fretted Industries, Inc., acquired the Washburn name in 1977 (for $13,000) when the Beckmens took their business in a different direction and so the Washburn name was returned to Chicago. With assistance from Ikutaro Kakehashi (founder of Roland Corporation), Schlacher was able to find instrument factories in Japan that could meet the desired standards.

Fretted Industries acquired other lines as well, such as Oscar Schmidt autoharps.

Schlacher bought out Johnstone in 1987, and changed the company name to Washburn International. A stateside manufacturing operation was opened in 1991 for higher-end, short-run, and one-off instruments, as well as development and prototyping. That year, a Chicago Tribune article confidently places Washburn "among the top three guitar manufacturers in the world," behind only Fender and Gibson.

On December 15, 2002, Washburn International announced that it had completed acquisition of U.S. Music Corporation and would be rolling its assets into that company in a reverse merger. Schlacher remained as CFO, appointing Gary Gryczan to COO; Gryczan had been Washburn's CFO from 1995 through 1998. The new USM's headquarters were in Mundelein (440 E. Courtland Street), which also housed the stateside Washburn luthiery, often referred to as "the USA Custom Shop." The USA Custom Shop was previously located at Elston Ave. and Springfield Ave in the 1990s in an old factory that was used as an icehouse after the great Chicago fire, it was rumored to be haunted by the victims whose bodies had been stored there.

Schlacher announced completion of selling USM to JAM Industries on August 24, 2009, and that he would be stepping away from his company after fully four decades: "We are pleased to join forces with a strategic partner like Jam Industries, that has a long, successful history in the music industry and has been a long-term business partner with U.S. Music for more than 20 years. It has been a thrilling and rewarding 40-year ride that has allowed me to realize my dreams and goals."

As R S Consulting, Schlacher remained a consultant to the musical-instrument industry and was an executive producer for a small-budget film.

The corporate offices of U.S. Music were relocated to Buffalo Grove, Illinois in 2012.

Very few modern Washburn instruments have been built by the company itself. It has relied on outside factories and luthiers to fulfill their designs and meet public demand.

By 1991, production of Washburn instruments had shifted almost entirely to Korea, built by Samick. When Samick opened their Cileungsi, Indonesia, facility in 1992, this factory also began to produce Washburn-branded instruments, generally identifiable by an "SI-" serial number prefix.

From 1992 to 2000, Washburn housed the USA Custom Shop in a factory at Elston Ave. and Springfield Ave. Grover Jackson ran production for the first half of the 90's and Larry English ran production for the second half of the 90's. At least two guitar heists occurred there when thieves backed a box truck through a wall and loaded the truck with guitars, getting away cleanly. Between 1994 and 2001, ten models of acoustic guitar were built for Washburn in the United States, five by Tacoma Guitars (Tacoma, Washington) and five by Bourgeois Guitars (Lewiston, Maine).

In 2012, when JAM Industries declined to renew the lease on the Mundelein facility, the Washburn luthiery closed. At the time, the Washburn facility was the ninth-largest employer in the village (the third-largest business), providing 180 jobs. The stated intent was to reopen at a smaller building in Buffalo Grove (1000 Corporate Grove Drive) but this did not materialize. A few Washburn models (particularly the N4) are produced in Cincinnati.

As of 2017, primary production has largely shifted from Korea to factories in Indonesia and China.

end of Wikipedia excerpt

My interest in Washburn International as a potential client started when they announced that they were beginning distribution of Mapex Drums for the United States. Mapex had been evolving in the North American market and was being bounced around through a number of distributors. Prior to Mapex having an affiliation with Washburn, they were unsuccessfully being distributed by Midco. Midco was an old-school music wholesaler in Effingham, Illinois, owned by Lowell Samuels. I spoke to Lowell about Mapex and learned that they were not really into full scale distribution, marketing and promotion of a professional drum line. I felt that Samuels was trying to convey, "Karl, do not get overly excited about it (Mapex Drums) because there may be a change very soon." I continued to monitor the Mapex distribution challenges and eventually it ended up in the hands of Washburn.

Washburn International was a true family business, with all four Schlacher family members working in the business. Rudy Schlacher was the patriarch, and the Schlacher family became the sole owners with his buy-out of a partnership in 1987. It evolved into a business doing $50 million worth of business annually selling Washburn, Oscar Schmidt, Soundtech professional audio, and Randall amplifiers. (They acquired Randall when the Guild Guitar Company was up for sale and Randall was spun-off separately) In the early days of Fretted Industries, Washburn was headquartered in Northbrook, Illinois. Decades later Washburn had a beautiful corporate headquarters in a business park located in the northern suburb of Vernon Hills, Illinois.

During the mid 1990s Washburn established an artist relations office in a small house near downtown Nashville. Nashville was known as Music City USA, and offered a direct connection and access to many of the country's top guitarists, top recording labels and a platform for Washburn's product diversification ambitions. This Nashville based A/R office provided promotion of Washburn products right in the back yard of the Gibson Guitar factory and headquarters located in Nashville. The Nashville office of Washburn had two artist relations representatives. One was Ken Austin, whom you will remember from the Pearl chapter. My mutual friendship and communications with Ken were still good.

Karl Dustman **Rudy Schlacher**

I arrived at Washburn on the heels of the April 1996 Crain's Business article and interview about Washburn and insights from President Rudy Schlacher. The article positioned Washburn as "one of the big three" Guitar manufacturers. I learned of some personnel changes within the Washburn Vernon Hills headquarters and that the company was searching for a Marketing Director. My original contact was with the company's short-term Executive Vice President Joe Baksha. My research into Washburn also indicated that the position of Marketing Director at Washburn was beginning to have the reputation of being a revolving door. People were coming and going on very short notice. Someone would be working in an office one day, and the next day when you arrive at the company, that office would be empty. Knowing this, I accepted this as a company trait and expected the unexpected. People were obviously dispensable and disposable. It was clear from the early discussions that the company's interest in me was my marketing background in many different product areas (including guitars) but certainly not any emphasis was placed on my drum and percussion background and experience.

Rudy Schlacher was interested in the concept of having a marketing director on a consultancy basis; it made things much easier to be able to simply not renew a contract instead of having to deal with the termination of a regular salaried employee. As hard as I might try and work for a client, I got the feeling that no one would ever really make Rudy happy in the position of marketing director. This was reminiscent of the Pearl experience. (In the end, my Washburn contract would be renewed multiple times over a three year period.) Rudy's wife, Marianna, signed my Consulting Contract without any revisions and I began getting involved in every product line on the very first day. The Marketing Director position was not newly created and the previous person held that position for about 2 years I was led to believe. Very little was ever brought-up or discussed about Washburn's previous marketing experts.

While I was immersed in all product lines, I became a Mapex Drum ally to Ken Austin in Nashville working on the Mapex product line. I helped him with some of his struggles in getting clear communication and directives about anything from Washburn headquarters. I sensed his frustration in trying to build a drum division within the Washburn product mix. Ken pressed onwards creating some wonderful full-page color Mapex Drum ads that were appearing in Modern Drummer magazine. I recall a very creative photo shoot where a Mapex drum set was positioned in his personal garage and all the various sports equipment were positioned to indicate being "cast-off for the enjoyment of playing drums". It soon became evident that Mapex did not really fit into what Washburn wanted to do. Washburn wanted a drum product line that would sell itself with very little time, effort or money put into the marketing and promotion. Mapex, as a newcomer to the American drum market, was just emerging and needed concentrated investments to bring the brand up to a house-hold respected and recognized brand. It was clear that the company just wanted to warehouse the Mapex product, have it sell itself, just coming in the warehouse back door and immediately turning around being sold and shipped at a profit to creditworthy retailers on a national scope. This was impossible and certainly naïve for handling a new brand of drums without any real marketing, artist relations, and so on. Mapex was floundering when I arrived as a consultant under contract in the early part of 1996. Within about six months of my arrival, Rudy decided to simply walk away from the Mapex distribution agreement. While I never had access to the distribution agreement, the decision to "liquidate the entire inventory" was just made one day.

This immediate decision one day on Mapex created an awkward situation for me in that Rudy Schlacher decided to cancel all the magazine advertising commitments he had made for Mapex. I found myself fielding phone calls from magazines who wanted to follow up on payment for full-page ads that the company had committed to, as well as future ad placements. Now it was my responsibility to inform the publications that Washburn was no longer the Mapex distributor and they should contact Mapex directly regarding payment for advertising invoices. I was getting notices for all of the full page Mapex ads and was instructed to not pay the invoice and to forward them to Mapex.

To the rest of the world, I was a Washburn employee; to the Schlacher family, but in reality I was a contracted hired marketing consultant. However, what evolved over time was good for me and the company. The many different projects I was working on for the company were such high visibility with the music products industry, the various trade magazines, the NAMM Show conventions and trade show exhibits, working directly with various high-level artists that Washburn kind of took on the visibility and feel of "Rudy and Karl". When questions or opportunities would come from all directions within the industry it would be turned over to Rudy, me, or Rudy's son Carl Schlacher for handling. Rudy liked steering the decision making process, but wanted others to do the implementation.

Time moved very quickly and I was immersed in everything that was thrown at me. I continued to live in two cities at once; Cleveland and Chicago. I was traveling back and forth every two weeks. Flights were still cheap, $95, and I could stay at my parents' home when I was in Chicago. I kept an automobile in Northbrook so I had access to getting around easily, including the "remote" parking lot at O'Hare airport and catching the 9:30 pm last United Airlines flight to Cleveland. I could pretty much be in two places almost at once. This got to be a regular commuting routine with the United Airlines flight attendants recognizing me on board almost every Friday evening heading to Cleveland.

Washburn had become one of the "big 3" guitar companies along with Fender and Gibson. They were like the Chrysler of the automotive "big 3" of Ford, GM, and Chrysler. Personally it felt good to be with a large company in the industry once again. Washburn exceeded Ludwig and even Pearl USA in annual sales and the marketing budgets I had to work with were reminiscent of earlier times.

Washburn was becoming somewhat of a clearinghouse for former Gibson Guitar personnel from various operations around the country, but mostly coming from Nashville. The first former Gibson sales director to come to Washburn that I already knew beforehand was John Hawkins, who I knew from the Gibson Pearl era. John was very supportive of my position within Washburn from the very beginning and clearly knew that there were going to be some roadblocks and speed bumps on our journey inside Washburn International. Hawkins (aka "The Hawk") communicated everything and anything on the sales marketing horizon so that he and I could help each other. This was reassuring from the beginning to have a sales director working with the internal marketing efforts.

As the Washburn sales director, John was overseeing a corporately owned dedicated sales force with multiple territories and sales quotas etc. I worked closely with John Hawkins for almost my entire first year with Washburn. Much to my amazement, one day I came in and John Hawkins was gone. Larry Volland, another Gibson executive vice president who formerly worked for Gibson President Henry Juszkiewicz, was now sitting at John Hawkins' desk. I did not really know

Larry well, but was aware of his background with Gibson and Dean Markley Strings and had crossed paths with him in the industry. Larry was closer in age to Rudy Schlacher, which enabled him to say things to Rudy that others would have had a hard time with. Volland was a sales leader that put tremendous value in people and their contributions to the company and sales goals. Unfortunately this "people value" was not a trait of Rudy Schlacher who could become somewhat abrasive. (Many of us recognized this and did not approve.)

I was directly responsible for the creation and completion of all of the marketing and product support materials for the various product managers. Bill Able was overseeing the entire Washburn guitar and bass product lines, Jeff Phillips oversaw the entire Soundtech Pro Audio product line, Rudy's son, Carl Schlacher, was overseeing the newly acquired Randall Amplifier product line development, and Tom was in charge of all Oscar Schmidt instruments including the Autoharps. The product managers did not report to me, but they all worked closely with me to arrange the product and brand support materials and the expertise required to have their product lines professionally marketed on a national scope. Dee Tatum was the International Sales Manager and I worked closely with he and his global distributors in various countries to make certain all the various graphic materials from the company were compatible for international distributor marketing campaigns and promotions.

Washburn Guitars was very much driven by professional high visibility guitar artists that endorsed the product. Fortunately Carl Schlacher was involved in every artist relationship and worked with them on advertising photography and approval processes.

This made my job that much easier because I did not have to deal with artist egos while getting artwork developed, approved and in-print in a timely manner. Many of these artists also had signature series instruments named after them, so the artist/company relationship was even stronger in these instances.

Key to my enjoyment of the Washburn contract and my success were the two very gifted full-time internal art directors working at Washburn. Both professionals knew graphic and design elements thoroughly, they each had creative ideas, and knew how to adapt to immediate and regular change. Both designers had been with the company a significant length of time and have seen various marketing directors already come and go a couple times. I guess this is why my first introduction by Rudy Schlacher on the first day grand tour was the art department. Vance Allen was the art director of the department, and Phil Carlson served as the assistant. Because Washburn employed this full time internal access to graphic design, advertising-catalog layout and creative work, the marketing department function of Washburn was capable of creating a tremendous amount of projects, advertisements, catalogs and trade show booth design elements. Having these two talented graphics people working for me was a luxury I was not accustomed to.

The marketing team included Carol Edwards who worked with Carl Schlacher on Washburn artist relations and assisted with the *In Tune* Washburn Newsletter, various consumer contests, and campaigns under the marketing umbrella. When Carol Edwards left the firm, Rudy's daughter, Lisa Schlacher became the marketing administrative assistant. Lisa was a great ally to have, as she was familiar with everything that I was working on, knew how hard I was working at it, and I'm sure some of all this got discussed over the dinner table at home. Lisa was a great partner to have in the marketing arena, as she knew how to get things done within the company and within the Schlacher family.

Summer 1996

IN TUNE NEWSLETTER

The Quarterly Bulletin Of Washburn International And Its Affiliated Companies

Washburn Presents Batten Custom Stage Series Guitar

Artist Hits The Road With Michael Jackson Tour

Jennifer Batten (inset) And Her New Custom Stage Series Guitar.

We recently had the opportunity to catch up with the world-class guitarist, Jennifer Batten. Jennifer is currently in rehearsal for her third world tour with Michael Jackson. The 1996 tour is shaping up to be two unbroken years on the road blanketing Europe, Asia and the South Seas (keep your VCR's poised for a potential HBO special). And while Jennifer has a gig most people would die for, she modestly states, "It's better than sitting at home, waiting for the phone to ring."

Her current solo project, **Momentum**, is a collection of original material, some written while on tour with Michael in 1992. Along with her signature guitar virtuosity, Jennifer adds a World Beat flavor to round out the diverse sonic character of the album. Look for a 1997 release date.

To assist Jennifer with her busy schedule, Washburn has prepared a going-away present. Based on the Stage Series, the handmade axe is stocked with Seymour Duncan pickups. Cosmetically speaking, the swamp ash body and natural matte finish are perfectly complemented by distinctive personal touches, like inlay work by Washburn's Yuriy Shishkov and the intricate depiction of an African tribal scene applied by an artist associate of Jennifer's.

For more information, write to:

Jennifer Batten Fan Club
P.O. Box 52107
Riverside, CA USA 92517-3107

Or for the WEB heads among us, Towanda (her dog's name) at:
http://musicianteractive.com/member/cgi-bin/gate2/mail/newmail.html

WASHBURN
What A Great Guitar Should Be

The longer I was at Washburn, the more I was beginning to know and learn what to expect. It would not be uncommon for Rudy to abruptly walk into my office and ask "what did you do today to make me money?" This became a regular interruption which could be interpreted as either; a) tell me what's going on in marketing or b) justify your existence and contract. In either case I started using a large blank white wall in my office to pin up almost everything that was "in process" and being worked on. This provided an immediate non-rehearsed show-and-tell answer I could use to explain what's going on in marketing. If Rudy had something to comment on, that would be his cue, and he took it regularly. I would then share this Schlacher concept with the Art Department and we would adjust and move forwards from there.

The annual NAMM Show conventions in Nashville and California were major projects, requiring massive amounts of time, money, and planning. The goal was to create elaborate trade show exhibits that would meet the expectations of Rudy Schlacher both aesthetically and in terms of generating sales. As a professional consultant I knew that very often the client would not know *what* they wanted in an ad layout, text, products exhibit, or brochure. I would have to reverse the exploration to determine what the client *did not want* in order to narrow the focus and determine what was needed.

One of the first areas of major involvement for me was getting the summer NAMM show display set up in Nashville. That involved a huge Washburn exhibit setup within a separate meeting room using rented slatwall exhibit partitions around the complete interior of the meeting room. Significant as this was, it was nothing in comparison to the efforts and expense that would be used at the Winter NAMM show of 1997. The Anaheim Convention Center was at that time going through a multi-year expansion and renovation, so the NAMM convention was moved to the Los Angeles Convention Center, located around the corner from the Staples Sports Arena.

Completely new exhibit booth graphics were needed along with new dealer in-store guitar kiosks. These were used as retailer guitar purchase incentives supplied to retailers free of charge. This encouraged qualifying and participating Washburn dealers to display six different Washburn guitars on small floor-stand kiosks. It was the marketing department that had to design the units, have them locally fabricated, and packaged in UPS size and weight cartons,

As the NAMM trade shows and exhibits evolved from one year to the next, the work involved in creating the exhibits and the changes in themes and graphics become more complex and elaborate. I began to see certain company behaviors that demonstrated my earlier statement about the company *not* placing value on the people within the organization. For the most part, I was always treated well and respected for what I was accomplishing for the company. I had open communications with the Schlacher family members and all the managers. While the company invested thousands of dollars on exhibits, advertisements, new graphics, and high visibility headline concerts during the convention, everyone was being placed in bottom-tier flea-bag budget hotels wherever there was a NAMM convention. These were absolutely the "bottom rung on the ladder" hotels and the cheapest possible rate that could be gotten through the NAMM Housing Bureau.

Anyone who remembers Anaheim, California NAMM shows remembers what the Jolly Roger Motel was like. These were the no-tell Motels around Anaheim. While they were relatively close to the convention center, they were not safe and many feared for what personal items were left in their motel rooms when they were working at the convention center. This same mental attitude about people and cost savings would be portrayed by the company in handling freight going to California. Sometimes to save on the convention center unionized freight handling costs, Washburn would ship 30-40 guitars to my motel room at The Jolly Roger. When I would get to my room after a day of setting up the exhibit, here was a mountain of guitar boxes stacked in my motel room. The following morning the guitars would have to be moved to the convention center using the rental van Carl Schlacher or someone would have rented. While some of these situations were caused by late samples arriving from Asia right before the convention, the real emphasis was Washburn's avoidance of the union handling of the product arriving for the exhibit. Mind you, this was a $50 million a year company.

Washburn was dedicated to creating completely new trade show exhibits at every major event. This demanded a tremendous amount of new graphic output. One example was the 40-foot long laminated graphic panels on all four sides of the exhibit. The internal art department created all of that. (The actual 40 foot-long color outputs were of course printed outside of the company.) While Rudy was the President and CEO of the company, he wanted the marketing director to direct the marketing. He considered himself a very hands-off type of president, yet I considered him very much hands-on and deeply involved in everything that was going on with marketing and advertising for all four product divisions.

National Sales Manager Larry Volland was experiencing the same level of involvement by Rudy. Sometimes the challenge was not in determining what it was that Rudy wanted; it was more a mission of finding out what he did *not* want. Whether this was marketing, sales management, advertising, or graphic design, much of the implementation was done by process of elimination. We would be able to find the path of least resistance, and get each project approved. This psychological approach meant that I even learned what colors Rudy preferred in the ads, in the exhibit graphics, in everything. He consistently liked and wanted a specific maroon color in everything, and it became known as "Rudy Red." This was a specific Pantone color number that the Art Department identified and regularly used as part of any art project that needed to get his approval.

I was always working with NAMM on negotiating for prime booth floor-space locations for the Washburn exhibit. The prime exhibit space was always the most expensive. Rudy felt entitled to prime space on the basis of all of the many NAMM conventions Washburn had participated in over the years. Rudy wanted to be portrayed in the NAMM conventions as one of the big three guitar companies along with Fender and Gibson. It became my job to make Washburn look like a "market leader" in all product categories without spending a lot of money. This was a constant challenge.

Over the years, Washburn became one of the companies that were known for hosting a large NAMM rock and roll concert for guests, retailers and the general convention public. These took place on Friday evening during the Anaheim NAMM convention. These Washburn events became known as NAMM-Jam concerts and would feature some high visibility "guitar-God artist" as the headliner. These concerts were held at one of primary convention hotels within close proximity of the convention center. They were extremely expensive and labor-intensive. Carl Schlacher was inevitably in charge of these because he was dealing closely with the artists. He had production company contacts in Anaheim so he would pull these concerts together through delegation to outside vendors and resources. I worked closely and successfully with Carl Schlacher. I had to; he was the next generation of Washburn International leadership despite his young age and basic business inexperience.

Carl often ended up with projects that were handed off to him from his father. This was certainly reminiscent of the Ludwig family and how Bill III would inherit delegated projects or assignments from Bill Ludwig Jr. I thought, "I've been here before and I know how to deal with a two-generation privately owned family business". Some of this project handing-off would in turn end up on my plate of responsibility. We all had to wear multiple hats while we were multi-tasking. Eventually, that happened with the Washburn NAMM JAM concerts. I was able to follow Carl's playbook and with the help and support of the people around me, I pulled it off. The January, 1998, Washburn NAMM Jam concert in Los Angeles featuring Washburn Artist Craig Chaquico and saxophonist Richard Elliot was an example of a hand-me-down project I inherited and successfully executed.

Washburn remained extremely visible in many events, activities and campaigns that were directed towards music awareness, music education and growing the market for the guitar. NAMM was in the process of building their Museum of Making Music in Carlsbad, California. The Washburn brand name on guitars goes back over a hundred years, and NAMM wanted to include some Washburn guitars in the museum on a loaner basis. I negotiated this out of Rudy's personal vintage guitar collection, arranging for two or three hundred-year old Washburn guitars to go on display within the NAMM Museum. The last time I was in Carlsbad, I noticed that those guitars were still on display in glass humidity-controlled display cases. That gave me a feeling of personal accomplishment, and of course Rudy was proud to see his guitars on display.

I was contacted by GAMA (Guitar and Accessories Manufacturers Association) about the placing of guitars in classrooms on an annual basis. GAMA wanted Washburn to be a part of this music advocacy effort to bring more guitar education into the school classroom. Rudy liked this investment in the future of guitar education and gave his approval to donate 50 guitars. This quantity which would equal what Fender and Gibson were each doing in support of the GAMA classroom initiatives. The donated guitars were instruments that had been classified as "seconds" because of minor imperfections or blemishes, but certainly worthy of donation to classroom school use.

Washburn was contacted by the Suzuki Rock and Roll Marathon of San Diego. This was an inaugural event for 1998 which would highly promote 25 to 30 live music bandstands with a variety of musical groups performing along the marathon race route through downtown San Diego. My brother was living in San Diego at the time, so I called him to ask about the event. He was very familiar with it and indicated that this was a very significant event for the San Diego area. The Rock and Roll Marathon management wanted to be able to give away 50 limited-edition Washburn acoustic guitars that would have the special Suzuki Rock and Roll Marathon logo, date and identification on the front of the guitar. I got the approval from Rudy, as he liked that kind of visibility and agreed to give them the 50 acoustic guitars. This donation was contingent upon Washburn being the exclusive guitar of the event and that neither Fender nor Gibson would be allowed to participate. This was a Washburn-only event and was highly successful as a brand awareness effort.

By the end of 1997, Washburn was doing some exciting things and the momentum was fast paced. There were new full color guitar catalogs coming out, complete new full-color guitar box-packaging, the Buzz Feiten Tuning System launch, new in-store merchandising aids for Soundtech and Washburn and of course the new and expanding affiliation with Paul Stanley of KISS. The project list was over flowing.

Rudy wanted a brand new January 1998 NAMM Show exhibit for Anaheim that would definitely bring unprecedented attention to the company and each of the Washburn product brands. I was directed to research three exhibit-building firms that could construct a suitable display within the design and graphic parameters I would provide. After many back and forth meetings and discussions with Rudy, the project was awarded to Tandem Design, located in Orange California. A new booth would cost $130,000, with the intent that this would be used and modified over a three to four year period. The firm's charges for delivery, set up and administration of all display supervision during the union labor set-up was in addition to the actual "construction amount". The exhibit would be outstanding in appearance and logistics, allowing all four product division to have adequate space and identification in the exhibit hall. The overhead banner would make the Washburn International identity unmistakable. I was very pleased to be leading this project, as I knew this would have lasting value in portraying my abilities and expertise, long after the Washburn project. This was a long and tedious project that started in early fall of 1997, through the January 1998 convention.

A Memorable Moment:

Going into the new display construction project, I knew that there would be "issues" in getting Washburn to systematically release payments for the $130,000 new exhibit. There were date and decision deadlines on the calendar all the way through the development and construction process. I worked closely with Tandem Design on a weekly basis leading up to the convention. The exhibit builder needed the $50,000 1st installment to move forwards. I went through the usual check request sequence for the $50k. There were weeks of procrastination by the company. Tandem Design eventually called and told me
"Karl, if we do not immediately receive the $50k deposit, we can *not* guarantee that the exhibit will be completed in time for the convention and we will not be held responsible". I understood that the firm's patience had been stretched to the limits. I walked into Rudy's office and communicated the circumstance and that he would only have an empty 60x60 foot section of bare concrete floor in the exhibit hall at the NAMM convention unless I had a $50k check sent for overnight delivery to the exhibit firm. I was surprised to have the check later that same afternoon. I had learned anew tactic with the Washburn operations. The threat of looking unprofessional, cheap, or ridiculous in the eyes of the entire music products industry scared the hell out them.

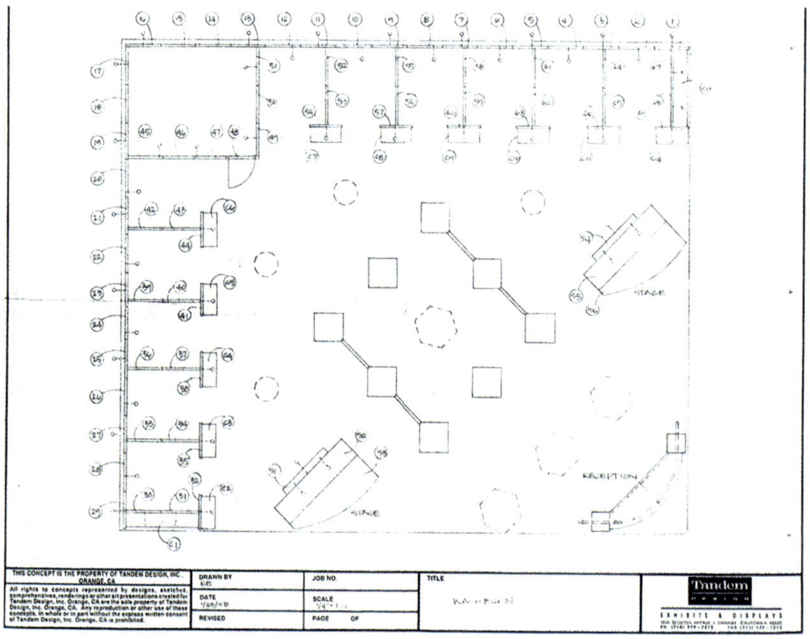

Blueprint, 1998 Washburn NAMM exhibit

1998
NAMM
WASHBURN
SoundTech
OscarSchmidt
Randall
Leading the Way in '98
WASHBURN USA CUSTOM SHOP
ARMADILLO
WASHBURN
What A Great Guitar Should Be
FINE STRINGED INSTRUMENTS
OscarSchmidt
BY WASHBURN
Autoharps

We came up with a new catalog for 1997-1998 that featured all new photography. I would go to Washburn's chosen product photographer, Paul Natkin in Chicago, which was a recommendation from Carl Schlacher. Natkin had done a lot of work for the various Rolling Stones tours and was highly respected in many musical circles. Natkin was used exclusively for all of the new photography images of the guitars as well as all product lines. We would take the guitars to Natkin's photography studio in Chicago. The respective product manager and one of the art directors would supervise the photo session. Keep in mind this was a period of time when film photography was being challenged by digital photography. Natkin was "old school" and preferred the traditional film photography for products because of the increased clarity based on technology at that time. Once the transparencies were received, they would be taken to Washburn's art department and they would turn it into a 25 or 30 page catalog. Those catalogs were expensive. In my opinion, these catalogs and the glamour product photography were some of the best Washburn printed pieces or catalogs the guitar market had even seen. These 40-page full color catalogs were expensive and looked like a Sotheby's Vintage catalog in quality.

The demand for the completely new Washburn Guitar catalog was huge and the company went through significant printing and re-printing costs. Eventually, halfway through 1998, the product line had changed enough to warrant a revised catalog and the decision was made to downsize to a more economical "pocket catalog", just like in the Ludwig chapter. We printed 150,000 copies of that catalog and wallpapered the world with Washburn pocket catalogs. The company wanted to make it available to retailers and individuals, anyone and everyone who was interested in Washburn guitars. . We tried to do creative things with the graphics.

1997 and 1998 brought out many new products and marketing campaigns. The Limited Edition D-97 acoustic guitar released only 1997 units for the global market. It also included a copy of the full color *History of Washburn* coffee-table collector's book along with a Certificate of Authenticity that was numbered and signed by Schlacher. We chose the "Rudy Maroon" ink color for the entire certificate.

WASHBURN
WORLD'S FINEST GUITARS
SINCE 1883
Limited Edition

Congratulations on your purchase of the 1997 Limited Edition Washburn acoustic guitar. Your 1997 Limited Edition is one of a select run of 1997 handcrafted instruments in the Washburn tradition since 1883.

Model D97Ltd. No. _____ of 1,997 Instruments

RUDY SCHLACHER, PRESIDENT

Washburn International 255 CorporateWoods Parkway • Vernon Hills, Illinois 60061-3109 • USA

Another example of the The Washburn Art Department's creativity was when Oscar Schmidt introduced the OG-2 Beginner's Guitar Kit. It included extra strings, polish, and a strap; everything that you would need in a guitar pack. They packaged everything it into a cool "graffiti" designed guitar carton for use underneath the Christmas tree. We followed the same unique special packaging on Washburn guitars and the Oscar Schmidt acoustic guitars.

Soundtech Pro Audio was a significant part of the Washburn company, revenue and product-brand offering. Soundtech received the same investments in full page color ads, a new catalog with all new product photography, and supporting wall posters.

For the background of many of the photographs, we used Washburn's small Chicago factory which was a custom shop. Fender and Gibson both had custom shops. Therefore Washburn had to have a "Custom Shop". Even though all of these companies were buying a tremendous quantity of guitar products from Asia, they each had the top-of-the-line, made-in-American instruments produced in their USA custom shops or factories. Grover Jackson ran the custom shop for Washburn in downtown Chicago. I do not know the terms of his parting, but eventually Grover Jackson was no longer there and Larry English, another former Gibson employee who came from Gibson's Montana factory, was brought in to run the Washburn Custom Shop. This was my first meeting and work experience with Larry English.

Early in 1998 It was decided by the Washburn art department that they wanted to shoot all the new items for the wearables Jam-Gear catalog in the Custom Shop.

The Jam-Gear product line was Washburn's wearables and promotional non-musical merchandising catalog to consumers. Jam Gear, was a very diverse product line and seemed to be a quite profitable brand identification product. For about a week the Washburn marketing department team moved into the Custom Shop late in the afternoon for doing the necessary product photography, all while not disturbing the Custom Shop's guitar manufacturing operations during the day. I was appreciative of the Custom Shop management for allowing us to move in for a week of late-day/evening photography within the various different manufacturing departs and expressed this gratitude regularly. Using the custom shop as a background for product allowed the product photos to include sawdust, c-clamps, work-benches, many different wood-working tools and machinery and so forth. The use of the Custom Shop in the background made each of the product photos that much more interesting to look at in the brand new color catalog.

The Jam Gear catalog project within the Custom Shop gave me an insight into new Washburn arrival Larry English. As experienced as I might have been by that point and to have almost encountered every type of individual in the music industry, I had never met a person who could be more downright rude and egotistically arrogant and condescending in demeanor and character. I wondered how Schlacher could have ever brought him into the company, as he irritated everyone he came in contact with in the company. I realized that Larry English was allowed to get away with this behavior because there was a side of Rudy Schlacher that a lot of people did not know; Rudy had a certain similar temperament and character. Schlacher would take great pleasure in startling the hell out of me saying something very off-the-wall or obscure, just to see my reaction. Eventually I just ignored this and stayed with the topic relating to professional business. Some of the things the he would say to female employees back then would end up in a lawsuit today under the heading of sexual harassment.

By June of 1998, Larry English was intent on taking over Washburn's entire marketing operation in addition to managing the Washburn Custom Shop in Chicago. I became aware of this through an internal proposal document authored by Larry English and addressed to Rudy and Marianna Schlacher. This document outlined specifically how English envisioned taking over the complete marketing department duties of all four product lines while also supervising the operations and production of the Chicago Custom Shop. While I knew there was some talk of the Custom Shop being relocated to the Vernon Hill headquarter operations building, I did not know the timeline for this possibility. It became apparent to me that the Larry English June 1998 proposal was being considered. This was a change that would have deep ramifications for many people, including myself.

The uprooting of the current successful marketing team and effort started in early summer with the abrupt decision by Rudy to terminate art director Vance Allen, effective immediately. It was my job to implement this dismissal under the explanation that "other arrangements for art direction have been made and Allen's professional services are no longer required". A two week severance check was issued and that was the end for half of the art department. In short order, Rudy started shopping outside advertising agencies to find one which would shoulder the responsibility of replacing the graphic design and artwork, previously led by long-time employee Vance Allen. With Phil Carson still in place as a "survivor" in the art department, Rudy selected an outside advertising agency of his choice and asked for "sample advertising comps" of their work. I would loan sample Washburn guitars to the outside agency for them to work with; they would photograph and submit renderings of what they felt the Washburn print image should be. I was so unimpressed with their work, I cannot even remember the name of the advertising firm.

The summer rolled forward with many projects and deadlines dealt with through non-traditional implementations and an "its good-enough" perspective. By early August it was time for me to submit a Dustman & Associates Contract Renewal for another six or nine month period. I was then advised by Marianna Schlacher that the company would not be renewing my contract at the end of August.

I didn't know how viable the Larry English marketing department/responsibility takeover was, but it was clear there would not be a place for me. English was successful in convincing Rudy that he could do all of the marketing by headquartering himself in the Vernon Hills main office location and that it would involve bringing in a number of Larry English's young, inexperienced, low-cost gophers to work under him in all the various aspects of the marketing and Custom Shop guitar operation.

IN RETROSPECT

The Washburn contract was a tremendous opportunity for me in a non-percussion environment. I made myself known and added contacts and credibility to my qualifications for future consulting projects. While I always learn a lot from each contract and client experience, I was disappointed to experience the complete lack of value placed on the *people* of Washburn. Disposable and dispensable are appropriate words to describe the mindset of the firm and the president. I found this disturbing, as I firmly believe a company and its products or services are only as good as it's people and leadership.

Ultimately, the Schlacher family got what they wanted in selling off the entire company, bringing obscurity to all four product brands and products for the new owners. I guess what goes around comes around. In 1999 Washburn was found guilty of two counts of mail fraud because they the removed all "Made in Korea" stickers from on Washburn guitars entering the United State from 1980 through 1994. This resulted in a fine of $880,000 plus $120,000 restitution to the USD Customs Service for unpaid import duties. The judgement also imposed five years of probation for Rudy Schlacher.

Client No. 7
Results Plus
Professional Development Workshops & Curriculums
Cleveland, Ohio

The completion of the Washburn contract in Illinois meant that I finally was able to stop commuting from Cleveland to Chicago and concentrate on Ohio-based opportunities. This allowed me to start professionally performing musically again. I was able to accept performance bookings and make commitments on the calendar because I was no longer out of town on business all week. This became a time of transition and research as I concentrated on diverse opportunities that could help me grow personally as well as professionally.

I was interested in learning about professional development and began to seek out some type of career advisor or "coach". I found a local firm called Results Plus which was about 12 miles from my home. This was a family-owned and operated professional development company based on the ideas and practices of coach and motivational speaker Dick Zalack. The firm was already successful and had workshops targeted to independent contractors, financial planners, insurance representatives, accounting firms, and entrepreneurial opportunists. While that may sound intentionally vague, it was really targeting people who were working for themselves in some capacity or were selling either a product or a service. Another target audience was the group of small to midsize company owners who wanted a certain amount of guidance in balancing their lives between professional and personal conflicts.

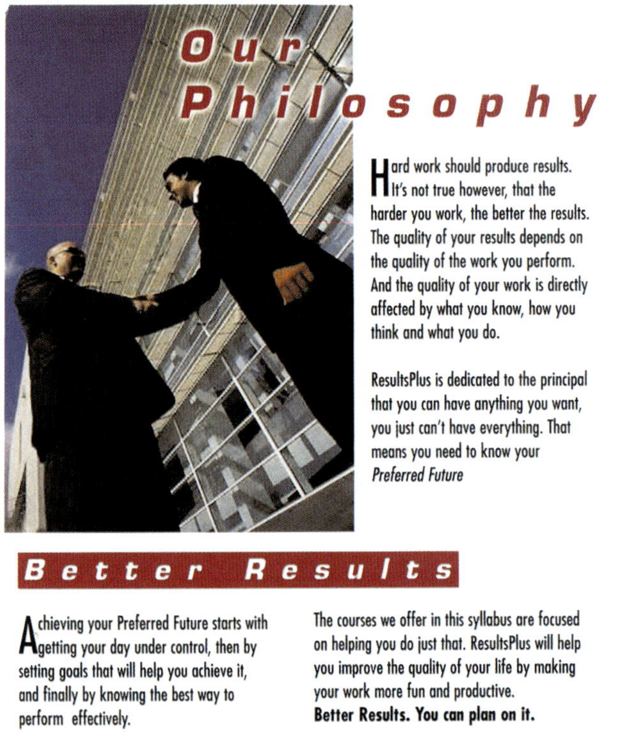

What started out as me investigating the company turned into them becoming interested in me.
Dick Zalack was traveling extensively all over the United States conducting workshops, guest speaking engagements, and platforms for selling his curriculums to firms on a broad scale. There was a need for an internal right hand man for the President and Founder, Dick Zalack. Zalack was the company creator, the main person and rainmaker as a motivational speaker. The company needed a director of business development; a marketing strategist to identify new markets and to provide executive briefings to prospective clients. The strategist would also be expected to strengthen/manage the internal independent telemarketing sales force.

I originally thought this could be a part time effort, allowing me to pursue other things and opportunities while budgeting a certain amount of time and effort on a weekly basis. It became clear from the very first one-on-one discussion that Results Plus had a pretty long list of things Zalack needed me to do in order to grow the company. I was intrigued by Dick Zalack's abilities and common sense aptitudes for business and creating a following for his curriculums and workshops. The foundation for the company was a very professional mindset but very small in size and revenues. There was a certain "fairness and honesty" to the company and the small team he had assembled, all of which probably were connected to Zalack's strong personal Christian values and trust in people. After dealing with the "disposable people mindset" at Washburn, this was refreshing. Zalack liked the consulting contract method of working together on a renewal-by-renewal basis. The downside for me was that this position had absolutely nothing to do with music or the music products industry, I thought.

I looked at this as an opportunity to do something totally different with the skill set I had developed and was a contract that would not require me to be there the rest of my life. I came into Results Plus under contracts set up for 6 to 9 months at a time. This project required me to learn the philosophies and content of all of the company's workshops, courses, and curriculums. This was no small task to learn the professional development "products" and sell them to prospective clients. Zalack could be on a national speaking tour during the week or presenting local or out-of-state multi-day workshops. This would involve a lot of "on the job training", listening, absorbing and interacting with clients that were already going through curriculums and workshop series. I saw the need for the special skills and talents I could bring to the company and felt that that the firm would benefit from my contributions.

One of Zalack's early clients was a professional advertising and public relations business owner, Randy Martin. I was instructed to work with Randy under this retainer, to create and develop any of the marketing and sales materials I would need for the Results Plus programs. This was a great tool to have timely access to creative graphic arts expertise. Randy and I worked well together, using Zalack as the sounding-board and final approval on materials we were moving forward with. I would pretty much be stationed at the company headquarters on a daily basis working on their marketing program strategies and business development initiatives.

We provide strategies for winning without losing at life!

RESULTSPLUS targets professionals like you who want to achieve better results. We help you avoid being consumed by distractions and other wasters of your time, energy, and creativity. We do this by helping you identify your key results areas and then showing you how to insulate them.

Our process centers on the development and alignment of core values in your personal and professional lives. Our process helps you clarify your goals, develop a track for accomplishing those goals, and maintain focus on managing your priorities while handling your responsibilities. All without sacrificing time for yourself and your family.

OUR OBJECTIVE is to equip people with a process that enables them to:

- Develop a Personal Strategic Plan
- Clarify Focus Results
- Recognize Barriers
- Overcome Those Barriers
- Monitor and Evaluate
- Implement Necessary Change

ResultsPlus serves successful senior executives, key administrators, middle management, and staff. We take individuals and whole teams from their present levels of success and achievement to the levels of success and achievement at which they strive to be. And we do that using a proven process that results in improved planning and decision making.

Results Mastery

A process that takes already successful business builders and aims them towards higher levels of personal and professional performance and achievement.

RESULTS MASTERY is a four phase, one-year program that will help you develop a 'Total Plan for Life.' It provides you with a foundation on which to build better results.

Through our well-defined process, Results Mastery will help you improve the balance in your life yet allow you to accept growth opportunities and challenges with a new level of confidence. The process will help you become a more well-rounded person and a leader who will increase the quality of their work and the quantity of time devoted to personal relationships.

THE RESULTSPLUS PROCESS focuses on:

- Thinking and Planning Tactically
- Thinking and Acting Strategically
- Capturing Your Niche Market
- Values Based Planning

And includes:

- A Personal Consultation in your office after each workshop
- Four Quarterly Energizers for evaluation and refocusing goals
- Unlimited Results Management Refreshers.

Results Mastery is the optimum ResultsPlus curriculum for the application of proven planning, organization, and productivity concepts.

Strategic Staff

A three-day session that will align your staff with the vision and values of you and your company, organization, or division while helping develop a strategic plan. Designed for the owner/Executive leader and key staff members.

THE KEY EXECUTIVE and the support management staff will learn the new laws and methods of doing business. You will create a blueprint for getting your day and work in order so that you may achieve the goals of the corporate strategic plan you will create. You will learn the difference between intention and method, how to plan and make decisions that support the core values of the entire organization.

DAY ONE (Key Staff Only)

- Mindset, Philosophy, Vision
- Align Values with Vision
- New Laws of Business
- Transformational Projects
- Mind Map, Business Model

DAY TWO (Key Staff Only)

- Tools, Methods, and Process
- Strategic Relationships
- Priority System
- Foundation Projects
- Refocus: Goals & Projects

DAY THREE (Executive & Key Staff)

- The Strategic Plan
- Values, Vision, Mission Alignment
- 3 and 5 Year Key Results
- 1 Year Goals and Barriers
- Implementation Process

Strategic Staff is an essential ResultsPlus curriculum for developing immediate and long-term Strategic Plans through management and staff development.

Strategic Results

A one-day business planning workshop that teaches teams to draft and implement their own value based work plans.

TEAMS LEARN the four steps of Strategic Thinking:

- Positioning the Organization
- Deciding Where to Focus Planning
- Planning Key Results, Problems, Goals & Action Plans
- Achieving, Implementation, Evaluation, Follow-Up

HANDS-ON PARTICIPATION on a One-Day Business Planning session that focuses on processes customized to your organizational values, mission, and strategic initiatives in order to develop, implement, and maintain a twelve-month company strategic plan.

Strategic Results is ideal for an entire company, single work unit, department, or division. Enables groups of diverse people to function as a cohesive unit.

Are you striving or thriving?

resultsplus™

BETTER RESULTS. YOU CAN PLAN ON IT!

330-225-1511

ResultsPlus
4178 Center Road
Brunswick OH 44212

The company was also looking to increase the number of professional independent telemarketing sales representatives. I would screen the prospective telemarketers and select ones for the necessary training. These were primarily commissioned sales people with minimal financial monthly retainers. This required finding those individuals who would use their relationship-building skills over the telephone. They also had to be people who loved talking to people all day on the telephone. Another requirement was a professional presence for making face-to-face appointments to explain and discuss the curriculums and workshops being offered. Selling intangible products like professional development courses, training and workshops is *not* an easy fast-track accomplishment. It takes time, tenacity, and persuasion to create and make the sale.

Sending sales development faxes in 2001 was still very much the norm. Everyone had a fax number and freely provided it to you for "fax harvesting". The internal Results Plus administrative assistant, Judy Nair, would spend a good amount of her work day sending out faxes to perspective clients to promote forthcoming workshops, executive briefings, and new courses being offered. Most northeast Ohio workshops would take place at the company's education center centrally located to all the major Cleveland area highways. This was a custom-built education training center, equipped with large comfortable classroom-style seating, complete equipped kitchen and audio-visual production capabilities. The surroundings were comfortable and excellent catered lunches were served. Participants were required to *turn off their cell phones* when attending sessions.This was all impressive and helped get people to attend and participate.

Email was just beginning to evolve. We were buying email address lists from prominent companies and various associations; mainly in the financial planner and insurance industries. (This methodology would become known as social media eventually.) These would be simple little messages sent out via email to draw attention. These messages would typically go out to about 5,000 email recipients on a monthly basis in attempts to develop interest in the workshops. These were day-long workshops. In some cases the participants would fly to Cleveland four times a year for a series of quarterly workshops. My time became half in the office and half in the education center working with the various workshops. The cost of the curriculums was from $1,600 to $2,400 per year. It was more than simple time management session that could be accessed for about $250; these were advanced coaching sessions in a classroom style. I felt that since I needed to understand the underpinnings of the content, I basically had to learn how to "drink the water in order to be able to sell the water." I became a practitioner of what we were preaching.

A Memorable Moment: September 11, 2001

Every American recalls and remembers where they were when the tragic events of this day hit the United States. I was working early in the morning at the Results Plus office on a variety of projects and assignments in preparation for the next day;s Results Plus executive briefing scheduled at a medical facility in Fairlawn, Ohio, about twelve miles from the office. We expected a diverse group of medical practice individuals, primarily administrative support specialists and hospital or private practice owners. This two-hour executive briefing would be conducted by Dick Zalack and attended by a number of Results Plus sales representatives. The goal was to generate enrollment in the four-session 12-month curriculum "Results Mastery". As the tragic events of the day unfolded, Zalack and I assessed whether or not we should go through with the planned next morning presentation. There was no cancellation notice from the hosting venue, so we decided to proceed as planned. Zalack was a "master" of getting people to open up and share their feelings and it seemed appropriate to go "off script" for the session. Those who did attend the executive briefing were in a daze of disbelief about what had taken place. They were walking robots and definitely not tuned in or receptive to a professional development presentation on determining their future. Zalack's Christian roots called for a minute of silence or prayer for all in the guest meeting room and then went into a person-by-person volunteer invitation to explore.... "What are you feeling, what are you thinking?" What happened in American shook the attending participants and humanity in general to the core of their values and faith.

The complexion of our workshop content and curriculums changed drastically after the September 11th events. A key element of every professional development self-assessment became "What is most important to you and why?" People were scared, stunned, afraid of what could happen next and whether it could happen to them. Priorities and emphasis in life for the participants changed dramatically. Success, money, prestige, titles, and accumulation of tangible property all gave way to a focus on defining how you want to be remembered. All of the warm fuzzy topics related to what is inside your heart, soul, and brain, started to become part of the curriculum. This shift in personal priorities and values became a significant part of life coaching. Finding and defining those important issues was basically what those sessions were all about.

Throughout the contract period I became fully invested in the content and value of the workshops. Designing and creating all the marketing materials used resulted in knowing the benefits of the workshop content and experiences. Client assessments became an added responsibility. I interviewed individuals to determine how well they were dealing with and employing the Results Plus curriculums. I would be one-on-one for about two hours with many individuals from the group of clients, trying to assess whether they were "getting it" (the curriculum systems and processes) These sessions became very personal to some and the confidentiality of the client meetings was essential in helping the clients to help themselves.

I learned that people seemed to open up and trust me with their inner feelings, conflicts and issues they were dealing with in their lives. This surprised me, but I appreciated the confidence it gave me as a result. While I did not always have solutions to the issues in their lives, I had a system for helping clients find, create, and implement a solution they would be able to live with.

Over the three years of this multiple-renewal contract I experienced a whole new understanding of what professional development means and became more comfortable than ever before about public speaking to any size audience in a small conference room or large event hall. The self confidence that this built in me could have not been achieved any other way than by "doing and leading others" to be the best company spokesperson and representative we could present. In associating with an extremely diverse client population in terms of age, background, profession, wealth-income and personalities, I became more of a "people person" than I could have ever imagined.

While this consulting contract had nothing really to do with the music business specifically. I learned a great deal about personal direction, public speaking, staying focused, project management, self assessment, sales candidate evaluation and creating a revenue-producing attitude. Everything I learned working within the Results Plus professional development organization I use and adapt every day.

ResultsPlus
Executive Briefing

We invite you and your
key managers to take
A Giant Step Forward

YOU'RE A BUSINESS BUILDER, A KEY management team player who seeks a higher level of performance and effectiveness. You want to achieve better results in every facet of your work and personal life, but you've discovered you can't do it alone.

You've reached a plateau in both your professional and personal life. It feels like you are standing still — stagnating; perhaps, even slipping backward! You see it; you feel it. But, you don't know exactly what to do about it. The things that used to motivate you no longer seem to work.

If that sounds like you, don't despair. There is a program that will help you return to your glory days. And then help you move beyond!

It's called Results Mastery.

Results Mastery provides the process to take your proven successful achievements and accomplishments and build on them. We assess your strengths, you assess your goals and dreams. Together, we build upon those skills and talents you've already mastered and provide a clear focus on the formula that will enable you to develop a 'Total Plan for Your Life.'

Results Mastery is a one year executive program that will help define, prioritize, and improve how you structure your time, energy, and creativity. Our different approach will help you manage every part of your life, accomplishing more with less frustration and anxiety.

With Results Mastery you will learn how to achieve a lasting balance in your life, while accepting challenges and growth opportunities with a new level of confidence. You will become a more well-rounded, multi-dimensional individual. You will discover how to have quality time at work and quantity time at home.

You will learn how to set intention-based goals instead of method-based ones; and create a strategic plan for your business.

Results Mastery will help you take more time off and earn more money while you do. You will discover you are now able to accomplish anything you choose, even implement what you learn in industry-related seminars!

Results Mastery is not available to everyone. To qualify, you must have been a successful business builder for at least three years. If you have been, then you and your managers are invited to attend our Executive Briefing and discover how Results Mastery can provide the process and plan to take you to higher level of effectiveness and success in your life.

Make the decision to invest just two hours of your time attending our Executive Briefing: Take A Giant Step Forward.

Start planning for the future now!

Call today to reserve your place
in our next Executive Briefing:
Take A Giant Step Forward

330-225-1511

resultsplus™
BETTER RESULTS. YOU CAN PLAN ON IT!
4178 Center Road
Brunswick OH 44212

Client #8
Innovation Drum Company

In 2002 I was approached by Steve Badalament in Detroit, who was the founder and president of Innovation Drum Company. He had a vision of, and passion for, quality American-made drums that he conveyed with unequalled enthusiasm and commitment. He wanted to take Innovation Drum from a boutique drum company to the next level by finding investment capital. His enthusiasm was contagious and he wanted me to become one of the company leaders. While I did not know of Steve Badalament before, he apparently knew of me and my background in the music products industry and percussion business.

Steve was a drum builder with extreme attention to quality and detail. Whatever he lacked in business knowledge and experience was made up for by his knowledge of drum building and the related skills. The company needed a professional business plan that could be presented to select possible investors and financial partners. In addition, the company needed a detailed marketing plan with related costs that encompassed everything the company would need to achieve national recognition in a highly competitive drum market.

I never considered allowing my Dustman & Associates consulting business to get involved in pro-bono assignments, as I could not afford to give-away my expertise, contributions and guidance. I agreed, however, to accept an equity position in the business in exchange for my guidance in obtaining the capital. There were many meetings, hours of telephone conversations, and meetings with the Innovation Drum Company endorsement artists. Sometimes the hype became overwhelming and I would caution Steve on avoiding being taken advantage of by so many people who saw his vulnerability and naiveté. This start-up capital challenge went on for years. Steve never really gave up, regardless of the setbacks and broken promises from many potential financial partners and institutions.

Innovation Drum Company eventually became involved in an economic development outreach initiative that was part of Sinclair Community College (SCC) called the AIM Center, (Advanced Integrated Manufacturing). This was sort of a small business incubator that encompassed many small start-up companies in the Dayton, Ohio area that could share their talents and expertise with each other while creating a positive outcome for the Community College and a success story for the city of Dayton.They wanted Steve to move his entire small drum building business and manufacturing operations to the AIM Center located on the campus of Sinclair Community College in a designated building. However at first, the concept of using the original Rogers Drums manufacturing building in Dayton was explored and considered. The entire building was vacant and available.

That Rogers building concept detracted from the synergy the College was trying to weave into the equation by having all these small start-ups collaborating under one roof,...or college project umbrella. The objective was that through this community college business development and economic outreach, Innovation Drum Company would be able to attract a $3 million dollar investment capital necessary to really put him in-business. This capital was a requirement to take Innovation Drum Company to the next level of success and stability.

Not every rainbow of outreached arms always turns to gold,... and Steve learned this the hard way. After Innovation Drum was completely moved to the community college's AIM Center, the relationship did not lead to what Steve Badalament needed, expected or had even hoped for. The end result of this venture was the company's shortly-thereafter move back to the original Detroit location they had just moved from. This was a disappointment for all connected with the project, the promotion and the planned success story of Innovation Drum in Dayton.

Affirmation:

"As the Stradivarius of snare drums this instrument represents a paradox in our industry. With most drums being mass produced, the quality of the instrument is getting lost in the supply/demand paradigm that pervades the current musical instrument manufacturing mentality. With the ***Innovation Drums®*** ***VFVSS™ Snare Drums***, we are offering the most discriminating artists their chance to own and play a truly world class instrument custom made to their exact specifications with unparalleled sonic and aesthetic beauty. In addition, we manufacture every component ourselves right here in the USA. We are the only drum company that can claim this. In a word, this instrument is a masterpiece! We handcraft each instrument one drum at a time. I am proud that this drum bears the Vic Firth name as it is synonymous with our commitment to unparalleled quality!"

The Snare Drum:

90% of a drummer's technique originates from the snare drum. It is the frame of reference of most every drummer. There have been many snare drums made by many drum companies throughout the years. Innovation Drum Company® comes from a proud tradition of great North American drum making to create the ultimate snare drum ever. Innovation Drum Company® proudly introduces the ***VFVSS™*** (Vic Firth Vertical Snare System) Snare Drums. The ***VFVSS™*** is a marvel of engineering and as such takes away all the issues that have plagued snare drums for years. The high level of engineering, raw materials, and strict manufacturing tolerances are all hallmarks of the ***VFVSS™*** and thus, enables the artist to focus entirely on their performance and not on the structure and function of their instrument.

Characteristics:

1). **Finest Raw Materials**
All components are made of the finest materials ever in the manufacture of drums. These include:

a). **Silica Bronze Drum Hoops**
These drum hoops are made of the same materials and processes that are used in the manufacture of the finest Church Bells. They are engineered, contoured, and perfectly in round. They are engineered to perform at least 100% more work load than could ever be asked of them, no matter what stress and tension they are under. More importantly, they produce a sound like no other drum hoops ever. THIS IS THE ONLY DIE CAST HOOP THAT IS TRULY IN ROUND AND WILL HOLD ITS TOLERANCE UNDER THE MOST STRENUOUS OF PLAYING SITUATIONS!

b). **Oil Pressed Tool Steels for all screw parts.**

2). **The Vic Firth Vertical Snare Strainer.** This strainer is made entirely of steel. The lever is machined to an exacting manufacturing tolerance which allows the snare wires to be lowered over 1.25" off the snare side drum head (in the disengaged position). Our strainer ***cannot*** disengage while in use and will only do so when the artist desires to lower the lever. This extremely low level of snare disengagement ensures that there will be no unwanted snare spray and parasympathetic snare vibration.

3). **Perfected Interlocking Tuning System.** In our Interlocking Tuning System the tension rods CANNOT POSSIBLY LOOSEN during performance and/or at any level of tension. This is the only lockable tuning system that doesn't employ unwanted jam nuts nor extra locking paraphernalia onto the tension rod. This system is built onto the tube lug itself and works 100% of the time. An industry first!

4). **Multi-Function Drum Key.** Our Multi-Function Drum Key employs some ideas from the past but has been completely re-engineered and redesigned to entirely new geometric dimensions. This system employs engineering that will, for the first time, ***effortlessly*** enable the drummer to:

a). Separately tune the ***top*** of the drum from the ***top***.

b). Separately tune the ***bottom*** of the drum from the ***top.***

and/or

c). Tune ***both the bottom and top drum heads simultaneously all from the top.***

5). **Internal and External Shell Isolation.** Complete external and internal shell isolation via custom made gaskets to ensure complete component isolation at every point of internal and external shell contact. Each gasket is custom made for a perfect fit.

VFID® 6"x14" Titanium VFVSS™ Snare Drum with 24 Karat Show Quality Gold Plating

VFID® 7"x14" Solid One Ply Rock Maple VFVSS™ Snare Drum with 24 Karat Gold Plating

VFID® 7"x13" Nine (9)- Ply Canadian Yellow Birch VFVSS™ Snare Drum with 24 Karat Show Quality Gold Plating (finished in Butter Green Dupont® Chromalusion™)

"It's about time that the snare drum be elevated to the level of a Stradivarius violin." Vic Firth

Steve continued building beautiful drums one by one for artists, collector and aficionados that wanted the best American-made drums available.

By 2008, Steve also got the ear and attention of Vic Firth. As a result, Innovation Drums became a part of the Vic Firth exhibit at the Anaheim NAMM show. Steve was allowed a certain small amount of floor space within the exhibit for a select number of his snare drums and the newly introduced VFVSS Snare Drums (Vic Firth Vertical Snare System). This whole concept seemed like it was not to the liking of the Vic Firth national educational manager and drum corps specialist, Neal Larrivee. In visiting the Vic Firth booth and seeing the strained atmosphere that Innovation Drums was placed in, I knew this relationship would not last long.

While I invested a lot of time and expertise in helping develop a complete professional business plan with a five-year and a ten-year vision, nothing seemed to click for Innovation Drum Company. He was just unable to generate the $3 million startup-expansion capital needed to create an actual drum production entity. The company went dormant for years. Then in 2019 Steve popped up again, asking for my continued help and assistance. He had a whole new circle of people interested in the company who were now willing and able to help him. He had legal advisors, accountants, and so on. By now, Badalament wanted to concentrate primarily on building state of the art snare drums with growth potential for complete drums sets in the near future.

Still, he needed capital. Despite the dedicated efforts and many conversations, it unfortunately did not happen for Innovation Drum Company. Innovation Drum Company stands in a ready-set-go position with bigger-than-life ambitions for the future. Steve and I remain friends and chat every now and then and he thanks me for my efforts over the years. If Innovative Drum Company had succeeded, I would have become one of the principals of the firm. The payback for all this pro-bono work have been having a piece of the Innovation Drum Company "action" without investing a dime. Who knows, this opportunity could resurface once again with a whole new dimension for quality American drum-building.

Client No. 9
Rick Latham Publishing

I knew of Rick as a student from North Texas State University and East Carolina University, where he had attended both Ludwig International Percussion Symposiums during the 1970s and 80s. Rick always was a personable and outgoing guy who helped me with the actual production of the symposiums in additional to being an enrolled participating symposium student. Little did I know back then that our paths would continue to cross for decades afterwards. Over the years I stayed in touch with Rick as I ran into him at NAMM shows and other industry events. Over time Rick developed a tremendous following as a player as well as an author of drum books.

In 2005 Rick was celebrating the 25th anniversary of his method book *Advanced Funk Studies*. The book had become one of the "drum learning bibles", accepted and respected by everyone.

Rick approached me about his need for an expert in public relations and marketing to support his efforts in putting together a 25th Anniversary celebration for the book as well as creating increased public awareness of him as a successful drummer. Rick engaged my services as a long distance client, contracted to create and implement targeted market development and promotions focusing on the new Rick Latham educational DVD as well as promoting the anniversary of the *Advanced Funk Studies* method book.

With a clearly defined contract agreement and understanding of what Rick wanted to accomplish, I immediately used my contacts and influence to get Latham featured on significant high visibility performance platforms that would increase his person-of-influence stature. I started working on the January Anaheim NAMM program as well as the January Jazz Educators Convention, the May Modern Drummer Festival , the November Montreal Drum Festival, and the November PAS convention in Columbus, Ohio. All of this took tremendous amounts of time, letter-writing, telephone calls and follow-up as well as calling in some industry I-O-U's. None of those programs automatically accept artists and contributions for their programming. I put in far more hours on the project than I invoiced Latham for. My accountant that handles the client invoicing kept reminding me that this was not a full time client. I did a lot of politicking to get Rick on the programs he really deserved being on. A key element to the success was working with Latham's respective companies and the brands he endorsed. This included Drum Workshop, Evans drum heads, Istanbul-Agop Cymbals, Carl Fisher Publishing, and Sennheiser Microphones. The projects I was proposing for Rick's appearances would all require funding, so I requested financial support from his product endorsement firms. I leveraged his popularity and industry-wide recognition with all the company and contact names Rick provided.

Some companies bought into the whole 25th Anniversary celebration idea completely, while others took a more reserved position of support. As an insight, companies like promoting an artist through the print advertisement of their products an artist uses and promotes. This is more "marketing tangible" than asking for cash to support a performance, anniversary celebration, or some high visibility event. It took constant follow-up to assemble the funding and company support to make invitations and key performances happen. In the meantime, Latham was working on the development and promotion of his own band, Rick Latham And The Groove Doctors, which included the all-star line-up of Ken Tussing, Vail Johnson, Albert Wing, Bob Luna and Mack Dougherty. The band had just completed a new recording, *Live And Loaded,* recorded live at world famous jazz club, The Baked Potato in Hollywood.

What Rick needed desperately was a professionally assembled artist bio media kit. With the materials Rick provided, I assembled a professional media kit in the format that is used within the mainstream music products industry. Half the success of any artist's public relations and visibility is having the professional tools to market and promote themselves. It is always easier to have someone else do the promoting about the artist, rather that the artist being perceived as "self promoting". The end of the one-year contract was completed with success and an increase in Latham's visibility and professional profile. He remains at the top of his performance and educational "game" building on the decades of his hard work and expansion into the international teaching and educational platforms he created in Italy and throughout Europe.

Today I remain in awe of the artistry and dedication Rick Latham brings to his trade as a professional musician and time-honored astute percussion educator. We remain friends and I was so appreciative to have Rick participate in the Percussion Marketing Council's International Drum Month campaign for 2020, Lesson With A Master.

L-R: Ken Tussing, Vail Johnson, Albert Wing, Rick Latham, Bob Luna, Mack Dougherty

Rick Latham and The Groove Doctors

http://www.groovedoctorsjazz.com

orignal logo

Client No. 10
Percussion Marketing Council,

2018 logo

(PMC)

The Percussion Marketing Council represents a relationship and working contract that was in place for 19 years. The PMC is the official music products industry's trade association representing the entire percussion product category, both acoustic and electronic, drum sets, hand drumming, accessories, printed and electronic educational materials and anything that supports the public's awareness of drums, percussion and the enjoyment of playing a percussion instrument.

It all started with International Drum Month in 1995. David Levine initiated the early stages of forming an industry-wide movement for percussion, very much like the International Guitar Month and others. This was an industry-wide promotion to generate interest and awareness in drums and drumming. The percussion industry liked the concept of having a non-profit organization that would promote drums and drumming throughout the year as a neutral organization without brand or company conflicts. The success of the annual International Drum Month traditionally held in November was the launching pad for creating a formal trade association named The Percussion Marketing Council. The beginnings were humble with only a few of the percussion industry's leaders getting involved.

Jerry Hershman had his own company handling other trade associations, Association Headquarters, and served as the director in getting the organization set-up legally with non-profit status founded in the state of New York. Various campaigns and promotions developed over the early times drawing attention to the percus-

PERCUSSION MARKETING COUNCIL

Roster as of May 17, 1996

Andy Borden
D'ADDARIO & Co.
595 Smith Street
Farmingdale, NY 11735
Phone: 1-516-391-5400
FAX: 1-516-391-5410

James Catalano
LUDWIG INDUSTRIES
600 Industrial Parkway
Elkhart, IN 46516
Phone: 1-219-522-1675 ext. 360
FAX: 1-219-295-5405

David McAllister
SABIAN, Ltd.
Main Street, Meductic
N.B., Canada EOH 1LO
Phone: 1-506-272-2019
FAX: 1-506-272-2040

Rob Birenbaum
DRUM HEADQUARTERS
7241 Manchester Ave.
St.Louis, MO 63143
Phone: 1-314-644-0235
FAX: 1-314-644-4373

Erik Paiste
PAISTE
460 Atlas Street
Brea, CA 92621
Phone: 1-714-529-2222
FAX: 1-714-671-5869

Rick Kowarek
VIC FIRTH,Inc.
65 Commerce Way
Dedham, MA 02026
Phone: 1-617-326-3455
FAX: 1-617-326-1273

Don Lombardi
D/W-DRUM WORKSHOP,INC.
101 Bernoulli Circle
Oxnard, CA 93030
Phone: 1-805-485-6999
FAX: 1-805-485 1334

George Barrett
PEARL CORPORATION
549 Metroplex Drive
Nashville,TN 37211-3140
Phone: 1-615-833-4477,x 3117
FAX: 1-615-833-6242

Steve Anzivino
YAMAHA CORP.OF AMERICA
3445 E. Paris Ave., PO Box 899
Grand Rapids, MI 49512
Phone: 1-616-940-4900
FAX: 1-616-949-7721

Bill Reim
HOSHINO (USA) INC.
1726 Winchester Road
Bensalem, PA 19020
Phone: 1-215-638-8670
FAX: 1-215-245-8583

Steve Beck
Percussive Arts Society
701 NW Serris Ave. 73507
PO Box 25, Lawton, OK 73502
Phone: 1-405-353-1455
FAX: 1-405-353-1456

John Sorenson
AVEDIS ZILDJIAN Co.
22 Longwater Drive
Norwell, MA 02061
Phone: 1-617-871-2200
FAX: 1-617-871-3984

Paul Damiano (Chairman)
KAMAN MUSIC DISTR.
PO Box 507
Bloomfield, CT 06002-0507
Phone: 1-860-243-7855
FAX: 1-860-243-7287

Pat Brown
PRO-MARK CORPORATION
10707 Craighead Drive
Houston, TX 77025
Phone: 1-713-666-2525
FAX: 1-713-669-8000

Jerry Hershman, Exec. Sec'ty
J & D MUSIC SVCS., LTD.
38 West 21st St., 5th Floor
New York, NY 10010-6906
Phone: 1-212-924-9175
FAX: 1-212-675-3577
e-mail: AssnHdqs@AOL.COM

Joe Andriano
L/P-LATIN PERCUSSION
160 Belmont Avenue
Garfield, NJ 07026
Phone: 1-201-478-6903
FAX: 1-201-772-3568

LLoyd McCausland
REMO,Inc.
12804 Raymer Street
North Hollywood, CA 91605
Phone: 1-818-983-2600
FAX: 1-818-764-1433

CONSULTANTS:

David Levine, Full Circle Management, 6057 Rhodes Ave., N.Hollywood, CA-91606-4627
Phone: 1-818-753-1310, FAX: 1-818-753-1313, e-mail: DLEVINE360@AOL.COM

Don Maggi, Intertainment, Inc., 50 Berman Way, Middletown, NJ 07748
Phone: 1-908-671-8566, FAX: 1-908-671-8597

sion industry and attracting other percussion related members.

By the fall of 2000, David Levine was seeking to step-out of the leadership of the organization. As a result, they placed a small advertisement in a music trade magazine seeking an executive director for this new music industry nonprofit trade organization. This would be a small part time position running the organization for the small but dedicated membership. I saw this as an opportunity for Dustman & Associates to connect with broader bases of contacts within the percussion industry. This organization was diverse in bringing a common vision and mission to the percussion industry while helping retailers in providing education and awareness to the general public. The end result of this industry-wide movement would be increasing the number of people playing percussion and increasing the demand for all percussion products. It also created a unified percussion industry voice (of the manufacturers, distributors, educational festivals, publishers and organizations) within the music products industry.

The PMC board voted to have me take this over beginning in 2001. I was required to attend the forthcoming NAMM convention in Anaheim where I would be introduced at the annual meeting as the new executive director.

I had just started the Results Plus Professional Development company Business Development contract. The PMC seemed like a logical solution to keeping my hand and name in the music business while I worked on a non-musical consulting contract in Cleveland. Results Plus was flexible in my time and travel and allowed me to included PMC activities and conventions in my calendar planning. This musical balance eventually became even greater as a result of forming Professional Percussion Products by appointment orchestral percussion showroom in Cleveland, opening in April of 2003.

PMC ANNOUNCES NEW EXECUTIVE DIRECTOR

Karl Dustman

Kevin Kearns, president of the Percussion Marketing Council announced the appointment of music/percussion industry veteran Karl Dustman as the new executive director of the organization.

"We have completed an extensive review and evaluation of candidates for this important position within our organization. We are very fortunate to have Karl accept this position and its' challenges. Karl will be working with both, the past executive director and organization founder, David Levine and myself to ensure a smooth transition," commented Kearns. "We are immediately concentrating on bringing Karl up-to-speed on our current and proposed programs for the coming year."

Since the organization's inception five years ago, the PMC provides a unified voice for the percussion industry within the total music industry. Many programs and activities have been implemented to grow the number of percussion players thus benefiting percussion retailers, instructors, publishers, and instrument manufacturers.

Dustman's thirty-five-plus year career has included executive positions with Ludwig, Gretsch, Pearl, and Sonor. He is currently heading his own Cleveland, Ohio based marketing communications firm, Dustman & Associates, now in its ninth year. The firm specializes in marketing/business development plans for clients both in and out of the musical arena. His musical clients include Baldwin Pianos, Washburn Guitars, Clevelander Drum, Amada Classical Guitars, and the Chicago Music Mart at DePaul Center.

"It was Karl's diverse musical, business, and marketing background that made him a perfect candidate for this challenging position," Kearns said. "Karl is recognized in the industry at all levels for his marketing, advertising, and educational programs that has touched percussion retailers, artists, educators, and promoted percussion in many diverse market development activities. He will be active in building strategic alliances with other music industry associations sharing common goals while searching outside of the traditional musical venues to increase the number of percussion players in all instrument categories."

As of press time, the PMC's activities for the year 2001 include;

- Frankie Muniz, from "Malcolm In The Middle" - various consumer and trade promotions centered on Fox TV's new star/talented drummer
- D.A.R.E. Program - developing a co-operative program along with Dallas Police Department drummer, Rick Flowers, that will introduce drumming's positive influences to the youth market and alternative pro-active recreation activities that reduce crime.
- Winterguard - developing a strategic affiliation with the indoor drumline competition.
- August Drum Daze - a late summer supplier/dealer promotion
- Festival Alliances program - which seek to incorporate PMC's Be A Player community outreach message into existing drum festivals throughout the world.

The PMC is funded by the drum industry, NAMM, and it's members. For additional information on PMC activities and membership, please contact the national headquarters at: PO Box 33252, Cleveland, OH 44133, tel: 440.582.7006, fax: 440.230.1346, e-mail: kbdustman@aol.com.

My plate of responsibility was more than full with a diverse assortment of business projects and assignments all requiring my devoted attention. The "part time" effort became more consuming as responsibilities were added such as new program design and creation, assuming all accounting functions, preparing the formal NAMM Foundation Grant applications and reports, etc. Kevin Kearns of Modern Drummer was President of the PMC at this time. I worked closely with Kevin to learn what the organization wanted, needed and what could be done to expand the growth potential for the organization. The Board provided assistance as well, even though most everyone was thoroughly absorbed in their full time employment and really became a sounding board as I requested their input on concepts, ideas and campaigns I was outlining for development.

I was creating programs of general population awareness. By mid-2001 we were getting ready to introduce and launch the Rhythm Of The Heart program which was geared to getting percussion retailers to host free drumming events which would create more new players within their regional market. The percussion industry was so busy competing amongst themselves for brand and product awareness that they were doing nothing collectively to grow the market and industry. That priority, (creating new percussionists) became the full time job of the Percussion Marketing Council. As an all-volunteer non-profit trade association there was a huge amount of work to do with limited resources of time, money and people.

PMC News

THE OFFICIAL NEWSLETTER OF THE PERCUSSION MARKETING COUNCIL • VOLUME FIVE • NUMBER FOUR

PMC'S RHYTHM OF THE HEART HELPS DEALERS DEVELOP LOCAL MARKETS

The Percussion Marketing Council has begun distributing it's "Rhythm Of The Heart " market development program. Interest in the program, which provides retailers with a step-by-step plan to bring together pro-active groups to promote percussion, is rapidly spreading across North America. "We've had inquiries and requests for the program guidebook from several dealers in the U.S. and Canada. We're very excited about the prospect of percussion dealers working together to put on these events," commented PMC executive director Karl Dustman.

"The PMC is interested in helping any retailer, or group of retailers, who wish to create and host a Rhythm Of The Heart local market development activity," Dustman continued. "This turnkey program is designed to guide one or more dealers in a local market on how to find, hire, and work with local percussion event facilitators to actually work the program. The best news for the dealer is that the facilitator's fee is paid for by the PMC."

"In designing this program and to assure its success, we knew we would have to create an all-encompassing program that outlined all the operational requirements and guidelines," Dustman said. "For all retailers and event coordinators, there is a guide that clearly identifies how to bring together multiple local drum and percussion retailers, teachers, players, artists, and educators to reach a large audience and create interest in playing a percussion instrument. By combining all local market interested parties, everyone wins when more people are interested in being a player."

PMC President Kevin Kearns added, "Dealers are busy running their stores. We knew that we needed to provide comprehensive marketing materials to help the local dealer groups and facilitators get the message out to broad audiences. Karl and his team have already produced full color "DRUMMERS WANTED" posters with blank imprint areas for specific local event date, time, and location information. A free 8-page booklet, *The Beginning Drummer,* has also been created. This booklet instructs the beginner on how to hold drumsticks, correct stroke movements, and simple rhythmic patterns. These starter booklets are intended for all age groups attending a Rhythm Of The Heart event, thus not only putting drumsticks in their hands for the very first time but showing them what to do with them."

Several events are planned for the remainder of this year and for 2002. The PMC is actively seeking other suitable hosting retailers and event facilitators to plan and implement Rhythm Of The Heart events. Requests for market development funding and support will be on a first-come-first serve basis, interested parties are urged to make inquiries as soon as possible.

To inquire about hosting a Rhythm Of The Heart event or for complete details on any PMC program, contact the PMC Headquarters office at: P.O. Box 33252 Cleveland, Ohio 44133, tel: 440.582.7006, fax: 440.230.1346, or e-mail: kbdustman@aol.com.

The PMC was evolving as the voice of the percussion industry and was sanctioned with the responsibility of trying to build better relations and compatibility with the Percussive Arts Society. This led to a rebirth of the PAS SMAC (Sustaining Members Advisory Council) to bring a voice and percussion industry representation to PAS through each of the on-going PAS Executive Directors, Randy Eyles, Michael Kenyon, Jeff Hartsough, and, currently, Joshua Simonds. The PMC became a rather politically charged voice in rebuilding the communications and bringing the industry and education efforts of PMC and PAS together. This alliance is crucial to the future viability of both the percussion industry and percussion education. This relationship strangthens and grows with each new executive director coming to the new Percussive Arts Society. I firmly believe this relationship between the two organizations will improve even further over the years to come.

The years moved forwards quickly with some PMC members leaving, some joining. There were always those consistent members who understood the importance of growing the market. If the PMC would not have taken the lead in this mission and purpose, no one would have. The programs, events and campaigns were always consistent in bringing attention to the enjoyment and fun in playing a percussion musical instrument. The mission is dedicated to creating new players and more customers for all the products and services through every music store, drum shop and private teaching studio.

Part of the mission was to unite the students, teachers, parents and percussion industry in supporting *new* customer percussion retailing on a national basis. Some PMC programs were more successful than others, but that is part of the learning curve and everything the PMC did built upon the previous successes and achievements.

A TRIP THROUGH THE PMC'S PAST, using the rear-view mirror...

Once I got through the first year of learning about the organization, working with and completing the NAMM Grant applications and required reports, I jumped into the many different priorities that the members and PMC Board envisioned for the future. The Rhythm of the Heart program was launched and we moved forwards with other initiatives.

HOW TO SERIES, from drum sets, cymbals and drum sticks....

Early on we had a Board that addressed their recommendations and needs for further discussion and exploration with the PMC membership. Out of those discussions the consensus was that a HOW TO PURCHASE series of neutral brochures or pamphlets should be created for mass distribution through percussion retailers and the new forthcoming website. Pat Brown from ProMark assumed responsibility for the Drum Sticks piece, Scott Donnell from Drum Workshop volunteered for the drum set portion and John De Christopher from Zildjian handled the cymbal selection piece. Included were various reference connections including the various PMC members that had products associated with the topic/product being written about. Thus each member got added visibility and support through these educational pieces.

I recruited the creative and graphic talents of previous Washburn Guitar Art Department designer Phil Carlson to handle the layout, graphics and creating camera-ready art for printing and publication.

FEMALE DRUM MARKET Hit Like A Girl, Drumming Is For Everyone

Concentration on growing the female drum market became a priority as market analysis demographics indicated that percussion retailers were missing fifty-percent of the drum market by ignoring the existing and potential female drummers. Most importantly, the entire market seemed to be alienating prospective new female customers of those young girls who wanted to learn and play drums but felt pushed away as, "drums are for guys". The 2002 International Drum Month campaign centered around this initiative with the trademark creation of Hit Like A Girl.

This created a frenzy of interest in various articles and pieces geared to helping the retailer develop this new market,... educating their sales people and realizing that most females wanted to be treated like "guy drummers" and not spoken down to. This was a very successful statement coming from the PMC and it seemed like the entire industry stood up and took notice. Eventually the PMC would sell the trademark for Hit Like a Girl to the female drummer contest by the same name. However, the female movement would surface again in the near future.

With the release and success of NAMM's Sesame Street Music Works project in 2002, the PMC created the Mommy & Me Early Childhood Music Program for pre-school children and their parents. The drum and drumming oriented initiaitive was supported with an assortment of printed and electronic materials that could be used by music retailers to promote the development benefits of drumming to pre-school children,...and their parents. Program co-creator, Jennifer Ritz from Latin Percussion had the goal of helping music retailers grow their markets with a most natural and accessible of all musical instruments; drums. The active music learning enviroment builds upon hands-on playing, learning and early positive experience with various percussion instruments. Available program components included: Program Guide and Instrument Selector, Take home Activity Sheet, and Certificate of Achievement.

Program creation that could bring together the educational community to local percussion retailers began within budget and time commitments. The early days of the PMC created programs, rolled them out for implementation and then evaluated the success and impact they had on creating more new players, drummers and customers for the local percussion retailer. Full page advertisements brought industry-wide awareness to the market development. Some retailers saw and experienced the educational value of using and implementing the various initiatives the PMC was creating, usually with financial support and funding from NAMM. Time would illustrate that the market needs to grow by creating more new players and drummers, as well as those just interested in percussion. As the percussion industry's official non-profit trade association, it was the organization's responsibility to make this happen through the support and resources of its members.

As programs evolved, more and different audiences and markets were being addressed. The media continued its support through full page advertisements with broader connectivity and diversification now included a re-emphasis of the female drum market and new programs; Percussion in the Schools and supporting Community Outreach Drum Circles.

The PMC branded all of this under the "Drumming Up Business" headline in hopes that all the different "program flavors" would attract the interest and implementation of the programs for the retailer, schools and recreation center venues.

The PLAYDRUMS initiative had two launching pads that evolved over time. Initially, Playdrums provided two separate "First free drum lesson" applications, one for drums set and the other for hand-drumming instruments like congas, bongos djembe etc. Percussion Retailers could download the complete program components free of charge from the PMC website or receive complimentary CD's with all program materials. The second phase expanded the concepts under "Community Outreach Engagement" a new focal point word in the music industry vocabulary. Basic program parameters were designed for retailers, festivals and recreation centers to host free drum lesson destinations. This expanded to providing a template for having a free drum lesson element constructed and offered during the various Percussive Arts Society DAYS OF PERCUSSION events that were growing in size, popularity and almost every state had a PAS chapter by now.

Roots Of Rhythm

Roots of Rhythm authored by Dr. Craig Woodson became one of the PMC's most sought after and promoted programs through the tireless efforts of Dr. Woodson. A multi-culture, cross-curricular integrated arts and academics program for primarily the 5th through 8th graders, classroom teachers and non-music teachers. The complete program offered fifteen separate chapters focused on unique cultures, history, geography and a suitable percussion instrument from around the world. The impact of this program over the ten years of its operation touched and impacted thousands of teachers and tens-of-thousands of students that received their very first introduction to drums and drumming, through Roots of Rhythm. This program continues today under the personal ownership and direction of Dr. Craig Woodson.

Developmental Drumming

Developmental Drumming expanded the childhood development program target further beyond Mommy & Me with a series of musical games and drumming activities for preschoolers, parents and caregivers. Further development of the program provided part-two targeted to the 5-7 year old market with the inclusion of drumming basics and World Drumming.

Girls Just Wanna Have Drums

Bentley Hall Public Relations became the official agency of record for the PMC in 2007. The emphasis on the female market received additional concentration under the careful guidance of Antoinette Follett and Honor Stockley handling the PMC account. The female drum market issue expanded with a whole new series of full page color ads and a color poster with twelve prominent female drummers supporting the cause and mission. The poster was an instant success and placed in popular demand when used and handed-out selectively at the various Percussion in the Schools events. Fact: 51% of the musicians in the US are female, roughly 44 million people. Of those 44 million people, 11 million are drummers.

Percussion In The Schools

Considered one of the PMC's most successful flagship programs, this grew out of the original BE A PLAYER program created and administered by long time PMC Board Member, Lloyd McCausland of Remo. Early on the PMC recognized that the school audiences were the most accessible to creative learning experiences by bringing percussion education into the classroom. Lloyd sought out qualified program facilitators that had contacts with various school districts and could get themselves booked for in-school hands-on percussion learning and playing experiences. I felt this program was still viable, needing expansion and a new name for the program. We started re-contacting and connecting with the past program facilitators to determine who is still interested and available from the original facilitator roster,while constantly seeking to add new and exciting program facilitators in all parts of the country that could present in-school general assemblies, in-classroom special events and bring percussion-playing to a whole new set of audience participants. Today, this remains a vibrant and accessible in-school program, with over twenty to thirty events per year, impacting twenty-thousand or more students annually.

Atlanta Percussion Trio; Karen Hunt, Scott Douglas, John Lawless

Hands on With Zig (Zig Wajler)

Dancing Drum, Steve Campbell & Lindsay Rust

Bob Bloom, Drumming About You

MARIA FLURRY …Sticks and Tones

Hannah Ford Welton

Matrix Percussion Trio Consisting of Joe Smyth, Todd London, Scot Corey

INDUSTRY SUPPORT

Percussion in the Schools receives tremendous support from the members and NAMM, providing educational support in the way of free drum sticks, beginner instruction books, DVDs and related information. An integral part of the message and connection is the NAMM Foundation materials connecting with parents, providing huge amounts of “Why Learn to Play Music” brochure to all audiences.

The PMC and NAMM create the spark to bring in new players, connecting the excitement and encouragement to the local music retailer to build the relationship and make a drum customer for life.

GOT STICKS? SELL DRUM STUFF? …
INTERNATIONAL DRUM MONTH unites entire percussion industry

International Drum Month remains one of the PMC's flagship programs from the very beginning of the organization in 1995. Creating separate TRADE and CONSUMER full page advertisements brought even greater attention to the annual public awareness campaign. In 2009 the bar was raised, creating a consumer response coupon for their first free pair of drum sticks and beginner instruction book, all supplied by the appropriate PMC members. Consumers had to get the coupon validated by the local music store or drum shop, allowing the retailer to harvest the names and e-mail addresses of the consumers that are participating in the free offering.

Hundreds of PMC "Care Packages" were mailed out to the consumers seeking to get started drumming with this "free stuff" campaign. The PMC was creating more new players, one drum and coupon,…at a time.

As the success of the International Drum Month grows from an annual "public awareness campaign", it makes a connection to the public and the percussion retailer. From,… HIT IT LIKE YOU MEAN IT,..evolves to ROADIE FOR A DAY contests…

2014
"Roadie" Launch

2015
Shannon Larkin

2016
Rich Redmond

2017
Matt Greiner

2018
Rick Allen

2019 Cindy Blackman-Santana

VANS WARPED TOUR summer First Free Drum Lesson Tents…on tour

Board of Advisor Billy Cuthrell opened the door of opportunity by introducing the PMC to the market development potentials of having the PMC 'First Free Drum Lessons" tents participate in the annual Vans Warped Tour summer tours. By providing this educational connection to local percussion retailers to host the Lesson Labs, the PMC brought thousands of new customers into the hands of percussion retailers that hosted and conducted these Lesson Labs in strategic cities of the Vans Warps Tour summer music festivals.

The integration of both electronic and acoustic drum sets in these lesson labs allowed multiple lessons to take place at the same time, it also allowed for better teacher-student interaction, hearing the rhythms and verbal instruction at the same time.

PMC Members provided swag, winning door prizes for consumer sign-up drawings and the retailer built a whole new contact base for follow-up and invitations for coming into the store to learn more while signing up for beginner drum lessons. Interesting that over fifty percent of the first-free-drum lessons were given to young girls….wanting to learn and play drums. Every PMC Vans Warped Tour city location provided 100 or more first free drum lessons per location. Six consecutive years of this PMC Vans collaboration created thousands of new players until the Vans Warped Tour management ended the events at the completion of their 25th Anniversary tour in 2017. Over the six years of collaboration, approximately five thousand individual first free five-minute drum lessons were given to the first-drumming experience tent guests.

DRUMS ACROSS AMERICA

2013 built upon the success of the Vans Warped Tour first-free drum lesson template. While the Vans collaboration lasted through the summer months, retailers could use the same PMC FREE DRUM LESSONS HERE TENTS…throughout the year to host their own regional events and promotions. The campaign became popular with those percussion retailers immersed in percussion education and equipped with active growing in-store private lesson practices. The PMC provided the portable highly decorated Lesson Lab Tents, free of charge for the dealer's event, further supported by complimentary drum sticks, educational instruction books, DVD's CD's and brand swag from PMC Members. Those retailers who invest the time and effort in conducting these events learned the success of creating new players, students and relationships.

I.R.C Music Indianapolis, during a PASIC convention

DRUM SET IN THE CLASSROOM

From the successes of the Roots of Rhythm program created by Dr. Craig Woodson, the membership drove the creation of this new program launched in 2016. The consensus was focused on creating more drum set players connected through the previous success of the in-school applications. In addition, the program for teachers and students participating in this curriculum would be geared towards developing the "everyone with a heartbeat is a drummer, they just don't know it until they sit behind a drum set". The feeling is that everyone wants to be a "rock star" and this grass roots program made everyone a drummer from the very beginning.

The program is one of the most successful due to the integration of both acoustic and electronic kits that illustrate the simple integration of drum set instruction into the classroom environment. The fact that the teachers (both music and non-music) want to "play drums" ignites the interest of the students and even encompasses recruitment of parents. At the same time, the Percussion Industry recognized the need for junior-size drums sets with significant sturdy quality, not toys. The market introduced a number of brands and models of smaller drum sets that 3rd graders could sit behind and feel comfortable learning and playing on. (Seems like we've had this discussion before with the five different sizes of Amada Classical Guitars through Geneva International)

MEDIA SUPPORT AND CONNECTION

The relationship the PMC has with the music industry media is essential to the success of the programs and connection with the music retailers throughout the country. Over the years the PMC has embraced those relations with all the magazines in electronic and print formats. The PMC would NOT be as successful if it were not for the support of, **The Music Trades, Music Inc, Musical Merchandise Review, Music and Sound Retailer, Modern Drummer, Drum Business and DRUM!.**

The efforts and leadership of the organization seemed to be winning support and visibility for the PMC within all of the trade publications. More and more editorial coverage, interviews and complimentary advertisements solidified the PMC with the media and all the trade publications. It also helped that many of the PMC board leaders were also the same individuals placing paid advertising insertions with each magazine.

The PMC received unprecedented support from the NAMM Foundation with annual grant approvals for a variety of market development initiatives, campaigns, and programs- all targeting the percussion retailer's connection with schools, teachers, parents and the percussion industry. The success of the PMC was evident in that it was the only trade association within the entire music products industry that ever received 18 years of uninterrupted financial support from the NAMM organization. That was not only because of my efforts, but also because the executive committee that was working with me within the organization.

I consistently tried to surround myself with those industry leaders that thoroughly understood the need for, and the mission of, the PMC. Everyone took their "brand-employer hat" off and concentrated on what was best for the industry and growing the demand for all percussion products. To this day I cannot thank the Executive Committee and Advisory Board enough for their support.

Special Guest Speaker Governor Mike Huckabee at the January 2014 PMC Industry-wide Members Meeting. Karl introduces Governor Huckabee to the enthusiastic audience of percussion retailers, industry, media and NAMM convention attendees.

A Memorable Moment:

The 2014 annual PMC Membership meeting in Anaheim, California was one of my favorite events with unprecedented planning and preparations. I was successful in working through NAMM to host Gov. Mike Huckabee as a featured guest speaker at the meeting. Huckabee had made numerous guest appearances at previous NAMM shows as a true music education advocate. After months of trying to confirm his availability to attend and speak at the meeting, we accomplished this with a tremendous attendance for his special presentation. The Executive Committee wanted to thank the Governor, by presenting a special PMC appreciation plaque and a very special Yamaha Bass guitar, arranged by Yamaha's Dave Jewell.

Huckabee's commentary to the audience was targeted to the importance of every child having the opportunity to learn and play music and that it is essential to every young person's educational experience which must include Music and the Arts. An avid musician himself, he recalled the years of playing he did growing up when he thought of himself as "wanting to be the fifth Beatle".

His gracious music advocacy message was encouraging to everyone in the room who heard him speak about music, life, and making a difference in the world.

PMC Executive Committee Member presentations to Governor Mike Huckabee: Stacey M. Clark with a thank-you presentation plaque, and Dave Jewell (far right) gave the Governor a Limited Edition Yamaha five string bass guitar.

Special Guest Speaker Governor Mike Huckabee at the January 2014 PMC Industry-wide Members Meeting. L to R, front: Dr. Craig Woodson, Brian LaRue, Stacey M. Clark, Governor Huckabee, Billy Cuthrell, Dave Jewell, Karl Dustman.
L to R, back: Brad Smith, Phil Hood

The visibility and opportunity the PMC provided me was essential to opening doors within the industry in general. Over the years I worked increasingly closer with the NAMM organization which also opened the door for my guest speaking presentation to the various audiences of the College Music Society.

The College Music Society (CMS) focused on providing career opportunities and insights in the music products industry. As this organization became more closely aligned with the NAMM Foundation, I worked more closely with both organizations. I was invited to provide multiple presentations during the January NAMM conventions, then became a guest speaker/presenter at the International Annual CMS convention in Santa Fe, New Mexico. My presentation, "Exploring Your Potential for a Career in the Music Products Industry" received positive recognition and led to invitations to speak and lecture at the Percussive Arts Society International Convention, The Chicago Drum Show, the University of Minnesota and Valparaiso University. While I was honored to be invited and in many cases receiving an honorarium, I was thrilled to see the interest in the music products industry from so many young people seeking careers in some form of music. Many of the young students I encountered were only prepared and supported for careers as a performance major or a teacher career path. I presented the thought of the *third* consideration, building a career track in the industry side of music making.

There were times when the years flew by at an astounding rate and there were other times where a certain stagnation seemed to creep in and it was time to ignite new programs and campaigns to re-build momentum and dedication in the mission of the organization. By the time the PMC approached the 25th anniversary of the organization in 2020, I had already been thinking about and working on the significance and recognition of this PMC milestone achievement for two years in advance. I had been regularly reminding the executive committee during each January's closed committee meeting of the forthcoming observance of the 25th Anniversary in 2020 and the need to make this a significant year of the industry's awareness about the PMC and its accomplishments over the past twenty-five years.

The executive committee created a tremendous year of noteworthy events, activities and a commemorative product drawing giveaway. There were consumer drawings for twelve free drum lessons at a percussion retailer of your choice, an online "Lesson with a Master", and 18 different commemorative percussion products each receiving the special limited edition PMC 25th Anniversary Commemorative badge affixed to the product. This took place during the entire year of 2020.

My decision to step down from the Percussion Marketing Council was implemented over a year in advance. The Executive Committee began their search for a replacement at the beginning of 2020 knowing this change would be taking place after 19 years of the organization's leadership which would end in January of 2021. My personal mission was accomplished, seeing and directing the organization through the successful completion of the 25th Anniversary year of 2020. I continue to work with my successor Antoinette Follett who took over at the beginning of 2021 and brings an amazing fresh direction and leadership to the PMC..

A Life-Changing Experience:

The Percussion Marketing Council made it possible for me to go to places and meet people I would have never dreamed of getting to work with within the music products industry. I have enjoyed the friendship and comradery of business professionals at all levels and spectrums of the industry. I have met and dealt with fantastic musicians and players, government leaders, industry icons, and personalities from all corners of the globe. The common thread that connected everyone and everything was a love for music and all the wonderful instruments and products that help the world enjoy and perform music.

Stepping down from the PMC role meant that Dustman & Associates would be able to pursue and enter into other marketing consulting contracts within the percussion industry or with other music product organizations. It also allowed me more time for local professional performance, more Mantovani Orchestra international concert tours and further consulting client diversification in an ever-changing business world.

Receiving a congratulatory engraved "thank you" cymbal from the Executive Officers of the Percussion Marketing Council; Dave Jewell, Stacey M. Clark, Jennifer Paisley and Brad Smith.

January 28, 2021.

Chapter 9

CODA... The Musical Momentum Continues Today and Tomorrow

Percussion is all about qualification and personality. The business of music has a diverse spectrum of requirements both in musical skills and understanding, but even more so a personal operating method that presents professionalism and self confidence in your abilities. Up to this point you have read about my career path through choices, opportunities and necessities that have all required tremendous adapting to circumstances and surroundings.

As time passes and the years move forwards I approached the new emerging twenty-first century with an inner renaissance of determination. Moving into the "fourth decade" at fifty-one years of age, I was able to create a mixture of many different projects and revenue-producing activities that became blended into one very busy schedule. The surprises beyond my imagination were about to begin. The passion for percussion and music would continue through every obstacle and challenge.

As mentioned, by now I had stopped the weekly commuting to Chicago and could now develop and return to regular musical performance in both orchestral percussion as well as my roots in performing on drums and vibes. This was a breath of fresh personal development, as I had let the performance element and proficiency slip while I concentrated on creating a career and leaving the "jobs" behind. I was also blessed with the ability to be selective in what clients and projects I wanted to take on and with whom. The Results Plus Professional Development client was progressing nicely, I was getting involved with the Cleveland Federation of Musicians locally, I was deeply involved in the Percussion Marketing Council, and I was ready for creating a completely new business that was going to take vast amounts of time, money, effort and all the expertise I had gathered over the many years in the music products industry.

Going Back to Church,...to make music

Even though I had been living in the Cleveland area since 1993, I had not had the time or opportunity to really create a momentum or contact list for becoming a working contracted musician. My percussion expertise as a musician was completely unknown within the market and I had to start from scratch by developing and promoting myself as a qualified professional musician. This takes time, vast amounts of time and determination in bringing your musical performance skills to the attention of those you want to work with and for.

The Musical Director of the Northcoast Brass Ensemble, Mike McGreen, was looking for an alternative timpanist to perform with the ensemble in all the various Cleveland area church performances they were contracted for. Church services, weddings, funerals, official installations, centennial ceremonies, and related events were all part of the timpani performance opportunities. In many instances printed music timpani parts did *not* exist for most of the music being performed. It was my job to create the timpani part that complimented the brass ensemble and/or vocalist/choir requirement. Timpani create the "musical drama" in church music and those who hear and feel it never want to perform without it.

The Northcoast Brass played together for years and became an in-demand group throughout the region. Soon other churches were learning of my timpani and orchestral percussion abilities and this escalated into additional engagements for my services. What helped from the beginning was the fact that I had a set of three portable fiberglass timpani. While there are a lot of percussionists that can play timpani, very few own or have transportation to bring their own timpani. These were reasonably lightweight and compact, so I could fit the complete set into a standard sedan. The drums could be moved in and out of small spaces and choir lofts and they were easy to tune and keep in tune. Properly maintained, this set of three kettles launched my entry into the church music making spectrum. This was a very civilized way to get back into organized professional timpani playing.

The success in the church community warranted serious consideration of, and investment in, a complete set of four Ludwig balanced action Professional Series timpani. I was successful in acquiring a slightly used set of timpani from Paul Yancich who took a set of four timpani in on trade from the The Cleveland Orchestra, Youth Orchestra. But now the problem was storing the timpani in a safe and accessible location when they were not being moved around in a rented U-Haul cargo van. Royal Redeemer Lutheran Church has one of the most widely known and respected music ministries in the area. I contacted the church's Music Director, Lee Zacharias, about the possibility of storing the set of four timpani somewhere in the church for a modest fee or donation to the church music ministry. His rent-free offer for storage was predicated upon me playing timpani and percussion for his forthcoming "God With Us" music cantata. I Agreed to this arrangement as an immediate but short-term solution for having safe and accessible storage of my new Ludwig Timpani. This quickly escalated into providing glockenspiel, chimes, and xylophone for the various church productions Zacharias was directing-conducting and hosting within this bustling Lutheran church. I became one of his "disciples in music" and as they say the rest is history. I remain close friends with Lee Zacharias to this day and he remains the only church music ministry that I provide occasional pro bono professional performance services.

The years passed with many performances through the calendar year and very hectic Christmas and Easter seasons. While the earnings were respectable, performing strictly church music was not my real ambition.

The end result of these church connections was the need and decision to acquire a complete percussion section instrument inventory that I use today in my contracted performances. I also am becoming one of the very few area professional percussionists who can bring an entire backline section of orchestral percussion instruments into any Northeast Ohio venue on a rental contract. Even today, performing timpani in church music remains a significant revenue producing activity built on years of relationships with all the prominent music directors. More constructive marketing, which opened more and more doors of performance opportunity. It's all about relationships.

Returning to Music Retail....... Why?

Early in the 2000, I knew Fred Marrick was looking to sell his longstanding Custom Music operation headquartered in a Detroit suburb. I had known Fred throughout the years primarily because of the KORI Mallet Instruments made in Japan which he was exclusively importing and marketing in the United States. Kori was an excellent Japanese product that was not reaching anywhere near its potential for market development. Despite my efforts to secure Custom Music and KORI as a client, Fred would not engage my marketing services. As I learned of his intentions for selling out, I crafted a proposal through my attorney to purchase the KORI distribution and inventory from him for a combination of cash and time-payments. This dialog went on for months without success. My marketing strategy was to have KORI mallet instruments as the centerpiece for a separate company that could be surrounded by other orchestral percussion products and brands.

At the same time, Paul Yancich had re-acquired the Clevelander Timpani product back from Richard Berger and the Grover-Trophy organization whom he had sold it to in the late 90's. Paul was now back in the timpani-building business, much against his long term desire to be out of the music product business and concentrate his complete efforts on the Cleveland Orchestra performance and touring along with teaching at the Cleveland Institute of Music. In continuing friendship and discussion, we both had a need for a professional outlet for our products and expertise. Paul's proposal for creating a by-appointment-only orchestral percussion showroom ignited a unique collaboration that provided solutions and a never-ending opportunity for product and brand expansion. Combining Paul's international recognition as a professional Principle Timpanist with one of the top five orchestras in the world, along with my extensive music products industry experience, seemed like a logical blending of two very different people and qualifications for creating a profitable small business.

PROFESSIONAL PERCUSSION PRODUCTS
A DIVISION OF DUSTMAN & ASSOCIATES

The business model was cast, and the official Professional Percussion Products opening celebration took place on April 1, 2003. Paul was influential in securing various brands of top quality-high-end orchestral percussion instruments and accessories for the showroom to stock and sell. Some product lines were opened as experimental consignment placements, others required outright purchased inventory. Because of my industry reputation I was able to secure every brand from every manufacturer we needed on "open account-net 30 day terms". This was unheard of for new entities starting out. The only exception to this start-up was Marimba One. We needed the brand and product to attract a serious conservatory-minded student and teacher. I purchased two five-octave instruments from Marimba One and mailed the company twenty thousand dollars up front. There was no turning back.

Paul's Clevelander Timpani, renamed Ohio Timpani, combined with Marimba One and Ludwig-Musser, became the three anchors of the new startup named Professional Percussion Products which was set up in a 1300 square-foot retail space.

The focus for this startup was attracting the 350 area-wide percussion majors to make appointments to vist the showroom to test, hear, play, and select the finest orchestral percussion products and brands available.

Jack Van Geem (center) with students at first showroom location 2003

Principle Percussionist of the San Francisco Symphony Jack Van Geem was in Cleveland for a guest performance with the Symphony when we hosted him for a Saturday afternoon Marimba One clinic, attended by all the area high school and college level percussion students. This was a huge success with standing room only for the two-hour presentation. We sold two Marimba One instruments as a result of this Jack Van Geem guest clinic presentation in the showroom. The word of mouth was working and we were making progress in attracting more new customers and students.

The showroom display and inventory led to more visitors and more demand for unusual products which required more time, money, and space. We always had area professional players and influential instructors stopping by.

Fernando Meza from the University of Minnesota and the Minnesota Orchestra created his own branded voiced set of signature marimba mallets. We sold these all over the world. Fernando remains a dear friend and supporter of Professional Percussion Products and his contribution to a quote on the back cover of this book is an appreciated compliment.

Peter Kogan, Principle Timpani with the Minnesota Orchestra, has been a longtime friend and partner in bringing his very special baroque style Klassischewienerpauken Timpani to the showroom in 2012. These unique instruments represent the finest baroque timpani available as re-creations of the original drums, updated and designed by Peter.

The demands of the business required attending and exhibiting at the annual Percussive Arts Society Conferences in Louisville, Nashville, and Indianapolis. This required a tremendous investment in exhibit space and the related fixed costs of hotel, food, and transportation.

4-page brochures were created. These were included with each order shipment, given to each visitor to the showroom, and as handouts at the various events that we would exhibit at.

Space in the original location was becoming too small. With the need to increase space and warehouse operations, the time to move-on had arrived. The new location provided more office and display space for hosting larger student groups at the showroom and in the various sound rooms. We then had separate testing rooms and areas, for timpani, orchestral cymbals, snare drums and all the Epstein, Vaughncraft, Equilibrium, Grover Pro and Treeworks accessories.

The commitment of time and money to selectively participate at various high visibility events included the Ohio State Chapter of the Percussive Arts Society at Youngstown State University, hosted by Dr. Glen Shaft. Then it was on to the Ohio Music Educators Association in downtown Cleveland. The need became clear to regularly participate in the Percussive Arts Society International conventions. This led to a Clevelander orchestral snare drum clinic presentation by Jack Bell, who had just retired from the Atlanta Symphony Orchestra.

Jack Bell, Atlanta Symphony Orchestra

Paul Yancich, Karl Dustman, Mark Yancich at exhibit

First PASIC exhibit, Louisville, Kentucky 2003

Most recent PASIC exhibit, Indianapolis, Indiana

As Professional Percussion Products now approaches its twentieth year anniversary, we have learned to adapt and adjust to the ever-changing demands of the customer base, the methods of marketing our products and services, and dealing with Internet competition. Today the business flourishes because of the emphasis on proprietary products that can be exclusively distributed or made to our exact specifications. The business remains the dominant resource for all imported Irish Super Kalfo calfskin timpani, snare, and bass drum skins. Our custom-made steel flesh hoops are fabricated here in Cleveland, and we offer professional calfskin head mounting services. Our own manufacturing of the official Dave Herbert Timpani Warm-Up Practice Pad since 2016 continues to grow in demand as we ship these around the world to timpanists of all ages, abilities, and performance platforms. We never stop learning, growing, or examining how we can be different from, and better than, everyone else.

(L-R) David Murphy, Principal Timpani of The Hour Of Power Orchestra, with Karl

During the Anaheim NAMM conventions, I would attend Sunday morning church services at the Crystal Cathedral in Garden Grove, just down the street from the Anaheim Convention Center. The regular Sunday services included a full scale 40-50 piece orchestra and 60+ member choir.

The music was breathtaking and something I looked forward to every year during the January NAMM convention. As time went on I introduced myself to the percussion section while carefully making them all aware of the Professional Percussion Products business and the orchestral percussion specialty we provided. While they had never heard of the showroom, they immediately became interested in the products and services we provided on a global basis. Timpanist David Murphy started ordering timpani sticks, and we began meeting after the service to talk shop. I arranged a complimentary NAMM Guest badge for him to attend the convention. Learning that I was a professional player he started inviting me to perform with the orchestra if I could arrive by 6:30 am for the closed rehearsal under then-conductor, Johnny Carl. I immediately accepted the kind invitation hoping I would receive the timpani parts for the entire one-hour program in advance. That did not happen. That year's NAMM convention was an experience. By the second day of the convention I had come down with the flu and was running a 102 temperature. There was no backing out on the planned Sunday performance, as Murphy had already advised the conductor, the other percussionists, and Reverend Schuller that I would be "sitting in on timpani" for that Sunday's live television broadcast. I was introduced as a musical guest from Rev Schuller's pulpit and featured on the huge in-church video screen. I prayed for divine intervention that I would not become even more ill during the rehearsal or broadcast performance. All went well with the performance; I survived without any musical or medical mishaps. David Murphy remains a dear friend and fellow musician to this day. While the Crystal Cathedral no longer exists, the memory of that outstanding professional orchestra and choir lives on in my memory forever.

The Hour of Power Orchestra and Choir, Johnny Carl, Musical Director, Karl as Guest Timpanist (far left)

Sharing people, business, and musicmaking skills with American Federation of Musicians

I started attending the various Cleveland Federation of Musicians annual Christmas parties, introducing myself to fellow members and the executive committee of the Local 4. Leonard DiCosimo still serves as President and was most gracious in welcoming me to their events, and inviting my participation in local musicmaking activities. He also became aware of the orchestral percussion showroom through our discussions about the availability of limited Percussion Marketing Council funds for the Percussion In The Schools program. My work at networking was neverending and I tried to get my name around in both union and non-union performance opportunities. Gradually this started paying off using a technique of sending congratulatory letters of appreciation to the conductors and executive directors for all the various concerts and performances I would attend. While conveying my "bravo" comments for the performance, I would also attach some introductory materials about my percussion skills and qualifications to compliment their percussion needs for the future. It's all about relationships.

Classics Restaurant in the Intercontinental Hotel was Cleveland's only Five Diamond restaurant in the entire city. I started going there for special family occasions and celebrations because of the elegant formal dining room and the featured live music. This wonderful music usually consisted of two extremely talented female violinists and an equally gifted pianist, Michael Leamon. They performed everything from classical to Broadway and everything from the Great American Song Book. I would request a table as close as possible to, or in front of, the musicians to see, hear, and experience everything. Michael would consistently hear my finger-drumming along on the table or playing ride cymbal parts or Latin shaker rhythms with his playing. Eventually we discussed having me playing "very soft" drums with him for two or three nights a week. A regular trio of piano, bass, and drums formed from this friendship and love for playing beautiful music in tuxedos for a very well established affluent dining room clientele. While we were not allowed to place a "tip glass" on top of the piano, the quiet monetary appreciation from the dinner guests was always beyond the norm. Unfortunately, the restaurant closed in 2006 and there will never be a formal Five Diamond restaurant in Cleveland again, offering this type of "black-tie music".

Frank Jacobs of the Summit Choral Society in Akron, Ohio, assembled a wonderful assortment of various themed concerts during the year, all performed in beautiful auditoriums, concert halls, or churches. Spectacular choral programming would include guest singers, dancers and various instrumentalists and full-scale orchestras. Upon receiving my "bravo complimentary letter" (that was accompanied by my professional musician introductory packet) after a Halloween concert, I got a call of inquiry about playing drums for the upcoming St. Patrick's Day concert. Extremely talented musicians, all familiar with traditional Irish music and the blazing tempos, were assembled. I learned the music and the meters, "by fire", bringing rock-solid rhythm to the group who were all seeking to rush even faster. I was included in almost every production until Jacobs' retirement from owning and running this wonderful choral performance group.

The drumming "actors" of the Crucible Production

The "Crucible" (By Arthur Miller) stage production was being prepared for professional presentation in one of the Cleveland's Playhouse Square theater district renovated theaters. The Director called for "traditional rope drummers" with drums depicting suitable rhythms and drums from the 1692 era. The "Rentals" tab on the showroom's website brought a call from the production manager seeking assistance with authentic rope drums that could be rented. In addition, he needed assistance with teaching the professional actors how to play whatever suitable rhythms would be appropriate for the specific scenes within the theatrical play. I had four Ludwig 16"x16" rope drums I purchased as "cast-offs" from the 1976 Ludwig Bicentennial drum production. These were perfect when equipped with multi-angle carry bars and white slings. I created the eight different rhythms that would support the characterization of the various scenes and taught the four drummer/actors how to hold the sticks and play the drums. I taught the rhythm by ear based on my demonstration of the rhythms. This relationship has expanded to numerous opportunities to provide rental instruments to the many different theatrical productions coming through Cleveland without timpani, chimes or whatever.

The Cleveland Federation of Musicians had Music Fund dollars available to invest in music educational activities and events throughout the Cleveland public and private schools. President DiCosimo knew of my vast assortment of percussion instruments and accessories in my personal collection. He also knew and recognized my passion for percussion and sharing this with young people. The PMC also had a small amount to co-fund some Percussion In The Schools presentations, all directed towards the mission of creating more interest in drums and drumming.

I was regularly contracted to bring in a large assortment of percussion instruments while also scripting a suitable educational program that would create interactive hands-on playing while teaching the students about the different drums and adapting this to various recorded popular tunes that the young students would already know. This expanded into multiple presentations throughout the school year in multiple locations. There is no substitute for seeing young students get excited about playing drums. This professional connection with the Cleveland Federation has opened doors of opportunity, securing a position on the Local 4 Music Fund Board and the foundation for many new friendships and partnerships for the long term future.

MANTOVANI ORCHESTRA
"The World's Most Elegant Pops Orchestra"

The invitation to go on an international concert performance tour through China for six weeks was the "invitation of a lifetime". Throughout my upbringing I was always listening to Mantovani recordings. They were played in our family home in my childhood. This was quite unusual for a young drummer growing up in the era of The Beatles, the British Invasion, and such. I have never known or felt such musical appreciation until I started rehearsing the three huge books of percussion parts being e-mailed to me in advance of the tour. I remain in awe of the orchestrations, the kindness of the musicians, and the overwhelming response from the audiences we experienced touring through China.

The five-week concert tour included eleven key performances in the most elegant and internationally recognized concert halls throughout China. Sold-out performances included Foshan, Shenzhen Concerthaus, Beijing National Opera, Xining, Lanzhou, Suzhou, Shanghai Poly Theater, Xiamen Grand Theater, Shanghai Oriental Arts Center and Guangzhou Grand Opera. The physical demands of the constant touring were challenging to everyone. We traveled by airplane and bus, and stayed in a different hotel just about every other night. The music and beautiful concert halls filled with Mantovani-adoring audiences was incredible. I have never been more musically prepared or more focused on the performance requirements for each piece of music.

Mantovani Productions President Ken Moulton and his tour and stage management team were a pleasure to work with. There is hope and anticipation of more touring in the future, despite the setback resulting from the sudden passing of orchestra conductor Charles Ellis. I stand ready to go and perform the ageless music of Mantovani at any time.

One percussionist for the three books of percussion parts and music. I was immersed, performing on an entire section of percussion instruments behind the huge orchestra. "Moving around quickly" garnered new meaning for me.

Performing "in tails" every night....

MOONLIGHT SERENADERS Big Band
Getting back into the "groove"

The amazing music of Glenn Miller, Tommy Dorsey, Benny Goodman, and Sammy Nestico takes on a whole musical experience when performed with Northeast Ohio's longest continuing performing big band in the region. With the band's record of over fifty years of performing the big band music of the 1940s and 50s, I knew I needed to be working with this band.

I loved the music, I knew the tunes by heart, and the sound of this band was beyond compare to the many other big bands I have heard over the years. I started following the band's performance schedule, showing up at many concerts and events, always saying hello to the principle players and expressing my desire to perform with the band as a full time regular member. My various letters of interest and support biographical packets were always appreciated, but there was never an opening for a drummer.

My opportunity as a drummer substitute developed with a call coming from the band manager, John Smith. I jumped at the opportunity to play with the band, even though I would be sightreading the drum parts. Knowing most of the tunes, I felt I could get through the three hour private function concert and dinner-dance without any major musical casualties. The success of this "sitting in" lead to discussions about bringing vibraphone and percussion to the band. Agreeing to write out all my own vibraphone parts derived from the piano, guitar, and lead sax/trumpet music, I embarked on a journey that will never end, just like the music that never dies.

The Moonlight Serenaders has become a part of my musical life and earnings. I use my marketing skills to develop many promotional materials and contacts for presenting and booking the band. They just don't write music like this anymore. We're always "In The Mood"!

Swing Era Big Band

Being contacted to be a substitute drummer for a couple months has never been a more rewarding and enjoyable experience. Those couple months turned into almost a year of reading some very challenging drum charts while getting my drum set skills back to where they were. The telephone call started with the leader's statement, "I have always really liked your drumming Karl". That was enough of an invitation for me to accept filling the drum chair for weekly rehearsals and scheduled performances. This relationship with the director started years ago through relationships founded on Professional Percussion Products servicing a local community band's percussion instrument needs and selling their old Musser 4.0 marimba on consignment. The music concentrates on the swing charts of Nelson Riddle, Frank Sinatra, Dean Martin, and Sammy Nesito. While the band is not getting rich or famous, the comaraderie of the instrumentalists and vocal soloists is amazing. This partnership is founded on a common love of the music and the opportunity for this middle-aged group of big band enthusiasts. I love rehearsing and performing with this band, built on musical relationships.

Karl, driving the 20 piece Big Band

Swing Era at Brother's Lounge Cleveland, Ohio

Business and Percussion do go together: Industry Relations with NAMM and PAS

In the music business, the future is built almost entirely on the present and the past. Not just in relationships, but in knowing and nurturing alliances and friendships that have mutual benefits to all involved. Early on in my career, I learned the value of professional organizations, both trade and educational, that can open doors of opportunity.

Attending industry events, supporting industry-wide campaigns, events, and promotions all bring together people of similar interests and backgrounds through a common thread of music making. Whether that connection is through musical instruments, publishing, music education, or the general population's musical awareness, everyone benefits when music becomes part of everyday life and employs creativity to reach every person who loves music.

Reconnecting at NAMM, Hannah Ford-Welton, PMC Facilitator, former drummer with Prince

Friendships go on forever, from the Ludwig Percussion Symposiums, Musser Artists, Dave Samuels and David Friedman, PASIC 2006

The NAMM Foundation opened the door of opportunity by inviting me to create and present a music industry presentation to the group of attending college-age students attending the convention, all studying music, as music business majors. Founded on my ease and confidence with public speaking through Results Plus, I built a program and following on a presentation I now market as, "Exploring Your Potential for a Career in the Music Products Industry". Based on the success of this and my direct background in marketing and sales, I was asked to create a broader presentation for all business majors. "Exploring Your Career Potentials in Sales and Marketing" was made available through my guest speaker services platform. This experience of sharing is one of the most fulfilling elements I have experienced in public speaking and business building.

The success of this topic and presentation has led to keynote addresses at NAMM Foundation events, College Music Society National Conferences, guest speaking engagements at leading colleges and universities along with invitations from the Percussive Arts Society and the Chicago Drum Show. Today there are more Music Business major curriculums than ever before, offering up-and-coming young people a *third* alternative career path, beyond the traditional performance and music education career paths.

I am positioned to be a contributor to this growing momentum as young people search for work in the music industry. I remain grateful for every guest speaker invitation I receive while realizing that everyone in the audience now knows who I am and how I can help them.

All through my career from the very first Percussive Arts Society Day of Percussion in December 1972, I have been a promoter and supporter of the Percussive Arts Society and its mission. I have intentionally sought to work closely with each PAS Executive Director over the past fifty years. It is my belief that the percussion industry cannot survive without the PAS and that PAS cannot survive without the percussion industry. Both are essential to having a demand for the products and the education on how to perform and teach with them. Having attended just about every PAS convention over the past fifty years, I realize more now than ever these alliances with all music-related organizations (like the Percussive Arts Society) can benefit every facet of the business and percussion performance world we live and work in. There was a time when a percussion student's membership in PAS was mandatory because of the educational value of the publications, news-bulletins and the annual PASIC conventions. While the "requirement" has been lifted, I encourage everyone reading this book to become a member of the Percussive Arts Society and to get involved in every element that you can learn from and contribute towards. I am honored to have served the organization for six years on the Advisory Board and continue my service to the Symphonic committee.

Post-presentation: coaching students on the industry, Anaheim, California NAMM convention

The NAMM organization (National Association of Music Merchants) has united the music products industry for more than one hundred years. From attending my very first NAMM Show in the Palmer House Hotel in Chicago as a young wanna-be musician studying percussion, I learned that NAMM *is* the music products industry. Everything and anything that goes into musical product merchandising involves the NAMM organization. Throughout my entire career I have worked closely with the NAMM organization, its various executive director leaders and dedicated staff. Every position I have held in every company, every independent client consulting contract have all involved working with NAMM as an integral part of my responsibilities.

Karl receiving the PAS recognition for serving six years on the Advisory Board, presented by Joshua Simonds, January, 2020

Over the years I have probably worked with every department and manager within NAMM on one project or another. The importance of relations and doing what you say you're going to do are essential in working with trade associations like NAMM and PAS. My

NAMM Grantee Summit at NAMM HQ, representing the Percussion Marketing Council

individual reputation was at stake every time I made a decision, a commitment or a promise, representing myself, my company or my client. I have never needed to ask for "forgiveness or a second chance".

Over the years I have served NAMM on their Recreational Music Committee, attended three separate NAMM FLY-INS marching on Washington DC for legislative Music Education Advocacy, and represented the Percussion Marketing Council at every NAMM Grantee Summit conducted at the NAMM Carlsbad, California headquarters.

Receiving a Music Industry Achievement award from NAMM during the January 2017 convention with Joe Lamond and Dan Del Fiorentino.

I continue my membership with NAMM as a voting Commercial Member through Professional Percussion Products. The umbrella we all work under in the music products industry would not be possible without the guidance and sustainability of the NAMM organization.

Percussion Marketing Council, Achieving the 25th Anniversary Celebration 2020 Goal

Nineteen years ago when I accepted the position as the organization's second executive director in 2001, I would have never dreamed that I would be leading the non-profit trade association through its 25th Anniversary year of celebration. I have met and worked with some of the finest individuals and companies in the entire music products industry. The fact that they are in the percussion category made them even that more special.

The journey through my years with the PMC has been extremely rewarding, both personally and professionally. I learned more from the people, situations and circumstances than could ever be put into words in any textbook. Remaining a neutral individual and not favoring one company, brand, or member over another was a full-time job. I believe in consensus decision making, not just for protecting myself, but always seeking membership input, guidance and direction from the Advisory Board and the Executive Committee. Directing an all-volunteer nonprofit organization is like leading a family reunion with distant relatives you have never met before.

It takes time to know the people, the personal agendas and how everyone can contribute to a common goal of growing the market for all percussion merchandise and services. This is a constant and neverending challenge and appears on the daily list of things to do.

The decision to step down from this leadership role was directly connected to the completion and achievement of a personal goal in seeing the organization through a successful 2020 25th Anniversary celebration year. 2020 was like no other year in terms of programs, campaigns and events, as well as dealing with the impact of Covid 19 through every facet of the organization. Having been through two previous years of industry-wide meltdown in 2001 and 2008-9, I was determined to see the PMC survive and thrive through the pandemic cause and effect.

The three elements for the 25th Anniversary celebration year consisted of:

- The Commemorative Product Giveaway, was supported by eighteen prominent members stepping up to make memorable product donations that were promoted throughout the year for monthly consumer drawings. Everything from snare drums, cymbals, bongos, electronic drum pads to educational book assortments were included in this unprecedented Commemorative Product Giveaway.
- Get Your Sticks Together provided for a monthly consumer winner to receive twelve free 30 minute drum lessons from their local percussion retailer, paid for by the PMC.

-Lesson With A Master brought together four internationally recognized professional drummers and teachers offering eight consumer winners the opportunity to have a one-hour on-line private lesson with the artist of their choice, paid for by the PMC.

In closing this relationship with the PMC, I am honored to have served the Percussion Industry and all the members of the Percussion Marketing Council for nineteen years. I am in debt for the opportunity to learn and grow while we all shared our passion for percussion and music making together each year.

Lesson With A Master Drummer
Rick Latham, Gordon Campbell,
Rich Redmond, David Stanoch

MY Great Expectations Can Become YOUR Expectations…..

Every person is gifted with a certain amount of creativity. However it must be exercised regularly,… every day … practicing your instrument, rehearsing a speech, designing a new self-marketing tool,.. creativity must be used in order to achieve anything.

Every new person you meet, every new situation or circumstance offers us a creative opportunity. Do not always seek the comfort zone but embrace and jump on these limited opportunities to develop your creative skills.

We all have a certain amount of ambition, we have dreams, desires and goals for what we want to accomplish and be recognized and remembered for. Take the time to define these important parts of our individual existence. Find what excites you the most and pursue it. Be constantly alert to the endless number of opportunities and possibilities around you, keeping LIFE and MUSIC open to everything that may appear on your personal radar.

A CLOSING THOUGHT…………..

Words are more important than facts. The purpose of this writing is to encourage, promote and inspire….. those who seek to understand and experience the Music Products Industry. There are no limitations where a career can take you, personally and professionally. This is a "people business" and I have been blessed with the opportunity to use and create a life-long business model that brought together every facet of music. I hope I have proven that,…"Business and Music DO go together".

Appendices

Business and Percussion *Do* Go Together

Karl Dustman

FROM THE VERY BEGINNING OF YOUR interest in music or percussion, you have come in contact with some facet of the Business of Music. Your first pair of drum sticks, practice pad, mallets or snare drum kit, all were marketed and sold through a retail music store. That person bought them from a distributor or wholesaler who bought them from a manufacturer. The cycle of how percussion products enter the American Free Enterprise system or network is not really that much different from many other consumer goods. However, musical instrument merchandise has had certain buying and selling traits that are unlike all other products.

Your experience as a musician/percussionist could very well open a career door of opportunity that you never realized could be available to you. However, as in anything else worth pursuing, the competition is fierce. In most cases, the number of positions that exist in the business are greatly outnumbered by the number of qualified people seeking them out. But before you take a *defeatist attitude,* let's look at a few basic understandings about the career opportunities in a field that could make significant changes in your life and chosen career development.

The Reasons for Considering the Music Business

On a broad scope, let us assume that you have achieved a fair amount of performance experience and completed studies in some form of higher education (2-4 years of college) and might already be working full-time or part-time utilizing those musical skills, inner talents and diligent hours of practice. You may already be teaching, at a local music store, privately in your home, or a combination of *non-musical* employment to pay the bills, and something else during the week or weekends that you love doing with music. But the next plateau of success, gratification, financial reward or use of your talent and/or education doesn't seem to be "happening," and there are no immediate prospects for improvement in the near future.

The Reasons for Considering the Music Business

On a broad scope, let us assume that you have achieved a fair amount of performance experience and completed studies in some form of higher education (2-4 years of college) and might already be working full-time or part-time utilizing those musical skills, inner talents and diligent hours of practice. You may already be teaching, at a local music store, privately in your home, or a combination of *non-musical* employment to pay the bills, and something else during the week or weekends that you love doing with music. But the next plateau of success, gratification, financial reward or use of your talent and/or education doesn't seem to be "happening," and there are no immediate prospects for improvement in the near future.

Before you *abandon* your dedicated desire to work in percussion and go into a totally different field of work or study, look into the possibility that the value of your musical performance or teaching background may have in the music business, or better yet, the percussion business. Keep in mind the competition, but you've already known what that is from your very first concert band contest, or section audition or entrance exam. It could also be that what you may lack in musical abilities, would be overshadowed by your positive *hidden business skills* or initiatives about which you never thought. You may be able to utilize more of your experience than you realize, and adapt it to a musical area closely aligned with the music business world.

Now think about all the *business people* you have met or know well that are involved in some aspect of *the industry.* Clinics you attended, artists you've met. PAS conventions you've attended, even the music store or drum shop that you patronize for your own equipment needs. These are all prospective *contacts* that could open some doors of opportunity for you in the business, or put you in contact with some of the *right people.* As with any competitive over-populated profession, openings or opportunities are rarely advertised.

Qualifications — Background Requirements

Before you present your interest in *the industry* to anyone, prepare yourself with the knowledge of what certain positions require and what strong personality or experience traits that you have which may match those requirements. Prioritize your best talents and skills as they relate to business, any business. Now, how can these skills be augmented by your achievements and success in music and/or percussion? The combination of these two areas has now created your first resume and *road map* for entering the Music Business. You must mentally redirect your focus toward business skills and development being more important than your musical background. You may also have to look at your appearance, first as a business person and eliminate some of the *artistic* forms of dress and behavior you have followed for years and to which you have become accustomed.

Karl Dustman

Your direct success from this point on is totally dependent upon how well you *market* yourself to the industry prospects. Consider that potential opportunities exist everywhere. Your perseverance, positive attitude, people-oriented personality and business *senses* are the key ingredients to getting your musical background and accomplishments even considered. Music is a *people* business. If you are not people-oriented, do not even consider the musical instrument business.

Entering the business at the beginning will generally only take place by your *selling yourself* to the right individual who has a need for a person with Personality and Percussion background. In many cases the way to a position you would like (and could provide enough monetary reward) may only be achieved by the *getting in through the back door* approach. Don't eliminate an opportunity just because you feel it doesn't utilize your background. Once you're in, you can continue to *sell yourself* for other more suitable positions after some experience while earning a company's recognition. This is true from working for a music store, publisher, manufacturer, importer/exporter or even talent/artist management. Don't set your expectations to be unrealistic. As a newcomer, only *you* know your worth. You'll have to prove it to others in the business.

As your search continues, so does your introduction to learning what is out there, what people are looking for, and what you have that they need. Focus on reading business information and world affairs. For example; foreign currency exchange rates directly effect the costs of many music instruments in the U. S. as more and more products are manufactured or assembled in foreign countries. Changes in taxes, shipping costs, government regulation, employment law/practices, the condition of the American Economy, unemployment rates,all affect the business of musical product marketing, sales and promotions. You need to become more aware of these areas' impact on the products with which *you* are looking to work.

The Sales Person in You

As a general rule, anyone in the business of music entered it through some sales experience or sales-related position. Any experience you have in selling anything to anyone will help you in this area. In turn, every position in the industry is filled with successful individuals who have been successful in selling in the business world. This is a requirement. In larger corporations, outside Sales Representatives are developed through inside customer service/sales-desk positions. Representatives were often retail sales people, former music store owners, or even prior music educators. But they all had the inner ability and desire to sell, and that helped to prepare them to enter the music business.

Most *inside* positions within companies are filled with people who were *outside* in some sales capacity or sales support position. There is no *inside track* to quick fame and fortune without experience, dedication or hard work, and sales achievement in some capacity.

You'll also find that anyone in top management positions, regardless of musical or nonmusical backgrounds, got there through proven success in selling: products, services, insurance, real estate, etc. Creativity in selling will open doors to advertising, public relations, promotions, artist relations, educational exhibits and many other areas within a company or organization. The better your sales background and business awareness, the better your chances of being considered for a position, or even being kept in mind for a future opportunity.

Skill and Luck...A Requirement

Being at the right place at the right time also applies to entering the music business. However, you can directly affect the *odds* by making yourself visible to the right people, following up with letters to the contacts you've made, and taking an active interest in learning everything you can about a company, its products, and the individuals who are responsible for that company's key areas. Find out about a company: is it being sold, merging with another, relocating, how stable are its sales and management work force, what does the average retail store owner think about the company in general? These questions and this type of investigation will help you focus your *skill* and *luck* on the right prospects for your entry into the business.

Present yourself and your skills as a business person, and put the musical side of your development as *the frosting on the cake*. It's difficult in this business to find many individuals who have the right *balance* of business and music backgrounds. Too much of one or the other will lessen the effectiveness of the position and your overall success within the company.

I often remember William F. Ludwig Sr.'s comments in his final days of daily work at the factory in 1972: "The last thing we need more of around the factory is Drummers!" That is still true today in our competitive business environment. However, the business still provides the same challenges and gratifications as it did when I entered the business through retail, twenty-five years ago.

Make your decision, plan your strategy, and get busy *selling*. It could be that an interesting career opportunity is closer than you think. And don't give up after your first or second meeting or introduction. Everyone in the business had to start *somewhere. When* and *how* is almost entirely up to your perseverance, abilities to market yourself and some proper planning. *GOOD LUCK!* ■

■

You can directly affect the "odds" by making yourself visible to the right people, following up with letters to the contacts you've made, and taking an active interest in learning everything you can about a company, its products, and the individuals who are responsible for that company's key areas. Conventions such as PASIC are a great place to start gathering information.

■

DRUM™
BUSINESS
Volume 2 Number 1
The Information Source For The Drum Industry
November International Drum Month

Selling To Schools Is Not So Elementary

by Karl Dustman

Every business is looking for additional sales opportunities to expand their customer base and profit potentials. This fall and winter one such opportunity may be right in your own backyard. Yes, even with many instrumental music programs seeing significant budget cuts, there's always going to be a "school-business pie." Are you getting a piece of it?

Your new retailing opportunity may be in recognizing that nine out of ten music educators have very little knowledge of percussion instruments beyond their basic schooling and "on the job experience." (Throughout this story we will focus specifically on junior-high- through college-level band and orchestra instrumental programs.) Combine this group with general music educators and you have a group relying on their very basic knowledge on how these percussion instruments operate, are cared for, or are performed on.

We will use this "window of opportunity" to explore how your percussion shop or department can be the solution to the music educator's weakness in percussion. Recognizing this opportunity and selling effectively to a school program and/or music educator is a careful combination of savvy professional skill, political astuteness, and hard work.

Defining Generalist Vs. Specialist

Your area music educators are currently being sold to and served by one of your local full-line general music stores. These generalist shops serve a wide variety of purposes, needs, and instruments. Very often the generalist shops are owned or operated by a former band director, stretching out into the "business side" of the music. It will be your responsibility and mission to set yourself ahead of the generalist and be recognized as a *percussion specialist*.

Begin by supporting the music educator with your specific percussion knowledge, showing an interest in his or her music program, and hopefully winning his or her respect and friendship. Service and support always has a higher priority than price alone. Much of this support can be augmented with resources from the percussion manufacturer. (More on that later.)

Convey your superior knowledge of product and problem-solving during every sale transaction to secure "after-market sales." You, as a specialist, will know better than anyone the newest of products, latest technologies, and common problem areas to address in advance. It is impossible for the music educator to assign a "value-added" to this intangible percussion support you offer. Great service and attention to detail sets you apart from the generalist's norm.

Employ all your creativity and imagination in presenting yourself as a superior source of information, assistance, and genuine interest, setting yourself apart from the "soup-to-nuts" type service of a generalist. Define the balance between letting the educator field-test new products for the manufacturers, and always trying to sell something. As a result of this "open communication," if there is a product need, only *you* will become the source for it. Have the solutions ready *first*, before others are even considered.

One primary example of your expertise could be in preparing the percussion equipment to "go on tour." Traveling can be a nightmare of adjustment, mishandling, and need for immediate parts. You're the resident expert: Prove this by showing your initiative to work with the students to ready the section for on-tour performance. You have the exclusive expertise far beyond a generalist who responds *after* something is lost, broken, or doesn't work.

Re-Engineering Your Selling Philosophy

Operating a retail store—where selling is a primary service to your customers—is very different from what is required to create a selling environment with the music educator. Your selling will not be done in the store, but more so on the phone and in person at the school.

If you're not up on current orchestral percussion, timpani, mallet instruments, etc., get with it immediately. You'll never sell big-ticket items if your knowledge stops with drumkits. Having a thorough knowledge of Latin percussion, world percussion, accessories, and special effects are all a part of *your* responsibility to the educator.

Still, the most effective form of school business development is maintaining a good rapport with all music educators. New and different ways of making their jobs easier will assure you a place in their merchant selection.

Don't forget that though the educator is your focus, each percussion *student* is also a potential customer for your store. Consider expanding your clinic offering from in-store events to school-district-wide events. Unusual topics like mallet-wrapping, head-tucking, and cymbal repair should all be included in your support function.

You might also want to consider using your accessory sales to get a chance on big-ticket purchases. We will touch more on the bid process later, but these accessory "bread and butter" items are daily reasons to be on the scene with the schools and educators.

It's very important to have a plan or purpose in mind every time you visit a music educator. Time should not be wasted "dreaming" about a product that is not in the immediate future. Create incentives for directors to attend in-store events, hopefully bringing with them all their percussion students.

Consider even an "open survey" that specifically inquires where and how the educator could use your specialized knowledge and service. This could include everything from tuning, repairs, and playing techniques to support, educational training, literature, and videos.

And finally, show your enthusiasm! Convey that your interest in the school goes beyond the next order. Get involved with school music support activities, band-parent associations, and fund-raising.

Put Yourself In The Instrumental Program

One of the best "windows of opportunity" to get into the school program is created when a new instrumental director or associate comes to the school district from another state. The playing field is now even with your competition, and you have a chance to "prove yourself" without previous comparisons.

A good way to get your foot in the door is to participate by attending concerts and regional and state competitions. Offer post-concert "congratulations" to the educators, and become the "drum guy" to the music educators and students. Offer repair-adjustment support when an ensemble attends a nearby festival that you plan on attending.

If possible, purchase a small advertisement in the school district's annual musical program book. Even if your ad is no larger than a business card, it represents your support and visible presence.

Student education is another way for you to hook up with the educators. Use your talents as a player and/or teacher to assist the non-percussion educator with the students. Practice sessions, drills, section rehearsals—these are all "support offers" that go *beyond* selling anything, but that build lasting relationships.

And don't make any excuses for details! You need to keep your act together. Besides the products you're trying to sell, you're also selling your detailed organization skills. Educators don't need to have complications due to somebody "dropping the ball" on a promise, deadline, or commitment.

With all the news on schools cutting back on music programs, don't abandon schools in your area that are slated to close the program or reduce the staff. Get resourceful to help save the program! Offer to hand out fliers or petitions, or cooperate with the band-orchestra parents' association. If the music program is saved and you visibly helped achieve the positive results, I guarantee you will be remembered when purchasing starts up again by the school and student musicians.

Your Suppliers Are Your Best Partners

The manufacturers and distributors of the products you carry are extremely interested in working with you to secure new school business. Just like you, they stand to gain. However, their resources are somewhat different.

You need to be creative. Provide the educator with manufacturer-produced educational materials on care and tuning, "how-to" literathing! You are *not* just a salesman.

Another way you can take advantage of the instrument manufacturer is by utilizing the manufacturer's local representative to call on school educators with you. By doing this you create a "triangular bond" of educator, manufacturer, and retailer. The representative can be most helpful in creating a "field-test" on new products needing actual playing-use testing. Educators and students love this insight to the music industry and welcome the chance to contribute to product development.

The manufacturer's representatives are always influential in getting drum corps, military sections, symphony players, and other notables to visit a school for "mini clinics." These guests are generally "free" during the day if they've got paid performances booked nearby in the evening or early morning.

If you find out about a school closing that cannot be saved, what about the percussion equipment in the school? Will this equipment be sold off, transferred to another school, or put in storage? This could be an ideal opportunity to pick up used equipment for resale, rental, or parts. You may also want to get the equipment "out of the school district" so that it does not eliminate a future potential sale. If the equipment has very little retail value, consider donating it to inner-city schools, hospitals, or institutions, thus taking the tax deduction.

Parent Nights—A Necessary Evil

If you haven't attended one of these annual events (generally conducted in September), do so as soon as possible. You will learn far more than I can briefly cover here.

Once you have introduced yourself to the music educator and established a rapport and purpose in his or her mind, you may be invited to participate in a "parent introduction meeting" at the school.

As a *specialist*, you must gear yourself to the "beginning drum" recruitment thought process. In some cases you may have to re-convince the parents to let their son or daughter play the drums. Use your "starting out" story to convey your close association with both student and parent perspectives. Calling upon your own beginning-drums experiences establishes the enrichment that music has brought you.

A couple of brief checklist things to remember must include:

1. Know what other full-line retailers will be exhibiting that evening and try to find out in advance what their snare-kit and bell-kit rental programs are.

2. Prepare your "Percussion Rental Program" clearly and professionally, focusing on service, drumkit incentives built around snares or bells, and competitive pricing. If allowed, mention supplemental availability (private lessons) from your store—but *only* if the educator is aware of your teaching service.

3. Convey your knowledge of and interest in the band method book that the student will be studying from. Your interest must go beyond the rental/purchase contract.

4. Create "parent take-home info packs" relative to having a "beginning drummer" in the house. Manufacturers print and provide a lot of this material. Make sure your store identification sticker or stamp appears on everything!

5. Record the name, address, and phone number of every parent and child meeting you have. Follow up during parent night, with each contact you make. If there is a signed contract, a "thank you" note is necessary. If a contract is pending, a phone call or follow-up note is appropriate.

This form of business is highly competitive. Show a few different snare or bell kits from the manufacturers you deal with, all at student/starter quality and prices. Parents never perceive that a snare kit/bell kit could cost or rent for the same thing or even more than a student-line band or string instrument.

The School Bid Process—A Fine Line

This topic warrants an entire separate article because of the complexity of the process and the vast amount of information there is to know.

You will hear that a good amount of the large school bids are price-factored at ridiculously low profit margins, just to secure the "school account business" for the future. There are high risks involved in bidding "lowest price" just to get the bid.

When you're ready for this aspect of school business, immediately involve your key suppliers to facilitate the completion of bid specs, delivery, and special school bid pricing.

Again, know your competition, get to know the school bid/purchasing director, and request insights from the music educator about the school purchasing process. Make certain he or she gets exactly what is wanted and not a substitute product. The educator will be most appreciative of your guidance and ability to correctly secure the needed material.

Summary

Selling and servicing schools is a very complex and time-consuming method of presenting your store and service. However, it is by far the most personally rewarding form of giving something of yourself and your business back to younger students and music education. If you went through a school music program when you were growing up and if it was your first introduction to studying a musical instrument, this process will be even more meaningful.

At first, the personal gratification of helping younger musicians will be the primary reward. As you further build this segment of your business, the additional sales and profits will start to appear on a monthly basis. New faces will be seen and new names added to your mailing list, and your community ties will develop far beyond your tax bill and operating license.

There is definitely a learning curve to your success rate based upon the time and energy you invest in this potential. As in any project, there will be discouraging signs early on that you are "not equipped" to create this additional growth and volume for your business. Don't give up! Get involved with outside sources to learn more. Join NASMD (National Association of School Music Dealers, [214] 233-9107). Their convention and publications can be of extreme value.

Through your close manufacturer ties, try to learn from NABIM (National Association of Band Instrument Manufacturers, [212] 924-9175) events and publications. They include active participation from the leading percussion manufacturers, and could be a great insight on music education support issues.

Do not look for immediate success in increasing your monthly sales projections by twenty-five percent the first month. This is a gradual building process that is "relationship founded" in working closely with the music education system, school boards, and supplier support.

And finally, don't wait until the next school year—start now! The "school bell of opportunity" is ringing, right in your neighborhood. Good Luck!

DRUM™

BUSINESS

Volume 2 Number 6

The Information Source For The Drum Industry

SCHOOL BIDS- The Thin And Narrow by Karl Dustman

The approach of the fall selling season and the re-opening of schools offers an ongoing seasonal opportunity for you as a percussion-specialist retailer to get in on annual school bid business. However, in my last article, "Selling To Schools Is Not So Elementary" (November—December '94 *DB*), we briefly touched on school bids and indicated that it takes more than just getting your store's name on the local school district's authorized bid list.

Why Go After Bid Business?

Any successful school service retailer will tell you that they have to walk a thin and narrow line on servicing and bidding on school musical equipment. Successful bidding very often is equated as *not losing* money, because of the close and minimal profit margins a retailer must sell at. In many cases, bidding is even considered a 'no-profit' area of the business. Yet it remains an essential part of music.

How? In two basic ways. One is to get a new store's "foot in the door" for future profits. The other is to create an environment of "business protection" with the exchange of dollars and additional volume between the store and the school. Bidding is the primary way that schools buy big-ticket items. A percussion-specialist retailer will not get even a piece of profitable accessory business unless you play in the "school bid league."

Another positive factor for the retailer who is actively involved in the local bidding process is in rentals. Successful bidding and servicing of a school program almost assures the eventual business through rentals to both the school *and* the individual students. For the percussion specialist dealer, it certainly would pay to be awarded a "break-even" bid on a set of four timpani or a set of chimes, for example, if you could be assured of getting all the future school's rental business and referrals while also becoming the supplier for all the snare and bell kits rented each fall season. It's widely known and accepted that bidding business and rental business go hand-in-hand when proper "people relations" are in place to secure this year-round business.

Outmaneuvering Mail-Order

If you stay close to your home selling area with local schools that you can work with on a regular basis, it becomes much more difficult for out-of-state competitors to come into the selling equation or for the schools to make major big-ticket purchases through mail-order catalogs. Of course there are always exceptions, but many school districts won't deal with a retailer who is not local and who is not prepared to assist when service or warranty matters come up. And we all know they come up regularly.

Consider your position—and the educator's—if something the school ordered and has been waiting for doesn't come out of the box from the factory exactly the way it was supposed to. Or if there were a substitution or the specifications changed. If you're servicing the school account correctly, the band director and the school administration will "work with you" to find a suitable solution that is reasonable for the buyer and seller of the percussion product. *You*, as the local percussion specialist, know more about the educator's needs than the friendly voice on the toll-free mail-order number quoting only price and availability information.

While price is very often the final factor as to which retailer is awarded the purchase order, very often there are "influence factors" that come into play for the music educator. "Who's going to help me with this expensive percussion stuff when it gets damaged or doesn't work properly?" At those times, the director is *not* looking for an 800 number that rings two thousand miles away.

The percussion-specialist retailer should be use, the potential for traveling, and the in-school movement, because you've been at the school. Out-of-town competitors and the mail-order houses barely know the instrument's effects to climate considerations, much less the performance requirements that these instruments will face over the years to come. A specialist must have the answers ready before the questions are asked. This is an essential selling principle of retailing and a requirement for the bidding process.

The ongoing complexity of the bidding process is very much attached to the "potential future for profitable business." If there is no possibility for building a long-term and further-developing relationship with the school district, you may decide to walk away from the bid without further considerations. However, once again, it comes back to relationships and realizing the *potentials*—something more than narrow price competitiveness and the very thin profit margins.

To avoid the pitfalls of the unprofitable business, be aware of the hidden potentials for losses resulting from the need for quick "overnight" bidding. In some cases the band director may have not used up the entire yearly budget and will be instructed to "use it or lose it." In your efforts to accommodate the request and make the sale, you may fail to take into consideration the true costs of the product and of delivering the big-ticket item. Consider, for example, a set of timpani. Either underestimating the shipping costs or forgetting them entirely could result in a *loss* rather than a profit.

Know The Exact Purchasing Specs—Or Else!

A primary component of successful bidding for the percussion product sale *must* include accurate information about what you are bidding on. Be specific about all the details concerning the brand of instrument, including exact model numbers, special finishes, colors, plating, cases, bags, and headprotectors. Without knowing these essential details you are blindly setting yourself up for a loss of time *and* money.

For example, a pair of 18" hand cymbals may seem very easy to order and select. But there are several factors to be considered, including weight (band, orchestra, or marching), brilliant or regular finish, bell/cup size—and even the type of handles. All these details will affect your costs from the manufacturer, which affects your bidding price to the school. Without this clarity, you may end up being awarded the bid and delivering the *wrong* product! If you allow this to occur, you have lost in many ways. You'll be late delivering the correct replacement product, which creates unhappiness with the customer. You may have to return the incorrect product to the manufacturer and incur re-stocking charges—or keep the wrong product in your inventory, tying up cash on a potentially slow-moving item. And let's not forget that you won't get paid by the school until you deliver the right product at the awarded price.

This clarity and definition of what *exactly* the school wants is regular protocol for bidding on everything from a triangle beater to a set of timpani. A single mistake or oversight will make the difference between your profiting or losing money on the entire process.

Defining "Or Equivalent"

The term "or equivalent" can be used anywhere on the bid paperwork, and it opens the door for any of your competitors to low bid on an item with an inferior product, brand, or model. Any time you see "or equivalent," the caution light must go on for you to research the item and establish the "best price" for the *real* item desired.

Very often the school administration issuing the bid knows very little about what they are putting out on bid. Administration support staffs purchase everything for the district and rely heavily on the information supplied to them from the music educator for musical purchases. Relationship building plays an integral role in allowing you to assist the educator in writing up the specifications for the bid, which will therefore contain the exact specifications, eliminating the need for "or equivalent" in the bid text.

In trying to build these partnerships with your area schools, enlist the assistance of the manufacturer's product manager. These factory specialists know all about "their" competition and will be able to provide specific features and terminology that will aid in bringing the bid in your direction. This manufacturer assistance can also help you eliminate certain brands that you do not carry, and can therefore "steer" the bid process to what you *do* carry.

Something as simple as size of casters on an instrument, bar-width in a certain octave range on mallet instruments, and kinds of snares, cases, and covers could all affect where the bid brand is specified.

Because of the wide variance of requirements in different states and parts of the country regarding rules on the bidding process, you need to fully understand the exact guidelines established for your school district. While learning and researching these rules and regulations, you must also be looking for the same "loopholes" that your competition may be aware of. The non-percussion retail merchant will be seeking to win the bid on lower prices—and perhaps on a lower-quality product than indicated.

Making certain you are specific about the product details with the educator and school program is very important, but it's just as important when dealing with your manufacturer/suppliers. Very often the manufacturer will have certain school-bid policies on payment terms, drop-shipping, special additional school discounts, and even the qualifying and non-qualifying of the item towards your store's account year-end volume rebates. A general music store that bids on everything very competitively may view his percussion bid business as zero profit, but he may decide to continue it just to increase his overall annual purchasing figure with a supplier—and therefore move his shop to a higher plateau of discount or rebate. This could affect his current year's purchases as well as his starting point for the following year.

The Intangible Ingredient: Service

Very often the percussion-specialist retailer can make the bid process a "win or lose" process based on one factor—*service*. While the bidding process is a year-round business activity, so is service. Often the decision as to who is awarded the bid goes beyond the cost factor. It may depend on who's going to service the instrument, who's going to adjust the product as it comes out of the carton, and who's qualified to know about the technical features and preventative maintenance years down the road.

I've seen actual printed qualifications in bids make specific references to "ability to service" the product. While this is very difficult to enforce, it does indicate a "window of opportunity" for you as a percussion specialist to establish your qualification, ability, and desire to service what you sell. Your "value added" could be something that means more than money. Because music educators generally know very little about the percussion products they purchase and have limited technical/mechanical background in how the instruments function, you must appeal to their needs *beyond* product costs and local delivery.

Common Bid Practices

Most bids are figured at your cost *plus* 10%. While there are some variations, this seems to be the norm across the country. Differences can be the results of freight costs on heavy big-ticket items, how a school district pays the invoice, or how some of the manufacturer incentives (that we've already mentioned) come into play in figuring your "real profit" from a sale. Generally the catalog houses will not go much lower than 10%.

If a manufacturer has changed a product and/or the price of an item that you have already bid on, in most cases the company will honor the original price if you supply them a copy of the bid awarded to you from the school. If the product change is significant enough to affect the decision process and bid specifications, discuss this with the school immediately to protect yourself, your customer, and your future business relations.

If an improvement has been made to the bidded product with little or no effect on the price, use this as a positive opportunity to keep the music educator informed, while again conveying that their percussion specialist is "working for them." You can also use this as a reason to "check in" and advise the educator on the delivery information and status on other pending purchases or decisions, without it sounding like a "sales call." This type of positive communication will have lasting impact on your business with the school and educator in the future.

Whenever you're trying to bid a situation as a newcomer to the school, try to determine in advance the relationship between the purchasing department (administration) and the music educator. Learn to know who's making the decisions about the bid and bidding list, as well as their policy on substitutions and what variances may be allowed within the bidding process. Try to determine how friendly—or unfriendly—the educator and purchasing manager are.

Music Educator Buying-Habit Profile

Through working with a particular school or music educator, you will start to develop a working profile as to how the school program functions and handles the bidding process. Each school may have their own methods and sequence of events connected with issuing and awarding bids. You, as an expert, can steer certain bidding "mechanics" to achieve maximum protection for your store in the process. A few of them are:

1. Watch out for the overnight bid process. If this occurs regularly, it indicates that the educator doesn't really have a handle on his annual operating budget. This also opens the door for bidding errors by the retailer in an effort to accommodate the urgency of not losing the budget funds. Rush bidding generally requires more time to process because of the urgency and sacrifice of letting other work sit while you attend to the bid.

2. Try to keep the product specifications simple and clear. Items that require special pricing and conversation with the manufacturer should be handled on a separate bid. Do not mix standard cataloged merchandise with special custom-order or unusual equipment. Also, try to avoid having small accessory items included on a major instrument bid purchase. This could have an extremely negative effect if a small accessory item is back-ordered and therefore holds up payment for the entire bid from the school.

3. Know when a bid will be issued, when it will be opened, and when the school will begin accepting bids. Timing is everything in working with a music educator. Try to find out what other firms will be bidding for the order and if there will be any out-of-state mail-order operations under consideration. Also, be sure to find out (or let the educator know) what importance is being placed on service, dealer prepping of the instrument as it comes out of the carton, etc.

Summary

Hopefully the insights discussed here have given you at least a broad overview of how to get into the business of school bids. As I mentioned earlier, you may determine that it's not right for your business. It *can* be a laborious process. The thing to keep in mind is that real success in achieving a place in the school bid process depends on your ability to handle details, work within close deadlines, and know your true product costs.

Rejection is also a part of the business. It may take three or four attempts for you to be taken seriously—to show that you are firmly dedicated in wanting a school's business. Understand up front that you will not automatically win all bids. The key here is to follow up after the loss to see who was awarded the bid, at what price, and where you perhaps went wrong. Use it as a learning experience.

If you are interested in the school bid business, get your name into the bidding cycle *now*. There isn't a particular season for entering or exiting. This is a business opportunity that's out there all year long!

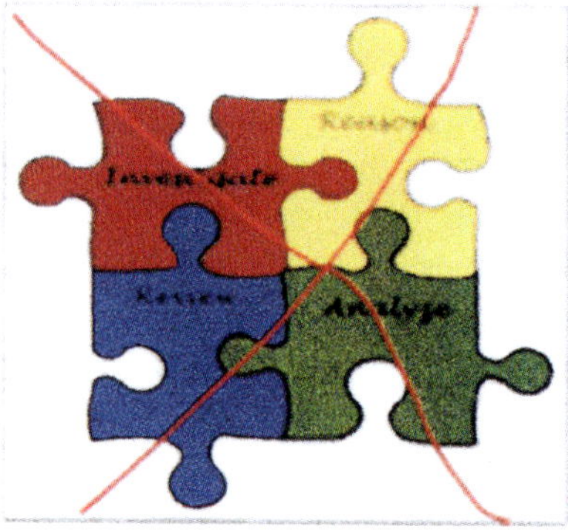

THE GREAT DEBATE;

MUSIC BUSINESS EDUCATION

QUESTION: WHAT IS THE BEST WAY TO LEARN THE MUSIC BUSINESS?

SO HOW DO YOU LEARN THE MUSIC BIZ?

1. Commit to learning,..... forever! Realize you will have to learn as much as you can, as fast as you can and through whatever means you can.

2. Learn to ask questions.... If you don't ask, you don't get,...and you don't learn.

3. MUSIC BUSINESS= NETWORKING, Surround yourself with more experienced people you can learn from, ask questions, be interested and polite,..the response with be extremely positive.

4. Find a MENTOR that takes interest in seeing you develop, can open doors and welcome a friendship, relating to the business segment you wish to enter. Fast-track learning is a result of having a mentor that is a serial "Doer".

YOU LEARN BY **DOING** IN THE MUSIC BIZ.. **(Investment of time, money and effort)**

- **Study "Music Business" at an accredited school, there are many**
- **On-Line music biz expert**
- **Free on-line services and blogs**
- **Go out and do it on your own**

SHOULD I GET A COLLEGE DEGREE IF I WANT TO WORK IN THE MUSIC BUSINESS?

- **Accounting, Budgeting, Marketing, Promotion, Website,.....are essentials in addition to the Music Business curriculum**
- **Get Involved in everything you can that is associated with your area of study and ambition.**

- **Completion of a DEGREE PROGRAM,.. demonstrates you have the essential skills to commit to tasks, completing projects, research new areas and understand the meaning of <u>commitment and perseverance</u>.**
- **Your <u>attitude, ambition and dedication</u> are your most valuable assets,...all developing while you're working at a DEGREE.**
- **Your PEOPLE SKILLS, is a platform for everything you do. If you can communicate verbally and in writing effectively,...others will LISTEN.**

<u>Bottom line</u>; Your Music Business degree is only worth what your ability is to <u>connect those curriculum skills</u> with the real-world elements of DOING, COMMUNICATING, and developing RELATIONSHIPS.

THE MUSIC BUSINESS,...is all about DOING....., its about RELATIONSHIPS,....its about NETWORKING..... Combine those character instincts and qualities along with a formal education and you have a winning combination for creating a path in the Music Business.

Dustman & Associates
Marketing Communications
P.O. Box 33252 Cleveland, Ohio 44133
Telephone: 440-582-7006 Fax:440-230-1346
e-mail: kbdustman@aol.com
Website: www.professionalpercussionproducts.com

"ME, INC."

A MINDSET,...A PHILOSOPHY,... AN ENTREPRENEURAL SPIRIT

PREPARING TO ENTER <u>THE MUSIC PRODUCTS INDUSTRY</u>

As the President and CEO of ME, INC,..... your goal and mind set is to market and sell your services as a <u>PRODUCT</u> to a select number of businesses and/or organizations directly engaged and related to career opportunities, positions or product categories within the <u>Music Products Industry</u>.

1. **Creating the Product:**
   - **Who Am I? Educator, Student, Music Retailer, Player, Teacher Arts-Curriculum, Administrator, Repair Technician**
   - **What <u>Unique</u> Qualities and Qualifications do I Offer? (*features-benefits*)**
   - **What type of Company could <u>USE</u> my expertise and background?**
2. **Marketing Yourself:**
   - **Getting noticed, developing Recognition as EXPERT in your field**
   - **Developing Word-Of-Mouth Silent Salesman connections**
   - **Creating events and accomplishments OTHERS will learn about**
   - **Designing your own <u>Elevator Statement</u> about YOU (the product)**
3. **Packaging Yourself:**
   - **How Do You COME ACROSS in your work, around people**
   - **Can You be JUDGED BY YOUR COVER? Do visitors want to learn and know more about you?**
   - **How does your APPEARANCE compliment and match the market and the "culture" of what you want to be doing?**
4. **Delivering The Product:**
   - **Ability to interact: VERBALLY, in WRITING, and IN PERSON**
   - **Professional ATTITUDE, APPEARANCE, APPETITE, (3-A's) for challenge,.... for opportunity**
   - **What AFFECT you have on people around you,..... Leader, Follower, Thinker, Joiner, Mixer, Joker**

THREE MAJOR <u>SEGMENTS</u> OF THE MUSIC PRODUCTS INDUSTRY

A) Manufacturing (domestic- international)

Product Design, Product Development,
Research & Development (new or existing products)
Marketing-Advertising-Trade Show, Public Relations
Educational Market Development/Church Market Development
Artist Relations, Educational Alliances
Sales (products-services) Sales Management (DSM)
Brand Management, Product Management, Specific Market Segment Management
Industry Relations, trade participation, representation
Marketing Communications/Public Affairs

B) Distribution/Wholesale

Product Line Manager
Sales to Music Retailers, Sales to OEM
Institutional Sales, Church, Hospital Sales
New Product Line Management-Development
Wholesale Catalog development for Merchant Distribution
Retail Consumer Mail-Order Specialty Catalogs, events, campaigns

C) Retail Dealer- Music Dealer- Merchant

Specific Department Management (brass-woodwind-band-string, combo, keyboard, sound reinforcement/amplification, lighting, acoustic fabrication)
In-Store Teaching Lesson Program (teachers, schedules, fees, contracting, recruitment)
Purchasing, School Bid Development & Completion/Compliance
Institutional Sales: Schools, Churches, Hospitals, Senior Centers, Community Cultural Arts Centers
Market Development- Adult combo, New Horizons Bands, Community Bands Summer Camps, Library Arts Programs, Player Fantasy Camps-Programs
Instrument Repair (specialty instrument or category)
Instrument Rental Programs, School Presentation
Sales-Marketing-Promotions-Advertising, Direct Marketing

WHAT ARE THE COMMON POSITIONS IN M.P.I. ...? THAT <u>CONNECT</u> TO ME & MY QUALIFICATIONS?

<u>**Preferred M.P.I. POSITION**</u>	<u>**Background-Education COME FROM.....**</u>
1. District Sales Managers (DSM)	Band Director, Retail Sales (musical/non-musical) Music Educator, Arts-Curriculum Director
2. Product Manager/Brand Manager	Retail Store Sales, Private Teacher, Player-Designer, Repair Technician
3. Marketing Manager	Related Product or Market Sales, Advertising
4. Artist Relations	Professional Player, Tour Management, Instrument Road Technician

THE ESSENTIAL SKILL SETS I NEED TO SUCCEED (in M.P.I.)

1. A **<u>Love for Music</u>**, making music and how **<u>PROFIT</u>** is the essential ELEMENT to make it all happen.

2. Knowing and understanding Business **<u>Basics</u>** of profit margins, mark-up, merchandising, competitive analysis, recognizing trends versus cycles. Understanding Balance Sheets, P & L... Statements..... are a plus!

3. **<u>Project Management</u>**, working alone or with a TEAM, steering, contributing and prioritizing

4. **<u>Organization, Prioritization</u>**.....are the key to getting things done, on-time and within budget. Without them,...you are "doomed"

5. **<u>BRING VALUE ADDED</u>**: "frosting on ***<u>YOUR</u>*** product" (AKA: What Makes You Better)

- Be involved in as many musical events and organizations as possible/feasible
- Join as many Business (musical & non-musical) organizations, (Rotary, Chamber of Commerce, AFM, NAfME,JEN, Church Music Ensemble, Community Band/Orchestra
- Personal Professional Development, Continuing Education, Interest Diversification
- Creative Writing, Business Letter Writing, Proof-Reading, Editorial experience, Contract Law
- Public Speaking, Power Point presentation
- Having a Mentor,......Being a Mentor

MR. PRESIDENT! OF <u>ME INC</u>.,....DON'T LEAVE HERE WITHOUT THESE "TAKE HOMES"...

1. **The MUSIC PRODUCTS INDUSTRY represents the largest number of entry-level career opportunities of the entire Music Business.**

2. **The Music Products Industry relies on MUSIC EDUCATION for stability, growth and development. MUSIC EDUCATION relies on the Music Industry to provide the instruments and related accessories to MAKE & TEACH Music for everyone.**

3. **The Music Products Industry is NOT a "Fall Back" for crowded performance stages or shrinking classroom music education programs,....its a PASSION WITH PURPOSE built upon your PLAYING A MUSICAL INSTRUMENT. <u>This is how YOU got started !</u>**

4. **Today's Graduating Music Students can develop <u>THREE Career Paths</u>.......**

   - **Professional Musical Instrument Performance (Entertainment)**
   - **Professional Music Education/Arts Education (Educational-Cultural Enrichment)**
   - **Music Industry,...... Focusing on <u>Music Products Industry</u> that are <u>REQUIRED</u> in both**

5. **All Music Making, begins <u>AT THE MUSIC STORE</u>**

Dustman & Associates
Marketing Communications
P.O. Box 33252 Cleveland, Ohio 44133
Telephone: 440-582-7006 Fax:440-230-1346
e-mail: kbdustman@aol.com
Website: www.professionalpercussionproducts.com

HOW TO MARKET YOURSELF,......EFFECTIVELY....

..........Like No One Else Can

1. **SEEK A STRATEGIC WAY TO CREATE & BUILD YOUR CAREER.**

    - Educate people about how you can help and what you bring.
    - Keep building your body of knowledge through professional development become a *sharing-mode*,... then you're in the "DRIVERS SEAT'.
    - Raise your hand!! Volunteer for new, different and difficult projects,...marketing yourself becomes a "**<u>learned automatic behavior</u>**" Attention INTROVERTS!

2. **NOBODY ELSE IS IN CHARGE OF YOUR CAREER, EXCEPT YOU!**
    Leaders regularly give themselves a "check-up", asking....

    - I'm happy in my job and position but how can I do it better?
    - How Do I continue to Learn, evolve and become a positive contributor?
    - How am I building my leadership profile,...and who will notice?
    - How can I develop the additional skill sets that will make me desirable for advancement?

3. **BUILD YOUR STRENGTHS, PROMOTE YOUR WORTH**
    - Clearly define what the **DREAM JOB** would look like in your mind,....but aim for the job, position, company etc,...that would give me access to ultimately what I want to do for a living.
    - Know the difference between a JOB,....and a CAREER.
    - Know what the skills and qualifications are for what you want to do. Determine how to CONNECT those skills and qualification to answer "WHAT WE'RE LOOKING FOR"....
    - Plug in the gaps in your knowledge,.... The results will change your vision from being tactics focused to more "results oriented'.

4. **GET SOCIAL,.... In all directions that interact with people YOU need to know, and they need to <u>learn about you</u>.**

    - Engage in meaningful conversation,..have a mission, purpose, agenda that is invisible to anyone you're speaking to.
    - Understand what the keywords are used by leaders in your field. Weave them into your natural vocabulary.
    - Think like an entrepreneur, NEVER as an employee. (ME, INC)
    - Stay connected with the right social media community that benefits YOU.

5. NETWORKING + INDUSTRY INVOLVEMENT = EASY MARKETING

- Find an individual that you feel represents the respect and recognition you would like to achieve, research and learn where and how that person developed.
- Build alliances out of camaraderie, similar interests and agendas that can open paths you never saw on your own.

- Create a personal **ACTION LIST** that is constantly emerging and developing as achievement is reached.

  a) Who do I want to meet that could help my ambitions and career?
  b) Who needs to know WHAT IAM,... and what I am doing now, the future...
  c) How do I get PUBLISHED?..... How do I get INVITED?..... How do others approach ME?

MARKETING YOURSELF, is all about leaving behind the COMFORT ZONES...and becoming stronger and more capable than we ever imagined.

Dustman & Associates

Marketing Communications

P.O. Box 33252 Cleveland, Ohio 44133

Telephone: 440-582-7006 Fax:440-230-1346

e-mail: kbdustman@aol.com

Website: www.professionalpercussionproducts.com

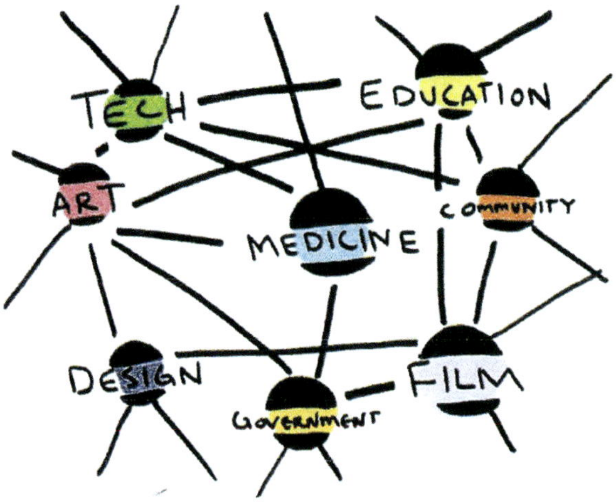

SALES & MARKETING PROFESSIONALS....

MAKING THE BUSINESS CONNECTION

1. HARNESS THE POWER OF YOUR PLATFORM

- Creating positive exposure for you as a credible expert and valued resource
- Producing positive name recognition for you, events, performances, published pieces.
- Providing your credible marketing support tools
- Appreciate every creative opportunity to get your name seen, heard, mentioned,....in a positive light supporting your abilities and talents.
- Develop career enhancing critical skills that increase in value over time and upward mobility.

2. WHAT IS ETIQUETTE?....WHY IS IT SO IMPORTANT TO YOU...

Background: The French are credited with creating early levels of ETIQUETTE in the mid 1700's as a social class status, separating upper, lower classes, blue collar, old money versus new money etc.

- It is how we ADAPT and fit into a particular situation, environment, demonstrating that we belong,....where you are.
- It allows the people around us to relax and be comfortable,...and content.
- Recognize and respect the difference atmospheres and environments,....learn to adjust, react, respond and fit....to where you are, what's happening,...and the positive impact and impressions YOU will have on others.
- Create <u>YOUR TRADTION</u>,... adapt, accept and encourage, be consistent, conscientious, considerate and courageous,....impacting everyone around you.

3. POLISHING YOUR NETWORKING IMAGE,....GET A MIRROR!

GOOGLE fact: 7% of what we communicate is through words we choose.
35% of what we communicate is through our visual appearance
58% of what we communicate is through non-verbal
(body language, facial)

Learn-know the differences: a) PEOPLE WATCHER-WALL FLOWER
b) N.E.X.T.....what can you do for me?
c) DRAMA QUEEN
d) THE CARD PUSHER
e) SETTLED IN & COMFORTABLE, (Me always first)

4. ACCELERATE YOUR SUCCESS (POTENTIALS),...BY GETTING ENGAGED.......(TOTALLY)

DEFINITION: Feeling motivated, applying your strengths, being committed to excellence, curious to learn and grow beyond any limitation.
FACT: 71% OF AMERICAN WORKERS,..... are NOT ENGAGED in their work.

- **Progressive companies focus on the "WHOLE PERSON"....at work, evaluating the mind-body connection and positive impact on the organization.**
- **Ownership of engagement is an individual responsibility, combined with enthusiasm and satisfaction.**
- **Uncover and applying individual strengths; THREE ESSENTIAL AREAS....**
  - a) **Clarify skills and strengths that make you feel strong and confident.**
  - b) **List you work responsibilities and top priorities to apply your strengths.**
  - c) **Being BOLD, and SPEAKING UP... in a positive pro-active manner.**

5. PRESENT YOUR BEST SELF (aka: "packaging the product")

KNOW the difference between a CAREER and a JOB. Are you STEERING or ROWING through life, your career,.....and how does this affect your happiness?

- **A CAREER/PROFESSIONAL is something you commit to for life, a passion, a purpose (It interests you, you enjoy it and rewards in a variety of ways)**

- **A JOB is something you go to,.... But is something you would NOT pick (paying bills, obligations, false perceptions)**

IN THE BUSINESS WORLD,.. Your ATTITUDE creates 100 percent of your HAPPINESS and PERCEPTION. **Check your ATTITUDE, setting an immediate tone:**

a) **Posture: how you sit, stand, walk illustrates what's going on inside**
b) **Eye Contact; seek out people awareness,... S & M professionals are supposed to LOVE people.... Direct eye contact and a firm hand-shake say a lot about you.**
c) **Anticipate Others Needs; be prepared, live-by a *just-in-case* mindset, use a how-can-I-help ? vision for the immediate moment and long-term relationship-building**
d) **Dress Up; First impressions are lasting impressions...know your environment. Successful, happy people are rarely *under-dressed*. Looking Good = FEELING good.**
e) **Be On Time (always); *"Time is Money",....* Yours and someone else's. DON'T WASTE IT!....The world will not wait for you,...as others will quickly take your place.**

6. PATIENCE, PERSISTENCE, PERSEVERANCE & PERSUATION.... ....SLOW AND STEADY WINS THE RACE

GOOD DAYS ARE EASY,.....How do you handle intensifying challenges?.... there is no light in the tunnel?.......your own sanity is being questioned,......are you on the wrong path?

- Congratulate Yourself, and acknowledge each and every small victory as a step towards a bigger goal. (write down your lists of wins, everyday)
- Learn From Your Lessons, know and understand why something went wrong and why something else worked better the 2nd time.
- Be Grateful, practice mentally being-thankful for people, events circumstances and outcomes you could NOT take for granted. Expecting GOOD THINGS to happen,....allows them to develop naturally, turning out better than expected.

MASTERING THESE SIX CHARACTER CONNECTIONS AS A WAY OF LIFE,...brings increased self assurance, awareness, satisfaction and confidence in doing the right thing at the right time for the right reason.

Dustman & Associates
Marketing Communications
P.O. Box 33252 Cleveland, Ohio 44133
Telephone: 440-582-7006 Fax:440-230-1346
e-mail: kbdustman@aol.com
Website: www.professionalpercussionproducts.com

MakingMusic
Connecting the world through music.

Exploring the Mystery of Playing Timpani (Kettle Drums)

MAKING MUSIC Magazine, May 2020

Timpani—An overview in understanding the instrument, technique and essentials

by Karl Dustman

Whether you're a music educator, band or orchestral student, conductor or composer, timpani has been one of the most mystical and misunderstood percussion instruments ever. Yet, it can be heard professionally performed in every type of music. From three hundred year old classical standard repertoire to marches, Broadway, pops, Latin and even big band jazz… timpani have been creating the drama, coming from the percussion section. So why is it that everyone is so afraid of these big, heavy shiny bowl-like drums, always placed at the back of the ensemble?

It is essential that all percussion students and educators know and understand the basic concepts in how these instruments work, how to perform on them, and that timpani are not just another drum. In this abbreviated overview, we will explore and discuss the essentials of this new understanding.

Proper Instrument Set-Up

Most schools use either a pair (29' & 26") or set-of-four drums (32", 29", 26", 23"). Traditional American set-up is the most common, largest drum on the players left, going to smallest drum on player's right. German set-up is found and used by most European orchestras setting-up the drums in reverse sequence. I recommend teaching and learning timpani set up in American sequence, like a piano.... the lowest notes are always on the left of the keyboard.

Player Standing or Sitting

Much has been said about the pros and cons of the timpanist sitting or standing while playing. In either case, a suitable adjustable height timpani stood should be a regular part of the percussion section, reserved exclusively for the timpanist. Personally, I prefer and almost always perform standing, as I can get a more controlled stick-impact placement, adjust the tuning pedals faster, see the music on the music stand better and have better eye-to-eye contact with the conductor. During long sections of counting measures of rest, the timpanist can "perch" on the timpani stool in an almost-ready position.

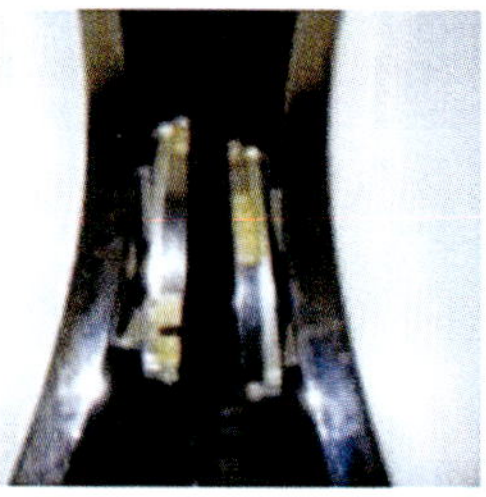

Tuning Gauges

Most professional timpani are equipped with some form of tuning gauges attached to the drum. These gauges can be a tremendous assist to the timpanist, providing the gauges are properly calibrated to the correct range of each drum, and the gauges work smoothly and properly. Music Educators must make certain that every student has a basic knowledge of Ear Training to establish the essentials in recognizing most common intervals and making adjustments to the tuning in each key-change tuning transition.

This Intonation Requirement is important for everyone playing timpani, as this instrument is considered a "pitched percussion instrument". Playing out of tune is unacceptable and can be eliminated with proper ear training from the very beginning.

Pedal Tuning

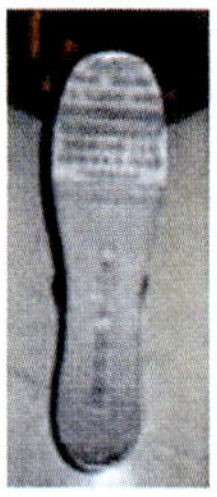

Each kettle has its own range generally a major 5th or 6th interval. When making adjustments in pitch, it is always best to "slide up" (depressing the toe of the pedal) to the note, rather than descending down to a desired pitch. The kettle needs to "be in tune with itself"... What's this mean? Balanced Action Pedal Tuning, refers to a balanced-equal tension between the HEAD tension and the Pedal SPRING tension in the silver adjustment knob located on the timpani base assembly. Pedal tuned timpani make all pitch adjustments by moving the pedal up or down. This has become a standard design, rather than the traditional-original pitch adjustments to the timpani head tension made with multiple "T"-handles around the top of each drum.

Each drum size (manufacturer & model) has a predetermined range that sounds best for each size kettle. The most common ranges should be memorized by the educator and player to help facilitate the fastest and most resonant pitches.

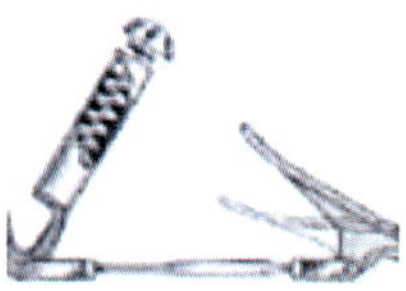

32" Heel down D....up to Toe down G
29" Heel down E,... up to Toe down B
26" Heel down A... up to Toe down E
23" Heel down D....up to Toe down A

Most common band and orchestra published music places the pitches of the individual timpani on the timpani part, but most will not specify which drum the pitch is suppose to be played on. By immediately knowing the ranges of the drums, and recognizing that the best resonance is in the middle of the range, the educator will be able to assist the student player in selecting "what pitch sounds best on what kettle size".

If the Balanced Action Pedal will not hold in place in either the HEEL DOWN or TOE DOWN position, the timpani head is NOT IN BALANCE with the correct range of that specific size kettle. This requires an adjustment to the timpani head tension around the perimeter and "big silver knob" at the bottom of the kettle, in front of the pedal toe. This is a fairly simple process, but requires considerably more space than we have in this overview. I will be happy to email you a PDF file, "Care and Tuning of Your Ludwig Timpani" by sending an email to kbdustman@aol.com. This two-page instruction prepared by the Ludwig Drum Company helps with many of the common timpani functions and adjustments.

Best Timpani Sound Production

Each kettle has a "sweet spot" which provides for maximum resonance, pitch clarity and projection. This is generally THREE inches from the edge of the drum. This is where the timpanist will strike the head 90% of the time, with the "beating spot" placed in-between the two closest tuning tension posts. Timpani sound and resonance is the result of many factors: sizes of the drum, fiberglass or copper kettles, extended head collar or non-extended collar, type of head material and thickness, acoustics of the hall, type of timpani sticks used, and the ability of the player to match the technique, volume, definition, and sound to the music being performed.

However the most common "sound production problem" is attributed to not changing the plastic timpani heads often enough. Plastic heads can go "dead" after a duration of stretching, vibrating and moving from one note to the other over time. Rule of thumb would be changing your timpani heads in a school setting at least every-other school year. Professional orchestras change their timpani heads every year. Locate a knowledgeable experienced person that can change timpani heads, calibrate the tuning gauges and refurbish internal mechanisms. I do this personally for many schools, colleges and universities throughout Northeast Ohio.

Much of the unwanted, persistent and annoying buzzing, squeaking and frustrating vibrations sounds are attributed to the lack of head lubricant on the underside of the head. The plastic head must move effortlessly and quietly over the timpani kettle-edge lip. Otherwise the plastic movement-friction will create a distracting sound whenever the pedal is moved up or down. Most rattles are created by loose tuning gauge letters or various nuts, bolts and washers that are part of the frame assembly that all loosen with time and continuous playing vibration. Again, a qualified professional timpani service expert is needed to resolve many of these issues common in all older well-played timpani.

I also recommend for educators and timpanists, the Mark Yancich 82-minute DVD, *Changing and Tuning Plastic Timpani Heads*. This is an excellent reference guide for everyone needing to know the basics of timpani sound production and how the mechanics of timpani really work. The entire series, *The Art of Timpani*, by Mark Yancich can be easily ordered through, www.professionalpercussionproducts.com/markyancich.html

Timpani Stick Selection

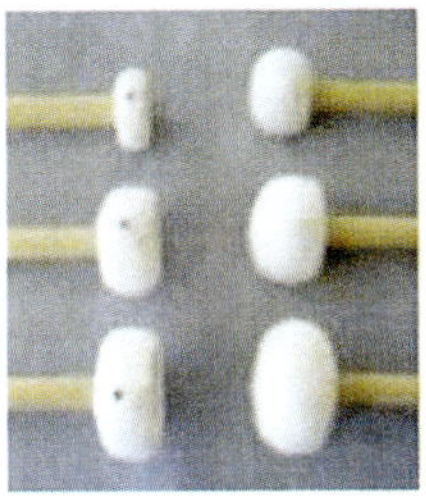

Much has been said, written and explained about all the differences in timpani sticks. Different handle materials, (bamboo, carbon fiber, cherry-wood, maple-wood) as well as all the different stick head covering materials, cores and related, (American Felt, German Felt, Cork, Flannel). This is why timpani stick selection remains a personal preference of the timpanist, and the sound the music conductor wants from the timpani. Different sticks provide different resonance, clarity, articulation and definition, which can change from one hall to another, differences in music composition, volume sensitivity and instrument placement onstage.

I recommend most students start with a three-pair essential of soft, medium, and hard. This can be selected from standard Roller Ball (right) or Cart-Wheel models, (left). I find that the Clevelander brand of timpani sticks with bamboo handles is an excellent choice, affordable and hand sewn in Cleveland, Ohio. These are easily available at www.professionalpercussionproducts.com.

Proper Timpani Stick Grip and Stroke

American, German, French,.... What's the difference? Again, this is a personal preference of the timpanist and what force or accent articulation is needed for the timpani part. Educators should be able to demonstrate the differences, French = thumbs-up, German = thumbs sideways (traditional matched grip) and American = somewhere in between the vertical French and the horizontal German.

The STROKE is very smooth, targeted and relying upon a rebound coming off the head. I refer to this as a WRIST MOTION similar to casting a fishing line, but only with the wrist moving. The timpani stick MUST be moved up from the timpani head immediately in a backwards "snap wrist action," allowing the head to fully vibrate and resonate.

How to practice timpani... without having timpani

There is a solution for this problem through the creation of the Timpani Warm-up Practice Pad, designed by Chicago Symphony Principle Timpanist David Herbert. A special pad material perfectly duplicates the timpani head feel and rebound, allowing professionals and students to practice timpani, anywhere at anytime.

This is perfect for developing even rolls, best sticking patterns between drums and practicing complicated musical passages with volume nuances.

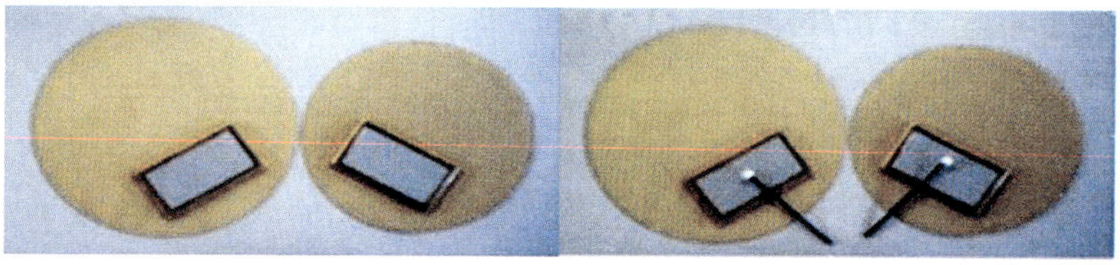

A logical solution to every timpani practice need would be to create two simple cardboard circles, 29" and 26" in diameter to simulate a full size timpani head, playing surface. By placing two of the D. Herbert Timpani Practice Pads at exactly the "sweet spot" playing location, the student has the visual connection to full size timpani heads, with the feel and rebound of a real plastic timpani head. Placement of both cardboard disks equipped with Herbert Timpani Pads on a standard 36" high kitchen counter or table, there is an immediate solution to practicing timpani at home or in a studio application. This brings immediate improvement to creating and practicing sticking patterns, cross-sticking needs and moving from kettle-to-kettle. These are perfect solutions for back-stage pre-performance wrist warm-up and audition waiting sequences before performance.

These Herbert Timpani Practice & Warm-up Timpani Pads are available at http://www.professionalpercussionproducts.com/davidherberttimpanipracticepad.htm

Recognizing these basic principles and challenges will equip the professional music educator, conductor, composer and percussion student,...with essential insights on how to set-up, tune, perform and maintain timpani as an integral instrument of the band, orchestra or any-size ensemble.

About the Author, Karl Dustman

Karl Dustman is a recognized professional Timpanist and Percussionist based in Cleveland Ohio. He performs regularly with many regional orchestras and ensembles in the area and tours internationally as principle Timpani-Percussionist with the world famous Mantovani Orchestra. He has been a featured guest performer with the Vienna Residence Orchestra and the Hour of Power Orchestra televised performances from the Crystal Cathedral in Garden Grove, California.

His published articles have appeared in Drum Business, Percussive Notes and various music industry trade publications in his capacity as Co-Executive Director of the Percussion Marketing Council for the past nineteen years. He has served on the Advisory Board and Symphonic Committee of the Percussive Arts Society.

His Music Industry guest speaker presentations have been part of the NAMM Foundation, College Music Society National Conference, the Percussive Arts Society International Convention and multiple university Music Business curriculums.

He is the founder and President of Dustman & Associates Marketing Communications, his twenty-nine year marketing consulting firm and Professional Percussion Products, the nation's first by-appointment-only orchestral percussion showroom resource serving all the major symphony orchestras, conservatories and professional percussionists around the globe. He makes in-school educational percussion presentations for the Cleveland Federation of Musicians throughout the Cleveland area and serves on the American Federation of Musicians Local 4 Music Fund Board of Directors.

He can be reached at kbdustman@aol.com

MAKING MUSIC MAGAZINE, May 2020

Drumming Up History

The Percussion Marketing Council Celebrates 25 Years of Advocacy

By Victoria **Wasylak**

For decades, the Percussion Marketing Council (PMC) has heralded May as International Drum Month, but for 2020, the PMC is taking their plans farther than ever before.

The quarter-of-a-century-old association has long served as an advocate for the percussion segment of the MI industry, working to create and maintain a nation of drummers and overall percussion players. Celebrating their 25th anniversary this year, the PMC looks back on their impressive history, while also keeping a firm grip on the future of the percussion industry.

"25 years ago, we had meetings like these in closets," executive director Karl Dustman told the PMC members gathered at the Hilton Anaheim's Vista Ballroom for their annual NAMM meeting on January 16.

That's not an exaggeration, either: the PMC initially started as International Drum Month, a month-long series of promotions to bring more players into the fold of the music industry and music education world.

In 1995, drum giants like Remo, Yamaha, and Drum Workshop commenced a campaign to push and raise awareness of the benefits of percussion education. After about two years, the companies formed an official non-profit trade association, keeping the already-existing International Drum Month in place as the centerpiece. As executive director, Dustman leads the PMC alongside additional board members with his 62 years of drumming experience and 54 years in the MI world.

"The fact that you're still in business, still growing, still being productive 25 years later, I think, is a key milestone," shares Dustman. "In this day and age, there are not a lot of trade associations within the music products industry that are having that type of track record. As an example, we lost the existence of the MDA (Music Distributors Association) just this year."

While growth remains an obvious and integral part of keeping any association running, Dustman says that diversifying their roster of members has also been key. From cymbals to vibraphones, there's much more to the percussion world than just drummers, and the PMC strives to represent all of them.

"It just cannot be a drum association for people playing drums – it involves every and all types of percussion musical instruments," he notes. "And the organization has diversified in its membership, and it has, in turn, diversified in its programs that it offers to grow that market. The newest entities coming into the percussion industry, they're looking for visibility. They're looking to be part of a big pool of manufacturers, distributors, publishers, and the little guys are looking for market visibility."

Citing electronic instruments and hand percussion as major movers and shakers in the industry these past few years, Dustman sees these areas as important components for growth. Electronic percussion, of course, offers players a quieter and more portable option, and hand percussion presents a great starting point for classroom players in schools for all ages.

"We're working closely with John Fitzgerald of Remo through our Hand Drumming For Life program, which is taking an organized industry and focusing on the recreational music element, specifically for percussion, and the music therapy element, specifically for percussion," Dustman says. "Both of those areas are using John Fitzgerald's expertise and contacts to get more drums and drumming into those hands for the first time. This is not preaching to the choir that already knows it. But what about all those perimeter organizations in medical treatment and various different diseases and so on, that can all use drums and drumming, more so than any other instrument, for a form of self-gratification and release?"

Sharing the unique benefits of drumming and percussion playing remain at the center of the association's mission, namely by homing in on the ease of playing and instant gratification for beginners of all ages.

Red Hot Chili Peppers drummer Chad Smith performs at a PMC assembly

"Immediately, drums are a physical exertion, and you don't have to read music at the beginning, you don't have to know rhythms," he adds. "It is the truest form of self-expression. From the very first moment that instrument is put in a person's hands, they want to play it. And it doesn't take a huge amount of expertise, other than self-expression, to receive immediate gratification. That's kind of our slogan: 'Everyone's a drummer with a heartbeat. They just don't know it until we put a drum in their hands.' And that's true with everyone that is breathing. You can't do that with a guitar, you can't do that with a piano, you can't even do that with a harmonica. But with a drum, you can achieve that immediate gratification and connection through self-expression. And there's not a wrong way of doing it."

For 2020, they've rolled out three new initiatives to enhance percussion education throughout the country. The first is called "get your sticks together," and offers players the chance to win 12 free drum lessons at the music shop of their choice. Each month of 2020, the PMC selects one random online winner to receive 12 free 30-minute lessons. In turn, the PMC will pay whichever retailer is identified on the consumer's contest entry form for a standardized flat private lesson rate.

"It could be a starter, or maybe it's somebody that's been playing for three or four years, and wants to get better," Dustman explains. "We don't care, as long as they're over the age of 10. We have in-store counter cards that invite their own studio students to sign up for 12 free drum lessons."

Also on deck for 2020 is an ongoing giveaway of limited-edition commemorative drumming and percussion products. Starting in this May's edition of International Drum Month, the PMC will hold drawings for items like one-of-a-kind snare drums, cymbals, cajons, conga drums, and bongos, all featuring special 25th-anniversary logo badges. Winners will be selected through the end of the year.

Finally, "lesson with a master" will also launch in May, offering chances for players to win a one-hour teleconference lesson with one of four internationally recognized drummers and celebrity artists. Rich Redmond, the drummer for Jason Aldean, Rick Latham, international drum educator, player, and teacher, David Stanoch, international educator and online video teacher, and Gordon Campbell, international celebrity artist, will all be available. These new initiatives for the May International Drum Month campaign will replace the widely-recognized Roadie for a Day contest.

"You need to liven things up every so often," Dustman notes. "And in doing that, we have completely redesigned International Drum Month for 2020."

Taking a page from one of their main inspirations – NAMM – the PMC has strived to make self-analysis one of their strengths, even if that means repurposing or stopping certain initiatives. One educational program called Roots of Rhythm was even sold to its developer, Dr. Craig Woodson, who now runs and independently owns the course.

The PMC program "Drums Across America" presents at Summer NAMM 2013 in Nashville

"We divested ourselves of it and replaced it with a drum set program based on his template, called 'Drum Set in the Classroom,'" Dustman says. "[Woodsen] wrote the program, he administers the program, he takes drum sets into the same classrooms that he used to take hand drums into. And now, he's teaching how to get drum set in classrooms, both acoustic and electronic kits."

As for what's hot now, Dustman says he's seen djembes and cajons captivate the industry in recent years, followed by the current trend of electronic percussion, including electronic drum kits and mallet keyboard instruments like the MalletKAT.

"What I do see evolving is that the manufacturers and brands that make these keyboard instruments - like a vibe, or a marimba, or a xylophone, or a glockenspiel. They [brands] are looking at this, because that is a direct extension of the Orff-Kodaly classroom instruction that has been going on for decades. So if somebody is learning on a xylophone, a glock, and so on, and they're just playing it on a little eight to 12 to 15-note classroom instrument, how do we keep that interest going? The answer is to have a two-and-a-half-octave electronic keyboard that can sound like any one of the mallet instruments that are out there in the percussion section. And I see that as an opportunity, and I see that those companies are signed up to attend our meeting."

Looking ahead at the coming years of the MI world, the PMC's focus is on keeping their growth consistent as they tackle the 2020s and beyond.

"If we were sitting around the conference table, we'd probably all unanimously say, 'Figure out a way to have this thing survive another 25 years,'" Dustman says. "But the real answer to that is to maintain the momentum. And the momentum increases, quite honestly, with each year."

Still, Dustman and the PMC practice their elevator pitch whenever possible – and since the percussion market hasn't bounced back the way that other MI segments have since the recession, there's no such thing as creating too many new players.

"The long-term established companies and brands spend all of their time, money, effort, and knowledge, trying to differentiate their brand from everyone else that is competing with them," he says. "They don't have the time or the expertise to devote to creating new markets, creating new players. And yet, the entire industry realizes that if we don't create more players, we are oversaturating the market with more supply than there is demand. The answer to this industry growth is to create more players, which become consumers for any and all percussion merchandise."

It all circles back to that one, determined slogan: "Everyone's a drummer with a heartbeat. They just don't know it until we put a drum in their hands." And as long as the PMC is around, the MI world might just see the largest generation of percussion players yet. MMR

Brad Smith (Hal Leonard), David Jewell (Yamaha), Stacey Montgomery-Clark (SABIAN), and Karl Dustman before the PMC's 2020 Winter NAMM gathering

INDEX

INDEX